HANDBOOK OF
MARRIAGE
COUNSELING
Second Edition

HANDBOOK OF
MARRIAGE
COUNSELING
Second Edition

Edited by Ben N. Ard, Jr.
and Constance Callahan Ard

SCIENCE AND BEHAVIOR BOOKS, INC.
Palo Alto, California: 1976

301.427
H 236

Dedicated to

W. C. McA.
and
M. M. A.

For support, backing, and encouragement over the years.

Contributors

Ard, Ben N., Jr., Ph.D. Professor of Counseling, San Francisco State University.

Ard, Constance Callahan, M.A. Licensed Marriage, Family and Child Counselor in private practice.

Bach, George R., Ph.D. Director, Institute for Group Psychotherapy, Beverly Hills, California.

Bedford, Stewart, Ph.D. Psychologist, Chico, California.

Blinder, Martin G., M.D. Psychiatrist, San Francisco; Medical Director, Family Therapy Institute of Marin, San Rafael, California.

Bowen, Murray, M.D. Clinical Professor of Psychiatry, Georgetown University Medical Center.

Branden, Nathaniel, Ph.D. Executive Director of the Institute of Biocentric Psychology, Los Angeles, California.

Ellis, Albert, Ph.D. Executive Director, Institute for the Advanced Study of Rational Psychotherapy, New York, New York.

Foley, Vincent D., Ph.D. Associate Professor, Department of Counselor Education, St. John's University, Jamaica, New Jersey.

Fowler, C. Ray, Ph.D. Executive Director, American Association of Marriage and Family Counselors, Claremont, California.

Goodwin, Hilda M., D.S.W. Assistant Professor in Family Study in Psychiatry, University of Pennsylvania School of Medicine.

Harper, Robert A., Ph.D. Psychotherapist and Marriage Counselor, Washington, D.C.

Hefner, Hugh M. Editor and Publisher, PLAYBOY magazine.

Hudson, John W., Ph.D. Professor of Sociology, Arizona State University.

Humphrey, Norman D., Ph.D. (Deceased) Formerly at Wayne State University.

Kaplan, Helen Singer, M.D., Ph.D. Director, Sex Therapy and Education Program, New York Hospital—Cornell Medical Center.

Kerckhoff, Richard K., Ph.D. Department of Child Development and Family Life, Purdue University.

Kirkendall, Lester A., Ph.D. Emeritus Professor of Family Life, Oregon State University.

Kirschenbaum, Martin, Ph.D. Co-Director, Family Therapy Institute of Marin, San Rafael, California.

Leichter, Elsa, M.S.S.A. Director of Group Therapy, Jewish Family Service, New York, New York.

Leslie, Gerald R., Ph.D. Chairman, Department of Sociology, University of Florida.

Lowry, Thea Snyder, M.A. Licensed Marriage, Family and Child Counselor in private practice, Kentfield, California.

Lowry, Thomas P., M.D. Psychiatrist in private practice in Kentfield, California.

Luthman, Shirley Gehrke, A. C.S.W., R.S.W. Co-Director, Family Therapy Institute of Marin, San Rafael, California.

Marsh, Donald C., Ph.D. Professor of Sociology, Wayne State University.

Morgan, Owen, Ph.D. Director, Center for Family Life Studies, Arizona State University.

Moxom, James E., M.S.W. Psychological Services, Los Angeles, California.

Mudd, Emily H., Ph.D. Formerly Director, Marriage Council of Philadelphia.

Neubeck, Gerhard, Ed. D. Family Study Center, University of Minnesota.

Nichols, William C., Jr., Ed. D. Editor, *Journal of Marriage and Family Counseling*.

Phillips, Clinton E., Ph.D. California Family Study Center, North Hollywood, California.

Rutledge, Aaron L., Th.D. Private practice, Grosse Pointe Psychological Center. Grosse Pointe Woods, Michigan.

Satir, Virginia, A.C.S.W. Family therapist; formerly Director of Training, Family Project, Mental Research Institute, Palo Alto, California.

Singer, Laura, Ed.D. President, Save A Marriage, New York, New York.

Stokes, Walter R., M.D. Psychiatrist, Stuart, Florida.

Vincent, Clark E., Ph.D. Director, Behavioral Sciences Center, Bowman-Gray School of Medicine, Wake Forest University, Winston-Salem, North Carolina.

Watson, Andrew S., M.D. Department of Psychiatry, University of Michigan.

Williams, John, M.A. Psychologist; Director, Northwest Branch, Institute of Rational Living, Seattle, Washington

Wyden, Peter. Executive Editor, *Ladies Home Journal*.

A Note to Students and Practitioners Who Have Bought This Book

Some thoughts on reading this book (with a low bow to Lord Acton):

* learn as much by writing as by reading: write in the margins;
* keep a journal of your reactions;
* do not be entirely content with any book or author; seek sidelights and contrasting views from others;
* have no "favorites" which blind your critical faculties;
* keep men and their ideas apart (avoid arguments *ad hominem*);
* guard against the prestige of "great names";
* see that your judgments are your own, and do not shrink from disagreement;
* no trusting without testing; test out a man's ideas before you trust them;
* never be surprised by the crumbling of an idol or the disclosure of a skeleton.

It is hoped that the following chapters, some of which are extracts from books and journals, will provide you with pegs (stout and well driven-in) on which you can hang your own further thoughts.

"Learning without thought
is labor lost;
Thought without learning
is perilous."

CONFUCIUS.

Contents

Foreword

Ben Ard: Handbook of Marriage Counseling

2nd Edition, 1976

Nearly a decade has passed since the publication of the first edition of this *Handbook of Marriage Counseling*. The social and demographic trends which seemed then to signal a profound shift in the nature of marriage and family life have accelerated. The demands for services of a marriage and family counseling nature have increased manyfold. Likewise, the demand for training of well-qualified marriage and family counselors has increased.

While not all of the trends noted a decade ago have continued exactly as anticipated, their general impact on the American family has been devastating. As a result of our unrealistic attitudes toward marriage, our Snow White/ Prince Charming expectations are rarely fulfilled much beyond the end of the honeymoon. In an earlier day, when religious and cultural authoritarianism required the maintenance of even a bad marriage, there was little recourse to alternatives. Although the poor man's divorce—desertion—has always been indulged in, divorce has become increasingly acceptable in the last generation. In an equalitarian society—at least in expectation, if not in practice—all members of the family unit expect this relationship to be personally gratifying and fulfilling. When it is not, dissolution is often the "treatment of choice" prescribed not by a well trained expert, but by the parties themselves as they seek the $5.00 remedy—do-it-yourself divorce. According to the latest figures, even in some of our wealthiest counties, more than 50% of the divorce actions filed are done without the services of an attorney by mutual consent of the couple themselves. We hold no brief for a bad marriage. Nor would we suggest that all attorneys are counselors—except "at law." However, in most cases the attorney does inquire into the circumstances leading a couple to file for divorce, including questioning them as to whether or not they have received any counseling. If they have not, and in the attorney's opinion it might be helpful, he will usually refer the couple. Lacking even such minimal intervention as this, when a couple files for dissolution by mutual consent, we have little reassurance that anything has happened except "desertion" of the relationship by both parties.

The proper function of the professional marriage counselor is not to save all marriages he/she sees, any more than it is to dissolve all those marriages in trouble which are referred for treatment. The marriage counselor is neither a savior nor a surgeon. Rather, he/she is a midwife, a listener, a coach, a clarifier, a wrestler, a nurturer, a confronter, and occasionally, an archaeologist. The marriage counselor's professional focus is the relationship between the marital partners and/or the family members. In order to focus effectively on those relationships, he/she must understand and confront the intrapsychic, as well as interpsychic phenomena encountered. In order to master the complex intricacies of the marital/family systems presented, he/she needs all the help available for training and supervision.

Some of the best help available is in this *Handbook of Marriage Counseling*. In its fifty chapters from forty contributors (including eleven new authors) will be found the most distinguished clinical professionals in the field of marriage and family counseling. In addition to the eleven new authors, seven of the chapters from the first edition have been extensively revised. While a few chapters from the first edition have been omitted due to space limitations, the Editor has rearranged and selected new materials which more than compensates for those omissions. Among the authors of the new chapters are Branden, Foley, Kaplan, Leichter, the Lowrys, Neubeck, Nichols, Phillips, and Singer.

While this volume is not an official publication of the American Association of Marriage and Family Counselors, the Editors and most of the contributors are A.A.M.F.C. members. Moreover, most of them have held positions of leadership within the Association; several of them are past-Presidents. Nearly every one of the authors who is an A.A.M.F.C. member holds the status of A.A.M.F.C. Approved Supervisor, and most are Fellows. Those contributors who are not A.A.M.F.C. members have equally distinctive credentials in their respective professional associations.

To this distinguished company of contributors is attached the indispensable professional reference materials including a subject/name index, an annotated bibliography, and seven "working" appendices for the professional marriage and family counselor.

The classic contributions combined with the most powerful newer statements of contemporary developments make this volume a most comprehensive and practical textbook on marriage counseling as a profession.

C. Ray Fowler, Ph.D.
Executive Director
American Association of Marriage and
Family Counselors

Preface

The field of marriage counseling has indeed "come of age," as was stated in the first edition of this *Handbook* in 1969. The profession has continued to grow by leaps and bounds, even with some set-backs. An increasing number of professionals now are involved in marriage and family counseling, and there seems to be an increasing demand for marriage and family counseling across the country and even around the world. Several states have passed laws pertaining to the certification or licensing of marriage and family counselors, and others are considering such laws. If all this can be said to show that marriage and family counseling is a profession (or at least is well on its way to becoming a profession), with a scientific body of knowledge, some relevant theory, a code of ethics, and some specific techniques, then there would seem to be a need for a handbook of marriage counseling which would incorporate these basic elements in an easy-to-get-at reference work.

This is what has been attempted in this book. The articles in this second edition of the *Handbook* represent a variety of points of view and are written by some of the outstanding professionals in the field. They have been purposely selected to present provocative, controversial, and contrasting points of view. A handbook does not *have* to be dull, dry, or boring. Hopefully the reader will not find this book has any such characteristics. But the proof is in the pudding: check it out, read it, and see for yourself.

In this second edition there are forty contributors, including eleven new faces. Several of the chapters from the first edition had to be omitted because of space limitations or newer developments. Seven chapters were extensively revised and brought up-to-date. New chapters by Branden, Foley, Kaplan, Leichter, the Lowrys, Neubeck, Nichols, Phillips, Fowler, Ben Ard, and Singer are included. The editors and the whole profession are indebted to the many contributors to this volume for their articles and to the others in the field who have contributed the many books and articles which have helped to make the field what it is today. It has been a privilege to work with many of these contributors personally and to correspond with others. It is hoped that the readers of this handbook, be they experienced counselors or beginning students, will enjoy some of the intellectual stimulation provided by interacting with the ideas of these leaders in the field of marriage and family counseling.

If this second edition continues to provide a ready reference for marriage and family counselors already practicing in the field and a stimulating introduction to the profession for the beginning student, it will have served its purpose.

San Francisco, California   Ben N. Ard, Jr.
1976   Constance Callahan Ard

Introduction

This handbook is intended as a fairly complete introduction to the field of marriage and family counseling. It obviously cannot realistically contain *all* the pertinent knowledge about marriage and family counseling, but it does represent some of the basic knowledge, an overview of the field, something of its history and development, some of the philosophy and value problems in the field, some of the relevant theory, a sampling of some of the techniques used in the field, discussion of many of the problems faced by the marriage and family counselor, some of the legislative considerations pertaining to marriage and family counseling, the code of ethics of the profession, and several articles dealing with practical help for the professional marriage and family counselor.

The articles are written by representatives of many professional fields, including psychologists, sociologists, psychiatrists, counselors, social workers, physicians, and writers. The field of marriage and family counseling is truly interdisciplinary. This is one of the strengths of the field as well as a source of problems at times. Sometimes practitioners with training in only one field (frequently from only one college or university, from teachers who represented only one point of view) end up with too narrow a view, i.e., assuming there is only one "right" way to do marriage and family counseling. If this handbook accomplishes nothing else, it should stretch the minds of those who might assume that there is only one approach or one technique that needs to be applied in marriage and family counseling. The professional marriage and family counselor, just because he or she deals with people in an area where narrow-minded values frequently prevail (and are the causes of many of the problems the counselor faces), particularly needs to have a broad, cross-cultural perspective if clients are to get the optimal help they need in our pluralistic, changing society.

In planning the contents of this volume, marriage counseling was conceived in the broadest possible sense. It was defined as any counseling with one or more clients dealing with problems related to marriage, i.e., problems about getting married (premarital counseling); staying married; getting out of marriage, getting divorced (divorce counseling); adjusting to the loss of a partner; sexual problems (premarital, marital, or extramarital); concerns about being a man (functioning as a man), husband, lover, father, friend; or as a woman, wife, lover, friend, mother. Consequently in the articles to be found in the following pages, the various contributors will deal with just these sorts of problems, along with others.

Some people in the field have tried to maintain a distinction between "marriage counseling" and "psychotherapy." In this handbook many of the authorities will not make this distinction, and so the reader will find in various of the articles the terms "marriage counseling" and "psychotherapy" used interchangeably. It is hoped that this will not bother the reader unnecessarily. Marriage and family counseling can be considered a special form of psychotherapy dealing particularly with the sorts of problems previously mentioned (marital, premarital, extramarital, post-marital, sexual, etc.), using specific techniques geared to the nature of the problems encountered. If the term "psychotherapy" bothers some people (as it evidently still does), what takes place can simply be called "marriage and family counseling," which to some people does not have the frightening overtones of "psychotherapy." So be it. It will be left up to the professional counselor to decide what labels to use for the work done. In this handbook, both terms will be used.

The handbook can be used in a variety of ways: as a textbook, to be read through critically and discussed; or as a reference work, to be kept handy on a nearby shelf in one's professional library for consultation when one wants to look up something about the professional code of ethics, legislative matters, a different theoretical approach, or a new technique one may wish to try with a certain client or group of clients. Even if the answer to a particular question cannot be found in these pages, probably more frequently than not one can find a resource or a professional person to whom one can write for further information and help. It is hoped that the indices and the appendices will prove of practical help to the professional counselor or the student who wants to look up what might be available on a particular subject.

The handbook will also be of value to anyone outside the profession who wants to know something about marriage and family counseling; or to the layperson who is concerned about some of the problems dealt with herein, is considering going to see a marriage and family counselor and wants to have some idea of what to expect, or is trying to do something on his own about adopting a new approach to some personal problem.

To each of the above readers, welcome to what is hoped may prove to be a stimulating experience. You may find much to agree with and possibly some to disagree with in the following pages. If the handbook stretches your mind in some new ways, causes you to think in ways you may have not thought before, it will have served a good purpose.

Overview

. . . imperfect human beings can be of therapeutic assistance to other imperfect human beings.

CARL R. ROGERS

This first section serves as somewhat of a panoramic overview of the broad field of marriage counseling. William C. Nichols, Jr. gives attention, in the first paper, to some of the major problems and issues the field faces and offers a suggestion concerning coordination and cooperation. He deals with the unsettled boundaries question and answers the question: who are the practitioners? He discusses briefly the professional organizations, related organizations and activities and asks two basic questions: what kind of preparation should marriage counselors have and also what kinds of theoretical orientations? Finally, he deals with values and ethics, and offers an idealistic proposal regarding cooperation and coordination in the field.

In the second chapter, Ben N. Ard, Jr. discusses some of the fundamental assumptions which seem, implicitly, to underlie marriage counseling. In most cases these assumptions are of the broadest, most general sort, but not everyone in the field of marriage counseling would agree with each of them. These assumptions, then, may serve as ideas to be examined. Assumptions are better when they are made explicit rather than implicit, and this article may stimulate some thought and discussion about what the major goals and aims of marriage counseling are.

One assumption which some people in the field might differ with or question holds that there is a reality different from distorted perceptions (e.g., illusions, delusions, hallucinations, projections, fantasies, etc). Some theoreticians deny any objective reality and rely only on the client's phenomenological field or subjective perceptions. The reader will have to decide for himself which assumption it is best for him to follow.

Another assumption which some might question is that the ultimate goal of marriage counseling is the *optimal* development of the *individual* client (rather than maintaining a marriage at all costs). Some marriage counselors might not agree with this individualistic approach. Again, each reader will have to decide for himself.

CHAPTER 1

The Field of Marriage Counseling:
A Brief Overview

William C. Nichols, Jr.

THE FIELD OF MARRIAGE COUNSELING
A BRIEF OVERVIEW

No longer is it possible—if, indeed, it ever was—to say, "Marriage counseling is . . ." and proceed to describe the field of marriage counseling in simple, precise terms. Marriage counseling in the United States has never been an easily defined and described field of endeavor, and the picture is even more complex today than it was in the past. It is exceedingly difficult for consumers of services to ascertain what they can profitably use from among the array of practitioner services being offered. To whom can they go and for what kind of help?

THE UNSETTLED BOUNDARIES QUESTION

Still a relatively new and emergent field after some four or five decades on the American scene, marriage counseling continues to present a virtual kaleidoscope of impressions to the critical as well as the casual viewer. Participation in professional organizations, practice as a marriage counselor, experience in training marriage counselors, examination of the literature on marriage counseling and allied endeavors, and general study of the field bring the definite impression here that while marriage counseling has attained unprecedented popularity in recent years it still tends to be an ill-defined field, meaning many different things to many different persons. There is much disagreement on what constitutes marriage counseling and the appropriate boundaries of the field.

Such disagreement and lack of clarity are not new. Study of the early writings on marriage counseling discloses that the field virtually was an inchoate mass. Confusion abounded. Arguments developed over the nature and focus of marriage counseling. Some of the key issues that emerged pertained to recognizing conscious versus unconscious motivations, practicing psycho-therapy versus counseling, focusing on the rela-

---

Reprinted with permission of the author and the publisher from *The Family Coordinator*, January, 1973.

tionship versus the individual personalities, being medically trained versus non-medically trained, and using primarily sociological versus psychological theory. That is, for example, disagreement developed over whether the person working in the field should attempt to deal with unconscious mental processes, be a psychotherapist, work only with the marital relationship, be medically trained, be trained basically in a group orientation, or conversely on each of these. Indicative also of the many differences of opinion and assortment of practices that prevailed were the eventual appearance of articles in question form: What is marriage counseling? Should marriage counseling become a full-fledged specialty? Should the marriage counselor ever recommend divorce?

Few of the questions raised in the earlier years have been resolved to the general satisfaction of those who offer their services toward the resolution of marriage problems. At the same time many of those questions have remained unanswered other, new matters have arisen to render the picture even more complex. For example, during the earlier stages of the development of marriage counseling, two major views prevailed as to what should be done to help persons suffering from marital discord. One held that marital difficulty stemmed from individual personality sources and that the help to be applied consisted of individual psychotherapy or counseling. The second defined the work of the marriage counselor as concerned primarily with the relationship of the marital dyad, the interaction between the spouses, and with the environment and external reality.

Before the very serious attempts of several clinicians and theoreticians to effect a synthesis between the "individual only" and "relationship only" approaches had an opportunity to bring about any general impact on the field of marriage counseling, a new emphasis had entered the picture. Many began to say that the term marriage counseling was too limited, that it was necessary to talk about marriage and family counseling or therapy, and that the treatment or counseling orientation must include not only a focus on marriage and marital interaction but also a focus on the family unit.

What are the boundaries of the field of marriage counseling? For purposes of legislation it is possible to delimit and delineate the field in various ways. Legislation may pertain to marriage counseling, marriage and family counseling, or as in one state marriage, family, and child counseling. For example, in the provision for certification of marriage counselors in Michigan the following definition appears:

> "Marriage counseling" means the providing of guidance, testing, discussions, therapy, instructions, or the giving of advice, the principal purpose of which is to avoid, eliminate, relieve, manage or resolve material conflict or discord or to create, improve, or restore marital harmony, or to prepare couples for marriage.

Such legislation and definitions do give a considerable amount of assistance in clarifying what the marriage counselor may do and how marriage counseling is construed by the legislature in a given state but do not begin to solve all the problems involved in delineating the field generally.

Marriage counseling sometimes is defined broadly as "what the marriage counselor does." This helps to a point. Marriage counseling certainly involves more than meeting with couples in a three-way session, the so-called conjoint interview. For that matter, marriage counseling is not identical with any particular mode of interviewing. The marriage counselor, depending on training and orientation, may work with individuals around marriage and family problems in addition to assisting couples and may work with married persons in group therapy, conjointly, or collaboratively with another counselor or therapist. He or she also may teach about sex education, marital adjustment, childrearing, and related topics, depending again on orientation, training, opportunity, and personal predilection. Some of these activities are marriage counseling activities and some are not; some are basically therapeutic and others primarily educational.

For those who function as marriage counselors four separate but related areas of clinical endeavor may be delineated: premarital, marital, postmarital, and family. The counselor may do a considerable amount of work in the area of preparation for marriage, some of which would most accurately be described as premarital education or guidance while some would fall under the heading of counseling. This work may be done with an individual or with a couple. In working with the marital dyad, the marriage counselor may utilize a variety of approaches, focusing on the interaction between the partners, on their individual needs and problems, or on both, depending again on the counselor's orientation and ability, as well as the needs of the marital partners.

When a marriage is broken by divorce or death, the task becomes that of burying the marriage, helping the individual deal with bereavement and grief, and in many instances aiding the person in preparation for remarriage. Divorce counseling may be regarded as a part of marriage counseling and as an entity in itself, having its own distinct focus and phases. Working with the family unit may come about as a result of parent-child problems or disturbances in the child's behavior made manifest in home, school, or community, or in combinations of all three of these as well as from an occasional instance in which marital problems are the initial focus and an extension of professional endeavor is then made into parent-child or family interaction and problems.

Under the rubric of marriage counseling fall a range of therapeutic endeavors from brief contact to longterm, intensive psychotherapeutic work with marital partners. Some work is of a crisis intervention nature, consisting of first aid for temporarily askew partners and marriages. Periodic supportive assistance is given in other cases. The referee and advice-giving roles sometimes are taken by marriage counselors. Some marriage counselors undertake the alleviation of practical, reality problems as part of their work with their clientele. Others consider the work of the marriage counselor or marital therapist as being confined to the interactive and interpersonal problems of the persons who have sought their services.

Clarification of the possibilities of assistance that marriage counselors or marriage counseling can realistically be expected to provide appears to be a significant need of the field. It is not a cure-all and has some definite limitations. Not all persons or marriages experiencing difficulty and discord can be assisted by marriage counseling any more than all individuals experiencing difficulty can be helped by personal psychotherapy. Determining and acknowledging the legitimate limitations and roles of marriage counseling, that it is not for all situations and cases but that it can be an effective modality when appropriately understood and employed, would be an important part of more adequately delineating the boundaries of the field.

WHO ARE THE PRACTITIONERS?

Deciding what marriage counseling is, however, is not the only problem that continues to face the field. Equally important is that of deciding who is a marriage counselor. As noted, there has been no accurate unitary description of the field and no single source of authority for either the marriage counselor or the public, several conflicting views of what constituted marriage counseling and who could practice having arisen during the past decades. The confusion continues to be compounded by the fact that working with marriage and family problems in some degree is an integral part of the work of many persons in one of the more established fields such as the ministry, medicine, law, social work, or clinical psychology. Some of these professionals now are given some training in dealing with marriage and family problems as part of their basic professional education, the amount and quality varying widely.

Whether or not they have even a basic orientation toward understanding and helping with family and marriage matters, however, professionals in all of these fields sometimes find themselves called on to respond to domestic problems. Occasionally representatives of one or more of these disciplines will continue to make manifest evidences of professional imperialism that would claim marriage counseling as the province of their particular profession. Thus far marriage counseling has continued to evade the attempts to make it the captive of any single profession and has continued along the line of developing as a field in its own right.

Today marriage counseling is an emergent profession, a quasi-profession, and an amateur activity, a field that is populated by highly skilled, clinically sophisticated practitioners at one extreme and by well meaning but incompetent amateurs at the other; by ethically and socially responsible professionals and unprincipled charlatans; by those who operate from a framework of explicit theoretical formulations and those who function intuitively without explicit theory; by some who give careful and major attention to intrapsychic processes and personality dynamics and by some who focus almost entirely on the marital relationship and the interspousal interaction; by some who rely on the insights of dynamic psychology and by some who deny that it has any meaning; by some who work almost entirely as marriage and family counselors or therapists and by others who do so only occasionally and incidentally; but some who are basically clinicians and by others who are primarily academicians; and by still other contrasting sets of orientation and practice.

Marriage counselors must be licensed or certified in three states: California, Michigan, and New Jersey. In those states some guidance is provided for the public as persons seek assistance for what they have defined as marriage problems. In theory the assistance may be greater than it works out to be in actual practice. A marriage counselor is one who is licensed or certified as a marriage counselor, but there are many shades of difference among those so licensed. Furthermore, exemptions of persons working in agencies or those who do marriage counseling as an "inherent" or "incidental" part of their work in an established professional practice may leave loopholes through which a considerable amount of incompetent and occasionally harmful marriage counseling activity occurs.

Regardless of the shortcomings of certification or licensure, such provisions in law do provide the public with some minimal guidelines and protection by preventing individuals who have not met the requirements set by the state from advertising their services. Otherwise those who seek the services of a marriage counselor frequently must take their chances without being able to secure guidance in locating a competent practitioner from the helping professionals with whom they are in contact or from other sources because nobody knows who the qualified marriage counselors are and how to avoid the incompetent.

Classified advertising in telephone directories under the heading of "marriage and family counselors" produces a confusing picture for the layperson, as well as for many professional persons, who seek to find a marriage counselor. Unless there is regulation through certification or licensure, it is very much the same whenever one examines a telephone directory from a city in north, south, east, or west: Individuals from various professions advertise themselves as marriage counselors. So do palmists. So do persons who claim degrees and qualifications that they may or may not possess. So do other individuals who may be untrained in any discipline. The major thing that many of them have in common is that they advertise their services as marriage counselors and, presumably, generally intend to collect a fee for whatever they do or promise to do.

Licensure or certification is no panacea. Practically speaking, the major outcome of legislative action and governmental implementation is more likely to be the determination of who shall practice and the elimination of some unqualified persons than it is to be the determination of the kind or quality of service that is available to the public. The latter questions are more likely to be decided by the quality and quantity of professional training that is available and secured and the actions of professional organizations in providing for continuing education, responsible practice, and public information and protection.

PROFESSIONAL ORGANIZATIONS

The major national organization exclusively for marriage counselors in the United States has long been the American Association of Marriage Counselors (renamed the American Association of Marriage and Family Counselors in 1970). Organized in 1942 in the northeastern part of the country, the association now spans the United States and includes between 1000 and 2000 members, a fraction of those practicing today. Its numerical strength is concentrated along the upper and middle east coast, in the midwest, and in California.

The AAMFC conducts an annual meeting in the fall of each year and a spring topical conference on a subject such as divorce or sexual behavior, as well as an occasional special conference or workshop, e.g., on training or licensure, and publishes a newsletter for its membership. It has long served as a standard-setting organization for marriage counseling, much of the early effort being done in cooperation with the National Council on Family Relations. Through its committees, AAMFC has continued to work toward the maintenance of standards for individuals who would practice as marriage counselors. It also sets standards for and approves training centers and has promulgated a code of ethics for marriage counselors.

Requirements for membership in the AAMFC and the conception of what should be minimal preparation for the marriage counselor have undergone change in recent years. For many years membership was granted on the basis of training in a profession such as law, medicine, psychology, the ministry, or social work, supplemented by additional specialized training in marriage counseling, plus several years of experience as a practitioner. In 1970-1971 an additional route into membership was opened: that of graduate education through the masters degree in a behavioral science, plus supervised work and experience acceptable to the organization's admissions committee. The organization also has begun to admit members on the basis of certification in their state of residence.

The concept of training in the AAMFC has been changed under the pressure of public demand for marriage counseling services. There is less emphasis on internship training in a formal training center such as in the pioneering program of the Marriage Council of Philadelphia (University of Pennsylvania) or in the formerly excellent but now defunct Merrill-Palmer Institute Counseling and Psychotherapy Training Program and more emphasis on supervised work in less formal settings. Although one primary motive for the AAMFC's recent establishment of an "approved supervisor" designation whereby individuals so named may provide supervision in marriage and family counseling under guidelines specified by the organization was to increase membership, the move can be viewed as potentially providing considerable benefit to the field and to the public generally.

Strong state organizations of marriage or marriage and family counselors, generally open to individuals licensed or certified in the particular state involved, exist in California, Michigan, and New Jersey. Although officers in both the California State Marriage and Family Counselors Association and the Michigan Association of Marriage Counselors have been active in the affairs of the AAMFC, neither state association is affiliated with the national organization. The large California association has been particularly active and publishes a *Marriage Counseling Quarterly*. State organizational affiliates of the AAMFC exist in several states such as North Carolina and Utah. The Middle Atlantic States Association and the Southwestern Association of Marriage and Family Counselors are regionally based affiliates.

Another national organization is the Academy of Psychologists in Marital and Family Therapy, established in 1962 as the Academy of Psychologists in Marriage Counseling. The name was changed in 1970. This organization is rather self-limiting in that membership is restricted to members of the American Psychological Association who generally must meet an additional requirement of state certification as a psychologist in their state of residence. The academy meets annually in conjunction with the American Psychological Association and publishes a *Newsletter* (journal) for its membership. Officers have mentioned that one goal is to become, in time, a division of the APA.

RELATED ORGANIZATIONS AND ACTIVITIES

Other clinically oriented organizations such as the American Group Psychotherapy Association and the American Orthopsychiatric Association regularly include sections on marriage and family counseling or therapy in their programs. Still others such as the more broadly based and educationally related National Council on Family Relations and the Groves Conference on Marriage and the Family devote portions of meetings to clinical issues pertaining to marriage and the family, the NCFR on a regular basis and the Groves Conference occasionally.

A note is in order with respect to what may be termed the family therapy movement. The principal source of national visibility for this movement is the excellent journal *Family Process*, published quarterly by the Family Institute of New York and the Mental Research Institute of Palo Alto, California. The movement also finds expression through these and other family institutes and workshops and symposia generally conducted by family therapists from such established training centers in family therapy.

The *Family Process* label of "multidisciplinary" and the explanation that it publishes "material in the broad area of family studies with particular emphasis on family mental health and family psychotherapy" provide some clues as to the character of the family therapy movement. Rather than moving in the direction of developing a new profession, the family therapy movement gives continued evidence of maintaining its multidisciplinary, as contrasted to interdisciplinary or new discipline, approach. Family therapy seemingly is regarded primarily as the work of practitioners in established professions rather than as a separate field in its own right.

This is a vitally important difference from the emphasis of the marriage counseling movement that has eventuated in licensure or certification in three states. Marriage counseling has been regarded as both a multidisciplinary field and an interdisciplinary, emergent field in its own right. Although a few individuals are actively identified with both the family therapy and the marriage counseling fields, there generally is little overlap between the two movements and informal efforts to secure a closer alliance have not been productive of tangible results to date. The latest developments point in the direction of an even closer linkage and identification of group therapy and family therapy.

The booming expansion in recent years of teaching, research, and counseling about human sexuality has produced activity and organizations that parallel and overlap the field of marriage counseling and the work of

the marriage counselor. Workshops and courses in sex education and counseling are conducted in increasing numbers in both academic and clinical
settings, in colleges, universities, and professional schools as well as in
hospitals, institutes, community mental health centers, and as a part of
the programming of professional organizations.

New emphases such as innovations in the treatment of sexual difficulties and dysfunction and the emerging practice of providing vasectomy
counseling furnish examples of activities that parallel and occasionally
overlap with the field of marriage counseling. The combination term sex
and marital counseling sometimes appears, particularly in medical settings.
The most accurate statement would be that sex education and counseling
form both a part of marriage counseling and a separate field of endeavor
in which the educational or counseling may be performed primarily with
individuals and not necessarily in relation to marriage or family problems
or functioning.

WHAT KIND OF PREPARATION?

Unfortunately, the majority of individuals moving into the practice of
marriage counseling probably continue to do so without any formal training or supervised experience in marriage counseling. For many of those
who are already functioning as clinicians in another field, the entry into
the practice of marriage counseling may represent a logical extension of
their work because of the needs of their clientele. Their movement may be
on the basis of attempted extrapolation from an individual therapy orientation and practice over to marital or from a family therapy orientation
and practice over to marital therapy. Sometimes the transition can be
made smoothly, sometimes it cannot.

Other professional persons who are not clinically trained in any field
continue to respond to the requests of their clientele for individual, marital, or family help, eventually coming to consider themselves marriage
counselors. Some individuals move into marriage counseling on the basis
of meagre training such as a brief workshop experience. The major way in
which persons from all of these categories learn how to function as marriage counselors may be by means of the same route that pioneer practitioners in any field learn, by trial-and-error and accretion of knowledge
through experience. Among the more salient reasons for the development
of this situation is the fact that popular acceptance of the idea that
marriage counseling can help with marital problems has created a demand
for such services that continues to exceed the supply of adequately prepared practitioners and the fact that there are multiple paths into practice
in a field that is still in a state of flux.

Marriage counseling has proceeded some discernible distances along
the road toward professionalization in the states in which there is licensure or certification. Nevertheless, the field has moved very slowly in the
direction of becoming a distinct profession, particularly in view of the
optimistic expressions of some marriage counseling leaders in the 1950s
and 1960s. Expectations concerning the development of doctoral programs in marriage counseling and a rapid and widespread movement of

states toward licensure have not been fulfilled. Instead, there are some indications that the major developments in the near future in the direction of degrees in marriage or marriage and family counseling will come at the masters level. The increase in the inclusion of didactic and clinical materials on marriage counseling in the curricula of professional education, such as in medical schools, can be viewed as both a parallel and a counteraction to the development of marriage counseling as a profession.

Marriage counseling has not developed consensus concerning a core of expert knowledge that it would deem necessary for practitioners in the field to master as part of their preparation. Put in another way, there is no general agreement in the field as to what the specialized training in marriage counseling should consist of, what the knowledge and training should include. Perhaps the most generally agreed upon idea is that the marriage counselor should have supervised experience in marriage counseling, in working with marital partners, and that at least one year of such supervised work is minimal or desirable. As for didactic work and course content, there do not appear to be any generally accepted guidelines, although various curricula proposals have been advanced over the years. Expansion of the concept of marriage counseling to include family counseling has resulted in further complications to the training and preparation picture.

The American Association of Marriage and Family Counselors has formulated for its voting members "standards of academic and professional standing, clinical competence and experience, and personal maturity and integrity." These standards have changed some over the years and depend for their meaning on the detailed materials developed by the organization through its committees. The AAMFC standards for preparation are far from being implemented throughout the field of marriage counseling, however.

What kind of preparation for what kind of practice or service? This is a major question facing the field of marriage counseling and therapy at this point. Is marriage counseling something to be done by established professionals who receive advanced training in the specialized area of marriage counseling or marital therapy? Is it something to be done by practitioners trained in a separate profession of marriage counseling? Is it something that can be done by members of established professions without further specialized training in marriage counseling? Is graduate work which includes some theory and practice in marriage counseling adequate preparation? Is it something to be performed by paraprofessionals? Is it all of these?

WHAT KINDS OF THEORETICAL ORIENTATION

Closely allied to the matter of preparation is the question of the kinds of theoretical orientation or orientations that underlie the practice of marriage counseling. To say that there is no theory in the field of marriage counseling is to err. To say that no single theoretical viewpoint has gained ascendancy over all others is to be more accurate.

There are many theoretical orientations employed by practitioners in the field of marriage counseling. For example, some of these are partial theories based on observations, formulations, and principles derived from study and work around limited aspects of marriage and marital interaction such as the handling of aggression. Others represent principles and approaches developed in individual or group psychotherapy with individuals or in laboratory and academic settings and subsequently applied to the marital dyad. Still others have been developed from extensive work with married persons or with families, new concepts and modifications being added to the original theoretical orientations of the clinician-theoreticians as a result of the accrued experiences.

There are psychodynamic, behavior modification, gestalt, transactional analysis, rational-emotive, symbolic interactionist, and other theoretical orientations and practices based on each of them. Adherents of each of these can claim success in helping to alleviate marital discord. Many practitioners are eclectic in both the positive and negative connotations of the term, practitioners who gather theoretical and practical concepts and practices from a variety of established orientations. At the same time there are practitioners who stumble along with an amalgam of ideas and techniques that bear little resemblance to any known theoretical viewpoint on either human personality or group life and interaction.

Although a few books on marriage counseling that attempt to set forth a combination of theory and practice have been produced in recent years, most of the printed material in this area has appeared in journals. Study of such material discloses that a considerable amount of work needs to be done in advancing the research and theory building aspects of marriage counseling. As is the case with many practical endeavors, there is a gap between what clinicians have evolved in terms of theoretical underpinning for the practice and what has found its way into print and the arena of scientific and professional discussion and debate.

The uses of short-term workshops and live demonstrations of theory and techniques in clinical meetings are currently in vogue as means of acquainting practitioners with new developments. How successful these are in conveying theoretical understanding along with technique to the observers is a question that bears examination. One can wonder whether such approaches meet the need for opportunity to study, discuss, and debate the merits and ramifications of the practices and their theoretical concomitants. At any rate, such means of educating practitioners would appear to be far more valuable as instruments of continuing education for those who already are working from an established theoretical base than as training for novices. For the immediate future, however, such brief exposures to theory and practice may be the only training that some practitioners are able to secure because of the shortage of training opportunities.

Marriage counseling resembles psychology, personality theory, psychotherapy, and other fields in being populated by a wide variety of theoretical orientations. A synthesis of theoretical viewpoints has not occurred in those fields and is not likely to take place in marriage counseling any more rapidly than it does, for example, in the more general field of psychotherapy. At this juncture in time there appears to be value in theoretical multiplicity, in the encouragement of the development and refinement of various approaches to understanding and dealing therapeutically, as well as educationally with marital and family discord and problems.

Theoretical multiplicity is not necessarily consonant with theoretical chaos or anarchy in a field. Not having a single universally accepted theory for marriage counseling does not mean that marriage counselors must work without theoretical underpinning. Instead, it may mean that practitioners have the opportunity to discriminate among choices of theoretical orientations, partial or incomplete though some of these may be, and select and use a theoretical approach that is compatible with their own training and personality. Although cross-fertilization is far from inevitable as an outcome of the encouragement of the development of several or many approaches, such theoretical multiplicity does provide opportunity for interaction among theories, theoreticians, and practitioners across a broad range of viewpoints.

VALUES AND ETHICS

Marriage counseling at the present time is experiencing considerable strain as the result of value divergencies and differences in outlook among its practitioners. While the sources of the conflicts that are occurring undoubtedly are complex and far-reaching in nature, some precipitating causes can be readily discerned. Changes such as altered attitudes and increased openness toward human sexuality, the appearance of variant forms and alternative styles of marriage and family living, changing attitudes toward divorce and remarriage, and other modifications in morals and mores have converged on marriage counseling with a collective impact that has produced cracks in old forms of service and modes of practice. These, in concert with a more general societal demand for action and immediate response, have faced marriage counseling with demands that the new behaviors and values be given a place in the spectrum.

What shall be the response of marriage counseling to such changes? Broadly speaking, shall the changes be embraced with open arms; held at arm's length, examined critically, and subsequently accepted, rejected, or ignored; or rejected outright and fought or disregarded? In brief, the practitioners of marriage counseling have open to them all of the avenues of response that are available to other individuals and groups facing sociocultural change and, in general, they seem to react in the same patterned ways that people typically respond to change. To the extent that marriage counseling is associated with the status quo and with traditional morality and values in relation to marriage and family life, the changes that take place present a threat. To those espousing different values, the changes that have occurred and are continuing to take place may represent something different, perhaps a welcome relief from oppressive social pressures.

Differences in value positions and conflicts in value preferences are nothing new in marriage counseling. What is new is the content of the questions being debated and contested. It is unlikely today that the question of whether the marriage counselor should ever recommend divorce would be debated in the program of an annual meeting of many national organizations representing marriage and family clinicians. The notion that the chief aim of marriage counseling is to "save the marriage" regardless of the nature of the marital relationship would not be accepted as widely and easily as it was in the past. Although many persons today still find divorce undesirable, the question among marriage counselors is more likely to be that of what kinds of counseling and educational services and programs are needed to assist those who are divorcing and remarrying than it is whether the marriage counselor should assist couples in making a decision to divorce.

Values and ethics tend to come together when marriage counselors face certain questions. For example, when they are met with the request for "marriage counseling" for unmarried couples who live together as well as when they are asked to provide marriage counseling for persons living in nontraditional forms of marriage, marriage counselors may face value conflicts and ethical dilemmas. Do they turn away those who are asking for help whose behaviors do not meet with their approval or offend their moral sensitivities? These, again, are not new questions for the field of marriage counseling, except for the fact that the particular content involved differs from that of the past. This same kind of ethical dilemma and value conflict faced practitioners in the past and will present itself in the future when the present content has been replaced by something that is not yet on the horizon.

For the present and immediate future there is need for the development of a strong code of ethics for the guidance of practitioners in the field of marriage counseling. The American Association of Marriage Counselors code is binding upon its members, but the AAMFC code, as has been recognized by the board and officers of the organization, represents a beginning more than a definitive product.

Among the ethical issues facing marriage counseling are those generally facing professions with regard to advertising and practice. These include how one presents himself or herself to the public as well as questions about such actions as pushing one's personal values upon clientele or using one's trusted position as helping person to try unproven techniques or questionable methods for dealing with marital discord on uninformed laypersons. Guidelines for the practitioner who is using physical techniques as opposed to verbal methods or who is attempting to be innovative in dealing with marital problems particularly appear to be needed. Other issues such as various practices of exploiting professional and organizational positions for commercial gain also require attention.

Value differences will continue to prevail in the marriage counseling field and well may become even more of an issue than they have been to this time. The major issue, however, does not stand forth as that of pluralism in values but rather that of whether some general agreement can be secured on ethical standards and significant efforts made to get these implemented in practice as normative for the field. Consensus on morality will not be forthcoming in a time of rapid and accelerating sociocultural change, but it should be possible for those practicing in a field that has some professional characteristics to secure some agreement on desirable practice, for their own interests if not for the protection of the public.

COOPERATION AND COORDINATION:
AN IDEALISTIC PROPOSAL

Stemming from diverse sources, growing at uneven rates, and moving in many directions, marriage counseling gives no sign of losing its great popularity in spite of its chaotic condition. It is here to stay. Nevertheless, to the concerned observer there are indications that cooperation and coordination in the field are greatly needed if the interests of both practitioners and the public are to be protected and advanced. Benign neglect of uncontrolled growth may lead to unnecessary malignancies. At the very least a considerable amount of waste occurs. Talent goes begging at the same time needs for service remain unmet. Interprofessional jealousies, professional imperialism, and, perhaps even worse, ignorance of happenings outside one's own professional domain continue to contribute to a lack of direction and focus. The reasons are legion why cooperation and coordination of effort are difficult to secure for this movement that simultaneously is galloping off in all directions like a herd of wild horses in some of its parts and languishing in a torpid state in others.

The first step toward bringing order out of chaos evidently has to be one that does not threaten very many vested interests. Attempts to secure amalgamation of existing organizations have not been fruitful. It does not seem likely that much progress is going to be made in this direction. At the same time the formation of still another organization in the marriage counseling or marriage and family field in the United States would represent basically a further splintering of the movement and the latest chapter in the continuing saga of the proliferation of associations in American life. The most productive effort at this time would seem to be one that permitted existing interests to come together for tentative exploration. Even the hope that this can be done probably is unrealistic. Nevertheless, here is a brief proposal toward that end.

A conference or series of conferences on marriage counseling and therapy—or marriage and family counseling or therapy—composed of representatives of professional organizations and professions whose members do marriage counseling; representatives of the field from states presently providing for or considering licensure or certification; representatives of training centers in marriage counseling; representatives of professional or graduate schools which include marriage counseling or marital and sex counseling in their curricula; representatives of family therapy; and representatives from the consumer public including both those with horror stories to tell and satisfied customers is proposed. The purpose of the conference or conferences would be to set forth and explore as fully as possible the issues facing this field including the problems and prospects with regard to cooperation and coordination of effort.

Some of the issues that appear to be facing the field as a whole— whether marriage counseling is perceived as a function of professionals from various disciplines or as a separate profession or both—pertain to the boundaries of this activity and the relation of marriage counseling to the broader fields of psychotherapy, education, and mental health; preparation and training; licensure; and a host of others including the vitally important but highly sensitive matter of insurance. Parts of these could be discussed and some changes effected with a minimum of threat to any of the vested interests.

This proposal does not call for the supplanting of any established professional or organizational activity but for a supplementing of such activity, again for the purposes of cooperation and coordination of effort. Given the nature and state of the field of marriage counseling, including the varieties of viewpoints that prevail and the public demands and expectations of service, there is need for coordination and cooperation along several different paths simultaneously. Some things can be handled on a national level and a conference for purposes of exploration would be helpful toward that end. Others can be approached through established organizations and agencies. Still other matters require the coordination of efforts and cooperation of interests in given geographical areas such as states.

Let's hope these wild horses get harnessed productively.

CHAPTER 2

Assumptions Underlying Marriage Counseling

Ben N. Ard, Jr.

Any growing science or profession, if it is to make sound progress, needs to question its basic assumptions and make them explicit rather than implicit. Assumptions influence procedures, techniques, methods, and ultimate goals, and for these reasons need to be brought out into the open and carefully scrutinized. This paper is offered as a preliminary discussion which the writer hopes will stimulate the thinking of anyone interested in this field.

There are several assumptions which can be seen as underlying marriage counseling. But before presenting some of them, it may clarify matters somewhat to state specifically just what marital maladjustment is understood to be in this context.

In the first place, marital maladjustment is frequently, but not necessarily always, one form of psychological maladjustment. Psychological maladjustment may be said to exist when the client denies to awareness various significant experiences or feelings, which consequently are not recognized and organized into his concept of himself, i.e., the gestalt of the self-structure (Rogers, 1951, p. 510). Potential guilt, tension, and/or anxiety arises from such a situation.

Healthy psychological adjustment may be said to exist, in these terms, when the concept of self is such that all the significant experiences and feelings of the client are, or may be, assimilated on a symbolic level into a consistent relationship with the concept of self (Rogers, 1951, p. 513). This psychological health or maturity, which is the framework within which the counselor sees the client, can be objectively determined, according to Erich Fromm. He says, "Man's main task in life is to give birth to himself, to become what he potentially is. The most important product of his effort is his own personality. One can judge objectively to what extent the person has succeeded in his task, to what degree he has realized his potentialities [Fromm, 1947, p. 237]." In other words, "A judgment that a person is destructive, greedy, jealous, envious is not different from a

Reprinted with the permission of the author and the publisher from *Marriage Counseling Quarterly*, 1967, 2, 20–24.

physician's statement about a dysfunction of the heart or the lungs [Fromm, 1947, p. 236]."

If marital maladjustment brings the client to the marriage counselor, with what assumptions does the counselor enter into marriage counseling?

1. *Anxiety, tension, guilt feelings, or concern over the relationship is the* immediate *driving force that motivates clients to seek marriage counseling.* A subsidiary assumption here is that where such anxiety or tension is not sufficient to cause clients much difficulty or worry, they are not at that time ready to move into and through marriage counseling or psychotherapy of any kind.

Where this tension or anxiety is sufficient to motivate the client, it causes him to bring into consciousness (i.e., become aware of) more and more of his significant experiences and feelings. Once they are conscious, the concept of self is expanded so that they may be included as a part of a consistent, total self-concept.

2. *Marital maladjustments and problems can be alleviated or worked through by using certain specific methods, knowledge, and techniques.* This would seem to be the fundamental assumption under which marriage counseling as such has developed as a psychological service which may be distinguished from other psychological services such as psychiatry, casework, and various forms of psychotherapy (Ard, 1955; Cuber, 1948; Karpf, 1951; Mudd, 1951; Mudd & Preston, 1950).

3. *Most, but not all, of the ways of behaving which are adopted by the client are those which are consistent with his concept of self.* Lecky (1945) and Rogers (1951) have developed the ideas related to this concept, which seems helpful and necessary if we are to understand and explain much of the psychological behavior of clients.

4. *There is a* reality *which is different from distorted perceptions as illusions, hallucinations, delusions, projection, fantasy, etc.* A clear (i.e., objective) perception of reality cannot, of course, be gained by anyone if he has psychological blinders on. However, given proper conditions, better perceptions of reality are possible, at least in some cases.

This concept is necessary for any understanding of psychological illness. Freud has pointed this out (1924, Volume II, pp. 277—82). Erich Fromm (1947) states that "the person who has lost the capacity to perceive actuality is insane [p. 89]." In other words, "when a person sees objects which do not exist in reality but are entirely the product of his imagination, he has hallucinations; he interprets events in terms of his own feelings, without reference to, or at least without proper acknowledgement of, what goes on in reality [p. 89] . . . . The insane person is incapable of seeing reality as it is; he perceives reality only as a symbol and a reflection of his inner world [p. 90]."

Maslow (1950), in his study of psychologically healthy people, found that one characteristic common to these self-actualizing people was a more efficient perception of reality. In other words, the neurotic is not only emotionally sick—he is cognitively *wrong.* The importance of this finding can hardly be overestimated. As Maslow has pointed out, if health and neurosis are respectively correct and incorrect perceptions of reality, propositions of fact and propositions of value merge in this area; and in principle, value propositions should then be empirically demonstrable rather than merely matters of taste or exhortation. For those who have wrestled with this problem, it will be clear that we may have here a partial basis for a true science of values, and consequently of ethics, social relations, etc.

5. *It is one of the aims of marriage counseling (or psychotherapy in general) to help the client perceive reality more accurately.* That is, the aim is to strive for a high degree of correspondence between perception and reality. The psychologically healthy people studied by Maslow (1950) were far more apt to see what is "there," rather than their own wishes, hopes, fears, anxieties, their own theories and beliefs, or those of their cultural group.

This fifth concept implies a subsidiary assumption, namely that conscious acceptance of impulses, feelings, and perceptions greatly increases the possibility of conscious control, thus enabling more adequate (i.e., intelligent) behavior.

6. *The client has the capacity, in most instances, to resolve his own conflicts, given certain circumstances (i.e., in this instance, good therapeutic conditions).* Good therapeutic conditions means here, the helpful atmosphere which obtains in the good marriage counseling relationship.

7. *Through procedures and techniques used in marriage counseling, which establishes a good therapeutic atmosphere, the client is encouraged to communicate (i.e., verbalize) his feelings and experiences, and will thereby gradually bring more and more of his significant feelings and experiences into the realm of awareness.*

In this regard it may be said that there is no sharp, clear dividing line between marriage counseling and psychotherapy. Marriage counseling shades into depth therapy in imperceptible degrees. Marriage counseling may include certain aspects or methods which are different from those seen in various kinds of psychotherapy (e.g., psychoanalysis and client-centered therapy), but marriage counseling also includes techniques and procedures which both these and other "schools" consider psychotherapy.

8. *There is a drive or tendency toward psychological health in most clients.* In other words, the organism has a basic tendency or striving to actualize (and therefore enhance) itself. In the majority of clients, the forward direction of growth is more powerful than the neurotic satisfactions of remaining immature and infantile. This drive moves the client in the direction of greater independence, self-responsibility, and autonomy (i.e., having all experiences available to consciousness). The client thus moves toward an increasing integration.

The best definition of what constitutes integration appears to be this statement that all the significant experiences and feelings are admissible to awareness through accurate symbolization, and organizable into one system which is internally consistent and which is, or is related to, the structure of the self (Rogers, 1951, pp. 513—14). The more that significant experiences and feelings are denied symbolization (i.e., awareness), or are given a distorted symbolization, the greater the likelihood that any new experience will be perceived as threatening, since there is a larger false structure to be maintained.

It is assumed, of course, that it is better to be mature than immature, psychologically healthy than unhealthy, spontaneous than rigid, relaxed than tense, etc. The client who satisfactorily completes marriage counseling (or psychotherapy) is more relaxed in being himself, more sure of himself, more realistic in his relationships. It is assumed that this is a good thing.

If the client is given the opportunity for a clear-cut choice between forward-moving and regressive behavior, this growth tendency will operate in most cases. This is why the counselor must help the client perceive accurately *all* the relevant factors in the situation. Unless experiences are adequately symbolized (i.e., verbalized), unless sufficiently accurate differentiations are made, the client may mistake regressive behavior for self-enhancing mature behavior.

These objectively derived standards for judging behavior in terms of psychological health come from the studies made by such men as Maslow (1950) and Fromm (1947). As the self-correcting science of human nature (psychology) gains better understanding of what mental health and psychological maturity are, we will have these qualities operationally defined.

9. *The optimal development of the individual's potentialities is the ultimate goal of marriage counseling.* From this statement it is obvious that marriage counseling cannot be interested in maintaining a marriage at all costs. This assumes by implication that divorce is sometimes a good thing. Fromm (1947) and Maslow (1950) have given the best descriptions of what we mean by the optimal development of the individual's potentialities.

10. *Marriage counseling is a good (i.e., worthwhile, helpful) thing.* All marriage counselors, it would seem, must make this assumption or they would not continue to offer the service.

All the above assumptions are interrelated. This is shown, for example, by the general tendency for clients to move in the direction of maturity *when the factors in the situation are clear*. This shows the function and necessity of the fourth assumption, regarding perceiving reality accurately. After the counselor has helped the client perceive reality more accurately, he relies on this tendency toward growth to move the client in the direction of maturity, mental health, psychological health, and well-being.

As the client perceives and accepts into his self-structure more of his significant feelings and experiences, he finds that he is replacing his previous value system, which was based so largely on introjections which have been distorted in their original perception and symbolization. These old values, based on distorted perceptions of reality, are replaced by new values, which are accepted because they are perceived as principles making for the self-actualization and enhancement of the person.

The greatest values for the enhancement of the person accrue when all experiences and all attitudes are permitted conscious symbolization, and when behavior becomes the meaningful and balanced satisfaction of *all* basic needs (these needs being available to consciousness). In other words, following marriage counseling (or psychotherapy), the individual is formulating his evaluations of experience on the basis of all the relevant data.

REFERENCES

Ard, B. N., Jr. Sex knowledge for the marriage counselor. *Merrill-Palmer Quarterly*, Winter 1955 *1*, 74–82.

Cuber, J. F. *Marriage counseling practice*. New York: Appleton-Century-Croft, 1948.

Freud, S. The loss of reality in neurosis and psychosis. *Collected Papers*. Vol. II. London: Hogarth Press, 1924. Pp. 277–282.

Fromm, E. *Man for himself*. New York: Rinehart, 1947.

Karpf, M. J. Some guiding principles in marriage counseling. *Marriage and Family Living*, Spring 1951. *13*, 49–51, 55.

Lecky, P. *Self-consistency: A theory of personality*. New York: Island Press, 1945.

Maslow, A. H. Self-actualizing people: A study of psychological health. *In* W. Wolff (Ed.), *Personality symposium No. 1*. New York: Grune & Stratton, 1950. Pp. 11-34

Mudd, E. H. *The practice of marriage counseling*. New York: Association Press, 1951.

Mudd, E. H. & Preston, M. G. The contemporary status of marriage counseling. *The Annals of the American Academy of Political and Social Science*, November 1950. *272*, 102–109.

Rogers, C. R. *Client-centered therapy*. Boston: Houghton Mifflin, 1951.

SECTION II

The Place of Philosophy and Values in Marriage Counseling

The first principle of sex education and marriage counseling gives attitudes precedence over anatomies.

ROBERT L. DICKINSON

In the quotation introducing this section, one of the early leaders in the field, Robert L. Dickinson, gives precedence to *attitudes* over anatomies, in both sex education and marriage counseling. This points up the need of carefully examining the place of "philosophy" and "values" in the profession of marriage counseling. Therefore, this section includes a wide variety of points of view regarding philosophy and values toward marriage, family living, love, sex, the "new morality," old and newer conceptions of conscience and superego, and even includes the "*Playboy* philosophy."

Marsh and Humphrey, in Chapter 3, discuss the question: What is the character of the boundaries within which "successful marital adjustment" occurs? Middle-class conventions seem to these authors to be the boundaries. Is conformity to middle-class conventions really the goal toward which marriage counselors should work? Are marriage counselors just trying to build more WASPs (people with conventional, middle-class, white, Anglo-Saxon, Protestant values)? Marsh and Humphrey raise the very basic question: how can marriage counseling (which is supposed to be an application of scientific principles, in addition to being an art) properly function when its major orientation is toward the mores of the conventional institutional family? Is middle-class morality the truly appropriate point of departure for all "marriage problem phenomena"? Does the baseline from which "success" in marriage is determined need to be that of middle-class morality and conventionality?

Chapter 4, by John Hudson, discusses value issues in marital counseling from at least four points of view: (a) the field of marriage counseling; (b) the definition of a marriage counselor; (c) the orientation of training of the marriage counselor; and (d) specific problems in the field of marriage counseling. Among the issues Hudson raises are: Should the marriage counselor limit himself to those marriage problems which are principally of a conscious or situational nature, or should he deal with problems involving personality disturbances and emotional conflicts which may involve the unconscious? Should marriage counseling have as one of its

23

central values "adjustment"? Should the marriage counselor ever recommend divorce?

Stewart Bedford discusses the "new morality" and marriage counseling in Chapter 5. How can a marriage counselor help individuals and couples make decisions regarding moral issues when the very term "moral" seems to be in a state of flux? Bedford takes the position that the marriage counselor needs to develop a framework for understanding (with the goal of accepting) the variations in moral codes that he is likely to encounter among his clientele. Perhaps most professionals would agree with the need for "understanding," but some might question the value of "accepting" all variations in moral codes. Bedford also discusses a value dilemma in a case involving artificial insemination.

In Chapter 6, Robert A. Harper looks critically at some of the general issues of morality in marriage counseling, particular expressions of which are encountered in actual counseling circumstances. The three broad areas of moral issues are divorce, parenthood, and sex. The reader will have to resolve for himself whether or not he agrees with Harper that the basic moral issue in marriage counseling is to help clients free themselves from a stagnant and unrealistic morality which blocks progress in love. Dr. Harper also makes some very important distinctions in this chapter between what is *moral, nonmoral, immoral, unmoral,* and *amoral,* and suggests that the marriage counselor should be *nonmoral.*

In Chapter 7, we have a presentation of a philosophy that has been very influential among many members of the younger generation (particularly among the college educated), namely the *Playboy* philosophy as espoused by Hugh Hefner, editor and publisher of *Playboy* magazine. Young people today are developing new ideas toward themselves, marriage, sex, and man-woman relations in general. These excerpts from the *Playboy* philosophy are a frank statement of a different point of view which underlies many people's beliefs about these matters. If certain young people are developing new philosophies, marriage counselors need to know about them.

In Chapter 8, Ben N. Ard, Jr. surveys all the possible stances the professional marriage and family counselor may take with regard to guilt in clients and specifically what the counselor can do about value decisions made traditionally by the conscience or superego. These are some of the knottiest problems a professional counselor can face and traditionally many counselors have tried to avoid facing these issues. Some readers may not like some of the suggestions made in this chapter but are urged to seriously consider better ways of making ethical or moral decisions and the question of what the counselor's responsibility is in helping clients to make better decisions—decisions which are less self-defeating.

CHAPTER 3

Value Congeries and
Marriage Counseling

Donald Chard Marsh and Norman D. Humphrey

What is the character of the boundaries within which "successful marital adjustment" occurs? The major underlying assumption of the typical marriage counselor appears to be that the best that can be done for a person "in trouble" is to aid him to be better able to bear the restrictions which middle-class society and culture impose upon him. The boundaries, in short, appear to be middle-class conventions, and success in marriage consists of conformity to them.

This also seems to be the verdict indicated by "objective research." Norman S. Hayner (1948) has derived a number of tentative conclusions drawn from the literature of marriage research. He indicates, among other things, that the longer the period of acquaintance, the better are the chances for a happy marriage. Companionship is a better basis for a stable relationship than romantic love; emotional maturity, rather than chronological age. Certain specific personality characteristics are associated with happiness in marriage. Optimists, those who are not dominant, those who are neither neurotic nor self-sufficient, and the like, are types that make good marriage partners. For happiness in marriage, personality needs should gear into each other. But dissimilarity of customs, religious background, and the like increase the risk of marital failure. While marriage problems center in the dynamic areas of sex, sex itself is secondary in import to personality factors in determining success of marriages. Occupations with small personal mobility and large impingements of social control are favorably associated with happiness in marriage. If both parents love their children, they provide a basis of emotional security for the children and for themselves.

From one perspective such materials would seem to add up to the fact that conformity to positive values of the middle class, to middle-class virtue, makes for happiness, or success, in marriage. But what of psychological factors? The literature also abounds in statements that cases of marital maladjustment can usually be traced to such factors as "emotional

Reprinted with permission of the authors and the publisher from *Journal of Marriage and the Family*, 1953, *15*, 28–34.

immaturity" on the part of one or both of the partners. The basic cause of such immaturity is felt to lie primarily in the person, who sometimes is also regarded as the consequence of the impress of his own parents' immaturity upon him. Psychological factors are thus often regarded as primary and causal. But, from another view, the "maladjustment" is manifestly relevant to certain cultural norms which are rarely questioned, let alone highlighted in the equation. Such an arrangement of conceptions is of questionable validity, for it makes the psychological factors primary, and themselves productive of states of tension, when by another construction, it is the cultural standard (normally, middle-class Protestant American morality, and more especially, virtue), which is the prime productive agent; and the so-called unhappiness and maladjustment, the psychological components, the actual consequence. As Jeurgen Ruesch, a psychiatrist, has noted, middle-class American culture is the "core culture":

> The American culture . . . can be described as that culture which is represented by the lower middle class, composed of people of Anglo-Saxon descent and of Protestant religion. It is the core culture . . . [which] set the cultural standards for the . . . country. All . . . immigrants were compelled to adapt to these standards. Public opinion in America is largely an expression of this core culture. We find it in novels, on the radio, in newspapers, public speeches and in the opinion of the man on the street [1948, pp. 126–127].

Certainly Mexican family organization, for example, and the culture it maintains, elicits different bases for "happiness" and "maladjustment" than those found in the United States. The question of the boundaries of successful marital adjustment devolves then, in part, into what is properly the independent, and what the dependent, variable: psychological make-up or cultural standard.

Yet, almost all of the adjustment-in-marriage studies, including those predicting adjustment, show relationships between what, in effect, is adherence to conventional standards of the middle class, and so-called success in marriage. Indeed, it would be very surprising if conventional middle-class persons, who were "well-adjusted," did not find themselves (or were not rated by friends) as correspondingly happy in their conventionalized states. To be unhappy would be to be "out-of-role," and the whole conditioning process would have gone for nought. But how adequate a criterion, except of conventionality, is a statement of happiness? As Erich Fromm (1949) has indicated: "What, for instance, do we know about the happiness of people in our culture? True enough, many people would answer in a public opinion poll that they were happy because that is what a self-respecting citizen is supposed to feel [p. 9]."

"Happiness" continues to be employed, however, as the criterion of success in marriage prediction, and as the major goal of the marriage counselor and client. To be sure, some criterion of success is necessary. But a criterion which would escape the endless circle of conventionality might be preferable and more useful. Much of the marriage prediction material appears to be measuring, scaling, and correlating several aspects

of the same phenomenon. A piece of middle-class conventionality is correlated with a part of adherence to the same morality; in effect with itself.

Emotional maturity (which is popularly indexed by the control of
affect, in such forms as not exhibiting temper, inhibiting jealousy without
manifest "projection," and the like) is also correlated with success in
marriage. But what passes for "emotional maturity" is often simply adult
middle-class moral excellence. A highly conventional middle-class person
possesses much middle-class virtue. Hence "becoming mature" and being
indoctrinated with middle-class morality, as they are utilized in the literature, are virtually the same thing. As Ruesch (1948) notes, "In the lower
class, where expression of anger is permitted, and where non-conformance
and rebellion are sanctioned by class ideals, there exist other means of
expressing conflicts [than by physical symptom formation] [p. 124]."

Kingsley Davis (1938) has long since demonstrated some of the relationships between the mental hygiene movement and the class structure.
C. Wright Mills (1943) has noted that the professional ideology of the
social pathologists stems in part from their social origins and the values of
their collective middle-class mentalities. Norton Springer (1938) indicates
that middle-class children tend to be better adjusted emotionally than
children on lower rungs of the status scale. Springer found that children
who come from middle-class families make more satisfactory behavior
adjustments than those who derive from a poor general social level. The
latter indicate more maladjustment and undesirable personal characteristics. He feels that emotional stability is closely related to the general social
status of the individual.

One may raise the question as to whether measures of emotional
stability, like measures of happiness in marriage, do not, at the same time,
largely measure middle-class morality, rather than scientific findings of an
objective character. Because of the widespread use by marriage counselors
of the findings of "objective studies," some of their assumptions and the
implications for theory and for practice must be examined.

The change which has been underway for the past fifty years in American family culture (from the Burgess perspective as distinguished from
Sorokin-Zimmerman viewpoint) has been that generally characterized as
the movement from an institutionalized form to one understandable in
terms of the central theme of companionship. While the stability of the
companionship type of relationship depends upon strong interpersonal
relations, the stability of the conventional type of family depended upon
such things as gossip, mores, public opinion, and the like. Granted that
there are still institutional aspects to the companionship type, and that
there were companionship elements in the institutional family, it is nonetheless useful to treat the two types more or less as opposites. Most family
counseling today, however, appears to be pointed toward the conventional
family rather than toward the companionship relationship, and counseling
invokes sanction from "objective" materials bearing on that somewhat
anachronistic organization.

This situation gives rise to the question as to how a marriage counselor can deal with a problem situation deriving from conflicts in the area of strong interpersonal relations. In short, while counseling is supposed to be an application of scientific principles, in addition to being an art, how can it properly function when its major orientation is toward the mores of the conventional institutional family? There is certainly a basic unreality in regarding idealized middle-class morality as the truly appropriate point of departure for all marriage problem phenomena, even though such conventionality may be bolstered by findings of so-called objective studies.

Persons in trouble normally need some other standard imposed upon them than that which has been largely responsible for their "problem situation." It is almost notorious knowledge that relief for the guilt-ridden alcoholic cannot derive from his knowledge of the actuarial tables on the "vice" of alcoholism, or from moral invocation to reform.

Under these circumstances what sort of "definition of the situation" (Volkart, 1951) is appropriate to the marriage counselor? The research investigator, and consequently the marriage counselor, has in large degree come to the point where he is faced with the fact that success-in-marriage is what success-in-marriage predictions predict. While this position may be tenable "operationally," it is manifestly untenable from anything but a naive operational viewpoint. Such a question also requires something more than the trite answer that the situation must be defined on a "case-to-case basis." The definition of the situation has significance not only for marriage counseling, but also for American social science. For implicitly the counselor's definition of the situation also concerns itself with whether social scientific marriage prediction and analysis deal even with the American sociocultural whole, or whether they are to limit their generalizations only to the plane of reference of the idealized morality of a single status grouping, which findings in turn it imposes on the totality of its materials.

Does the baseline from which "success" in marriage is determined need to be that of middle-class morality and conventionality? Even within the American status structure there are other bases from which the data of the marriage counselors' "generalized other" may be drawn. (This extension of the term "generalized other" derives from the discussion in Mead, 1934.) The family, for that matter even the *good* family, might conceivably be something quite different from the middle-class conventional family.

Many persons in our society basically and ordinarily identify with "unconventional" subcultures. To be sure, some of these subcultures move in the direction of fulfilling personal sense satisfactions, rather than developing stable social relations. Other "deviant" relationships become quite stable. But it is with just such problems that the marriage counselor frequently must deal. The actuarial materials on happiness in these areas today do not exist.

A social segment in every metropolitan area, for example, works in downtown offices and shops and tends to find its sex partners, and to evolve stable social relationships, through association developed in downtown bars. How significant are factors such as residential propinquity or church attendance for success in the companionship type of marriage derived from these groupings? Such persons, participating as they do in a greater variety of subcultures than conventional middle-class persons, appear to be capable of much "multivalence." They consequently are able to emphasize one tradition and its dominant values in one circumstance, and a quite contrary tradition in another, without notable inner conflict, and with the several sets of values quite real and significant for adjustment to stable sex roles. Were the marriage counselor to define this situation with the criteria of middle-class conventionality in judging problems and probabilities for success in such unions, he would tend to do scientific violence to an equivalent reality. It would, however, be analogous to the case workers doing relief work early in the Depression, who asked themselves what there was in clients' psychological make-ups which prevented them from getting employment.

The instruments developed for the actuarial prediction of success in marriage never take into account such common phenomena in American married life as the "phantom lover." The phantom lover performs all sorts of services, including the sex act, in such fashion that amazing "happiness" accrues to some women, and he is rarely matched by, unless he is imaginatively combined with, his "surrogate," the actual husband. Middle-class morality does not countenance the existence of such a fantasy. It therefore never finds its way into the instrument from which predictive tables are derived. In view of the tendency toward homogamy in actual unions, and the tables indicating improbability for success the greater the discrepancy in cultural and religious background of mates, it would be interesting to determine the extent to which phantom lovers are of other ethnic and religious backgrounds.

The problem faced by the marriage counselor is thus, from a scientific viewpoint, at least twofold. The marriage bond and family relationship may not always be adequately defined in terms of what *ought to be* from the viewpoint of middle-class conventionality. And the counselor has little of an actuarial sort to guide him for other forms of relationship. He may even lack scepticism of the utility of his own values, which a knowledge of cultural relativity potentially could give him.

Under the circumstances how much "scientific" education for marriage is feasible? As Willard Waller (1951) said some years ago, "Various 'educational' programs have been devised in order to promote better family life. Many such programs are definitely harmful, since their effect is merely to strengthen the existing mores and to accentuate the conflicts of persons unable to live within the mores. . . . Where such educational programs are based upon the scientific study of the family, and the possibility of changing mores instead of conforming the individual to them is not excluded, they may be helpful [pp. 600–601]."

Programs of education for marriage, and marriage counseling as a field, obviously need now to recognize, as social case work in part has come to recognize in the past ten years, that something other than the standards of middle-class conventionality may be imposed on clients and students, and that success in marriage will have to be defined in terms of the several cultural traditions of the persons addressed. The areas of the "generalized other" must be examined until the most usual and tolerable locus of the person is determined.

Without a broad exploration of the anthropological literature bearing on the variety of fulfillments of personality needs, at least the lesson of Freud's rather obvious dictum, that the illicit sex relationship of the lower-class girl living on the ground floor of the Vienna apartment house will have quite different significance for her than the equivalent experience of her middle-class counterpart on the second story, must be taken into account. Cultural tradition molds sex roles and marital difficulties and, for that matter, marital counseling. But marital counseling potentially could escape it.

REFERENCES

Burgess, E. W., & Cottrell, L. S. The prediction of adjustment in marriage. *American Sociological Review*, 1936, *1*, 737–751.

Christensen, H. T. Family size as a factor in the marital adjustment of college couples. *American Sociological Review*, 1952, *17*, 306–312.

Davis, K. Mental hygiene and the class structure. *Psychiatry* 1938, *1*, 63.

Fromm, E. Psychoanalytic characterology and its application to the understanding of culture. *In* S. Stansfeld Sargent & Marian W. Smith (Eds.), *Culture and personality*. New York: The Viking Fund, 1949.

Hayner, N. S. The sociologist views mariage problems. *Sociology and Social Research* 1948, *33*, 20–24.

Mead, G. H. *Mind, self and society*. Pp. 154ff. Ed. by C. W. Morris. Chicago: University of Chicago Press, 1934.

Mills, C. W. The professional ideology of social pathologists. *American Journal of Sociology* 1943, *49*, 165–180.

Ruesch, J. Social technique, social status and social change in illness. *In* C. Kluckhohn & H. A. Murray (Ed.) *Personality in nature, society and culture*. New York: Alfred A. Knopf, 1948. Pp. 126–127.

Springer, N. Influence of general social status on the emotional stability of children. *Journal of Genetic Psychology*, 1938, *53*, 321–327.

Volkart, E. (Ed.) *Social behavior and personality: Contributions of W. I. Thomas to theory and social research*. New York: Social Science Research Council, 1951.

Waller, W. *The family: A dynamic interpretation*. Rev. by Reuben Hill. New York: Dryden Press, 1951.

CHAPTER 4

Value Issues in Marital Counseling

John W. Hudson

A consideration of the value issues in the field of marriage counseling must include looking at the problem from at least four points of view: (*a*) the field of marriage counseling; (*b*) the definition of a marriage counselor; (*c*) the orientation and training of the marriage counselor; (*d*) specific problems in the field of marriage counseling. In this chapter I will attempt to deal with each of these areas and some of their value implications in some detail, with the hope of raising questions which will encourage further inquiry by the reader.

The forces which converged to bring about the formalization of the field of marriage counseling included: (*a*) the marriage education movement, with its emphasis on getting to know the prospective marital partner and understanding the personality factors necessary for marital success; (*b*) the sex education movement and the research in animal and human sexual behavior; (*c*) the increased complexity of modern, urban living. Many individuals, including teachers, ministers and physicians, had been engaged in marriage counseling as the direct result of the requests of the groups with which they were working.

"A particularly important development in the field of marriage counseling in the United States was the organization in 1942 of the American Association of Marriage Counselors, the first national group to recognize marriage counseling as a distinct social and scientific discipline [Stone, 1957]." In its early years the American Association of Marriage Counselors met with the hope of meeting more effectively the needs of those seeking their help. Marriage counseling was viewed principally as a specialized field designated to deal with problems which were primarily on the conscious level. Cuber (2), in his article "Functions of the Marriage Counselor," lists the four functions of the marriage counselor as: (*a*) the advice-giving function (the giving of information, sometimes technical and sometimes lay); (*b*) the decisional function (assisting the client in making a decision); (*c*) the definitional function (if some act comes to be defined as "bad," "sinful," or "indecent," and then, somehow, one commits that act, he may acquire a serious maladjustment); (*d*) reorganization of be-

---

Reprinted with permission of the author and the publisher from H. L. Silverman (Ed.), *Marital Counseling*. Springfield, Ill.: Charles C Thomas, 1967. Pp. 164–176.

havior (this type of case frequently grows out of the preceding type and becomes possible only when the client has already partly defined the given behavior as wrong or inexpedient but cannot break the old "habit" by mere volition alone). Clark Vincent, commenting on Cuber's article, points out that the marriage counselor performing functions (*a*) and (*b*) would define marriage counseling in a manner different from the counselor performing primarily the function in the fourth category. Cuber set forth what was then, and continues to be, one of the major value and philosophical issues in the field of marriage counseling—the value issue concerning whether the marriage counselor should limit himself to those marriage problems which are principally of a conscious or situational nature or whether he will deal with problems involving personality disturbances and emotional conflicts which may involve the unconscious. The lines here are fairly well delineated. They seem to arise from whether a marriage counselor can be effective in many of the situations with which he is confronted without going into what has historically been the province of the psychologist and psychiatrist. Marriage counselors themselves are divided on this question. Each side has its vociferous spokesmen.

Laidlaw (1957), then chief of psychiatry at Roosevelt Hospital, New York, and past president of the American Association of Marriage Counselors, gave his point of view at the 1949 meeting of the American Psychiatric Association:

> Marriage counseling is a form of short-term psychotherapy dealing with inter-personal relationships, in which problems relating to marriage are the central factor . . . it is an approach carried out essentially at a conscious level. . . . If, as therapy progresses, unconscious factors are discovered which necessitate long and involved psychotherapeutic techniques, the case ceases to be in the field of marriage counseling.

Foster (1950), formerly director of the marriage counseling service and training program, Department of Social Applications, the Menninger Foundation, stated in 1950: "Marriage counseling is primarily and essentially an educational job."

The New York Academy of Sciences, recognizing the need for clarification of the fields of psychotherapy and counseling, established five commissions to explore the subject. The following statement is relevant here:

> We can express the difference in emphasis, then, by saying that counseling looks more often toward the interpretation and development of the personality in the relations characteristic of specific role-problems while psychotherapy looks more often toward the reinterpretation and reorganization of malignant conflictual elements within the personality through the relation with the therapist [Perry, 1955].

As recently as 1957, marriage counseling was placed by Mace in the general category of one of "the services which help the individual, at the conscious level, to achieve a better understanding of himself and of his destiny. This broad category includes all functionally directed education—teaching, preaching, and propaganda. It also includes all counseling in the generally understood meaning of the word."

In *Marriage Counseling: A Casebook*, edited for the American Association of Marriage Counselors, the authors state:

> The marriage counselor can best make his important contribution by equipping himself to function not as a pseudo-psychiatrist or analyst, but as one who has made a special study of the problems and interpersonal relationships of family life: the bonds, loyalties, and conflicts; the loves, rivalries, and hostilities; the need for identification and dependence, on the one hand, and the conflicting desire for independence, on the other; the wish for security and the urge for adventure; in brief, the stresses and strains involved in membership in a marriage and a family, and the psychosocial factors and influences of such membership on the personality [pp. 40–41].

The authors of the *Casebook* define marriage counseling:

> Marriage Counseling may be defined as the process through which a professionally trained counselor assists a person or persons to resolve the problems that trouble them in their interpersonal relationships. The focus is on the relationship between the two persons in marriage, rather than, as in psychiatric therapy, the reorganization of the personality structure of the individual.

Throughout the literature there are also individuals who point out: (a) that marriage counseling is a form of psychotherapy; (b) that the effective marriage counselor needs to be able to recognize and differentiate between psychotic and neurotic problems; (c) that many of the difficulties within marriages are the result of personality conflicts within or between marriage partners; (d) that the marriage counselor will be dealing with problems of the unconscious as well as the conscious, and at times will be involved in efforts at basic personality reorganization. Spokesmen for the marriage counselor's functioning as a psychotherapist have become more outspoken as the profession has developed.

Stokes (1959), psychiatrist and marriage counselor, in his discussion of an article entitled "The Orientation and Focus of Marriage Counseling," states:

> Marriage counseling is a form of individual psychotherapy in which there is a special concern with the ways in which marriage partners interact with each other. . . . Although I deeply believe in marriage counseling as a worthy and needed profession, I would reject the idea that my primary interest is really counseling in marriage. It so happens that marriage is the chief proving-ground of emotional maturity, as well as the arena in which the parent-child relationship so critically affects the emotional development of human beings. Therefore it is in marriage that the symptoms of emotional immaturity and neurosis most strikingly appear. . . . Thus I see the marriage counselor of the future as primarily a student of the human life cycle, with emphasis upon its emotional aspects. He will be a therapist concerned with the application of his knowledge to all members of the family, at every age [p. 25].

Rutledge (1963), director of marriage counseling and psychotherapy training at the Merrill-Palmer Institute and former president of the American Association of Marriage Counselors, has long been a champion of the idea that marriage counseling represents the most advanced and highly technical form of all psychotherapies. Commenting in *Marriage and Family Living*, Rutledge says:

> It is deceptive to believe that the marriage counselor does not deal with the unconscious just because he does not intend to. Clients bring themselves, including their unconscious motivation, to the counseling hour, whether they come for personal problems or because of marital difficulties. This certainly means the counselor should have a basic understanding of, and be able to recognize, evidences of the unconscious in the daily married life and in the counseling session [p.28].

Whitlock (1961), in a discussion of "The Use of Dreams in Premarital Counseling" went a step further in his opinion of the counselor's dealing with the unconscious:

> (1) The use of dreams in counseling and therapeutic contacts is a legitimate function for many specialists in human behavior, not just for the psychiatrist or psychoanalyst, as has often been claimed. (2) This automatically underlines the fact that, whether or not they know it, all counselors are dealing with unconscious material [p. 260].

Ellis (1962), in his discussion of the use of rational-emotive psychotherapy as a technique for use in marriage counseling, states:

> Very possibly, most of these troubled individuals should come for intensive psychotherapy rather than for "counseling," but the fact is that they do not. It therefore behooves the counselor, and especially the marriage counselor, to be enough of a trained and experienced therapist to be able to deal adequately with the individuals who come to him for help . . .

Albert (1963), in his article in *Marriage and Family Living*, adds a significant note in his conclusions:

> But it does appear highly worthwhile to urge that universities and other training centers require that marriage counselors-in-training receive a thorough grounding in motivation, personality development, abnormal psychology and diagnostics, as well as a working knowledge of psychoanalytic theory (including, perhaps, not only Freudian concepts but also such more recent approaches as those of Sullivan, Reich, Rogers and the Neo-Behaviorists). This would be in addition to courses in the specific area of marriage counseling, and such other relevant subjects as family dynamics and the sociology of the family.

Obviously, a marriage counselor with the type of training that Albert is recommending is not going to limit himself to advice-giving and dealing with only conscious, reality-oriented problems. The philosophical and value question of the role of the marriage counselor is at present unclear. The field of marriage counseling and its practitioners are faced with the value question of whether marriage counseling is to remain primarily an educational, advice-giving, reality-oriented service for "normal" people or whether it is to be a profession of highly trained, competent therapists prepared to deal with a wide variety of marriage problems, including those which have their roots in individual personality disturbances.

Marriage counseling from its inception has been a multidisciplinary profession. Among others, the disciplines have included psychology, sociology, medicine, social work, law, and religion. Each profession has been adamant in insisting upon the importance of its own special contribution to the field of marriage counseling. We find the psychologist frequently emphasizing psychological factors; the physician emphasizing physiological factors; the minister, spiritual factors; the sociologist, cultural factors; etc. Although specialized internships and training in marriage counseling may reduce these tendencies, it is usually not difficult to spot the principal theoretical bias of the marriage counselor. Undoubtedly, one of the major factors which contributes to a counselor's theoretical bias is the lack of a systematic theoretical structure for marriage counseling.

Related to the theoretical bias of the counselor are the methods and techniques of counseling and psychotherapy that he employs. We find individual marriage counselors who are identified with the Freudian approach, the Rogerian approach, Ellis's approach to psychotherapy, as well as with many others. Initially, most psychotherapeutic approaches were designed to be used in working with an individual client; consequently, they must be modified when applied to the interpersonal marital situation.

It is not the purpose of this chapter to analyze the underlying value assumptions of various theoretical approaches. It should be clear to the reader that a marriage counselor operating from a Freudian frame of reference, with its emphasis on instincts, drives, repressions, and unconscious conflicts, is going to reflect a different set of values than the therapist who operates from a Rogerian point of view. Marriage counselors who utilize Rogers' system will turn more to their own thoughts and attitudes. Rogerians hold to the value that the thoughts and feelings the therapist has toward the client are the most crucial antecedents to effective therapist behavior. Rogerians assume that "if the therapist holds the 'right attitude,' if he has a fundamental faith in the patient, the appropriate statements and expressive gestures by the therapist will follow [Ford & Urban, 1963]." If the marriage counselor subscribes to the theoretical position of Ellis's rational-emotive therapy, he will take a more active and direct role than either of the counselors described in the preceding therapeutic approaches. It is clear that the choice of personality theory and the method and techniques for the marriage counselor are not based solely on an objective analysis. His choice reflects his own conscious and unconscious values and biases.

Most schools of psychotherapy agree that the ideal theoretical model describes the counselor as one who: (a) takes a serious interest in the client and gives him his undivided attention: (b) does not respond or react to either the client's affectionate or hostile feelings; (c) does not pass moral judgment; (d) maintains neutrality both affectively and intellectually; (e) keeps his own emotional life separate from that of the client's; and (f) keeps his own biases and predilections out of the counseling situation. Obviously, as all ideal models are theoretical, it is highly doubtful that any counselor can measure up to the foregoing list. There is also the question of whether the counselor who holds rigidly to these standards can be effective.

The marriage counselor is a product of his culture and, as such, reflects his own values in the counseling relationship (whether he is aware of it or not). It is important, for both theoretical and therapeutic reasons, for the marriage counselor to be cognizant of his values and how they operate in the therapy. If the marriage counselor risks revealing himself from behind the professional shroud of the passive, reflecting, nonjudgmental mummy, it is inevitable that he will express his values, attitudes, and opinions on a wide variety of subjects. This is particularly true when working with married couples, as the basis for much marital disharmony lies not only in the neurotic pattern of the individuals involved but in their philosophical and value conflicts. The philosophical and value conflicts of husbands and wives arise frequently from their different sociocultural backgrounds. The marriage counselor first must face the fact that he is a human being and, as such, holds values. Second, if he is going to be effective in his counseling, much of his therapy with couples is going to involve the exploration and discussion of values, including many of the therapist's. Third, the counselor will consciously or unconsciously communicate his own values, and it may as well be done openly. Fourth, the more open the counselor is regarding his own values, the freer and more spontaneous the counseling can be.

A factor which influences the value position of the marriage counselor is that marriage counseling has tended to be problem-oriented and has directed its attention principally to the resolution of conflict situations. Although it is not explicitly stated, it is clear from reading the literature in the field of marriage counseling that one of the central values is that of adjustment.

This concept is not unique to the field of marriage counseling, but is particularly significant for the marriage counselor because he is frequently working with two or more individuals. In many cases the marriage counselor cannot hold equally to the value of the integrity of both individuals where adjustment is the value. It makes a difference whether one is talking about adjustment in terms of the integration of self or adjustment in terms of the compromising of self for the value of others. The value of adjustment seems to have been adopted by many marriage counselors. Where adjustment means the acquisition of new knowledge or skills which will further facilitate the growth and development of an individual, it may be appropriate; but where adjustment means the compromising of self-values for the values of others for the sake of a marriage or family, the value is dubious.

Green (1946) states; "Therapists who advocate any specific type of adjustment are prone to sociological naivete. The institutional bases of their own specific values are shifting ground so rapidly in modern society that it is a rare combination of value and structure that is itself in adjustment." The conflict between self-values and the values of others is many times erroneously thought to be resolved by the marriage counselor by shifting the focusing of the counseling from the individual to the institution of marriage. Adjustment may become an end in itself without regard to the individual. The "well-adjusted" person is all too frequently seen as the individual who adapts himself to any situation, person, or marriage for the sake of avoiding personal or social disorganization. When the focus is shifted from individual values to the institutional values of marriage and family, it may implicitly or explicitly convey to the client that there is a value which transcends his personal wishes or desires. This may represent an unconscious rejection, on the part of the marriage counselor, of divorce as an acceptable solution to marital discord.

It is important for the marriage counselor to be aware of his position on the value issue of divorce. Much harm can be done to an individual by the counselor who insists that the only satisfactory solution to marital conflict is adjustment and reconciliation. He is apt to find himself in the position of contributing to far greater personal and family disorganization by his unrelenting value stand. An obvious case is the situation involving the married couple where one of the partners finds the marriage relationship to be no longer meaningful and wishes a divorce so that he can pursue his own personal interests. This picture may be further complicated where there are children. If the counselor is committed solely to the values of marriage and the family, he is apt to violate the integrity of the individual wishing to get out of the marriage, viewing his behavior as neurotic, disturbed, or immature.

Although the professional code of ethics of the American Association of Marriage Counselors does not state saving marriages as one of the goals of marriage counseling, the individual counselor may nevertheless find himself in this position, as the result of his own personal values or those which are imposed upon him by the agency for which he works or by the client who seeks his help. Because the marriage counselor is working within an interactional system—that is, the relationship between husband and wife, as well as other family members—he may be less able to disregard the effects of one individual's behavior on another.

One of the clearest statements of the value issue of divorce is made by Stokes in the February 1959, issue of *Marriage and Family Living*:

> I have small concern with the preservation of the marriage as such. My primary focus is upon the dignity and satisfactions of the individual spouses and only secondarily upon the sociological values associated with the marriage. I cannot conceive of accomplishing enduringly successful marriage counseling upon any other terms.
>
> I suspect that because marriage has been for so long entrenched as a religious sacrament, many marriage counselors still feel impelled to preserve marriage at any cost. . . . I often have a feeling that too much emphasis upon the sociological factors and values of marriage is just a rationalized hangover from the ancient mystical concept of marriage as an inviolable sacrament [p. 25].

Rutledge (1963), in his article, "Should the Marriage Counselor Ever Recommend Divorce?" says:

> If a marital diagnosis reveals that continued marriage of a couple not only promises nothing in the way of a healthy relationship but points to marked personality destruction for one or both, it is the marriage counselor's responsi-

bility to underline this prognosis. To be sure, one of the couple must make the decision to separate or not to separate, to divorce or not to divorce. But the counselor may be derelict in some cases unless he gives his professional opinion of the advisability of ending, with as little hurt as possible, a relationship that can bring only continued destruction of personality.

Barrier discusses Rutledge's article, quoting Section 14 of the proposed Code of Ethics of the American Association of Marriage Counselors which states:

> While the Marriage Counselor will feel satisfaction in the strengthening of a marriage, he should not feel obliged to urge that the married partners continue to live together at all costs. There are situations in which all resources fail, and in which continued living together may be severely damaging to one or several persons. In such event it is the duty of the Counselor to assess the facts as he sees them. However, the actual decision concerning separation or divorce is a responsibility that must be assumed by the client, and this should be made clear to him. If separation or divorce is decided upon, it is the continuing responsibility of the Counselor to give further support and counsel during a period of readjustment, if that appears to be wanted and needed, as it often is.

Barrier concludes her discussion of Rutledge's article with the statement: "It is not the role of the marriage counselor to recommend dissolution of the marriage [p. 325]."

In the thirteen years that I was affiliated with the Marriage Counseling Service and Psychotherapy Training Center of the Merrill-Palmer Institute, I was repeatedly struck with the infrequency with which divorce was recommended as a solution to an unsatisfactory marriage. With the system of courtship and mate selection that is used in our culture, it would seem that a certain percentage of individuals seeking the services of marriage counselors would be poorly mated and that, unless the counselor were committed solely to the values of adjustment or the sacredness of the marriage relationship, divorce would more frequently be recommended.

Related to the counselor's value system is the setting in which the counseling takes place, and this may influence the investment that the marriage counselor makes in the individual client. If he is in private practice, the selection of clients is more apt to be based on values reflecting his own financial welfare, professional status, prestige, and personal and therapeutic biases than if he operates in an agency setting where his salary is fixed. In an agency the size of his case load, the clients, and his preferences for particular types of marriage counseling problems may not be given consideration. The counselor working in an agency may find himself under more direct supervision, and his personal investment in his clients may not be as great. If the counseling is part-time and an adjunct to his primary responsibility, it will have an effect on the relationship between the marriage counselor and his client. The college teacher who does counseling as an outgrowth of his teaching is faced with different value issues than the minister who does counseling as part of his pastoral functions.

The teacher is frequently faced with the value dilemma of separating the roles of the critical evaluation and judgment of academic performance from the accepting, nonjudgmental role of counselor. The minister may find himself caught in a value dilemma arising out of theological precepts and religious convictions. When his theological precepts and religious convictions clash with the reality situations of his counselees, the minister may have to sacrifice either religious values or secular values.

Fees are one of the major value dilemmas for the marriage counselor. The problem of fee-setting is one which many counselors would prefer to avoid. In agencies it is frequently handled by administrative decision, but for the private practitioner there is no neat, ready-made solution. In discussions with many marriage counselors (both those working in an agency setting and those in private practice), I wonder at their inability to face this issue squarely. The amount of uncollected fees frequently equals the sum of a few years' annual collections. The counselor who has difficulty in setting and collecting his fees has many "valid" explanations. He may rationalize his failure to deal realistically with the issue on vague therapeutic grounds. He may set his fees low because of doubt about his own adequacy, or he may set his fees arbitrarily high on the sole assumption that if an individual is unwilling to pay a high fee, he is not sufficiently motivated to get help. There is little doubt that money has a variety of meanings to individuals, including marriage counselors, but it is an integral part of the counselor-client relationship and, as such, must be dealt with realistically. The arbitrary setting of fees without regard to the financial situation of the client, excessively large uncollected fees, refusal to see an individual at a reduced fee—all reflect value conflicts of the marriage counselor.

The sources of the marriage counselor's referrals pose value questions which cannot be dismissed casually. The marriage counselor may find himself being cast in the role of a clearing house for lawyers, courts, and physicians. He may find himself being used by other professional persons who are attempting to avoid their responsibility in helping their clients to face crucial issues. Under certain conditions referral to a marriage counselor may be a form of coercion. The coercion may be by a spouse, lawyer, physician, or other professional. Care must be taken by the counselor not to impose his value of counseling on the person. It is important to know the terms under which the client presents himself to prevent being caught in a power struggle. A value dilemma may arise if a client has been under some other therapist's care prior to his coming to his present counselor. If one uses the simple interpretation that this is a form of resistance or hostility on the part of the client toward his previous therapist, the value issue is resolved. It may be that the client is resistant or hostile, but there are other valid reasons for changing therapists. Among other valid reasons for changing therapists include: (a) inability to establish rapport with previous therapist; (b) fees of previous therapist prohibitive; (c) transportation to and from previous therapist inaccessible; (d) time of appointments inconvenient or not feasible for client; (e) previous therapist's theoretical and psychotherapeutic techniques unacceptable to client; and (f) incompetency of previous therapist. Care must be taken at all times to insure the rights of the client to choose his therapist.

Depending upon the particular state in the United States, or upon professional affiliations of the marriage counselor, he may or may not have privileged communication. The issue of privileged communication is being clarified for the marriage counselor in many states which have certification or licensing acts. Although this handles the technical problem, it does not handle certain value issues that arise in marriage counseling. Because of the unique position the marriage counselor occupies, he frequently becomes apprised of information which may seriously affect a marital relationship. In most situations he is committed to the confidentiality of interview material given by each spouse. Situations arise where he might be able to facilitate the relationship or help to avert unnecessary complications if he were to divulge information given in confidence. Where privileged communication does not exist, it is important to inform the client in order to avoid future complications or legal involvement.

SUMMARY

Part of the reason for the formation of the American Association of Marriage Counselors and for its rapid growth arose from one of the assumptions of analytic therapy which had generalized itself into almost all psychotherapies. The assumption is that effective therapy can take place only in those situations where the relationship between the therapist and the client is not encumbered or complicated by contacts with any other members of the client's family. This position has been carried to ridiculous lengths by some therapists, including the refusal to talk to or see any other member of the family, even when permission has been granted to the therapist by the client. Some of the pioneer marriage counselors recognized that the interaction of husbands and wives frequently brought about problems which could be resolved only by a therapeutic approach to the couple rather than to an individual.

In recent years there has been an increasing recognition on the part of marriage counselors that values are both implicitly and explicitly operative in the counseling relationship. The very notion of counseling implies a value system. The particular theoretical orientation of the practitioner carries with it certain value assumptions. The circumstances under which the therapy occurs may denote certain value considerations which are functioning for both therapist and client. The value issues with which marriage counselors are faced become increasingly complex when the therapy involves a married couple.

The value position of the marriage counselor is probably more complex than that of any other individuals working in the helping professions. This comes about partly as a result of: (a) confusion in the minds of the individuals seeking the services of the marriage counselor regarding the role of the marriage counselor; (b) the orientation or capacity in which the marriage counselor functions; (c) the particular theoretical framework of counseling to which the marriage counselor subscribes; and (d) the source of referral. One of the best methods a marriage counselor may employ in examining his own values is the careful questioning of the underlying assumptions he makes to support his diagnosis of the individuals he is seeing. Psychological jargon and diagnostic categories are all too frequently rationalizations for more fundamental personal values on the part of the counselor. Whenever a marriage counselor finds himself viewing all marital conflict as the result of immaturities, neurotic patterns, personality disorders, or psychopathology, he is probably deluding himself regarding his own objectivity and value positions. Marriage counseling has adapted the methods and techniques of individual psychotherapy and has principally relied on existing theories of personality development. As a consequence, the marriage counselor must frequently force the problems arising out of marital interaction into theoretical systems which were originally constructed to explain individual behavior. The methods and techniques of therapy which he employs are likewise those originally designed for application to individuals.

. With the implementation of standards of training and the establishment of training centers the professional marriage counselor is coming into his own.

Marriage counseling is evolving from an educational advice-giving, conscious, reality-oriented service to a scientific, highly specialized form of psychotherapy. The prestige of the profession is reflected in the increased number of individuals now referring to themselves as marriage counselors with psychological or sociological backgrounds, rather than as "psychologists or sociologists who do marriage counseling."

The further growth of the profession will hinge on the effectiveness with which we marriage counselors can deal with value issues, not only those of the client but, more importantly, our own.

REFERENCES

Albert, G. Advanced psychological training for marriage counselors—luxury or necessity? *Marriage and Family Living*, 1963, *25*, 181–184.

Cuber, J. F. Functions of the marriage counselor. *Journal of Marriage and Family Living*, 1945, *7*, 3–5.

Ehrlich, D. & Wiener, D. N. The measurement of values in psychotherapeutic settings. *Journal of General Psychology*, 1961, *64*,, 359–372.

Ellis, A. Reason and emotion in psychotherapy. New York: Lyle Stuart, 1962.

Ford, D. H. & Urban, H. B. *Systems of psychotherapy*. New York: Wiley, 1963.

Foster, R. G. Marriage counseling in a psychiatric setting. *Marriage and Family Living*, 1950, *12*, 41–43.

Ginsburg, S. W. Values and the psychiatrist. *American Journal of Orthopsychiatry*, 1950, *20*, 466–478.

Green, A. W. Social values and psychotherapy. *Journal of Personality*, 1946, *14*, 198–228.

Greene, B. (Ed.) *The psychotherapies of marital disharmony*. New York: Free Press, 1965.

Laidlaw, R. W. The psychiatrist as marriage counselor. In C. E. Vincent (Ed.) *Readings in marriage counseling*. New York: Crowell, 1957. p. 52–61.

Leslie, G., Neubeck, G., Greene, K., Hill, T. & Luckey, E. Who are your untreatables? *Marriage and Family Living*, 1960, *22*, 333–341.

Mace, D. R. What is a marriage counselor? In C. E. Vincent (Ed.) *Readings in marriage counseling*. New York: Crowell, 1957. p. 29–35.

Mudd, E., Karpf, M. J., Stone, A. & Nelson, J. F. (Ed.) *Marriage counseling: A casebook*. New York: Assn. Pr., 1958.

Mudd, E. H. The practice of marriage counseling. New York: Assn. Pr., 1951.

Perry, W. G. On the relation of psychotherapy and counseling. *Annals of the New York Academy of Sciences*, 1955, *63*, 319–432.

Rutledge, A. L. Should the marriage counselor ever recommend divorce? *Marriage and Family Living*, 1963, *25*, 319-326.

Schofield, W. Psychotherapy: *The purchase of friendship*. Englewood Cliffs: Prentice-Hall, 1964.

Stone, A. Marriage education and marriage counseling in the United States. In C. E. Vincent (Ed.): *Readings in marriage counseling*. New York: Crowell, 1957, p. 12-19.

Stroup, A. L. & Glasser, P. The orientation and focus of marriage counseling. *Marriage and Family Living*, 1959, *21*, 20-25.

Whitlock, G. E. The use of dreams in premarital counseling. *Marriage and Family Living*, 1961, *23*, 258-263.

CHAPTER 5

The "New Morality" and Marriage Counseling

Stewart Bedford

How can marriage counselors help individuals and couples make decisions regarding moral issues when the very term "moral" seems to be in a state of flux? How can marriage counselors help clients face moral decisions in a time when there are such ideas as "the new morality"? As a start toward answering these questions, I would suggest a careful and rational look at some of the issues and questions involved.

To me, "the new morality" is an effort to redefine ground rules of living that can apply to the new territories being mapped out by the advances currently being made in the fields of science, industry, marketing and communications (to name only a few). Marriage counselors working in today's society might well be aware of these changes and the resulting implications for the various moral codes held by their clients. Understanding these changes could make it easier to help clients maintain identity and perspective while also accepting the fact that they are, first of all, human beings and second, that they are members of a complex society.

I believe that the human being is a creature with a limited repertoire of instinctual behavior patterns, but nonethcless a biological being with basic biological needs and drives. I am assuming that these drives and needs are natural and inherent and therefore neither bad nor good *per se*—just there, and a part of being biological creatures.

Since we, as human beings, do not have extensive instinctive patterns of behavior, we are dependent on creating and learning patterns of behavior that help us adapt to changing and diversified environments. In fact, some people believe that a unique characteristic of human beings has been our creativeness and ingenuity in adapting to environmental change. We are inventors, innovators, and improvisors. We have fantasy and imagination. We have the power to be creative and, as a result, we have created a part of the environment in which we live—especially that which we call "society."

Our ingenuity has produced the automobile with rapid and mass travel—and smog, and highway congestion, and freeways, and the necessity for developing a maze of legal rules and regulations for driving.

Our medical scientists have brought many deadly diseases under control—to a point that "death control" makes it highly desirable that we take a new look at our opinion on "birth control."

Other scientists have extended our maps of space to new and fantastic dimensions and have taken more than preliminary steps to add the dimension of space to our immediate environment. As a result, we as individuals have had to fit our fantasies about God being "up there" to "out there" to "just where"?

Paleontology, anthropology, and archeology, with a big assist from physicists, have pushed the date of human origin back hundreds of thousands of years. At the same time fellow scientists in the biological and chemical fields have come extremely close to the creation of life itself.

Behavioral scientists, neurologists, and physiologists have done extensive work in mapping the mind, motivation, and behavior of human beings and have shown us among other things that we are not entirely conscious of all motivating factors and thinking involved in our reactions and behavior.

Biofeedback research has made it possible for us to monitor some of our body functions and in turn to become more responsible for what our bodies do and how we respond to the world about us.

Biological scientists have developed "the pill," artificial insemination, and the ability to implant a fertilized ovum from one female to the womb of another. The pill has allowed women one more degree of freedom, and artificial insemination and ovum-planting have raised intricate and yet unanswered legal questions of parental rights and identity.

Other scientists and teams of scientists have clearly shown that we as human beings could conceivably control and direct our future evolutionary changes. Scientists (and others) have suggested that in the future, we as human beings might well: consider requiring governmental permission for conceiving children; establish semen banks with stock taken from our great men; establish deep freeze storage for some individuals who die from currently incurable disease so that their lives could be restored at some time in the future; and that we utilize suspended animation to send space travelers far into outer space to inhabit other planets.

These changes and projected changes wrought by science and industry would appear to me to make it imperative that we as human beings take a very careful look at our framework for making moral decisions—for the decisions related to these changes involve moral as well as scientific issues.

We, as human beings, might be well advised to consider the fact that we are apparently writing scientific and industrial change with one hand while with the other hand we are writing such statements as "the earth is flat and square, and on each corner sit giant storks that deliver new human beings already clothed." We might also be well advised to listen to the feedback we get from our young adults which says, "You, Dad, are the one who is square, and in each corner of your squareness there are lies and myths that tell us that we can trust no one older than ourselves."

Marriage counselors might be well advised to understand the effects of scientific change on moral decisions if they are going to be effective in helping clients integrate their moral decisions with a rapidly changing environment. To help clients, marriage counselors might develop a framework for understanding the variations in moral codes that they are likely to encounter in their clientele. Here, it might be helpful for counselors to learn to differentiate between moral codes and laws that are based on moral codes. Understanding the difference between moral codes and moral laws makes it easier to help clients understand and define alternatives when the clients are faced with moral decisions. Marriage counselors, in understanding the difference between moral codes and moral laws, might then be in a better position to help their clients predict and understand the consequences related to various alternatives open to them in decisions with moral implications.

Moral codes in this context can be defined as rules developed by individuals or groups of individuals to encompass their own philosophies and/or religious beliefs.

Laws based on moral codes—*moral laws*—might be defined as governmental rules that incorporate the moral codes of some individuals or groups of individuals into the law of the land.

Recognizing these differences (particularly where harm to others and the infringement of the rights of others *is not involved*) is helpful in helping clients understand their reactions and anticipated reactions to their decisions relating to moral codes and moral laws.

For the violation of a moral code, the client (a couple or an individual) might anticipate expulsion from the group that made the rule. This would then involve the loss of privileges and benefits from remaining in good standing in the group and whatever this meant to the client.

If the client violated a moral law, he might anticipate some governmental penalty in addition to being penalized by his group. The difference here would be important in terms of helping the client define his apprehension in terms of reality factors.

For example, suppose that as an individual I join a group that has a rule that I cannot kiss my child on Sunday. I know that if I violate this rule (moral code), I risk losing membership in this group. If I am excluded from this group, I lose benefits, fellowship and support of the group (nutty though it might be), but I go about the business of living as best I can in a free society.

If on the other hand, a group becomes powerful enough to get a law enacted that says I cannot kiss my child on Sunday (a law reported to be on the books of one of the Colonies in 1644), my freedom—if I kiss my child on Sunday—is in jeopardy whether I am a member of the group or not.

In the first situation, the thoughts behind my emotional reactions probably would relate to the value of the group to me (both real and fancied). In the second situation, the thoughts might relate to the value of freedom and the monetary value of the penalty. A counselor, trying to help me ferret out the thoughts associated with these two situations might have an easier time of it if the differentiation between moral code and moral law were made.

It would seem to follow then, that marriage counselors might benefit from an increased awareness of another facet of "the new morality," namely, that some states in the union have been making an effort to

eliminate laws involving sexual behavior between consenting and competent adults.

In the United States today, state laws are the principal laws dealing
with sexual behavior. Almost without exception, these state laws have
grown out of English common law. English common law in turn, was
based on ancient, Judeo-Christian moral codes.

History tells us that the United States was the first nation to organize
its government by a written constitution. The Constitution and the Bill of
Rights were written by our founding fathers who had ample evidence of
the dangers of governmentally-dictated religions. These founding fathers
wrote into the Constitution and Bill of Rights the principle of separation
of church and state. In this respect, our founding fathers helped define a
part of the framework of this "new morality" currently being defined in
changes developing today. I feel that we as marriage counselors might well
benefit from thinking about some of these issues as we counsel with our
clients and help them struggle with the many moral problems with which
they are frequently faced.

CASE ILLUSTRATION

In way of illustration of some of these ideas in the context of marriage
counseling, let us assume that we are counseling a couple who were unable
to have a child by natural means. They have had medical consultation and
know that: The woman is fertile; the man is sterile but capable of having
sexual relations; artificial insemination would in all probability result in a
successful pregnancy if the sperm of a man other than the woman's mate
were used.

The couple are active members in a religious group that classifies
artificial insemination as adultery. The religious group classifies adultery
as a serious enough sin that it requires expulsion from the group and the
foregoing of all the privileges, including entrance to the promised land.

To complicate matters (we didn't really expect a simple case did we?),
the couple live in a state that allows artificial insemination even though
there is a law against adultery on the books in the state.

To further complicate matters, the mates are both young, healthy,
financially sound, and they both love children as well as each other. Both
individuals want very much to have a child; and they both prefer one that
would be at least "part theirs," as compared to one that they might adopt,
while still remaining in good standing in their church.

This is clearly a dilemma with scientific, moral, and possibly legal
implications. Both parties are apprehensive and have guilt from even
thinking about the possibilities. How can we as mature and rational marriage counselors help them see as many aspects of their dilemma as possible so that they can make as rationally sound a decision as possible?

Using some of the framework discussed, I would try to help them
outline as many alternate solutions as they could in considering ways out
of their dilemma. I would also try to get them to anticipate what they
would think of themselves, or in a sense, what they would tell themselves

about the consequences of the various alternatives (Ellis, 1962). I would point out to them that scientific advancement had made it possible to have alternatives open to them that were not available at the time the religious restrictions were formulated by past religious leaders. I would point out that from a legal standpoint they would probably not be violating any state criminal laws, although some question might be raised in the future if either of them wanted out of the relationship. I would make a strong suggestion that they seek legal counsel regarding these legal questions, again to help them have the best information to aid them in making their decision. I would try to have them come up with their definitions of some of the terms (such as *adultery*) as they considered semantic and theoretical discrepancies. I would also try to have them define what their particular brand of religion meant to them and what being expelled from the religion would mean. I would try to help them differentiate between rational and irrational apprehension by helping them see and define differences between practical (reality-oriented) and theological implications of the various alternatives open to them. In short, I would try to help them evaluate the information available to them, including the information that they were giving to themselves in their own interpretations of their dilemma.

I would feel that the framework of the new morality would offer them new degrees of freedom to make their decision on the basis of the knowledge available to them today as well as the knowledge available to them from yesterday. As a marriage counselor, I would feel that this could be beneficial to them, to their progeny, and to society in general.

REFERENCES

Ellis, A. Reason and emotion in psychotherapy, New York: Lyle Stuart, 1962.

CHAPTER 6

Moral Issues in Marital Counseling

Robert A. Harper

Moral issues in marital counseling are usually most effectively dealt with by transforming them into nonmoral issues. Does this mean, then, that the marital counselor contributes to the undermining of morals in marriage? No, it means only that we must spend some time at the outset of this chapter in defining the terms we shall use in trying to understand moral issues in marital counseling.

Morality is that quality of behavior that makes it right or wrong. *Morals* is a term which refers to the alleged rightness or wrongness of specific standards or of concrete behavior. When we label certain behavior of an individual or group as *moral*, we are judging it to be in accord with a code of conduct with which the individual or the group is identified.

One of the difficulties in contemporary American society, composed of persons from widely varying cultural backgrounds, is that morality is a very complicated matter. It is difficult or impossible for the marital counselor who serves a heterogeneous group of clients to be a *moralist*—that is, a student and teacher of morals, one who moralizes. So to function he would have to be an expert on the widely varying moral codes of the persons who consult him. Moralists usually must confine themselves to their own particular constituency: the rabbi of an Orthodox temple may be in a sound position to give moral advice to Orthodox Jews, but his moral counsel may not be well received by Reformed or Conservative Jews, let alone gentiles; the minister of Missouri Synod Lutherans does not pass muster as a moralist for even other brands of Lutherans; and so on. Obviously, a marriage counselor cannot wear all sorts of moralistic cloaks for persons of various religions, nationalities, social classes, and other groups of varying moralities.

Even if it were possible, however, for a marriage counselor to be the expert defender of all the multitudinous varieties of moral codes, it would not be desirable. For the greatest effectiveness of help in marital counseling, we would contend, the atmosphere is not desirably moral, immoral, unmoral or amoral, but *nonmoral*. Let's look at the important distinctions in these terms.

Reprinted with permission of the author and the publisher from H. L. Silverman (Ed.), *Marital Counseling*. Springfield, Ill.: Charles C Thomas, 1967. Pp. 325–335.

We have already discussed *moral* marriage counseling. *Immoral* marital counseling would carry the meaning of recommending that individuals violate whatever moral codes to which they subscribe. This is obviously as difficult (and more undesirable) for the marital counselor as trying to be a positive moralist.

Unmoral marital counseling would be the kind provided by a person who lacks understanding of morality. The fact that the marital counselor can function most effectively by not being a moralist does not mean he lacks understanding of the nature and importance of morality in human behavior, nor that he lacks sympathetic understanding of moral conflicts of his clients.

Amoral marriage counseling would be the sort in which the counselor would advocate or function in accordance with a doctrine that exhalts the right of persons to disregard moral codes of all kinds. This would be the Nietzschean superman type of counseling, a type which, so far as we know, has never been advocated by any sane professional person.

Nonmoral marital counseling, however, simply contends that the criteria of right and wrong are not appropriately or helpfully applied to the problems presented in the counseling setting. A request the writer has heard many hundreds of times from couples in marital counseling is: "Just tell us which of us is right and which of us is wrong." And the appropriate answer invariably is that there is no right side or wrong side in marital disagreement—just *different* sides.

Why is this nonmoral position so important? The practical reason is that in marital counseling we are looking for *solutions* to problems. *Differences* between couples can, with the help of the counselor, be understood, reduced, compromised, and sometimes even removed. But so long as we look for right and wrong, we remain stymied by moral judgments rather than problem solutions. When the husband and wife, along with the marriage counselor, try to understand rather than judge, differences can usually be dealt with effectively.

It is important for the reader to realize that the very nature of a moral judgment is such that there is nothing to be understood: the matter is either right or wrong, and the person is either being good or bad. Negative moral judgments toward others come out in the form of contempt, condescension, scorn, ridicule, and even horror and loathing; and toward oneself in the form of guilt, shame, defensiveness, and inferiority feelings. Positive moral judgments toward others are expressed in uncritical admiration, fawning, idealization of character traits, and flattering judgmental generalizations; toward oneself in smugness, conceit, or pride.

Both negative and positive moral judgments, then, are obviously not to be encouraged in a situation where a marriage has encountered problems. Such feelings as those we have just listed block understanding of the ongoing process in marriage and prevent husband, wife, and counselor from working out daring and imaginative ways of improving the relationship.

Because marriage counseling is no place for making moral judgments does not mean, however, that there are not many moral issues to be dealt with in the process of counseling. If the counselor does not moralize, how can he help with these issues? He can encourage the clients to engage in rational evaluation, realistic appraisal, and critical conceptual thinking, instead of looking for moral edicts which cover their problems.

In actual counseling situations, such rationality and realism must be geared to the specific situations faced by the particular couple with whom the counselor is working. It should be of some value for us in this chapter, however, to look critically at some of the general issues of morality, particular expressions of which are encountered in actual counseling circumstances. As we do so, we shall be able to observe some of the differences in perspective between this method and one based on uncritical moralizing about the same issues.

The reader's attention is called at this point to the understanding that the questions raised and the assertions made about moral issues in the rest of this chapter are to be taken as stimulating to his critical conceptual thinking. They are not to be considered new moral dogma, but a challenge to develop creative, flexible, reality-oriented attitudes about some of the moral issues which occur in many contemporary marriages.

The three broad areas of moral issues that we shall now consider are divorce, parenthood, and sex. These are probably the three foremost clusters of long-standing moral judgments which have beclouded critical conceptual thinking about marriage.

DIVORCE

Although the morality about divorce is gradually changing in many subgroups of our society, a large percentage of Americans have been indoctrinated from a very early age in home, school, church, and various other settings to feel that any person who gets a divorce is a failure and a sinner. To their conditioning regarding failure and sin are added a jungle of legal technicalities and outright humiliations for many of the hundreds of thousands of American couples who seek divorce each year. When, then, some of these men and women indicate anxiety, confusion, and other emotional disturbances, the moralists like to point to such symptoms as proof of their thesis that divorce is automatically and inevitably a terrible thing.

Obviously, the marriage counselor's role is to help people to think through whether or not divorce is for them a more desirable course of action than a continuation of their particular marital relationship. It is relevant, then, to ask ourselves if, from a nonmoralistic point of view, divorce must be inherently "a terrible thing."

A rational study of divorce would seem to suggest that divorce might be thought of as an essential component of democracy. Just as there should be, in a democracy, no major abridgements of freedom of speech, assembly, and worship (including, as some moralists like to forget, freedom *not* to worship), just as there should be no attempt to prevent a person from *responsibly* taking and quitting a job rather than remaining forever in his first job, so, a critical conceptual judgment would seem to tell us, there should be no interference with a person's *responsibly* entering or leaving a marriage, rather than remaining forever in his first marriage.

All human freedoms are subject to irresponsible misuse, and divorce is certainly no exception. In the hands of the irresponsible, divorce can be cruel, exploitative, tragic. In the hands of the responsible, divorce can be humane, kind, spirit-freeing. No one wants to abolish or drastically curtail the use of automobiles because they can produce tragedy in the hands of the irresponsible. Some can be prevented from using automobiles because they are permanently too irresponsible; others can be educated to use them responsibly. Most people can probably be educated to use both marriage and divorce responsibly. This is one of the marriage counselor's functions.

It is sometimes contended that divorce is always irresponsible for a couple who has children. If moralistic attitudes are put aside, however, it is difficult to find a marriage which, on realistic grounds, should be maintained strictly *because* of children. When two people have reached a point where their marriage has for them lost all possible positive value and is steadily accumulating negative values, what of a constructive nature is likely to accrue for children by the maintenance of that marriage?

Many moralists point to statistics about delinquency and broken homes. There are a number of fallacies concealed in such statistics, but the fact most relevant here is that when two people have decided that their marriage is dead and that they will stay married *only* for the children, that home is already broken in an emotional sense. There is no evidence to support the assertion that it is the physical parting of the parents that hurts the children. Or, put differently, there is no evidence that emotionally estranged parents who stay physically in the same house for the sake of their children really do their children any favor.

Faced with the moral issue of impending divorce with children involved, the marriage counselor can often help the couple to remove or reduce some of the undesirable effects of the earlier emotional break in the marriage and to protect the children from some of the unnecessary consequences of the physical break of separation and divorce. To help in this way, the marital counselor will have many specific things to work out with the couple regarding their particular children, but certain general understandings can also be helpful.

One helpful understanding is that we have been so propagandized by the picture of children who are mourning their departed parents that we often overlook certain counterbalancing pieces of reality. For example, children are very conservative, for they are—reasonably enough for chronological children—quite insecure in the world. Hence, they tend to oppose anything that strikes them as a threat to their security systems, as a major change in the status quo. If Daddy has been little more to the children than an emotional stranger seen only briefly on weekends or holidays, they will nevertheless fight bitterly, forlornly, tragically, to retain his fleetingly familiar presence. But once Daddy is gone, even if he has been a more constructive influence than the father just described, children quickly adjust to life without father. They adjust *unless* Mother indicates (and perhaps Daddy, too, in the course of his visits with them) that something horrible has happened. "This is a terrible, terrible tragedy," say the parental emotional messages.

Children are, of course, excellent emotional mirrors. It is probable that we could reinforce in our children the feeling that *any* kind of change in the status quo is tragic, calamitous, unbelievably awful, providing we gave them the same sort of treatment we often do on the matter of divorce. Most of us, by way of illustration, have seen children temporarily indicate every bit as much disturbance over some such situation as a rip in a teddy bear as over a parent's departure from the home. The main difference is that they do not get the same reinforcement of their feelings of great tragedy from the adults around them on ripped teddy bears as they do on broken marriages. Hence, teddy-bear tragedies tend to be transitory, and parental divorce tragedies tend to get lasting reinforcement not only from their parents, but from neighbors, teachers, clergymen, and others.

Marriage counselors can do a great deal, then, even in the unfortunate situations where emotional divorce has already occurred, in helping parents to overcome some of the emotional damage they have already done to their children, and in helping them to avoid doing additional damage with separation and divorce. Responsibly and intelligently planned divorce need not be terrible and tragic, even when children are involved.

PARENTHOOD

Even in the face of the ever-more-threatening problems associated with excessive world population, and with tremendous deficiencies in the genetic quality and environmental training of high percentages of human beings born year by year, moral myths about parenthood go relatively unchallenged in our society. To stimulate critical thinking about the usually unquestioned points of view about parenthood, the marriage counselor must sometimes strongly state radically different views. The following assertions are beliefs held tentatively by the writer (subject to correction by much-needed research), but they are made in the form of rather unqualified assertions for the sake of clarity, readability, and, hopefully, startling challenge to prevailing prejudices about parenthood.

1. The only time reproduction is truly desirable for the children, for the married couple, and for the general society is when: (*a*) the husband and wife are considerably above average in such traits as mental and physical health, intelligence, emotional and social maturity, and creative and adaptive skills; (*b*) the marriage is a happy one; and (*c*) both the husband and wife not only want children in a sentimental sense, but are eager to make parenthood a main enterprise in their lives, and include in their eagerness a realization that this task means a lot of hard study, hard work, and sacrifice of many other satisfactions. While some of these parental traits are not easily determined by existing evaluative methods, just the setting up of even roughly determined standards of the sort

described would help to combat the moral myth that parenthood is a process to be entered into by the relatively stupid, ignorant, and undedicated.

2. Very few people meet all three of the foregoing criteria (*a*), (*b*) and (*c*). There is a fair number of healthy, intelligent, mature, creative, adaptive people who are quite successful in business or professional activities but think that marriage and parenthood can be successfully pursued as an avocation to which they give little time and attention and for which they have little or no preparation. The facts are that, in order to be even moderately successful in marriage and parenthood, under contemporary social circumstances, a great deal of time and energy and skill are required. Often indifference, at worst, or unskilled goodwill, at best, are all basically competent people offer family life; they have already given most of their available time, energy, and talent to out-of-home careers.

3. The minority of couples who do fairly well in fulfilling the standards mentioned are likely to have their happy marriages made happier by children. In fact, for this minority, the joyful labors of parenthood probably bring as deep a sense of creative achievement as is available in life.

4. Under present-day social conditions, ancient conceptions about *duties* or *rights* about having children are quite inappropriate. "Be fruitful and multiply" is exceedingly poor advice with increasingly excessive world overpopulation and accompanying problems. Concerning the matter of *duty*, married couples who choose not to have children are being much more dutiful citizens in the light of contemporary realities than those who do have children. The former are at least not adding to the overall weight of population or of the social and psychological problems which tend to arise from duty-inspired offspring. As for any *rights* that genetically, sociologically, and psychologically unqualified people may have to enter parenthood, these are privileges which have been socially granted and which may be socially removed. All individual rights are subject to the limitations set by the welfare of the society to which the individual belongs. And the welfare of the world society—that is, of all mankind—it becomes increasingly clear, depends upon drastic reduction in quantity and improvement in quality of population.

5. Just from their own vantage points, happy couples who do not prepare themselves seriously and well for the hard work and real sacrifices of parenthood are often in grave danger of having their previously sound marriages undermined by the arrival of children and the accompanying increase in life's stresses. Couples who have consulted the writer as a marriage counselor not infrequently mention that their troubles either began with, or were markedly increased by, the arrival of children.

6. Even more definitely, couples who were already quite unhappy prior to children are likely to find that the additional burdens of parenthood bankrupt their marriage and broaden and intensify their unhappiness.

7. Many of the people who urge married couples to have children and try to make them feel guilty if they do not are actually resentful of the

freedom and enjoyment of life indicated by some childless couples. "I am tied down with a life I find difficult and not very enjoyable with children (doing my duty); why shouldn't you be likewise?" are the thoughts which often lie behind the spoken "Nothing like children to make life worthwhile." Such propagandists for reproduction are malefactors, not benefactors, of the couples, of children thus reproduced, and of mankind in general.

Such observations as the seven just made are apt to be judged as very radical and misanthropic by some persons, but any less severe approach to the responsibilities of parenthoood seems to the writer to disregard current social reality. Realistic perceptions of existing world circumstances add up to the generalization that whenever parenthood is an involuntary function and/or one for which the individual is grossly unsuited, ill effects are very likely to ensue for all parties concerned.

Both the matter of desire and competency for parenthood are, however, relative. No parent is wholeheartedly happy about his role as a parent, and certainly no parent is perfectly equipped for the responsibilities of parenthood. But surely people who are functioning as parents predominantly contrary to their wishes and skills do injustice to themselves, their children, and their society.

There is a condition which accompanies some brain injuries and diseases psychiatrically referred to as *anosognosia*, the denial of illness. A patient with anosognosia may be paralyzed in his right arm, for example, and yet stoutly deny the existence of the paralysis. He apparently so reorganizes his perception that he is able to "remove" the paralyzed limb from his field of perceived reality. He is afraid to face the reality of paralysis; he feels comfortable in denying reality.

The denial of the difficulties, the burdens, the displeasures of parenthood (or, at least, the denial of their very formidable nature), we would suggest, involves much the same psychological process as the denial of illness in the brain-injured. This might be considered an instance of *moral anosognosia*. Many people are afraid to face the unhappy realities of parenthood; they feel more comfortable in denying these realities, in believing the myth that having children is a sure route to happiness and the good life.

SEX

The traditional moral outlook on sex, of course, is more irrational than that on any other single topic with which the marriage counselor has to deal. In critically rethinking some of the moral issues connected with sex, the reader will find in the following assertions about sex an outlook that differs radically from the conventional ones.

1. Realistic evidence seems to point to the desirability not only of fully educating children about sex, but of making contraceptive and prophylactic information and equipment completely available to all persons who reach the age of possible fertility. The writer does not mean making it discreetly possible for the young person of more than average

intelligence to worm such information and equipment out of the sexual black market. He means that it would be desirable to encourage young people to procure contraceptive and prophylactic knowledge and equipment. It is difficult to see what other purpose unwanted pregnancies and venereal disease serve in our society today than to punish or threaten to punish people who sexually function contrary to the ancient superstitions which constitute our premarital moral code.

It is undoubtedly true that some of the more guilt-ridden and faint-hearted youth are deterred by fear of pregnancy, of venereal disease, and of the alleged wrath of a vindictive Jehovah from engaging in premarital sexual intercourse. But they then often pay the lifetime price of anxiety and guilt about even marital sex, which seems a peculiar reward for touted virtue. Other costs of the deterrence program on young people who proceed with premarital sex are such things as: untreated venereal disease which fans out in a wide circle of infection; illegitimate children; guilt-ridden, resentment-filled shotgun marriages; sojourns in humiliating, morality-dripping homes for unwed mothers; illegal abortions; and a number of other priceless products of puritanism. It is only because we keep reciting rigidly to ourselves the moral ditty about the catastrophic nature of premarital coitus that we cannot even clearly see, let alone do anything constructive about, our completely unnecessary, utterly idiotic premarital sexual morality.

2. The writer thinks it would be desirable to educate young people frankly in how to use sex as an important part of their skills in interpersonal relations. The suggestion here made is not only to stop teaching them that premarital sexual intercourse is bad, but to teach them how to exercise their own critical faculties about deciding under what sorts of circumstances and with what sorts of partners it is likely to be functionally desirable for all parties concerned. We should try to educate them to develop the kind of maturity and experience and the kind of love and understanding of themselves and others to work out their widely varying self-guides for sex functioning along with other kinds of social functioning. The writer would trust young people, thus educated, to have considerably superior judgment in such matters to the second-hand judgments that come to them from the ready-made codes of moralists.

3. If we take a critical and rational look at abortion, here, too, we shall emerge with different ideas than the moralistic one that "to take a human life is always bad." We shall question, first of all, whether the life to be taken may be correctly considered human in light of what we know in modern sociopsychological terms regarding the postnatal development of human nature out of interpersonal relations. We shall ask, further, what is most desirable for all parties concerned in a specific situation: the potential human being, the mother, the father, and other people directly involved?

Under such changed approaches to abortion, our answer would at times be, if we were thinking instead of moralizing, that the greatest practical desirability would be to destroy the embryo or fetus. At other times, let it develop. But we would be humanizing the concept of therapeutic abortion to take into account the social and psychological, not just the physical, consequences of both continued and interrupted pregnancies.

Such a view of abortion, moralists say, would bring about loss of respect for human life. The writer believes it would do quite the contrary, in other words, increase respect for human life and for every human representative of that general life. Entrance into human life would become less the product of unhappy chance and increasingly the product of man's well-worked-out plans, his best critical judgment.

4. A sex ethic should be constructed solely for the welfare of living and future human beings and not to please our ancestors or any assumed supernatural beings or functions. What Moses, Jesus of Nazareth, Freud, and other respected figures from the past had to say should be taken into account for any leads they may provide us, but their points of view should be subjected to the same rational inspection as any other points of view. And any scientific evidence available (which in a sexually rational environment would become increasingly so) should take precedence over opinion from any source.

5. A rational sex ethic would be based on principles that derive from our knowledge of psychological, sociological, and biological facets of human behavior, and would not concern itself with moral edicts or mystical or spiritual observations. Since our present empirical observations, including the growing clinical information of motivations outside the individual's conscious attention, are still crude and relatively unsifted, our sex values need to be particularly tentative and flexible, subject to change as we acquire new knowledge about human behavior and as social conditions alter human needs.

6. Our system of values for sex would in no way unfairly discriminate against males or females. It would be basically the same for both sexes with differences, if any, designed strictly for the necessary protection of the males or females.

7. The system of values would likewise obviously exclude any other type of discrimination, such as that of race, creed, religion, color, or socioeconomic status.

8. A rational sex code would likewise not discriminate against children and adolescents except in instances where their welfare is demonstrably involved, where their sex-love activities need to be limited for the actual protection of *their* health and well-being, and *not* for the protection of adult moral prejudice.

9. A realistic system of values regarding sex must take into account the fact that reproduction is a natural, though fortunately relatively infrequent, result of human sexual activity. Marriage and family laws under such a system would be primarily concerned with the encouragement and enforcement of proper care and protection of children, rather than with the hemming-in of adults with rules which do not bear on anyone's welfare.

10. Such a system of values would be based on the biopsychological fact that sex is fun for human beings. Nature has provided the healthy

male and female with sexual dynamisms, which, unless restrained and perverted by social conditioning, provide the user with great pleasure. Probably more consistently enjoyable sensations proceed from the relatively unhampered erotic relationship of a man and a woman than from any other life activity. Any system of values which fails to take into account the outstanding fact that sex is pleasurable will be unrealistic, irrational, and contrary to human welfare (much of our conventional sex morality is testimony to this point).

11. The kind of system of values we have been discussing would view as criminal and legally punishable only those forms of sex activities in which one individual forces his attentions on an unwilling participant, willfully harms another, annoys others with his activities, or takes advantage of a minor. Other sexual deviations than these, however neurotic, should be considered eccentricities or illnesses, not crimes.

12. Finally, a system of values for sex, along with those for parenthood and divorce which we barely touched upon, must be woven into an all-encompassing system of values which helps each individual toward increasing fulfillment of his various capacities, especially his capacity to love. Mature love means the development of concern, understanding, esteem, and responsibility for all human beings, including oneself. No one achieves such love perfectly, but our efforts urgently need to be directed toward helping more individuals to progress in loving themselves and others.

The basic moral issue in marriage counseling is to help clients to free themselves from a stagnant and unrealistic morality which blocks progress in love. Many self-styled God-fearing people in our various social groups are also thought-fearing, love-fearing, science-fearing, and life-fearing people.

Although the social system of the West contains in many respects the same destructive components as the social system of the Communist East, we are still permitted greater individual freedom and nonconformity. It is still possible, although difficult, for persons who have feelings of concern, understanding, esteem, and responsibility for the human race to use opportunities within such institutions as the school, the home, the church, industry, labor, and government to foster the growth of love and care and their necessary companion, critical conceptual judgment.

As marriage counselors we have not only opportunities but profound responsibilities to stimulate ourselves, our clients, and others with whom we relate to question, to think, to examine the reality of our social life— including the marriage and family mores to which we have so stubbornly, so unthinkingly, so compulsively locked ourselves in what may well be a death embrace. These moral matters take priority, in the writer's opinion, over many of the other issues with which we have concerned ourselves as marriage counselors, for these matters are near the core of our continued existence as a civilization.

CHAPTER 7

Excerpts from the *Playboy* Philosophy

Hugh M. Hefner

"... *PLAYBOY'S* aims and outlook have been given considerable comment in the press, particularly in the journals of social, philosophical, and religious opinion, and have become a popular topic of conversation at cocktail parties around the country. . . . We have decided to state our own editorial credo here.

"What is this 'particular point of view,' then, that *PLAYBOY* shares with its readers? *What is a Playboy?* . . . He can be many things, provided he possesses a certain *point of view*. He must see life not as a vale of tears, but as a happy time; he must take joy in his work, without regarding it as the end and all of living; he must be an alert man, an aware man, a man of taste, a man sensitive to pleasure, a man who—without acquiring the stigma of the voluptuary or dilettante—can live life to the hilt. This is the sort of man we mean when we use the word *playboy* [December, 1962] . . . ."

"A major part of *PLAYBOY'S* spectacular success is directly attributable to our being a part of the new generation, understanding it, and publishing a magazine with an editorial point of view that our generation can relate to [December, 1962] . . . .

"The opposition to *PLAYBOY* is prompted by the significant element of puritanism that still exists in the United States. *PLAYBOY* offends some people, and makes others uneasy, because they think of sex as something either so sacred or so profane that it has to be hidden away in a dark room; they object to sex being frankly depicted or described in public [December, 1964] . . . .

"*PLAYBOY* is editorially interested in precisely those aspects of life that the Puritan was most against: sex, first and foremost, of course. But also our more general emphasis on pleasure and play; as well as the notion that the accumulation of material possessions can be a positive addition to the other interests in life. . . .

"If we were not sexually oriented, there would be no criticism. It is our positive approach to sex that distresses some people. . . .

"Since one of the things *PLAYBOY* is especially concerned about is the depersonalizing influence of our entire society, and considerable editorial attention is given to the problem of establishing individual identity, through sex and as many other avenues of expression as may be available in a more permissive society, it is wrong to suggest that we favor depersonalized sex. Not unless, by depersonalized sex, we are referring to any and all sexual activity that does not include extensive involvement, commitments, and obligations. In this sense, it is true, to the extent that the magazine emphasizes the pleasures rather than the problems of sex, and focuses on that period of life in which real personal involvement is not yet desirable—a time of transition into maturity, prior to accepting the responsibilities of marriage and family.

"I certainly think that personal sex is preferable to impersonal sex, because it includes the greatest emotional rewards; but I can see no logical justification for opposing the latter, unless it is irresponsible, exploitive, coercive or in some way hurts one of the individuals involved. . . .

". . . we are among the most outspoken advocates of a more healthy, open, and positive outlook on sex. We treat it with humor, which helps to take the onus off it; we place our emphasis on approval rather than negation; and we attempt to treat sex in as attractive and appealing light as possible [December, 1964] . . . ."

"Kinsey found 'premarital sex statistically increased a woman's chances of getting married and of making a success of her marriage.' . . . Kinsey found 'considerable evidence' that sexual experience prior to marriage contributed 'to the effectiveness of the sexual relations after marriage' [July, 1963] . . . .

"The simple act of sex performed prior to marriage does not, per se, increase the chances of a successful marriage, of course. It is the attitudes that lead to the act that will determine how well a person adjusts both to sex and to marriage. There is a good deal more to sex than just the learned physical techniques (although the techniques themselves are largely underrated in our society and a majority of adults live out their lives with only the most rudimentary knowledge of this most vital of all human activities). Sex is often a profound emotional experience. No dearer, more intimate, more personal act is possible between two human beings. Sex is, at its best, an expression of love and adoration. But this is not to say that sex is, or should be, limited to love alone. Love and sex are certainly not synonymous, and while they may often be closely interrelated, the one is not necessarily dependent upon the other. Sex can be one of the most profound and rewarding elements in the adventure of living; if we recognize it as not necessarily limited to procreation, then we should also acknowledge openly that it is not necessarily limited to love either. Sex exists—with and without love—and in both forms it does far more good than harm. The attempts at its suppression, however, are almost universally harmful, both to the individuals involved and to society as a whole.

"This is not an endorsement of promiscuity or an argument favoring loveless sex—being a rather romantic fellow ourself, we favor our sex mixed with emotion. But we recognize that sex without love exists; that it is not, in itself, evil; and that it may sometimes serve a definitely worthwhile end.

"We are opposed to wholly selfish sex, but we are opposed to any human relationship that is entirely self-oriented—that takes all and gives nothing in return. We also believe that any such totally self-serving association is self-destructive. Only by remaining open, and vulnerable, can a person experience the full joy and satisfaction of human experience. That he must also, thereby, know some of the sorrow and pain of this world is without question, but that, too, is a part of the adventure of living. The alternative—closing oneself off from experience and sensation and knowledge—is to be only half alive. The ultimate invulnerability is death itself.

"This is not at odds with what we have previously expressed about the need for a greater *enlightened self-interest* in society. Too many people today live out their entire existence in a group, of a group, and for a group—never attempting to explore their own individuality, never discovering who or what they are, or might be. Searching out one's own identity and purpose, taking real pleasure in being a person, establishing a basis for true self-respect—these are the essence of living.

"We believe that life can be a greater pleasure if it is lived with some style and grace and comfort and beauty, but we do not believe that these are the all of it. It is possible to become so caught up in the trappings—both the form and the accouterments of living—that the real satisfactions become lost. Each man—and woman—should try to know himself, as well as the world around him, and take real pride in that knowledge. . . .

". . . if we truly respect ourselves, it is impossible not to respect our fellow man as well. . . .

"What we believe in, first and foremost, is the individual—and his right to *be* an individual [July, 1963]."

"It is our view that man is a rational being and while his heredity and environment play a major role in setting the pattern of his life, he possesses the ability to reason and the capacity for choice, not granted to lower animals, whose response to life is instinctually predetermined. The use, or lack, of use, of his rational mind, is, itself, a choice, and we favor a society in which the emphasis is placed upon the use of reason—a society that recognizes man's responsibility for his actions. . . .

"We believe in a moral and law-abiding society, but one in which the morality and the laws are based upon logic and reason rather than mysticism or religious dogma. . . .

"We believe that a society that emphasizes the individual and his freedom, is based upon reason, and has happiness as its aim is an ideal society and the one to be strived for. . . .

"This, then, is the foundation of our philosophy—an emphasis on the importance of the individual and his freedom; the view that man's personal self-interest is natural and good, and it can be channeled, through reason, to the benefit of the individual and his society; the belief that morality should be based upon reason; the conviction that society should exist as man's servant, not as his master; the idea that the purpose in man's life should be found in the full living of life itself and the individual pursuit of happiness [December, 1963]."

CHAPTER 8

The Conscience or Superego in Marriage Counseling

Ben N. Ard, Jr.

When clients come to a marriage counselor for professional help, they frequently are facing what have been called "moral dilemmas." They need help in resolving questions involving very basic issues centering around "right" or "wrong" behavior. Because so many "moral" issues are raised in marriage counseling, the professional marriage counselor needs to be quite clear about how such moral issues are best resolved.

Some of the problems clients may face can involve such moral issues as (1) whether or not one should marry anyone of another faith or race; (2) whether or not premarital intercourse is ever acceptable (if so, under what conditions?); (3) whether masturbation is wrong or not; (4) whether certain, if any, birth control methods are right or wrong; (5) whether certain "thoughts" are immoral, sinful, or not; (6) whether certain forms of behavior are sins against God or not; (7) what sorts of sexual behavior are "normal," "abnormal," "sinful," "perverted" or not; (8) whether extra-marital intercourse is ever justified or not (or whether it, in and of itself, justifies divorce); (9) whether an abortion should ever be considered or not; and (10) whether separation or divorce should ever be considered or not (if so, under what conditions?).

There has been some developing interest in the areas of values and morals in psychotherapy (Buhler, 1962; London, 1964), but there has not been sufficient discussion of what marriage counselors (who face particularly difficult value dilemmas in their practice) should do with regard to the conscience or superego in their clients. For purposes of smoothness and clarity, we will use "conscience" throughout this chapter as an interchangeable term with Freud's "superego."

The marriage counselor might take several possible stances with regard to these moral issues so often raised in marriage counseling.

1. He may refuse to discuss "moral matters" and refer all such problems to the religious leader considered appropriate for the clients in question (minister, priest, or rabbi).

---

*Reprinted with permission of the author and the publisher from the *Marriage Counseling Quarterly* Vol. 5, No. 1, Fall, 1969 and from H. L. Silverman (Editor) *Marital Therapy* (Thomas, 1972).

2. He may strive by a variety of methods to reinforce or strengthen the clients' previously existing moral values so that the clients may have the moral resolve to decide what they already know (in some sense) is right.
3. He may teach the "proper" religious values which the clients may not know and thus provide the clients with the means to resolve the moral dilemmas at hand.
4. He may try to always remain philosophically "neutral" and never say or do anything which would influence the clients in any particular direction on any moral issue.
5. He may strive to lessen the severity of the superego (following Freud's suggestions) and make it more "benevolent" or "tolerant." (But after the client has transferred the authority of his superego to the psychoanalyst, later the client reintrojects his own superego, according to this view.)
6. He may strive to eliminate entirely the traditional ways of deciding so-called moral issues (eliminate the conscience) and help the client develop more rational ways of deciding ethical questions.

The first stance, or the "refer" stance, seems on the face of it to get the marriage counselor off the hook, so to speak. But it really is no ultimate solution. The marriage counselor simply cannot continue to function as a marriage counselor if he merely refers all moral problems to religious leaders. Sooner or later the marriage counselor is going to have to get down to brass tacks and wrestle with the moral issues raised by his clients.

The second stance of strengthening the clients' previously held values is no real solution either, in many cases, since one of the main reasons the clients are in the marriage counselor's office is that their previously-held values have not led them to any resolution.

The third stance of teaching proper religious values may be acceptable to counselors who only see clients of their own religious faith. But it is hardly a solution for the professional marriage counselor who sees a variety of clients in this pluralistic society of ours.

The fourth stance of trying always to remain philosophically "neutral" is probably one of the most popular among marriage counselors these days. Several authorities in the fields of counseling and psychotherapy have suggested that the counselor or therapist not get involved in moral issues and should remain philosophically "neutral" on all such matters (Browning & Peters, 1966). However, to leave all moral decisions up to the client presumes that the client already has an adequate way of resolving moral dilemmas. Specifically, this means the counselor will rely on the client's conscience to resolve all his moral dilemmas. In what follows, the fundamental assumption that the conscience is the best (or, as some assume, the *only*) way to resolve moral issues will be critically examined.

An extended discussion of the philosophical basis for making value judgments will not be possible in the present context. The interested reader may wish to consult several authorities in the field. Some authorities have suggested that all moral judgments are of an emotional (subjective) nature rather than a rational, cognitive, objective, or scientific nature (Stevenson, 1944). Others have maintained that it is possible to begin thinking about the development of an objective, scientific standard of ethics (Maslow, 1959; Otto, 1949; Fromm, 1947; White, 1948).

From ancient times, descriptions of human nature have contained many concepts to explain a particular portion of man's personality, variously called his "moral reason," "divine reason," "moral sense," or *conscience*. Philosophers and religious writers have held forth at length about this "moral faculty." Some conceived of conscience as an organ implanted in man by God to guide his conduct and show him what is right. The "voice of conscience" was thought of as the "voice of God." It was thought that man was born with this conscience.

Under such conditions, it is hardly surprising that little critical thinking was done about the conscience. Who could presume to criticize "God's handiwork"? But gradually, as a more scientific way of looking at man developed, closer, more critical views of man's conscience began to appear (Aronfreed, 1968; Knight, 1969).

Freud introduced a three-part division of the human personality: the id, ego, and superego; the id being the unconscious part of the personality, the ego being the reality-oriented, conscious, cognitive part of the personality. The superego corresponded (in a loose sense) to the older concept of conscience. The superego is basically unconscious, although occasionally conscious.

Freud did agree, to some extent, with earlier religious views that the conscience (or superego) was the basis of morality (Symonds, 1946, p. 292). But this raises a very basic question: is the superego a sound basis for morality?

As Grace Stewart put it, we need to question seriously the superego as our only or best guide.

> For conscience has so often been called the voice of God that we might well examine it rather as the voice of the parent and his group and age. Conscience has, in such philosophies as Kant's, been exalted as man's greatest good. We might well ask ourselves whether it be not sometimes as much an evil as a good; whether there be not better guides, guides more reliable and more humane (Stewart, 1951, p. 72).

While Freud introduced some scientific thinking into how the superego developed (discarding the former assumption that we are born with a fully-developed conscience), he, too, saw no other way to make moral decisions than through the superego. He described the superego as "a memorial of the former weakness and dependence of the ego and the mature ego remains subject to its domination. As the child was once compelled to obey its parents, so the ego submits to the categorical imperative pronounced by its superego (Freud, 1927, p. 69)."

Freud was critical of former conceptions of conscience.

> The philosopher Kant once declared that nothing proved to him the greatness of God more convincingly than the starry heavens and the moral conscience within us. The stars are unquestionably superb, but where conscience is con-

cerned God has been guilty of an uneven and careless piece of work, for a great
many men have only a limited share of it or scarcely enough to be worth
mentioning (Freud, 1933, p. 88).

But Freud saw no alternative to the superego in making moral decisions. He considered the superego natural, normal, and good. He also said,
"The fear of the superego should normally never cease, since it is indispensable in social relations in the form of moral anxiety (Freud, 1933, p.
123)."

The next basic question which each counselor must decide for himself
is, what shall be his goal with regard to the superego or conscience?
Should he try to strengthen the superego/conscience (particularly if it is
weak or nonexistant? Or should he, along with Freud, try to lessen its
severity? (This is the fifth stance we mentioned earlier.) Or should he try
to change it at all?

What happens to the superego in psychoanalytic therapy is not always
crystal clear, to say the least. The final disposition of the superego in
therapy should give us some better idea of its necessity for mentally
healthy, psychologically mature individuals.

Judging from the literature on the subject, as one psychoanalyst himself admits, additional clarification is needed on the problems of assessing
the precise results of analytic therapy in terms of the superego (Bergler,
1952, p. 349). The general agreement seems to be: the superego becomes
milder, more "tolerant" or "benevolent." But Bergler said,

> Personally, I doubt the direct applicability of the quality of benevolence to a
> monster such as the superego, whether the individual's state of health be that
> of health or neurosis. I would rather say that psychoanalytic therapy changes
> the technique of torture. The alleged "benevolence" of the post-analysis super-
> ego seems to me to be a mirage (Bergler, 1952, p. 349).

Another analyst, Erik Erikson, has spoken of a "workable equilibrium" or "balance" between the ego and the superego (Erikson, 1950, pp.
367–368). Still another analyst, Flugel, has said that in psychoanalysis
"the superego is required to undergo changes which result in a weakening
in the power of at any rate its deeper layers (Flugel, 1945, p. 176)."

During therapy the patient is said to transfer to the analyst the authority of his superego (Freud, 1949, p. 77). Eventually, however, in the
course of treatment, the "transference" is resolved, "so that the patient
loses his dependence on the analyst, that is, he reintrojects his superego
(Flugel, 1945, p. 177)."

Freud said that in therapy the analysts are, among other things, "attempting the gradual demolition of the hostile superego (Freud, 1949, p.
75)." One might read this as an attempt to demolish the superego entirely,
except for that preceding adjective "hostile." Perhaps Freud only meant
to demolish the *hostile* superego. But this implies there is a non-hostile
("benevolent") superego, which is not so, according to Bergler (vide
supra).

Elsewhere, Freud said that in analytic therapy "we find ourselves
obliged to do battle with the superego and work to moderate its demands
(Freud, 1930, p. 139)." In still another place, Freud stated that the objec-

tive of therapeutic efforts is "to strengthen the ego, to make it more independent of the superego (Freud, 1933, p. 111)." Here again we note the crucial word "more" in front of independent. Evidently Freud did not attempt to make the ego entirely independent of the superego. So it would seem that we must conclude that Freud considered the superego still necessary, even after successful analysis.

Apparently Freud was led to postulate the necessity of the superego by his conception of the nature of man in relation to society. According to Freud, the first society was formed by setting protective taboos against the so-called instincts of incest and murder. Man conformed only out of fear. Culture is thus a kind of rigid police system imposed upon man. Thus, *according to Freud*, man is "good" *only* because of his helplessness and dependence on others. This is certainly an attitude which is still prevalent in our society today, as Clara Thompson has pointed out. But, as she clearly stated,

> It leaves out of consideration entirely the possibility that some things may be bad for man even though they are socially approved, and that some things socially disapproved may be good, and it implies that there are no socially constructive tendencies unless the police force, society, insists upon them (Thompson, 1950, pp. 138–139).

Thus, Freud's view of the nature of man (that it is essentially, or ultimately evil), led to the view that society must restrict man. This fatalism is reflected in the therapy of Freud and those who followed him unthinkingly. With the Freudian point of view, "the best that can be done for a man is to make him more able to accept the restrictions of society (Thompson, 1950, p. 152)."

Not all of those who followed Freud did so in an unthinking manner, however. And this leads us to the final stance for the marriage counselor, which is that of eliminating the conscience. Some recent theorists have felt there is no necessity for slavishly following Freud's views of human nature, nor the goals of therapy following therefrom. A different point of view derives from the "cultural school," as exemplified by Erich Fromm and Karen Horney. For example:

> With the new point of view the goal of therapy is different. The aim of the "cultural school" goes beyond merely enabling man to submit to the restrictions of his society;... it seeks to free him from its irrational demands and make him more able to develop his potentialities and to assume leadership in building a more constructive society (Thompson, 1950, p. 152).

In her book *Conscience and Reason*, Grace Stewart (1951) has provided a very insightful and critical review of the superego concept. At one point she seemed to feel that we would be better off without any superego:

> It would seem that if one grows up in a community which has no sense of sin, and if in consequence no stern parental rule makes one take into oneself and establish in one's own mind a stern superego, then a considerable amount of strain, anxiety, dominance, condemnation, competitiveness, ambition and war will naturally and inevitably be eliminated (Stewart, 1951, pp. 146–147)."

The next question is, what about the future? What should be the counselor's aim with regard to the superego? In stating the object of therapeutic efforts, Freud said, "Where id was, there shall ego be (Freud, 1933, pp. 111–112)." Fenichel (1945, p. 589) thought that his dictum should be supplemented. We should *also* say that "*where superego was*" (that is, the automatic autonomy of unreasonable guilt feelings, the principle of talion, revenge, and automatisms), "*there shall ego be*" (that is, a reasonable handling of reality). Fenichel commented that such an additional "shall" runs against socially-determined barriers (Fenichel, 1945, p. 589). That is a masterpiece of understatement.

Perhaps one of the clearest statements of what a counselor can aim for (if he wishes to adopt the sixth stance we mentioned earlier) is the one given by Karen Horney:

> Freud can aim merely at reducing the severity of the superego while I aim at the individual's being able to dispense with his inner dictates altogether and to assume the direction of his life in accordance with his true wishes and beliefs. This latter possibility does not exist in Freud's thinking (Horney, 1950, p. 375).

Some of these professional insights were anticipated somewhat by that perceptive young man, Mark Twain's Huckleberry Finn, who said,

> It don't make no difference whether you do right or wrong, person's conscience ain't got no sense and just goes for him anyway. If I had a yaller dog that didn't know more than a person's conscience does, I'd pizon him. It takes up more room than all the rest of a person's insides, and yet ain't no good nohow. Tom Sawyer says the same (Quoted in Huxley and Huxley, 1947, p. 124).

Since marriage counselors must deal with a variety of problems that clients bring in which are, ultimately, reducible in the main to *ethical* or what have been called "moral" issues, counselors must be explicitly clear in their own minds and in their relationships with their clients about how such issues are best resolved. Turning such dilemmas over to the client's conscience is really not a very satisfactory solution.

Whatever the problem may be, divorce, extra marital relations, certain sexual behaviors within the marriage, the handling of money or other marital "rights," the conscience may be the major factor in the client's *having* the problem in the first place. Turning the client back to his conscience is of very little fundamental help to him, particularly if the reason he feels guilty and is in the counselor's office in the first place is because of the unquestioned assumptions of his conscience.

Camilla Anderson, a psychiatrist, has suggested that man's propensity for making *moral judgments* is the basis for much of his human trouble (Anderson, 1957). As the present writer has discussed in other contexts (Ard, 1967), counselors need to get away from such concepts as "sin" (Mowrer to the contrary notwithstanding), and help clients come to rational conclusions that will not be as self-defeating as turning back to the conscience.

As Huxley so succinctly put it,

> Once we realize that the primitive superego is merely a makeshift developmental mechanism, no more intended to be the permanent central support of

our morality than is our embryonic notochord intended to be the central support of our bodily frame, we shall not take its dictates so seriously (have they not often been interpreted as the authentic Voice of God?), and shall regard its suppression by some more rational and less cruel mechanism as the central ethical problem confronting every human individual (Huxley & Huxley, 1947, p. 256).

REFERENCES

Anderson, C. *Beyond Freud*. New York: Harper, 1957.

Ard, B. Nothing's uglier than sin, *Rational Living*. 1967, Vol. 2, No. 1, pp. 4–6.

Aronfreed, J. *Conduct and conscience*. New York: Academic Press, 1968.

Bergler, E. *The superego*. New York: Grune & Stratton, 1952.

Browning, R. L., & Peters, H. J. On the philosophical neutrality of counselors, in Ard, B. N., Jr. *Counseling and psychotherapy: classics on theories and issues*. Palo Alto: Science & Behavior Books, 1966.

Buhler, C. *Values in Psychotherapy*. New York: Free Press of Glencoe, 1962.

Erikson, E. H. *Childhood and society*. New York: Norton, 1950.

Fenichel, O. *The psychoanalytic theory of neurosis*. New York: Norton, 1945.

Flugel, J. C. *Man, morals and society*. New York: International Universities Press, 1945.

Freud, S. *The ego and the id*. London: Hogarth Press, 1927.

Freud, S. *Civilization and its discontents*. London: Hogarth Press, 1930.

Freud, S. *New introductory lectures on psychoanalysis*. New York: Norton, 1933.

Freud, S. *An outline of psychoanalysis*. New York: Norton, 1949.

Fromm, E. *Man for himself*. New York: Rinehart, 1947.

Horney, K. *Neurosis and human growth*. New York: Norton, 1950.

Huxley, T. H., & Huxley, J. *Touchstone for ethics*. New York: Harper, 1947.

Knight, J. A. *Conscience and guilt*. New York: Appleton-Century-Crofts, 1969.

London, P. *The modes and morals of psychotherapy*. New York: Holt, Rinehart & Winston, 1964.

Maslow, A. H. *New knowledge in human values*. New York: Harper, 1959.

Otto, M. *Science and the moral life*. New York: New American Library, 1949.

Stevenson, C. I. *Ethics and language* New Haven: Yale, 1944.

Stewart, G. *Conscience and reason*. New York: Macmillan, 1951.

Symonds, P. M. *The Dynamics of human adjustment*. New York: Appleton-Century-Crofts, 1946.

Thompson, C. *Psychoanalysis: evolution and development* New York: Hermitage, 1950.

White, A. B. *Ethics for unbelievers*. London: Routledge & Kegan Paul, 1948.

Theoretical Issues and Viewpoints

> *. . . I am distressed at the manner in which small caliber minds immediately accept a theory–almost any theory–as a dogma of truth.*
>
> CARL R. ROGERS

The following section deals specifically with several different theoretical approaches to marriage and family counseling. Following this section is still another section on conjoint marriage counseling (Section IV), which has developed particular theoretical approaches of its own. Of course, group marriage counseling (Section V) has particular theoretical concepts arising from the nature of its parameters. In a sense, the whole handbook is sprinkled with various theoretical approaches to the different sorts of problems in marital, premarital, sexual, and other areas. But in the following section several outstanding authorities discuss in depth a variety of theoretical issues and viewpoints.

Hilda Goodwin and Emily Mudd, in Chapter 9, discuss various indications for marriage counseling, along with some of its methods and goals. Specifically, these authors examine the values sought in contemporary marriage, the basic concepts in counseling practice, the definition of marriage counseling, the goals of marriage counseling, the indications for marriage counseling, the structure and process of counseling, desirable gains in marriage counseling, and the future of marriage counseling.

In Chapter 10, Constance Callahan Ard discusses a frequently-overlooked matter of fundamental importance in marriage counseling: the role of nonverbal communication. Much of the literature in the field of marriage counseling deals with verbal communication and its interpretation so marriage counselors need to be aware of the added information they can make use of in the nonverbal communication evidenced by their clients.

Aaron Rutledge, in Chapter 11, discusses male and female roles in marriage counseling. Are there some particular problems in marriage counseling which should be handled by a female? By a male? By both a male and a female working together as a professional team?

In Chapter 12, Ben N. Ard, Jr. discusses the rational-emotive approach to marriage counseling, spelling out some of the basic ideas of a provocative approach initiated by Albert Ellis. RET (rational-emotive therapy) is presented as an approach to marriage counseling which

deserves consideration, despite the fact that it introduces some controversial techniques and methods, such as vigorously attacking the irrational,
unquestioned philosophical assumptions or ideas of the clients. Other new
ideas of RET are the techniques of confrontation, confutation, deindoctrination, re-education and a unique contribution of "homework
assignments." Although many of these ideas may appear too radical to
some readers, each of them can well be considered as a possible tool in the
marriage counselor's armamentarium.

In Chapter 13 Murray Bowen discusses the use of family theory in
clinical practice—the current status and possible future of the family
movement, his own theoretical and clinical orientation, family theory, and
the clinical use of family psychotherapy.

In Chapter 14, Clinton Phillips presents an eclectic approach to
marriage counseling theory, incorporating concepts of synthesis, eclecticism, systems theory and paradox.

Gerhard Neubeck, in Chapter 15, presents a humanistic approach in
the final chapter of this section.

CHAPTER 9

Marriage Counseling: Methods and Goals

Hilda M. Goodwin and Emily H. Mudd

The term "marriage counseling" has, over the years, been used to describe a wide variety of activities. Today the problem of defining what is meant by marriage counseling becomes a first essential of any discussion. Not only is there no clear definition of what constitutes a marriage except in the legal and religious sense, but there are no clear-cut or agreed-upon factors essential to a satisfying marriage for all individuals in our multi-pronged, rapidly changing society (Womble, 1966). Thus, one finds many different theoretical formulations, methods, and goals as the bases for a therapeutic approach to a troubled relationship between husband and wife. These varied approaches include "Haley's Marriage Therapy [Haley, 196?]," the psychodynamic approach to the individual problems of husband and wife (Greene, 1965), "role theory (Stein, 1959)," the transactional approach of Grinker (1961) and associates, and the sundry methods of working with a marriage reported by members of the interdisciplinary American Association of Marriage Counselors (Mudd, Karpf, Stone, & Nelson, 1958). At times the ideas advanced by these various theoretical formulations restate established principles of therapy or counseling without identifying them as such, and essentially offer new perspectives rather than new principles or facts.

In addition to the theoretical and conceptual differences, we find many variations in the structure of marriage counseling. Some counselors prefer to see only one member of a marriage, having the other partner work with someone else; others may see one partner primarily and the other spouse occasionally; still others may decide to work with the partners in individual and occasional joint interviews; others may prefer only joint interviews with the two spouses. More recently, group marriage counseling, involving either one spouse or at times both spouses, further complicates and enriches the picture.

Many similar problems are presented in therapy of the whole family. Even the question of how one defines the family unit is a moot one

Reprinted with permission of the authors and the publisher from *Comprehensive Psychiatry*, 1966, 7, 450–462.

(Christensen, 1964). Does one conceive of it empirically to at times involve an apparent outsider who is in reality a functional part of the family group, or do we hold to the theoretical unit of the nuclear family? There are many variables in considering any one of these family units. A family unit changes with time and has a different structure, a different function, different boundaries, and the members have different psychological needs, depending upon where the family is in the life cycle. This is also true of marriage, which, as Otto Pollak has indicated (Pollak, 1965), has many varied psychological orientations, functions, and kinds of reciprocal relationships between the spouses. Thus, in considering any specific marriage, it becomes essential to consider the psychological factors, the ego strength of the partners, the sexual factors, the economic factors, and the situational factors. In addition, the particular function of the marriage at the time help is sought, the past experiences of each spouse, and the nature and areas of current disfunctioning are essential factors for consideration.

We would define marriage as a partnership between two individuals which carries with it commitment, not only to each other, but to the third entity of the marriage, the marital relationship. This partnership, hopefully, will offer each spouse certain specific satisfactions and values (Mace & Mace, 1960). A primary satisfaction sought in many of today's marriages is the meeting of each partner's emotional and affectional needs—the fulfillment of which every individual seems to strive for, to be the most beloved or the most important adult to some one other person. Beyond this, marriage offers satisfaction for sexual desires and activities within a relationship that carries religious, social, and cultural acceptance, thus alleviating feelings of guilt and anxiety in this vital area of living. A third value consists of a way of life, recognized by the community, which is distinctly different from that enjoyed by a single person or by individuals living in other kinds of liaisons. The fourth value is a stable situation in which to work and plan *with someone* toward future living, having a companion with whom one may grow old and share disappointments, dissatisfactions, and frustrations as they are met in day-to-day living. An additional satisfaction for many couples is the projection of life into the future through their children. This carries an ongoingness in living that, in this day and age, may not be so readily available either through a religious philosophy or other media. However, it is our impression that many marriages today tend to remain stable only as the partners are able to offer at least minimal gratifications of each one's emotional needs. It is when either spouse begins to feel that his or her emotional needs are not met, and the rewards of marriage are not sufficient, that frustration, rejection, and conflicts emerge.

BASIC CONCEPTS IN COUNSELING PRACTICE

One of the basic concepts that determine both theoretical formulations and methods of working with marriage partners is related to balance within the reciprocal marital interaction. So long as there is an adequate dovetailing of each partner's needs and acceptable patterns of reciprocity in meeting them, the union seems to remain stable. We do not mean to imply that the marital partners are in any sense divorced from the larger environment, nor that there cannot be problems concerning children, in-laws, money, sexual adjustment, etc., arising within the marriage. How-ever, it has become evident in our years of clinical experience that when there is a fundamentally positive reciprocal base for meeting each other's emotional needs, the capacity for problem-solving within the family remains high.

It is generally recognized that each partner carries into marriage many unresolved needs from childhood, and may attempt to have these satisfied by the spouse. However, it is not the type of need that is definitive, but whether the needs of the partners coincide and result in mutuality in emotional support and affection as the central components of the rela-tionship. Thus, every marriage should be approached by the counselor as a unique organization of two individuals who have brought certain specific needs and desires to the situation, certain concepts of the marital roles of each, certain methods of communication, certain reciprocity in the shar-ing of responsibility, and varying degrees of commitment to the union.

Many people seeking assistance comment about difficulties in com-munication. It soon becomes apparent that part of the difficulty is not necessarily in the lack of verbal ability, but in the fact that the words used carry within them not a "dictionary meaning," but the meaning of the experiences behind the words to the person who is using them. This was illustrated vividly in a group of graduate "trainees" when a Protestant theologian spoke with great reverence of the word "cross" at Easter and of the redemption significance it had for him. A Jewish theologian in the same group listened and then replied that this word held a far different meaning for him. He explained that during his boyhood in a ghetto in Europe the marching of a group of Christians toward the ghetto and the infliction of severe punishment on the members of the Jewish race were symbolized for him by the cross the group carried as it came toward the ghetto (Goodwin, 1964). This same use of words to carry the emotional meaning of experience is part of the communication problems within any marriage situation. In a similar way idiosyncrasies of behavior, social manners, dress, tones of voice, and recognition of ceremonies communi-cate the meaning of the experiences behind them along with the present response.

The term "counseling" has been used to describe a variety of activities over the years and therefore carries different connotations to persons of different professional and experiential backgrounds. As the term "counsel-ing" is used in this article, it is regarded as a learned art in which a professionally trained person has acquired certain basic knowledges, atti-tudes, and skills and has integrated these into a disciplined capacity to use himself therapeutically with individuals or couples seeking help with intra-personal or interpersonal problems of adjustment. Their basic knowledges would include an understanding of physiological and personality growth, of psychodynamic theory, of cultural and ethnic factors as they affect the unique marital partners, of role interaction, of relationship theory, and of counseling skills and process. An understanding of the many facets in marriage—including the affectional, sexual, economic, ethical, and religious—is important (Goodwin & Mudd, 1964).

All of these factors bring important influences to bear on the behavior of both spouses and of the counselor as they relate to each other, and all influence the type, degree, and success of communication between the three. As the counselor deals in verbal and nonverbal communication, he will need to be expert in understanding language as it is related to thinking, feeling, and behavior, and he will need to be aware that the language which is characteristic of his own social position may facilitate or handicap the understanding he is attempting to achieve with his clients. It is also important that the counselor be related to the psychological processes involving circular transactions between the partners and between himself and the partners.

Marriage counseling differs from individual counseling in that the focus is upon the marital relationship and the circular interaction between the partners rather than on the specific intrapsychic forces within the individual partners. At times, as indicated by the process and content, a counselor may work with an individual on his intrapsychic difficulties as they relate to a particular area of difficulty in the marriage, with the focus moving back and forth between childhood needs and patterns of relating as they were developed in the past and are inappropriate in the current marital situation (Goodwin, 1957).

We would define complementarity of roles to mean that each person automatically acts in conformity with the role that he is expected to assume by the partner, and the disequilibrium occurs when for some reason or another this complementarity is disturbed, and the expectations of each from the other are disappointed, with the resultant tension, anxiety, and frustration occurring. Spiegel (1957) defines role as "a bold directed pattern or sequence of acts tailored by the cultural process for the transactions a person may carry out in a social group or situation [p. 1]." When role complementarity is established, the marriage presents stability and harmony, and is conducive to further work toward unifying the marital relationship.

GOALS OF MARRIAGE COUNSELING

Recognizing the complementary nature of the needs and patterns of behavior of the two marital partners as they are reflected in the reciprocal marital interaction, one of the essential goals of marriage counseling is to help the troubled partners come to some understanding of the interlocking and intermeshing nature of their problems. Through a compassionate and empathetic relationship with a marriage counselor, the partners are helped to some awareness of the ways in which their own feelings, attitudes, demands, expectations, patterns of relating, and responses affect this circular interaction. A second goal may be to help the partners come to terms with the satisfaction that may be realistically possible in adult life within the specific existential situation of their marriage.

The basic goal in marriage counseling is, therefore, not to effect any drastic change in the personality structure of either partner, but to help each to perceive his own reality, the reality of the partner, and that of the marriage more clearly. Where possible, counseling would assist each spouse to shift in his demands and patterns of relating sufficiently so that each may achieve at least minimal satisfactions and rewards within their particular marriage. In some instances counseling may help the couple clarify their inability to effect a satisfactory adjustment in this marriage, and a decision to seek psychiatric help for basically crippling personality characteristics may be made and referral effected for one or both partners. In certain instances a decision to terminate the marriage may be constructive and may be the final choice of one or both spouses.

The degree of change and the depth to which it may occur depends upon the individual's personality structure, its flexibility, the person's other assets, and the motivation to change. In some situations a very slight shift in each partner may permit the other spouse to receive sufficient gratifications out of the relationship to effect a satisfactory modification in the marital balance. In other situations in which the individuals exhibit greater flexibility in coping with change, are more open to their own and others' feelings, and have some capacity for genuine feeling communication, considerable growth toward maturity and toward a mutually supporting marital balance may occur.

There are a variety of sources in the United States where marriage counseling can be found. Among these are the member agencies of the Family Service Association of America, church-associated clinics, independent organizations, university services, as well as facilities offered in the private practice of psychiatrists, psychologists, social workers, teachers, ministers, and lawyers. Marriage Council of Philadelphia offers a clearly defined service, that is, psychologically oriented counseling help, either premarital or postmarital, to couples who are experiencing difficulties within their relationship (Mudd, 1951). With the current dissemination of knowledge on personality and on interpersonal dynamics, and with the mass media emphasizing the desirability of securing psychological help for troubled marriages, application for marriage counseling defines, to a degree, where the marital partners place their problems and where they are willing to begin to work on them. For those couples who perceive their difficulties as lying within the relationship, marriage counseling help is indicated. If there is pronounced intrapsychic illness in either or both partners, a referral for psychiatric care is indicated.

Marital conflict may begin at any stage of a marriage; in some situations it may precede the actual marriage ceremony. Today, with the increased number of situations in which pregnancy may precede the marital ceremony, conflicts may exist prior to, or from the date of, marriage. These may be engendered by the couple's feeling of loss of choice (although this may be denied in various ways), by the insecurity this loss

creates concerning the partner's feelings about the spouse and the marriage, and by the necessity for changes in plans and for the assumption of
responsibilities for which neither partner was prepared. For these and
other unready couples, there are a number of life tasks to be accomplished
before a unity and mutuality in marriage can be achieved. Each partner
may need help in separating from the parents, in achieving a sense of
personal identity, in understanding and accepting the roles of husband and
wife, and in developing an identity as a married couple. In such situations
marital counseling can often facilitate a couple's growth toward maturity
and a mutually satisfying marital realtionship.

Another indication of the need for help with a marriage relationship
may be found in the couple who are experiencing difficulty in "communication." Broken down, this usually means that the differences or conflicts
have been denied. Each partner has suppressed his angry or negative feelings and has withdrawn more and more from the relationship. When this
occurs, satisfactions and gratifications diminish until the accumulation of
irritations and resentments break into the open and threaten the marriage.
At such a period couples may seek help. More recently we are finding an
increase in applications from couples approaching retirement and the ending of active life (Mudd, Mitchell, & Taubin, 1965). Old conflicts and
difficulties tend to be exacerbated as life fears increase, and, as a result, a
heavier demand for security and reassurance is placed on the partner.
These couples utilize short-term individual and joint marital counseling
very effectively.

Marital counseling is also sought by those individuals, either or both of
whom have already obtained individual psychiatric help with some abate-
ment of their own personal discomfort, but without observable improvement in the marital relationship. In other instances one marriage partner
may be involved in individual therapy, with the result that the other
partner feels isolated and confused concerning changes in the spouse
which result in modifications in the marital interaction. The isolated
spouse may, under such circumstances, seek marital counseling for himself, or this may be suggested by the psychiatrist. We have found that it is
helpful to such partners to be involved together in a marital counseling
group. Other couples for whom group marital counseling may be the
treatment of choice are those individuals who experience little anxiety
concerning their own adjustment, shift very slowly or not at all in individual counseling or therapy, but are unhappy in their marriage, and tend to
almost totally project blame and responsibility for the difficulties and the
necessity for change onto the spouse. We have found group marital counseling an effective method for working with such situations (Linden,
Goodwin, & Resnik, 1966).

STRUCTURE AND PROCESS OF COUNSELING

Within our conceptual framework, we see marital difficulty arising, as
indicated earlier, out of the reciprocal interaction of the two unique
human beings who are the marital partners and who create in the process a

third entity, the marital relationship, with its rewards and gratifications, its frustrations and hostilities. Thus, the essential center of interest in counseling with a marital pair is on the reciprocal dynamics of the marital relationship and what each partner puts into this, rather than specifically on the intrapersonal conflicts of each. However, the concept of "marital relationship," like most labels for human behavior, does not imply a continued or a consistent state of being, but a relationship which changes from day to day. At best, marital partners are intimately related to each other occasionally and at certain points in time, rather than with continuous awareness as many couples seem to expect.

There are inevitable periods when either spouse, engaged in the problems and tasks of daily living, needs to be to a degree disengaged. There is, however, a guideline that can be useful to beginning counselors—that is, the relative degree of mutuality there is in a relationship. Mutuality as used here would imply a recognition by each of the separateness as well as of the unity of the partner, and that he or she has responsibilities, wants, and needs of his own which coexist with those of the marriage. Each can perceive the other as a separate person and have concern and caring for the partner rather than expecting him or her to exist solely as an extension of himself or for his own satisfaction. This may be contrasted with the inordinately self-centered persons who have little or no ability to perceive the other as a separate individual but who expect an idealized happiness to be created for them by the spouse, who supposedly exists solely for them and for their satisfaction. Any failure of the spouse to meet the needs of such partner is considered as selfish and hostile.

The average couple will fall toward the middle of a continuum from a mutual capacity for caring and concern for each other to the other end of the scale where there is self-centeredness and inability to relate to another person or his needs. It thus follows that, in working with any couple, one has to take into consideration the specific individuals, the kind of reciprocal interaction flowing back and forth between them, and what possible solution one can work toward with this particular couple. The specific partners, their personality structures, dynamics, interrelationship, and chronicity of difficulties do determine, to a degree, the process and goal of counseling. In 66 percent of cases served at Marriage Council, follow-up contacts four years later indicated that the situation for which assistance had been sought had been resolved or modified (Ballard & Mudd, 1957). In certain cases a constructive goal can be to help the partners recognize that this union cannot give them or their children the kind of satisfactions desired. Support of their choice toward separation is seen as more desirable than a continuing destructive relationship between them. In other cases the goal may be to help either one or both partners accept the need for individual psychiatric help. This happens in approximately 10 percent of Marriage Council's cases.

Marriage Council has, over the years, offered individual counseling to marital partners and within the past several years has offered group marriage counseling to certain selected couples. Throughout, it has been the agency's philosophy to make every effort to work with both partners, and through experience over the years we have found it more helpful to have the same counselor work with the two marital partners. This enables the counselor to experience, directly and intuitively, nuances in feeling and behavior within individual and joint interviews that are not possible when two counselors see the spouses separately. In individual counseling each partner is seen on a weekly basis for approximately fifty minutes, and joint as well as individual interviews are held in initial contacts and as indicated thereafter by the process of counseling. In other situations, where it seems that group counseling might be a more efficient way of working with the couple, this is suggested and the couple is assigned to a group totaling not more than six couples, led by a man and a woman as co-counselors.

Of central importance to working with marriages are the personality and characteristics of the counselor, his orientation, and his basic background knowledge. It is important that the counselor be a person with capacity for depth in relationship. In our method of approach, capacity to form a relationship not only to one person, but to the two partners as a marital pair, is essential. This includes keeping as a basic concern the couple's interrelationship with each other without becoming over-identified with either one. It has been our experience that technical training and knowledge is not adequate in working with marital relationship problems. It is a definite advantage for the counselor, to whom a couple can relate and with whom they can work honestly and sincerely on their difficulties, to have had a certain amount of life experience which helps him in attaining perspective on the couple's situation. The counselor needs to see himself as an enabler using his knowledge and skill in the process of helping the partners to clarify the source of their difficulties, rather than as an authoritative person with a definite concept of what every marriage must be. Since marriage is a factor in every counselor's life, either through his parental situation or in his own life experience, the problem of over-identification with one spouse or the other is a difficult one. It is important, therefore, that the counselor be aware of his own attitudes and philosophy toward marriage, and be willing and able to examine his own part in the counseling process actively and continuously as he works with marriage problems.

In individual counseling, as the process moves beyond the initial stage of identifying the problems, of determining when they began and how the couple has tried to handle them, part of the focus is on helping the partners clarify what it is they want in marriage. Are their goals realistic or unrealistic? Is what they desire possible in an adult relationship, or is this an inappropriate need brought over from childhood that cannot be met realistically in a marriage? (Glasser, 1965).

The attempt is made in counseling to help the couple reduce the intensity of the conflict by verbalization, by helping the clients to deal with their feelings of hostility and guilt, and by strengthening their self-esteem, thus reducing their need for holding to rigid defenses. As the couple becomes related to the counselor as an empathetic, responsible adult who cares what happens to his clients, each client is helped to look at his own pattern of relating and behavior, and to determine how this affects the marital interaction. Gradually the client comes to see the other partner and the self more realistically. Inevitably, each member of a marital pair comes to counseling feeling that the change needs to be in the other partner. It relieves both guilt and anxiety to help them understand during the early interviews that the primary difficulty lies not in either person, but in the circular interaction that takes place between them—the failure of each to meet in a way that is satisfying for the other the kinds of needs and wants that each has (Sullivan, 1950).

Joint interviews are useful in helping clients to connect with their circular interaction. During the joint interview the interaction of the couple in its destructive phases may be demonstrated, and the counselor takes responsibility for enabling the partners to evaluate what has been occurring between them and the effect it has had on each. As each spouse is able to see the part each has played in their joint difficulties and to express angers, frustrations, and resentments, hostility is reduced and more positive feelings, hopefully, may begin to emerge. Essentially the counselor has both a therapeutic and a re-educational function as he helps the couple see the ways in which they behave destructively and find other more constructive types of reacting.

As stated earlier, the process may involve many variations, depending upon the character structure and capacity of the partners. In certain situations an ego-supportive and reality-oriented approach by the counselor may be the treatment of choice. "Borderline" clients, or clients suffering from various degrees of ego defect, constitute a large proportion of the clients who come today to social agencies for help with problems of interpersonal difficulties. Invariably the problem is perceived as a situational or interpersonal one, with little awareness of the part played by intrapsychic difficulties. Since these clients are struggling with a high degree of ambivalence, are apprehensive, distrustful of relationship, and have frequently been disappointed in prior attempts to secure therapeutic help, the management of the counselor-client relationship assumes great importance.

Our approach at the Division of Family Study* and Marriage Council* is based on a nurturing relationship with an active reaching out and interest in helping the partners and a genuine responsiveness to the feelings of each. Because of the weak ego strength of many clients, focus within interviews is kept on solving the current reality and relationship problems with which the client is struggling, and efforts are directed toward improving ego strength and functioning. Effort is directed toward helping these clients to know more clearly what they feel, and to connect their ways of behaving with the response they receive. There is a different use of techniques; that is, the counselor names and "talks to" *feeling* rather than working toward helping the client understand the *why* of the feelings he experiences. It is equally important to help these clients develop more

---

*Division of Family Study in Psychiatry, University of Pennsylvania School of Medicine; and Marriage Council of Philadelphia.—*Editors*

accurate perception of reality and more skill in reality testing. The counselor in these situations, without implication of criticism, helps the partners to review conflicts and incidents step by step, tentatively raising questions concerning each partner's perception of the incident, other possible interpretations of it, and the way it may have been perceived by the other. Movement will be slow, but small gains in constructive ego functioning may shift the balance in the marriage and set in motion a more positive spiral of interaction, which in turn often effects constructively other interactional relationships of the client (Parad & Miller, 1963).

In 1958 group marriage counseling, involving four to six married couples (eight to twelve individuals) in the same group, was instituted at Marriage Council, and has continued to be one method in the treatment of certain types of marital difficulty: for example, couples where one or both are "acting out" their difficulties; couples where one or both partners are unaware or afraid of feeling; couples where one partner views self as the victim and the spouse as the offender; couples where one or both has had prior individual counseling or psychiatric therapy, with perhaps some personal gain, but no perceptible improvement in the marriage; couples where there is extreme use of projection and denial as major defenses; and marriages in which a partner is an excessive drinker (Linden et al., 1966).

Focus in groups, as in our individual counseling, is on the reciprocal interaction between the partners, rather than on the individual's intrapsychic conflicts. Content of group discussions may vary within wide limits, and is often characterized by excursions into past individual or marital history as related to each person's current marital difficulties. However, the ongoing focus and central theme is on the reality of the day-to-day, interspouse relationship, individual striving, role expectations, obvious psychological defenses, and conflicts as seen in the marriage. Each partner's characteristic pattern for satisfying his own needs, as well as modes of response to the demands of the spouse, emerge in the group process.

Groups are led by male and female co-counselors who carry in the role of counselors certain responsibilities. These include maintaining the focus of group effort on the interrelationship between marital partners, creating a group "climate" of acceptance, developing a group orientation through mutual trust and the factor of universalization. This process is conducive to expression of both positive and negative feelings and attitudes. It stimulates and supports group interaction rather than communications directed toward the co-therapists. The group members are thus enabled to respond to each other intellectually and affectively. The co-counselors assist the group to recognize distorted feelings, warped attitudes, specialized behavior, and ideational content through clarification, paraphrasing, and simplification. They aid the development of group process through the support of individuals or of their comments. They assist participants in identifying and dealing with either positive or negative feelings toward the co-counselors which have their roots in the past and are inappropriate in relation to the present situation. In these various processes the marital partners become aware of their neurotic interlocking patterns of need and response.

As indicated earlier, there is no effort in our approach to work deeply on the intrapsychic problems or conflicts of any individual partner, but instead to help them become aware of the way in which their own wants, needs, and patterns of relating affect their marital relationship. Through this approach the major changes that may occur will be in the circular interaction between the husband and wife, and collaterally, after this first step occurs, changes are often apparent in other relationships of each partner: to their children, their parents, their business associates. However, changes may be carried to considerable depth, depending upon the partner's personality and capacity.

In situations where marriages have benefited, there will be better communication with more honesty and more directness, less hostility, less actual conflicts; and when conflict arises, each partner will tend to examine his or her own part in it more quickly, and the conflict will then be resolved within a shorter time. Couples will have found a better way of talking about and resolving their problems. Some change in their concept of their own and their spouse's role and more realistic perception of the partner and of his wants and needs and of the individual self occurs. Defenses of denial and projection are used less extensively, and there is an acceptance of more responsibility for self-discipline and control of own behavior with greater tolerance for both the self and the spouse in the human quality of their interaction. As each learns a little more about the self and the partner, there tends to be a reawakening of the earlier, more positive relationship, and some conviction about the other's care and concern is revived.

It seems of considerable significance that the changes described in the way in which partners hopefully will handle their daily relationships after counseling are almost identical with the processes of problem-solving and conflict resolutions reported by one hundred couples who consider their marriage and family relationships successful and whose communities concurred in this estimate. Apparently healthy couples, whose reciprocal interaction is mutually satisfactory, have spontaneously arrived at these processes as realistically practical and constructive.

THE FUTURE OF MARRIAGE COUNSELING

Marriage counseling has become one aspect of the day-by-day work of professional persons from a variety of backgrounds, primarily social work, psychology, the ministry, medicine, and education. Since the first services in marriage counseling were initiated in the United States in 1931, among those interested there has been a gradually increasing exchange of data based on experience. Articles and books, and more recently a systematic review of cases from members of the American Association of Marriage Counselors, have been published. Some forty-one cases in which there was follow-up contact after the close of the case were reported in *Marriage*

Counseling: A Casebook, edited by a committee of the association. After analyzing these cases, the conclusions of the committee as formulated in 1958 still seem pertinent to further developments in this specialization (Mudd et al., 1958).

> When the Committee undertook to prepare this casebook there was no evidence available as to whether or not there were common denominators between theory and practice in the field of marriage counseling. Nor was it known how specifically any school of psychological thought might affect or differentiate methods and techniques employed by counselors with their clients. The close relationship between some of the more general principles and procedures in marriage counseling, on the one hand, as stated in Chapter 2 ("Principles, Processes, and Techniques of Marriage Counseling") and, on the other, the methods actually used by marriage counselors in practice as presented in the case material seem to have important implications for the present status of marriage counseling as well as for the future development of this field. The high degree of correlation between these general principles and the case material indicates that although the field is relatively new, there has already been developed a considerable amount of generally accepted practice, whether such practice is consciously related to formulated theory or not.

The world of 1966, and specifically the conflictual involvements within the United States and internationally, focus increasingly on the problems of human beings caught in a culture pervaded by scientific discoveries and technological innovations (Lee, 1966). It is almost a platitude to reiterate that "the conduct of human affairs, in contrast to progress in science and technology, has suffered from reliance upon generalities, superstitions, fallacies, and prejudices. There is all too little pertinent research concerning man's relation to his fellows and few guides to aid in the attainment of creative, cooperative, and mutually constructive interaction (Mudd, 1966). Marriage counseling can serve as a beginning guide.

Marriage counseling deals with the most intimate interpersonal relations of men and women. It also deals with one of the smallest social systems in which the dynamics of interpersonal conflict resolution can be observed and studied. It furnishes data as yet little explored or utilized in careful research. It is now incumbent upon man to learn how his own behavior with his fellow man can be modified to accommodate to the exigencies of tomorrow.

On the basis of our counseling experience, we suggest that conflict resolution in various groups might benefit from the use of the conceptual framework and the processes of the counseling session: the unpressured, unaccusing atmosphere, the give and take, the catharsis, the perspective, and the support of efforts at new and mutually acceptable behavior and interaction.

REFERENCES

Ballard, R. G. & Mudd, E. H. Some theoretical and practical problems in evaluating effectiveness of counseling. *Social Casework*, 1957, 10.

Christensen, H. T. (Ed.) *Handbook of marriage and the family*. Chicago: Rand McNally, 1964. Chap. 22.

Glasser, W. *Reality therapy*. New York: Harper & Row, 1965. Chap. I.

Goodwin, H. M. The nature and use of the tri-dimensional relationship in the process of marriage counseling. Unpublished doctoral dissertation, Univ. of Pa., 1957.

Goodwin, H. M. Marriage counseling and the minister. *J. Religion Health*, 1964, *3*, 1.

Goodwin, H. M. & Mudd, E. H. Concepts of marital diagnosis and therapy as developed at the Division of Family Study, Department of Psychiatry, School of Medicine, Univ. of Pa. In E. M. Nash, L. Jessner, & D. W. Abse (Eds.), *Marriage counseling in medical practice*. Chapel Hill: Univ. of North Carolina, 1964.

Greene, B. L. (Ed.) *The psychotherapies of marital disharmony*. Glencoe, Ill.: Free Press, 1965.

Grinker, R. R., et al. *Psychiatric social work—A transactional casebook*. New York: Basic Books, 1961.

Haley, J. Marriage therapy. *Arch. Gen. Psychiat.*, 1963, *8*, 213-234.

Johnson, D. *Marriage counseling: Theory and practice*. Englewood Cliffs, N. J.: Prentice-Hall, 1961.

Klemer, R. H. *Counseling in marital and sexual problems*. Baltimore, Md.: Williams & Wilkins, 1965.

Lee, A. McC. *Multi-valent man*. New York: George Braziller Publisher, 1966.

Linden, M., Goodwin, H. & Resnik, H. Group psychotherapy of couples in marriage counseling. Paper presented at Annual Meeting of the American Psychiatric Association, May 13, 1966, Atlantic City, N. J.

Mace, D. & Mace, V. *Marriage East and West*. New York: Doubleday & Co., 1960, Chap. 2.

Mudd, E. H. *The practice of marriage counseling*. New York: Association Press, 1961.

Mudd, E. H. Conflict and conflict resolution in families. In S. Mudd (Ed.), Conflict resolution and world education. Vol. III. The Hague, Netherlands: World Academy of Art and Science, 1966.

Mudd, E. H., Karpf, M. J., Stone, A., & Nelson, J. F. (Eds.) *Marriage counseling: A casebook*. New York: Association Press, 1958.

Mudd, E. H., Mitchell, H. E., & Taubin, S. R. Leisure and retirement. In *Success in family living*, New York: Association Press, 1956. p. 192-209.

Parad, H. J., & Miller, R. R. *Ego-oriented casework*. New York: Family Service Association of America, 1963. Chaps. 2, 7-9.

Pollak, O. Sociological and psychoanalytic concepts in family diagnosis. In L. Green (Ed.) *The psychotherapies of marital disharmony*. Glencoe, Ill.: Free Press, 1965. Chap. II.

Satir, V. *Conjoint family therapy: A guide to theory and technique*. Palo Alto, Calif.: Science and Behavior Books, 1964.

Spiegal, J. P. The resolution of role conflict within the family. *Psychiatry*, 1957, *20*, 1.

Stein, H. D. Sociocultural concepts in casework practice. Smith College Studies in Social Work, Feb. 1959. p. 63-75.

Sullivan H. S. Psychiatry: introduction to the study of interpersonal relations. In *A study of interpersonal relations*. P. Mullahy (Ed.), New York: Hermitage Press, 1950. p. 98-121.

Womble, D. L. Preparing for marriage tomorrow, in *Foundations for marriage and family relations*, New York: Macmillan, 1966. p. 523-548.

CHAPTER 10

The Role of Nonverbal
Communication in
Marriage Counseling

Constance C. Ard

Human beings are verbal animals. Even when they are not talking, they are more than likely thinking to themselves in sentences (Ellis, 1962; Ellis & Harper, 1961). So much of human behavior involves verbal interaction that it is easy to overlook the importance of *nonverbal* communication.

The scope of nonverbal modes of communication would include or involve any physical movement or gesture of any portion of the body—facial expressions, glances of the eyes, hand and arm movements, the manner in which an individual sits or walks, and what he expresses as he does these things (Bell, 1886; Spencer, 1910; Allport & Vernon, 1933; Birdwhistell, 1953; Barbara, 1956; Davitz, 1961; Dittman, 1962; Satir, 1964; Ekman, 1964, 1965; Rosenfeld, 1965; Wachtel, 1967). The tone of voice, how one touches another, the manner and style of dress, and the texture of skin around the eyes suggest additional modes of nonverbal communication. All personal mannerisms help to express how the individual feels towards himself, people, and life. In other words, his projection of self-worth and the values he holds may be indicated by his nonverbal communication. Many facets which an individual uses for means of nonverbal communication can be controlled—that is, if he is aware he is communicating nonverbally. Others cannot be controlled that easily. The latter could include a person's facial expressions and the eyes.

> Above all, the therapist must regard behavior and action as baselines of reality and must consider words—including his own—as secondary. If discrepancies arise between talking and doing, action always speaks louder than words. Once the patient has learned to observe action and to base his conclusions upon actions rather than words, he has a basis on which to function [Ruesch, 1963, p. 135].

There is a flaw here, however, in the implied suggestion to accept actions at face value, for there is no suggestion that the therapist verbally

Ard, C. C. Use of nonverbal communication in marriage counseling. *Marriage Counseling Quarterly*, 1968–69, 3–4, 32–45.

and logically "checks out" the nonverbal behavior or actions. Merely accepting the apparent meaning of nonverbal behavior could lead to misperception and projection. Nonverbal communication tends to be less guarded than verbal communication. This is accentuated and reinforced through our training in verbal communication, whereas nonverbal communication is generally disregarded or even discouraged (Beckman, 1963). Because of our careful censorship and control in the use of language, our true ideas and feelings can be camouflaged. Therefore, nonverbal behavior tends to be the more reliable form of communication (i.e., more likely to express one's "true" feelings or thoughts).

Professor Jerome Bruner of Harvard suggests that too much emphasis is placed on verbal communication: ". . . verbalization is not the only way people learn or know [Middleman, 1968, p. 80]."

Hall (1959) suggests that the "counseling interview is primarily vocal communication between two people. Not what the person says, but how he says it—his intonation, rate of speech, and other expressive behavior—are the chief sources of information for the interview [p. 148]."

I once had a client who could not (or preferred not to) look at people when they talked. She related that she could not concentrate as well. She also had the tendency not to "get involved" or want to care about others. "People-watching" was enjoyable for this client, but seldom did she look at people who were talking. She had had very little practice in how to handle and cope with people, men and women alike, who wanted to get close to her emotionally. During several interviews, her nonverbal communication was more clear and unguarded than her verbal communication. Part of her "homework" during the week was to practice looking at her boyfriend as he spoke to her, then "check out" her own thoughts and reactions about what she was hearing and observing from him. After several months of listening to and observing significant others, including her boyfriend, she was able to act more comfortably with the increased personalism of these relationships.

Each of us brings his own unique background of experiences to an interpretation of nonverbal cues (Wendt, 1962). This is why it is so important to check out these nonverbal cues by any means (e.g., stop assuming and start asking, check out one's perceptions with others, etc.). Satir (1964) suggested that feelings could be related to facts by asking for specific examples or documentation of each nonverbal behavior the client is referring to. For example, "the therapist can ask the client for data which help to support his perceptions: 'How do you know she doesn't care what you do?' or 'What does he do that makes you feel he is mean?' [p. 170]." She goes on to say that "the nonverbal is a less clear or explicit communication, so it requires greater attention [p. 78]."

It is interesting to note that nonverbal forms of communication are an infant's first means of expression. As the child begins to grow and "mature," nonverbal communication still persists; but due to our cultural demands, verbal communication moves into the spotlight. When nonverbal communication is placed in a secondary position, not only is a child's skill hampered in the area of communication, but his personality growth may be affected by diminishing his sensitivity to the natural and social environment, his ability to think critically, and his potential for creativity (Beckman, 1963). As we continue up the path of "maturity," many adults develop a sort of mask, behind which they conceal their true feelings and thoughts. Over the years the mask tends to become one with smaller holes, which can narrow the vision of the beholder.

A possible reason why some individuals may tend to overlook or not be aware of nonverbal communication is its covert nature. With friends and acquaintances we may disagree with a statement that has been made, but seldom do we comment about facial expressions, smiles, etc. Within the counseling arena, however, incongruent nonverbal communication should be questioned in a similar fashion to illogical verbalizations.

Ethnic and class groups differ both in the primary modes of nonverbal behavior and in the extent of their reliance upon nonverbal communication.

William Webster (1967) has observed that when counseling with adult Spanish-Americans and Negroes, the "hands and arms are very important adjuncts to the ability to communicate effectively [p. 1]," whereas counselors possessing middle-class standards generally do not use their hands or arms to communicate to any great extent.

Rowe, Brooks, and Watson (1960) suggest that people unfamiliar with American Indian gesture language are able to understand, through gestures alone, what is being communicated.

Chagall has said, "In mixed company, women practice a sort of visual shorthand, which later, they will laboriously and at great length decode in the company of other women."

Delaney (1968) suggests that "there is no mystical construct necessary for the understanding of emotions communicated by facial expression, hand gestures, and feet and body movements. This communicative ability to express oneself without the use of words is common to all men, cutting across cultural ties [p. 315]." (Cf. Vinacke, 1949; Vinacke & Fong, 1955.)

Other research (Ekman, 1965) on nonverbal behavior suggests that the direction of an individual's motives are indicated through facial expressions while manifestations of intensity of motivation can be observed in the gestures of the lower body. Arthur Rogers (1968) provides an illustration which was made possible through the use of a videotape:

> A young woman viewed herself on a videotape—with the sound turned off. Her gestures were alternately wide open, with hands extended to people, and closed off and restricted (all within the course of a few minutes of speech). Here gestures epitomized her central concern at the time. "That's it," she said. . . . "I don't know whether to be open or closed [p. 39].

The use of the video tape when counseling with married couples presents a vast source of the "here and now" behaviors and verbalizations.

One can record the nonverbal as well as the verbal then immediately playback the information and "check it out" with the client. (See also Chapter 48, "Information-Gathering Techniques of Value in Marriage Counseling.")

NONVERBAL COMMUNICATION IN THE COUNSELING SESSION

How and why is nonverbal communication an important aspect in marriage, family, and child counseling? In the pages to follow I will describe the relationship of this introductory material to the counseling task. Illustrations have been drawn from the experience of colleagues as well as from my own clients and research.

When a new client comes to the office for marriage counseling, a handshake usually takes place. The handshake between the marriage counselor and his client is an indicator of some nonverbal communication. This was illustrated in an episode in the comic strip *Peanuts* (Schultz, 1966): Lucy is playing the role of the psychiatrist, whose help costs in this instance, 5 cents. (Don't let the cost fool you!) She has her hand extended to her client, good ole Charlie Brown, who asks, "What are you doing?" Lucy responds, "I want to shake your hand. . . . A doctor sometimes can tell a lot about a patient merely by shaking his hand. . . ." They shake hands. Lucy remarks: "Mercy, I can't believe it." "What's the matter?" asks Charlie. Lucy continues, "It's fantastic! I never would have believed it. The things you can learn about someone just by shaking his hand!" Charlie asks, "What's the matter?" Lucy responds, "I can't tell you. . . . This is one of those things that can never be discussed with a patient! It's much better that you don't know. Actually, I still can't believe it. I just can't believe it. . . ." As Lucy walks away Charlie is left standing, responding with his mouth wide open, "AAUGH!"

I suggest that as a counselor one *must* share these insights because they can be valuable in helping clients better understand their own behavior.

Let us consider some case illustrations of how married couples react to, or function with, nonverbal communication. One couple seen for marriage counseling devoted much talk to the areas of affection and making love. There were complaints that the husband was more affectionate before marriage than after; that he "stroked" his mate more while courting and "whispered sweet nothings in her ear"; but now that he has her "hooked," he can "relax". And she had assumed that after they were married and had a child, certain of his annoying behaviors would change—they did not, they were just more frequent.

Throughout the period of counseling I saw this couple together several times and observed that *nonverbal* cues were being exchanged. They usually sat apart from each other. When one partner did not like something the mate said, sharp glances of the eyes and a general tightness of the body would follow. I asked them if they were aware of this nonverbal behavior and how it seemed to reinforce what they were saying verbally. At times they were aware of it, but they did not "check it out." They reported just feeling "hotter under the collar." In fact, one reaction of the husband was to light another cigarette and look down or away from his wife while he continued to speak. We proceeded to work on what each person expected from the other in terms of *nonverbal* affection and reinforcement, as well as *what* they were saying to each other and *how* they were saying it.

Another couple was experiencing a different kind of communication difficulty. This couple communicated more on the nonverbal level than on the verbal. At times, they caused each other psychological hurts, as each neglected to check-out the messages that were received. Other times one partner would take a change in the tone of voice of the spouse as a personal affront, while the sender of the message would be unaware of a tone change. This couple was given a "homework" task of answering a nonverbal worksheet which caused them to stop and analyze how they were interacting, as well as how they interacted with their children. After several sessions and several weeks of working daily on their given homework, they began to improve in their accuracy of both nonverbal and verbal communications. This helped to foster a freer, healthier relationship. They were instructed also to "stop assuming and start asking," which became easier with practice.

In the two examples cited, it was evident to the counselor that there was a great deal of nonverbal exchange, but the couples were unaware of it or did not check out what meanings they were perceiving. It appears to me, that in addition to various "homework" assignments which can help the couple learn how to communicate (on all levels) more congruently, the use of the video tape also could help the couples increase their awareness of the multiple channels of their communication. The video tape provides an immediate and accurate feedback which can be rerun as often as necessary.

Alger and Hogan (1967) suggest that by viewing videotape playbacks married couples can develop an "increased awareness of the activities and feelings of both marital partners [p. 1426]." This procedure would help them to become more aware of the many different messages they are sending. For example "one husband asked that the tape be stopped and said to his wife, 'You know, when you were talking there, I was feeling very tender and concerned and loving toward you, and yet as I see myself on the TV, I see that no one would ever know I was feeling that way by my bland look.' His wife then spoke, and as she did, tears were in their eyes. 'I didn't feel your caring then, but I feel it now' [Alger & Hogan, 1967, p. 1427]." This example illustrates how the nonverbal and verbal messages sometimes do not complement one another. By each person's becoming more attentive to his spouse's total communication or to the relationship between the nonverbal and verbal communication, errors are less likely to occur, and the partners can become more congruent if they continue to practice and work on their new knowledge.

Carl Rogers (1961) offers some food for thought regarding the ability to recognize congruence and incongruence within individuals, which could be applied to the marital situation:

With some individuals we realize that in most areas this person not only consciously means exactly what he says, but that his deepest feelings also match what he is expressing, whether it is anger or competitiveness or affection or cooperativeness. . . . Obviously, then, different individuals differ in their degree of congruence, and the same individual differs at different moments in degree of congruence, depending on what he is experiencing and whether he can accept this experience in his awareness, or must defend himself against it [p. 342].

Problems regarding "body language" between spouses come up quite often in sexual relations. Communicating through touch is often related to love-making. Mating is, according to Frank (1958),

tactile communication, reinforced and elaborated by motor activities and language, by concomitant stimulation, visual, auditory, olfactory, gustatory, and the deeper muscle senses, combined to provide an organic-personality relationship which may be one of the most intense human experiences . . . [p. 61].

Frank's theory of "tactile communication," in summary, suggests that "the skin functions as the organ of communication—both as a receptor and transmitter of messages. . . . In many interpersonal relations, tactile language functions most effectively and communicates more fully than vocal language [p. 35]."

Frank also states that "the elementary sexual process of the human organism may be transformed and focused into an interpersonal love relationship with an identified person to whom each is seeking to communicate, *using sex not for procreation . . . but as another language*, for interpersonal communication [p. 61]."

One particular couple I saw was faced with such a situation. The husband, in this case, had been approached by another woman desiring to have sex with him. There had been available opportunities for this new twosome to go to bed, but they stopped at the heavy petting stage. The wife knew about the other woman; in fact they were friends. There was no desire on either the husband's or the other woman's part to have sex relations for procreative reasons, only to partake in another form of communication.

Another example of a breakdown in nonverbal communication between partners appeared in the couple who had been married for twenty years. When questioned by the marriage counselor, the husband was unable to report whether or not his wife ever had had orgasm. This is a strong indicator of going-through-the-mechanical-motions of sex, but never being aware of, or "tuned in" to, the many nonverbal cues or indications present in the love-making experience.

To help illustrate a few of the tactual difficulties some people experience, perhaps Rollo May's (1966) statement would be appropriate:

It is a strange fact in our society that what goes into building a relationship—the sharing of tastes, fantasies, dreams, hopes for the future, and fears from the past—seems to make people more shy and vulnerable than going to bed with each other. They are more wary of the tenderness that goes with psychological and spiritual nakedness than they are of physical nakedness in sexual intimacy [p. 21].

NONVERBAL COMMUNICATION IN CHILDREN

Children tend to use nonverbal communication automatically until adults interfere or fail to respond. Most children are very adept at communicating and reading nonverbal communication.

Much has been written discussing therapy with children. Moreno (1946), Moustakus (1953), and Axline (1947) are a few who have written about, and worked with, children in play therapy. Play therapy gives the child an opportunity to act what he is thinking and feeling in the "here and now."

It would be helpful when working with children in play therapy to have intermittent periods for verbal discussion of some of the child's nonverbal behavior, to describe it and perhaps interpret together its meaning and use. Beier (1966) has suggested that children may use facial expressions, gestures, and silences to express their emotions. Also valuable within the child's communicative framework are his toys. Children learn rather quickly that certain behaviors will elicit certain adult responses, including specific uses of toys.

Examples of how a child might communicate two different messages would be his verbal expression of warmth toward a person while his body was very tight and rigid; his saying everything is fine while he's sobbing; saying that he does not have a stomach ache while he is clutching at his stomach; and when questioned regarding a fight with a boy at school, giving a verbal response "no" about his involvement while his facial expressions say "yes" he was involved and his voice pitch changes. When a child's nonverbal and verbal communications are in conflict, they call for further checking out by the receivers.

Nonverbal communication can be said, then, to have a prime position in the family structure of interaction. How might a greater awareness of nonverbal communication help the members of a family unit? There are several ways. It can help parents to understand their children and spouses to understand one another by providing an additional avenue of communication. Attention to nonverbal communication may help family members understand nonfamily persons better (e.g., friends, people with different cultural backgrounds, etc.). Even though children are frequently ahead of adults in understanding nonverbal communication, children can still benefit from being helped to "read" siblings' and parents' nonverbal behavior more accurately. Attention to one's own nonverbal communication may help each individual family member to understand himself better, especially those messages he is communicating to others without awareness. In so far as family members can improve their skills at understanding nonverbal communication, they will probably increase their ability to get their wants, needs, and desires met more adequately, inside the family as well as outside. They probably would be more creative and more spontaneous in their nonverbal reactions, so the quality of their interpersonal relations in general should increase due to the increased variety of their behaviors.

Adults who use nonverbal communication often seem unaware of doing so. They seem to be poor at interpreting cues of their own because they are unaware of other adults' nonverbal communication. Some use this ability easily and readily with children but not with other adults. It is as if they do not have the time or patience to do so with adults. The family counseling setting can provide an excellent opportunity for family members to learn how to recognize the various types of messages they are sending. It would also provide family members the opportunity to learn how to "check-out" certain nonverbal messages, instead of falling into the "over-psychologizing" trap. There may not be some deep, dark, negative reason for a person's behavior—Freud notwithstanding—and reading interpretation *into* behavior can be a serious mistake.

Modes of nonverbal communication in a family group probably allow adults to teach children indirectly what to believe and how to behave. Beier (1966), in dissecting the "anatomy of a message," distinguishes between a "persuasive" message, in which "the sender codes his message in full awareness of what he is doing," and an "evoking" message. Beier goes on to say, "Repeated persuasive messages will create certain value systems in the child without his ever becoming aware of where he learned these values [p. 12]."

Satir (1964) explains how the counselor can relate silence to covert controls: The counselor says, "I saw you looking at mother. Were you thinking she didn't want you to speak? Maybe you think if you speak you'll get clobbered. We'll have to find out what makes it so unsafe to talk [p. 167]."

When the counselor is working with a family unit, video tape is again valuable. More than likely the family members are unaware of the discrepancy between their nonverbal and verbal communications. The video tape can record these discrepant responses, and then be replayed, dissected, and clarified by the family members. It would provide them with a close and immediate look at *what* and *how* they are saying something and how other members of the family react—nonverbally as well as verbally. Hopefully, this will help sharpen each person's awareness of his unique behaviors and how he functions within his family. If adults and children alike can learn how to express appropriately what they think and feel, even on controversial issues or in once taboo areas, then the nonverbal communication would be a means to support the growth of creative, spontaneous, healthy interpersonal behavior.

A QUESTIONNAIRE ON NONVERBAL CUES

I prepared a list of questions regarding nonverbal cues and responses, which was sent to parents but elicited very little response. This indicated to me that many parents are not aware of these nonverbal cues. This questionnaire has been given as a homework task to couples who are having communication difficulties. My goal is that by pondering the questions and searching for answers, the couple will show a valuable carry-over into their personal interactions. The questions are:

What differences have you noted in your individual children's abilities to "read" you nonverbally? How do you as parents interpret or "check out" this nonverbal communication?

In what manner does your child interpret or "check out" nonverbal communication? Does he/she experiment, try different behavior?

Can you tell your child's inner feelings from the way he/she sits in your lap, or leans against you, or touches you (i.e., interacts nonverbally)? Are these messages the same for each child (if there is more than one)? Do they change over time?

Before your child learned to talk, what were some of the best indications that he/she gave to you of his/her desires, feelings, wishes, and needs?

In what ways do children communicate nonverbally among themselves? Are they better at this than adults?

What part of your child's or spouse's body most clearly gives away (i.e., nonverbally) their innermost state?

What changes in nonverbal communication have you noticed in your children as they progress from infancy, through childhood, adolescence, and into maturity?

What are the first signs you notice in your spouse or children that foretell "trouble ahead"?

Can you recall an instance when you received two conflicting messages— one verbal, one nonverbal? Which is a more reliable indicator of the sender's inner state? Why or how do you know?

Do any members of your family (spouse or children) tend to give nonverbal cues to their psychological state (for example, a visible build-up of tension) before they reveal it to you verbally? How do you know?

Are there any nonverbal signs by which you are able to understand your spouse better? Please describe them.

Can you describe an instance of a nonverbal cue which told you a different message than the verbal message that your spouse was giving to you at the time?

What signs does your spouse evince (other than verbal communication) which are "dead give-a-ways" of his/her inner state (e.g., wiggle feet; pull ear; drum on table)? What do these signs mean?

Do you and your spouse have any nonverbal cues or signals which you use to communicate in situations where you do not want other people to catch your meaning (e.g., at parties, in front of children, etc.)?

Parents, and children alike need to sharpen their level of awareness as to what they are saying, both with their words and with their body language. If more attention were devoted to this within the family unit, fewer breakdowns in communication would be presented to the marriage and family counselor. The assistance of the counselor in teaching the family how to look more carefully and listen more thoroughly to the body and verbal exchanges could be indeed an enriching and growing experience.

Just as a painting is more than the sum of its physical ingredients, so true meaning is often found only in the Gestalt of a total communicative action; that is, in the combined effect of its words, sounds and movements, but not in the communication significance of any single element by itself [Knapp, 1963, p. 153].

In the process of evaluating ourselves and our relationships to the world about us, we tend to rely on words rather than facts. The healthier and the more aware a person is, the more accurate a map he creates of himself, and the more he "knows himself," as he is and not as he feels he should be. A map can never represent all of its territory; one's self-evaluation in and of itself omits certain details of one's actual self—we never know ourselves completely [Barbara, 1956, p. 289].

Our work as counselors, psychologists, psychiatrists and physicians working with couples, families, and children needs a closer examination. What are *we* saying, and how are *we* saying it?

REFERENCES

Alger, I. & Hogan, P. The use of videotape recordings in conjoint marital therapy. *American Journal of Psychiatry* May, 1967, *73*, 1425-1430.

Allport, & Vernon, P. *Studies in expressive movement.* New York: Macmillan, 1933.

Axline, Virginia. *Play Therapy.* New York: Houghton Mifflin, 1947.

Barbara, D. A. The value of nonverbal communication in personality understanding. *Journal of Nervous and Mental Disease* 1956, *123*, 286-291.

Beckman, D. R. The fifth language arts: non-verbal communication. *Elementary English*, February 1963.

Beier, E. G. *The silent language of psychotherapy.* Chicago: Aldine, 1966.

Bell C. *Anatomy and philosophy of expression as connected with the fine arts.* (7th ed.) London: G. Bell & Sons, 1886.

Birdwhistell, R. *Introduction to kinesics.* Louisville, Kentucky: University of Louisville Press, 1953.

Davitz, F. & Davitz, J. L. Nonverbal vocal communication of feeling. *Journal of Communication*, June 1961, *11*, 81-86.

Delaney, D. J. Sensitization to non-verbal communications. *Counselor Education and Supervision* Spring, 1968, *7*, 315-316.

Dittman, A. T. The relationship between body movements and moods in interviews. *Journal of Consulting Psychology*, 1962, *26*, 480.

Ekman, P. Body position, facial expression and verbal behavior during interviews. *Journal of Abnormal and Social Psychology*, 1964, *68*, 295-301.

Ekman, P. Communication through nonverbal behavior: a source of information about interpersonal relationship. In S. S. Tomkins & C. B. Izard (Eds.), *Affect, cognition and personality.* New York: Springer Press, 1965. Pp. 390-442.

Ellis, A. *Reason and emotion in psychotherapy.* New York: Lyle Stuart, 1962.

Ellis, A. & Harper, R. *A guide to rational living.* Englewood Cliffs, New Jersey, 1961.

Frank, L. Tactile Communication. *ETC.*, Autumn, 1958, *16*, 31-79.

Fretz, B. Postural movements in a counseling dyad. *Journal of Counseling Psychology*, 1966, *13*, No. 3.

Hall, E. *The silent language.* Conn.: Fawcett, 1959.

Knapp, P. *Expression of the emotions in man.* New York: International University Press, 1963.

May, R. An antidote for the new puritanism. *Saturday Review*, March 26, 1966.

Middleman, R. R. *The non-verbal method in working with groups.* New York: Association Press, 1968.

Moreno, J. L. *Psychodrama.* New York: Beacon House, 1946.

Moustakas, C. E. *Children in play therapy.* New York: McGraw-Hill, 1953.

Rogers, A. H. Videotape feedback in group psychotherapy. *Psychotherapy: Theory, Research and Practice*, Winter, 1968, *5*, 37-39 (1).

Rogers, C. *On becoming a person.* Boston: Houghton Mifflin, 1961.

Rosenfeld, H. Gestural and verbal communication of interpersonal affect. Paper read at Midwestern Psychological Association meetings, 1965.

Rowe, F., Brooks, S., & Watson, B. Communication through gestures. *American Annual of the Deaf*, 1960, *105*, 232-237.

Ruesch, J. The Role of communication in therapeutic transactions. *The Journal of Communication*, September, 1963.

Satir, V. *Conjoint family therapy: a guide to theory and technique.* Palo Alto, Calif.: Science and Behavior Books, 1964.

Schultz. *Peanuts*. San Francisco *Chronicle* (United Feature Syndicate, Inc.), November 6, 1966.

Spencer, H. *Principles of psychology*. Vol. 2. New York and London: Appleton Press, 1910.

Vinacke, W. E. The judgment of facial expression by three national-racial groups in Hawaii: I. Caucasian faces. *Journal of Personality*, June, 1949, *17*, 407–429.

Vinacke, W. E., & Fong, R. W. The judgment of facial expressions by three national-racial groups in Hawaii: II. Oriental Faces. *Journal of Social Psychology*, May, 1955, *41*, 185–195.

Wachtel, P. L. An approach to the study of body language in psychotherapy. *Psychotherapy: Theory, Research and Practice*, August, 1967, *4*, 97–100 (3).

Webster, W. Gestures in Counseling. *Newsletter of the California Counseling and Guidance Association*, February, 1967, 7, 1–3 (3).

Wendt, P. R. The language of pictures. In S. I. Hayakawa (Ed.), *The use and misuse of language*. Greenwich, Conn.: Premier Book, 1962.

CHAPTER 11

Male and Female Roles in Marriage Counseling

Aaron L. Rutledge

In no other relationship do the two-sided needs of humanity—i.e., the need for individuality and the need for nearness through relationship—find such opportunities for fulfillment and for threat as is present in modern marriage. The way this drama of need is lived out will be vitally related to the role perception of husband and wife.

Once men were men and women were women and both were glad of it, or so the popular songs would have it. It seemed enough for the dictionary to define *male* as the sex "which begets young" and *masculine* as denoting that which is opposite to female, especially vigor, strength, and independence. *Female* described that sex which "conceives and brings forth young," and *feminine* delineated those qualities which are opposite to male; i.e., those deeper, more tender, more gracious qualities.

Today the picture is not so clear. Separately and collectively, the many social forces making for the revolution and evolution in the American family scene during the last half-century have torn down the distinctions in male and female roles. In the emancipation of women the only way many knew to become "equal" was to become "male." Usurpation of the male role became the goal of the day, not true self-determination. Thus history has witnessed a few generations of lost women who have in turn helped produce generations of inadequate males. Slowly, some women are finding their way out of this morass into an awareness of selfhood that permits the flexibility to find one's way through the varied and cyclic course of life. More slowly, men are beginning to rediscover themselves and become more adequate mates and fathers of children.

But the sources of confusion have not been put to rest. For thousands of youth the stereotype of the patriarchal family is taught at one level, the highly distorted democratic ideal at another, and what is practiced may be hardly recognizable from the viewpoint of either. The conflict between these positions, within the individual and between the couple, comes to fruition in the marital stress or apathy which leads to the counselor's office.

Reprinted with permission of the author and the publisher from *Pastoral Psychology*, October, 1962.

Let us examine a few of the ways in which perceptions of what is male and female influence marriage relationships, especially as seen in the re-enactment of sibling and parent-child conflicts, in contrast with adult man-woman relationships.

I. *Sex against sex, or sibling rivalry.* Along with learned stereotypes of what is male and female, together with the fact of conflicting and overlapping stereotypes, an individual may react as if men and women were different kinds of creatures, either to be avoided or used as pawns in life's struggle. This can amount to the worst aspects of extreme sibling rivalry in a marriage, with sides chosen along sexual lines.

These stereotyped expectations, full of inconsistencies, become the major tools whereby two immature adults put on costumes and enter into the contest of marriage to see who can get the most out of it, with little ability to live spontaneously or to share. When children are born to such a spurious union, they become further sibling competitors in the juvenile tug of war for "my way, my rights, my pleasure, my, my . . . mine."

Example: A wife is highly offended that her husband has a girl friend. She misses the contest-oriented life which they once enjoyed. Early in marriage she changed jobs repeatedly to keep a salary larger than his. He traded cars to keep a flashier model than hers. She excelled at polo, but he continued to fall off the horse. Then it was swimming. She outdistanced him and became the rescuer when he almost drowned. He couldn't hit a barn with a scatter gun, whereas she scared him to death clipping cigarets from his lips at ten paces with a pistol. It does not make sense to her that he has surrendered in despair and spends hours just holding a woman's hands listening to music.

The *punching-bag marriage* is based on the philosophy, or rather, con-ditioned reflex, that those of one sex are superior creatures, should get their rights, punish when these are challenged or neglected, and administer additional beatings just to keep the inferior one in line. In the middle-class families where physical violence is taboo, verbal or emotional assaults may be perfected to an art. This demands a somewhat masochistic mate or one who is conditioned to expect and endure the mistreatment, if not "enjoy" it.

In this master-slave relationship in which one exists to serve the other, we see women in the ascendant position as often as men. A common occurrence just before such a couple comes for counseling is that these roles have shifted or been seriously challenged.

II. *The pseudo-therapeutic marriage*, or the reform-based relationship, is another expression of counterfeit marriage. The extent to which some human beings need to remake things is astounding. Some refinish old furniture, some overhaul automobiles, and some get married. This recon-struction may be assumed to be either a male or a female prerogative, although it tends to be generalized. He is going to remake her personal habits or housekeeping. She is going to change his drinking habits, religion, or smell. This phenomenon is seen in many marriages of quite sophisticated people, particularly in its "therapeutic" expression.

When democracy or equality is the ideal, each one may set about to change the other through "understanding and love," but to change him nevertheless. Their primary motivation in coming for counseling is the desire to find another method which will guarantee to change the mate. Such an experimental attitude usually fails because of essential nonparticipation in the marriage relationship as a committed adult.

Example: A professional man brings his wife, saying: "I married a Ph.D. becuase I wanted intellectual companionship. She's a bore—prattling about babies, cooking, and the neighborhood. . ." "No! I don't want her to work. I want her to take classes, read intellectual material—higher criticism, semantics, cybernetics . . ." "No. I don't want counseling for myself. You work with her; see me occasionally to tell me what you have learned that I can use to change her."

III. *The parentified marriage.* The central task of growing up is to find one's identity as a human being. This can force the child into trying on various stereotypes of male and female in order to gain from the parents the emotional sustenance so necessary to preserving himself as an entity, however segmentalized or crippled it may leave him.

In the absence of a warm relationship between two adults which would manifest itself in every facet of life, including the sexual, the child is likely to become aware of, and identify with, only the *parental* aspects of being adult. This can lead to a "parentified" type of marriage in which the roles are those of a pseudo child-parent relationship. One of the couple, needing to be an adult through "parenting" another, chooses (or is chosen by) a mate who needs to preserve the only "role" he knows, that of a child. These dynamics become endlessly complicated in that one who fits into either of these patterns is likely to have unconscious needs to play the opposite role. This means that even in a neurotic way the mates cannot be adequate for each other. These marriages make possible a socially acceptable survival, but such child's play is a poor substitute for relatively unencumbered and spontaneous interaction of two "whole" adults. A few common situations illustrate the phenomena.

The *mother-son marriage* is a common expression of the parentified relationship. This is the woman who as a girl saw or experienced only the mothering type of femininity. Mother's affectional and sex life, her relating as a total adult, were absent, hidden, or danger-fraught. As a result the girl was conditioned to express her adulthood only through being a mother, desiring both to emulate and to displace her own mother. Marriage becomes a chance for her to get a family for whom she can be a mother. She chooses a man who has to be a boy or needs primarily to be mothered. And there are many such candidates, products of unhappy marriages of crippled men and women. The male child of an unhappy woman is particularly vulnerable, catching the hatred she has for self and for husband because of her unhappy lot.

There may be enough drive toward healthy relations and enough desire to get away from the slavery to his own mother, to push such a youth toward marriage. Yet he has to marry a mother figure, not an adequate, total female.

Many such marriages seem to work quite well for months or even years, depending upon the degree to which the two sets of needs complement each other. A shift in need patterns brings acute conflict. Typically, this woman seeks help because her once fine husband has become a terrible husband. He is drinking, refusing to come home at night, gambling, or "running around." In an oversimplified way, this is what has happened. The marriage was "good" because she served well as the mother he needed, at the same time finding her chief satisfaction in that process. But she has become either such a poor mother that he must rebel or such a good mother that he has grown. When little boys grow, the next step is adolescence and adolescent rebellion. Now he is "sowing wild oats." Good mother to her little-boy husband, she cannot tolerate being a mother-wife to an adolescent-husband. She tightens the reins and he kicks over the traces all the more.

This dilemma, perhaps forcing into consciousness for the first time some of her unrealized potential as a woman, leads to further stress in the marriage. In other marriages, through the process of daily living, the wife grows into a more complete woman and then finds herself endlessly frustrated because the husband cannot shift roles and become an adequate adult male lover and companion.

These marriage types are commonly described as "neurotic complementarity." One person, feeling inadequate and incomplete, unable to live a whole life, finds another who can complement or complete the syndrome of personality need. A woman with strong repressed needs to rebel against what she perceives as the strictures of femaleness, chooses a man who becomes alcoholic, has affairs, or is sexually perverted. She may protest this male freedom or failure and yet wear the robe of female martyrdom with agonizing pride. The fact that she is living out vicariously the repressed side of her crippled self often becomes evident when, through counseling, he begins to make rapid changes toward health. She protests that counseling is making him worse, or she has an affair, begins to drink excessively, or to use drugs, or becomes mentally ill.

Of course, this whole picture may be seen with the wife as the actor-outer and the husband the martyred member of the conspiracy in neurotic living, in which one is the hell-raiser and the other the protector of home, ideals, mores, religious ideals or law, but who, in reality, is just as sick.

IV. *Marriage as adult self-fulfillment.* The complementarity of marriage is by no means limited to the neurotic or crippled components of personality. The basic biology of life is a complementarity of male and female. Such pairing of opposites to gain greater fulfillment permeates the entire life of man. Similarities in appearance, race, religion, education, and social class, although slowly breaking down, have tended to be the rule. However, it becomes increasingly evident that at the emotional level it may be the differentness of the other person, promising to meet unfulfilled personality needs, which really leads to marriage. This is the reciprocity of healthy nearness, two distinct individuals simultaneously making the life of self and of the loved other more complete through spontaneous giving, receiving, and relating. (See Winch's theory of *complementarity*, Jung's concept of *anima* and *animus*, and Rutledge's concept of *nearness*.)

Our culture will not return to clearly defined roles for men and women. Rather, there will be less and less distinction between what is male activity and what is female activity. But, as people become healthier specimens of human nature, the absence of rigid distinctions in function will make less and less difference, and greater flexibility will lead to more creative self-fulfillment through marriage.

ROLE IDENTIFICATION OF THE COUNSELOR

It may be redundant to say that counselors are only human, but an honest attempt should be made by each professional to locate himself and his marriage in the above preview of the kinds of dynamics with which he must work. Psychotherapeutic assistance for the counselor often is indicated, and would speed the process of self-understanding in almost every case. To be blind to these factors in himself, to live a haloed existence as mate and as counselor, is certain to result in client injury if not personal involvement that will threaten his career.

I. *How are responses determined by the counselor's own gender?* It is difficult to say whether the relation between the counselor's biological gender and his responses (whether verbal or emotional) is superficial or fundamental. It is a fact that he is male, or she is female. Yet, if the counselor is fairly healthy and aware of self, responses are less likely to be basically altered by the fact of gender. However, the effect of attitudes and feelings about the fact of gender are crucial. The counselor may have such fixed notions of what is expected in male or female behavior that he judges the client accordingly. Even if he controls himself to the point of saying nothing, his reaction will have registered upon the client. The effect may be essentially the same whether he feels judgmental or just becomes tense because the experience has activated his own sore spots about the "maleness" or "femaleness" within his own personality.

Circumstances can aggravate this problem. For instance, most of the marriage counseling done by a pastor will be requested initially by wives. There are more women than men actively involved in church activities. This loyalty naturally gives the pastor a deep appreciation of women, and may add up to a somewhat solicitous interest in their welfare. This can be quite complicated if, as many clergymen and other counselors do, he neglects his own wife under the guise of serving God, the Church, and Humanity. He can project upon the client's husband his own guilt, as well as hostility, because of his religious apathy. Thus the counselor's total attitude is colored by the preconceptions of an errant male. The husband's experiencing of this as rejection reinforces his own beliefs that his story won't be appreciated and he refuses to return for more of the same. Counselors with problem wives—whether naggers, frigid, or sexual actor-outers—may reject problem behavior of women to such an extent that the female client is repulsed, or guilt elements and other isolated factors are blown up out of proportion.

II. *How is this communicated to the client?* Distorted conceptions of what is male and female in general, and the counselor's biases in particu-

lar, may be verbalized to the client. "Most men are that way, you know."
"Women have to be the understanding ones, you know." However, of
much greater concern are the subtle ways in which the artifacts of male-
female evolution are reinforced through stereotyped attitudes unconsciously applied.

Communication of attitudes and feelings is effected through all the
senses, not merely verbal exchange. Verbal communication becomes
heavily laden with the symbolic, and what is not said may become more
powerful than that which is put into words. Stereotyped reactions in an
emotionally charged atmosphere may be reinforced by symbolic expressions and by nonverbal messages through bodily tensions, emanations, and
movements.

III. *The client's use of role perceptions.* A client may misuse the
counselor's own conceptions of himself as male or female. Similarly the
client may misuse the counselor's role as perceived by the client. Confusion is compounded when both sets of perceptions are serious distortions
of reality.

A counselor may perceive of himself as the great father and protector
of mankind. A client who needs to be protected may fall into an incapaci-
tating dependency upon such strength, and cast the counselor in the role
of father or mother. Contrariwise, another person may be repelled because
this threatens to expose the dependency needs which are being fought and
repressed. Whereas the perception of the counselor as an aggressive male
lover may drive one woman away, it will seduce another into an erotically
tinged *affaire de thérapie* and lead to further alienation from the husband.

The female counselor who has an undue need to "mother" clients will
attract some and drive away others. The web of possessiveness, solicitous-
ness, and unnecessary assumption of responsibility for the client can
entrap many crippled personalities. When the health within the client
begins to assert itself it is difficult for that counselor to let go and extend
the freedom necessary to grow.

The ersatz masculinity or femininity of a counselor may repel or
fascinate a client, either one to his detriment. One woman refused to
return to a counselor after three sessions. She thought him "sincere and
no doubt well-trained, but he's more nervous than I am. He either chain
smokes or drinks coffee throughout the sessions, or drums incessantly on
the desk." Further exploration of her feelings revealed: "He is uncomfortable as a man in the presence of a woman. I don't think he likes being a
male."

Other clients, with greater need to distort and reinforce stereotype
identifications will adopt the mannerisms, habits, language, and beliefs of
the counselor's reactive way of life. Often this intensifies marital conflict
because the mate cannot change to meet the new role, and is made
increasingly uncomfortable by invidious comparisons to the counselor.

The counselor who is an ineffectual representative of his own gender is
particularly at a disadvantage with a client with homosexual tendencies.
He threatens to remind the latent or unhappy overt homosexual client of
his own inadequacy and pain at a deeper level than can be faced. Or, the

confirmed homosexual sees through the counselor and approaches counseling with attitudes of disdain, exploitation, or homosexual love.

COUNSELOR-CLIENT IDENTIFICATION

Thus far we have been describing the neurotic transference and countertransference of the counseling relationship, along with the intricate involvements of male-female role perceptions. Actually, whether the counselor is male or female is relatively insignificant in helping most clients. A healthy counselor can experience a wide range of human emotions, thoughts, and feelings. Contrary to stereotypical thinking, the ability to express or understand aggression, strength and courage; or gentleness, tenderness, and love; or scorn, guilt, and hatred are not gender based. They are human and equally available within men and women.

The first level of experiencing a counselor may well be at the "transference" level; i.e., the client imputes to the professional what he expects, both positively and negatively, based upon past experiences. He needs either to lean on, or to fight, an authority figure, so he casts counselor in the role of father or mother. He needs to work out unresolved feelings about siblings, so he sees the counselor as brother or sister in either the "palsy-walsy" or competitive sense. Religious terminology—father, padre, brother, sister, mother, etc.—provides the pastoral counselor ready-made vehicles through which unresolved conflicts can be worked through to healthier concepts of self. The concept of "doctor" serves a somewhat similar function.

A client may be concerned at first with the sex of the counselor. For a while he may identify so strongly as to desire to be of the counselor's sex, or to be like him in other ways, or he may react to the opposite extreme. But such role concepts and expectations are merely symptomatic of deeper needs. These needs are always twofold: at one level, he wants to play-act a habitual role with someone who will accept it, or to be given a more effective part to play in the drama of marriage—in three easy lessons. But at another level the need is to discover the birthright sold for a mess of role-playing pottage, and become the fulfilled person one was meant to be. It is here that the counselor's *being* speaks louder than what he says, cutting through the babble of client confusion, and calling forth the unrealized potential as a human.

As the client gains insight through *being accepted as he is*, with all his shortcomings, he has conflicting urges to defend what he is and to become different. At first this may mean becoming like the counselor—a particularly difficult time in marriage counseling. The client of the same sex as the counselor may become so "therapeutic" in aping the counselor as to make life intolerable for the spouse. The client of the opposite sex to the counselor can find a perfect escape from the pain of personal understanding and growth: "My counselor accepts me as I am, why can't my husband?" "Why can't my husband be like my counselor? So patient, kind, understanding, so male!" Such thoughts further contaminate the marriage as the counselor becomes the "other person" in the marriage triangle.

Although this fantasy can be used as an aid to counseling, it must be guided skillfully. Many a counselor meets the challenge of his life as he tries to navigate the ship of therapy between the Charybdis of the client's surging emotional and sexual needs on the one hand, and the Scylla of his own unmet needs on the other.

Back to our individual client who is now trying to become like his counselor. The next cycle of counseling is to help him clarify this need to change, to see it as the desire to become his own unrealized self, not a carbon copy of anyone else. He should be aided in identifying with the counselor, not as a person, but as a representative of the process of becoming, growing, and living effectively.

Whatever the route followed in getting there, most successful marriage counseling goes through the steps of each person's unraveling and becoming able to use insight in these areas: experiencing, although not necessarily understanding, a real person through the relationship with the counselor; gaining some basic understanding of what oneself is like, a little of why, and some beginning acceptance of responsibility for the past and the future; understanding of the mate's feelings and reactions, and giving him some right to be what he is and to feel what he feels; gaining some insight into the nature of the marriage relationship, the interactive process. Then, and usually only then, does the marriage show genuine improvement.

CHAPTER 12

The Rational-Emotive Approach to Marriage Counseling

Ben N. Ard, Jr.

Mark Twain, that perceptive observer of human beings, once said, "We all do no end of *feeling* and mistake it for *thinking*." Throughout the history of counseling and psychotherapy, from Sigmund Freud to Carl Rogers, the major emphasis has been on the clients' irrational impulses and *feelings*, rather than on what they *think*. However, there has developed a new approach in counseling and psychotherapy which goes against this trend.

One of the most provocative and challenging approaches to marriage counseling developed in recent years is the rational-emotive approach originated by Dr. Albert Ellis, a psychologist and marriage counselor who is Executive Director of the Institute for the Advanced Study of Rational Psychotherapy in New York City. Other contributors to this developing approach have been Robert A. Harper (1960), Ben Ard (1967, 1969, 1971, 1974), Virginia Anne Church (1974), and Diamond and Songor (1972), to mention just a few.

We may divide reasons for unhappy marriages roughly into two main causes: real incompatibility between the spouses, or neurotic disturbances on the part of either or both the husband and wife which make them think and act in such a manner that fundamental incompatibilities appear to exist between them (Ellis & Harper, 1961). *Incompatibility* means truly irreconcilable differences in the basic attitudes, ideas, values, and interests of the marital partners. The main remedies here consist of striving for mutual interests. This is often quite difficult because sometimes the differences are irreconcilable. Then the realistic alternative is divorce (Ellis & Harper, 1961). A rational approach in this latter instance is for the marriage counselor to help his clients get through the divorce without unnecessary feelings of bitterness, resentment, failure, and guilt.

But what is a rational approach to marriage counseling for those couples who do not have irreconcilable differences, but rather neurotic disturbances which are affecting their marriages? Rational-emotive therapy (often called "RET" for short) is well-fitted for couples who do not believe that they are emotionally disturbed but who know that they are not functioning adequately in some specific area of life, such as their

103

marriage. Possibly many of these troubled people should come for intensive, long-term psychotherapy rather than for marriage counseling, but the fact is that they do not (Harper, 1960). It therefore behooves the marriage counselor to be enough of a trained and experienced psychotherapist to be able to deal adequately with the people who come for help (Ellis, 1956). If the marriage counselor knows and practices the essentials of RET, he or she will be well prepared in this regard (Ellis, 1962).

Most couples who come for marriage counseling are victims of what has been fairly aptly called "neurotic interaction" in marriage (Ellis, 1958). Such "neurotics" are individuals who are not intrinsically stupid and inept, but who *needlessly* suffer from intense and sustained anxiety, hostility, guilt, or depression. Neurotic interaction in marriage arises when a theoretically capable husband and wife actually behave in an irrational, marriage-defeating (and self-defeating) way with each other. If the theses of RET are correct, then marital neurotic interaction arises from *unrealistic* and *irrational ideas, beliefs,* or *value systems* on the part of one or both of the marriage partners; and it is these beliefs and value systems which therefore must be concertedly *confronted, challenged* and *changed*, if neurotic interaction is to cease.

What are some of these basic irrational ideas or beliefs that are common among clients of marriage counselors? One of the main irrational beliefs that people use to upset themselves with is the notion that it is a *dire necessity* for an adult human being to be *approved* or *loved* by almost all the significant other people he or she encounters; that it is most important what *others* think of the person instead of what the *person* thinks of himself. The ancient Greek Stoic philosopher Epictetus once gave us some words of wisdom that are perhaps relevant here: "If any one trusted your body to the first man he met, you would be indignant, but yet you trust your mind to the chance comer, and allow it to be disturbed and confounded if he revile you; are you not ashamed to do so?" (Quoted in Oates, 1940, p. 475.)

Applied to marriage, this irrational idea means the "neurotic" individual firmly believes that, no matter how he behaves, his mate, just because she *is* his mate, *should* love him; that if she does not respect him, life is a catastrophe; and that her main role as a wife is to help, aid and succor *him*, rather than to be an individual in her own right. This leads to obvious conflicts in marital relationships.

The second major irrational belief which most "neurotics" in our society seem to hold is that a human being *should* or *must* be *perfectly* competent, adequate, talented, and intelligent—and is utterly *worthless* if he or she is incompetent in any significant way. Perfectionism and striving constantly for "success" are rampant in much of our society.

A third irrational assumption of the majority of "neurotics" in our culture is that they *should* severely *blame* themselves and others for mistakes and wrongdoings; and that punishing themselves or others will help prevent future mistakes. The concept of sin runs very deep in our culture. Many people are very upset by the behavior of other people, even when that behavior does not needlessly or gratuitously harm them. We need to return once again to the wisdom of Epictetus: "For no one shall harm you, without your consent; you will only be harmed, when you think that you are harmed (Oates, 1940, p. 476)."

A fourth irrational assumption which underlies and causes emotional disturbance is the notion that it is horrible, terrible, and catastrophic when things are not the way one would like them to be; and that one should not have to put off present pleasures for future gains. These ideas cause untold havoc in many marriages.

A fifth and final irrational belief which we shall consider here is the mythical supposition that most human unhappiness is *externally* caused or forced on one by the outside people and events; and that one has virtually no control over one's emotions and cannot help feeling bad on many occasions. Actually, of course, virtually all human unhappiness is *self*-caused and results from unjustified assumptions and internalized sentences stemming from these assumptions, such as some of the beliefs we have just been outlining. Another Stoic philosopher, Marcus Aurelious, put the matter most succinctly: "If thou art pained by any external thing, it is not this thing that disturbs thee, but thy own judgment about it. And it is in thy power to wipe out this judgment now (Oates, 1940, p. 550)."

It is a staunch contention of Albert Ellis, then, that a seriously neurotic individual possesses, almost by definition, a set of basic postulates which are distinctly unrealistic, biased, and illogical (Ellis, 1975). These ideas or beliefs are implicit if not explicit in the person's behavior.

If what has been said so far is reasonably accurate, then the solution to the problem of treating neurotic interaction in marriage would appear to be fairly obvious (Ellis & Harper, 1961). If neurotics have basically irrational assumptions or value systems, and if these assumptions lead them to interact self-defeatingly with their mates, then the marriage counselor's function is to tackle not the problem of the marriage, nor of the neurotic interaction that exists between the marital partners, but rather the problem of the irrational ideas or beliefs that *cause* this neurosis. This consists largely of showing each of the marital partners who is neurotically interacting (a) that he has some basic irrational assumptions; (b) precisely what these assumptions are; (c) how they originally arose; (d) how they currently are being sustained by continual unconscious self-indoctrination; and (e) how they can be replaced with much more rational, less self-defeating philosophies (Ellis & Harper, 1961).

In the rational-emotive approach to marriage counseling (as opposed to other approaches), there is an attempt to help the disturbed individuals acquire *three levels of insight* (Ellis, 1962). Insight Number 1 is the usual kind of understanding of which the Freudians make much: the individual's seeing that his *present* actions have a *prior* or *antecedent* cause.

An additional and unique contribution of RET, however, is that it does not stop there but goes on to further insights. Insight Number 2 concerns the understanding that the irrational ideas acquired by the individual in his past life are *still existant*, and that they exist today because he himself keeps *reindoctrinating himself* with these ideas, consciously or unconsciously.

And finally, Insight Number 3 is the full understanding by the disturbed individual that *he simply has got to change his erroneous and illogical thinking*, if he wants to get better. Unless the client, after acquiring Insights Numbers 1 and 2, fully sees and accepts the fact that for him to get better *there is no other way* than his forcefully and consistently attacking his early-acquired and still-heartily-held irrational ideas, he definitely will not overcome his emotional disturbance.

The rational-emotive therapist, then, adds to the marriage counselor's other methods the more direct techniques of *confrontation, confutation, deindoctrination,* and *re-education,* as well as a unique contribution known as "*homework assignments*." These techniques, while they may go against the teachings of some other approaches, probably account for the effectiveness and elegant solutions arrived at through the rational-emotive approach.

Confrontation means facing the client with the self-defeating irrational ideas, premises, or assumptions which are implicit in his behavior. The marriage counselor needs to be well trained and experienced in what has been called the Socratic dialogue. That is, the counselor needs to know how to ask questions that get at the philosophical assumptions of the clients.

Confutation means that the marriage counselor needs to have the question-asking skills of a good Philadelphia lawyer as well as good training in logic and the scientific approach. He needs to be able to show the client where he is mistaken in his assumptions, premises or basic values, and particularly in his illogical thinking or overgeneralizations.

Deindoctrination means that the counselor needs to help the client get rid of the irrational assumptions, ideas and conclusions that he has previously been indoctrinated with by, usually, his parents and the unquestioned assumptions of the society in which he lives. This is hard work and takes time. It is difficult, but not impossible.

Re-education is the final or ultimate technique the marriage counselor uses to help the client develop a more rational philosophy of life, one less self-defeating than what has guided the life-decisions previously made. This is the basic function of psychotherapy: re-education.

"*Homework assignments*" are perhaps the fundamental tool or technique that the rational-emotive approach relies upon to get the clients to question and challenge and change their self-defeating philosophies. Clients, if they are going to *get better* rather than just temporarily *feel* better in the therapeutic hour, need to risk themselves during the other hours of the week and try out what they are learning in therapy. Homework assignments can involve actual try-outs of new behavior, checking out one's self-talk by filling out homework assignment sheets about critical events and their reactions to them. Also "bibliotherapy" is used. This means reading some books that may help the client move faster and more efficiently through his or her problems.

A whole series of books have been specifically written to help clients look at their problems and learn more effective ways of dealing with them. Ellis and Harper's *A Guide to Successful Marriage* (1961) can prove very helpful in marriage counseling. Ellis' other books are helpful with clients who are single again (1970, 1963a, 1963b), who are having sexual problems (1960), and who decide to stay married to a neurotic partner (1975). Ard's book on treating psychosexual dysfunction (1974) is intended to help the intelligent layman clear up misunderstandings in the sexual area.

More concretely, in applying rational-emotive therapy to marriage counseling, each spouse is shown that his disturbed behavior arises largely from underlying unrealistic beliefs; that these beliefs may have originally been learned from early familial and other environmental influences but that they are now being maintained by *internal verbalizations* (or *self-talk*); that his marriage partner, in consequence, is rarely the real cause of his problems; that he himself is actually now creating and perpetuating these problems, that only by learning carefully to observe, to question, to think about, and to reformulate his basic assumptions can he hope to understand his mate and himself and to stop being unilaterally and interactionally neurotic (Ellis, 1962, p. 211).

Whenever marriage counseling clients can be induced to *work* at changing their underlying neurosis-creating assumptions, significant personality changes ensue, and their interactions with their mates, families, or other intimate associates almost always improve. More specifically, this work usually consists of: (1) fully facing the fact that they themselves are doing something wrong, however mistaken their intimates may *also* be; (2) seeing clearly that behind their neurotic mistakes and inefficiencies there invariably are important irrational, unrealistic *philosophic assumptions*; (3) vigorously and continually *challenging* and *questioning* these assumptions by critically examining them and by actively doing deeds that prove they are unfounded (homework assignments); (4) making due allowances for the intrinsic differences and frustrations of certain human relationships such as monogamous marriage; (5) learning to keep their mouths shut when one of their close associates is clearly behaving badly, or else to objectively and *unblamefully* point out the other's mistakes while constructively trying to show him or her how to correct them in the future; and (6) above all, continually keeping in mind the fact that a relationship *is* a relationship, that it rarely can spontaneously progress in a supersmooth manner, and that it must often be actively worked at to recreate and maintain the honest affection with which it often starts.

While the ideas of the rational-emotive approach are considered heretical by many in the field of marriage counseling who have emphasized the importance of *expressing feelings* rather than *thinking rationally*, we may turn once more to the ancient Greek philosopher of Stoicism, Epictetus, who as usual gets to the crux of the matter very quickly: "What disturbs men's minds is not events but their judgments on events . . . . And so when we are hindered, or disturbed, or distressed, let us never lay the blame on others, but on ourselves, that is, on our own judgments. To accuse others for one's own misfortunes is a sign of want of education; to accuse oneself shows that one's education has begun; to accuse neither oneself nor others shows that one's education is complete (Oates, 1940, p. 469)."

Put in simple A-B-C terms, it is rarely the external stimulus situation, A, which gives rise directly to an emotional reaction, C. Rather, it is almost always B—the individual's beliefs regarding, attitudes toward, or interpretation of, A—which actually leads to his reaction, C.

Our job as marriage counselors, then, is to help clients see for themselves that it is necessary for them to work on the B step; on their assumptions or internalized sentences, rather than railing at the external past situation, A, or wallowing in their own miseries at C. If we can get our clients to work on their assumptions and challenge their self-defeating values, they can develop more rational and therefore more self-satisfying philosophies and lives.

REFERENCES

Ard, B. N., Jr. The A-B-C of marriage counseling. *Rational Living*, Vol. 2, No. 2, pp. 10–12, Fall, 1967.

Ard, B. N., Jr. Communication in marriage. *Rational Living*, Vol. 5, No. 2, pp. 20–22, Spring, 1971.

Ard, B. N., Jr. Treating psychosexual dysfunction. New York: Jason Aronson, 1974.

Church, V. A. Rational therapy in divorce practice. *Rational Living*, Vol. 9, No. 2, pp. 34–38, Fall, 1974.

Diamond, L. & Songor, E. Eight rational principles of effective communication in relationships. *Rational Living*, Vol. 7, No. 1, pp. 36–38, Spring, 1972.

Ellis, A. A critical evaluation of marriage counseling. *Marriage and Family Living*, 1956, 18, 65–71.

Ellis, A. Neurotic interaction between marital partners. *Journal of Counseling Psychology*, 1958, 5, 24–28.

Ellis, A. *The art and science of love*. New York: Bantam Books, 1960.

Ellis, A. *Reason and emotion in psychotherapy*. New York: Lyle Stuart, 1962.

Ellis, A. *Sex and the single man*. New York: Lyle Stuart, 1963a.

Ellis, A. *The intelligent woman's guide to man-hunting*. New York: Lyle Stuart, 1963b.

Ellis, A. *Sex without guilt*. Hollywood: Wilshire Books, rev. ed., 1970.

Ellis, A. et al. *Growth through reason: verbatim cases in rational-emotive therapy*. Palo Alto: Science & Behavior Books, 1971.

Ellis, A. *Humanistic psychotherapy: the rational-emotive approach*. New York: McGraw-Hill Paperback, 1974.

CHAPTER 13

The Use of Family Theory in Clinical Practice

Murray Bowen

In little more than one decade, family psychiatry has evolved from the relative unknown to a position of recognized importance on the psychiatric scene. The term "family therapy," or some variation of it, is known to the informed lay person. What is the origin and current status of the "family movement"? I believe it is a "movement," which I shall attempt to convey in this paper. Since there is disagreement even among leaders of the family movement about some of the critical theoretical and therapeutic issues, any attempt to explain or describe the family movement will represent the bias and viewpoint of the author. In this paper I shall present some of my ideas about circumstances that gave rise to the family movement and some ideas about the current status and future potential of the movement. The main body of the paper will be a presentation of my own theoretical orientation, which provides a blueprint for the clinical use of family psychotherapy.

I believe that the family movement began in the early and mid-1950's and that it grew out of an effort to find more effective treatment methods for the more severe emotional problems. In a broad sense, I believe it developed as an extension of psychoanalysis, which had finally achieved general acceptance as a treatment method during the 1930's. Psychoanalysis provided useful concepts and procedures for the mass need of World War II, and a "new" era in psychiatry began. Within the course of a few years psychiatry became a hopeful, promising specialty for thousands of young physicians. Membership in the American Psychiatric Association increased from 3,684 in 1945 to 8,534 in 1955. Psychoanalytic theory had explanations for the total range of emotional problems, but standard psychoanalytic treatment techniques were not effective with the more severe emotional problems. Eager young psychiatrists began experimenting with numerous variations in the treatment method. I believe the study of the family was one of these new areas of interest.

Reprinted with permission of the author and the publisher from *Comprehensive Psychiatry*, 1966, 7, 345–374.

There are those who say the family movement is not new and that it goes back twenty-five years or more. There is some evidence to support the thesis that current family emphasis evolved slowly as the early psychoanalytic formulations about the family were put into clinical practice. In 1909 Freud (1949) reported the treatment of "Little Hans," in which he worked with the father instead of the child. In 1921 Flugel (1960) published his well-known book, *The Psycho-analytic Study of the Family*. There was the development of child analysis and the beginning of the child guidance movement, in which it became standard procedure for a social worker or second therapist to work with parents in addition to the primary-psychotherapy with the child. Later, the child guidance principles were adapted to work with adults, both in inpatient and outpatient settings, in which a social worker or second therapist worked with relatives to supplement the primary psychotherapy with the patient. With these early theoretical and clinical awarenesses of the importance of the family, there is accuracy to the statement that "family" is not new. However, I believe that the current family direction is sufficiently important, new, and different to be viewed as a movement. I shall review some of the theoretical and clinical issues that seem important in this development.

Psychoanalytic theory was formulated from a detailed study of the individual patient. Concepts about the family were derived more from the patient's perceptions than from direct observation of the family. From this theoretical position, the focus was on the patient and the family was outside the immediate field of theoretical and therapeutic interest. Individual theory was built on a medical model with its concepts of etiology, the diagnosis of pathology in the patient, and treatment of the sickness in the individual. Also inherent in the model are the subtle implications that the patient is the helpless victim of a disease or malevolent forces outside his control. A conceptual dilemma was posed when the most important person in a patient's life was considered to be the cause of his illness, and pathogenic to him. Psychiatrists were aware that the model did not quite fit, and there were attempts to tone down the implicit starkness of the concepts, but the basic model remained. For instance, the concept of the unconscious postulated that the parent could be unconsciously hurtful while trying to help the child. This was different from what it would be if the hurt had been intentional or an irresponsible act of omission, but it still left the parent as "pathogenic." There were efforts to modify diagnostic labels, and there were even suggestions that labels be discarded, but a *patient* requires a *diagnosis* for his *illness* and psychiatry still operates with a medical model.

One of the most significant developments in the family movement, which distinguishes it from previous "family" work, is a change in the basic treatment process. Since the beginning of psychoanalysis, the analysis and resolution of the transference has been viewed as the primary therapeutic force for the treatment of emotional illness. Though modified by different "schools," the "therapeutic relationship" is the basic therapeutic modality used by most psychiatrists. The confidential, personal, and private nature of the relationship is considered essential for good therapy. Over the years there have been methods, rules, and even laws to guard this privacy. Since the beginning of the child guidance movement there have been efforts to involve the family in "treatment," but the "therapeutic" patient-therapist relationship was protected against intrusion and the family assigned secondary importance. Among those who initiated the current family movement were psychiatrists who, in addition to the patient's dilemma, began to pay more attention to the family side of the problem.

I believe the current family movement was started by several different investigators, each working independently, who began with either a theoretical or a clinical notion that the family was important. As the focus shifted from the individual to the family, each was confronted with the dilemma of describing and conceptualizing the family relationship system. Individual theory did not have a conceptual model for a relationship system. Each investigator was "on his own" in conceptualizing his observations. One of the interesting developments has been the way investigators first conceptualized the system and the ways these concepts have been modified in the past ten years. There were terms for the distortion and rigidity, the reciprocal functioning, and the "interlocking," "binding," "stuck togetherness" of the system. The following illustrates some of the terms used by a few of the early investigators. Lidz and Fleck (1957) used the concept "schism and skew," and Wynne and his co-workers (1958) used the concept "pseudomutuality." Ackerman, one of the earliest workers in the field, presented a conceptual model in his 1956 paper, "Interlocking Pathology in Family Relationships." He also developed a therapeutic method which he calls "family therapy," which might be described as observing, demonstrating, and interpreting the "interlocking" to the family as it occurs in the family sessions. Jackson and his co-workers (Bateson, Jackson, Haley & Weakland, 1956) used a different model with the concept of the "double bind." As I perceived his original position, he used communication theory to account for the relationship system and individual theory to account for functioning in the individual. His "conjoint family therapy," which I interpret as the joining of individuals in family therapy, would be consistent with his conceptual scheme. I conceived of a preexisting emotional "stuck-togetherness," the "undifferentiated family ego mass," and developed a therapeutic method for which I have used the term "family psychotherapy," which is designed to help individuals differentiate themselves from the "mass." Other investigators used a spectrum of slightly different terms to describe and conceptualize the same family phenomenon. As the years pass, the original concepts tend to be less "different."

CURRENT STATUS AND POSSIBLE FUTURE OF THE FAMILY MOVEMENT

The family movement is currently in what I have called a "healthy, unstructured state of chaos." The early investigators arrived at "family therapy" after preliminary clinical investigation and research. There may have been one exception to this general statement, recounted by Bell (1961), one of the earliest workers in the field. He misinterpreted a statement about psychotherapy for the family, following which he worked out his own plan to begin seeing family members together. After the idea of "family therapy" was introduced, the number of family therapists began to multiply each year. Most went directly into family therapy from their orientation in individual theory. Group therapists modified group therapy for work with families. As a result, the term "family therapy" is being used to refer to such a variety of different methods, procedures, and techniques that the term is meaningless without further description or definition. I consider this "healthy," because once a therapist begins seeing multiple family members together, he is confronted with new clinical phenomena not explained by individual theory, he finds that many previous concepts have become superfluous, and he is forced to find new theoretical concepts and new therapeutic techniques. The increasing number of family conferences become forums for discussion of experiences and acquiring new ways to conceptualize the family phenomenon.

A high percentage of therapists are using the term "family" to designate therapy methods in which two or more generations (usually parents and children) attend the sessions together, the term "marital therapy" when two spouses are seen together, and "individual therapy" when only one family member is seen by the therapist. The one most widely held concept of "family therapy," both within the profession and by the public, is that of entire families (usually parents and children) meeting together with the therapist while the family acquires the ability to verbalize and communicate thoughts and feelings to each other, with the therapist sitting alongside to facilitate the process and to make observations and interpretations. This I have called "family group therapy." In my experience, this can be amazingly effective as a short-term process for improving family communication. Even a slight improvement in communication can produce dramatic shifts in the feeling system, and even a period of exhilaration. I have not been able to use this as a long-term method for resolving underlying problems.

Although the family movement may continue to focus on "therapy" for many years to come, I believe the greatest contribution of "family" will come from the theoretical. I think the family movement rests on solid ground, that we have hardly scratched the surface in family research, and that "family" will grow in importance with each passing generation. The study of the family provides a completely new order of theoretical models for thinking about man and his relationship to nature and the universe. Man's family is a *system* which I believe follows the laws of natural systems. I believe knowledge about the family system may provide the pathway for getting beyond static concepts and into the functional concepts of systems. I believe that family can provide answers to the medical model dilemma of psychiatry, that family concepts may eventually become the basis for a new and different theory about emotional illness, and this in turn will make its contribution to medical science and practice.

THEORETICAL AND CLINICAL ORIENTATION OF THE AUTHOR

The primary goal of this presentation is to describe a specific theoretical and therapeutic system in which family theory serves as a blueprint for the therapist in doing family psychotherapy and also as a useful theoretical framework for a variety of clinical problems. A family orientation is so different from the familiar individual orientation that it has to be experienced to be appreciated. It is difficult for a person who thinks in terms of individual theory, and who has not had clinical experience with families, to "hear" family concepts. Some are better able to hear abstract theoretical ideas while others hear simple clinical examples. The first part of this section is designed as a bridge between individual and family orientations. To provide a variety of bridges, it will include a spectrum of clinical observations, broad abstract ideas, theoretical concepts, and some of my experiences as I shifted from an individual to a family frame of reference.

My family experience covers twelve years and over ten thousand hours of observing families in family psychotherapy. For the first five years of family practice I also did some individual psychotherapy, and I had a few patients in psychoanalysis. The term "family psychotherapy" was reserved for the process when two or more family members were seen together. The technical effort was to analyze the already existing emotional process between the family members and toward keeping myself emotionally disengaged, which I called "staying out of the transference." This will be discussed later. During those years I used the term "individual psychotherapy" for the process when only one family person was seen. I had not dealt with my own emotional functioning sufficiently nor developed techniques to avoid a transference, and there was the "either-or" distinction between family and individual psychotherapy. I considered it *family* when the emotional process could be contained within the family, and *individual* when this was not possible. During those years, another evolutionary process was taking place. After having spent thousands of hours sitting with families, it became increasingly impossible to see a single person without "seeing" his total family sitting like phantoms alongside him. This perception of one person as a segment of the larger family system had governed the way I thought about, and responded to, the individual, and it had changed my basic approach to psychotherapy. For the past seven years my practice has been devoted entirely to "family" psychotherapy, although about one-third of the hours are spent with only one member of a family. The volume of clinical experience has been in private practice where an average clinical load of forty families are seen with a maximum of thirty hours per week. In past years only a few families have been seen more than once a week, and an increasing number do as well with less frequent appointments. It has been difficult to communicate the notion of avoiding a transference and "family" psychotherapy with only one family member. It is my hope that this can be better clarified in this paper.

A number of facets of the human phenomenon come into view in observing family members together that are obscured with any composite of individual interviews. Any person who exposes himself to daily observations of families as they relate to, and interact with, each other is confronted with a whole new world of clinical data that do not fit individual conceptual models. I use the terms "relate to" and "interact with" because these are a few of the inadequate terms that have been used to describe the family phenomenon. Actually, family members are *being*, and *doing*, and *acting*, and *interacting*, and *transacting*, and *communicating*, and *pretending*, and *posturing* in such a variety of ways that structure and order are hard to see. There is something wrong with any single term that has been used. To this point, family research has gone toward selecting certain areas for detailed, controlled study. In 1957 one of my research associates (Dysinger) did a study called "The Action Dialogue in an Intense Relationship," which was an attempt to blank out words and do a coherent "dialogue" from one period of gross action between a mother and daughter. Birdwhistell (1952) and Scheflen (1964) have made a significant contribution in their precise definition of "kinesics," "body language" system, automatic in all relationships. One of the popular areas for study has been "communication," which on the simplest level is verbal communication. There have been the linguistic studies and the different communications that are conveyed by nuances in tone of voice, inflection, and ways of speaking—communications that each person learns in infancy and uses without "knowing" he knows it. Bateson, Jackson, and co-workers (Bateson, *et al.*, 1956), from analysis of verbal communication, developed their concept of the "double bind," which has to do with conflicting messages in the same statement. There is also the area of nonverbal communication and extrasensory perception, which operates with fair accuracy in some families. There is an advantage in using terms such as "communication" or "transactional" system in that each lends itself to more precise research analysis. The disadvantage is in the narrowness of the concept and the necessity of using a broad interpretation of the concept. For instance, under "communication" theory it becomes necessary to assume the full range of verbal, action, nonverbal, extrasensory, and feeling communication, plus other modalities such as a visceral response in one family member to anxiety or a mood shift in another. However one approaches the family, each investigator has to choose his own way of conceptualizing the family phenomenon.

One striking group of clinical patterns, present to some degree in all families, will provide a brief view of the family relationship system. These follow the general pattern of the family process that diagnoses, classifies, and assigns characteristics to certain family members. Observations may prove reasonably consistent, periodically consistent, or inconsistent with the family pronouncements about the situation. The "family projection process" by which a family problem is transmitted to one family member by years of nagging pronouncements, and then fixed there with a diagnosis, has been discussed in detail in another paper (Bowen, 1959). Family assignments that overvalue are as unrealistic as those that devalue, though the ones that devalue are more likely to come within the province of the psychiatrist. The diagnosed one may resist the family pronouncement and precipitate a family debate; or he may alternately resist and accept; or he may invite it, at which time the assigned characteristic becomes an operational *fact*. Family debates on subjects such as "rejection," "love," and "hostility" will force the therapist to reevaluate his own use of such terms. As I see "rejection," it is one of the most useful mechanisms for maintaining equilibrium in a relationship system. It goes on constantly between people, usually unmentioned. At one point in the family process someone makes a fuss about "rejection" and the debate starts. At a point when rejection is present throughout the family, the one who claims "rejection" is usually more rejecting of the other, rather than the obverse being true. Positive statements about the presence or absence of "love," with reactions and counterreactions, can occupy the scene while there is no objective evidence of change in "love" within the family. Whatever love *is*, it is factual that many family members react strongly to statements about it. The misuse and overuse of the concept "hostility" is another in the same category. The same can apply to terms such as "masculine," "feminine," "aggressive," "passive," "homosexual," and "alcoholic."

The use of the term "alcoholic" provides a good example. In one family, two generations of descendants referred to a grandfather as alcoholic. He had been successful and fairly responsible except to his wife, who was a very anxious woman. He found reason to stay away from her and he did drink moderately. The wife's label was accepted by the children and transmitted to the grandchildren. A recent consultation with another family illustrates another aspect of the problem. A wife had presented the details of her husband's alcoholism. I asked for the husband's view of the problem. He agreed he had a real drinking problem. When asked how much he drank, he flared with, "Listen Buster! When I tell you I have a drinking problem, I mean it!" When asked how many days he had lost from work because of drinking, he said, "One! But I really hung one on that time." It can be grossly inaccurate to assign *fact* to statements such as, "He was an alcoholic." It can be accurate and also convey a *fact* about the relationship system if such statements are heard as, "One family member *said* another was an alcoholic." This applies to the entire spectrum of terms used in the family relationship system.

I would like to present the concept of the family as a system. For the moment I shall not attempt to say what kind of system. There is no single word or term that would be accurate without further qualification, and qualification would distort the *system* concept. The family *is* a system in that a change in one part of the system is followed by compensatory change in other parts of the system. I prefer to think of the family as a variety of systems and subsystems. Systems function at all levels of efficiency from optimum functioning to total dysfunction and failure. It is necessary also to think in terms of overfunction, which can range from compensated overfunction to decompensated overfunction. An example of this would be the tachycardia (overfunctioning heart) of an athlete in strenuous physical activity, to tachycardia that precedes total heart failure and death. The functioning of any system is dependent on the functioning of the larger systems of which it is a part, and also on its subsystems. On a broad level, the solar system is a subsystem of the larger system, the universe. The molecule is one of the smallest defined subsystems. On another level, the process of evolution is a system that operates slowly over long periods of time. There is sufficient knowledge about evolution to recognize the general patterns of its function, but there is much less knowledge about the larger systems of which evolution is a subsystem. We can look back and make postulations about the factors that influenced past evolutionary change, but our lack of knowledge about the larger systems reduces us to guessing about the future course of evolution.

From observing families I have attempted to define and conceptualize some of the larger and smaller family functioning patterns as they repeat and repeat, and as old patterns tone down and new ones become more prominent. The research started with schizophrenia in which one family member was in a state of total dysfunction and collapse, and the patterns so intense they could not be missed, but it required work with the entire range of human dysfunction to see the patterns in broader perspective. One of the most important aspects of family dysfunction is an equal degree of overfunction in another part of the family system. It is factual that dysfunctioning and overfunctioning exist together. On one level this is a smooth-working, flexible, reciprocating mechanism, in which one member automatically overfunctions to compensate for the dysfunction of the other, who is temporarily ill. Then there are the more chronic and fixed states of overfunctioning and dysfunction in which flexibility is lost. An example would be the dominating (overfunctioning) mother and passive father. The overfunctioning one routinely sees this as necessary to compensate for the poor functioning of the other. This might be valid in the case of temporary illness in one spouse, but in the chronic states there is evidence that the dysfunction appears later to compensate for overfunction in the other. However it develops, the overfunction–dysfunction is a reciprocating mechanism. In previous papers (Bowen, 1959, 1960) I called this the "overadequate-inadequate reciprocity." Symptoms develop when the dysfunction approaches nonfunctioning. Families often do not seek help until flexibility of the system is lost and the functioning of one member is severely impaired. When the mechanism advances beyond a certain point, anxiety drives the mechanism toward panic and rapid increase in both overfunction and dysfunction. The increased pressure can "jam the circuits" of the disabled one into paralyzed collapse. Even at this point, recovery can begin with the slightest decrease of the overfunctioning, or a slight decrease in the dysfunction.

Some of the main functional patterns observed in families have been formulated into component concepts that comprise the family theory of emotional illness. It would be more accurate to say "family dysfunction." The broad family patterns of emotional illness are also present in physical illness and social dysfunction such as irresponsible behavior and delinquency. The component concepts (subsystems) are among those I believe to be the most critical variables in human dysfunction. Symptoms in any part of the family are viewed as evidence of dysfunction, whether the symptoms be emotional, physical, conflictual, or social. There have been most promising results from the effort to view all emotional symptoms as evidence of family dysfunction rather than as intrapsychic phenomena.

The "therapist" also fits into this concept of the family as a system. This is a combination theoretical-therapeutic system in which theory determines therapy, and observations from therapy can in turn modify the theory. The original design, reported in another paper (Bowen, 1961), has been continued, although both the theory and therapy have been constantly modified. From the early days of the research there was increasing emotional detachment from the families. The more one observes families, the easier it is to detach from the narrow conceptual boundaries of individual theory; and the more one detaches from individual theory, the easier it is to see family patterns. The early family psychotherapy was predominantly observational, with questions to elicit more information about the observations. Over the years, "research" families have done better in family psychotherapy than those for whom the primary goal was "therapy." This helped establish a kind of orientation which has made all families into "research" families. It has been my experience that the more a therapist learns about a family, the more the family learns about itself; and the more the family learns, the more the therapist learns, in a cycle which continues. In the observational process with early families, some were able to restore family functioning without much "therapeutic intervention." The most successful families followed remarkably consistent courses in accomplishing this. Thereafter, it was possible to "intervene" and tell new families about successes and failures of former families and to save the new families endless hours and months of trial-and-error experimentation. In broad terms, the therapist became a kind of "expert" in understanding family systems and an "engineer" in helping the family restore itself to functioning equilibrium.

The overall goal was to help family members become "system experts" who could know the family system so well that the family could readjust itself without the help of an outside expert, if and when the family system was again stressed. It is optimum when the family system can begin a shift toward recovery with the important members of the family attending the hours. There were those in which the family became "worse" during the therapy, the "helpless one" becoming more helpless in response to the overfunctioning of the other. Some would struggle through this period and then move toward recovery; others would terminate. In these situations, it was found to be more profitable to work with one side of the reciprocity until the family was able to work together without increasing the "bind." It is far easier for the overfunctioning one to "tone down" the overfunctioning than for the poorly functioning one to "pull up." If the overfunctioning one is motivated, I see this one alone for a period of "family" psychotherapy in which the goal is to free the immobilized system and restore enough flexibility for the family to work together. From my orientation, a theoretical system that "thinks" in terms of family and works toward improving the family system *is* family psychotherapy.

With this theoretical-therapeutic system, there is always the initial problem of the therapist establishing the orientation of the system. Most families are referred with a diagnosis for the dysfunction. They think in terms of the medical model and expect that the therapist is going to change the diagnosed family member, or the parents may expect the therapist to show or tell them how to change the child without understanding and modifying their part in the family system. With many families, it is surprisingly easy for the therapist to establish this family orientation in which he stands alongside to help them understand and take steps to modify the system. To help establish this orientation, I avoid the diagnosis of any family member and other medical model concepts such as "sick" or "patient." I persistently oppose the tendency of the family to view me as a "therapist." Instead, I work toward establishing myself as a "consultant" in family problems for the initial interviews, and as a "supervisor" of the family effort for the long-term process. When the therapist allows himself to become a "healer" or "repairman," the family goes into dysfunction to wait for the therapist to accomplish his work.

From this discussion of the family as a system, I have avoided saying what kind of a "system." The family *is* a number of different kinds of systems. It can accurately be designated a social system, a cultural system, a games system, a communication system, a biological system, or any of several other designations. For the purposes of this theoretical-therapeutic system, I think of the family as a combination of "emotional" and "relationship" systems. The term "emotional" refers to the force that motivates the system and "relationship" to the ways it is expressed. Under relationship would be subsumed communication, interaction and other relationship modalities.

There were some basic assumptions about man and the nature of emotional illness, partially formulated before the family research, that governed the theoretical thinking and the choice of the various theoretical concepts, including the notion of an "emotional" system. Man is viewed as an evolutionary assemblage of cells who has arrived at his present state from hundreds of millions of years of evolutionary adaptation and maladaptation, and who is evolving on to other changes. In this sense, man is related directly to all living matter. In choosing theoretical concepts, an attempt was made to keep them in harmony with man as a protoplasmic being. Man is different from other animals in the size of his brain and his ability to reason and think. With his intellectual ability he has devoted major effort to emphasizing his uniqueness and the "differences" that set him apart from other forms of life, and he has devoted comparatively little effort to understanding his relatedness to other forms of life. A basic premise is that what man thinks about himself, and what he says about himself, are different in many important ways from what he *is*. Emotional illness is seen as a disorder of man's emotional system, and man's emotional system is seen as basically related to man's protoplasmic being. I view emotional illness as a much deeper phenomenon than that conceptualized by current psychological theory. There are emotional mechanisms as automatic as a reflex and that occur as predictably as the force that causes the sunflower to keep its face toward the sun. I believe that the laws that govern man's emotional functioning are as orderly as those that govern other natural systems and that the difficulty in understanding the system is governed more by man's reasoning that denies its existence than by the complexity of the system. In the literature there are discrepant views about the definition of, and the relatedness between, *emotion* and *feelings*. Operationally I regard an *emotional* system as something deep that is in contact with cellular and somatic processes, and a *feeling* system as a bridge that is in contact with parts of the emotional system on one side and with the intellectual system on the other. In clinical practice, I have made a clear distinction between feelings, which have to do with subjective awareness, and opinions, which have to do with logic and reasoning of the intellectual system. The degree to which people say, "I feel that . . ." when they mean, "I believe that . . ." is so commonplace that many use the words synonymously. However valid the ideas behind the selection of these concepts, they did play a major part in the choice of concepts.

An attempt has been made to keep terminology as simple and descriptive as possible. Several factors have governed this. The effort to think of the family as a fluid, ever-changing functional system was impaired by the use of the static, fixed concepts conveyed by much of conventional psychiatric terminology. Early in family research, the loose use of psychiatric terms, such as "depressed," "hysterical," and "compulsive," interfered with accurate description and communication. An effort was made to prohibit the use of psychiatric jargon within the research staff and to use simple descriptive words. This was a worthwhile discipline. It is difficult to communicate with colleagues without using familiar terms. An effort was made to bridge this gap by the sparing use of familiar terms. In the early years I worked toward some kind of correlation of family concepts with psychoanalytic theory. In writing and professional communication, the use of certain familiar terms would evoke vigorous discussion about the proper definition and use of terms. When the discussions went beyond productive exchanges of views and into nonproductive cyclical debates that consumed both time and energy, I elected to describe the family phenomenon in terms that did not stir up debates, to advance the research as far as possible, and to leave integration of individual and family concepts for some future generation. Although there are inaccuracies in the use of the term "family psychotherapy," I have retained it as the best working compromise between the theory and the practice, and for describing it to the professions to which it is related.

THE FAMILY THEORY

The central concept in this theory is the "undifferentiated family ego mass." This is a conglomerate emotional oneness that exists in all levels of intensity—from the family in which it is most intense, to the family in which it is almost imperceptible. The symbiotic relationship between a mother and child is an example of a fragment of one of the most intense versions. The father is equally involved with the mother and child, and

other children are involved with varying lesser degrees of intensity. The
basic notion to be conveyed at this moment is that of an emotional
process that shifts about within the nuclear family (father, mother, and
children) ego mass in definite patterns of emotional responsiveness. The
degree to which any one family member may be involved depends on his
basic level of involvement in the family ego mass. The number of family
members involved depends on the intensity of the process and the functional state of individual relationships to the central "mass" at that moment. In periods of stress, the process can involve the entire nuclear
family, a whole spectrum of more peripheral family members, and even
nonrelatives and representatives of social agencies, clinics, schools, and
courts. In periods of calm, the process can remain relatively contained
within a small segment of the family, such as the symbiotic relationship in
which the emotional process plays back and forth between mother and
child, with the father isolated from the intense twosome.

The term "undifferentiated family ego mass" has been more utilitarian
than accurate. Precisely defined, the four words do not belong together,
but this term has been the most effective of all in communicating the
concept so that others might "hear." Also, the four words, each conveying
an essential part of the concept, have provided latitude in theoretical
extension of the idea. Clinically, the best examples of the relationship
system within the undifferentiated family ego mass are conveyed by the
more intense versions of it, such as the symbiotic relationship or the
"folie a deux" phenomenon. The emotional closeness can be so intense
that family members know each other's feelings, thoughts, fantasies, and
dreams. The relationships are cyclical. There is one phase of calm, comfortable closeness. This can shift to anxious, uncomfortable overcloseness
with the incorporation of the "self" of one by the "self" of the other.
Then there is the phase of distant hostile rejection in which the two can
literally repel each other. In some families, the relationship can cycle
through the phases at frequent intervals. In other families the cycle can
stay relatively fixed for long periods, such as the angry rejection phase in
which two people can repulse each other for years, or for life. In the
rejection phase, each can retreat into a similar emotional involvement with
another family member or with certain other people outside the family.
Within the family emotional system, the emotional tensions shift about in
an orderly series of emotional alliances and rejections. The basic building
block of any emotional system is the triangle. In calm periods, two members of the triangle have a comfortable emotional alliance, and the third,
in the unfavored "outsider" position, moves either toward winning the
favor of one of the others or toward rejection, which may be planned as
winning favor. In tension situations, the "outsider" is in the favored position and both of the emotionally overinvolved ones will predictably make
efforts to involve the third in the conflict. When tension increases, it will
involve increasing outside members, the emotional circuits running on a
series of interlocking emotional triangles. In the least involved situations,
the emotional process shifts about in a subtle process of emotional responsiveness, which might be compared to an emotional chain reaction. These

mechanisms can be defined in the later stages of family psychotherapy, in which it is possible to analyze the family emotional system. For instance, a smile in one family member might initiate an action response in another, and this initiate a reverie about a dream in another, which is followed by a "change the subject" joke in another.

There are three major theoretical concepts in the theory. The first has to do with the degree of "differentiation of self" in a person. The opposite of differentiation is the degree of "undifferentiation" or "ego fusion." An attempt has been made to classify all levels of human functioning on a single continuum. At one end of the scale is the most intense version of the undifferentiated family ego mass in which "undifferentiation" and "ego fusion" dominate the field and there is little "differentiation of self." The symbiotic relationship and the "folie a deux" phenomenon are examples of clinical states with intense ego fusion. At the other end of the scale the "differentiation of self" dominates the field, and there is little overt evidence of ego fusion. People at this end of the scale represent the highest levels of human functioning. Another concept has to do with the relationship system *within* the nuclear family ego mass and the *outside* emotional forces from the extended family emotional system and from the emotional systems of work and social situations that influence the course of the process within the family ego mass. Important in this concept is the "family projection process," by which parental problems are transmitted to their children. The patterns of this process have been incorporated into a third concept, which deals with the multigenerational interlocking of emotional fields and parental transmission of varying degrees of "maturity" or "immaturity" over multiple generations. For practical purposes, the term "family ego mass" refers to the nuclear family which includes the father, mother, and children of the present and future generations. The term "extended family" refers to the entire network of living relatives, though in the everyday clinical situation this usually refers to the three-generation system involving grandparents, parents, and children. The term "emotional field." refers to the emotional process in any area being considered at the moment.

The Differentiation of Self Scale is an attempt to conceptualize all human functioning on the same continuum. This theory does not have a concept of "normal." It has been relatively easy to define "normal" measurements for all areas of man's physical functioning, but attempts to establish a "normal" for emotional functioning have been elusive. As a baseline for this theoretical system, a detailed profile of "complete differentiation of self," which would be equivalent to complete emotional maturity, has been assigned a value of 100 on a scale from 0 to 100. The lowest level of "no self," or the highest level of "undifferentiation," is at the bottom of the scale. Some of the broad general characteristics of people at the various levels of the scale will be presented.

People in the lowest quarter of the scale (0 to 25) are those with the most intense degree of "ego fusion" and with little "differentiation of self." They live in a "feeling" world, if they are not so miserable that they have lost the capacity to "feel." They are dependent on the feelings of those about them. So much of life energy goes into maintaining the relationship system about them—into "loving" or "being loved" or reaction against the failure to get love, or into getting more comfortable—that there is no life energy for anything else. They cannot differentiate between a "feeling" system and an "intellectual" system. Major life decisions are based on what "feels" right or simply on getting comfortable. They are incapable of using the "differentiated *I*" (I am—I believe—I will do—I will not do) in their relationships with others. Their use of "I" is confined to the narcissistic, "I want—I am hurt—I want my rights." They grew up as dependent appendages of their parental ego masses and in their life course they attempt to find other dependent attachments from which they can borrow enough strength to function. Some are able to maintain a sufficient system of dependent attachments to function through life without symptoms. This is more possible for those in the upper part of this group. A "no self" who is sufficiently adept at pleasing his boss might be considered a better employee than if he had some "self." This scale has nothing to do with diagnostic categories. All in the group have tenuous adjustments, they are easily stressed into emotional disequilibrium, and dysfunction can be long or permanent. The group includes those who manage marginal adjustments and those whose efforts failed. At the extreme lower end are those who cannot exist outside the protective walls of an institution. It includes the "dead enders" of society, many of the lower socioeconomic group, and those from higher socioeconomic groups with intense ego fusions. I would see the hard core schizophrenic person at 10 or below on the scale, and his parents at no more than 20. In family psychotherapy, I have yet to see a person in this group attain a higher "basic" level of differentiation of self. Many attain reasonable alleviation of symptoms, but life energy goes into getting comfortable. If they can gain some symptom relief and a dependent attachment from which they can borrow strength, they are satisfied with the result.

People in the second quarter of the scale (25 to 50) are those with less intense ego fusions and with either a poorly defined self or a budding capacity to differentiate a self. This has to be in general terms because a person in the 30 range has many of the characteristics of "lower scale" people, and those between 40 and 50 have more characteristics of a higher scale. This scale provides an opportunity to describe "feeling" people. From 50 down it is increasingly a *feeling* world except for those at the extreme lower end who can be too miserable to feel. A typical *feeling* person is one who is responsive to emotional harmony or disharmony about him. Feelings can soar to heights with praise or approval or be dashed to nothingness by disapproval. So much life energy goes into "loving" and seeking "love" and approval that there is little energy left for self-determined, goal-directed activity. Important life decisions are based on what feels right. Success in business or professional pursuits is determined more by approval from superiors and from the relationship system than the inherent value of their work. People in this group do have some awareness of opinions and beliefs from the intellectual system but the budding "self" is usually so fused with feelings that it is expressed in dogmatic authoritativeness, in the compliance of a disciple, or in the opposition of a rebel. A conviction can be so fused with feeling that it becomes a "cause." In the lower part of this group are some fairly typical "no selfs." They are transilient personalities who, lacking beliefs and convictions of their own, adapt quickly to the prevailing ideology. They usually go along with the system that best complements their emotional system. To avoid upsetting the emotional system, they use outside authority to support their position in life. They may use cultural values, religion, philosophy, the law, rule books, science, the physician, or other such sources. Instead of using the "I believe" of the more differentiated person, they may say, "Science has shown . . ." and it is possible to take science, or religion, or philosophy out of context and "prove" anything. It is misleading to correlate this scale with clinical categories, but people in the lower part of this segment of the scale, under stress, will develop transient psychotic episodes, delinquency problems, and other symptoms of that intensity. Those in the upper range of the scale will develop neurotic problems. The main difference between this segment and the lower quarter of the scale is that these people have some capacity for the differentiation of selfs. I have had a few families in the 25 to 30 range who have gone on to fairly high levels of differentiation. It is a situation of *possibility* but *low probability*. Most in this range will lose motivation when the emotional equilibrium is restored and symptoms disappear. The *probability* for differentiation is much higher in the 35 to 50 range.

People in the third quarter of the scale (50 to 75) are those with higher levels of differentiation and much lower degrees of ego fusions. Those in this group have fairly well-defined opinions and beliefs on most essential issues, but pressure for conformity is great and under sufficient stress they can compromise principle and make feeling decisions rather than risk the displeasure of others by standing on their convictions. They often remain silent and avoid stating opinions that might put them out of step with the crowd and disturb the emotional equilibrium. People in this group have more energy for goal-directed activity and less energy tied up in keeping the emotional system in equilibrium. Under sufficient stress they can develop fairly severe emotional or physical symptoms, but symptoms are more episodic and recovery is much faster.

People in the upper quarter of the scale (75 to 100) are those I have never seen in my clinical work and that I rarely meet in social and professional relationships. In considering the overall scale, it is essentially impossible for anyone to have *all* the characteristics I would assign to 100. In this group I shall consider those that fall in the 85 to 95 range which will include most of the characteristics of a "differentiated" person. These are principle-oriented, goal-directed people who have many of the qualities that have been called "inner directed." They begin "growing away" from their parents in infancy. They are always sure of their beliefs and convictions but are never dogmatic or fixed in thinking. They can hear and evaluate the viewpoints of others and discard old beliefs in favor of new. They are sufficiently secure within themselves that functioning is not affected by either praise or criticism from others. They can respect the self and the identity of another without becoming critical or becoming emotionally involved in trying to modify the life course of another. They assume total responsibility for self and are sure of their responsibility for family and society. They are realistically aware of their dependence on their fellowman. With the ability to keep emotional functioning contained within the boundaries of self, they are free to move about in any relationship system and engage in a whole spectrum of intense relationships without a "need" for the other that can impair functioning. The "other" in such a relationship does not feel "used." They marry spouses with equal levels of differentiation. With each a well-defined self, there are no questions or doubts about masculinity and femininity. Each can respect the self and identity of the other. They can maintain well-defined selfs and engage in intense emotional relationships at the same time. They are free to relax ego boundaries for the pleasurable sharing of "selfs" in sexuality or other intense emotional experience without reservation and with the full assurance that either can disengage from this kind of emotional fusion and proceed on a self-directed course at will.

These brief characterizations of broad segments of the scale will convey an overall view of the theoretical system that conceives all human functioning on the same continuum. The scale has to do with *basic* levels of differentiation. Another important aspect has to do with *functional* levels of differentiation which is so marked in the lower half of the scale that the concept of *basic* levels can be misleading. The more intense the degree of ego fusion, the more the "borrowing" and "lending" and "giving" and "sharing" of self within the family ego mass. The more the shifting of "strength" within the ego mass, the more likely the marked discrepancies in functional levels of self. The occasional brief shifts are striking. One of the best examples of this is that of the regressed schizophrenic person who pulls up to resourceful functioning when his parents are sick, only to fall back when they have recovered. Other shifts are so fixed that people wonder how one spouse so strong would marry another so weak. A striking example of this is the overadequate husband who might function well in his work at perhaps 55 on strength from a wife housebound with phobias, excessive drinking, or arthritis and a functioning level of 15. In this situation, the basic level would be about 35. Fluctuations in the upper half of the scale are present but less marked, and it is easier to estimate basic levels. People high on the scale have almost no functional shifts. Other characteristics apply to the entire scale. The lower the person on the scale, the more he holds onto religious dogma, cultural values, superstition, and outmoded beliefs, and the less able he is to discard the rigidly held ideas. The lower a person on the scale, the more he makes a "federal case" of rejection, lack of love, and injustice, and the more he demands recompense for his hurts. The lower he is on the scale, the more he holds the other responsible for his self and happiness. The lower he is on the scale, the more intense the ego fusions, and the more extreme the mechanisms such as emotional distance, isolation, conflict, violence, and physical illness to control the emotion of "too much closeness." The more intense the ego fusions, the higher the incidence of being in touch with the intrapsychic of the other, and the greater the chance that he can intuitively know what the other thinks and feels. In general, the lower the person on the scale, the more the impairment in meaningful communication.

Relationship System in the Nuclear Family Ego Mass

An example of a marriage with spouses in the 30 to 35 range will convey an idea of several concepts in this theoretical system. As children, both spouses were dependently attached to parents. After adolescence, in an effort to function autonomously, they either denied the dependence while still living at home, or they used separation and physical distance to achieve autonomy. Both can function relatively well as long as they keep relationships distant or casual. Both are vulnerable to the closeness of an intense emotional relationship. Both long for closeness but both are "allergic" to it. The marriage for each duplicates essential characteristics of former ego masses. They fuse together into a "new family ego mass" with obliteration of ego boundaries and incorporation of the two "pseudo selfs" into a "common self." Each uses mechanisms previously used in their families of origin in dealing with the other. For instance, the one who ran away from his own family will tend to run away in the marriage. The most common mechanism is the use of sufficient emotional distance for each to function with a reasonable level of "pseudo self." The future course of this new family ego mass will depend on a spectrum of mechanisms that operate *within* the family ego mass, and others that operate *outside* in their relationships within the extended family system.

Within the family ego mass, spouses use three major mechanisms to control the intensity of the ego fusion: (1) *Marital conflict* in which each spouse fights for an equal share of the common self and neither gives in to the other. (2) *Dysfunction in one spouse.* A common pattern is a brief period of conflict followed by one spouse's reluctantly "giving in" to relieve the conflict. Both spouses usually see self as "giving in," but there is one who does more of it. In another pattern, one spouse volunteers to be the "no self" in support of the other on whom they become dependent. The spouse who "loses self" in this mechanism may come to function at such a low level that they become candidates for physical, emotional, or social illness. There are some marriages that continue for years with one functioning well and the other chronically ill. (3) *Transmission of the problem to one or more children.* This is one of the most common mechanisms for dealing with family ego mass problems. There are a few families in which ego mass problems are relatively contained within one of the three areas. There are a few with severe marital conflict but no impairment of either spouse and no transmission to the children. There are also a few with no marital conflict, no dysfunction in either spouse and in which the entire weight of the marital problem goes into one child. There may be no significant symptoms until after adolescence, when the child collapses in psychotic dysfunction or other dysfunction of comparable degree. In most families, the problem between the spouses will be "spread" to all three areas. The few families in which the problem remains contained in one area are important theoretically. The fact that there are some families with intense marital conflict and no impairment of children is evidence that marital conflict does not, within itself, cause problems in children. The fact that serious impairment of children can develop in calm, harmonious marriages is further evidence that impairment of children can occur without conflict. The degree of the problem between the spouses can be assigned quantitative measures. The system operates as if there is a certain amount of "immaturity" to be absorbed by the system. Large quantities of this may be "bound" by serious dysfunction in one family member. One chronically ill parent can be a kind of "protection" against serious impairment of children. In the area of transmission to children, the family projection process focuses on certain children and leaves others relatively uninvolved. There are, of course, families in which the "quantity" of immaturity is so great that there is maximum marital conflict, severe dysfunction in one spouse, maximum involvement of children, conflict with families of origin, and still free-floating "immaturity."

The mechanisms that operate *outside* the nuclear family ego mass are important in determining the course and intensity of the process *within* the nuclear family. When there is a significant degree of ego fusion, there is also a borrowing and sharing of ego strength between the nuclear family and the family of origin. In periods of stress the nuclear family can be stabilized by emotional contact with a family of origin, just as the nuclear family can also be disturbed by stress in the family of origin. In general, the intensity of the process in a nuclear family is attenuated by active contacts with the families of origin. There is one striking pattern illustrated by the following example: The father separated himself from his family when he left for college. There was no further contact except infrequent, brief visits and occasional letters and Christmas cards. He married a wife who maintained close contact with her family, including frequent exchanges of letters and gifts, regular family reunions, and visits with scattered members of the clan. Five out of six of the father's siblings followed the same pattern of separating from the family of origin. The mother was one of five siblings, all of whom married spouses who were brought into the emotional orbit of her family. This pattern is so common that I have called these *exploding* and *cohesive* families. The spouse who separates from his family of origin does not resolve the emotional attachment. The old relationship remains "latent" and can be revived with emotional contact. Through the "active" relationship with the cohesive family, the nuclear family system is responsive to emotional events within the cohesive extended family. There are other nuclear families in which both spouses detach themselves from families of origin. In these the spouses are usually much more dependent on each other, and the emotional process in the family tends to be more intense. The average family in which both spouses are emotionally separated from families of origin tend to become more invested in the emotional systems of work and social situations. An example is a family in which the principal outside emotional tie was the father's long-term emotional dependence on his boss at work. Within weeks after the sudden death of the father's boss, a teen-aged son was in serious dysfunction with a behavior problem. A brief period of "family" psychotherapy with the father alone restored the family emotional equilibrium sufficiently for the parents to work productively together toward resolution of the parental interdependence. Knowledge of the relationship patterns in the extended family system is important in understanding the overall problem and in devising a family psychotherapy program.

Multigenerational Transmission Process

One of the important concepts of this theoretical system is the pattern that emerges over the generations as parents transmit varying levels of their immaturity to their children. In most families the parents transmit part of their immaturity to one or more children. To illustrate this multigenerational pattern in its most graphic and extreme form, I shall start with parents with an average level of differentiation and assume that in each generation the parents project a major portion of their immaturity to only one child, thereby creating maximum impairment in one child in each generation. I shall also assume that in each generation one child grows up relatively outside the emotional demands and pressures of the family ego mass and attains the highest level of differentiation possible in that situation. It would be essentially impossible for this pattern to occur generation after generation, but it does illustrate the pattern. The example starts with parents at 50 on the scale. They have three children. The most involved child emerges at 35 on the scale, much lower than the basic level of the parents and a fairly maximum degree of impairment for one generation. Another child emerges with 50, the same basic level of the parents. A third grows up relatively outside the problems of the family ego mass and emerges with a level of 60, much higher than the parents. In considering the child at 35 who marries a spouse in the 35 range, the personality characteristics of this marriage would vary according to the way this family ego mass handles its problems. A maximum projection family would have a calm marriage and almost total preoccupation with the health, welfare, and achievement of the most involved child, who could emerge with a level as low as 20. They could have another who grew up outside the family ego mass with a level of 45, much higher than the parents. To have two children, one at 20 and another at 45, is hardly probable. The child at 20 is already in the danger zone and vulnerable to a whole spectrum of human problems. In his early years he might be an overachiever in school, and then in the postadolescent years go into an emotional collapse. With special help he might eventually finish school, spend a few aimless years, and then find a spouse whose "needs" for another are as great as his. At this level of ego fusion the problems are too great to be contained in one area. They will probably have a variety of marital, health, and social problems, and the problem will be too great for projection to only one child. They might have one child at 10, another at 15, and another who grows up outside the family mass to a level of 30, much above the basic level of the parents. The ones at 10 and 15 are good candidates for total functional collapse into states such as schizophrenia or criminal behavior. This illustrates former statements that it requires at least three generations for a person to acquire the level of "no self" for a later collapse into schizophrenia. In the average situation the immaturity would progress at a much slower rate. Also, in every generation there are children who progress up the scale, and in the average family the upward progression is much slower than illustrated in this example.

It is emphasized that the scale level figures used in the preceding examples are to illustrate the broad principles of the theoretical system. The shift in functional levels in the lower half of the scale is so responsive to such a variety of hour-to-hour and week-to-week shifts, through good years and bad, that approximate levels can be established only after having awareness of the particular variables most operative over a period of time for a given family. It is the general level and the pattern that are most important in the clinical situation. The levels in the multigenerational concept are strictly schematic and for illustrative purposes only. The postulations for this concept were derived from historical material covering three to four generations on approximately 100 families, and ten or more generations on eight families.

There is one other theoretical concept that I have combined with my own work that is used with every family in psychotherapy. These are the personality profiles of the various sibling positions as presented by Toman in *Family Constellation* (Toman, 1961). I consider his work one of the significant contributions to family knowledge in recent years. He presents the thesis that personality characteristics are determined by the sibling position and the family constellation in which one grows up. I have found his personality profiles to be remarkably accurate, especially for people in the mid-scale range of my Differentiation of Self Scale. Of course, he did his study on "normal" families and made no attempt to estimate other variables. He also did not consider the personality alterations of the child who was the object of the family projection process. An example of the shift is a family of two daughters. The older, the one most involved in the family emotional system, emerged with the profile of a younger "baby." The younger daughter, who was less involved in the emotional system with the parents, emerged with more of the characteristics of an older daughter. Most of his profiles contain a mixture of the adult and the infantile characteristics. The higher a person on the scale, the more the adult qualities predominate; the obverse is also true.

CLINICAL USE OF FAMILY PSYCHOTHERAPY

I hope that the theoretical concepts help the reader think more in terms of family systems rather than diagnostic categories and individual dynamics. Each point in the theory has application in clinical evaluation and in family psychotherapy. This section will be presented in three main parts: (1) survey of the family fields, (2) the process of "differentiation of self" in family psychotherapy, and (3) family psychotherapy principles and techniques.

Survey of the Family Fields

This is a term used to designate a family "evaluation" process used in the initial interview with every family I see. It is designed to get a volume of factual information in a brief time. The information is used with the family theory for a formulation about the overall patterns of functioning in the family ego mass for at least two generations. The formulation is used in planning the psychotherapy. Initially, it required a number of hours to get this information. With practice, and the careful structuring of the interview, and an average uncomplicated family, it is possible to do a survey adequately for planning the psychotherapy in one hour. This is different from the kind of "evaluation" in which the therapist may spend several hours with all family members together to observe the workings of the family relationship system. In the training of young therapists, considerable experience in observing multiple family members together is essential. It is not possible to *know* a family without direct clinical observation, and it is not advisable to work with segments of families until one has a working knowledge of the whole. For the average family, the initial interview is with both parents, who can usually provide more information than one. In addition, it provides a working view of the marital relationship. If there is evidence that marital discord might interfere with the fact-gathering, I often ask to see the one parent who has the most knowledge about the family. Some interesting developments come from this. Most families seek help when there is dysfunction in one or more of the three main stress areas of the nuclear family system: (1) marital conflict, (2) dysfunction in a spouse, or (3) dysfunction in a child. To illustrate this survey, I shall use a family referred for a behavior problem in a teen-aged child.

In surveying the family fields, I first want to know about the functioning in the nuclear family field, and then how the functioning of the extended family field intergears with the nuclear field. A good starting point is a chronological review of the symptom development in the teen-aged child, with specific dates and circumstances at the time of each symptom eruption. Many symptomatic eruptions can be timed exactly with other events in the nuclear and extended family fields. The parents might report the child first played hooky from school "in the eighth grade," but it would convey much about the family system if one knew the day he played hooky was the day his maternal grandmother was hospitalized for tests for a feared cancer. Information about feeling and fantasy systems of other family members on that day would be helpful if it could be obtained.

The second area of investigation is the functioning of the parental ego mass since marriage. This emotional unit has its own system of internal dynamics that change as it moves through the years. The internal system also responds to the emotional fields of the extended families and to the reality stresses of life. The goal is to get a brief chronological view of the internal system as it has interresponded with outside forces. This might be compared to two constantly changing magnetic fields that influence each other. The internal functioning is influenced by events such as closeness or distance and emotional contact with extended families, changes in residence, the purchase of a home, and occupational success or failure. Major events that influence both emotional fields are births within the central ego mass and serious illness or death in the extended family. Functioning within the ego mass can be estimated with a few questions about stress areas, which are marital conflict, illness or other dysfunction, and projection to a child. A change in stress symptoms might be related to internal dynamics or external events. The dates of changes are important. A change from a calm to a conflictual relationship might be explained by the wife as "the time I began to stand up to him," when it would in fact be timed exactly with a disturbance in an extended family.

Important ego mass changes accompany the birth of children. The birth of the first child changes the family from a two-person to a three-person system. At an important event such as this, it is desirable to do a "fix" on the entire family system, including place, date, ages of each person in the household and the functioning of each, and a check on the realities in the extended families. It is desirable to get readings on the feeling-fantasy systems of various family members at stress points, if this is possible. A check on the family projection process is often easy by asking about the mother's fantasy system before and after the birth of the child. If it is a significant projection process, her worries and concerns have fixed on the child since the pregnancy, her relationship with this one has been "different," she has long worried about it, and she is eager to talk about it. An intense, long-term, projection process is evidence of a deeper and more serious problem in the child. A projection process that started later, perhaps following the death of an important family member, is much less serious and much easier handled in family psychotherapy. A projection process, usually between mother and child, *changes* the internal functioning of the family system. This much psychic energy from mother to child will change the psychic energy system in the family. It might serve to reduce marital conflict, but it might also disturb the husband to the point he would start spending longer hours at work, or he might begin drinking, or have an affair, or become emotionally closer to his parents. This survey is followed to the onset of symptoms in the child for which there are already nodal points that may be connected with dates and events in the parental relationship. The survey provides a picture of general functioning levels, responsiveness to stress, and evidence about the flexibility or rigidity of the entire system. It also provides a notion about the more adaptive spouse, who is usually the more passive. The adaptive one is much more than one who "gives in" on a controlled surface level. This involves the entire fantasy, feeling, and action system. A spouse who develops physical symptoms in response to an emotional field is in a "cell to cell" adaptiveness that is deep.

The next area of investigation is the two extended family fields, in either order the therapist chooses. This is similar to the nuclear family survey except it focuses on overall patterns. Exact dates, ages, and places are very important. The occupation of the grandfather and a note about the marital relationship and the health of each grandparent provides key clues to that family ego mass. Information about each sibling includes birth order, exact dates of birth, occupation, place of residence, a few words about spouse and children, a note about overall life course, and frequency and nature of contact with other family members. From this brief information, which can be obtained in five or ten minutes, it is possible to assemble a fairly accurate working notion about the family ego mass, and how the nuclear parent functioned in the group. Siblings who do best are usually least involved in the family emotional system. Those who do poorly are usually most involved. Distance from other family members and quality of emotional contacts with family provide clues about the way the person handles all emotional relationships and whether this tends toward an "exploding" or "cohesive" family. A high incidence of physical illness often occurs in those with low levels of differentiation of self. The sibling position is one of the most important bits of information. This, plus the general level of family functioning, makes it possible to postulate a reasonably accurate personality profile to be checked later. In general, a life style developed in the family of origin will operate in the nuclear family and also in family psychotherapy.

Surveys of the family fields follow the same pattern for other problems, except for different emphases. Certain areas may require detailed exploration. It is always helpful to go back as many generations as possible. The overall goal is to follow the total family through time with a focus on related events in interlocking fields. The lower the general level of differentiation in a family, the greater the frequency and intensity of the related events. A secondary dividend of a family field survey is the family's beginning intellectual awareness of related events. The family emotional system operates always to obscure and misremember and to treat such events as coincidental. Family replies to an effort to get specific dates might go, "That was when he was about . . . 11 or 12 years old," and, "He must have been in the fifth grade," or, "It was about five or six years ago." It requires persistent questioning and mathematical computation to get specific information. The obscuring process is illustrated by a family in family psychotherapy. Ten days after the wife returned from her mother's funeral, her daughter developed nephritis. Some weeks later the wife was insisting that the daughter's illness preceded her mother's death. The husband's memory and my notes were accurate. In theoretical thinking, I have never been willing to postulate causality or go beyond noting that such events have a striking time sequence. I believe it may have to do with man's denial of dependence on his fellowman. I avoid glib dynamic speculations and record the family explanations as, "The family member said . . ." I have never been able to use the related events early in psychotherapy. Early in family psychotherapy there was the temptation to show this to the family after the initial interview. Some families found reason to never return. My goal is to keep asking questions and let the calendar "speak" when others are able to "hear."

The family field survey is primarily for the therapist in knowing the family and how it operates, and in planning the psychotherapy. If the symptoms develop slowly in the nuclear family, it is likely to be the product of a slow buildup in the nuclear family. If the symptoms develop more quickly, the situation deserves a thorough exploration for disturbance in the extended family. If it is a response to the extended family, it can be regarded as an "acute" situation and it is fairly easy to restore the family functioning. The following is an example of multiple acute problems following a disturbance in the extended family.

A 40-year-old woman was referred for a depression for which hospitalization had been suggested. Her husband belonged to a "cohesive" family of six siblings, all of whom lived within a few hundred miles of their parents. Two months before, his 65-year-old mother had a radical mastectomy of breast cancer. Two weeks after the operation, one of the husband's sisters had a serious automobile accident which required months of hospitalization. Six weeks after the operation, one of the husband's brothers had a son arrested for a series of delinquent acts, the first of which had occurred two weeks after the operation. After an initial interview with the depressed wife alone, the husband and wife were seen together. A few hours with the process focused on feelings about the mother brought rapid relief of the depression and set the stage for long-term family psychotherapy with both together.

The Process of Differentiation of a Self

The basic effort of this therapeutic system is to help *individual* family members toward a higher level of differentiation of self. An emotional system operates with a delicately balanced equilibrium in which each devotes a certain amount of being and self to the welfare and well-being of the others. In a state of disequilibrium, the family system operates automatically to restore the former togetherness equilibrium, though this be at the expense of some. When an individual moves toward a higher level of differentiation of self, it disturbs the equilibrium and the togetherness forces oppose with vigor. In larger emotional systems, an individual may seek an ally or group to help oppose the forces of the system, only to find self in a new undifferentiated oneness with his allies (even a sect or minority group within the larger system) from which it is harder to differentiate than from the original oneness. Any successful effort toward differentiation is for the individual alone. Some of the forces that oppose the "differentiation of self" will be described later. When the individual can maintain his "differentiation" stand in spite of opposition, the family later applauds.

One of the important concepts in this theoretical system has to do with "triangles." It was not included with the other concepts because it has more to do with therapy than the basic theory. The basic building block of any emotional system is the "triangle." When emotional tension in a two-person system exceeds a certain level, it "triangles" a third person, permitting the tension to shift about within the triangle. Any two in the original triangle can add a new triangle. An emotional system is composed of a series of interlocking triangles. The emotional tension system can shift to any of the old preestablished circuits. It is a clinical fact that the original two-person tension system will resolve itself automatically when contained within a three-person system, one of whom remains emotionally detached. This will be discussed under "detriangling the triangle."

From experience with this therapeutic system, there are two main avenues toward a higher level of "differentiation of self." (1) The optimum is differentiation of a self *from* one's spouse, as a cooperative effort, in the presence of a potential "triangle" (therapist) who can remain emotionally detached. To me, this is the "magic" of family psychotherapy. They must be sufficiently involved with each other to stand the stress of "differentiation" and sufficiently uncomfortable to motivate the effort. One, and then the other, moves forward in small steps until motivation stops. (2) Start the differentiation alone, under the guidance of a supervisor, as a preliminary step to the main effort of differentiating a self *from* the important other person. This second avenue is a model for family psychotherapy with one family member. A third avenue is less effective: (3) the entire process under the guidance of a supervisor who coaches from the sidelines. Direct use of the "triangle" is lost, the process is generally slower, and the chances of an impasse are greater. As a general comment about "differentiation," the highest level of differentiation that is possible for a family is the highest level that any family member can attain and maintain against the emotional opposition of the family unit in which he lives.

Family Psychotherapy Principles and Technique

My optimum approach to any family problem, whether marital conflict, dysfunction in a spouse, or dysfunction in a child, is to start with husband and wife together and to continue with both for the entire period of family psychotherapy. In most families, this "optimum" course is not possible. Some 30 to 40 percent of "family" hours are spent with one family member, mostly for situations in which one spouse is antagonistic or poorly motivated, or when progress with both is too slow. The method of helping one family member to "differentiate a self" will be discussed later. The method of working with the two parents evolved from several years of experience in which both parents and symptomatic child (usually postadolescent behavior and neurotic problems) attended all sessions together. An average course would continue a year or more. Family communication improved, symptoms disappeared, and the families would terminate, much pleased with the result. There was no basic change in the pattern of the parental relationship, postulated to be fundamental in the origin of the problem. On the premise that the entire family system would change if the parental relationship changed, I began asking such parents to leave the child at home and to focus on their own problems. These have been the most satisfying results in my experience. Many of the children who initiated the family effort were never seen, and others were seen only once. The parents who achieved the best results would continue about four years at once a week for a total of 175 to 200 hours with better results than could be achieved with any other psychotherapeutic method in my experience. The children were usually symptom free in a few weeks or months, and changes have gone far beyond the nuclear family into the extended family system. The time has been so consistently in the four-year range that I believe it might require this amount of time for significant differentiation of self. Some people can spend a lifetime without defining themselves on numerous life issues. I am now experimenting with less frequent appointments to reduce the total amount of time.

The basic process of working with husbands and wives together has remained very much the same over the years with some different emphases and modifications in theoretical concepts. In the past I stressed the communication of feelings and the analysis of the unconscious through dreams. More recently, it has been a process of watching the step-by-step process of externalizing and separating out their fantasy, feeling, thinking systems. It is a process of knowing one's own self, and also the self of the other. There have been comments such as, "I never knew you had such thoughts!" and the counterresponse, "I never dared tell anyone before, most especially *you*!"

The following is an example of two small "differentiation" steps with the emotional response of the other. One wife, after many hours of private thinking, announced, "I have decided to take all the thought, time, and energy that I have devoted to trying to make you happy and to put it into trying to make myself into a more responsible woman and mother. Nothing I tried really worked anyway. I have thought it out and I have a plan." The husband reacted with the usual emotional reaction to an "I" position by the other. He was angry and hurt. He ended with, "If I had realized it would come to this after fifteen years, I can tell you one thing, there never would have been a wedding!" Within a week he was happy with his "new" wife. Some weeks later, after much thinking by the husband, he announced, "I have been trying to think through my responsibilities to my family and to work. I have never been clear about this. If I worked overtime, I felt I was neglecting my family. If I spent extra time with the family, I would feel I was neglecting my work. Here is my plan." The wife reacted with emotion about his real selfish lack of concern finally showing its true color. Within a week that had subsided.

As spouses change in relation to each other, they disturb the emotional equilibrium in families of origin where there are the same emotional reactions and resolutions as between themselves. Most of these spouses have become the most responsible and respected in both extended family systems. The emotional opposition to change also occurs in social and work emotional systems. The main point to be communicated here is that a change in "self" disturbs the emotional equilibrium and evokes emotional opposing forces in all interlocking emotional systems. If two spouses can make the primary changes in relation to each other, it is relatively easy to deal with the other systems.

One of the most important processes in this method of psychotherapy is the therapist's continuing attention to defining his "self" to the families. This begins from the first contact, which defines this theoretical and therapeutic system and its differences from others. It proceeds in almost every session around all kinds of life issues. Of importance are the "action" stands which have to do with "what I will do and will not do." I believe a therapist is in a poor position to ask a family to do something he does not do. When the family goes slowly at defining self, I begin to wonder if there is some vague, ambiguous area of importance about which I failed to define myself.

At this point, I shall describe *family* psychotherapy with one family member. The basic notion of this has to do with finding a way to start some change in the deadlocked family; with finding a way to get into contact with family resourcefulness and strength, and to get out of contact with the sickness morass; and with getting some differentiation to rise out of the family quagmire. Actually, if it is possible to get some differentiation started in one family member, it can loosen up the entire family system. Communication of this idea has been difficult. To those who use a medical model and consider the therapeutic relationship the basic healing force in emotional illness, the idea is erroneous. I have used several different concepts in trying to write about the idea and a number of different angles in trying to teach it. There are those who heard it as "treating the healthiest family member instead of the patient, on the grounds that the healthiest is more capable of modifying behavior." This is an accurate description of the goal, but it uses a "health" concept in the place of "sickness," which is still a medical model. A therapist who attempts to "treat" the healthiest with his medical orientation could either drive him away or make him into a "patient."

The conflictual marriage provides one of the best examples of working with one spouse. This is a clinical situation in which the emotional system is already fairly well locked in dysfunction before the partners seek help. A fair level of overt conflict is "normal," and it has to reach a relative state of dysfunction before they seek help. The marriage began with an almost idyllic model in which each devoted a high percentage of "self" to the happiness and well-being of the other. This I have called a "fraudulent" emotional contract, in which it was realistically impossible for either to live up to the agreement. With this arrangement, the functioning of self *is* dependent on the other and, in that sense, any failure in happiness or functioning *is* the fault of the other, The emotional investment in each other continues, only it shifts into negative energy that accuses, indicts, and diagnoses. I believe the conflictual marriage is an enduring one because of the energy investment. The amount of *thinking* time that goes into the other is probably greater than calm marriages. With the intensity of emotional interdependence and the ability to utilize conflict, the conflictual spouses usually do not seek help until adaptive mechanisms are jammed. In a high percentage of conflictual marriages, I see one spouse alone for a few months to a year before calm working together is possible. Choice about the one to see first is easy when one is motivated and the other antagonistic. It is a little different when both are seen together and the repetitious "accuse the other—excuse self" continues in the interview. If they have any capacity to stop the cycle and look at the pattern, I continue with both together. If a vigorous effort to help them contain the cycle is not successful, I say that I consider this cyclical and nonproductive, that I am not willing to spend time this way, and that I want to see the healthiest, best-integrated one alone for a period of time to help this one gain some objectivity and emotional control. A request for the "healthiest" establishes a different orientation and changes their long-term diagnosing, "You are the sick one who needs a psychiatrist." I do not see spouses alternately. It invites "triangling," neither really works at the problem, each expects the other to do it, and each tends to justify self to the therapist. My "I" stands, all based on experience, are in terms of what I will do and will not do, and are never in terms of "what is best."

Since the process of working with one family member alone is similar in all situations, I shall describe the effort with the conflictual spouse in some detail. The early sessions go into a detailed communication of an orientation with the use of clinical examples and a blackboard for diagrams. In broad terms, the concept is one of withdrawing psychic energy from the other and investing it in the poorly defined ego boundaries. It involves the idea of "getting off the back" of the other (by reducing the "other-directed" thinking, verbal and action energy which is designed to attack and change the other) and directing that energy to the changing of self. The changing of "self" involves finding a way to listen to the attacks of the other without responding, of finding a way to live with "what is" without trying to change it, of defining one's own beliefs and convictions without attacking those of the other, and in observing the part that self plays in the situation. Much time is devoted to establishing the therapist's self in relation to the one spouse. These ideas are passed along for their possible use in defining a "self." He is told that others have found some of them helpful; that the effort will fail if he tries them without incorporating them into "self" as his own beliefs; that he would be unrealistic to try something he could not really believe in; and it will be his responsibility to find other ideas and principles if these do not fit with his own "self." He is assigned the task of becoming "research observer" and told that a major part of each hour will go into his report on his efforts to see self. I tell him about the predictable stages he can expect if his efforts are successful in defining "self" and containing the critical actions, words, and thoughts that have been trying to direct the life of his spouse. If he is successful at this, the first reaction will be a version of, "You are mean, selfish, and vicious; you do not understand, you do not love, and you are trying to hurt the other." When he can listen to the expected attack without reacting, a milestone will have been passed. Then he can expect a withdrawal from the other which emphasizes, "To heck with you. I do not need you." This will be the most difficult stage. He might get depressed and confused and develop a whole spectrum of physical symptoms. This is the reaction of one's psyche and soma as it cries out for the old dependence and togetherness. If he can live with the symptoms without reacting, he can expect the other to make a new and different bid for affection on a higher level of maturity. It is usually not many days after that before the other spouse asks to take the therapy hour, and often not many hours before they can finally work together.

The life style of this low level of "differentiation" is the investment of psychic energy in the "self" of another. When this happens in the therapy, it is transference. A goal of this therapy is to help the other person make a research project out of life. It is as important to keep "self" contained with the therapist as the other spouse. If the person understands the life-goal nature of the effort, and that progress will slow down or stop with energy invested in the "self" of the therapist, he is in a better position to help keep the energy focused on the goal. If progress does stop, the family psychotherapy is shifted to a similar effort with the other spouse. It is not possible to use this "differentiation of a self" approach with two spouses. It results in intense "triangling."

Work with one sick spouse depends on the problem and which one seeks help. If the well one seeks help, the "sick" one is near collapse. With these I work toward avoiding a relationship with the sick side of the family, and work toward relating to the well one about his problems with the sick one. Some of these families achieve remarkable symptom relief with a few appointments, but these people are not motivated for more than symptom relief. When the "sick" one seeks help, I maintain a detached, "Let's examine this and understand your part in the family problem." The cells of the "sick" spouse literally go into dysfunction in the presence of the other spouse, especially in those with severe introjective and somatic dysfunctions. If the other spouse is brought in too early, the therapy effort may terminate within a few hours. A goal is to propose "family" early and wait until the "self" of the sick one can operate in the presence of the other without going into dysfunction. There have been some excellent long-term results which include about six months with the sick one and some two years with both. Problems such as impotence and frigidity belong more in the area of relationship functioning. These can usually be converted to "family" within a few hours and the response has been good. Impotence often disappears within a few weeks and frigidity is rarely mentioned after a few months. Most of these go on with long-term family therapy for two years or more.

The problem of the "triangled" child presents one of the most difficult problems in family psychotherapy. From the initial family survey can come a fair estimate of the intensity of the process. If it is not too severe, the parents can focus on their own problems immediately, they almost forget about the child and, suddenly, he is symptom free. Even with severe "triangling," I do a "trial run" with both parents together to test the flexibility in the parental relationship. In the severe "triangling" or projection of the parental problem to the child, the parents are not able to leave the child out of their feelings, thoughts, and actions. There are the less severe versions in which parents try hard to work on their problem but the relationship between them is dull and lifeless. Life and self are invested in the child. The "gut reaction," in which a parent's "insides tie into knots" in response to discomfort in the child, is common. After several years of symptom-relieving methods, including working with various combinations of family members, I began what I have called "detriangling the triangle." This is too complex for brief discussion but it involves helping one parent to establish an "I" position and to "differentiate a self" in the relationship *with the child*. If there is another "magic" in family psychotherapy, it is the family response when one parent can begin to "differentiate a self" from the amorphous "we-ness" of the intense undifferentiated family ego mass. One bit of clearly defined "self" in this sea of amorphousness can bring a period of amazing calm. The calm may quickly shift to other issues, but the family *is* different. The other parent and child fuse together into a more intense oneness that alternately attacks and pleads with the "differentiating parent" to rejoin the oneness. If the differentiating one can maintain a reasonable "I" for even a few days, there is an automatic decrease in the intensity of the attachment between the other two and a permanent decrease in the intensity of the triangle. The second step involves a similar effort by the other parent to "differentiate a self." Now the parental relationship has come a little more to life. Then there is another cycle with each parent separately, and then still more life and zest between the parents. Differentiation proceeds slowly at this level of ego fusion, but there have been a few of these families that have gone on to reasonable levels of differentiation.

There are several other configurations of family psychotherapy with one family member, but this provides a brief description of the basic principles. It is used when the family system is so stalled that efforts to work with the multiple family members increase the dysfunction, or when work with multiple members reaches a cyclical impasse. The effort is to help one family member to a higher level of functioning which, if possible, can restore function to the family system.

REFERENCES

Ackerman, N. Interlocking pathology in family relationships. In S. Rado & G. E. Daniels (Eds.), *Changing concepts in psychoanalytic medicine*. New York: Grune & Stratton, 1956.

Bateson, G., Jackson D., Haley, J., & Weakland, J. Toward a theory of schizophrenia. *Behav. Sci.*, 1956, *1*, 251–264.

Bell, J. E. Family group therapy, Public Health Monograph 64, 1961.

Birdwhistell, R. *Introduction to kinesics*. Louisville, Ky.: University of Louisville Press, 1952.

Bowen, M. Family relationships in schizophrenia. In Auerback (Ed.), *Schizophrenia–An Integrated Approach*. New York: Ronald Press, 1959.

Bowen, M. A family concept of schizophrenia. In D. Jackson (Ed.), *The Etiology of Schizophrenia*. New York: Basic Books, 1960.

Bowen, M. Family psychotherapy. *Amer. J. Orthopsychiat.*, 1961, *30*, 40–60.

Bowen, M. Family psychotherapy with schizophrenia in the hospital and in private practice. In I. Boszormenyi-Nagy & J. L. Framo (Eds.), *Intensive family therapy*. New York: Harper & Row, 1965.

Dysinger, R. The action dialogue in an intense relationship. Paper read at Annual Meeting, American Psychiatric Association, Chicago, 1957.

Flugel, J. C. *The Psycho-analytic study of the family*. London: Hogarth Press, 10th Impr., 1960.

Freud, S. Analysis of a phobia in a five year old boy. In *Collected papers*. Vol. III. London: Hogarth Press, 1949.

Lidz, T., Cornelison, A., Fleck, S., & Terry, D. The intrafamilial environment of the schizophrenic patient: II. Marital schism and marital skew. *American Journal of Psychiatry*, 1957, *114*, 241–248.

Scheflen, A. The significance of posture in communication systems. *Psychiatry*, 1964, *26*, 316–331.

Toman, W. *Family constellation*. New York: Spring Publishing Co., 1961.

Wynne, L., Rykoff, I., Day, J., & Hirsch, S. Pseudo-mutuality in family relations of schizophrenics. *Psychiatry*, 1958, *21*, 205–220.

CHAPTER 14

Toward a Theory of Marriage and Family Counseling: Systems Eclecticism

Clinton E. Phillips

Introduction

My greatest hope for this paper is that it will lay a groundwork for a theory of Relationship Counseling. However, I don't think I am able to do that at this time. Perhaps no one is. I will, however, attempt to develop a theoretical orientation to counseling which I would like to call *Eclectic*. Yet, there is some difficulty with this term because eclecticism in its past usage has not implied the *synergistic* and *serendipitous* aspects of systems theory which I am introducing. I shall have to settle for *Systems Eclecticism* until a better word or phrase comes along. There are four major aspects to this orientation: Synthesis, Eclecticism, Systems Theory, and Paradox.

Eclecticism becomes respectable when, around a systems framework, we can see more clearly how a treatment model such as operant conditioning is not really contradictory to the concepts of gestalt methods. We can see that transactional analysis can be used with an existential approach. In other words, rather than believing with some of the old timers, who said, "My way is the way and the only way, and you will reach the psychotherapeutic heaven when you treat people in the ways I have outlined to you," we believe now that they were talking about and teaching useful theory and methodology which applies to one or two levels of human experience. We now know that experiences are conceptualized in different ways, and that each theory and method of counseling which has been shown to be valuable for large numbers of people is valid in its own right *at that level*. Apparent contradictions turn out to be straw men, as we suspected all along. Eclectic counselors have been pragmatic in their application of several modalities, with success, in spite of the "contradictions." They were only logical contradictions which can now be resolved with paradox theory and the use of logical types theory (Watzlawick, et al, 1967, 1974.).

Semantics

Because words are not things (Hayakawa, 1964), it is necessary to remind ourselves at the outset that we are using words to express experience, and that although we are using process words, neither are they things. The words "synthesizing," "cognating," "emoting" and "acting" are only efforts to convey process meanings, not to delineate things.

Synthesis

As I use it here, synthesis means more than putting together human thinking, feeling, and emotion as processes. It refers to all the processing of human experience which is involved in "making sense out of" both environmental and internal stimuli which are mediated by what psychologists refer to as the processes of cognition, emotion, and action. Too often these processes of thinking, feeling, and behaving are thought of and spoken of as if they were unitary and separate from each other in the human experience. In other words, one thinks without reference to feeling or behaving, etc. These processes are also too often thought of as things or entities. They are not. They are high-level abstractions; they are concepts, semantic constructs which are useful in describing *somewhat* distinct but overlapping processes.

Such compartmentalization is, of course, not reality. We are actually always "putting together" these and other aspects of the human experience into a whole, or a series of holistic *intentions*, or trial runs. We mentally explore alternatives by way of processing input, feedback, and trial syntheses of our cognitions, our emotions, and our behaviors. This "mind-body" synthesizing is synergistic and serendipitous—it brings together facets of experiences and often something new arises out of the amalgam experience. The better terms to catch more nearly the meaning of these experiences are process terms such as *synthesizing, cognating, emoting,* and *behaving.*

In this context, I am using the term "synthesis" in the sense of bringing together or putting together in a meaningful way; it is used to imply the organization of data, out of which something new may arise. Although newness is not stressed at this point, I believe that the eclectic counselor is generally more responsive, flexible, and creative in relation to client needs than one devoted to only one of the present day "schools."

Later in the paper, synthesis is used in a more technical sense where it implies that a process of mental activity is always going on which includes "creative" processing of cognition, emotion and behavior. Synthesizing is given necessary and equal, even prior status to the processes of thinking, feeling, and behaving in the human experience. It is the mental and body activity of being alive to, responding to, reacting to and planning for coping with the human environment, including the internal environment.

Eclecticism

This word means that I will draw from several schools of psycho-therapeutic thought, theory, methodology, and application to treatment; many of these will not be mentioned in this paper. As a rule, marriage and family counselors (MFC) use a great variety of counseling skills, methods, and techniques. They draw upon such diverse tools as come from social interaction theory, psycho-drama and role-playing, gestalt therapy theory, behavior modification or learning theory, psychoanalytic theory, dynamic or ego-psychology, small group theory, transactional analysis, individual psychology and many, many more.

There is a second reason for an eclectic orientation. It is not just to put "schools" together. They belong together—in fact, they cry out to go together—the similarities are so great and so obvious, only the words are different. The contradictions are not what they seem to be. They may appear to be contradictory or opposite, when indeed they are simply operating at and emphasizing a level of experience which appears to be contradictory to another theory because one is, let's say, emphasizing the *feeling level* of experience while the other "school" is emphasizing the *rational level* of experience.

My approach to this theoretical orientation is pragmatic. In other words, I begin with what counselors do, and I do not begin with a philosophic "given" or *a priori* position, or truth, and develop a grand or inclusive theory from it. I do not think that that approach is possible or reasonable. I do think on the other hand that the surest way to fail at theory building is to begin that way. It is safer to begin with a pragmatic orientation which answers the question, "What do most MFC counselors actually do in their counseling of couples and families and what theoretical orientations best explain these behaviors?" Perhaps an even better way of stating the question is, "What goes on in the interaction between counselors and clients which brings about change in the behaviors of the clients?"

I am deliberately eclectic in my approach to counseling in much the same way as is Frederick Thorne. (See Ch. 13, Corsini, 1975.) I differ from Thorne in my eclecticism and will indicate some of these major differences later. The overriding question is, how come other theories and methods work if any one of them has all the answers?

Let us look briefly at the paradox of competing counseling theories. Perhaps you have asked yourself, "Why are there different schools of psychology?" "Isn't there some truth in most, if not all, the various approaches to counseling?" I am convinced that human behavior and the motivations for human behavior are complex enough to require a broad perspective; a broad theory of psychology. A larger perspective is obviously needed than that of any one school and Frederick Thorne has spent many years developing his Integrative Psychology plus a deliberate eclectic approach to counseling or psychotherapy, or "psychological case handling" as he calls it.

A larger perspective is gained when we realize that all of living is a *process of decision-making and paradox*. Around this central concept we will develop a bit of a philosophy of man, a psychology of process human development, and an eclectic theory of counseling and psychotherapy. Contrary to most psychotherapy theorists who stress one view of man, these various theories of psychotherapy are helpful in that each of those we have studied makes very real contributions to an understanding of man and of the ways he can change. Instead of one way being the *only* true way, each adds something to the understanding of man, and each suggests ways (methods, skills, and techniques) of treatment which are useful to the eclectic counselor or psychotherapist.

Some behavior modifiers are becoming increasingly eclectic in their approach to psychotherapy. Lazarus (1973, 1974) is foremost in this regard. He writes that in treatment we must include sensations, perceptions, emotions, cognitions, behaviors, and interpersonal relationships, with or without drugs. He uses the acronym BASIC ID to express these modalities as follows: *B*ehavior, *A*ffective processes, *S*ensations, *I*mages, *C*ognitions, *I*nterpersonal relationships, with or without *D*rugs. He says that each modality must be paid specific attention if long lasting results from psychotherapy are to come about. He stops short of calling himself eclectic.

Another behaviorist, Meichenbaum, stresses cognition as the best way to enter the behavioral process for change. (In press.)

Neither Lazarus nor Meichenbaum is yet systems-oriented in his theory.

In spite of all the claims of each school of psychotherapy, no one of them, nor for that matter, any two of them, have all the answers to the human condition. A proof of this lies in the simple fact that one "school" of therapy has about as high a success rate as another, plus the fact that some people change with gestalt treatment while others do not, whereas some people change with behavior modification treatment while others do not. Furthermore, some people who have not changed with one method, two methods, or three methods, respond quickly enough to another method.

It is also interesting for our argument that a counselor can use both behavior modification methods and gestalt methods in the same hour (or session) with an individaul, couple, or family, and both methods can be helpful to the people involved. These theories are seen as quite different from each other and the "purists" among them claim the other school of thought is wrong. But that is not true because both work. It is not true because the process of human living and development is such that people are ready for different things at different times depending on their accumulated experience, the circumstances, and on the "personalities" of the people around them at any one time. People can also integrate and synthesize operant methods at the behavioral level *without* understanding the "whys" (they are acting "on faith"), and in the same hour of counseling "get with their feelings" and create a new type of relationship with family members without having to "think" in any organized way about their feelings and without having to explain what they did in any sense whatsoever. "It just happened—it went together," it synthesized. True, all levels of experiencing are present in an event, but with different degrees of awareness and of emphasis. At one time the cognitive level is primary, at another time, feeling or behavioral, or all three, but the individual is also synthesizing experience throughout.

As much as we are all indebted to Frederick Thorne, his concerns, and his writing, the eclecticism I am presenting here is not his (Corsini, 1957). I differ with Thorne on some fundamental issues which should now be summarized.

Frederick Thorne

Thorne makes use of his knowledge of different "schools" for both diagnosis and treatment. (In this approach the different schools are simply "seeing" different facets of the same behaviors.) These same schools see behaviors selectively—often deliberately so—while ignoring other behaviors, so that a linear diagnosis can be made. The result is that "significant" behavior is labeled in terms of one of the schools, and then a treatment modality is designed to change that particular behavior complex.

From a systems point of view, each school suggests entering the individual's complex personal and interpersonal system at points idiosyncratic to the school's frame of reference, rather than from the individual's frame of reference. Often this is done by relabeling the client's complaint. This is wasteful of energy and money, and often is the reason for counseling failure; the client could not follow the counselor's diagnosis or relabeling of his complaints. He then quits counseling or sought out someone who could communicate with him in terms he could understand.

My theoretical orientation is systems and process-oriented, whereas Thorne's orientation is linear and additive (Corsini, pp. 445–6).* In spite of his understanding of the integrating tendency of man, he comes out at the end making a diagnosis and treating the diagnosed "condition" as if it were a thing:

> Theoretically the eclectic has the best chance of being methodologically broad enough to comprehend the almost infinite complexity of behavior causation and to *diagnose what needs modification* (p. 463). (Italics mine.)

Thorne also writes:

> Eclecticism derives from the systematic study of *causes and effects* and applies behavior modification methods following *diagnosis in individual prescriptions to specific clinical problems* with unique configurations of etiological factors. The eclectic method thereby becomes a basic scientific approach to the problem of *matching* suitable clinical methods to the needs of specific cases (p. 445). (Italics mine.)

Thorne objects to structural and trait psychology on the one hand, but appears to be contradictory to this position in his great emphasis upon *diagnosis* of the "psychological state" of the individual. He even raises diagnosis to a high level priority in "psychological case handling," whereas my approach avoids diagnosis as far as possible. Once again, diagnosis is static and linear pigeonholing of people and consequently often misleading to the counseling process, if not outright damaging to people. To label a "psychological state," that is, to diagnose, becomes a semantic trap in no real sense different from labeling or diagnosing in the traditional sense of trait psychology. Thorne would therefore treat or "handle" one *thing* at a time (singular), (the most important first—but by whose definition? Probably the counselor's!). But I am stressing the systems and process nature of counseling activity in which the counselor enters the

---

*The references to Thorne are to be found in his chapter "Eclectic Psychotherapy" in Corsini, R. J., *Current Psychotherapies*.

system and interacts mostly in those areas (plural) where the most pains (plural) are being communicated. All of this is done without diagnosing or labeling anything and with the client(s)' cooperation, feedback, and involvement (synthesizing), etc. Then, if the client wants to change some things about himself, his behaviors and the results he gets from other people, then the counselor's activities (interventions) are designed to aid in bringing about a change. This counselor activity is often done as a second order level intervention which shifts the client's whole experience to a different, and one hopes more acceptable level of functioning with self and/or others (Watzlawick, et al, 1974). In Thorne's terms, however, the counselor would, let's say, apply *either* T.A. *or* gestalt *or* psycho-analytic *or* some other method to an individual case for a particular result.

Thorne believes that his eclectic method can become a "science" in the same sense that the physician can diagnose a particular form of cancer and then prescribe a known treatment (somewhat apart from other factors in the system). This form of eclecticism (linear and additive) is unacceptable for reasons of the pragmatics of human experience and the system demands as already stated.

Thorne also postulates that we can have no truly eclectic psychology and psychiatry until we know how the brain works. I disagree that this is a necessary condition because we are dealing with much more than how the brain works in such social and interactional aspects as marriage relation-ships, family living and group behavior. The more we understand human communication, the paradoxical nature and functioning of language, the system processes of interaction adjustment and how the entire body records, stores, and retrieves information, the better able the counselor is to intervene for change purposes, whether he understands how the brain works or not (Bandler and Grinder, 1975).

Thorne has set forth a number of principles and concepts which are convincing for an eclecticism in counseling and psychotherapy. One of the most important of these concepts is what he called *unification* and later on *integration*.

Thorne defines integration as: " . . . the level of organization at which the organism is able to mobilize all its resources in a functionally autonomous manner in coping with the life situation of the moment."

From a process point of view, the above definition is deficient because (a) it focuses on the individual's coping ability without reference to his social support systems and, (b) it does not include a recognition of the potential for serendipitous outcomes, or newness arising out of the interactions and processes.

However, Thorne's concept of integration is similar to what I call *synthesizing*. The whole of man is involved in processing and making sense out of experience and in decision-making, activity, and commitment of self to action or inaction. (See Sommerhoff, 1974, and Konorski, 1967.)

Sommerhoff writes: " . . . that no part of the brain acts in isolation and no aspect of brain function is unrelated to another or to the organization of the brain as a whole (1974)."

Also . . . "Although, therefore, from the nature of the case the relation between a mental state and the associated behavior disposition is a close one, *it is not a logical one.* In consequence, it is logically possible to be in pain and not show it and, conversely, to show pain behavior and not to be in pain. In other words, it is possible to pretend (1974, p. 63)." (Italics mine.)

And . . . "The critical characteristic of mental states, as we have seen, is their privacy. In the last analysis the distinctions between different mental states are based on *subjective self-categorizations* and we have no direct access to the mental state of another individual except through his introspective utterances (1974)." (Italics mine.)

Thorne says of this human experience: " . . . that the central process of the organism is unification (integration) and that attempts to break up this central process by elementaristic operational methods inevitably result in loss of functional unity of the whole integrative process (p.454). He fails, however, to carry this concept forward into a systems orientation. Thorne nevertheless has called attention to the very important fact of human experience, namely that there is a constant process of unifying and integrating going on and that it cannot be reduced to its parts without great loss of information. He also has outlined ways in which man integrates experiences but he does not reach a systems orientation in his work.

Thorne and Nathan (1970) have written on "Systems Analysis Methods for Integrative Diagnosis," but this article is only an attempt to apply systems *methods* to diagnosis. It is still a linear application of system and does not deal with the synergistic and "spin off" capabilities of man's mind at work.

A great deal of space has been devoted to Thorne because (a) it is important to show the very real differences between his eclecticism and mine and (b) he is the leading proponent of the old eclecticism and deserves credit for his contributions to the data of eclecticism as well as his original and creative thinking. In my view, being eclectic after Thorne provides the client with far superior service than one (or even two) "schools" of counseling and psychotherapy. However, there is another step to be taken now. We must build on Thorne and go beyond him to a thorough Systems Eclecticism.

System Theory

Family system theory, one of the descendents of general system theory, has provided much of the structure or framework for my theoretical orientation. I agree with David Olsen and Carlfred Broderick that system theory is more of a framework for theory than it is a theory in and of itself (Broderick, 1969).

Von Bertalanffy has called attention to the necessity of system-type thinking and process thinking in a number of intellectual and academic fields. System theory is mechanical but process-oriented and has its easiest and simplest application in physics and thermodynamics. System theory indicates in a rather straightforward way that it is important to note that elements, in relation and in interaction with each other, have an effect on one another in a systematic manner and that these effects or results are not summative. Rather, the whole (of the interacting parts and the environment) is more than the sum of its parts. The system of interacting parts and its environment is an *added* feature to the sum of parts.

When applied to human experience, this system organization is better described by a group of process concepts such as analyzing, evaluating, and synthesizing of input of thinking, feeling, and behaving. It is the whole of man at work; it is the "mind" always taking in information, while thinking, feeling, and behaving in the form of evaluating and estimating possible outcomes of various actions all at the same time. The individual or family is never just thinking, or never just feeling, or never just behaving. The processes which we label thinking, feeling and behaving are labeled in this manner due to the limitations of language and the need to conceptualize human experiencing. We see how difficult it is to describe process as compared to linear and "thing" oriented concepts of human experience. Philosophers, semanticists, and language theorists as well as psychologists have long been aware of the unity of mind and body and still we have continued to dichotomize by labeling mental functioning as consisting of three *things*: thought, feeling, and action, while the rest of the body experienced other functions. These must now be thought of as part of a functioning organizational whole. We cannot divide the mind from the body. We cannot even be contented with the concept of synthesis as a fourth element, for it is not an element, or thing, any more than thinking, feeling, and behaving are things. The functioning "mind" is a human experience in which the processes of thinking—feeling—behaving—analyzing—evaluating—predicting—synthesizing and more, are all occurring pretty much as the process of one experience.

It is important that both individuals and families be seen as systems and as open systems. The individual's experience of himself is a complex of activities as outlined above which not only takes into account his various internal processes, but also includes his responses and reactions to both the people environment as well as the physical environment around him. What he will do with himself in response to all of these is often not predictable because he, as an open system, is more than the sum of his "parts" and processes, and all the parts and processes may never be known. The products and outcomes are the essence of human creativeness. Something new has been added by virtue of the serendipitous results of the "mental" capabilities of synthesizing experience so that there *is* something new under the sun.

Now what is true of individuals is true of the husband-wife relationship, the diadic relationship, and family and group relationships as well, namely that these are open systems which themselves are engaged with each other in processes of reacting to one another and groups of others while feeling, thinking, calculating, monitoring, estimating, and predicting outcomes, etc., so that the outcomes of relationships are not yet completely predictable.

Equifinality

A system concept of importance in relationship counseling theory is equifinality. This means simply that certain results or out-puts of a system may come from different sources or "causes." Some parents and family life circumstances can turn out drug or alcohol abusers, but so may other kinds of parents in altogether different kinds of life circumstances. Whereas very similar families to both the above do not produce any drug or alcohol abusers.

If the subject matter of general system theory is, as von Bertalanffy says, the "formulation of principles that are valid for 'systems' in general, whatever the nature of their component elements and the relations or 'forces' between them" (1968), then it can be stated that the subject matter of family system theory is the formulation of principles that are valid for families in general, whatever the nature of their component elements and the relations between them.

Also, the subject matter of counseling system theory is the formulation of principles that are valid for counseling in general whatever the nature of their component elements and the relations or forces between them. The principle of wholeness requires that all counseling methods that work, or seem to work, be integrated into this counseling theory. Hence the logical requirement for a pragmatic system eclecticism. Even "contradictory" methods (schools) must be included if they are shown to be of value to some people in changing their lives. This is accomplished by reference to logical types and paradox theory when we show that the various schools and their methods are a part of a class of logical objects and that they are not therefore mutually exclusive of each other and contradictory, but rather complimentary. When these different views of man are seen from this frame of reference we have more wholeness and similarity than separation and difference. (Watzlawick, et al, 1975.)

Paradox

Language is central in human interaction and cannot be dispensed with, and yet there is much in language that is paradoxical in its expression. Thought and language contain much about their structure and expression that appear as paradox. Not everyone agrees as to the logic of language and certainly not everyone is logical or consistent in his thinking or in the manner of his expression. However, some order can be made of dysfunctional communication patterns in human interaction and an understanding of paradox is helpful in this respect (Watzlawick, et al, 1967 and 1974).

Paradox, or seeming opposites, is a constant part of the ongoing, living process. We are faced with paradox from the beginning to the end of our lives. Life itself is not real without death. Death is then a part of life; a seeming paradox. Life has no meaning without death, and death has no meaning without life. Notice also the lack of choice in life and death. They are givens. Much of our living process is that way. Paradox is always with us, and it is a part of life which demands process, that is, the synthesizing of thinking, feeling, and behaving in our efforts to make decisions and choices.

Perhaps because some things are inevitable, in the languages of the Western world, we have been taught to think in either-or terms (Hayakawa, 1964), that is, thinking in paradoxical terms is a part of our language and culture and thought patterns. For example, we are taught about heaven and hell, good and evil, a thing is either this or that, etc. It is little wonder then that psychological theorists were prone to stress *either* behavior *or* feeling *or* thinking in their approaches to man.

By simply violating the rules of this Aristotelian logic we can create other alternatives and solve our problems in new and different ways—at least in different terms. We can say that neither feeling, thinking, behaving nor any other part process has primacy in understanding or changing man, but that they all go together to make a whole. We can also say that a person is processing or synthesizing experience all the time and that the counselor's task is to enter the client's field of experiencing *at the levels* and with *the languages* which are most useful to the client. Operant behavioral methods might be quite meaningful to a couple's change process, while in the same hour both can experience deep feelings of anger, love, respect, and appreciation from a behavioral exercise, or the other way around. In other words, it becomes rather meaningless to attempt to explain change from only one level, behavioral, when much, much more is being experienced by the couple.

Theory of logical types also helps us to understand and to make use of methods to bring about change. A mechanical example is useful at this point. Two *levels* of change are described: (1) When an automobile's transmission gears are hand-shifted from first through fourth speeds, it is quite a different change from the use of the auto (2) on a stationary block with the transmission locked into one gear and the running mechanism transformed into a mill saw. In the latter, the *change* occurred from outside the system, whereas in the former the change was within the system.

The change occurring from within is called *first order level* change (in which nothing of the system changes) and the change which occurs from without is called *second order level* change, and the system is changed. The latter is usually the goal of counselors and psychotherapists (Watzlawick, et al, 1974).

For example, a client may want his wife to stop drinking. Rather than advise him to remind her more of how much he and their children love her and how she is ruining her health, etc., which is *first order* change, he might well be advised to buy her liquor and to encourage her to drink, then simply pay *no more attention whatsoever* to her drinking. That is *second order level* change. Only then is his wife likely to change. The paradoxical aspect is that if A wants B to change, A must change first and change with radically new and different behavior, on the *second order level*. Something *new* must be added to the system. For more on second order level change also see Ashby, 1956.

Reframing. To conceptually change the meaning of an event or a situation is to reframe it. Reframing is, therefore, closely related to second order change. For example, the counselor might reframe a husband's nagging and critical behavior both to himself and to his beleaguered wife as his only way of expressing his deep love and concern for her. Both are better off when they understand and accept this "what" description of the husband's behavior than to try and find out "why" he nags and complains to her. Reframing is not a search for "why" but rather a new and more accurate description of what is going on in a relationship (Watzlawick et al, 1975).

Watzlawick et al (1967, 1974) and Haley (1963) have discussed the theory and practice of paradox and they should be read in order to follow the brief treatment of paradox theory here. Paradox will be discussed further under the next heading where intervention, paradox, and systems orientation to counseling are considered together.

Application to Counseling

In system theory terms it does not matter much where the family therapist enters the system for intervention (equifinality), but rather that he enter at a level which is understood or is acceptable to the client(s) with the realization that the counselor has, by virtue of being a part of the environment, become a meaningful part of the system in process. The counselor is not external to the husband-wife, or family system but is now a part of it. Their combined interactions tend to bring about something new in both the clients' lives and experiences as well as in the life and experience of the counselor. System theory requires, and counselor experience indicates, that the family system does not change when "more of the same" is tried or prescribed or when less of the same is tried or prescribed. Rather change occurs when a new and radical shift takes place, usually to a new level of functioning. Behavior is then carried out by one or more of the counseling team, which includes both clients and counselors (Watzlawick, et el, 1974).

As mentioned in our discussion on eclecticism, no one "school" has the one approach to counseling that works for everyone. Nor does logic require us to deal with the "schools" as contradictory, with one right school and the rest wrong. We may proceed to another level of reasoning and the problem is resolved by seeing each school's contribution to human experience as partial understandings, and rather valid at the level of the view. For example, Perls' insistence upon the prime gestalt at the feeling level for therapeutic change is only one facet of human experience and his partial theory and method work a great many times because (a) the gestalt therapist is skilled; (b) he is able to enter the client(s)' system with the feeling emphasis at an appropriate time; (c) the client is sensitive and adjusted his experiential field in order to "get with the counselor"; (d) the client carries out other behaviors which bring him to a new level of social psychological functioning; and (e) other processes.

In the same manner, the rational-emotive therapist is entering the person's or the family's system at a point that makes enough sense for the clients to make use of the intervention. However, to enter the system through "reason" is no more necessary than it is necessary to enter it through feeling or behavior in order for change to take place. The fact is that all human "mental" processes are having their "say" in the entire experience anyway, no matter what the R-E-T therapist "thinks," or convinces his client to think.

I agree that among the many "mental" processes which integrate or synthesize human experience that thinking, feeling, and behaving as concepts have served a useful but somewhat outmoded function. The schools of psychotherapy are easily classified under these concepts, as below. They ought not to stand alone, for together they reflect facets, aspects, and levels of a holistic view of the human experience.

COGNITION	EMOTION	ACTION
Adlerian	Gestalt	Behavior Modification
Ego Psychology	Humanistic Psychology	Sociodrama
Psychoanalysis	Existentialism	Psychodrama
Rational/Emotive	Neo-Reichian	Biofeedback
Reality Therapy	Feeling Therapy	Role-Playing
Transactional Analysis	Client-Centered	

Some of these schools overlap with one another somewhat and each also deals with cognition, emotion, and action, but only after having entered the human (system) experience through one of the "philosophical doors," either thought, feeling, or behavior. Whichever process given primacy by the founder of the school is then stated to be *the given* of human experience and is raised out of process into a static position of "thing" or "element" at a higher level of abstraction than the experience itself.

Psychoanalysis serves as a good example. Freud is said to have discovered the unconscious—at least he brought the power of the unconscious process or deeper feelings (emotion) of mankind to the forefront of attention in his day. He then proceeded to abandon his discovery because he was a rationalist, that is, he continued (unconsciously) feeling-wise, to be a part of his time so that he analyzed the patient (use of the cognitive process) and *he told the patient what the patient was feeling*. Control of the emotions by the patient, in psychoanalytic terms, comes about as a result of an understanding (and some "working through" never defined) in the office relationship (transference) with the analyst. The patient's feelings thus change and he is presumed to *behave* differently with other people. This essentially rational approach works with some people some of the time even with the most rational of analysts. This is not because the philosophy (rationalistic) is correct, but because of the interactions (systems operations) between the analyst and the analysand, together with the good sense and intelligence of the patient. He can then use all facets of his human experience of monitoring, analyzing and synthesizing, feeling, behaving, internal feedbacks, the feedbacks from his people and physical environments, predictions, calculations, and estimates as a part of his day-to-day life and "existence."

Perls made and many other gestaltists make the same kind of mistake psychoanalysts make when he emphasized *feeling* to the virtual exclusion of analyzing and synthesizing the various internal and external human processes. It is difficult to understand how the genius of the various founders of schools could have overlooked what appears to be so obvious—the systems operations and relationships among all these processes. I do not understand how Perls could have so easily negated or relegated to minor positions thinking and behavior in his gestalt psychology.

The behaviorists have been no different. They emphasize either behavior, or the behavior of others to the near exclusion of any "mental" functions.

This can no longer be done. It is time for a systems eclecticism which takes the individual, the family, his groups and society into account (in the broadest sense) as open systems in order to bring the most appropriate and efficient therapy to clients.

Watzlawick et al (1974) discuss the problems of persistence and change and the paradox of *plus ça change, plus c'est la même chose* (the more things change, the more they remain the same). Individuals and families have a tendency to change in the process of growth and development to a point, but some of them get caught for varying lengths of time in a pattern of behaviors within themselves and/or toward others which are experienced as painful. Some of these people seek counseling in order to change.

However, it is easier to say, "I want to change," than it is to change. We tend to persist in old and familiar behavioral patterns in spite of pain. It is often easier to bear the pain of the familiar than to bear the "pain" of change. In families the hope seems to be "you change" while "I will remain the same." From a systems point of view change usually does not come about easily in therapy. Systems tend to maintain a steady state or homeostasis.

If a spouse nags more (or less), the nagged-about behavior, say drinking or over-eating, does not diminish. Only a new order of behavior (change) *on the part of the complaining spouse*; such as stopping nagging altogether, or leaving the relationship, will likely bring about change in the partner. Two things have occurred. The paradox is that (a) the one who wants change in the other must change radically and himself go to another level or order of behavior and (b) the spouse who has not asked to change is changed by his reactions to the other's change.

These dramatic changes don't usually come about easily or immediately. However, when the first spouse to change persists in the change, the second spouse can only make adjustments to that change.

Another facet of this paradox which is important to consider is that of prescription of the symptom. Most of the traditional and classical therapies work against the symptom, either directly as in operant conditioning or indirectly as in the insight therapies (by understanding and thereby removing the cause of the symptom). The therapeutic use of paradox often dictates that the counselor should understand the symptom and then proceed to prescribe it. In this way, the control of the symptoms is now in the hands of the counselor. And when the client is told he must practice all the symptoms, paradoxically he now gives it up. The client's previous feeling of having no control over his symptom turns out not to be true; all the result of the use of paradox by prescribing the symptom.

We have shown that human experience is very much an open system of internal and external processes which are synthesized by the whole person in relation to his meaningful groups and other environmental pressures around him. Also, we have seen that many counseling methods work because of a multitude of different factors operating differently at different times within the clients' fields and within the counselor's.

Step Analyses of the Approaches of "One School" Counselors Vs. "Two or More School" Counselors, and the "System Eclectic"

One School Approach

1. Hear the problem in terms of the school—listen for what is "behind" the presenting problem.
2. Make a diagnosis in terms of the school, having decided what the "real" problem is.
3. Proceed to treatment in terms of teaching the client to think, or feel or act in ways consistent with what the school teaches is optimum functioning. In the process the client must learn a vocabulary and new ways of talking to the counselor before he can benefit from the counseling.
4. Most useful when client identifies himself as having a problem which he feels is idiosyncratic to himself, is highly intelligent, and possesses lots of spare time and money to spend on therapy.

Two or More Schools Approach (À la Thorne)

1. Hear the problem in terms of (a) what lies "behind" the problem and (b) in terms of the schools in which the counselor is trained and which throw most light on the problem.
2. Make a diagnosis in terms of one of the schools having decided what the "real" problem is and which approach best fits the "real" problem.
3. Proceed to treatment in terms of teaching the client to think or feel or act in ways consistent with the diagnosis and the school of thought which supports the diagnosis. Behavior change is the primary goal. The client learns the necessary vocabulary and concepts in order to communicate most effectively with the counselor and in order to most effectively change his behavior.
4. Most useful when the counselor is flexible and tends to search for understanding (explanation) of client's problem within the counselor's range of eclectic background of schools. (More likely to be helpful to client than "one school" approach.)

System Eclectic Approach

1. Hear the problem in terms of how the client describes and perceives his problem. It is absolutely necessary to understand the *client's* language and other messages. The system eclectic counselor usually chooses to use the *client's* language in order to develop a common ground of understanding. (This gives a new definition to what is commonly called rapport.) The counselor also models flexibility and does not require the client to change even his language.
2. The counselor attempts to understand how (not why) the client's problem is supported and maintained by his own synthesizing, cognating, emoting, and behaving processes. The client is simultaneously seen as an open system and the above-mentioned processes are seen as bases for the client's problems. They are

supported and maintained by external systems of interpersonal relationships without which the client's problem would likely subside in intensity to the point where it might be manageable and tolerable. Then the patient would not likely need outside counseling aid.

3. The counselor's treatment is intervention in the individual, couple, or family open system at whatever point makes sense to counselor and client, usually around one of the presenting problems (pain) in the here and now. In the counseling hour it is likely that a number of different methods, cognitive, emotive, and behavioral, will be used with some emphasis upon client(s)' finding solutions to their problems. If the client adds new concepts and words to his vocabulary it is incidental to the processes which occur in system and the various methods terms. These are kept at a minimum and it is hoped that explanations are given in terms which are already a part of the client's vocabulary.

System eclecticism suggests some hypotheses for research.

HYPOTHESES

1) That eclectic counselors, à la Thorne, are more effective than counselors of "one school." This will be true because the eclectic counselor and his clients will more likely match up their common experiences and there will be more flexibility of communication and consequently understanding between them than with one-school counselors. In the latter instance the client must adjust to the counselor's system in order for there to be a match-up; that is, the client is forced to enter the counselor's system rather than the other way around. When successful, the client is more flexible than the counselor!

2) That systems eclectic counselors will be more effective than either "one school" counselors or eclectic counselors, à la Thorne. This will be true for at least two reasons: (a) systems eclectic counselors more readily understand the person(s) involved in the pain which brought them in for counseling and treat them as a part of the interpersonal process systems they are involved in, and (b) the clients do not have to adjust to pre-set explanations offered by the counselor's school or schools of thought.

The systems eclectic counselor uses the language and orientation of the client and thereby is more readily accepted into the client's system. The client does not have to hold his pain until he first learns the new language of the counselor. The client also does not have to hold his pain until the counselor makes an exhaustive study of his symptoms and then arrives at a specific diagnosis of his "psychological state" and then chooses a method or school which, hopefully, will "cure" the client.

3) That the appropriate comparisons of outcome studies are between "schools" and systems-eclectic counselors rather than between such modes of therapy as, for example, gestalt vs. R.E.T. or individual vs. group counseling.

These are only a few of the hypotheses to be developed from this paper. Others can and will be generated as time and opportunity permit.

REFERENCES

Ashby, R. W. *An introduction to cybernetics*. London: Chapman and Hall, 1956.

Bertalanffy, L., von. *General system theory*. New York: G. Braziller, 1968.

Broderick, C. *A decade of family research*. Minneapolis: NCFR, 1969.

Haley, J. *Strategies of psychotherapy*. New York: Grune-Stratton, 1963.

Hayakawa, S. I. *Language in thought and action*. New York: Harcourt, Brace and Co., 1964.

Konorski, J. *Integrative activity of the brain*. Chicago: University of Chicago Press, 1967.

Lazarus, A. A. Multimodal behavior therapy: treating the BASIC ID. *Journal of nervous and mental disease*. 1973, *156*, 404–411.

Lazarus, A. A. Multimodal therapy: BASIC ID, *Psychology today*. 1974, 7, 59–63.

Meichenbaum, D. Theoretical and treatment implications of developmental research on verbal control of behavior. In press.

Sommerhoff, G. *Logic of the living brain*. New York: John Wiley & Sons, 1974.

Thorne, F. C. & Nathan, P. E. Systems Analysis methods for integrative diagnosis. *Journal of Clinical Psychology*, *26*:3–17.

Thorne, F. Eclectic psychotherapy, in Corsini, R. J. *Current psychotherapies*. Itasca, Ill. F. E. Peacock Publishing, Inc., 1975.

Watzlawick, P. et al. *Pragmatics of human communication*. New York: W. W. Norton and Co., 1967.

Watzlawick, P. et al. *Change: Principles of problem formation and problem resolution*. New York: W. W. Norton and Co., 1974.

CHAPTER 15

Toward a Theory of Marriage Counseling: A Humanistic Approach

Gerhard Neubeck

If marriage itself can be considered as the last stronghold of amateurism, marriage counseling is usually regarded as an activity that is eclectic, but in the unfavorable sense. Paul E. Meehl in his introduction to *Therapeutic Psychology* (Brammer and Shostrom, 1960) referred to this kind of eclecticism in respect to psychotherapy saying, "Most of us, if we hear a psychotherapist described as being eclectic, tend immediately to think of someone who has not been trained to do anything particularly well, and whose cognitive activity with respect to the technology he practices is either muddled or nonexistent." Gerald Manus, (1966) in his provocative paper, "Marriage Counseling: A Technique in Search of a Theory," makes this point in specific reference to marriage counseling when he claims that there is no succinct and consistent theory underlying this vast and, at least in the United States, widely demanded service. Gerald Leslie, (1964) suggests that a synthesis of concepts must be found to develop a theory of marriage counseling. My "thinking out loud" here is a stab in that direction. Another way of saying it is that a great many marriage counselors probably counsel "by the seat of their pants" and it is time to think more precisely about why they are doing what they are doing. To try to "put it all together," going with the popular slogan, to assemble all the strains which have led to the establishment of the marriage counseling phenomenon becomes not merely an intellectual exercise but a vital action to assure practitioners about the soundness of their practice and consumers that they are up against better than chance.

To produce the kind of synthesis Leslie is writing about requires two main strains as the obvious components. One is the developing rationale about marriage not only as a social institution but also as a system of personal relationships. The other is the conceptual framework on which therapeutic psychology, to use Brammer and Shostrom's term, is based.

Reprinted with permission of the author and the publisher from *The Family Coordinator*, January, 1973.

A COUNSELOR AT WORK

Shall we look at a typical marriage counselor, regardless of disciplinary affiliation? (From this point forward in mentioning marriage counselors I am going to use both masculine and feminine pronouns.) He or she is engaged in an initial appointment with Mrs. M. who is in her middle thirties. Upon the invitation of the counselor Mrs. M. reveals that her husband frequently comes home very late from the office—he is a businessman, eats his dinner alone since the family ate earlier, and then retreats to his den where he listens to his hi-fi. Later on she may join him in the den but there rarely is meaningful conversation. (Her term) More or less every weekend they have sexual intercourse in what she describes as a perfunctory fashion. This whole state of affairs is extremely unsatisfactory to her and she has developed migraine headaches. When she told her physician a bit about the marriage he had recommended marriage counseling. Our marriage counselor perhaps, having been in practice for some ten years, had heard this kind of report before. Let us tune in on his or her mental processes now and then examine how these processes were generated.

Our counselor has been trained in a number of ways which most likely circumscribe the counseling situation. We are observing a trained counselor here rather than a self-styled one of course. First of all he or she is located in an office, a private one or one connected with what I will broadly call a mental health facility. The door to the office is closed to safeguard privacy. There is usually a desk in this room, rarely a couch, and Mrs. M. who is most times called a client with the exception of medical settings where she is known as a patient will sit either across or by the side of the desk. The atmosphere can be seen as rather informal. In most cases money is exchanged for this interview which usually lasts a few minutes short of an hour. The counselor probably has a note pad available and makes an occasional entry. While this is a quite typical counseling situation, there are, of course, many variations and even deviations from this type of an encounter. I am going into these details because I want to point out that the manner in which these interviews are conducted is not an accidental one but has definite roots.

The marriage counselor had suggested to Mrs. M. earlier that she begin by relating what had brought her there. Now he or she listens while Mrs. M. tells of her concerns. Occasionally the counselor will ask a question, reflect a thought of Mrs. M.'s, and encourage her to bring out as much as is possible for her to specify. As she unfolds her story the counselor is busy formulating a number of hunches about her, her husband, the relationship between the two, and the general family situation and, in addition, is likely to think about Mrs. M.'s feelings during the time she is making these revelations. The counselor also possibly is cognizant of how she or he feels toward this new client, but these impressions usually are not shared with the client.

This process will be repeated when Mr. M. is present for his interview with the marriage counselor and again when the pair—as is the preference of most marriage counselors today—are both seen together. When the partners are seen together the counselor who has had the advantage of individual sessions will observe the interaction between Mrs. and Mr. M. more keenly to see if any of the hypotheses developed earlier are substantiated or at least somewhat supported by the couple's behavior. (When a couple have been seen together for the very first interview the counselor obviously has had much less evidence about them individually to produce a useful set of hunches.) Some counselors will have seen the results of psychological tests by the time the joint interview occurs and their deliberations about the marital interaction may have been shored up by these more objective data.

In other words, as we review this process, our marriage counselor behaves in the tradition of counselors, psychotherapists, helping-profes-sion-workers—name them that you will—whose general aim is to alleviate the stresses and misfortunes of their clients, but in this particular case focusing on marital malfunctioning. The marriage counselor is also aware that being married constitutes a persistent problem-solving situation which demands a variety of skills regardless of the background and personality of either husband or wife, and that marriage is not located in a vacuum but in the latter part of twentieth century American society.

Based on what is present from her or his counseling training, theoretical orientation, and experience—that is, how and what to say, what not to say, what physical distance to keep or not to keep, how to make use of all the verbal and nonverbal behaviors available for this interaction and the counselor's emerging ideas of how and why this woman and this man have ended up with their "problem," the counseling will then proceed.

Our counselor is a counselor who is immersed now in this marital matter if not morass; that is his or her metier now, that is the river to swim in, the air to breathe, and, if you please, the mess to mix in. But how has the counselor become a counselor and what options have been available to him or her in order to explain, make sense, understand why marital pairs behave the way they do? These are the major questions which I wish to pursue now, firmly believing that these two strains must be welded together and cannot be understood, the one without the other. Yet they need to be taken up here by themselves before they can be superimposed upon each others.

COUNSELING: SOME BACKGROUND

Counseling is essentially a process of planned intervention into the life of other persons. This intervention is benign and solicited by the person or persons to be counseled. In contrast to other interventional processes such as punishment and, often, teaching and medicating, the counseling condition can only be established as a result of a contractual agreement between those to be counseled and the counselor. Following an individual's recognition, however dim, on either an external, behavioral or an internal, emotional level that he or she wishes to make changes and is not capable of executing these changes alone, this person turns to someone who has a designation somewhere along a specific professional category, a counselor.

For most of its existence this interventional process has been closely allied to what has been called the mental health movement, even though in its beginning it can be seen as coming from the quite universal human tradition of charity. Originally charity may have been a human emotion exercised on a private basis, but through the ages and across many societies it eventually became institutionalized. On an economic level social welfare programs or outright socialism were later substituted to alleviate the inadequacies which originally had called for the expression of charity. But on a non-economic level, cutting across class or other distinguishing characteristics, difficulties of coping with social, that is, human relationship, problems in both agrarian and industrial societies arose and multiplied.

Social work as a profession in the United States, originally established to deal more with economic inadequacies, was caught up in the maelstrom of psychoanalytic concepts of intervention, linking coping problems with physiological/psychological states or intimating that it was not a coping situation but one in which the individual was failing to make necessary adjustments to the outside world and in the process evoking stress. Out of these considerations a number of interventional techniques, usually called treatment or therapy developed and this, in turn, gave rise to the mental health concept. Psychologists also joined this trend and, in fact, brought it to its ultimate flowering, particularly as a result of federal supports shortly after World War II when the Veterans Administration established clinical services which later were emulated in public and private agencies throughout the country. Counseling has continued to flourish.

While psychoanalytical explanations of human behavior originally were the mode, social and behavioral scientists—often those who themselves were practitioners of this interventional process called therapy or counseling—soon developed new ideas about how human beings came to act the way they did and how to intervene into these behaviors and help persons alter or modify them. At first there came variations on classic Freudian concepts, then outright rejection of them, and finally entirely new explanations of what made people function and how they could be aided in changing feelings as well as behaviors. Also a great deal of attention began to be given to look upon the counselor not only as an objective "other" but also as a person who had become an agent for the client, one who would invest his or her total self in behalf of the individual who had come for help. Increasingly, attention was also paid to the counselor as a person whose feelings and ideas must be an important factor in the interventional activity.

This is not the place to list, much less discuss, the various therapeutic or counseling approaches which have appeared on the scene. Useful compilations are available, among them Harper (1959) and Brammer and Shostrom (1960). Whatever version of the workings of human personality and concomitant interventional systems we are confronted with, no single explanation that has stood up to rigorous scientific testing has emerged. As yet it has not been possible to explain once and for all what human behavior is like or what it takes to change it. In fact, there is still considerable doubt whether a universal answer to understanding personality is ever going to be found and, whether the interventional processes of counseling or therapy are effective at all as compared to the individual's effort in his or her own behalf. Changes have, in fact, been considered as coming spontaneously, no active interference having been practiced. Yet counselors are keeping busy in a wide variety of settings (Brammer and Shostrom, 1960, 5).

THE GROUP

Up to this point it should be noted my reference to the counseling situation and the explanations surrounding it generally has assumed this to be a phenomenon of a therapist or counselor interacting with one individual, the client or patient. (The latter term an obvious throwback to the biological or sickness allusion.) This kind of intervention concentrates on how the intervener is to be instrumental in assisting the individual to alter feelings and behaviors. These feelings and behaviors, to be sure, concern those of others—women, men, children—the gamut of social and personal others. The relationships to those others were occasionally informal but more often intimate or institutionalized as in occupational settings, but most of all in the central societal units of marriage and family. (That the interventional activity can also take place in groups—group counseling or group therapy—does not alter these aims and purposes.)

It was in the settings of marriage and family that it dawned on the conceptualizers and practitioners alike that the individual, while never losing his or her individuality, was, however, not a single independent unit but that feelings and behaviors most of the time were connected to if not governed by others who had entered into or been established with the individual in relationships which made them part of a social system. As marital partners they had entered into this bond voluntarily; as children they had had no choice. Marital and family life could now be seen as involving its members in reciprocal behaviors, and conflict situations that arise in these systems—inevitably it seems—call for resolution or at least alleviation; that is why husbands and wives are turning to a marriage counselor for help.

A plethora of explanations for the phenomenon of marital interaction and conflict are available today and are based on more or less sophisticated theories, some of which are tested and replicated but most of which have not been validly—that is, scientifically—established. For some time it had been taken for granted, however, that marriage was a paradisical state and that one who could not fit into it comfortably must be deficient in some way or deviant. Spouses were then "treated" by practitioners to make themselves over to fit better into or adjust to this state. What this view of marriage failed to take into account was that this paradisical state was, after all, not a pure state but was made up of the behaviors of its two participants. Even if it were possible for a spouse to alter her or his responses, the "state" might not be affected at all unless the other spouse would react in an equally effective fashion. This is not to say that an individual spouse might ot be deficient in his or her emotional or behavioral repertoire but that these deficiencies do not exist in a no-mans-land (no-womans-land?); they occur in the day-by-day marital relationship.

The list of theories attempting to delineate marital interaction is long but this is not the place to either enumerate them or critically comment on them. The most useful summary can be found in Olson (1970). While some marriage counselors undoubtedly interpret the husband-wife interaction which they are exposed to strictly according to one or another of these theories, it is likely that they do modify certain aspects of the concepts if the concepts do not happen to explain a specific emotion or action. Many counselors have arrived at an amalgamation of the various conceptual frameworks and practice an eclecticism that is based on sophistication rather than ignorance.

Having a counselor who is trained in, oriented toward, and experienced in a certain counseling technique as well as armed with explanations about the marital system and its stresses, do we know now all about what goes on in the process of counseling a marital pair? Do we know enough when we report that a marriage counselor wedded to a transactional approach and skillful in directional techniques of counseling is different from one who believes in neurotic interaction and is a Gestalt therapist? I think not!

We have failed to observe that in establishing a situation in which there is more than one person present—in the case of client and counselor a dyad, and the case of the two spouses a triad—an entirely new phenomenon has come upon the scene, a group. The new group that comes into existence has a life of its own as much as it is anchored in the background described earlier. Counseling sessions with both wife and husband together have become a practice ever more popular with marriage counselors and the three-person group can now be seen as the major thrust in the interventional enpterprise. In this respect it must be mentioned that the marriage counselor continues to act as the agent for both spouses, at least as long as they want him to, as long as they wish to preserve their own marital contract.

THE TRIAD

This then is the welding of all that has been discussed so far. What happens in this triad consisting of the two spouses and the counselor? Here is our counselor behaving as a counselor in the aforementioned tradition and interacting with a marital pair which is presenting and acting out as well their interpersonal stresses and conflicts. What is it that takes place in this confrontation? The moment of importance has come: if we can find a rationale for this interaction we may have made some progress toward an overall explanation.

The triad situation alters the traditional one-to-one session in obvious fashion. One, the counselor is no longer dependent on impressions or interpretations of marital interaction by one or both of the spouses or reports about behaviors and perceptions of either husband or wife with regard to these behaviors; instead, the counselor now can bring both his cognitive and affective self to bear on either or both of the pair. In addition, the counselor also has become a participant-observer and active member in a new interaction, now unavoidably and constantly adding her or his behavior to that of the couple. As an observer he is cognizant of the marital interaction, but this recognition goes side-by-side with an awareness of behaviors and feelings between either of the spouses and himself or herself. In the actual exchange of words and gestures between the counselor and one of the pair, it always had to be taken into account that the other member of the pair is present and is perceiving these behaviors and feelings in his or her own subjective way. Asked to intervene, the counselor becomes an intruder, establishes a co-existence for a time with the marital pair, and while not contractually married to either of the spouses, becomes in a number of ways an intimate and certainly an instrumental person in their life.

Out of this situation emerges an intricate process which I believe lies at the heart of marriage counseling: here are the marital partners acting out their stresses and conflicts and the counselor gets into that act bringing her or his behavior into their system, and in the wake of this interference then originates a new system. This causes now an assymetry which, in turn, results in coalitions that produce unequal power. These dynamics are affected by other factors such as age, gender, verbal facility, affectual traits, cognitive ability, erotic if not sexual attraction and, indeed, projections which hang impressions about other individuals on the triadal members. But one thing remains steady: the focus of all this activity is on the two clients and how they can produce changes in feeling and/or behavior in order to alleviate their marital stress. Perceptions and interpretations by all three group members are open to question according to previously agreed upon ground rules. Verifications or misunderstandings are thus picked up, aired, and then incorporated into the cognitive or affective repertoire. (Or, of course, they may not be thus handled.) Hopefully, and usually, counseling is then regarded as successful.

Does it matter to us if the counselor is a persuader or reflector, shaper or cajoler, listener or manipulator, toucher or distancer; the counselor may act in one or in a combination of those approaches; it is his or her very participation in the group that is the instrument of change. The counselor may teach or exhort, be a model of expressing certain behavioral modes, or be passive, whisper or shout, weep or laugh. (This small group interaction has been excellently summarized by Bales, 1950.) It is how his or her responses are incorporated into the network of pain responses, what the partners as individuals and in their interaction do with these counselor behaviors, that makes the difference for learning.

The counselor throughout these interchanges brings to bear upon the situation—we must not lose sight of that—his or her informed understanding of marital dynamics. That is the ticket for being a marriage counselor in the first place, and clients expect to have that kind of expertise available to them. (Interestingly enough, this expectation does not seem to include a confidence that marriage counselors must be able to lead a satisfactory marital existence for themselves; some counselors are not particularly successful in their own marital life, but this seems to have had little affect upon their popularity.) What is asked of the practitioner is that he or she possess an understanding of marital dynamics and put them somehow across to the marital partner counselees.

The triad operates primarily in the offices of counselors, although occasionally the three-person interchange has been transferred to the natural habitat of the spouses, usually their home. The interactional focus is retained even when the so-called professional setting is not. The focus may be slightly diluted at times by some social byplay, eating or listening to music for instance, but these activities seldom deter from the prime thrust, that of intervention. During the course of counseling often the counselor even though not present in person, "shadows" the marital interaction, as if indeed he or she were present.

People who have come together in this purposeful way by their very presence are compelled to establish new relationship patterns through learning how to negotiate, mostly via words, of course. (To some degree this explains why counseling has been more popular among those groups in society which are verbally inclined.) As the three group members have come together they have brought to this new interchange their own behavioral repertoire which in the case of the marriage counselor, as I have pointed out, is the sum of her or his training, experience, cognitive and effective know-how, and in the case of the clients their accumulated set of understandings—often misunderstandings—and ingrained response sets. Out of this mix now emerges a pooling of behaviors and emotions, perhaps a contrasting or pitting them against each other, but in some way or another a utilization of them to produce changes.

QUESTION

This paper has been entitled, "Toward a Theory of Marriage Counseling." Have I pointed the way in a more precise fashion than it has been done before to make it possible to develop a theory *sui generis*? I hope that I have and that someone else now can put these markers together to go all the way.

REFERENCES

Bales, R.F. A set of categories for the analysis of small group interaction. *American Sociological Review*, 1950, *15*, 257–263.

Brammer, L. M. and E. L. Shostrom. *Therapeutic Psychology*. Englewood Cliffs, New Jersey: Prentice-Hall, 1960.

Grey, A. L. (Ed.) *Man, Woman, and Marriage: Small Group Process in the Family*. New York: Atherton Press, 1970.

Harper, R. A. *Psychoanalysis and Psychotherapy*. Englewood Cliffs, New Jersey: Prentice-Hall, 1959.

Leslie, G. R. The field of marriage counseling. In Harold T. Christensen (Ed.), *Handbook of Marriage and the Family*. Chicago: Rand McNally, 1964.

Manus, G. I. Marriage counseling: A technique in search of a theory. *Journal of Marriage and the Family*. 1966, *28*, 449–453.

Olson, D. H. Marital and family therapy: Integrative review and critique. *Journal of Marriage and the Family*. 1970, *32*, 501–538.

Conjoint Marriage Counseling

> *"Before I built a wall, I'd ask to know*
> *What I was walling in or walling out*
> *And to whom I was likely to give offense.*
> *Something there is that doesn't love a wall*
> *That wants it down."*
>
> ROBERT FROST, "MENDING WALL"

During its early years, marriage counseling placed considerable emphasis on seeing individual spouses separately, although there has long been a practice of seeing both spouses together at times. Some theoreticians would claim that marriage counselors have generally failed to develop the potential inherent in joint interviewing, while family therapists have made increasing use of it.

Members of the various helping professions are developing a body of theory and approaches which might be called "conjoint marriage counseling." However it is labeled, conjoint marriage counseling is seen differently by different practitioners. In this section, four representatives of four different professions (a sociologist, a psychiatrist, a social worker, and a psychologist) discuss different aspects of this recent trend in marriage and family counseling.

Gerald R. Leslie, a sociologist, describes conjoint therapy in marriage counseling in Chapter 16. Leslie states that conjoint therapy aids in the identification and working through of distortions, helps hold transference and countertransference in check, quickly brings marital conflicts into the open and into counseling sessions, and emphasizes current relationship problems. Leslie concludes, however, that conjoint therapy is not a panacea and is probably inappropriate with some clients and problems.

In Chapter 17, psychiatrist Andrew S. Watson states the premises about the marriage relationship, then the strategic and practical goals of a conjoint treatment of marriage partners are described. The dynamics of transference-countertransference are conceptualized and techniques of interpretation are set forth. Despite Watson's statement that it is not yet possible to specify contraindications for conjoint counseling, each professional marriage and family counselor will want to think through the implications of this fast-growing approach very carefully.

In Chapters 18 and 19, Virginia Satir, a social worker and author of the book *Conjoint Family Therapy* (1967), discusses the concepts of therapy and the role and technique of the therapist in conjoint marital therapy. Satir bases her approach on communication theory as previously developed by such men as Ruesch, Bateson, and Jackson.

In the final chapter of this section, Ben N. Ard, Jr., presents a critique of communication theory in marriage and family counseling. Several basic questions are raised, including a critical examination of some of the basic assumptions of communication theory. Will all marriages improve if marriage counselors help their clients "communicate" better (or more)? In Ard's view, improving communication alone may not necessarily maintain a marriage, or even improve it. Unquestioned values, exceptions, premises, and assumptions need to be critically examined for their consequences, he suggests, and fatalistic defeating ways of interacting. *What* is communicated may be, on occasion, more important than *how* it is communicated.

CHAPTER 16

Conjoint Therapy in Marriage Counseling

Gerald R. Leslie

The term "conjoint therapy" has been popularized more by family therapists than by marriage counselors. After a long period of failure to appreciate fully the potential inherent in joint interview techniques, it appears that conjoint therapy may become a major approach to marriage counseling in the relatively near future.

It is ironic that marriage counseling and family therapy should have developed along such separate but parallel lines. Both are twenty years old, plus or minus a few years. Both developed rather quietly as far as the outside world was concerned. And both had terrific impact upon the small group of "insiders" who called themselves, respectively, family therapists and marriage counselors. Some members of both groups, it might be added, have seen themselves as doing the ultimate in pioneering work in counseling and psychotherapy. If their claim is granted, the further plaudit may be added that modesty has not always been one of their primary virtues.

THE DEVELOPMENT OF FAMILY THERAPY

If the author sees it adequately, family therapy developed largely within psychiatry. Some child psychiatrists, particularly, were moving in the direction of family therapy during the 1940's (Burlingham, 1951). Therapy with children often revealed that the child's difficulties reflected emotional problems in the mother, or, more radically, conflict between the parents. The analytic taboo against the therapist's having contact with other members of the patient's family was not as strong in child psychiatry, and therapy with the child often led to therapy with the mother. While some psychiatrists religiously referred other family members to different therapists, some began to experiment with, and to see virtue in, having the same therapist work concurrently on different aspects of a family's problems. Eventually, this led some therapists to seeing whole families in joint-interview situations (Shellow, 1963).

Reprinted with permission of the author and the publisher from *Journal of Marriage and the Family*, 1964, *26*, 65–71.

Other psychiatrists working specifically with schizophrenic children were moving in the same direction (Bowen, 1960). They began to work with schizophrenic families. Scattered groups over the country developed their own approaches to family therapy, often unaware that others were proceeding along similar lines. First there were guarded conversations at professional meetings, then formal papers on family therapy, and subsequently the family therapy "movement" appeared full-blown and in print.

Some of the developments in psychiatry toward family therapy do not fall neatly into the two patterns described so far. The best known work outside these two groups probably is that of Nathan Ackerman (1958). Ackerman made the jump from individual to family therapy earlier and more aggressively than most. Other psychiatrists working in a variety of settings groped through stages such as the concurrent analysis of married couples and the stereoscopic technique (Martin, 1953) toward analysis of the family neurosis (Grotjahn, 1960).

As radical as these developments appeared to many psychiatrists, a sociologist-observer sees in them at least two other things. One is that, in spite of the drastic shift in definition of the diagnostic and treatment unit, there remains a strong emphasis upon a biologically based concept of illness, and analysis of the interaction between family members tends to be structured in terms of "cure" of the ill members (Parsons & Fox, 1952). Psychiatrists do operate as physicians, with the result that both organic problems and psychopathology are more conspicuous among their patients than among the clients of many nonmedical therapists.

The second striking thing is the conspicuousness of what sociologists and anthropologists call simultaneous invention (Ogburn, 1926). Pioneers in therapy methods, as evidenced by the fact that there were so many of them working relatively independently of one another, appear very much to have been products of their time.

THE DEVELOPMENT OF MARRIAGE COUNSELING

Not only were there convergences toward family therapy within psychiatry, but the parallel movement called marriage counseling was developing at the same time. In some respects, marriage counseling was ahead of its psychiatric counterpart, but in other respects, it gradually fell behind.

During its early years marriage counseling probably was unique in the degree of its focus upon relationships. It came into existence to treat relationship problems rather than personal problems (Leslie, 1965). Diagnosis and treatment planning involved two persons *and* a relationship. For a while, there was an attempt to adapt the old bio-medical model to marital conflict, and people wrote and spoke of "sick" marriages. This model was so inappropriate, however, that it soon was discarded for a more broadly applicable one.

Marriage counselors came to view marital interaction as constituting a social system (Parsons, 1951). In this framework, the person is no longer the basic unit of analysis, and less priority is assigned to personality factors. Both personality and relationships are conceived as entities, each being composed of simpler elements or systems and each having dynamics of its own, such that neither is completely reducible to the other. These systems are interpenetrating, of course. Social systems are composed of roles; and conversely, roles, as configurations of behavior, are components of personality.

As a system the marital relationship is viewed as having unique properties resulting from the impingement of two personalities upon one another in a particular social context. The relationship possesses dynamic force in its own right and influences the way in which personality is manifested. A man who has neurotic difficulties, for example, may or may not give malignant expression to those difficulties depending upon the kind of woman he marries and the resulting relationship between them. Moreover, to "cure" his neurosis may upset the relationship between the partners to the point where either or both manifest symptoms more disabling than the original ones. Marital diagnosis involves making integrated appraisals of both partners and the relationship so that treatment of the partners may be coordinated and gains in one area of personal or marital functioning used to reinforce gains in other areas of living.

From the beginning marriage counselors typically worked concurrently with both partners to a relationship. The early marriage-counseling literature is replete with assertions of the advantages inherent in such a procedure. Though social workers had long assigned one worker to entire families, the emerging family therapists generally had not reached this point.

Curiously, however, marriage counselors failed to see the full potential in having the same counselor work with different members of the family. This failure is reflected in the traditional marriage-counseling approach to the use of joint interviews. The literature stresses the usefulness of initial joint interviews for diagnostic purposes and then generally urges their discontinuance until counseling is nearing its terminal stages (Skidmore & Garrett, 1955). The impression is created that more systematic use of joint interviews is apt to be unproductive and to bog down in quarreling and recrimination.

Thus, even while marriage counselors were trumpeting the uniqueness and advantages of their approach, they lagged in developing it. The emerging family therapists, to whom the idea of conjoint therapy originally was anathema, were more creative. For approximately the past ten years, marriage counselors have been gradually awakening to the fact that someone has stolen their thunder. Gradually, they are now exploring the marriage counseling use of conjoint therapy. The thesis of this paper is that the implications of conjoint therapy for marriage counseling are considerable and that most of the limitations on such use are yet unknown.

CONJOINT THERAPY IN MARRIAGE COUNSELING

The term conjoint therapy is not precise. Its essence is the systematic use of joint interviews in which the counselor simultaneously interviews two or more persons, usually the marital partners. In purest form conjoint therapy involves *all* interviews being conducted as joint interviews, with neither partner being seen in individual sessions. The author and his colleagues have been doing some experimentation with this pure form of conjoint therapy and are finding it feasible in a small proportion of cases. Occasional couples whose problems are acute rather than chronic, who focus consistently on a particular problem area, and who are both motivated to strengthen their relationship by working out their problems appear to be good risks for pure conjoint therapy.

In this experiment, most of the counselors most of the time prefer to do some individual interviewing of the partners early in counseling. At these individual sessions, excessive hostility to the other partner is drained off through catharsis, "privileged" communication permits the revelation of attitudes and behavior that would not be revealed with the partner present, and thorough diagnostic study of each of the two partners is done. When the counselor believes that the couple can work productively in joint sessions, conjoint therapy becomes the sole or major technique for most of the counseling process. The joint interviews become the major vehicle for insight development, and further individual interviews are used only when anxiety in one of the partners mounts to the point of interfering with progress in the joint interviews.

The experimenters have not yet determined whether the alleged advantages in this combination of joint and individual sessions are really advantages to the clients. Few would question the legitimacy of the cathartic and personality-assessment functions of the individual interviews, but there is some doubt about the need of counselors to "know the whole story" through the revelation of material that is not to be shared with the partner. That counselors feel more comfortable when they know more about the clients may partly reflect the counselor's discomfort in working with the unfamiliar new technique of conjoint therapy. A less charitable interpretation would stress the elements of psychological voyeurism inherent in marriage counseling (Grotjahn, 1960) and indicate that the counselor's need to know is not necessarily consistent with his clients' welfare. More experience with conjoint therapy should illuminate this question, but in the meantime experience indicates that some individual interviews mixed with more frequent joint interviews may be the most widely applicable form of conjoint therapy.

Finally, conjoint therapy shades off into traditional marriage-counseling technique when joint interviews become occasionally interspersed among individual interviews. For purposes of this paper, the term conjoint therapy will be used to refer to the first two patterns only.

Effects upon the Counseling Process

Much has been written about the psychotherapeutic process. The intention of this paper is not, however, to survey or analyze that literature. Suffice it to say that, through accretion and reinforcement, a body of principles has become widely accepted without those principles having been subjected to controlled empirical test. The following discussion of effects of conjoint therapy upon marriage counseling process is of the same order. To persons with comparable backgrounds of training and experience, it should make sense or at least provide thought for discussion. To determined unbelievers, none of that which follows can be adequately proven.

The identification of distortions. In marriage counseling, as in psychotherapy generally, clients present themselves to the counselor in ways that involve considerable distortion. The identification and working through of these distortions is an involved problem even when the clients are essentially healthy, and it may be prolonged where there is much pathology.

Many clients distort consciously and perhaps willfully. Virtually all clients—indeed, all people—have done many things of which they are not proud and which they do not wish to reveal to others. Desiring and needing acceptance from the counselor, they conceal information that might threaten that acceptance. Even when clients are able to avoid the temptation of deliberate concealment, they are prone to present themselves in one-sided, biased fashion. No matter how hard they try to be objective, they are too immersed in their conflicts to see themselves in adequate perspective. It is common in marriage counseling to hear the same relationship described by husband and wife in such different terms that the counselor must force himself to realize that the clients are talking about one another. And finally, of course, there are distortions that derive from repression. These may be mere fragments, or they may be systematic and comprehensive. Obviously, they present the greatest difficulty.

Individual psychotherapy may proceed for months without the therapist being able to break through the barriers presented by these distortions. It is the author's experience that in conjoint therapy such distortions tend to be fewer and less extreme and that clients cling to them less tenaciously. When one counselor is seeing both partners, and when, at least part of the time, they are being seen in joint sessions, there is less possibility of, and less need for, concealment. Each partner is forced to hear descriptions and interpretations of his behavior that differ from his own. Furthermore, the rapport that develops between each client and the counselor is not based upon such a partial, favorable revelation of self. The clients confirm directly that the counselor can accept them in spite of the things that they wish to conceal.

Just as surely, the unwitting distortions of each partner are quickly revealed. Whether these are merely problems of perspective or whether they result from repression, neither partner can escape at least the fact that distortion is occurring. To the likely criticism that such rapid confrontation is apt to result in even more serious symptoms, the author can only reply that he has not usually found it so. Ackerman's (1958) observation that so-called family secrets, allegedly very dangerous, are neither very secret nor especially dangerous is pertinent here.

The situation in traditional marriage counseling practice when the counselor must lengthily unravel and work through distortions with each partner before bringing them together is largely cut short. What might otherwise take months is frequently accomplished in a very few sessions.

Moreover, the counselor in conjoint therapy is not placed in the position of having constantly to restructure his relationship with each of the partners.

The handling of transference and countertransference. The author uses the terms transference and countertransference very broadly. The transference neurosis of classical psychoanalysis is included but extended to embrace all distortions of the counselor-client relationship. As with distortions in the clients' productions discussed above, transference distortions may occur at different levels, ranging along a continuum, perhaps, from the mildest sort of personalizing of the relationship to the full-blown transference neurosis.

Some degree and some form of transference is exceedingly common in marriage counseling. On the other hand, permitting the development of an integrated transference neurosis is not necessary for the satisfactory resolution of much marital conflict, and the working through of such a relationship unnecessarily lengthens the counseling process. Marital conflict does not usually derive directly from unresolved pre-oedipal situations, and the conscious problem-solving abilities of most marriage-counseling clients are considerable.

Even in conventional marriage-counseling practice, incipient transference reactions tend to be held in check because the participation of the other spouse discourages the development of a "private world" between counselor and client. In conjoint therapy the physical presence of the other partner is an even more effective deterrent. Each spouse's tendencies to maneuver the counselor into private roles run head up against the counselor's relationship with the other partner. Thus too much regression is discouraged, and the partners are encouraged to work on their problem at more current relationship levels. Where the counselor still becomes a parent surrogate, he is more likely to become a joint parent and to reinforce the relationship between the partners.

With some marriage-counseling clients, transference becomes pronounced even in conjoint therapy. The interplay between counselor and two clients occasionally gets exceedingly complicated. Traditionally-oriented therapists to the contrary notwithstanding, this writer finds that most counselors handle these multiple transference situations about as well as they handle other transference problems. The added burden of having to work through distortions with both partners is at least partly offset by the lower probability of the counselor becoming unwittingly caught up in either pattern of distortion. Not only do many common forms of transference become very obvious to the counselor doing conjoint therapy, but many common forms of countertransference are quickly identified as well.

The drawing-out of conflict. A third effect of the systematic use of conjoint therapy in marriage counseling is to bring the marital conflict into the open and into the counseling sessions. Herein lies both a major advantage of conjoint therapy and a major source of resistance to its use by some counselors.

Marriage counselors long have recognized that when hostile spouses are seen jointly, they are apt to begin to fight. Conventional practice is based upon the assumptions that if the clients are permitted to fight, their relationship will deteriorate and the counselor will lose control of the counseling sessions, and that, as he loses control, he loses his ability to aid the clients. Two of these assumptions may be challenged, and the third may be shown to have little to do with conjoint therapy *per se*.

It is true that many couples in joint session will fight. It does not follow, however, that the fighting need produce deterioration of the marital relationship. For the question is not whether the couple will fight, but only whether they will fight in the presence of the counselor. They have been fighting at home and will continue to do so. Moreover, while the deteriorating effect of the conflict upon their relationship is what brings them into counseling, the ability of most couples to tolerate prolonged, severe conflict should not be overlooked. They are both afraid of their conflict, and they are accustomed to living with it. When a counselor excludes that conflict from the counseling sessions, he may inadvertently heighten the clients' fears. On the other hand, when the counselor can accept the conflict without alarm, the effects of the conflict upon the partners tend to become less malignant.

There is no good reason why conflict in the counseling sessions should cause the counselor to lose control. The counselor permits the expression of other feelings without losing control because he does not become embroiled in those feelings. But when clients begin to fight, they may trigger both anxiety and hostility in the counselor. Counselors themselves may be rather controlled people to whom outbursts of direct hostility are threatening and whose own tendencies to respond in kind, or perhaps to withdraw, are uncomfortably close to the surface. When this happens or when the resulting anxiety is communicated to the clients, the counselor may indeed lose control of the sessions and the confidence of the spouses. But this is a counselor problem, not a characteristic of conjoint therapy as such. Not only do many counselors quickly become comfortable with conflict in the counseling sessions, but they learn to use it to advantage.

Direct alteration of interaction. Whereas under conventional marriage-counseling procedure there may be prolonged inconsistency between the behavior of clients in the counseling sessions and their behavior in relation to one another outside the sessions, conjoint therapy admits the counselor directly to current squabbles. When the partners find that the counselor can empathize with each of them without taking sides, they can become more objective about both the partner and themselves. Each can be helped to make tentative gestures toward a less hurtful pattern of interaction and find that the other partner reciprocates. This process, in time, becomes cumulative and circular. Gradually, the couple can be led out of conflict according to dynamics analogous to those which led them into it originally.

The partner's interaction during the sessions provides a model for interaction between sessions. Each partner becomes, with the counselor, a kind of co-therapist working throughout the week. Because both partners are involved, alliances within the triad are avoided. More of the responsibility for solving their problems is shifted to the clients, where it belongs. Less dependence upon the counselor is encouraged, and eventually less weaning away from the counselor is required.

Focus on current relationships. A final distinguishing feature of conjoint marriage counseling, and one that has been implied above, is the emphasis it places on current relationships. The term "current" does not connote momentary, ephemeral, or trivial here. Roughly, it marks off the period from the time of marriage forward. Spouses seen together do not receive great encouragement to relive their early family experiences. The emphasis is upon what hurts them as a pair. They will, naturally, ferret out the bases for their conflicts both in what has occurred between them and in the fund of experience which each partner brought into the marriage. They will develop insight into the effects of childhood experience, but the emphasis is upon the contribution of childhood experience to the marital conflict and not upon early frustration or personality impairment as such.

By implication, personality reconstruction is not a primary goal in marriage counseling. Most couples become more comfortable with their own dynamics, with those of the partner, and with the common product. That change is inherent in this process is obvious. There is no sharp line between marriage counseling and reconstructive therapy. But there are differences of degree and emphasis. The point is simply that with a marriage counseling emphasis, conjoint therapy has many advantages that are just beginning to be appreciated.

Limitations in the Use of Conjoint Therapy

Limited successes with conjoint therapy should not blind its users to its limitations. The temptation is there, but to portray conjoint therapy as a panacea will only bring discredit upon it and delay its taking its proper place in the therapeutic arsenal. Unfortunately, the full limitations upon the use of conjoint therapy are not yet known. There follow some suggestions regarding these limitations based upon the author's own experience.

Lack of counselor preparedness. Most professional marriage counselors received their training in the tradition of individual psychotherapy which emphasized the exclusiveness of the counselor-client relationship and which stressed the alleged dangers involved in becoming entangled in the clients' conflicts. Consequently, few of them have much skill in the conduct of joint interviews, and their first efforts along these lines frequently result in disappointment. The resulting threat to professional self-concept encourages the rejection of the technique rather than acknowledgment of the need to develop new skills.

Beyond this, conjoint therapy is inherently more demanding upon the counselor. He must respond continuously and rapidly to an exceedingly broad range of stimuli. He must almost simultaneously hear, accept, and reflect the communications of both partners; he must protect each partner; and he must continuously support the relationship. It is demanding work for which some counselors may not be suited.

There also may be limitations upon the number of such interviews that any counselor can successfully complete in the course of a working day.

Lack of client preparedness. Clients as well as counselors have problems. Some client problems undoubtedly make the systematic use of joint interviews inadvisable.

Among marriage-counseling clients, the problem of motivation is important. If it is true that marriage-counseling clients "hurt less," on the average, than psychiatric patients and sometimes have to be "coaxed" to work concertedly on their problems, the more rapid confrontation inherent in conjoint therapy may tend to drive some of them out of counseling. Since the prognosis for such clients is not usually good, it may be asked whether this is really a disadvantage.

There is a more subtle problem related to the nature of the clients' motivations. It may be assumed that a disproportionate number of persons who seek out a marriage counselor need to work out their difficulties within the context of marriage. But some marriage-counseling clients come specifically seeking support for the dissolution of an intolerable relationship. At various levels of consciousness, these motives may be mixed and confused. Clients who are committed to separation may only be handicapped by joint sessions. Those whose motivations need to be worked through and clarified may be worked with far more efficiently in individual sessions.

There are also forms of client maladjustment that militate against the use of conjoint therapy. How many such patterns there are and how severe the illness must be are not yet known. Two examples recur in the author's own practice. Not surprisingly, clients in whom there are integrated paranoid features tend to interpret the conjoint situation as conspiratorial. Whether these delusions could eventually be worked through in conjoint therapy is less relevant than the fact that whatever advantages ordinarily accrue to conjoint therapy are lost in this instance.

Similarly, clients who have suffered such severe early deprivation that they are seriously crippled emotionally cannot participate actively in conjoint therapy any more than they can in individual therapy. When such persons are brought into conjoint therapy with hostile partners, the overwhelming need for protection of the disabled spouse blocks the development of the desired cumulative circular interaction.

CONCLUSION

This has not been a comprehensive discussion of conjoint therapy in marriage counseling. Such would require a substantial monograph rather than a brief article. Moreover, most of the pages for that monograph could not yet be written. The message of this article is really very simple. Marriage counselors have been slow to recognize the congruence of conjoint therapy with their basic orientation to counseling. Experiments with it indicate that it perhaps has more advantages for counselors than for the psychiatrists who originated it. Fascination with a new technique, however, should not obscure the fact that psychotherapy is a wondrously complex process which persistently defies universal solutions.

REFERENCES

Ackerman, N. *The psychodynamics of family life*. New York: Basic Books, 1958.

Bowen, M. Family psychotherapy. *American Journal of Orthopsychiatry*, 1961, *31*, 40–60.

Burlingham, Present trends in handling the mother-child relationship during the therapeutic process. *The Psychoanalytic Study of the Child*, 1951, *5*, 31–37.

Can one partner be successfully counseled without the other? *Marriage and Family Living*, February 1953, *15*, 59–64.

Grotjahn, M. *Psychoanalysis and the family neurosis*. New York: W. W. Norton, 1960.

Haley, J. Observation of the family of the schizophrenic. *American Journal of Orthopsychiatry*, 1960, *30*, 460–467.

Leslie, G. R. The field of marriage counseling. In Christensen, H. (Ed.), Handbook on marriage and the family. New York: Rand-McNally, 1965.

Martin, P., & Bird, W. An approach to the psychotherapy of marriage partners. *Psychiatry*. May 1953, *16*, 123–127.

Mittelman, B. The concurrent analysis of married couples. *The Psychoanalytic Quarterly*. April 1948, *17*, 182–197.

Ogburn, W. F. The great man vs. social forces. *Social Forces*, December 1926, *5*, 225–231.

Parsons, T. *The social system*. Glencoe, Ill.: The Free Press, 1951.

Parsons, T., & Fox, R. Illness, therapy, and the modern urban American family. *Journal of Social Issues*, 1952, *8*, 31–44.

Shellow, R. S., Brown, B. S., & Osberg, J. W. Family group therapy in retrospect: Four years and sixty families. *Family Process*, March 1963, *1*, 52–67.

Skidmore, R., & Garett, H. The joint interview in marriage counseling. *Marriage and Family Living*, November 1955, *17*, 349–354.

CHAPTER 17

The Conjoint Psychotherapy of Married Partners

Andrew S. Watson

Since the appearance in 1956 of Eisenstein's *Neurotic Interaction in Marriage*, publication of papers and books on the treatment of family and marriage problems has mounted. While for many years social workers and others have done "marriage counseling," psychiatrists only recently have started to work actively in this field, or at least to report their work in publication (Grotjahn, 1959, pp. 90–104). The impact of psychoanalytic theory and practice on the concepts and techniques of psychotherapy has tended to focus on the treatment of individual patients and has aimed at altering intrapsychic as well as external adaptation through manipulation of the psychological process. This has brought excellent therapeutic results in certain categories of patients, but many others have not been treated or their treatment has failed. Frequently this has been accounted for by judging them as "untreatable," or by deciding that the psychotherapeutic method was poorly applied. It appears that many of these conclusions were arrived at largely by assumption, since there is not only little objective data to support such a view, but also increasing evidence to the contrary.[1] Clearly, adaptive potential and versatility seem to be consistently underestimated by professionals.[2] Likewise, the literature reveals that there is good reason to search further for causes of family disruption using the psychodynamic concept of homeostasis as a launching point (Bell, 1961, pp. 4–5, 48–52; Jackson, 1959, pp. 122–141; and Bowen, 1961, pp. 40–60). In this paper, I will endeavor to explain and conceptualize my recent treatment efforts with family and marriage problems.

---

[1] For example, studies of the placebo effect demonstrate that even very "sick" psychotics have considerable capacity to improve with nothing more than the increased attention paid them in the context of research operations (Frank, pp. 65–74).

[2] See the work of Berlien on military adjustment.

Reprinted with permission of the author and the publisher from the *American Journal of Orthopsychiatry*, 1963, *33*, 912–922.

Several specific premises regarding the nature of marital unions will be utilized but not explicitly substantiated here. They are:

1. That marriage partners choose each other for highly specific, conscious and unconscious reasons. This selection represents the summation and gratification of normal and appropriate goals, as well as various neurotic and symbolic needs that must be met either intrapsychically or socially (Ackerman, 1958, pp. 148–149; Bell, 1961, pp. 4–5, 48–52; and Sherman, 1961).

2. Both partners enter into a mutually "satisfying" interlocking homeostatic balance (Basamania, 1961, p. 22, and Jackson, 1959, pp. 129–145). Despite external appearances to the contrary, they reach a state of psychological equilibrium that "gratifies" both mature and neurotic needs for both partners (Kubie, 1956). One of the treatment objectives in this kind of therapy will be to elucidate the details of this interlocking system, in order to open up the possibility for a different and more appropriate adjustment between them.

3. This homeostatic relationship may also be viewed as a mutually shared communication system involving many verbal as well as nonverbal communication devices (Grotjahn, 1960; Jackson, Riskin, & Satir, 1961). Therefore much characterological interchange will take place, and this will lead inevitably to the necessity for emphasizing the interpretation of character manifestations in this form of treatment.[3]

4. Any therapeutic disruption in the psychological homeostasis of one partner in the marriage will inevitably force upon all other members in the family an alteration in their psychological adjustments. For this reason, it appears that often the most efficient way to impinge upon the interlocking adjustment of the partners is to have both participate in the insight-producing process. This would simultaneously tend to bring about revised homoeostatic techniques for each. The family anxiety level may be kept closer to optimal limits than often occurs when individuals are treated separately and only one member has opportunity for, and access to, insight-producing experience (Ackerman, 1961, pp. 61–64).

These, then, are the premises on which this form of treatment is based. In addition, all the basic hypotheses of psychodynamic theory are utilized and woven into the treatment situation.

TECHNIQUE

There have been several recent papers describing the treatment of marriage partners in various kinds of combinations and with various goals. For example, Ackerman (1958) used "interpretive family treatment," while Hambridge (1959) used "simultaneous analysis of marriage partners" to designate such procedures. Greene (1960) describes "concurrent analysis," and Martin and Bird (1959) describe "concurrent psychotherapy," but in neither case are both partners present at the same time. Geist and

---

[3]As Reich puts it, *how* material is stated is as important as *what* is said, and is the focus for interpreting character defenses.

Gerber (1960) as caseworkers shying away from the word "therapy," call their technique "joint interviewing," as does Sherman (1959). Carroll (1960, pp. 57–62) employs "family unit therapy."

Since none of these adequately designated an insight-producing psychotherapy focused on interpretation of transferences and carried on by a single therapist with both partners simultaneously present, I sought a new designation.

The meanings of the word "conjoint" seemed to satisfy the above requirement. No sooner had the expression "conjoint treatment of marital partners" been coined, when the excellent paper, "Conjoint Family Treatment," by Jackson and Weakland (1961) appeared in print. Correspondence with Jackson revealed that this term had been used in an earlier paper (1959, pp. 122), which I had not yet seen.

In conjoint psychotherapy, both marriage partners are seen together, and the strategic goal of the interpretive process is to work through the central neurotic distortions of their interlocking adaptive and communication systems. This involves interpretation of the multiple transferences, utilizing all the traditional psychoanalytic concepts of personality dynamics. Because of the more complex transaction in these sessions, several specific procedures are followed.

It will be clear to all sophisticated in the theory of psychotherapy that there is an extremely complex interlocking system of transference-countertransference operations present in a therapeutic setting where three individuals participate. Because of this fact, it is essential at the very beginning of treatment to understand thoroughly the characteristics and etiology of each partner's psychological participation.

When the decision has been made to treat a couple conjointly, both parties will be interviewed separately for two or three sessions in order to obtain a thorough anamnesis and diagnostic formulation. Following the suggestion of Saul, an effort is made to isolate and formulate the core psychodynamic forces operating in each spouse and relate them to precise etiological data. Early memories are obtained; family backgrounds are explored with emphasis on recollections and thoughts about significant family members; dreams and other specific historical details needed to develop the diagnostic formulation are collected. By the time these interviews are concluded, the therapist should be able to make at least a well-educated guess about the meaning of the various communications that will be present during the course of treatment. Just as the significance of communications becomes more clear as individual psychotherapy progresses, so they will become more meaningful in the course of conjoint treatment.

Some may leap to the assumption that patients in this kind of treatment setting will not talk freely about the details of their fantasy life, but this has not proved true. It is my impression that freedom to communicate in such treatment is more often than not a function of the therapist's comfort and countertransference than it is of the patient's inhibition. As Ackerman (1958) has stated, "These so-called secrets turn out not to be real secrets at all. Far more often they are common family knowledge surrounded by a tacit conspiracy of silence [p. ix] ." I share this view, and when the basis for the conspiracy is worked through, the participants have no further need to avoid free discussion or free association.

As the exploratory sessions with each partner are drawing to a close, it is usually in order to make some general statement to each about specific adaptive techniques that appear to create their difficulty. Then, when both are brought back into the conjoint setting, they will have some anticipation about their own contribution to the marriage problems.

As in all psychotherapy, conjoint treatment starts where the patients want it to start. They may or may not talk about themselves, their children, or a multitude of other problems. Material is not judged "good" or "bad" but as communication relating to the significant problems or resistances. Associations are interpreted in the same way as they are in any other form of psychotherapy. However, one factor controls the interpretive choice made at any given time: *All interpretations will focus on those aspects of the material and dynamics that relate to the process of communication between the spouses.* In other words, in selecting which of several alternative interpretations to make, the therapist will choose the one that is related dynamically to the cause of the communication distortion in the marriage. Material mainly relevant to only one partner will not be interpreted.[4]

As material is brought up by one or the other partner and its meaning is interpreted in the presence of both, it helps the listening or observing spouse to impersonalize communications and progressively see them as a function of his partner's psychic problem. This distance-producing measure facilitates improvement in the ego's perceptive capacity, progressively decreases the narcissistic identifications between the partners, and thereby improves their capacity to communicate rationally and resolve mutual problems more objectively. For example, if psychological closeness is ego-threatening to a husband, any demonstration of closeness and intimacy by his wife will cause him to withdraw and she will usually interpret this as personal rejection. When this maneuver manifests itself and is interpreted in treatment, the husband can learn to understand why he "needs" to withdraw. At the same time, the wife is learning why she views such reactions as personal and, progressively, how to objectify the meaning of the withdrawal.

Another important aspect of this technique is that the therapist must observe strict strategic neutrality. He will interpret objectively whatever he sees in the behavior of both spouses, and from time to time will focus his attention on one more than the other. Over the course of treatment, however, he will not ally with one party more than with the other. This is especially important in the beginning phases of treatment, and it is essential to establish this fact clearly to both participants. For the first several hours, this necessitates shifting interpretive focus back and forth between

---

[4]This focus is concurred in by Bell (1961, pp. 4–5), Carroll (1960, p. 60), Ackerman (1961, pp. 65–66,), Jackson & Weakland (pp. 36–38) and others.

the partners, so that hours end with each receiving approximately equal attention from the therapist. Interpretation should also balance in terms of their positive and negative implications to the partners.

After setting forth to both partners the psychological premises stated above, the therapist then encourages the unfolding of the marital problems. Usually this happens quickly and in very vivid form. As in all transference-oriented treatment, it is possible to see at first hand the nature of the psychological participation of both partners. The therapist need not speculate about what has happened at home, since he may directly observe the interaction between them, as well as their individual transferences to him. Especially in the early phases of treatment, this is excellent material to focus upon, since it gives patients insight into the goals of treatment, provides them with sufficient gratification to offset some of the anxiety this technique produces, and thereby creates "hope" that the treatment will be worthwhile. Such an attitude is a crucial element for effective therapy (Carroll, 1960, p. 59; Chance, 1959, pp. 151–154).

One of the principal tactical advantages of this kind of treatment lies in the fact that it is possible to make an interpretation to one spouse, though its main impact is directed toward the other one. If there is strong resistance or ego vulnerability in one, a correlated interpretation can be made to the other spouse, thus turning the interlocking nature of the marital neurosis to therapeutic advantage. For example, if there is a provocative-masochistic tendency in one, coupled with sadistic-criticalness in the other, either side of this emotional axis may be interpreted. Both hear the interpretation and perceive it in terms of their own dynamics. If they have a psychological need to do so, they may, temporarily at least, be permitted to view this as "the other person's problem." Such displacement-potential is useful for regulating the timing of interpretations, while permitting the therapist to deal with current pertinent material. This considerably increases therapeutic flexibility.

This approach stirs up active psychological participation in the couple, with mounting anxiety usually related closely to the emotional stalemate that brought them to therapy. It is important to give reassurance during the early stages, while they are in the process of discovering their own powers to sustain such discomfort. The therapist, during his early experience with this form of treatment, will likewise reverberate to the patient's anxiety, until he too finds that it is possible to carry out and control such therapy. Ultimately, his calmness and comfort in participating in this process, more than anything else, provide patients with the will to explore and accept what had been frightening in the past and had always caused avoidance and reinforced repression (Bowen, 1961, p. 56).

Another characteristic of this technique is the degree of participation in the process by the therapist. In most one-to-one psychotherapy, the therapist can remain essentially passive, only occasionally making interpretive or confronting remarks. In conjoint treatment, where interpretation often centers upon some character manifestation, the "action" is fast-moving and the therapist will by necessity bring himself more into view (Ackerman, 1961, pp. 63–64; Jackson & Weakland, 1961, pp. 38–39).

Also, as interpretations are made, he may "lend" his identity by way of references to personal experiences that serve to underscore his awareness of the problems as well as his belief that they may be resolved. This can be analogized to the ego support rendered by parents to their children as they encourage the annexational identifications that press them forward in their exploration and mastery of reality. Though this kind of support is more specific and tangible in conjoint treatment, it is certainly present at least by implication in the most classical psychoanalytic process. In fact, one might say that one of the criteria for psychoanalysis is the capacity on the part of the patient to perceive this fact. If patients cannot, some alternative approach must be taken (Erickson, 1956).

From the supervisory observation of residents utilizing this kind of therapy, it is clear that there are many "styles" in which it can be conducted. However, in comparison with other forms of therapy carried out by the same resident, there is likely to be much more activity exhibited in conjoint treatment. Needless to say, this has countertransference implications. For example, it has been stated that many who practice psychotherapy do so in order to participate vicariously in the emotional life of others (Szasz, 1956; Wheelis, 1956).The essentially passive relationship of the therapist to his patient in most kinds of psychotherapy permits such participation while retaining relative noninvolvement. To whatever degree this need is present in a given therapist, he will be strongly disinclined to utilize such procedures as conjoint therapy. The corollary probably is also true, that the more actively inclined will find this method holds special attraction. (In assaying any psychotherapeutic process, it is obviously important to take into account the therapist's conscious and unconscious attitudes about "how" and "what" therapy "will work" (Frank, 1961, pp. 114–141).

Once this treatment technique has been elected, it should be the dominant therapeutic mode, at least until the interlocking psychological problems of the couple have been resolved. However, on occasion one spouse may try to use the therapeutic situation to act out neurotically, in a way that would create individual problems and disrupt the timing of the therapeutic process. Such maneuvers should be blocked promptly by the therapist through interpretation. If such acting out cannot be checked within the conjoint sessions, there is reason to see that spouse individually sufficiently often (usually one to three sessions) to clarify and obviate the motives for such masochistic moves. Any reactions stirred up in the partner *not* seen alone must be dealt with actively, and occasionally he, or she, too must be seen alone in order to retain balance.

After the conjoint sessions have been reinstituted, the material that came out in the individual meetings can usually be worked slowly into the discussions. Sometimes these separate sessions turn out to have been flanking moves to avoid a conjoint issue. In such a case it must be so interpreted to the partners, and the therapist should view the separation as a tactical miscalculation.[5] At other times enormously valuable material

---

[5]Some therapists such as Bell (pp. 24–28) would refuse altogether to see one family member alone. This has not been a problem in our work,

emerges which, when dealt with conjointly, moves therapy forward precipitously because of the therapist's deepened understanding and the patients' added insight.

TECHNICAL PROBLEMS

The main problems arising in conjoint treatment are the product of the more complex transference-countertransference reactions. Clearly, conjoint therapy should not be undertaken unless the therapist can comprehend quickly what is going on in the sessions and can think freely about the material in precise psychodynamic terms. So much occurs during the conjoint sessions that the therapist has no time to pause and reflect at length before dealing with the material. Neither can he sit by and wait for multiple confirmations of the psychodynamic theme before he decides to make an interpretation. To do so puts him far behind the affectively significant events, and he may never come abreast of the significant transactions. While there will be much reiteration of material, the same timing problem will always exist.

Obviously there are two sets of transferences, as well as two sets of countertransferences (I say "sets" deliberately, to reflect the overdetermined imago present in any individual's repetition-compulsion). Because of the presence of both marital partners and the more realistic presentation of problems, there is an increased risk of the therapist's unconsciously identifying with one or the other spouse. However, by being aware of this hazard and through more active involvement in the therapeutic process, there is greater opportunity for empathic identification and a quicker grasp of the problems unfolding before and with him. Under these circumstances it is neither possible nor effective to have long periods of silence nor to avoid finding answers to specific reality problems. This does not mean that the goal is simply to gratify. Rather, the exploration for answers is carried on in a way that impinges dynamically on the neurotic process of the couple. The *act* of mutual exploration is contrived to clarify the defensive maneuvers of each spouse in such a way as to increase insight and maturation even as a problem is being solved (Grotjahn, 1959, pp. 100–101). Obviously this is different from the kind of communication used in more typical psychotherapeutic interpretation. It appears, however, that its dynamic effect is similar. Defensive distortions are forced into sight where their current implications can be subjected to reality testing and possible revision.

Another common countertransference anxiety in conjoint treatment arises when the partners begin to make threatening remarks about getting a divorce, or some other offer to act out. Because both partners are present to witness the intense affect unleashed, and because it may readily be interpreted as more than mere transference, the therapist is likely to wonder if he may not have a tiger by the tail. These occasions may be turned to good therapeutic advantage, but only if the therapist is comfortable in taking them up and working them through. He may very easily assume that he has been the cause of such an upset. While this is obviously not true, the physical presence of both partners with their emotional reactions to the therapeutic situation makes this distortion easy to believe.

The therapist is also likely to react with deep concern to other kinds of highly charged material as it emerges and creates the specter of serious trouble between the partners. As noted above, such material is not truly secret, and its revelation presents an opportunity to clarify issues that have too long been hidden just deeply enough to prevent resolution and yet cause marriage difficulties. To date, there have been no instances in which truly damaging material has arisen. Rather, it has been confirmed that the information was "known" by both parties beforehand.

TECHNICAL ADVANTAGES

Though it is often stated that the psychotherapist presents no value judgments to his patients, I do not accept this view. For example, whenever it is decided that there has been a neurotic distortion such as projection, a value judgment about reality has been made and, along with it, an estimate of the degree of distortion. All this is inferred from what the patient has said, which places a large analytical task upon the therapist. Though he does have access to transference reactions with which to check out impressions of extra-therapy behavior, there is always the possibility of error due to observational bias, as well as the likelihood that some reactions to the therapist will be different in kind from those to other persons in the environment. In conjoint therapy there is the immediate advantage of direct observation of the participants in the family problem. This facilitates more objective evaluation of the partners' behavior and limits the need to judge distortion from more indirect data. This frees the therapist's energy to deal with the complexity of the process, and well offsets the disadvantages arising from the increased distortion potential caused by the complicated interaction.

Another marked advantage of this technique results from the pressure it places on the couple to re-examine their reality testing. When an interpretation is made to one spouse, the other has the opportunity to hear it, remember it, and reintroduce it, during the interim between therapeutic sessions. This provides the therapist with a working assistant for each of the partners, who will constantly reinforce the interpretation he makes during therapy sessions. While there is a possibility and even a probability that interpretations will be used for nontherapeutic purposes, the general summation effect is reinforcement of, and mounting pressure toward, increased reality testing by both spouses. In most individual psychotherapy there is a strong tendency for the patient to leave the hour and fall back into archaic patterns of problem-solving and old ego defenses. Ever so slowly the therapist breaks into the automaticity of the defense system, to bring about broadening of the reality-testing and subsequent improvement in the patient's capacity to synthesize and manipulate current experience. The speed with which conjoint therapy improves reality-testing is a distinct advantage. There is, in addition, the marked ego satisfaction that comes from the fact that both spouses are participating jointly in the solution of common problems. Here there is no untreated spouse to build up fantasies of being conspired against by the therapist (Ackerman, 1961, pp. 57, 64; Ackerman, 1959, p. 111; Brodey, 1959). Instead, there is the clear opportunity to work with the partner and share in the resolution of difficulties. Thus one of the principal problems in treating a married person may be avoided.

Another advantage in conjoint treatment is that insights are gained in the very context from which problems arise. This removes much of the need to translate from transference back to reality, since reality and transference are close together in time and content and therefore more accessible to perception and learning. Such contextual analysis appears to enhance markedly the speed of such learning, even while maintaining the advantages of individual treatment to ferret out and clarify neurotic distortions. This avoids vicarious guilt in one partner for gaining something the other is not getting, and facilitates the forging of a new ego ideal that can be held jointly by both (Ackerman, 1959, pp. 115–116).

The final advantage I would like to comment on is economic. There is ample evidence that the decision of *who* gets psychotherapy depends to a large extent on economic status (Chance, 1959, Ch. 7; Hollingshead & Redlich, 1958). Obviously, if the multiple parties to a marriage problem may be successfully and simultaneously treated, the saving of professional time will have at least two immediate and practical reverberations for this group of patients:

1. Therapy will become at least twice as available, which is important in the face of an absolute shortage of treatment personnel.

2. The cost of treatment to such a couple may be halved, which can extend the availability of treatment to many who cannot now afford it.

There are other economic effects in conjoint treatment. Several writers have commented on the speed with which this process works, and I concur fully with such observations (Bell, 1961, pp. 49–50; Bowen, 1961, pp. 57–58). Psychodynamic elements that ordinarily take months to raise to awareness sufficient for their being re-examined and reality-tested emerge and are effectively altered in a matter of four or five sessions. While these new insights are not fully integrated in such a short time, the improved adaptation that re-evaluation of attitudes and feelings carries with it begins and gains momentum. Patients can then return to their own reality-testing and experience-gathering with a likelihood for continued maturation.[6] This accelerated process, if the passage of time demonstrates that gains are maintained, will result in much saving of expensive professional time as well as many direct and indirect economic and social gains for patients.

---

[6]It seems appropriate here to quote part of a footnote from Freud's Rat-man case:

"It was impossible to unravel this tissue of phantasy thread by thread; the therapeutic success of the treatment was precisely what stood in the way of this. *The patient recovered, and his ordinary life began to assert its claims: there were many tasks before him, which he had already neglected for too long, and which were incompatible with a continuation of the treatment.* I am not to be blamed, therefore, for this gap in the analysis. The scientific results of psychoanalysis are at present only a by-product of its therapeutic aims, and for that reason *it is often just in those cases where treatment fails that most discoveries are made.*" (Italics added.)

INDICATIONS

To discuss indications for conjoint therapy at length would be premature. However, there are several specific situations in which they seem clear-cut:

1. In those family relationships where the commonly held distortions are so gross and so reality-disruptive that speed in checking family disintegration is a critical factor, conjoint treatment seems to offer an ideal way in which to slow down the destructive neurotic process and provide a chance to resolve at least the surface problems before they destroy the marriage, and often the children.

2. This technique is especially well suited to cases in which the problems are largely of an acting-out, characterological nature. It helps greatly in "trapping" these maneuvers where they can be seen, interpreted, and attached to some of the underlying neurotic dynamisms and affects. This makes it very useful in just that type of case in which the parties are "poorly motivated" and "not ready" for treatment. Once they are seen in this therapeutic setting, they may very quickly be led to "discover" reasons and feelings to justify continuing.

Various writers have proposed narrower indications than these, such as the presence of children, and the absence of psychosis. I myself have not felt these limits to be necessary, and successful treatment has been carried on outside of them.

The question arises as to how far conjoint treatment can be carried. The answer to this is not yet clear, since various cases have proceeded (and are proceeding) to the handling of all levels of psychopathology from superficial to deep. It does appear, however, that when the focus of psychological emphasis shifts away from elements of mutual emotional cathexis to the partners, if further therapy is needed it should move to individual sessions. There is reason to believe that one should not leap too quickly to this alternative, since it is clear that even dreams and fantasies among marriage partners have a high degree of mutuality. These facts seem to indicate that there will be far-reaching therapeutic potential for conjoint psychotherapy.

Contraindications

As with the discussion of indications, it is not yet possible to set forth any specific contraindications. Couples have been treated who were grossly psychotic or involved in the weirdest varieties of reality difficulties, as well as more run-of-the-mill and superficial problems. If reality is not too far out of hand, it appears possible to utilize this kind of treatment advantageously. Neither have any situations arisen in which it was felt that this method was "dangerous." The question of contraindication, then, must also remain open until further experience has been accumulated.

Conjoint psychotherapy of marriage partners seems to hold promise as a means for therapeutically intervening in many problems that have formerly defied success. The principal bar to utilization may rest more in countertransference problems than it does with difficulties experienced by patients. Its main prerequisite is the capacity to understand psycho-dynamic events with facility so that therapeutic interventions may be made promptly and in the context of the early appearance of material. To date, a precise statement of indications and contraindications may not be made.

REFERENCES

Ackerman, N. W. *The psychodynamics of family life.* New York: Basic Books, 1958.

Ackerman, N. W. The psychoanalytic approach to the family. In J.. H. Masserman (Ed.), *Individual and familial dyanmics.* New York: Grune & Stratton, 1959.

Ackerman, N. W. A dynamic frame for the clinical approach to family conflict. In *Exploring the base for family therapy.* New York: Family Service Association of America, 1961.

Basamania, B. W. The emotional life of the family: Inferences for social casework. *American Journal of Orthopsychiatry,* 1961, *31*, No. 1, 74–86.

Bell, J. E. Family group therapy. Public Health Monogr. No. 64, Washington, D. C.: U. S. Government Printing Office, 1961.

Berlien, I. C. Psychiatric aspects of military manpower conservation. *Journal American Psychiatric Association,* 1954, *111*, No. 3, 91–99.

Bowen, M. Family psychotherapy. *American Journal of Orthopsychiatry.* 1961, *31*, No. 1, 40–60.

Brodey, W. M. Some family operations and schizophrenia. *Archives of General Psychiatry,* 1959, *1*, 388–389.

Carroll, E. J. Treatment of the family as a unit. *Pennsylvania Medical Journal,* 1960, *63*, No. 1, 56–72.

Chance, E. *Families in treatment.* New York: Basic Books, 1959.

Eisenstein, V. W. Neurotic interaction in marriage. New York: Basic Books, 1956.

Erikson, E. The problem of ego identity. *Journal of American Psychoanalytic Association,* 1956.

Frank, J. D. *Persuasion and healing.* Baltimore, Md.: Johns Hopkins Press, 1961.

Freud, S. A case of obsessional neurosis. In *Collected Papers,* Vol. 3. London: Hogarth Press, 1950.

Friend, M. R. The historical development of family diagnosis. *Social Service Review,* 1960, *34*, 11–12.

Geist, J., & Gerber, N. Joint interviewing: A treatment technique with marital partners. *Social Casework,* 1960, *41*, No. 2, 76–83.

Greene, B. L. Marital disharmony: Concurrent analysis of husband and wife. *Diseases of the Nervous System,* 1960, *21*, No. 2, 73–78.

Grotjahn, M. Analytic family therapy: A survey of trends in research and practice. In J. H. Masserman (Ed.), *Individual and familial dynamics.* New York: Grune & Stratton, 1959.

Grotjahn, M. *Psychoanalysis and the family neurosis.* New York: W. W. Norton, 1960.

Hambridge, G. The simultaneous psychoanalysis of marriage partners. Paper read at meeting of the American Psychoanalytic Association, Philadelphia, 1959.

Hollingshead, A. B., & Redlich, F. C. *Social class and mental illness.* New York: John Wiley & Sons, 1958.

Jackson, D. D. Family interaction, family homeostasis and some implications for conjoint family psychotherapy. In J. H. Masserman (Ed.), *Individual and familial dynamics.* New York: Grune & Stratton, 1959.

Jackson, D.D., & Weakland, J. H. Conjoint family treatment. *Psychiatry,* 1961, *24*, Suppl. 2, 30–45.

Jackson, D. D., Riskin, J., & Satir, V. A method of analysis of a family interview. *Archives of General Psychiatry,* 1961, *5*, 322–324.

Kubie, L. S. Psychoanalysis and marriage. In V. Eisenstein (Ed.), *Neurotic interaction in marriage.* New York: Basic Books, 1956.

Martin, P., & Bird, H. W. A marriage pattern: The "lovesick" wife and the "cold sick" husband. *Psychiatry,* 1959, *22*, 246.

Menninger, K. Hope. *American Journal of Psychiatry,* 1959, *116*, 481–491.

Reich, W. *Character analysis.* New York: Orgone Institute Press, 1949.

Saul, L. J. The psychoanalytic diagnostic interview. *Psychoanalytic Quarterly,* 1957, *26*, No. 1, 76–90.

Sherman, S. N. Joint interviews in casework practice. *Social Work,* 1959, *4*, No. 2, 20–28.

Sherman, S. N. Concept of the family in casework theory. In *Exploring the base for family therapy.* New York: Family Service Association of America, 1961.

Szasz, T. On the experiences of the analyst in the psychoanalytic situation. *Journal of American Psychoanalytic Association,* 1956, *4*, 204–208.

Wheelis, A. The vocational hazards of psychoanalysis. *International Journal of Psychoanalysis,* 1956, *36*, 171–184.

CHAPTER 18

Family Communication
and Conjoint Family Therapy

Virginia Satir

1. In this chapter, I should like to state in a general way some ideas about psychic health and illness in order to show their relevance to the interactional approach of family therapy. I also want to present my own picture of what a family therapist is and does, since he becomes, to an important degree, a model for his patients' subsequent behavior.

   I am not trying to present a "philosophy of therapy." These ideas appear to me as working tools, helpful in organizing my own way of handling therapy, or as a conceptual core around which therapeutic growths may be structured, rather than as a system of thought possessing value in and for itself.

2. The most important concept in therapy, because it is a touchstone for all the rest, is that of *maturation*.

   a. This is the state in which a given human being is fully in charge of himself.
   b. A mature person is one who, having attained his majority, is able to make choices and decisions based on accurate perceptions about himself, others, and the context in which he finds himself; who acknowledges these choices and decisions as being his; and who accepts responsibility for their outcomes.

3. The patterns of behaving that characterize a mature person we call functional because they enable him to deal in a relatively competent and precise way with the world in which he lives. Such a person will—

   a. manifest himself clearly to others.

Reprinted with permission of the author and the publisher from Virginia Satir, *Conjoint Family Therapy* (rev. ed.). Palo Alto, Calif.: Science and Behavior Books, 1967.

b. be in touch with signals from his internal self, thus letting himself know openly what he thinks and feels.
c. be able to see and hear what is outside himself as differentiated from himself and as different from anything else.
d. behave toward another person as someone separate from himself and unique.
e. treat the presence of different-ness as an opportunity to learn and explore rather than as a threat or a signal for conflict.
f. deal with persons and situations in their context, in terms of "how it is" rather than how he wishes it were or expects it to be.
g. accept responsibility for what he feels, thinks, hears and sees, rather than denying it or attributing it to others.
h. have techniques for openly negotiating the giving, receiving and checking of meaning between himself and others.*

4. We call an individual dysfunctional when he has not learned to communicate properly. Since he does not manifest a means of perceiving and interpreting himself accurately, or interpreting accurately messages from the 'outside, the assumptions on which he bases his actions will be faulty and his efforts to adapt to reality will be confused and inappropriate.

   a. As we have seen, the individual's communication problems are rooted in the complex area of family behavior in which he lived as a child. The adults in the family provide the blueprint by which the child grows from infancy to maturity.
   b. If the male and female who were his survival figures did not manage jointly, if their messages to each other and the child were unclear and contradictory, he himself will learn to communicate in an unclear and contradictory way.

5. A dysfunctional person will manifest himself incongruently, that is, he will deliver conflicting messages, via different levels of communication and using different signals.

   a. As an example, let us take the behavior of the parents of a disturbed child during their first interview with the therapist. When the therapist asks what seems to be the trouble, they practically deny that there is any.

      M: Well, I don't know. I think financial problems more than anything . . . outside of that, we're a very close family.

      F: We do everything together. I mean, we hate to leave the kids. When we go someplace, we take the kids with us. As

*This description of maturity emphasizes social and communication skills rather than the acquisition of knowledge and recognized achievement, which in my view derive from the first two.

far as doing things together as a family, we always try to do that at least once a week, say on Sundays, Sunday afternoon, why we always try to get the kids together and take them out for a ride to the park or something like that.

b. In words, they imply that there is no reason why they should be in a therapist's office. But their actual presence there, and the agreement they have already made to enter therapy, amount to an admission of the contrary. And the father presents a further contradiction when he reduces his claim that the family does "everything" together to a statement about the rides they take on Sunday afternoons.

6. In addition, a dysfunctional individual will be unable to adapt his interpretations to the present context.

a. He will tend to see the "here and now" through labels which have been indelibly fixed in his mind during the early part of his life when all messages had survival significance. Each subsequent use of the label will strengthen its reality.

b. Therefore, it is conceivable that he will impose on the present that which fits the past, or that which he expects from the future, thus negating the opportunity to gain a perspective on the past or realistically shape the future.

—For example, a school-age girl was brought into therapy because she was acting strangely and talking in riddles. When the mother was asked, "When did you notice that your child was not developing as she should?" she replied, "Well, she was a seven-month baby, and she was in an incubator for six weeks." The child's present and past difficulties were thus connected in a very illogical fashion.*

—Later she said that after she brought the baby home from the hospital, "She wouldn't give me any reaction, just as though she couldn't hear. And I'd take her around and hold her next to me, and she wouldn't pay any attention, and I know it upset me, and I asked the doctor and he said it was nothing, she was just being stubborn—that's one thing that sort of stuck in my mind with her."

—By using the word "stubborn" for the baby's indifference, the mother has given the baby a label that does not suit the context of babyhood. It implies that the child can be held accountable for willfully refusing to return the mother's love. Later on, the

---

*The communication aspects of this situation Jackson has labeled "past-present switches." Thus, the answer to the therapist's question, "How out of all the millions of people in the world did you two find each other?" may be as useful in family diagnosis as psychological testing. This question allows the spouses to describe their present relationship under cover of talking about the past. For further examples of this phenomenon, see Watzlawick's *An Anthology of Human Communication* (1964).

mother applies the same explanation to the child's strange behavior.

—By using the label "stubborn," and by implying in her first statement that the child's difficulties have a physical cause, the mother is able to absolve herself of blame; in fact, she has a double coverage. It is hard for such a mother to see her child's present problems objectively because she has already imposed her own interpretation on them.

7. Finally, a dysfunctional individual will not be able to perform the most important function of good communication: "checking out" his perceptions to see whether they tally with the situation as it really is or with the intended meaning of another. When two people are neither of them able to check out their meanings with each other, the result may resemble a comedy of errors—with a tragic ending. Here is one possible misunderstanding between a husband and a wife:

> *Report*: W: "He always yells." H: "I don't yell."

> *Explanation*: W: "I don't do things to suit him." H: "I don't do things to suit her."

> *Interpretation*: W: "He doesn't care about me." H: "She doesn't care about me."

> *Conclusion*: W: "I will leave him." H: "I will leave her."

> *Manifestation*: Wife uses invectives, voice is loud and shrill, eyes blaze, muscles stand out on base of neck, mouth is open, nostrils are distended, uses excessive movements. Husband says nothing, keeps eyes lowered, mouth tight, body constricted.

> *Outcome*: Wife visits divorce lawyer. Husband files a countersuit.

8. Difficulty in communicating is closely linked to an individual's self-concept, that is, his self-image and self-esteem.

   a. His parents may not only have given him inadequate models for *methods* of communication, but the *content* of their messages to him may have been devaluating.
   b. In order to form his self-image, the child has a demanding task. He must integrate messages from both parents (separately and together) telling him what to do with aspects of living like dependency, authority, sexuality and coding or labeling (cognition).
   c. If the parents' own attitudes are uncertain, or if they disagree with each other, the messages the child takes will be equally confused. The child will try to integrate what cannot be integrated, on the

basis of inconsistent and insufficient data. Failing, he will end up
with an incomplete picture of himself and low self-esteem.

d. In addition, the child's parents may depreciate his self-esteem
more directly. He looks to them to validate his steps in growth; if
these are not acknowledged at the time they occur, or if they are
acknowledged with concomitant messages of disgust, disapproval,
embarrassment, indifference or pain, the child's self-esteem will
naturally suffer.

9. Low self-esteem leads to dysfunctional communication:

a. When there is a conflict of interests. Any relationship presupposes
a commitment to a joint outcome, an agreement that each partner
will give up a little of his own interests in order to reach a wider
benefit for both.
   —This outcome is the best objective reality that can be arrived at
   in terms of what is possible, what is feasible, what fits the best
   all the way around.
   —The process used for reaching this outcome depends on the self-
   concepts of the persons engaged in it. If their self-esteem is low,
   so that any sacrifice of self seems intolerable, it is likely that the
   process will be based on some form of deciding "who is right,"
   "who will win," "who is most loved," "who will get made." I
   call this the "war syndrome."
   —If a person operates by means of this war syndrome, it is inevitable that his ability to seek objective information and arrive at
   objective conclusions as to what fits will be greatly impaired.

b. Dysfunction in communication will also follow when the individual is unable to handle different-ness.
   —An individual who has not achieved an independent selfhood will
   often take any evidence of different-ness in someone he is close
   to as an insult or a sign of being unloved.
   —This is because he is intensely dependent on the other person to
   increase his feelings of worth and to validate his self-image. Any
   reminder that the other is, after all, a separate being, capable of
   faithlessness and desertion, fills him with fear and distrust.
   —Some couples express their objections to each other's different-
   ness freely and loudly (the "teeter-totter syndrome"), but
   others, less secure in this area, prefer to pretend that different-
   ness does not exist.
   —With such couples, communication becomes covert. Any message
   which might call attention to the self as a private agent, with
   likes and dislikes, desires and displeasures of its own, is suppressed or changed. Wishes and decisions are presented as if they
   emanated from anywhere but inside the speaker himself; statements are disguised as symbolic utterances; messages are left
   incomplete or even not expressed at all, with the sender relying
   on mental telepathy to get them across. For example, a couple

who overtly behaved as if they had absolutely no problems responded in therapy to the "How did you meet?" question as follows:

H: "Well, we were raised in the same neighborhood."

W: "Not exactly the same neighborhood" (*laughs*).

This slight modification on the wife's part presaged many revelations of serious division between them.

10. Thus far we have been talking about dysfunctional behavior rather than the symptom that calls attention to it. What is the connection between them?

    a. Dysfunctional behavior is, as we have seen, related to feelings of low self-esteem. It is, in fact, a defense against the perception of them. Defenses, in turn, are ways which enable the person with low self-esteem to function *without* a symptom. To the person himself and to the outward world, there may appear to be nothing wrong.

    b. But if he is threatened by some event of survival significance, some happening which says to him, "You do not count; you are not lovable; you are nothing," the defense may prove unequal to the task of shielding him, and a symptom will take its place.

    c. Usually it is only then that the individual and his community will notice that he is "ill" and that he will admit a need for help.

11. How, then, do we define therapy?

    a. If illness is seen to derive from inadequate methods of communication (by which we mean all interactional behavior), it follows that therapy will be seen as an attempt to improve these methods. The emphasis will be on correcting discrepancies in communication and teaching ways to achieve more fitting joint outcomes.

    b. This approach to therapy depends on three primary beliefs about human nature:

        —First, that every individual is geared to survival, growth, and getting close to others and that all behavior expresses these aims, no matter how distorted it may look. Even an extremely disturbed person will be fundamentally on the side of the therapist.

        —Second, that what society calls sick, crazy, stupid, or bad behavior is really an attempt on the part of the afflicted person to signal the presence of trouble and call for help. In that sense, it may not be so sick, crazy, stupid, or bad after all.

        —Third, that human beings are limited only by the extent of their knowledge, their ways of understanding themselves and their ability to "check out" with others. Thought and feeling are inextricably bound together; the individual need not be a prisoner of his feelings but can use the cognitive component of his feeling to free himself. This is the basis for assuming that a human being can learn what he doesn't know and can change ways of commenting and understanding that don't fit.

12. This brings us to a discussion of the role of the therapist. How will he act? What picture will he have of himself?

   a. Perhaps the best way that he can see himself is as a *resource person*. He is not omnipotent. He is not God, parent or judge. The knotty question for all therapists is how to be an expert without appearing to the patient to be all-powerful, omniscient, or presuming to know always what is right and wrong.
   b. The therapist does have a special advantage in being able to study the patient's family situation as an experienced observer, while remaining outside it, above the power struggle, so to speak. Like a camera with a wide-angle lens, he can see things from the position of each person present and act as a representative of each. He sees transactions, as well as the individuals involved, and thus has a unique viewpoint.
   c. Because of this, the family can place their trust in him as an "official observer," one who can report impartially on what he sees and hears. Above all, he can report on what the family cannot see and cannot report on.

13. The therapist must also see himself as a *model of communication*.

   a. First of all, he must take care to be aware of his own prejudices and unconscious assumptions so as not to fall into the trap he warns others about, that of suiting reality to himself. His lack of fear in revealing himself may be the first experience the family has had with clear communication.
   b. In addition, the way he interprets and structures the action of therapy from the start is the first step in introducing the family to new techniques in communication.
   c. Here is an example of how the therapist clarifies the process of interaction for a family:

   Th: (*to husband*) I notice your brow is wrinkled, Ralph. Does that mean you are angry at this moment?

   H: I did not know that my brow was wrinkled.

   Th: Sometimes a person looks or sounds in a way of which he is not aware. As far as you can tell, what were you thinking and feeling just now?

H: I was thinking over what she [his wife] said.

Th: What thing that she said were you thinking about?

H: When she said that when she was talking so loud, she wished I would tell her.

Th: What were you thinking about that?

H: I never thought about telling her. I thought she would get mad.

Th: Ah, then maybe that wrinkle meant you were puzzled because your wife was hoping you would do something and you did not know she had this hope. Do you suppose that by your wrinkled brow you were signalling that you were puzzled?

H: Yeh, I guess so.

Th: As far as you know, have you ever been in that same spot before, that is, where you were puzzled by something Alice said or did?

H: Hell, yes, lots of times.

Th: Have you ever told Alice you were puzzled when you were?

W: He never says anything.

Th: (*smiling, to Alice*) Just a minute, Alice, let me hear what Ralph's idea is of what he does. Ralph, how do you think you have let Alice know when you are puzzled?

H: I think she knows.

Th: Well, let's see. Suppose you ask Alice if she knows.

H: This is silly.

Th: (*smiling*) I suppose it might seem so in this situation, because Alice is right here and certainly has heard what your question is. She knows what it is. I have the suspicion, though, that neither you nor Alice are very sure about what the other expects, and I think you have not developed ways to find out. Alice, let's go back to when I commented on Ralph's wrinkled brow. Did you happen to notice it, too?

W: (*complaining*) Yes, he always looks like that.

Th: What kind of a message did you get from that wrinkled brow?

W: He don't want to be here. He don't care. He never talks. Just looks at television or he isn't home.

Th: I'm curious. Do you mean that when Ralph has a wrinkled brow that you take this as Ralph's way of saying, "I don't love you, Alice. I don't care about you, Alice."?

W: (*exasperated and tearfully*) I don't know.

Th: Well, maybe the two of you have not yet worked out crystal-clear ways of giving your love and value messages to each other. Everyone needs crystal-clear ways of giving their value messages. (*to son*) What do you know, Jim, about how you give your value messages to your parents?

S: I don't know what you mean.

Th: Well, how do you let your mother, for instance, know that you like her, when you are feeling that way. Everyone feels different ways at different times. When you are feeling glad your mother is around, how do you let her know?

S: I do what she tells me to do. Work and stuff.

Th: I see, so when you do your work at home, you mean this for a message to your mother that you're glad she is around.

S: Not exactly.

Th: You mean you are giving a different message then. Well, Alice, did you take this message from Jim to be a love message? (*to Jim*) What do you do to give your father a message that you like him?

S: (*after a pause*) I can't think of nothin'.

Th: Let me put it another way. What do you know crystal-clear that you could do that would bring a smile to your father's face?

S: I could get better grades in school.

Th: Let's check this out and see if you are perceiving clearly. Do you, Alice, get a love message from Jim when he works around the house?

W: I s'pose—he doesn't do very much.

Th: So from where you sit, Alice, you don't get many love messages from Jim. Tell me, Alice, does Jim have any other ways that he might not now be thinking about that he has that say to you that he is glad you are around?

W: (*softly*) The other day he told me I looked nice.

Th: What about you, Ralph; does Jim perceive correctly that if he got better grades you would smile?

H: I don't imagine I will be smiling for some time.

Th: I hear that you don't think he is getting good grades, but would you smile if he did?

H: Sure, hell, I would be glad.

Th: As you think about it, how do you suppose you would show it?

W: You never know if you ever please him.

Th: We have already discovered that you and Ralph have not yet developed crystal-clear ways of showing value feelings toward one another. Maybe you, Alice, are now observing this between Jim and Ralph. What do you think, Ralph? Do you suppose it would be hard for Jim to find out when he has pleased you?

14. The therapist will not only exemplify what he means by clear communication, but he will teach his patients how to achieve it themselves.

    a. He will spell out the rules for communication accurately. In particular, he will emphasize the necessity for checking out meaning *given* with meaning *received*. He will see that the patient keeps in mind the following complicated set of mirror images:
    —Self's idea (how I see me).
    —Self's idea of other (how I see you).
    —Self's idea of other's idea of self (how I see you seeing me).
    —Self's idea of other's idea of self's idea of other (how I see you seeing me seeing you).

Only if a person is able to check back and forth across the lines of communication, can he be sure that he has completed a clear exchange.

b. The therapist will help the patient to be aware of messages that are incongruent, confused or covert.

c. At the same time, the therapist will show the patient how to check on invalid assumptions that are used as fact. He knows that members of dysfunctional families are afraid to question each other to find out what each really means. They seem to say to each other: "I can't let you know what I see and hear and think and feel or you will drop dead, attack or desert me." As a result, each operates from his assumptions, which he takes from the other person's manifestations and thereupon treats as fact. The therapist uses various questions to ferret out these invalid assumptions, such as:

"What did you say? What did you hear me say?"

"What did you see or hear that led you to make that conclusion?"

"What message did you intend to get across?"

"If I had been there, what would I have seen or heard?"

"How do you know? How can you find out?"

"You look calm, but how do you feel in the stomach?"

d. Like any good teacher, the therapist will try to be crystal-clear.
—He will repeat, restate and emphasize his own observations, sometimes to the point of seeming repetitious and simple. He will do the same with observations made by members of the family.
—He will also be careful to give his reasons for arriving at any conclusion. If the patient is baffled by some statement of the therapist's and does not know the reasoning behind it, this will only increase his feelings of powerlessness.

15. The therapist will be aware of the many possibilities of interaction in therapy.

a. In the therapeutic situation, the presence of the therapist adds as many dyads (two-person systems) as there are people in the family, since he relates to each member. The therapist, like the other people present, operates as a member of various dyads but also as the observer of other dyads. These shifts of position could be confusing to him and to the family. If, for example, he has taken someone's part, he should clearly state he is doing so.

b. The therapist clarifies the nature of interchanges made during therapy, but he has to select those that are representative since he can't possibly keep up with everything that is said. Luckily, family sequences are apt to be redundant, so one clarification may serve a number of exchanges.

c. Here is an illustration of the way the therapist isolates and underlines each exchange.

—When the therapist states, "When you, Ralph, said you were angry, I noticed that you, Alice, had a frown on your face," this is an example of the therapist reporting himself as a monad ("I *see* you, Alice; I *hear* you, Ralph"), and reporting to Ralph and Alice as monads (the use of the word *you*, followed by the specific name). Then, by the therapist's use of the word *when*, he establishes that there is a connection between the husband's report and the wife's report, thus validating the presence of an interaction.

—If the therapist then turns to the oldest son, Jim, and says, "What do you, Jim, make of what just happened between your mother and father?" the therapist is establishing Jim as an observer, since family members may forget that they monitor each other's behavior.

—When Jim answers, everyone knows what his perception is. If it turns out that Jim's report does not fit what either Alice or Ralph intended, then there is an opportunity to find out what was intended, what was picked up by Jim, and why he interpreted it that way.

16. Labeling an illness is a part of therapy that a therapist must approach with particular care.

a. A therapist, when he deals with a patient, is confronting a person who has been labeled by others or by himself as having emotional, physical or social disorders. To the non-therapeutic observer, the behavior which signals the presence of a disorder is usually labeled "stupid," "crazy," "sick" or "bad."

b. The therapist will use other labels, like "mentally defective," "underachieving," "schizophrenic," "manic-depressive," "psychosomatic," "sociopathic." These are labels used by clinicians to describe behavior which is seen to be deviant: deviant from the rest of the person's character, deviant from the expectations of others, and deviant from the context in which the person finds himself.

c. The observations made by clinicians over the years have been brought together under a standardized labeling system called the "psychiatric nomenclature." It is a method of shorthand used by clinicians to describe deviant behavior.

d. These labels often presuppose an exact duplication of all the individuals so labeled. Over the years, each of the labels has been given an identity, with prognosis and treatment implications based on the dimensions of that identity.

   e. If a therapist has labeled a person "schizophrenic," for instance, he may have based his prognosis of that person on his ideas about schizophrenia, rather than on an observation of a person who, among other labels like "human being," "Jim," "husband," "father," "chemist," has the label "schizophrenic."

   f. But neither the clinician or any other person has the right to treat him only in terms of the label "schizophrenic" while losing sight of him as a total human being. No label is infallible, because no diagnosis is, but by identifying the person with the label, the therapist shuts his mind to the possibility of different interpretations which different evidence might point to.

   g. The therapist must say to his patient, in effect: You are behaving now with behavior which I, as a clinician, label "schizophrenia." But this label only applies *at this time, in this place*, and *in this context*. Future times, places and contexts may show something quite different.

17. Let us close this discussion of the role of the therapist with a look at some of the specific advantages family therapy will have compared to individual or group therapy.

   a. In family therapy, the therapist will have a greater opportunity to observe objectvely. In individual therapy, since there are only two people, the therapist is part of the interaction. It is hard for him to be impartial. In addition, he must sift out the patient's own reactions and feelings from those which might be a response to clues from the therapist himself.

   b. The family therapist will be able to get firsthand knowledge of the patient in two important areas.
     —By observing the individual in his family, the therapist can see where he is in terms of his present level of growth.
     —By observing a child in the family group, the therapist can find out how his functioning came to be handicapped. He can see for himself how the husband and wife relate to each other and how they relate to the child.
     —This kind of firsthand knowledge is not possible in individual therapy, or even in group therapy, where the individual is with members of his peer group and the kind of interaction that can be studied is limited to this single aspect.

18. As a therapist, I have found certain concepts useful, somewhat like measuring tools, in determining the nature and extent of dysfunction in a family.

   a. I make an analysis of the techniques used by each member of the family for *handling the presence of different-ness*. A person's reaction to different-ness is an index to his ability to adapt to growth and change. It also indicates what attitudes he will have toward other members of his family, and whether he will be able to express these attitudes directly or not.

—The members of any family need to have ways to find out about and make room for their different-ness. This requires that each can report directly what he perceives about himself and the other, to himself and to the other.

—Example: Janet misses her hatpin. She must say, "I need my hatpin (clear), which I am telling you, Betty, about, (direct), and it is the hatpin that I use for the only black hat I have (specific)." Not: "Why don't you leave my hat alone?" or "Isn't there something you want to tell me?" or going into Betty's room and turning things upsidedown (unclear, indirect, and unspecific).

—As I have said before, when one of the partners in a marriage is confronted with a different-ness in the other that he did not expect, or that he did not know about, it is important that he treat this as an opportunity to explore and to understand rather than as a signal for war.

—If the techniques for handling different-ness are based on determining who is right (war), or pretending that the different-ness does not exist (denial), then there is a potential for pathological behavior on the part of any member of the family, but particularly the children.

b. I make what I call a *role function analysis* to find out whether the members of a family are covertly playing roles different from those which their position in the family demands that they play.

—If two people have entered a marriage with the hope of extending the self, each is in effect put in charge of the other, thus creating a kind of mutual parasitic relationship.

—This relationship will eventually be translated into something that looks like a parent-child relationship. The adults, labeled "husband" and "wife," may in reality be functioning as mother and son, father and daughter, or as siblings, to the confusion of the rest of the family and, ultimately, themselves.

—Here is an oversimplified example of the way things might go in such a family:

Suppose Mary takes over the role of sole parent, with Joe acting the part of her child. Joe then takes the part of a brother to their two children, John and Patty, and becomes a rival with them for their mother's affections. To handle his rivalry and prove his place, he may start drinking excessively, or he may bury himself in his work in order to avoid coming home. Mary, deserted, may turn to John in such a way as to make him feel he must take his father's place. Wishing to do so but in reality unable to, John may become delinquent, turning against his mother and choosing someone on the outside. Or he may accept his mother's invitation, which would be to give up being male and become homosexual. Patty may regress or remain infantile to keep her place. Joe may get ulcers. Mary may become psychotic.

—These are only some of the possibilities for disturbance in a family that has become dislocated by incongruent role-playing.

c. I make a *self-manifestation analysis* for each member of a family. If what a person says does not fit with the way he looks, sounds and acts, or if he reports his wishes and feelings as belonging to someone else or as coming from somewhere else, I know that he will not be able to produce reliable clues for any other person interacting with him. When such behavior, which I call *"manifesting incongruency,"* is present in the members of a family to any large degree, there will be a potential for development of pathology.

d. In order to find out how the early life of each member of a family has affected his present ways of behaving, I make what I call a *model analysis.*

—This means that I try to discover who the models were (or are) that influenced each family member in his early life; who gave him messages about the presence and desirability of growth; who gave him the blueprint from which he learned to evaluate and act on new experience; who showed him how to become close to others.

—Because these messages have survival significance, the ways in which they are given will automatically determine the way the individual interprets later messages from other adults, who may not be survival-connected but who may be invested with survival significance, like spouses, in-laws or bosses.*

19. The ideas in this chapter have been discussed out of the context of ongoing therapy, where they belong. In the next chapter, I hope to show more specifically how I, as a therapist, incorporate them into the action of therapy.

REFERENCES

Watzlawick, P. *An anthology of human communication.* Palo Alto, Calif.: Science and Behavior Books, 1964.

---

*While there are obvious connections between this theory and both the analytic concept of transference and the Sullivanian concept of parataxic distortion, there are also differences. In particular, instead of inferring from the transference the probable nature of the individual's early environment, I use the information about his past to evaluate the survival significance of his current messages.

CHAPTER 19

Techniques of Conjoint
Family Therapy

Virginia Satir

1. The therapist must first create a setting in which people can, perhaps for the first time, take the risk of looking clearly and objectively at themselves and their actions.

   a. He must concentrate on giving them confidence, reducing their fears, and making them comfortable and hopeful about the therapy process.
   b. He must show that he has direction, that he is going somewhere. His patients come to him because he is an expert, so he must accept the label and be comfortable in his role.
   c. Above all, he must show patients that he can structure his questions in order to find out what both he and they need to know.

2. The patient is afraid. He doesn't dare ask about what he doesn't know; he feels little, alone, and frightened.

   a. He suffers from the Crystal Ball Syndrome: "I'm supposed to know. But I am little and can't ask. Yet I am big and omniscient; I can guess. You, the therapist, should be able to guess too."
   b. He suffers from the Fragility Syndrome: "If I ask, the other person will fall apart. If I ask, I will get an answer that will make *me* fall apart."
   c. He suffers from Fear of the Unknown. Pieces of the past are missing or can't be looked at. This or that is forbidden territory.
   d. He doesn't know what it is he doesn't know; he feels hopeless. He has been operating from insufficient information for a long time. He feels that there is no point in continuing the struggle.
   e. He can't ask about what he doesn't know; he feels helpless. Sick people can't be direct about what they want. They can tell about what hurts, not about what is wrong.

Reprinted with permission of the author and the publisher from Virginia Satir, *Conjoint Family Therapy* (rev. ed). Palo Alto, Calif.: Science and Behavior Books, 1967.

f. He fears that therapist will lie to him; he feels suspicious. He assumes that others know and won't tell; that others see and hear everything. ("Ma always knew when I was in the cookie jar. So others know what is inside of me.")

3. The therapist is not afraid.

   a. He does dare to ask questions, and the way he frames them helps the patient to be less afraid as well.
      —The therapist asks what the patient can answer, so that the patient feels competent and productive.
      —The therapist engages the patient in a history-taking procedure to bring out details of family life. This makes the patient feel he knows things the therapist doesn't know, that he has something to contribute. (Patients get very involved in building this factual history of their own past. They argue with each other about the facts, correct the therapist, and so forth.)
      —The therapist asks questions which the patient can emotionally handle at the time, so the patient can feel he is in control.
   b. The therapist doesn't know what it is he doesn't know, but he knows how to find out and how to check on his knowledge.
      —The therapist does not assume anything. He must not think he knows more than he does. All he can assume is that there is a body before him; it is breathing; it is a male or a female of certain age.
      —If the therapist operates from assumptions without checking on them, he is often wrong. He must question his patients constantly:

      "Does she like being beaten, or not?"

      "Did they ever get to the movies?"

      "What does 'Well, sort of' mean?"

      —He must question his own assumptions too. Does their coming late to the appointment mean they are "resisting" or not? (There is a story about a man accused by the therapist of "resisting" therapy because he arrived late for the therapy hour. Later the therapist discovered the man had been held up by a serious accident on the freeway.)
   c. The therapist can ask about what he doesn't know; he knows how to get facts.
      —Facts about planning processes: "Did you get to the movies as you planned?" or, "Did you ever get the bread on the table?"
      —Facts which reveal loopholes in planning. For instance, the mother complains that her children don't do chores. The therapist finds by questioning that she never tells them what to do; all the instructions are in her head.

—Facts about perceptions of self and other: "How did you expect he would react?" or, "What did you assume she thought?"

—Facts about perceptions of roles and models: "Who does what in your house?" or, "How did your dad handle money?"

—Facts about communication techniques:

"You weren't sure what he meant? What was it about his behavior that made you uncertain?"

"What did you say to him? What did you say back to her?"

"Did the words coming out of his mouth match the look on his face?"

"Did you try to get your point across? How? Then what did you do?"

—Facts about how members express sexual feelings and act out. The therapist doesn't give double-level messages to patients to the effect that he really wants to hear about these subjects more than any other. His questions concern everyday living, *including* sex activities and periods of acting out. When discussing sexual material, the therapist does so in an open, concrete, matter-of-fact way. He treats this subject like any other. He says: "What way is it?" not, "Who is to blame?"; "How does that go?" not, "Why don't you respond?"

d. The therapist does not fear the patient is lying to him; he is not suspicious. He realizes the patient is not deliberately withholding information or misrepresenting it. He is responding to a vague fear of blame and low self-worth.

4. The therapist shows the patient how he looks to others.

a. The therapist rises above the cultural prohibition against telling others how they manifest themselves:

"Your nose is bleeding."

"Your slip is showing."

"You seem to want to be friends with him but you don't act the way you say you feel."

"You seem to want to succeed but you act as though you might be afraid to try."

b. The therapist realizes that people are grateful to be told how they manifest themselves.

"We all need three-way mirrors. Yet we assume that others see in us what we feel we are manifesting."

"We can give information if we do it in such a tone that our good will is clear. Clarity of intent gets across if our words, face, tone of voice, are all of a piece."

But such information must also be given in an appropriate context, in an appropriate relationship. The telling must not be overdone, and good things must be told too. For example, a husband had a glob of something on his shoe. He and his wife sat through a whole therapy session with me. Finally the wife mentioned it to her husband. He asked her why she hadn't told him, and she said she didn't want to embarrass him or hurt him. Also, she thought he knew about it. He was angry that she hadn't told him. Even though the news we get from others may be uncomfortable, we prefer that to not knowing the impression we give.

c. The therapist can also put the tape recorder to good use. Playing back tapes of previous conversations (which were openly recorded, of course) can be a good way of showing people how they sound and look to others, as well as making it easier for patient and therapist to study the interactions of therapy. In addition, the positive moves of patients can be pointed out to them while playing back tapes.

5. When the therapist asks for and gives information, he does so in a matter-of-fact, nonjudgmental, light, congruent way.

a. The therapist verbally recreates situations in order to collect facts. He has a flair for acceptance and imagination:

Th: Now let me see. There was no bread. What did you do for bread that night?

W: Well, we didn't have any.

Th: Well, then you didn't get enough to eat. Now let's take a look at what you were trying to do. You wanted food on the table and it wasn't there. And you thought Harry was going to bring it. Your husband is telling you that you don't keep him informed, and you are telling him he doesn't care what happens in the house, what happens to you. Let's see where this all started. Here you are, Harry, coming in the door wondering if dinner's cooked. And your wife is thinking, "We don't have any bread . . ."

b. By showing he is easy about giving and receiving information, the therapist makes it easier for the patient to do so.
   —I can ask—so can you.
   —I can give information—so can you.
   —I can receive information—so can you.

—I can give a clear message—so can you.

(But the therapist must beware of the inappropriate light touch. One time a trainee-therapist sat with a smile on her face while a patient was telling her about very painful material. The trainee's consultant-observer pointed this out to her after the session was over. She was unaware that she was doing this, and said she guessed she always smiled when things were painful to cover up what she was feeling inside. The therapist must be congruent in his behavior.)

6. The therapist builds self-esteem.

   a. The therapist makes constant "I value you" comments along the way:

      "You're a responsible person."

      "You have feelings too, you know."

      "You can want things for yourself, can't you?"

   b. The therapist labels assets. The patient is like a grocery store after an earthquake, with unlabeled goods lying all around. The therapist takes a tally for the patient; what is in stock, how it might be sold. The therapist says:

      "You showed you could do that quite well."

      "You never allowed yourself to develop that, did you?"

   c. The therapist asks the patient questions he can answer.
   d. The therapist emphasizes that he and his patients are equals in learning.
     —By asking questions, he tells his patients: "You contribute to what I know." (Family members check each other on facts and this should be encouraged.)
     —He admits that he can make mistakes: "I goofed on that. I'm sorry," or, "I forgot. It was careless of me. I should have remembered."
     —By his actions, he tells his patients, "I share what I know." The therapist shares as much of his assumptions and knowledge as he can, but at the right time and in an appropriate manner.
   e. The therapist includes himself as a person whose meaning can be checked on: "I will try to be perfectly clear. You check me if you don't follow me."
   f. The therapist takes the family's history and notes past achievements.
   g. The therapist begins to accentuate the idea of good intentions but bad communication:

"I think Mother and Dad very much want to get across their messages, but somehow something seems to stand in their way."

"In this family I see everyone wanting to report on what they see and hear and on what they wish for, but somehow behaving as though others won't hear."

"There is no lack of good intentions, good wishes in this family. But somehow everyone seems to have trouble making these wishes clear."

"I don't think for a minute that anyone in this family wants to give pain to others. But when comments are made, they always seem to come out in the form of accusations."

"Why is it that members of this family don't seem able to give open reports to each other on what they see and hear?"

h. The therapist asks each family member what he can do that brings pleasure to another member:

"What can you do, Joe, that you know ahead of time will bring pleasure to Mary?" (and vice versa)

"What can you do, Johnny, that will bring big smiles to Mother's face?"

By these questions the therapist not only further delineates family rules, but he helps each member to see himself as others see him. Maybe Johnny says (about his father): "I can't do anything to please him." Maybe Joe says (about what he thinks his wife wants of him): "Just bring in the money." Maybe Mary says (about what Joe wants of her): "Just keep him fed."

i. The therapist is human, clear, direct. Love is not enough. The therapist works for maximum adaptability by helping the family to feel they are likeable. He raises their capacity to give and minimizes their sensitivities to painful subjects, thereby decreasing the necessity for defenses.

7. The therapist decreases threat by setting the rules of interaction.

a. The therapist sees to it that all are present: "We need your reaction, experience, on this," or, "Only you can tell us what you saw and heard."

b. He makes it clear that no one is to interrupt others:

"You're all talking at once. I can't hear."

"I guess Johnny will have to speak for five minutes, then Patty can speak for five minutes."

"You're hurting my eardrums."

c. He emphasizes that no one may act out or make it impossible to converse during the session:

"I have to hear in order to do my work."

"You got your point across. Now let's get to work."

"No wonder you have not been able to work this out. Nobody is listening to anybody else."

"Now I know how deeply you feel about this. There's no further need to show me."

"When you can talk in an adult manner, then come back and we'll get to work. Until then we will have to terminate therapy."

d. He makes sure that no one is allowed to speak for anybody else:

"When you speak, speak for yourself only."

"Let Johnny speak for himself. You can't be an authority on Johnny."

"Have you ever crawled inside another's skin and looked at a thought? You can't do it. Neither can I. We have to check."

"You can collect evidence on his behavior and on what he says and see if they fit. You can then ask about it. But only he can explain why his messages didn't fit."

"Did you ever *ask* what he meant by what he said? Or did you just guess?"

e. He tries to make everyone speak out clearly so he can be heard.

f. He makes direct requests to people to speak up:

"I'm a little deaf. Not very deaf, but a little deaf. You're going to have to speak up."

"We don't want to miss what you have to say."

"Maybe you feel that what you have to say isn't important."

g. He kids:

"Cat get your tongue?"

"Know the language?"

"You need practice in exercising that lower lip."

h. He relates silence to covert controls:

> "I saw you looking at Mother. Were you thinking she didn't want you to speak?"

> "Maybe you think if you speak you'll get clobbered."

> "We'll have to find out what makes it so unsafe to talk."

8. The therapist decreases threat by the way he structures the interviews:

a. The therapist announces that therapy is aiming toward a concrete goal and will have a definite end.

   —At the very beginning he sets boundaries: "This is not going to be an open-end process, one which may drag on indefinitely. The total number of interviews within which we shall try to work will be . . ."

   —He may also set more limited deadlines: "At the end of five sessions, we shall re-evaluate to see what has been accomplished, where we need to go."

b. The therapist plans the interviews so that the family will understand that he sees them as a *family* and is not taking anyone's side.

   —He may begin therapy by seeing the two mates, the "architects" of the family, or he may see the whole family together. But whenever he starts with a new family, he wants to see them all together at least once, even when the children are too young to enter therapy, in order to understand the operation of the family and what each person's place in it is.

   —He never sees the I. P.* and his parents alone, as this would only reinforce the common assumption that the I. P. is the root of the family's trouble.

   —He never sees any unit other than the parents alone before he and the family are clear on the whole family's way of operating. Doing so before this understanding is reached may make the therapist appear to be in a coalition with certain family members, or getting privileged data which may be kept from other members. The therapist must guard against any actions which might be taken by the family as a message about "who is to blame," "who is loved most," "who is sick," etc.

   —After the operation of the family is made explicit to the therapist and the family, he can see individuals on a basis understood by everyone to pertain to some work relating to a marital pair, an individual, the sibling unit, and so forth.

   —The therapist singles out units when it seems practical or feasible. Sometimes family members are away for business or camp and seeing the separated units comes about naturally. If he sees anyone separately, it is always with the idea of reporting back to the family group what he and they have "discovered."

_____
*Identified Patient.

9. The therapist decreases threat by reducing the need for defenses.

   a. In my opinion, the dysfunctional family operates within a reign of terror, with all members fearing they will be hurt and all members fearing they will hurt others. All comments are taken as attacks on self-esteem. Therefore, the therapist must reduce terror. Defenses, as I see them, are simply ways of enhancing self-esteem and defending against attacks on self-esteem. So the therapist does not have to "destroy" defenses in order to produce change. He exerts all his efforts to reducing terror, reducing the necessity for defenses.

   b. The therapist asks each family member what he can do that brings anger from another member:

   > "What can you do which you know, as sure as sure, will make Dad blow his cork?"

   > "What can you do, Mary, that will make Joe especially mad?"

   Such questions further delineate family rules and prohibitions. They help family members make covert rules overt. They also continue to decrease fears about showing anger.

   c. The therapist interprets anger as hurt:

   > "Well, as far as I am concerned, when a person looks angry, this simply means he feels pain inside. In some way he feels his self-esteem is in danger."

   > "We will have to work out ways so that you can all give clear messages without feeling you will hurt other people's feelings."

   > "Dad may look angry but he is really feeling some kind of pain and hurt. He will have to give a clearer message about his pain, so that others will know what is going on inside him."

   d. The therapist acknowledges anger as a defense and deals with the hurt:

   > H: It's all I can do to keep from killing you!

   > W: You're a mean old man!

   > Th: Now I know how deeply disappointed you both are. Things have turned out so differently from what you hoped. Let's see what happened which has prevented the two of you from having joy and pleasure in your lives.

   e. The therapist shows that pain and the forbidden are all right to look at:

"Did you see your parents' pain? Were you able to relieve it?"

"So your dad had a wooden leg. You couldn't talk about that, could you? That was painful for your family to talk about. Why?"

"So Roger was adopted. Did you know this, Roger? What did Mother tell you about it? Why weren't you able, Mother, to tell Roger this?"

f. The therapist burlesques basic fears in the family:

"Mother and Dad won't drop dead if you simply comment on what you see and hear."

"You must think that Mother and Dad are pretty fragile creatures. They look like pretty strong people to me."

"You seem to act, Mary, as if Joe will fall apart if you simply report on what you have observed."

By burlesquing, or by painting the picture ad absurdum, the therapist helps decrease overprotective feelings and feelings of omnipotence, thus further reducing the need for defenses.

10. The therapist decreases threat by handling loaded material with care.

a. He handles loaded material by careful timing, going from least-loaded to most-loaded.
 —He goes from a history of the past, how couples first met, what they saw in each other, to the present interaction.
 —He starts with a discussion about the parents of origin and leads on to a discussion about the present parents.
 —The timing of questions is done by the order in which they are asked during the history-taking:

"What did your parents do for fun?"

"How were your parents different from each other?"

"Were your parents able to disagree?"

"How did your parents disagree?"

"What do *you* do for fun?" etc.

b. The therapist switches to less loaded material when things get hot.
 —To one subject rather than another (this depends on what in the family is the most loaded material).
 —To the past rather than the present: "How did money-handling go in your family when you were a kid?"

c. The therapist handles loaded material by generalizing what one expects to see in families:

> "It is not unusual for families to hurt, have pain, have problems, fight."

> "When one person in a family is hurting (or angry, or frightened) all are feeling the same way."

> "When one person in a family is hurting, all share a responsibility in that hurt."

d. The therapist handles loaded material by relating feelings to facts.
—He asks for specificity, examples, documentation: "He beats you sometimes? How often?" or, "He sort of cheats? What do you mean?"
—He asks about data that patients use to support their perceptions: "How do you know she doesn't care what you do?" or, "What does he do that makes you feel he is mean?"
—But he does not ignore the real things to which patients are responding. He must be careful not to analyze a perception without checking it out against reality.
—Neither does he wallow in feeling or allow others to do so. He must also keep from analyzing feelings separate from the context of interaction.

e. He handles loaded material by using his own personal idiom.
—He uses slang: "Dad hit the ceiling then, huh?" or, "I guess the fur flew then."
—He uses profanity, vulgarity: "All right. So he acted like a bastard that time," or, "You must have been mad as hell."
—He avoids pedantic words and psychiatric jargon. He uses "self-esteem" instead of "poor sex identity"; "count" and "valued" instead of "acceptable"; "lovable" instead of "loved," etc.

f. He handles loaded material by translating hostile behavior and feelings:

> "So you felt unlovable."

> "So you felt attacked."

> "So what came out of your mouth didn't match the pain inside. How come?"

g. He handles loaded material by preventing closure on episodes and complaints (besides, he often has insufficient data from which to evaluate what feelings are about): "As we go along this will become clearer," or, "We can learn more about that."

11. Let us now move forward to seeing how the therapist re-educates patients for adulthood, for accountability.

a. The patient constantly gives clues that he does not feel accountable:

> "I can't do it." (I am little, insignificant.)

> "They won't let me do it." (Others are bigger than I am. I am a
> victim.)

> "You made me do it." (I fix accountability in you.)

> "Yes, I do it, but can't help it. I don't know why." (I fix
> accountability inside me, but I am not related to myself.)

> "I did it because I was drunk (amnesic, crazy)." (I was not
> me.)

> "I didn't mean to do it." (I was not me.)

> "I did it because I love you." (Blackmail Syndrome.)

b. The therapist uses certain techniques for restoring the patient's
feeling of accountability.
—He reminds the patient of his ability to be in charge of himself:

> "Who eats for you?"

> "Who goes to the toilet for you?"

> "You can decide, you know."

> "You don't have to rob yourself, you know." (To a patient
> who wants to quit school.)

> "How did it happen, if you didn't mean to do it?"

> "Others can't see your inside wish. They can only see the
> outward behavior which gives a clue to the wish. You have to
> make your wishes clear."

> "You invested that person with authority over you. Why did
> you give your authority away?"

> "You made an agreement with him that he would control you.
> Does this have to go on?"

> "What stands between you and your ability to control Mary?"

—The therapist checks back always on pronouns to see who did
what to whom. Schizophrenics, for instance, never say exactly
who did what. They say: "Children shouldn't do such and such."
The therapist pins the patient down: "You mean Johnnie?" The
therapist makes the patient's covert accusations overt so that
they can be dealt with and so that he can check if the pronouns
are accurately placed.
—The therapist deals with tattletalers:

S:　(*to mother*) I'm going to tell on you.

Th:　Now I think you want to get Ma in trouble. Does this happen at home? How come you parents are in a position where your kids can get one of you in trouble?

* * * * * * *

M:　My husband drinks.

Th:　(*turns attention to what wife can report on herself*) Do *you* drink?

* * * * * * *

D:　(*discrepancy watcher*) He gets ten cents. I only get five cents.

Th:　You want to make sure you get your share of things. That you don't get robbed or left out.

　　—The therapist deals with spokesmen:

　　　"How does it happen that you have to be a spokesman for Johnny? He can speak for himself. Let's ask him about this."

　　　"Does this go on at home? People speaking for other people? How do you suppose this came to be?"

　　—The therapist deals with acting-out of children. He doesn't turn to the parents; he asks the child, "How come?" He reminds the child that he has a choice about his behavior. He isn't a victim. He can influence his environment.
c. The patient-therapist relationship itself highlights problems of accountability.
　　—The patient behaves in a certain way. He acts as if he is stuck with that behavior, can't help it. If the therapist, too, treats this behavior as separate from the person, he is saying to the patient, "I expect you to have no controls." So he highlights the behavior as belonging to the person, and he sets up behavior treatment goals.
　　—The patient expects the therapist to be a great white father or mother from whom all things flow. He expects the therapist to take charge. The therapist does take charge, but does not treat the patient like a child or expect him to behave like one. He treats the patient like an adult and expects him to behave like an adult. He does not violate the adult label.

—The therapist is not indispensable to the patient, though he may need to think he is. He is not like the parent of the schizophrenic who says: "You can't feed yourself. You need me to live." So he doesn't give to patients in a "feeding" and "draining" kind of way. He only makes it possible for them to give to themselves and get from other family members.

12. The therapist helps the patient to see how past models influence his expectations and behavior.

   a. He reminds patients that they are acting from past models:

   "I would expect you to be worried about that. As you said, your dad never..."

   "Your mother handled money that way. How *could* you have learned other ways?"

   "Now it sounds to me as if you are giving the same kind of message to him that you saw your mother give to your dad. Yet you didn't like the way your mother and father handled things and are struggling hard to do it differently. Let's see what may be standing in your way."

   b. The therapist openly challenges expectations: "Do you really believe that all children should be beholden to their parents?"
   c. The therapist reminds patients that they married each other for the very qualities about which they are now complaining. "Now this is what you said you liked about your wife. I wonder why you don't like it now?"
   d. The therapist highlights expectations by completing communication:

   Th: (*to Johnny*) Do you like spinach?

   S: No.

   Th: Did you know your mother thought you did like spinach?

   S: No, but I didn't want to hurt her feelings.

   Th: (*to mother*) Did you ever ask him if he liked spinach?

   M: No, I thought all men did. Pa did.

   e. The therapist highlights expectations by exaggerating them: "*Your* Pa did it, so *naturally* all men do it!"

13. The therapist delineates roles and functions.

    a. The therapist recognizes roles himself, in addressing and treating a family.
    —He calls couples "Mother" and "Dad" when referring to them as parents and by their first names when referring to them as individuals or as husband and wife.
    —In history-taking, the therapist includes members in a relevant order. He takes the father first, as head of the house, and next, the mother. He then takes the oldest sib first, saying to the younger ones: "Wait a minute. You haven't arrived yet. You haven't been born!"

    b. The therapist questions patients about their roles:

> "You wear three hats—individual, marital, parental. I can see the parental, but where are the other two?"

> "Before marriage you were Miss So-and-So. What happened to her?"

> "Why do you have to get permission?"

> "Are you Daddy's wife?"

    c. The therapist can teach explicitly about roles. He lists three roles on the blackboard: individual, marital, parental. He does this so that patients will see that they have a choice as to how they will treat each other. If the therapist makes patients aware of how they are responding and shows them other ways to respond, they can then choose among these ways. Creativity in living is having a wider choice of alternatives.

14. The therapist completes gaps in communication and interprets messages.

    a. The therapist separates the relationship part of a message from its content. Patients usually confuse the two and talk about relationships in "content" terms:
    —"This coffee is no good" is a patient's way of saying, "You are no good."
    —"Glasses get dirty" is a schizophrenic's way of saying, "You can't see straight."

    b. The therapist separates comments about the self from comments about others. Patients usually confuse the two, and can't figure out which part of an interchange tells them something about the speaker and which part is addressed to them.
    —"I'm tired" can be a statement about the speaker's fatigue. It can also be a question: "You too?" It can also be a request: "Help me!"

—So when the patient tells the therapist what B said, the therapist asks what the patient got out of B's message.

c. The therapist points out significant discrepancies in communication:

F: I feel fine.

Th: You look awful. How come you say you feel fine when you look awful. Can't you allow yourself to feel like hell?

* * * * * * *

F: (*to child, whose symptom is related to the father's delinquent behavior*) Be good and I'll be back soon.

Th: (*to father*) I think there were two parts to that message which perhaps confused her. You said to be good very loud and clear, but you did not tell her where you were going and when you would be back. Did the second message come through equally loud and clear?

d. The therapist spells out nonverbal communication:

Th: (*to Johnny*) You looked to your mother first, before answering. I wonder if you feel you have to get permission to speak.

Th: (*To Patty, who takes her father's hand during an argument between her mother and father*) Are you telling your dad that you sympathize with him?

* * * * * * *

Th: (*in reference to seating pattern*) You all act as though you would like to get as far away from him [me, her] as possible.

e. The therapist spells out "double-level" messages:

D: (*to mother*) May I go to school?

M: (*to daughter*) When I was a little girl, I never had an education.

Th: (*to mother*) Now your daughter asked you if she could go to school and I'm wondering if she got an answer from you. Should she go to school or shouldn't she?

15. In general, here are my criteria for terminating treatment.

    a. Treatment is completed:
      —When family members can complete transactions, check, ask.
      —When they can interpret hostility.
      —When they can see how others see them.
      —When they can see how they see themselves.
      —When one member can tell another how he manifests himself.
      —When one member can tell another what he hopes, fears, and expects from him.
      —When they can disagree.
      —When they can make choices.
      —When they can learn through practice.
      —When they can free themselves from harmful effects of past models.
      —When they can give a clear message, that is, be congruent in their behavior, with a minimum of difference between feelings and communication, and with a minimum of hidden messages.

    b. Another set of criteria for terminating treatment is when the adult male and female as husband and wife can:
      —*Be direct*, using the first person "I" and following with statements or questions which:

Criticize	Find fault
Evaluate	Report annoyance
Acknowledge an observation	Identify being puzzled

      —*Be delineated*, by using language which clearly shows "I am me" and "You are you." "I am separate and apart from you and I acknowledge my own attributes as belonging to me. You are you, separate and apart from me, and I acknowledge your attributes as belonging to you."
      —*Be clear*, by using questions and statements which reflect directness and the capacity to get knowledge of someone else's statements, directions, or intentions, in order to accomplish an outcome.

    c. In short, treatment is completed when everyone in the therapy setting can use the first person "I" followed by an active verb and ending with a direct object.

CHAPTER 20

Communication Theory in Marriage Counseling: A Critique

Ben N. Ard, Jr.

Faulty communication (frequently, lack of communication) would seem to be one of the major reasons why so many families do not function at their optimal level. Counseling with married couples, as well as with parents and children, has led many people in the various helping professions to the general conclusion that lack of effective communication lies at the root of many a family's problems (cf. Ruesch & Bateson, 1951; Satir, 1964; Watzlawick, Beavin, & Jackson, 1967). Thus faulty communication can justifiably be labeled "the rock on which families founder."

By communication I mean any messages conveyed in whatever way from one person to another. Communication does not refer, thus, to verbal, explicit, and intentional transmission of messages alone; the concept of communication is intended to cover here, as in other discussions in the field (cf. Ruesch & Bateson, 1951, pp. 5–6), all those processes by which people influence one another—verbal and nonverbal, explicit and implicit, clear and unclear, intentional and unintentional, aware and unaware, pathological and healthy.

There would seem to be little doubt that communication difficulties lie at the heart of many a family's problems. Most workers in the helping professions could probably agree on this basic point. Where disagreements might begin to appear, however, is on how professionals can best be of help in working with families with problems.

What communication problems (quarrels, for example) frequently turn out to be are disagreements about the nature of the relationship involved, rather than conflicts over the specific content or apparent messages being communicated. As Watzlawick, Beavin, & Jackson (1967) have found,

> ... it seems that the more spontaneous and 'healthy' a relationship, the more the relationship aspect of communication recedes into the background. Conversely, "sick" relationships are characterized by a constant struggle about the nature of the relationship, with the content aspect of communication becoming less and less important [p. 52].

Presented at the National Council on Family Relations' annual conference, August 17, 1967, at the San Francisco Hilton Hotel.

Communication difficulties in families frequently began before the family in question was even a functioning unit. Communication gets off to a bad start during the dating period: expectations of what each *assumes* will be the "proper" behavior of the other are rarely ever explicitly spelled out. As one moves through dating, the engagement period, and into marriage (with its marital roles and, later on, parental roles), these expectations change (often, again, without being explicitly discussed). As Don Jackson (1965) has observed,

> Couples . . . who engage in wondrously varied behavioral ploys during courtship, undoubtedly achieve considerable economy after a while in terms of what is open to dispute, and how it is to be disputed. Consequently they seem . . . to have excluded wide areas of behavior from their interactional repertoire and never quibble further about them [p. 13].

Some of this is perhaps good, but some of the results may turn out later on to be detrimental to the marriage. For example, a couple during courtship may discover that they have differences regarding their respective views and values concerning religion. But, as often happens in our culture, these religious differences may not prove very detrimental during the courtship phase. Because the girl, for example, may want so badly to get married, she may "conveniently overlook" the differences regarding religion. In an attempt to avoid facing a very touchy issue, the couple may avoid all discussion of their basic values in this area. Yet when children come along and questions must be decided about their religious training, then it is frequently too late to find out that there are basic, fundamental differences in values which cannot be resolved.

To turn to another illustration, one couple married and only later found out that they differed in a very fundamental way about race questions. He was a segregationist while she was an integrationist, and they lived in a southern town where the election of the sheriff turned on just this issue. They tried seemingly endless communication on this issue to no avail; neither could change the other. So they agreed that this subject was never to be a topic for dinner table conversation because it ruined too many dinners. In other words, they did not communicate any more about race relations. But they agreed that each had the right to go out and work for the election of his respective candidate for sheriff.

Ruesch and Bateson (1951) have maintained that the definition of a relationship depends not merely upon the skeleton of events which make up the interaction but also upon the way the individuals concerned see and interpret those events. "This seeing or interpretation can be regarded as the application of a set of propositions about the world or the self whose validity depends upon the subject's belief in them [p. 220]." For example, "if each comes to believe in the hostility of the other, that hostility is real to this extent and to the extent that each acts upon its belief [p. 222]."

But we need to avoid the phenomenological trap this sort of theorizing can lead us into, if we are to be of most help to clients with such problems. The fact that a husband feels he has justification for jealousy

does not tell us in fact whether or not the wife has done anything to
justify his jealous reaction. Feelings are not enough to base one's actions
on; one needs still to check the reality involved, not merely one's feelings.
Reality is a "bad word" to many in the helping professions today, but I
am suggesting that we counselors need to get that concept back into our
thinking, if we are to be of more effective help to clients.

With the recent emphasis on communication as the most important, if
not the key, factor in marriage counseling, joint conferences with both
partners in a marriage are sometimes thought to clear up misunderstandings stemming from lack of communication. But the joint conference can
become the means of further separating spouses instead of bringing them
together. Husband and wife may make wild accusations and say cutting
things to each other. Once these things are said in the presence of a third
party, even a professional person, they tend to become fixed and to take
on a different significance and value. A joint conference can provide an
ideal opportunity for both parties to say things to punish and hurt each
other which neither will forget because of the presence of a third party
(cf. Mudd et al, 1958, p. 52).

Much of the therapeutic help that has been heretofore offered to
families has been based (implicitly, at least) on the assumption that if
spouses can become fully aware of the communication pattern they are
caught in, this "insight" will "cure" the problem. However, even when
both spouses are evidently fully aware of their pattern, this awareness
does not help them in the least to do something about it (cf. Watzlawick
et al, 1967, p. 87). The prevailing emphasis on nondirectiveness or permissiveness has held up therapeutic progress. Clients have to be encouraged,
persuaded (even directed!) to *do* something about the pattern in which
they appear to be caught (cf. Ellis, 1966).

There is an assumption among many people in the family life field
that "there is no difficulty that enough love will not conquer." But love
alone is not enough, and will not conquer all difficulties.

An analogous assumption seems to be implied in recent communication theory, namely, that "there is no difficulty that enough communication will not conquer." But communication alone, no matter how effective, will not conquer all difficulties, either.

Improving communication, in and of itself, will not always maintain a
marriage. Too much uncritical reliance on the assumptions of recent communication theory, including this basic one, will not necessarily provide
the best therapy for husbands, wives, and families in need of help.

As an illustration of the absurd lengths to which couples can go in
non-communication, one married couple I know have eaten steaks cooked
rare for many years—each spouse *assuming*, without checking, that the
other preferred his steak cooked that way. Frequently where there is lack
of communication, there are *unquestioned assumptions* that need to be
looked into—in this instance the assumption that a "proper" spouse will
defer to the other and eat his food the way the other prefers. (Self-sacrifice
is a very basic unquestioned value in our middle-class culture.)

My own research study of married couples who were followed through twenty years of marriage indicated, among other things, that even those couples who maintained their marriages over twenty years had problems communicating with each other about such simple matters as their desired frequency of intercourse (Ard, 1962). The husbands consistently *under-estimated* their wives' preferred frequency of intercourse, while the wives consistently *overestimated* their husbands' preferred frequency.

Turning to relations between parents and children, there is a serious and apparently growing communication gap between generations; of late this seems to be particularly so regarding drugs and sex. Many young people seem to be operating on the unquestioned principle of protecting their parents from uncomfortable truths (i.e., truths which the youth assume would make their parents uncomfortable). This principle of protecting others from uncomfortable truths, whether it be between parents and children or between spouses, is a very shaky basis on which to maintain an effective relationship.

The unquestioned assumption underlying much of this "spare the parents uncomfortable truths" sort of thinking is the middle-class cultural premise that we should bend over backwards never to "hurt" those who love us or gave birth to us. But to hide behind that "honor thy father and mother" bit and on that basis to refuse ever to discuss our basic differences with our parents or children surely is self-defeating.

When a parent who has not resolved all of his own sexual problems suspects his youngsters of having sexual thoughts or indulging in sexual behavior which he defines as "sinful," it frequently arouses too many anxious feelings which he may try to pacify (often unknowingly) by clamping down tighter controls on the young, or by blindly denying the evidence before his eyes of his youngsters' sexual maturity (Ard, 1967a).

As a further commentary on the sad state of communication within American marriages, I would like to relate the reaction to a recent paper I presented at a conference on "Teen-age Marriage and Divorce" (Ard, 1967b). I suggested many things, but the one thing all the newspapers picked up was one suggestion to the teenage husband, to wit: "Now that you have married the girl, try to make friends with her." I was only suggesting that too many young men marry girls with whom they are passionately involved but with whom they are not really friends.

This evidently startling idea was picked up out of all the other things that were said and played up by editors and headline writers across the nation. The attention this idea received is a commentary upon either the editors and headline writers and/or the sad state of communication in our American marriages.

Much of the recent interest in communication theory has, understandably, emphasized verbal communication. But *nonverbal* communication needs attention as well, for several reasons. For one thing in early childhood the primary tools of communication are nonverbal. Long before a child communicates verbally, he functions on the basis of communication skills which are chiefly nonverbal. Much of the most significant communication throughout life remains at a nonverbal level. Too much of what in the past has been assumed to be "intuition" or some "sixth sense" has really been just very perceptive nonverbal communication. Sherlock Holmes can teach us more in this regard than a passel of mystical seers.

Perhaps an illustration of how nonverbal communication works would clarify matters here. If a wife notices a pained expression flicker across her husband's face during dinner table conversation, she might assume that he was expressing (nonverbally) a negative reaction to the topic or situation being discussed. And she might be right. But there is a possible danger here, if she does not check out her assumption: her husband may merely be having gas pains. If so, she would have been "over-psychologizing," and that can get people into deeper trouble very quickly!

In the recent study of communication the emphasis has been on the *how* of interaction rather than the *why*. So we get extensive studies of "communication systems" (families?) which go into the matter as if they were studying computers, using terms such as "feedback loops" and "input-output systems." The proverbial man from Mars could observe a computer system and possibly figure out *how* it works, but he still would not know *why*, which is a different sort of question entirely. I hope research in this field of family communication, in its great surge of interest in the *how*, never forgets the importance of also asking *why* (cf. Watzlawick et al, 1967, pp. 130–131).

There seems to have developed, in recent communication theory, a tendency to "explain" pathological behavior—for example, that resulting from a double-bind pattern, where messages are paradoxically contradictory—as the *only* thing the persons involved could do. Schizophrenic behavior is all that can be expected from a child reared in a double-binding schizophrenic family, it would seem, according to the theory. The schizophrenic behavior (communication pattern) is seen as "appropriate" (cf. Watzlawick et al, 1967, pp. 212–213, 217).

This sort of theorizing would seem to be a fatal flaw, a self-defeating trap, a fatalistic determinism in the very field (counseling and psychotherapy) where the possibility of promoting better ways of responding is our only justification for existence as a profession. If the faulty communication was "all that the identified patient could do under the particular circumstances," then it would seem difficult to help him see that in the future (after counseling or psychotherapy) there would be another alternative, a better way of reacting, when in contact with schizophrenic people who do give out contradictory messages.

If families are not to founder on the rock of faulty communication, they need to become more aware of their problems in communication. As Watzlawick et al (1967) have put it,

> What we can observe in virtually all these cases of pathological communication is that they are vicious circles that cannot be broken unless and until communication itself becomes the subject of communication, in other words, until the communicants are able to metacommunicate [p. 95].

We need to get family members to check their premises (cf. Branden, 1966), to question their definitions, to challenge their assumptions (cf. Ellis, 1966), and to look into the objective validity and consequences of their basic values.

Unfortunately, too much of the professional help provided for families in trouble does not seriously question the cultural premises or values which are at the base of many apparent "communication" problems. Too often the typical American counselor or therapist permits the client to make some minor movements away from the cultural premises (through the counselor's "permissiveness") but *ultimately* helps the client to *adjust to* the cultural premises. As Ruesch and Bateson (1951) have put it, "Though on the surface it looks as if the patient had moved away from the cultural premises by talking about feelings and thoughts, he is in reality finally adjusting to the surroundings in which he lives [p. 133] ." In another passage Ruesch and Bateson state that "the American therapist's aim is to socialize the patient. This is done by making the patient accept the fact that the group acts as a censor of his action [p. 167] ."

If clearing up communication problems leads to a forthright facing of value conflicts, then this is, indeed, a step in the right direction. But we must follow through if there is a difference in assumed values and get the participants to challenge and question their values, if these values are the conventional ones in our culture, which are self-defeating and largely definitional.

Because values have been seen by many in the helping professions as "off limits" (i.e., the professional is supposed to be "neutral" or not to deal with the client's values), we have avoided dealing with the basic problem underlying communication difficulties: differences in basic values (which are rarely examined or questioned, even when they are self-defeating). Ellis and Harper (1961a, 1961b) have provided some helpful suggestions on just what sort of values these frequently are in our culture, as well as some ways of helping the client eliminate his reliance upon them.

Values are even more basic than mere communication, and in a sense, logically prior to communication. If conflicts in a family are assumed to be due to a lack of communication (which is often true), or due to faulty communication (also often true), we may still be led down a blind alley by assuming that if we merely improve the communication in the family we have solved the problem. The most effective communication can lead to the break-up of a family because the basic values are ultimately in conflict. We need to get at the basic values of people in conflict, whether they be spouses or parents and children, and see if these values need to be changed or not, rather than merely going along with those conventional values that are assumed without question by most people in our culture, including the helping professions, who should know better. (cf. Maslow, 1959).

In conclusion, if families are not to founder on the rock of faulty communication, counseling and psychotherapy should get beyond merely improving communication within the family (important as that will always continue to be) and get at the basic values involved in family conflicts. Families and individuals often integrate their lives on levels that are not ultimately satisfactory but which only give the *illusion* of well-being (cf. Browning & Peters, 1966, p. 189). It is the counselor's professional responsibility to see these hidden, assumed values and to warn families and individuals of their possible consequences.

BIBLIOGRAPHY

Ard, B. Sexual behavior and attitudes of marital partners. Unpublished doctoral dissertation. Ann Arbor: University of Michigan, 1962.

Ard, B. Do as I do, be as I am: The bruising conflict. In S. M. Farber & R. H. L. Wilson (Eds.), *Sex education and the teenager*. Berkeley: Diablo Press, 1967. Pp. 78-88. (a)

Ard, B. Gray hair for the teenage father. In S. M. Farber & R. H. L. Wilson (Eds.), *Teenage marriage and divorce*. Berkeley: Diablo Press, 1967). Pp. 95-104. (b)

Branden, N. Psychotherapy and the objectivist ethics. In B. Ard (Ed.) *Counseling and psychotherapy: Classics on theories and issues*. Palo Alto: Science and Behavior Books, 1966. Pp. 251-269.

Browning, R. L., & Peters, H. J. On the philosophical neutrality of counselors. In B. Ard (Ed.), *Counseling and psychotherapy: Classics on theories and issues*. Palo Alto: Science and Behavior Books, 1966. Pp. 187-195.

Ellis, A. The essence of rational therapy. In B. Ard (Ed.), *Counseling and psychotherapy: Classics on theories and issues*. Palo Alto: Science and Behavior Books, 1966. Pp. 94-113.

Ellis, A. & Harper, R. A. *Creative marriage*. New York: Lyle Stuart, 1961. (a)

Ellis, A., & Harper, R. A. *A guide to rational living*. Englewood Cliffs, N. J.: Prentice-Hall, 1961. (b)

Jackson, D. D. The study of the family. *Family Process*, 1965, *4*, 1-20.

Maslow, A. H. (Ed.) *New knowledge in human values*. New York: Harper, 1959.

Mudd, E., et al (Eds.) *Marriage counseling: A casebook*. New York: Association Press, 1958.

Ruesch, J., & Bateson, G. *Communication*. New York: Norton, 1951.

Satir, V. *Conjoint family therapy*. Palo Alto: Science & Behavior Books, 1964.

Watzlawick, P., Beavin, J. H., Jackson, D. D. *Pragmatics of Human Communication*. New York: Norton, 1967.

Group Marriage Counseling

No man is an island, entire of itself;
Every man is a piece of the continent,
  a part of the main;
If a clod be washed away by the sea,
  Europe is the less,
as well as if a promontory were,
as well if a manor of thy friends, or
  of thine own were;
any man's death diminishes me,
because I am involved in Mankind;
and therefore never send to know
  for whom the bell tolls;
  it tolls for thee.

JOHN DONNE

In view of what appears to be a constantly increasing need for marriage counseling, and the apparent reality that there probably will never be enough competent, professionally-trained marriage and family counselors to meet this pressing need, there would seem to be an obvious point in considering group marriage counseling as one alternative to serving the growing number of people who are having difficulties with marriage.

Blinder and Kirschenbaum (a psychiatrist and a psychologist), in Chapter 21, provide a discussion of the technique of married couples group therapy and a brief review of some of the previous work in this highly valuable field.

In Chapter 22, Elsa Leichter presents her approach to the treatment of married couples groups.

The Technique of Married Couple Group Therapy

Martin G. Blinder and Martin Kirschenbaum

In the past decade, a score of papers have appeared describing the experiences of various workers in treating married couples in groups. Most have been pleased with their experiment; a few have had serious reservations.

A review of the literature by Gottlieb and Pattison (1966) revealed that most objections to the treatment of married couples, within or outside a group setting, stemmed from unnecessarily narrow commitment to psychoanalytic theory rather than from pragmatic considerations. The more operational concerns of those with an interpersonal or transactional approach—namely, that such treatments might result in either inhibition of group process by defensive pairing of the spouses in an anxious coalition against attempts at exploration of their neurotic interaction, or contrariwise, the destruction of a marriage through premature dissolution of the neurotic ties binding the couple together, intensification of neurotic acting-out, or release of quantities of long repressed hostility incompatible with conjugal living—were not borne out in practice.

Leichter (1962) found that married couple group therapy enabled the spouse to serve as an auxiliary ego, expanded "the mate's ego capacity to deal with conflictual material," reduced the spouse's investment in maintaining his partner's pathology, and loosened the pathological symbiotic ties, resulting in the emergence of the marital partners as individuals.

Hastings and Runkle (1963) found that the resolution, within the group, of marriage neuroses initially used by the couple as resistance to therapy served to open new channels of communication and paved the way for amelioration of marital conflict at home.

Gottlieb and Pattison (1966) found that the group made possible mobilization of hope for marital rehabilitation; a permissive atmosphere for open scrutiny of supposedly hidden family "secrets"; recognition of angry outbursts for poorly executed and misperceived attempts at intimacy; provision of a model for healthy and constructive disagreement via open discussion of differences between cotherapists; acceptance of a measure of personal freedom and self-determination in the spouse (individuation) in place of defensive and unhappy symbiosis ("unity

Reprinted with permission of the authors and the publisher from *Archives of General Psychiatry*, 1967, *17*, 44–52.

identity"); disruption of marital games and parataxic distortions peculiar to a couple consequent to their crossmarital projection onto other group members who refuse to respond in the expected way; exposure to, and development of, alternative and more adaptive patterns of marital interaction; replacement of irrelevant marital disputes by more direct, appropriate, and constructive means for expression of painful intrapsychic conflicts; explicit rendering of nonverbal obstructions to clarify conflict; an increase in the capacity to grasp the spouse's thoughts and feelings ("correction of manifest communication distortion"); adoption of more realistic expectations of what narcissistic gratification marriage can and cannot provide ("correction of neurotic distortion"); and finally, recognition (if not always a thorough working-through) of the multifaceted manifestations of transference. While these workers focused primarily on neuroses manifested by marital disharmony, the effects of their therapeutic techniques were profound in other areas of the patients' lives, with these areas providing an increasing portion of the grist for the group's mill.

Neubeck (1954), Perelman (1960), and Von Emde Boas (1962) are among the more enthusiastic of others who have found married couple group therapy an effective treatment modality. Blinder et al (1965) have reported encouraging experiences with groups consisting of seven to eight entire families.

RATIONALE

Marriage may be viewed as the purposeful, highly specific selection of a mate on the basis of various conscious and unconscious criteria, in the hope of gratifying the mature and neurotic needs of both partners. A marriage may be expected to disappoint its participants when many of the following exist reciprocally:

Perceptual distortions. "Mates in dysfunctional marital pairs see their spouses as they expect them to be rather than as they really are and treat them accordingly [Satir, 1965]." They may, for example, misperceive them as significant and conflictual persons in their past; they may persist in seeing their spouses in roles better fitting their own unexpressed hopes than the spouses' actual capabilities; they may attribute to their spouses many of their *own* unconscious attitudes which in turn are internalizations of important childhood figures, or they may project onto the spouses those aspects of their own personality that rebel against these introjects. All of these leave to the misperceived and unsuspecting spouse the impossible task of resolving the residua of upheavals in his partner's parental home. Because communication between the partners is faulty, neither recognizes the part his misperceptions play in the conflicts that inevitably result.

Disturbances in communication. Partners may act upon unwarranted assumptions about each other's wishes or feelings, and are then hurt when the spouse acts contrary to expectations. They fail to correct their misapprehensions because (a) it has rarely occurred to them to check them out explicitly with the spouse; (b) they lack or are afraid to use the verbal techniques with which to do so; (c) they are more comfortable altering their perceptions to fit their expectations; (d) they fail to recognize or correctly interpret crucial nonverbal cues; and (e) messages they consider universally clear are, in fact, idiosyncratic to themselves.

Frustrated dependency needs. The inevitable failure of any marital union to meet lifelong narcissistic yearnings for all-absorbing, unconditional love often is reflected in the development of psychosomatic symptoms.

This failure may also result in states of chronic, irrational anger frequently punctuated by acute episodes of rage. Such may be a woman's response to her husband's efforts to meet his own dependency needs while seemingly ignoring hers; such may be the feelings of a man whose wife's very presence threatens his independence, thereby augmenting his dependency yearnings to an intolerable degree.

There may be rejection of a spouse upon whom despised dependency feelings have been projected. This is the mechanism that may lie behind a compulsive husband's intolerance of his wife's feminine emotionality, or a "phallic" wife's denigration of her husband's "failure to be a real man."

Alcohol abuse is another common consequence of frustration of dependency needs. Typically, a husband will struggle with unacceptable, unmet dependency yearnings, which are usually kept repressed because of the threat their recognition would constitute to his sense of masculinity, but which are permitted expression through episodes of total alcoholic helplessness, a helplessness mercifully kept from clear representation in consciousness by the fact of his intoxication. The alcoholic's spouse typically defends against recognition of *her* dependency by compensatory aggressive, controlling, domineering, and militantly abstinent behavior, which provides her a reassuring semblance of strength and independence, but also serves, self-defeatingly, to force her spouse to greater alcohol abuse and a proportionately reduced capacity to meet directly her dependent needs. Convinced by her own childhood experiences that no support or security may be had from an adult relationship with a man, and offering her husband scant opportunity to persuade her otherwise, she snatches what moments she can of a sense of mature womanhood by unconsciously acting to keep her husband a child. (The alcoholism-abstinence roles are easily exchanged in a married couple; the dynamics are then sex-reversed but otherwise identical.)

Threats to adaptive defenses. A functional marriage provides each partner a measure of security he cannot readily attain alone. Partners in a dysfunctional marriage, however, often inadvertently fail to support each other's defenses against anxiety because their self-esteem is so low that each is too desperately seeking relief for himself to notice the anxiety of the other; because each is unable to distinguish between behavior that buttresses the other's security system and that which may be perceived as a threat; because of the misbelief that what is helpful to one partner can only be obtained at the expense of the other; because the anxiety felt by one partner may be so severe as to cause him to distort, misuse, reject, and in other ways disqualify, (i.e., render ineffective) the help his spouse may willingly provide; or, because the partners feel compelled to obtain security from the knowledge that each can control the other, rather than from the unifying, pleasurable process of reaching mutually satisfying goals through cooperation and a sharing of skills.

Many pathological interactional forces making for a conflictual, unhappy marriage do not necessarily jeopardize its stability; indeed, neurotic bonds may at times be stronger than healthy ones. The marriage that seriously threatens the individual security system of its participants, however, is likely to be fragmented and short-lived.

Fears of the unfamiliar. There are those for whom the unpredictable, however painful, is relatively less discomforting than the unknown, whatever hope it may hold for the future. Accordingly, these people unconsciously select marriage partners with whom they can live out the same unresolved conflicts they have known in their childhood homes, and who embody introjects of the same elements that obstructed resolution of the parental conflict. Though they secretly hope this time for a different outcome, they continue in the old, familiar, but unproductive pattern. Should their first marriage dissolve, they would more often than not recreate it with other partners selected according to the same unconscious criteria, as in the case of the woman who marries and divorces a succession of alcoholics.

Obviously, the degree to which a spouse can play into his partner's basic conflicts depends somewhat on that partner's ability to blindly project onto the spouse what he wishes to see. Nevertheless, people tend to select repetitively and with uncanny accuracy spouses who do to some extent conform, or can be pressured into conforming, to their concept of what he or she must be like. One cannot long project a round picture on a square screen. For example, a woman chooses to marry a man she hopes will *not* treat her as her father did, but she expects from past experience that he, "being a man," *will*. Often, the husband does indeed behave like her father, because she either unconsciously selects him for that reason or acts to make him conform to her expectations. She can live with him, however unhappily, because she was trained to deal with this behavior as a child, perhaps by developing somatic complaints, perhaps by acting-out, or by withdrawal. She may complain vociferously about her husband's behavior and seek treatment for her own symptoms. When therapeutic pressure is applied, however, to change the homeostatic equilibrium from the level of her expectations to the level of her hopes—to the unfamiliar— she becomes anxiously aware of how much she prefers that the marriage continue in the old way, with both partners perpetuating a pattern already present in their parental homes, and now, to a greater or lesser extent, in their own. If at first present to a lesser extent, their overreactions to each other will soon make it a greater one.

In their efforts to maintain the familiar pathological equilibrium, spouses will sabotage their partners' attempts to remove the very symptoms that appear to cause so much dissension between them, lest this clear the field for exposure of their own pathology. (The man whose wife ceases to be frigid may suddenly find himself impotent; the woman whose husband's headaches no longer confine them to the house may for the first time be confronted with the fact of her own agoraphobia.) They will see in their spouses' attempts at healthy individuation a threat to their own autonomy, and set up elaborate family rules that suppress overt expression of innocent differences. They will be intolerant of the inevitable episodes of nonpathological regression so often prerequisite to subsequent spurts of growth or change in fixed attitudes. And, of course, the spouse's entrance into therapy for treatment of "his" or "her" problems seems quite acceptable until the spouse actually begins to change, and consequently, upset the couple's neurotic equilibrium.

Thus, conflictual marriages may occur between those who appear "good matches" as well as between those who do not. If the spouses are very much alike, they may still lash out at characteristics in the other despised in themselves, or they may attempt to preserve, to the detriment of the marriage, the other's nonadaptive defenses because of the protection they afford the apparently asymptomatic mate. If they are not alike, conflict usually arises not from the differences themselves, but from the threat these pose to self-esteem and established patterns of behavior, or from efforts to force the other into a more familiar mold.

CLINICAL ILLUSTRATIONS

These five interlocking motifs coalesce into a complex of reciprocal neurotic patterns that cause marital disharmony ranging from occasional sexual failure to divorce. The example that follows is the annotated and somewhat telescoped transcript of a "simple" exchange between Mr. and Mrs. C near the start of a married couple group session. Difficult, perhaps, to assimilate outside the context of the couple's history or the flow of the group, it nevertheless illustrates how these five patterns serve as a frame of reference for the couple's every transaction.

Mrs. C's harsh, overcritical parents have left her with a chronic sense of inadequacy. She characteristically projects this punitive introject of her parents onto her husband and consistently reacts with further loss of self-esteem to that which she misperceives as originating in him, as illustrated by her reply to Mr. C's first statement.

Mr. C: The roast didn't turn out as well tonight.

Mrs. C: I spent literally hours working on dinner, and all you have to say is I'm a bad cook.

In this example Mrs. C has made an incorrect assumption about her husband's attitude—an assumption she fails to check out. In point of fact, however, she has unconsciously selected in Mr. C a man who tends to be somewhat critical, as was her father, in the hope that this time there will be a better outcome—that she will win the man's unqualified affection and approval. Thus, although he is indeed a screen for his wife's projections, Mr. C is in "reality," somewhat demanding.

Mr. C: "I *don't* think you're a bad cook, but I *do* expect you to prepare a good meal without a lot of fuss.

Mrs. C: Well, I wouldn't need to "fuss" if you came home on time once in a while instead of wasting half the night at the bar with your cronies.

Mrs. C also projects onto her husband those aspects of her own personality that secretly rebel against her punitive introjects; and so, she chastises *him* for irresponsibility—irresponsibility conceived within her own mind but attributed to her spouse. She has also expressed a dependent need for her husband's attention and, in an idiosyncratic way, a wish that things be better between them.

Mr. C perceives her remarks as an attack on the self-assertiveness he may need to ward off despised feelings of dependency engendered by contact with his wife.

> Mr. C: Maybe I get a lot more out of spending the evening with Charlie instead of coming home to this every night. If only we could have a little peace in the house.

The husband has also sent an idiosyncratic message that he wants things to be better between them, but at this point, a suggestion that Mrs. C give up maladaptive but comfortably familiar behavior is not likely to meet acceptance. Now, in full rebellion against the real and fantasized demands of her husband, she rejects him completely.

> Mrs. C: Oh, why don't you eat out with them from now on?

Thus we see how a complex set of interactional distortions has transformed a mutually desired joint outcome (a pleasant, intimate meal together) into disappointment and pain for both partners.

PROCEDURES

Many of the methods used in individual, family, and traditional group therapy will serve the leader of a married couple group in good stead. There are, however, a number of techniques either unique to married couple group therapy or of special importance here. These are discussed in the sequence in which they are commonly used during the course of treatment. (Illustrative examples are drawn from one of the author's groups consisting of four couples (Anna and Alan A, Betty and Boris B, Carla and Courtney C, and Dora and Daniel D), here labeled alphabetically according to increasing age, ranging from the early 20's [Mr. and Mrs. A] to the late 50's [Mr. and Mrs. D].)

Four couples are usually selected for the group. There follows a series of four or five conjoint interviews with each couple separately so that the therapist can more quickly establish rapport and obtain diagnostic impressions. (Throughout the course of treatment patients are also seen alone, as necessary.) At the first group meeting the therapist has the patients introduce themselves; the method each member chooses to disseminate this simple information is often a harbinger of things to come.

The therapist then asks each couple their previous day's fears and fantasies as they contemplated coming to their first group session. This leads to an inquiry as to how each couple views the problems that impelled them to seek treatment. Care is taken not to *prematurely* force members, convinced that "their problem" consists entirely of the other spouse's symptoms, into accepting the therapist's concept that the ill partner is symptomatic for them both.

As soon as the couples start to feel comfortable about the group situation, the question of confidentiality, etc., one couple is chosen by the therapist for the group's initial focus. A relatively nonthreatening area of likely conflict, such as "getting Johnny to bed," "making out the budget," or "sitting down to eat" is used as a vehicle to begin exploring this couple's characteristic pattern of neurotic interaction. Such exploration becomes meaningful to the rest of the group as soon as the therapist begins to deal with some of the universal dynamics described in the preceding section, at which point the therapist may ask: "Has any other couple (or person) had an experience such as the one we just heard?"

In succeeding sessions the therapist notes and, where appropriate, comments on disturbed patterns of communication, distortions of perception, and erroneous assumptions. Whenever, for example, a spouse characteristically speaks for the other or reacts very strongly with anger, silence, or anxiety to another's seemingly innocent statements, the therapist intervenes and has the group examine the interaction.

In example 1, the therapist asks Betty B, whose husband Boris consistently speaks for her, to comment on her husband's assertions.

Example 1:

Boris: (*Referring to his wife*) It's a great struggle for her to come to this group. She always feels uncomfortable talking here.

Therapist: There is something in the group, Betty, that makes you uncomfortable?

Betty: Not particularly, Doctor, but if he doesn't get to speak everything on his mind he gets very antsy so I just sit and listen.

Therapist: Did you know that, Boris?

Boris: (*To wife*) She was always afraid to recite in class.

Betty: Oh, that was 15 years ago.

Therapist: Perhaps, Boris, there are other assumptions you have made about your wife—her silence and other habits—that bear checking out.

The group sessions provide many opportunities for the therapist to demonstrate how poorly the unverified assumptions of one partner coincide with the thoughts of the other. Gradually, the verbal spouse grows reluctant to speak for his more reticent mate (who soon becomes less reticent) and begins verifying his suppositions before making any authoritative statements.

When a spouse's reactions to his mate's seemingly innocent remarks seem inappropriately vehement, the therapist inquires as to what in his mate he was responding. His answer is then compared with the observations of the group, which may reveal an area of perceptual distortion in the responding mate or the unintended transmission of disqualifying nonverbal messages from the stimulus partner.

Example 2:

Courtney: I never saw a woman give so much to her kids as Carla.

Carla: Damn it, Court, will you lay off that? (*Silence. Carla sits sullenly; Courtney is crestfallen.*)

Therapist: Carla, I can see Courtney has really gotten to you, I wonder what he did that you were responding to?

Carla: He's just setting me up so when Joey [their son] disappears again for a week, I feel . . . (*starts to cry*).

Dora: It sounded to me, Carla, that Courtney was only trying to be nice.

Carla: I know that sarcastic grin.

Courtney: Sarcastic grin? I'm just being pleasant.

Boris: You did have a big grin on your face.

Therapist: When Courtney smiles, Carla, you think what he is saying is insincere? Or what?

Similarly, the therapist would actively intervene when a mate is noted to be constantly struggling to offer his spouse something she continually rejects. Such unhappy transactions are readily traced to the mate's misperception of what he thinks his spouse wants, setting the stage for his spouse's refusal of whatever he offers.

The therapist can use a particular couple's manner of speaking to stimulate other group members to examine their own verbal transactions. For example, some couples use pronouns in an idiosyncratic way which serves to hinder rather than facilitate communication. In the illustrative group, the therapist had frequent occasion to point out that Mr. and Mrs. B used "he" and "she" rather than "you" and "I" (as in example 1), whenever talking to the group about themselves, a form of address well suited to destroying intimacy and to the creation of false assumptions.

Mr. and Mrs. C had a somewhat different pronoun problem. Mrs. C typically would switch persons so frequently as to make her statements quite ambiguous, a communicative defect conducive to paranoid responses from her puzzled spouse.

Example 3:

Carla: (*To husband*) *You* ruined all of my plans, and then *he* storms out.

Mr. C is the subject of both angry phrases. His wife, however, has shifted her frame of reference in midsentence here, as she would often do when anxious. In this instance, the therapist intervened to reduce her anxiety and then suggested how she might make herself clearer.

The group also provides the therapist many opportunities to point out how partners send each other paralyzing double-bind messages, as in the case of the wife who repeatedly told her husband to bring her little gifts from time to time "without her asking"; or that of the husband who would demand that his wife "speak her mind freely," but would consistently compliment her effusively just before she spoke, effectively seal-ing-in any anger toward him that she might have wanted to express; or that of the wife who also begged for her spouse's full expression and then suddenly "felt faint" were he to say something she considered unkind.

Examination of these sorts of transactions brings the topic of "covert communication" into focus. By seeing how other couples disqualify verbal messages (as in the above examples), members of the group can under-stand how their own apparently innocent requests for or transmission of information can contain threats and other suppressive maneuvers aimed at the spouse. Once the group has given up preoccupation with the defense of one spouse or the other on the basis of mere explicit content and has begun to recognize disqualifying nonverbal cues, messages with multiple meanings, and other obstacles to clear and accurate transmission of intent, it is time for the major task of the married couple group therapist, "dis-crepancy analysis."

Discrepancy Analysis. Several family incongruencies lend themselves to group treatment. The first of these is that which occurs between what the partners *hope* to obtain from each other and what they have come to *expect*, either through bitter experience in their own home, current distorted perceptions, or their own subversive activities. A woman may hope for warmth and explicit expression of concern and affection from her husband, but has learned to expect only irritable indifference; for his part, there may be hopes for harmony and smiles of wifely contentment, but expectations of only complaints and criticism. Their mutual dis-appointment and subsequent attacks on the disappointing object (the offending spouse) are apparent in their arguments with each other and with other members of the group.

Dysfunctional couples will have arguments in most of the major areas of marital contact, such as raising children, spending money, achieving sexual gratification, etc., but these topics are merely vehicles for expres-sion of a basic discrepancy that transcends any operational differences of opinion. At an appropriate time the therapist can intervene and dissect out the primary recurrent discrepancy underlying most of these argu-ments. He can reveal to the couple and the group that they are not really talking about the budget, for example, but about unmet, deep-seated emotional needs; he can trace the historical roots of these needs and elicit similar experiences from other members of the group; finally, he can engage them in finding better ways to meet these needs than that of fruitless and largely irrelevant arguments.

Example 4:

> Anna: Sometimes, as soon as Alan comes home, he walks past me right to the frige, takes a can of beer and goes upstairs to play the guitar. He doesn't say hello to me or Tommy, he doesn't ask how we are, or say how he is, he just goes upstairs and plays that thing all night as loud as he can.
>
> Alan: I play it for about an hour, and I just play it loud enough to hear.
>
> Anna: Oh, come on! Last night you played it so the house shook.

Alan: Well, you kept on bugging me.

Therapist: What do you mean by "bugging me," Alan?

Alan: She kept on coming up and giving me things to do.

Anna: I just asked you if you were coming down to dinner.

Alan: Yeah, come to dinner—and call Professor Roberts, and put a light bulb in the hallway. . . .

Therapist: Let's stop things for a second, Alan. First, I think this is the first we've heard, isn't it, of your being an avid musician?

Alan: (*Laughs*) I'm not actually, but nothing works better than that in cooling me off after ten hours in the drugstore. I'm so prickly I don't want to talk to anyone or be with anyone. . . .

Therapist: So then, playing is some sort of outlet for you—sort of makes you human again?

Alan: Yeah, if she'd just. . . .

Therapist: Well, let me hold things for just a second. Now Anna, if I understand you, by the time Alan gets home you've got quite a few things that have to get done.

Anna: Yes. Well, not really.

Alan: Oh boy!

Carla: Why are you so pissed off, Alan?

Courtney: He doesn't like to do a bunch of shit when he gets home, [after] working ten hours.

Therapist: Well, let's see if we can find out. Okay, Anna, you get upset with Alan because he plays the guitar instead of some other things?

Anna: It's just that I would like him to show once in a while that he knows he is married and has a wife and a son and a home. . . .

Alan: I know I've got them. I work hard enough. . . .

Anna: . . . he just walls himself off in the bedroom with that guitar.

Therapist: Walls himself off?

Anna: Like nobody else exists.

Therapist: Nobody else?

Alan: If I don't wall myself off, ten minutes after I start playing she is in there, telling me to do this or do that.

Dora: She just wants to see you, Alan.

Alan: I just as soon not be seen some nights—'til I unwind.

Therapist: Now, let me see if I understand; Anna, you don't object so much to the guitar as you do to the fact that it seems to exclude you and the family—which is really you again; and Alan, you want a little time to yourself to sort of settle down after your latest battle with the drugstore.

Alan: Yeah. I'm a lot nicer when I'm settled down, aren't I, Anna? (*Anna nods.*)

Therapist: So, Alan, you hope to settle down so you can make things go smoother with Anna, and Anna, you want to be with Alan in hopes that he will share things with you and make you feel more—more married?

The therapist has now isolated the hopes of both partners and can proceed to explore their expectations. In the example given, it came out that Anna's family had been deserted on three separate occasions by her father, the family broken up, and Anna placed several times in a foster home. She expected Alan to leave her, too, and interpreted his need to isolate himself briefly and work off his anger and frustration as a threat to the marriage. Alan, for his part, had spent his childhood meeting the incessant and arbitrary demands of his parents, particularly his mother, in whose shop he had worked since the age of 7. He characteristically anticipated that Anna also would make unreasonable demands upon him, in the name of family unity or "helping the weaker sex," and misinterpreted her requests for recognition accordingly. The therapist was able to use the A's to show the group how both partners hoped for a satisfying relationship but anticipated its ruin, one by loss of a spouse and the other by oppression.

In the next session, Dora and Daniel volunteered that they thought they had a similar quarrel each morning at breakfast. The group was able to discover that Dora hoped for warmth and affection before her husband left for work but expected rudeness, which she would often prophylactically ward off with criticism the moment her husband entered the room; Daniel also hoped for warmth and affection but expected only criticism, which he defended against by sullen withdrawal, regardless of his wife's mood.

The transactions of these couples were also examined for a discrepancy between *intent* and *performance*. Both couples intended to bring about a more harmonious marital relationship, but performed in such a way as to accomplish the opposite. Alan's attempts to prevent his tension from adversely affecting his wife served only to drive him further away. Dora and Daniel, too, strove for intimacy in a self-defeating manner.

In these situations, the therapist is able to detoxify the conflict by relabeling it as *an attempt to achieve intimacy* rather than a wish to inflict pain; once having accepted this relabeling, the couples are able to examine, nondefensively and without rancor, the effects of their present efforts, and explore alternative means which might be available for achieving their desired goals. Each participant's alternatively trying his old and then his new techniques for achieving an understanding with group members other than his spouse is often an enlightening experience.

The last, but probably most fundamental, discrepancy to be worked through is that existing between the partners' "survival myth" and "survival reality" (Gehrke & Kirschenbaum, 1967). Many marriages operate on the mutual assumption that open expression of conflict, the possession of feelings contrary to those of the spouse, or a desire for some measure of individual development independent of the spouse constitutes a withdrawal of love. Furthermore, the partners see any alteration in the marital equilibrium as a dire threat to their continued existence (the survival myth). They have never been taught, or have rejected, the survival reality, which is that a marriage is a union of two separate *individuals* who, though they frequently come to amicable agreement and compromise, nevertheless bring to the marriage different sets of values and a potential for different kinds of growth; that honest expression of these differences and the opportunity for independent growth are essential to a viable, healthy relationship; and that marriage is a unique, dynamic, and flexible interpersonal exchange subject to constant variation, many layered shifts, and the ebb and flow of feeling.

Betty and Boris, for example, maintained that they never argued, agreed on everything, and came to the group only to ensure that Betty would have a professional contact established should she have another "nervous breakdown." They were so protective of each other in their efforts to present a united front that they had effectively sealed themselves off from any other adult relationships outside of those forced upon them by membership in the group. When a group member would comment that it seemed in a particular instance that the B's did not really see eye to eye, they would become quite anxious and change the subject. Gradually, the therapist was able to reassure the B's that they indeed had each other, that they need not cling so tightly, that an occasional expression of "I" feelings did not mean the death of the "we" feelings. This interpretation was also helpful to Betty, providing her another example upon which to base her growing understanding that her husband's need for individual expression did not mean he was growing away from her.

The therapist next explores the parental roots of the group's dysfunctional behavior (*model analysis*). The extent to which the therapist may be active when using this technique is demonstrated in the following example.

Example 5:

During the tenth hour Anna began crying, whereupon Alan could be seen to pull away from her. In the process of examining this transaction with them, the therapist asked the following questions (replies are deleted for the sake of brevity).

"Alan, did you notice Anna was crying? What did it make you feel? What did you make of it? How did you arrive at that? Anna, did you notice Alan's response? What did it make you feel? What did you make of it? How did you arrive at that? What did you make of what Alan has said? What did you expect from Alan? Where did you learn what to expect from men?" (There followed a discussion of Anna's childhood and her feeling that only by tears could she give vent to her angry disappointment at her father's having left her alone.) "Alan, when Anna started crying, what did you want to do? I wonder how it comes about that you cannot do that? Anna, can you think of what might be getting in Alan's way?" (To group) "I'd be interested in some other responses to Anna's tears."

"Alan, someone you love is crying; you want to embrace her and cannot. I wonder if you expect a negative outcome if you should try and reach out to her? Has this happened to you before?" (There followed a discussion of Alan's childhood, with the group members as well as the therapist asking pertinent questions, in which Alan revealed that when all else failed, his mother would manipulate him to do her bidding by loud sobbing.) "Has anyone else in the group had a similar experience with his parents?"

The group was next asked what techniques Alan might try in order to achieve a more satisfying outcome (e.g., touching his wife, asking her what is bothering her, giving some clear sign of his concern). Having understood what is holding him back, he should be in a position to try other modes of behavior. Anna, too, aware now of the effect tears have on Alan, can with group support begin to look for other ways of having her needs met.

In all sessions the group is encouraged to comment when one spouse causes the other to turn away. Among the most frequently visible devices partners inadvertently use to destroy marital intimacy is that of role confusion. Couples frequently will misuse, in the group, the occupational roles they inappropriately impose upon their marriage. One woman, a teacher, lectured the group pedantically as she always had her husband; one man, a graduate student in psychology, was more of a therapist to his wife than a husband. Such interaction opens the door to exploration of "How comfortable are we in the role of wife and husband; Where did we learn the skills and how well did we learn them?"

A word about group resistances is in order at this point; a number occur repetitively in a married couple group. They make take the form of unspoken rules such as, "We can talk about feelings but we don't show our feelings here." The therapist can prevent the group from suddenly shifting focus away from a couple at a critical moment in favor of an intellectual discussion by demonstrating that the group will not fall apart if feelings come out, and that the therapist himself is not above showing what he feels inside.

In the same vein is the rule: "We never attack our parents." Inevitably, certain couples are assigned parental roles and are then vigorously protected by the group from honest examination of their conflicts. The therapist must demonstrate by his manner that objective inquiry into a couple's defense system is in no way an attack. A point must be made of supporting any group member who attempts to break these oppressive, upspoken rules. Other more general group resistances quite common to married couple therapy groups have been cheerfully catalogued by Berne (1966).

One modus operandi that stands out in examination of almost any group session is the therapist's persistent and deliberate relabeling of potentially destructive action according to its positive intent (e.g., Mrs. X's repeated "helpful" comments on her husband's driving are an attempt to make meaningful contact with him), in contrast to more psychoanalytic interpretations of intent which may often be negative (e.g., Mrs. X's repeated helpful comments about her husband's driving serve to cover the murderous impulses she has about him).

In married couple group therapy, positive interpretation of intent serves to turn the patient from defensive and fruitless justification of his dysfunctional goals to constructive participation in group process, through which he is freed to examine the effect of his behavior and to experiment with alternatives. Giving the spouses more benevolent views of their marital interaction liberates the psychic energy with which they may change. It is difficult to react in a blind, angry fashion to a stimulus no longer perceived as hostile. The therapist, it is hoped, is no Pollyanna, but a perceptive observer who struggles to seek the words that will enable his warring, stalemated patients to recognize the relatively benign wish lying behind the most misguided dysfunctional behavior.

SUMMARY

An interpersonal theory of disturbed marital interaction views marriage as the purposeful, highly specific selection of a mate on the basis of various conscious and unconscious criteria, in the hope of gratifying both the mature and neurotic needs of its participants, who can expect disappointment when there are many reciprocal perceptual distortions, disturbances in communication, frustrated dependency needs, threats to adaptive defenses, and fears of the unfamiliar. The therapy group obtains for its members a healthier marital equilibrium through correction of these perceptual and communicative errors, alleviation of reciprocal anxieties, analysis of discrepancies, and facilitation of intimacy. The therapist's persistently positive interpretation of intent serves to turn the patient from defensive and fruitless justification of his dysfunctional goals to constructive participation in group process, through which he is free to examine the effects of his behavior and experiment with alternatives.

REFERENCES

Berne, E. *Principles of group treatment.* New York: Oxford University Press, 1966.

Blinder, M. G., et al. "MCFT": Simultaneous treatment of several families. *American Journal of Psychotherapy*, 1965, *19*, 559–569.

Gehrke, S., & Kirschenbaum, M. Survival patterns in family conjoint therapy: Myth and reality. *Family Process*, 1967, *6*, 67–80.

Gottlieb, A., & Pattison, E. M. Married couples group psychotherapy. *Archives of General Psychiatry*, 1966, *14*, 143–152.

Hastings, P. R., & Runkle, R. L. An experimental group of married couples with severe problems. *International Journal of Group Psychotherapy*, 1963, *13*, 84–92.

Leichter, E. Group psychotherapy with married couples: Some characteristic treatment dynamics. *International Journal of Group Psychotherapy*, 1962, *12*, 154–163.

Neubeck, G. Factors affecting group therapy with married couples. *Marriage Family Living*, 1954, *16*, 216–220.

Perelman, J. L. Problems encountered in psychotherapy of married couples. *International Journal of Group Psychotherapy*, 1960, *10*, 136–142.

Satir, V. Conjoint marital therapy. In B. L. Green (Ed.), *The psychotherapies of marital disharmony.* New York: The Free Press, 1965.

Von Emde Boas, C. Intensive group psychotherapy with married couples. *International Journal of Group Psychotherapy*, 1962, *12*, 142–153.

CHAPTER 22

Treatment of Married Couples Groups

Elsa Leichter

For at least the last decade, the treatment of married couples groups as a therapeutic method increasingly has been used in the spectrum of marital therapy. There are still therapists—chiefly from the orthodox psychoanalytic school of thought—who work with one married partner exclusively and refuse even to talk to the spouse. Some find cooperative work by two therapists with each partner useful. However, an increasing number of therapists, whose major focus is on the marital relationship as such, treat the couple as a unit. In the treatment of married couples in groups two major categories can be found:

1. Parents groups, often as an adjunct to therapy of the child, where the major goal is some modification of the parental functioning of the couple.

2. Married couples groups proper in which the change of the marital relationship as such is the goal of therapy, but the treatment of the couple takes place within the structure of the group.

This article will focus on two major aspects of the treatment of married couples groups:

1. On the fact that the process in the married couples group is largely affected by its structure: Some characteristic treatment problems and process phenomena in married couples groups are quite different from other therapy groups in which the participants have no relationship other than in the treatment group.

2. On the necessity to differentiate between the various married couples groups according to the social and chronological stages of the marriage. Furthermore, the approach of therapists with a family orientation to see "significant others" together with the married couple in family interviews as an occasional supplement to the treatment in the married couples group will also be touched upon.

Reprinted with permission of the author and the publisher from *The Family Coordinator*, January, 1973.

THE SPECIAL CHARACTERISTICS AND TREATMENT
PROBLEMS OF ALL MARRIED COUPLES GROUPS

A married couples group consisting of four or five couples is drastically different from other therapy groups with eight to ten participants who are strangers to each other. Each couple brings to the married couples group a joint history, a past, and they share a very powerful reality from which they come to the group session and to which they return to live with each other for a week till the next session. Thus, one can safely say that the married couples group consists of four or five subgroups which in fact must and, indeed, does have a strong impact on the developing group and treatment process.

Perhaps the most important is the expectation and hope of what group treatment will offer: Whereas in other therapy groups the expectation is some change of the self (even though wishes for magic may be at play), the couples usually are expecting change of the mate rather than of themselves. This is so in spite of the fact that in the initial treatment contract between therapist and couple there has to be a modicum of acceptance of the thought that the marital relationship needs modification, something which ought to imply that each partner has to take some responsibility for his own behavior and attitudes in the marriage.

Undoubtedly, in therapy groups of individuals there is also a good deal of projecting and blaming of outside forces for one's difficulties. However, in the married couples group, the projection is on the "present other"—the marital partner—and the demand that he or she change to meet the needs of the mate are all acted out in the group. Even though the mate is right there in the room, he or she will be "talked about" in terms of severe complaints, if not real attacks, or the marital partners will be involved repeatedly in a circular fight in which neither takes any self-responsibility. At the same time, group and therapist are not allowed to "get in."

Absences from the group have quite specific ramifications in a married couples group, since one partner's resistance or inability to attend a session often leads to the absence of the mate. This is especially true in the early phase when the couple interprets the idea of the "marital relationship being the focus of therapy," as meaning that in the group they must be a symbiotic unit and either be there together or not at all. This distortion, however, signifies more than just that.

If the nonattendance of the session is a reflection of resistance by one of the marital partners, there is a good chance that there will be a strong pull to keep the other, also, out of the session whether it is to punish the group, and (or) the therapist, or to prevent the mate from moving in a direction that is very upsetting. However, occasionally one partner may wish to attend a session without the mate (and then will find a way of preventing the mate from coming), in order to use such a session for the purpose of sharing with the group something about himself or herself, which he does not want the mate to know. While the accumulation of secrets between group and one of the spouses obviously is not desirable therapeutically, the one session without the mate can make it possible for the partner to test out the group's reaction in greater safety before he ventures letting the partner into the secret, if such, indeed, is at all feasible.

When more than one couple are absent from a session the group may seriously feel that its survival is threatened and the therapist (unless experienced and fairly clear about the dynamics of the absences) may easily merge with the group's anxiety and sense of abandonment instead of enabling the group to deal with its "crisis." Dealing with its "crisis" often means talking about what happened in previous group sessions that led to the absences and, perhaps, more importantly, giving the group a chance to express feelings of dissatisfaction about treatment to each other or to the therapist, which due to their hostile nature had been censured heretofore. The more such communications are permitted in the group, the less it is probable that its participants will act out, either through absenting themselves and pulling their partners along or literally through "sitting on their anger."

Even if couples do not act out through absenting themselves from the group, they do have to live with each other day and night, and delayed or postponed reactions to the mate about what occurred in a given group session can be powerfully punitive and retaliative. The mate may have ventured for the first time to confront his partner with anger or hurt for what the partner has been doing to him or depriving him of. However, the partner's punitive and retaliative reaction literally can throw the mate back in his attempt to break through a pathological pattern of interaction and take some time till he recuperates and can take a chance again.

Yet, such confrontations are necessary, because in order to achieve the capacity to give, to relate, and to love, one also has to achieve the capacity to let oneself feel and where possible to express appropriate anger. Where anger goes far back into early childhood it takes usually the form of rage, a diffuse sense of hostility, and is largely irrational. In the therapy situation, the attempt is to convert rage into anger which can be expressed about a specific situation and about and, most importantly, toward a specific person. If this anger eventually is received without counterhostility, and the individual gradually learns to separate his or her childhood rage from appropriate potent anger, some of the bound-up inner energies are freed and can be used for more truly intimate relationships.

All therapy groups allow for a large range of interaction between the participants. Sometimes there is criticism that individuals are exposed to too much attacking. This may be true in some groups where "expression of anger" seems to become a purpose in and of itself. For a truly therapeutic group, however, the capacity to love better, rather than to hate better, is the goal.

In the married couples group, this whole issue has added a special significance, since the goal of "learning to love better" (if at all possible) is aimed at five dyadic highly rigidified subsystems in the group. The group as a whole gives each individual the opportunity to interact in any way with others, including the therapist and through the feedbacks he gets gradually to learn new and more appropriate patterns of relating. In essence, a married couples group tends to operate as a "third family," which in the last analysis means that it gives each individual and couple another chance to come to life and to grow, whereas the real family (primary or present) has had a growth-thwarting effect. This is true of all therapy groups, but again the fact that each individual comes as part of a couple has its own significance. In a sense, the group as a whole represents the transferential mother. Wishes and expectations are directed at it, and dissatisfactions, as well as feelings of disappointments are equally directed at "it," "them," "the group." ("They don't understand," "they always interrupt me," "they ignore me," or "the group is wonderful, the only place where you can be real honest, etc.")

In the early group process especially, the need to share time and attention with others tends to be experienced as deprivation or as in real families as a feeling that there is not enough to go around. Thus, sibling rivalries are stimulated in regard to "preferred" individuals and (or) "preferred couples." Sometimes it can happen that a couple will not return to the next session because "our marriage, or we, are not as interesting as the other couples," or "we cannot be as aggressive as couple X, Y, or Z." Interestingly, however, sibling rivalries often develop between marital partners themselves, which may rather dramatically reflect their rivalrous relationship on the outside. Feelings such as "he is pulling the wool over your eyes," "you are always picking on me, but let her get away scot free," are frequently expressed. Later, when change in one of the partners occurs the spouse frequently reacts with jealousy and denial of the change. (As indicated earlier, there is almost always a reaction to the change because it upsets momentarily the marital equilibrium.)

In the group, unlike in the primary families, these feelings are allowed full expression and each individual in the group has the opportunity of finding out his own particular way of coping with such feelings. For example, in the couples group the person who, due to anger, does not come to the next session often is the husband or wife who "pack their suitcase" at the slightest provocation (and for comparable reasons: "Not getting enough"). This connection can be made particularly well within the group situation.

The therapist quite naturally at times becomes an important object of dissatisfaction, this dissatisfaction often is transferred onto the group peers—siblings, as frequently happens in families. If the messages or behavior seem to indicate such a move, redirecting of the anger for "unmet needs" onto the therapist in the presence of the group can have considerable therapeutic value. There has to be much freedom and acceptance for the irrational demand to be brought out: The "hungry" client or couple need first be "heard" and "received" on the child level and helped to get connected emotionally with that needy, but unacceptable part of themselves. Only then can they move on to some acceptance of the reality that what they are demanding nobody can give, and this most decidedly includes the marital partner. Essentially, all of this means that some shift of the transference from the partner onto the group or therapist takes place and, finally, one comes to better terms with what can be realistically expected from the spouse.

For the married couples group, the just described aspect of the group process has very specific implications. One has to distinguish between the partner and the group while one individual goes through a period of heightened anxiety. The partner often gets terribly frightened, fears the mate may fall apart, and does all he can to reassure, deny, and to censure. Often he gets quite angry at the mate, the therapist, or the group. His aim is to stop what seems to be quite a threat. The group—even though some individual in it can get almost as frightened as the marital partner—can be invaluable in supporting both partners in this difficult phase of allowing one partner to express anxiety and to live out strong feelings as painful connections are made. At the same time, the group is able to sympathize with the other partner's reaction, helping him see it for what it is and intervening in his attempts to stop his mate. If this is done in a supportive manner—and often the help of the therapist is needed there as he interprets angry interruptions as a reflection of apprehension or anxiety— the partner gradually becomes enabled to see the mate in a truly new light, namely as a person with his own needs and vulnerabilities. Equally important, he finally realizes that the group is working for rather than against him, the latter reaction being based on the threat which any shaking up of the marital equilibrium entails.

In this important process, then, each couple, almost like a pair of siblings, gradually experiences the group as the "good third family" which, different from their primary families, allows and, indeed, welcomes growth for each of them individually and for both of them as a pair. Their "joint growth" is finally most strikingly reflected in their ability and readiness to leave the group, and to take on jointly the responsibilities of marriage. However, before this commitment is made by the marital partners, they are given a chance to consider honestly the question of whether they wish to remain married. The author has observed that sometimes the final step of a desirable separation is taken very soon after the group therapy experience ends.

MARRIED COUPLES GROUPS IN DIFFERENT STAGES OF LIFE CYCLE

Even though there are universal themes pertaining to all married couples groups, there are significant psychosocial differences among married couples in consecutive states of the marital relationship which are reflected in the group treatment process psychodynamically as well as in terms of the actual content of the ongoing group sessions.

Young Married Couples

Young married couples often find themselves in a peculiar state of transition. Considering the long period of at least economic dependence on the parents, they are, during the early stages of marriage, still struggling to achieve separation from their primary families and in this struggle, dependency needs and independent strivings are in conflict with each other. Whereas in many other cultures, the continuing close tie to the primary family is most decidedly considered "normal," in the American middle-class culture the young married couple is expected to have achieved separation to a considerable extent. The inner conflict thus is intensified by societal expectation which is guilt-provoking and for some young couples only serves to prolong the struggle.

While there are some young couples who want treatment out of a mutual recognition of danger signals and out of a joint desire for growth so as to get ready for children and/or to make life altogether more satisfying, the majority of young couples come for help because of severe clashes from the start of marriage which threaten to produce total breakdown. Unlike couples in later stages of marital development, these younger couples, as a rule, are not yet really married except in the term's most external connotation. Their ties to their respective primary families are often extremely strong and one can rightfully state that the couple plus their parents constitute the *de facto* family. Just as in later marital stages the children are the focus of the difficulties, in this early period of marriage, parents and in-laws become objects of marital strife and hostile dependency. They are in the kitchen and the bedroom of the young people, and often there is actual involvement in the occupational and working level.

It appears that two types of young couples in particular have the greatest difficulty with a relatively healthy separation from the parental family:

1. Those who have lived in a symbiotic type of family and literally cannot cut the umbilical cord.

2. Those who came from "undernourishing" isolated families in which a sense of great emotional deprivation was experienced, including those who due to a tragic reality situation suffered an actual loss of parenting—mothering.

Usually and unfortunately, such young people tend to pick marital partners who are equally deprived. This similarity may in the courtship period produce a pseudo-closeness and warmth which are taken for "love." As such young people enter marriage, they find it extremely difficult to make the transition from the hierarchical relationship in which the parent was the predominant emotional provider to the marital peer relationship in which the mutual give-and-take has to be balanced. The more deprived the marital partner is, the more he will tend to perceive the spouse as if he were a parental figure. In such cases, need clashes with need. What started as a hopeful relationship quickly deteriorates, leaving the couple bewildered and disappointed in a largely transferential relationship, making it psychologically impossible even to grasp the needs of the partner, let alone meet them. With such couples, many practitioners are tempted to separate the marital partners and to treat them each individually, since the individual emotional disturbance is more than obvious. Yet, the reality of the marriage exists, even if it is a marriage of two immature, disturbed young people, who, through their circular interaction, feed into and add to each other's pathology.

A married couples group can be an excellent medium of treatment for such couples as a wide range of content and process themes are touched off and focused on. Almost every piece of even the most specific discussion content, such as money or occupation, has psychological implications. Some aspect of the transferential relationship of the couple enters into the seemingly topical discussion. It is thus worked on in many different ways, with the hope that eventually the marital relationship may to the extent possible grow into a more adult relationship with the give-and-take more evenly balanced.

Some of the specific content themes in the young married couples group are in the area of money and occupation—"working as a team to get jobs done"—and sex. Discussions of parents and in-laws can be very specific in terms of actual experiences and relationships, but appear in less concrete terms in the here-and-now interactions and transactions of the therapy group.

Occupation and Money. One of the very powerful topics in all married couples groups is money; but for young couples this has a very distinct flavor, since the partners for the first time have to share the responsibility for money management which gets them immediately from the romantic aura of the courtship relationship into one of the "nitty-gritty" aspects of marital life. When both partners are working in the early phase of marriage, some of the difficult interactional issues may not appear in full strength. Frequently, there are intense involvements with parents and in-laws in this period. The mate may have been chosen less for his own personal attractiveness than for the family (parents) he has. The young man often actually may be working for his father, or father-in-law, and the question of how he is recompensated and treated can be fraught with tremendously intense emotions. These factors are, of course, interwoven with his sense of self-esteem which can be easily threatened and yet he is stuck in a situation which he hates. The wife, thus, can find herself between husband and primary family and more often than not will tend to side with the primary family. In other situations the wife may continue to accept regular material gifts from her family, gifts which allow for luxuries that the husband would not be able to meet. The interactional pattern in relation to this is contradictory: on one hand, the couples are in a silent pact to accept the gifts (and dependence) and, on the other hand, there is mutual resentment. The husband's sense of self-esteem is deeply threatened, since even where there may be a fairly good income, he cannot compete with the extras which the in-laws have to offer. For the wife, this constellation provides a good reason to undermine the husband and to hold him in contempt.

Usually it is not difficult for a married couples group to recognize some of the paradoxical, contradictory aspects of the marital interaction. Since the subject of money and money making is of much interest to most couples, many identifications and alliances—often men with men and women with women—take place in the married couples group. Thus, men who may be relating to their own "overdemanding" or "dissatisfied" wives with "passive withholding" have a chance in the married couples group to react to other men's wives who show similar tendencies and "let them have it." This prepares the men for the eventual confrontation with their own partners. On the other hand, the men can take a man to task if they feel he lets his wife "step all over him." To give an example, it emerged in a married couples group that the wife continuously overspent and contracted debt which her husband then had to meet grudgingly. The group, especially the men, confronted the husband with his passivity which reflected itself also in his tendency to fall asleep in the group. It became clear that the wife substituted money for love since she had an absentee husband. On the other hand, it became equally clear that the wife took rather powerful, childish revenge on her husband for his neglect of her. Each of the marital partners, and occasionally both together, went through a period of strong anger with the group, including temporarily staying away from the session. Gradually, however, the couple reached the point of courageous, open confrontation of each other. As an outcome of this, the wife went to work and helped with the repayment of accumulated debts, and the husband not only stopped sleeping during the group session but generally showed more aggressiveness and vitality.

The group can often prove a great reality-tester and can in some respects be more down to earth than the therapist when it comes to the reality aspects of money and income. It is quite helpful to put couples in the group who are economically and occupationally quite heterogeneous. Many fantasies can be diminished by the presence of seemingly "success-ful" couples, whose greater affluence obviously has not been the answer to all problems. On the other hand, the less "successful" and even less-educated couple may in the area of perception and emotional availability be quite ahead of their fantasized "superiors."

Teamwork. Literally, these young couples have to learn how to live together as a pair, to become a team that can get jobs done, rather than getting stuck in clashes around each necessary task. This involves profound emotional questions, especially the deeply unresolved depen-dency needs and excessive, infantile demands of each other which make teamwork impossible. One of the most poignant comments in this respect was found by the author in a psychosocial description of a young couple. "They can't get together on anything. They want to have coffee together, but argue about which room. They want to have sex, but cannot agree on a time. Therefore, neither sex nor coffee occurs."

In a couples group, such specific areas of breakdown can be dealt with in a very specific way through identifications on one hand and recognition of the irrational handling of specific situations on the other hand. Thus appropriate reactions or responses on the part of other couples, or individuals, whose own irrationality is not identical, are helpful elements in the group interaction. They can open up for other couples new insights into their own areas of functional breakdown.

Sex. In young married couples groups the question of "sex" naturally looms very large. Where the marital relationship is largely transferential, much of the sexual conflict between the partners has strongly oral connotations. Sex then becomes the object of demand and withholding.

In therapy groups of young couples, the sharing of sexual problems is, as a whole, fairly easy and almost "comes natural." To some extent, this serves as a defense for the group, the couple, or one of the marital partners to cover up the underlying need for parenting, or the use of sex as a binder of anxiety: These underlying needs are the real secrets because they are invested with shame and guilt and usually are kept out of awareness. Thus, group, couple, or individual resistance emerges more powerfully when these connections are beginning to be made.

There are, however, real sexual secrets, which have to do with actual experience. Since the couples are young, earlier sexual experience is not as far removed in time as it may be the case for couples in the later stages of marriage. The secrets have usually to do with more or less traumatic childhood experiences, not infrequently of an incestuous nature. As all secrets, they are accompanied by a sense of shame and guilt and frequently are not known to the partner. When one individual in the group gets ready to reveal the forbidden actions of their childhood, the group experiences first anxiety and then great relief. These revelations are accompanied by either sobbing, tears, or giggling, as the group as a whole relive pieces of their childhood that had remained hidden from outside knowledge. Subsequently, many secrets of this nature come to the fore from other group members.

The whole area of sexual secrets, including the practicing of some sexual perversions, and sexual fantasies can be dealt with in a group quite effectively. The mate, while perhaps shocked at first, begins to understand and appreciate some of the partner's idiosyncrasies in their sexual relationship. The constellation of the group with the "parent-therapist" who takes an uncritical attitude and in fact welcomes the bringing out of heretofore hidden material—be it fact or fantasy—and the sharing of comparable experiences and their mutual accpetance among peers has a deeply therapeutic potential. Usually, these discussions lead once more to the never ending topic of the "nonprotective" parents (primary families) who ignored and looked away from what was happening to their young children.

Primary Families. The relationships to parents is a continuing theme in the married couples group. It is a very complicated but most important subject of concentration. The complexity is due to the fact that behind each couple are two sets of parents, dead or alive. These discussions take place on many levels, but essentially the group treatment endeavors to help all group members to move from extreme, often very irrational attitudes toward, and perceptions of parents and parents-in-law to more realistic ones which eventually allows for healthy separation.

A couple's respective relations with, and feelings about parents and in-laws can create rather complicated marital interactions. For example, while there may be denial and idealization in relation to one's own parents, the in-laws may be the recipients of the projection and/or transference. This can drive the partner into a defensive position on behalf of his "attacked" primary family, which then prevents him from dealing in a realistic manner with his own feelings toward his primary family. Some mates deny their feelings of anger or rage toward in-laws as much as toward their own parents; in situations where the partner is able to express angry feelings or unhappiness about early deprivation he is criticized or censured by the mate for such unacceptable emotions. Yet, in the whole area of relations and reactions to primary family, the married couples group has the advantage that the partners often do have more realistic impressions than the spouse of the latter's parents and actually often know some significant background facts. Thus, the marital partners frequently are mutually able to debunk some of each other's distortions, but for this the help of the group is quite important: By having some added facts at its disposal, the group can support the partner's more objective perceptions of his in-laws while empathizing with the defensive reactions of the mate.

Hopefully, all group participants eventually can move from their extreme (transferential) positions to more realistic and mature ones in which neither total denial of anger nor total rage are necessary any longer and the parents are finally viewed as "people" with their "good" and their "bad" features.

Some group therapists with a family therapy orientation occasionally may invite the couples' parents into the group, allowing the group to gain a direct objective view of these people rather than being left with distortions which are often hard to unravel. In addition to the regular weekly group meetings other therapists prefer to have family interviews with the two generations from time to time, often including siblings of the younger pair. The purpose is not only diagnostic but most decidedly to give the family a chance to get more meaningfully involved with each other, where and if possible.

Couples Groups in Later Stages of Marriage

The couple who are parents are in a very different developmental stage of the marriage and the group process reflects this fact. Naturally, many of the themes discussed earlier, such as money and occupational difficulties, are also prevalent in this type of group. But often emotional and behavior patterns are more rigidified and there is more resistance and denial as character defenses are more habitual. There is often also more hopelessness with regard to the possibility of change.

On the perhaps more positive side, couples with children—except for the most disturbed families—usually have found a way of functioning and operating. Some teamwork must be there for the couple to perform the parental functions on at least a minimum level. These couples survived the early marriage, often quite well, even though if the beginning of the marital difficulty is retraced one can find with some couples that the arrival of the first child—something which always shakes up the dyadic balance and requires a readjustment on the part of both marital partners—was where the serious difficulty all started. In many cases, however, the problem could be kept "under wraps" till the children reflected some of the pathology of their parents and added to it so that eventually a full-grown family pathology became evident.

Very often in married couples groups in which the couples are parents, the original presenting difficulty was a child rather than the marital relationship. In fact, children are all too often used to perpetuate the myth of the happy marriage or are blamed for the marital disturbance. In order to get such couples into a married couples group, a therapeutic process in which the whole family, i.e., the couple/parents, the disturbed child, and well siblings are seen and worked with together, has proved to be most helpful. As a result of such a process, the decision may be reached that the parents as a marital pair should use the help of a married couples group in order to concentrate on themselves and their relationship rather than exploiting a child to maintain the myth that everything else would be fine if only the child changed. What other treatment decisions are made depends on what the family needs and is prepared to do. By all means, however, even if treatment of the family is broken up into several parts, from time to time members ought to be brought together for testing of changes and for direct involvement with each other in a structured therapeutic milieu. Occasionally, after an intensive period of family therapy, couples join married couples groups as a next step in the total treatment process.

Fewer couples in this category come for help with the marriage *per se*. As with younger marriages, there may be couples who face their mutual difficulty and really are motivated toward help. They may maintain that the children are not affected, are doing well, etc. The practitioner with a family orientation still will try to meet with the whole family even if only for the purpose of arriving at a more reliable understanding of the marital disturbance. Such interviews often bring out some hidden disturbances in the children, as for example, a reversed structure in the family in which the children carry the parental function in many ways lest their family go to pieces. The family interviews thus can serve as fact finders leading where possible to preventive steps with regard to the children, who can be greatly relieved by having someone become aware of their burden.

Married couples groups thus frequently are composed roughly of those couples who originally came about a child—but were helped through a process to recognize and to take at least minimal responsibility for some underlying disturbance in their own relationship—and of those who asked for help with the marriage claiming correctly or incorrectly that the children were fine. Such a total group can be quite helpful to each of its subgroups. Those couples who acknowledge the marital difficulty and often are locked in a pattern of circular accusation without taking any real responsibility for the effect this has on the children get into a conflict situation with the subgroup whose pull continues to be in the direction of the children with a concomitant minimization of marital difficulty. The latter subgroup often can break into the circular process of the former quite effectively through: (1) their articulated reaction of the effect on them (from feelings of exclusion to feelings of fear about the violence of the attacks) and (2) identifying with the other subgroup's children, who may well react similarly to their parents' destructive behavior.

If this process is to be productive, the arousal of guilt toward the children is necessary before these couples can begin to shift from their self-centered accusatory system toward taking more responsibility in their role of parents. On the other hand, couples in an open marital struggle sense the denial of those who pretend that "all is well in the marriage" and through their challenges bring the underlying marital difficulty into sharper focus. The conflictual interplay between the two subgroups tends to be quite dramatic. Thus the married couples group seems a particularly good medium for enabling the partners to decrease their respective areas of denial and projection.

Again, other themes which are focused on in the young married couples groups are very much in the picture here also, but with a somewhat different slant. For example, there are still unresolved ties to primary families, often highlighted by the existence of the children and their parents' feelings about being parents when they are still so much in childlike relationships to their own parents. The wish for mothering from the partner is often reflected by powerful sibling rivalries with one's own children. On the other hand, involvement with the mate (including sex) is avoided by concentration on a child or on the children.

The latter point brings to mind a couple who came for help because their fifteen-year-old son had become heavily involved with alcohol and drugs. They were also complaining about their younger eleven-year-old daughter who was not living up to potential scholastically and having trouble making friends. Initially, the family was worked with as a unit. After a period of intensive family therapy the marital partners were ready for concentration on their marriage in a married couples group. (Both children who had gained a lot in family therapy simultaneously were ready to get appropriate treatment for themselves.) The husband had been sexually impotent for three years, and the wife felt extremely rejected by her spouse. This difficulty fed into her long-standing self-image of being unattractive as a woman. The "deadness" in the marital relationship was reflected in a family gloom and doom which had its serious impact on the children. The husband found it easier and less threatening to have a sort of love affair with his daughter than with his wife. The mother grew intensely jealous of the girl and increasingly upset about the son's use of drugs and alcohol. Her rage and fury were directed at both children but the girl, as a female rival, bore the brunt of her mother's hysterical outbursts.

In the married couples group, the problem of the couple was reenacted: There was very little interaction between the marital partners: The husband displayed a rather passive, lecturing kind of stance; he could express his seething rage only through taking little stabs at the therapist or others, chiefly because nobody could give him "answers." The wife went through periods of seeming calm in which, however, she accumulated anger, which then exploded. She would yell hysterically at the group or the therapist and run out of the room, claiming she got nothing and accusing the group and the therapist of letting themselves be seduced by her husband's "smart alecky" intellectualizations, which, in truth, was the only way in which he could cope with his sense of helplessness and impotence.

One of the major goals of the treatment process was to offer new life to this "dead" couple. The group became the third family in which they initially behaved as they had with their primary families and as they behaved with each other at home, the latter meaning that they were quite isolated from each other. The husband gradually was helped to acknowledge his seething rage within the transferential situation of the group, i.e., he learned how to recognize that his barbs, his sarcasm, his tendency to put others down—including the therapist—were expressions of profound hostility for what felt to him like unending deprivation. With the female therapist he could get to some rather powerful feelings about his exploitative, nongiving mother. Subsequently, he went through a period of expressing anger directly at the women in the group. Especially, when the anger was appropriate, he was encouraged by the therapist, who welcomed the emergence of his "male aggressiveness." When at last he became ready to communicate directly, even though angrily, with his oversensitive wife her first reactions were typical of her: She became hysterical. Yet, she had been complaining she wanted her husband to be "a man" in more than one respect.

At that critical juncture, when the newly found male aggressiveness was still not quite integrated and could easily revert back to the old, familiar pattern, the wife was sufficiently supported by the group in her understandable reaction to her husband's anger because of many "old sins." This, in turn, left the therapist free to put out a clear challenge to the woman: "You can't have it both ways; if you want a man, you must let him be a man." At an earlier point in process, she had similarly challenged the husband: "If you want to have a wife, you cannot expect her to be your mother, who still cuts your food. You have to choose between the roles of little boy and husband. You can't have it both ways." (At an earlier point in group treatment, all wives had ganged up against the female therapist, who encouraged potent, male aggressiveness, which none of them could tolerate at first; their own fantasy about their husband's maleness actually being the wish that the husband should find a way of being a man [whatever that meant] and yet do the woman's bidding.) The couple began to have sexual intercourse again when they were able to have meaningful communication with each other, and both also had changed their respective roles as parents, moving essentially away from helplessness to some sense of mastery.

This example, although necessarily quite sketchy, was intended to bring out many of the points repeatedly made in this article. The obvious point that couples who are parents, can be in quite different stages of the ongoing life process of the marriage needs to be stated firmly. It is important to take into consideration whether they are just starting parenthood and are themselves quite young or whether they are approaching middle age, biologically and emotionally (menopause!); whether they are the parents of several children; and whether one or more of these children has reached adolescence or young adulthood. When exactly did the difficulty reach the point that the family could not contain it any longer? Was it as soon as the nurturing of the first baby became an added function in family living? Was it when the child began to leave the symbiotic mother/child relationship and started "walking" away? Was it when the adolescent became an object of sexual attraction for the parent of the opposite sex? Was it when the husband and wife found themselves facing each other and old age after their children left?

While the writer so far has made a strong distinction between couples groups in the various stages of married life, in actual practice the lines of distinction cannot really be drawn so sharply. In fact, many therapists find it quite fruitful to have more heterogeneity in their married couples groups. It is obvious that the latter structure can heighten the transferences and the conflicts, as the young couples often tend to identify with the children of the middle-aged couples, relating to the latter as if they were their parents. Yet, eventually and gradually they can learn to grasp the feelings and reactions of parents who are as vulnerable to the hurts from their children as is true the other way around.

SUMMARY AND CONCLUSIONS

It seems important to remember that the institution of marriage is now in a state of great flux. Since this is happening in the immediate present, it is not possible as yet to relate it with a sense of perspective. The author is reminded of the time—some years ago—when the adolescent scene was beginning to change, not only leaving the parents but the whole adult generation bewildered and frightened. Today, the drug culture is making itself intensely felt in every social system that adolescents are part of, including the therapeutic systems (private practices, agencies, clinics).

The following outside developments are beginning to be reflected especially in young marriages and have begun to become part of the content in the married couples groups:

1. The use of drugs by couples on a social level (similar to the use of alcohol).

2. The switching of partners (swinging), often as a means of getting "turned on" for marital sex.

3. Women's Liberation Movement; its repercussions and influence are beginning to make their imprint in married couples groups in which some of the arguments of the movement are used as a weapon in the battle between the sexes.

All of this is still only to a small extent part of the general culture of the married group therapists, however, to see some of the signs that may eventually end the traditional structure of marriage. Moreover, since therapists are a part of the total society, they tend like many others to react with shock and rather judgmental attitudes especially to the "swingers." Obviously such reactions do not serve to help the group members with their own similar attitude of strong disapproval. Therapists need to keep in mind, whatever their personal values may be, that couples engaging in drug-taking or couple mixing would not seek help if there were not some dissatisfaction with or even unhappiness about their current life situation. This, rather than their unacceptable behavior, makes it possible for the married couples group and the therapist to help the marital partners to achieve the kind of relationship which is mutually more satisfying and offers some stability and security to the next generation.

In terms of optimal treatment goals which, of course, have to be modified according to the couple's capacity to change—both partners need to become aware of and emotionally connected with some of their own unresolved infantile needs and those of the mate. They have to learn to know and to respect the partner's sensitive and vulnerable spots rather than constantly hitting the mate "below the belt." Only if this occurs can the treatment of married couples groups result in true mutual caring in the marital relationship.

REFERENCES

Arden, F., Jr., & MacLennan, B. W. Some dynamic factors in marital group therapy. *International Journal of Group Psychotherapy*, 1962, *12*, 355.

Dicks, H. V. Marital tensions. In *Clinical studies towards a psychological theory of interaction*. New York: Basic Books, Inc., 1967.

Gallant, D. M. et al. Group psychotherapy with married couples: a successful technique in New Orleans alcoholism clinic patients. *Journal of the Louisiana Medical Society*, 1970, *122*, 41–44.

Gottlieb, A. & Pattison, E. M., Married couples group psychotherapy. Archives of General Psychiatry, 1966, *14*, 143–152.

Gurman, A. S. Group marital therapy: clinical and empirical implications for outcome research. *International Journal of Group Psychotherapy*, 1971, *21*, 174.

Hooper, D., Sheldon, A. & Koumans, A. J. R. A study of group psychotherapy with married couples. *International Journal of Social Psychiatry*, 1968, *15*, 57–68.

Kohn, R. Treatment of married couples in a group. *Group Process*, 1971, *4*, 96.

Lebedun, M. Measuring movement in group marital counseling. *Social Casework*, 1970, *51*, 35–43.

Leichter, Elsa. Group psychotherapy of married couples groups: some characteristic treatment dynamics. *International Journal of Group Psychotherapy*, 1962, *12*, 154.

Leichter, Elsa. The interrelationship of content and process in therapy groups. *Journal of Social Casework*, 1966, *47*, 302.

Liberman, R. Behavioral approaches to family and couple therapy. *American Journal of Orthopsychiatry*, 1970, *40*, 106–118.

Olsen, E. The marriage—A basic unit for psychotherapy. *American Journal of Psychiatry*, 1971, *127*, 945–947.

Perlman, J. S. Group treatment of married couples. A symposium, I. Problems encountered in group psychotherapy of married couples. *International Journal of Group Psychotherapy*, 1960, *10*.

Reckless, J. A. Confrontation technique used with married couples in a group therapy setting. *International Journal of Group Psychiatry*, 1969, *19*, 203–213.

Sherman, S. Group counseling. In Eisenstein, V. W. *Neurotic interaction in marriage*. New York: Basic Books, Inc. 1956.

Targow, J. G. & Zweber, R. V. Participants' reactions to treatment in a married couples group. *International Journal of Group Psychotherapy*, 1969, *19*, 221–225.

Premarital Counseling

Keep your eyes wide open before marriage, half shut afterward.

BENJAMIN FRANKLIN

If marriages are to be better in the future than they have been in the past, education for marriage and premarital counseling would seem to be among the necessary steps. Many marriage counselors do premarital counseling and would like to do more, since prevention of marital difficulties may be more effectively handled in premarital counseling rather than in attempts at patching up a deteriorating marriage, if not an already broken marriage.

In Chapter 23, Owen Morgan, a psychologist, presents some points for premarital discussion in groups coming together for premarital counseling. Dr. Morgan has led many such discussions when he formerly worked at the Merrill-Palmer Institute in Detroit. Each person leading such group discussions in premarital counseling may want to develop different topics and approaches, but Dr. Morgan gives us some thought-provoking suggestions.

Nathaniel Branden, a psychologist, in Chapter 24, provides a defense of the concept of "romantic love." Some people would say that the concept of romantic love explains why people get married. Some authorities in the field seem to think that the romantic notions of love cause more problems than anything else in many people when they are considering marriage. Branden discusses the concept of romantic love in a provocative article.

In Chapter 25, Ben N. Ard, Jr. discusses the many and varied attitudes toward love and aggression in our culture and specifically deals with the perils of loving. "Love" is not all "peaches and cream," it would seem, nor is it all candlelight, roses, dances, perfume, and candy. These attitudes toward love (and its opposite, aggression) influence men and women in the continuing "battle between the sexes," and influence how they relate to each other in and outside of marriage. The attitudes toward "romantic love" expressed in this article may be disagreed with by many people. Each reader is urged to think through the implications of the various views expressed about "romantic love" and come to his or her own conclusions, after having considered all the relevant data. Do counselors have to be able to distinguish between "sick" and "healthy" love?

In Chapter 26, Albert Ellis discusses a rational approach to premarital counseling. Some of the questions that need to be dealt with in premarital counseling are: "Is my fiancée the right person for me?" "Should I have premarital sex relations?" "How can I find a suitable mate?" "How can I overcome my sexual incompetence or my homosexual leanings before I marry?" Dr. Ellis discusses how these and other questions can be handled in premarital counseling according to the principles of "rational psycho-therapy." Dr. Ellis puts his ideas into a basic A-B-C schema which can be adopted and tried by any marriage counselor in his or her practice, or even put into practice by any interested person in his own private life. The theory and practice of rational psychotherapy are applied to two cases of individuals who were seen for premarital counseling.

In Chapter 26, Lester A. Kirkendall, a psychologist, takes a courageous look at contraceptives for the unmarried. This is a controversial topic and one on which many people have conflicting views. Dr. Kirkendall gives the reader a chance to honestly examine and think about what some people would consider unthinkable. With the advent of the pill and the loop, the topic of contraceptives has received much more attention in all the mass media. Unmarried as well as married people will have to come to some decision regarding contraceptives. Kirkendall's article may provide a thoughtful and provocative first step into this difficult area.

In Chapter 28, Clark Vincent, an authority on sociological aspects of premarital and extramarital pregnancies, discusses counseling in such cases. Several topics are discussed, including cases involving unmarried mothers, counseling with the young unwed mother, counseling with the unwed's parents, whether or not there should be a marriage, decisions concerning the baby, unmarried fathers, married and divorced "unwed" mothers, the divorced unmarried mother, and, finally, maintaining the context in counseling with such cases.

CHAPTER 23

Some Points for
Premarital Discussion

Owen Morgan

This chapter is prepared with the purpose in mind of passing on in written form some of the things I would hope to talk over with young people who seek premarital consultation. None of them are meant as the "pronouncements," which they might appear to be without any opportunity for discussing them together, but primarily as something to stimulate thinking and for people to use as they relate to the meanings which their own experiences have for the two of them. My hope would be that reading this might prompt young people to talk with some professional person—counselor, family life educator, clergyman, or physician—who is specifically trained in helping people as they move into marriage.

Ultimately, the discussion will deal with specific aspects of the sexual relationship in marriage. These are by no means necessarily the most important aspects; in fact, my own feeling is that, important as they are, they are secondary to the deeper meaning of marriage. People get married primarily because of the human quest for love, belonging, intimacy (in the general sense), the need to be needed—in other words, because of the desire to live significantly with someone they love. Even in cultures where there is a great deal of sexual freedom outside of marriage, people still do marry. Some one figured it up and concluded that less than one-tenth of one percent of the average couple's time is spent in any kind of direct sex play (although broader ramifications of sexuality certainly run through much of marriage). It is the meaning which a husband and wife have to each other in all aspects of their living together that determines the success of a marriage. Sometimes people forget this. For example, some writers have asserted that much marital difficulty stems from sexual maladjustment due to disparity in the size of sex organs. It is true that "bigness" and "littleness" have a lot to do with marital success, but it is the bigness or littleness of people as persons, and not that of physical anatomy, which is more likely to play the greater part in most cases.

You may wonder, then, why the sexual relationship in particular is given so much attention in this discussion. It is largely because there is less likelihood that people marrying have had a good opportunity for learning in a sensible way about this part of marriage, and especially because many couples are likely to have more difficulty learning to communicate with each other in this area. Also, each of the partners will be likely to have had more previous experience with other aspects of the marriage relationship, since scarcely anyone has lived in isolation. After all, marriage is primarily a human relationship—one which is more intimate, more permanent, more continuous, more rewarding, sometimes more frustrating and disappointing, but in very few ways entirely different from other kinds of relationships (sex and parenthood roles tending to be major exceptions). For example, there are many ways in which living with a roommate is similar to marriage, and in general one of the best indications for predicting the likelihood of success in marriage is the way each of the parties has been able to get along with the people he or she has lived with, played with, and worked with up to this time. This is, of course, barring any specifically warped attitudes or behavior patterns concerning the ways in which marriage *is* different, either in degree or kind.

Thus, human relations skills, attitudes, personality and behavior patterns constitute the basic equipment a person brings to marriage. Emotional maturity (bigness rather than littleness, being as concerned with the welfare and happiness of another as with your own, having given up childish ways and adopted those of an adult, not *having* to have your own way); adaptability or flexibility as contrasted with rigidity; having a purpose in life, hopefully somewhat similar to that of your mate; and the capacity to both give and receive love, warmth, and understanding—these are the keystones on which marriages stand or fall. Such human relations skills as the ability to communicate and talk out your feelings and thoughts, hopes and aspirations, problems and disappointments with each other in ways which are neither personally threatening nor defensive, are also mighty valuable assets. Obviously the ability to *listen* with understanding to each other is important, too. None of these behavior characteristics or skills can be acquired merely by will or resolution alone. They are much more basic than some of the other things we will talk about here. Sometimes it may be possible for a person or a couple, realizing their importance and the need to work to develop them, to do so in the process of being married and living together. Usually, though, habits, personality patterns, and ways of looking at life have been going in certain directions long before marriage enters the picture. There is no point in *blaming* anyone for lacking these qualities, for rare indeed is the person who is like he is just because he decided he would be that way. This does not mean that no one has any responsibility for his behavior, but understanding and basic acceptance constitute the atmosphere which fosters growth rather than blame or guilt. And it is not safe to rely on the marriage relationship to modify ways of behaving and responding. When a person recognizes a need for real growth, recognition of this need being an important first step, it is wise for him to talk and work with someone trained to give help of this kind.

It may well be that the most important factor of all in determining your qualification for marriage is the way you feel about being *you*—the degree to which you feel comfortable in your own skin.

There are some common misconceptions about marriage which we might stop to consider. The first concerns what happiness lies waiting for you in marriage, just lying there for you to stumble into. A couple finds in marriage pretty much just what they put into it—themselves—for their own personalities and the resulting relationships are the ingredients. Foolish indeed is the unhappy single person who concludes that all he needs to be happy is a trip to the altar. Another misconception is that love is all that counts. True, love is essential, but marriage isn't all "moonlight and four roses"; there is a lot of down-to-earth working together in the everyday realities of living. Besides, it is practically impossible to love each other all the time; there are times when every married couple gets fed up with each other, at least momentarily, just as almost all parents sometimes get fed up with their children (and vice versa)—clear to the ears. It is quite important to realize this, for many young people get hit over the head hard with it, both in marriage and in parenthood, and are likely to think it is because they are "bad" or "abnormal" people, not realizing that others experience the same thing. There are bound to be irritations, upsets, conflicts, disappointments, and frustrations. A successful marriage is not characterized by an absence of all conflict and difficulty, but rather by the ability to work through them.

Still another false assumption is that the honeymoon will be the best time of the marriage and sexual utopia—or any other kind. A further misconception is that you don't have to pay for what you get in marriage. There is a lot of give and take, and the person who isn't equipped or prepared to give up a lot for the very great potential satisfactions is in for a rude awakening, just as is the person who thinks there is something magic about a thirty-minute wedding ceremony which automatically assures everlasting satisfactions for the couple without any further effort on their part. In summary, marriage quite likely provides greater opportunity for the deepest satisfactions known to humans, but it quite likely provides greater disappointments and frustrations, too. In other words, it may well be true that the range of meaningful experiences is wider in marriage because the intensity and continuity of the relationship is greater.

Any new venture requires adjustments, and marriage is no exception. People should not expect to immediately shuck off their old habits of living as single individuals and start automatically to live as a married couple. Building a sense of "we-ness" along with "I-ness" is probably the most important task facing the couple. There are practical things to learn and to work out in this respect. For example, if a person is used to sleeping alone, sleeping with anyone else—man, woman, or beast—may take some getting used to. An instance has been reported of one brand new bridegroom who spent the latter part of his wedding night huddled up on the floor next to the radiator with his overcoat over him because there wasn't much else he could do after his wife stretched herself out diagonally across the bed, all wound up in the blankets. (Veteran husbands might have some suggestions here, but the bridegroom wouldn't even have considered them so few hours after the wedding ceremony!)

In planning the wedding and all the activities leading up to it, some thought can very wisely be given to the fact that utter exhaustion is not the best condition for launching wedded life.

A honeymoon which, regardless of its length, provides an element of unhurried relaxation and privacy is helpful in beginning this venture. It is a good idea to have done some planning ahead of time, but not so rigidly as to rule out flexibility. (It is, by the way, a good idea to let some responsible person know something of your likely whereabouts in case of an emergency at home.) The honeymoon and early stages of marriage might best be considered merely as a continuation of the "courtship plane," rather than assuming that this is to be the peak of marital bliss.

Popularly anyway, the honeymoon is thought of as having a large and important sexual component. Again, this is partly because it is more likely to be a new experience and one for which the couple has presumably been waiting. Even if there have been premarital sexual experiences, there can be more freedom and completeness now. Not that this is all the bride and groom have been waiting for, but in most of the other areas there is at least more of an overlap with previous experience. Of course, even without a premarital sexual relationship per se, there is still some overlap, unless we make an arbitrary and artificial distinction between sexual intercourse and all other forms of loving relating, including in most cases a certain amount of erotic play. Still, there would usually be *more* of a difference between what is *to be* experienced and what *has been* experienced during previous years of the person's life in the sexual area than in other realms.

Sex, like marriage, is essentially another kind of a *human relationship*, although physically more intimate than most others. (It should be noted here that it is entirely possible [a] for sexual intercourse to occur without any real relationship or psychological intimacy, and [b] for two people to be deeply and personally intimate without any sexual behavior at all.) My own definition runs something like this: "Sex is a good and delightful way for a couple to express their love for each other and to have fun together—and when they are ready (ideally, that is) to become parents. It is essentially another way of relating to, and communicating with, each other." In all aspects of this very human relationship, but even more particularly in sex, such qualities as love, consideration, understanding, patience, and mutuality are most significant. These qualities are much more important than specific knowledge about sexual anatomy or techniques. In the sexual relationship there is a potential for fulfillment and completion that is not likely to be duplicated elsewhere in life, and it is in the meaning which this holds for the particular couple, rather than physical sensations as such, that the core of the experience lies.

It is unreasonable to think that all couples can learn to relate sexually with utmost effectiveness in the early weeks of marriage. There may be an instinctual basis, but loving is partially an art, which requires the development of understandings and skills that can come only through experience over a period of time. Any universal expectation of sexual bliss during the honeymoon leaves the door wide open for disappointment. In fact, some couples may have relatively little success at first, but patience and a reasonable lack of haste and urgency are likely to pay dividends later. Being able to talk with each other and to help each other is especially important here. There is really no valid reason to think that the wedding night is a complete failure if either fatigue, miscalculated menstrual schedule, or what have you, happens to postpone for a brief time initiation of intercourse itself. Usually this wouldn't be the case, but in instances where it is, there's lots of time a-waitin'.

Presumably the bride and groom will have seen a physician for a general examination and premarital consultation. He has checked, along with other things, the condition of the hymen and taken steps to remedy or show the girl how to remedy the situation if such steps are needed. With the kind of life girls live now, the use of tampons, more frequent and earlier pelvic examinations, etc., many brides need no medical help here, though they have not had previous sexual experiences.

For most couples in this day and age, having a choice about when a pregnancy is to occur is important. This is another matter in which the physician's help should be sought. He is the one who can provide not only the prescription but also the education and guidance for the couple in the most effective use of whatever means of family planning they choose. In many metropolitan areas a local agency affiliated with the national Planned Parenthood organization provides excellent help for couples with family planning if they do not consult a private physician for this purpose. This consultation should take place at least several weeks before the time when sexual intercourse is begun. If the rhythm method is to be used, medical guidance is particularly important in order to maximize the reliability of this method, which even under medical supervision is by no means completely reliable.

In only an artificial way can the sexual part of marriage be separated from the rest of the relationship. It is an integral part of a whole network of relationships in the marriage. It is a very important part, but like any of the others, it needs to be viewed in the perspective of the total meaning which living and loving together have for any particular couple. Frequently, one or the other of two extreme points of view is encountered. The first would hold that sex is the crux of marriage and that almost everything that goes on rests on the sexual basis. The other would maintain that this aspect of marriage really hasn't much significance at all and that we should think as little of it as possible. Neither of these positions seems at all tenable. Marriages built on sexual attraction alone, unless the rest of the relationship grows, are likely to be shallow and hazardous. On the other hand, if sex has no significance, then men might just as well marry men and women marry women. When unfortunate negative attitudes and a too-often appalling lack of information don't distort the potentials of the sexual relationship, it can make marriage a more delightful and a more meaningful kind of life, adding zest to the experience of living together through the years. (In *The Happy Family*, by David Levy and Ruth Munroe, the chapter on "Sexual Satisfaction" depicts the variety of meanings which the sexual relationship can have.) Once again though, it is the satisfaction and meaning found in all aspects of living together which is the ultimate criterion for our marriages today, so no one particular area can be considered by itself. There have been marriages in which sexual activity was *in*voluntarily ruled out which were more satisfying to the partners than *some* in which it served as a major focal point. The ideal would seem to be making the most of *all* potential avenues of sharing, communication, and joy, including of course the sexual channels.

Just as attitudes concerning roles of men and women in general have been modified through the years, so have those about sexual relationships. Today there is more thought given to making them a more mutual kind of experience, as in other relationships. This is in contrast to traditional views which held that sex was something of an obligation for wives and a right for husbands. Women were not supposed to really find any pleasure in sex, but it was their duty to "submit" in order to satisfy their husbands. Actually, in recent years this pendulum may have swung too far in the opposite direction, with many articles in popular journals carrying the implication that husbands are usually "at fault" if their wives don't find some sort of ethereal and superhuman ecstasy.

The criterion for success in sexual living should be much the same as for the marriage in general—the satisfaction of the partners involved rather than merely the kind or intensity of sensations. Some people may think that a "democratic" type family, with a balance of power, mutual participation in decision-making, etc., is the only thing; but if some families prefer another sort and are happy with that, then more power to them (and less to anyone who tries to show them how miserable they are)! Since the relationship between expectations and fulfillment is important in determining "satisfaction" (e.g., when you expect a movie to be really out of this world and find it only mediocre, you are more disappointed than if it hadn't been given such a buildup), let's take a moment to discuss the reasonableness of expectations about marriage. What we say here is important for marriage in general, not just for some isolated segment of it.

It is difficult to avoid something of a dilemma here, for expectations can be either too high or too low. Not knowing anything about what to expect nor how to enhance the experience can detract from satisfactions, too. For example, to carry the analogy of a movie further, a person who had never experienced a movie before and had ltttle idea of what to expect might go to a drive-in theater and see the film without knowing he was supposed to make use of any audio device. He might enjoy the *seeing* of the show, not realizing that it could have been even better. It might not be accurate to say that he was dissatisfied, yet we would likely agree that he was sort of missing the boat. On the other hand, if this person always expected to hear stereophonic sound or to have cool breezes blow on him when mountain scenes were shown, he might well be disappointed. Similarly, if wives are led to anticipate the earth trembling, stars quivering, bells playing heavenly tunes and the aforementioned indescribable ecstacy, they may feel cheated in their actual sexual experience and think they are unhappy in their marriages. Again our contention that happiness in marriage cannot be measured only in terms of physical sensations. On the other hand there is little valid reason to assume that eventually the sexual experiences can't be mutually enjoyable instead of just for one to enjoy and the other to tolerate. Even if the wife herself doesn't care whether she really gets involved and is relatively satisfied with nothing more than the feeling that, "It's so nice that I can provide satisfactions for my husband whom I love so much," there is still the husband's feeling to think about. If he is satisfied with this, too, then none of the rest of us has any business complaining, but *he* may prefer something besides sole satisfaction for himself. The average wife would probably find some satisfaction in just watching her husband enjoy a meal she had prepared. But wouldn't it be reasonable to think that the husband might enjoy the meal more if they ate together and both enjoyed it? This is what is meant by "mutuality," and it is likely to be fostered by the participation in, and enjoyment of, the sexual relationship (and others) by both parties. (A good reading reference here is the chapter "The Art of Loving" by Dr. Kenneth Walker in the book *Men: The Meaning and Variety of Their Sexual Experiences*, edited by A. M. Krich.)

Now that the idea of mutuality and enjoyment together of married life has been stressed, the following paragraphs are offered in the hope that they may contribute to these goals in the sexual relationships.

In the majority of cases the husband's sexual response, at least in the early years of marriage, will be "nearer the surface" and perhaps will be more readily called into play than the wife's. There is some question as to whether this is due to the nature of the two sexes or is related to the teachings of our culture. There is nothing at all "wrong" if this is reversed, but it is more usual to find it as stated. This means, for one thing, that the husband may initially be interested more often than his wife. It is a rare marriage indeed where the sexual desire of husband and wife fit exactly the same pattern. Again, in some cases the frequency of desire may be reversed, but usually the other way around, at least in the earlier stages of marriage. Kinsey found that males reached the peak of sexual desire in late teens or early twenties, females in late twenties or early thirties. Again one is led to wonder whether this is strictly physiological or may be due to a later sexual awakening for women in our culture. At any rate, one or the other will sometimes be initially interested in sex play at times when the partner's attention is on something else altogether. However, if both partners maintain what could be called an attitude of "receptivity," i.e., a willingness to get involved in love-making and to permit words, caresses, etc., which will enhance interest and arousal, it will usually be possible for both to be caught up in the "spirit of the game" with something other than apathy or indifference. The emphasis is not meant here to be just on physical love-making or mechanical techniques, but includes warmth, responsiveness, and love in a broader sense. One writer (English, 1953) stresses the importance of seeing the capacity in men for tender love instead of *just* a passionate desire.

Another important difference often found between male and female sexual response—and one closely related to that described above—is that in many cases the husband can initiate, engage in, and complete his sexual "cycle" much more quickly than can his wife. It was because of a failure to recognize this that wives often used to have little part in the sexual relationship other than merely providing satisfaction for their husbands. One person has described this in terms of an analogy with a mile race between the typical husband and wife—pointing out that unless the husband either gave his wife a head start or stopped to let her catch up, he would usually finish way ahead of her. In sexual terms the finishing would be the sexual climax or orgasm. Because of the physiology involved, it is practically impossible for the husband to undertake intercourse until he is sexually aroused and has the resulting erection. This situation does not necessarily hold true for the wife, inasmuch as it is at least physically possible for her to engage in intercourse without being aroused, just as it is possible for her to continue after a climax (though perhaps not so enjoyably as before). In fact, there may be times when a couple has intercourse wherein the wife doesn't really get involved at all, and this may be less disturbing for her than a situation wherein she becomes highly aroused but finds that her husband has finished and she is left "in mid-air." The latter point makes it important to realize that sex play is not limited to intercourse as such—especially to intercourse in one particular way—and that at particular times mutual satisfaction is more likely if couples are willing to vary their pattern.

This might be a good point at which to say something about the sexual climax, for it is around this phenomenon that much confusion and misinformation have been in evidence. Actually it would make more sense to talk in terms of *contentment* and *relaxation*, for these are better operational terms for the goal, especially if we add the term *satisfaction* to the other two. However, since so many people ask questions specifically about the nature and significance of the *climax*, the following information is given: In the male this comes at the point of ejaculation of the seminal fluid containing the sperm cells. In the female there is no corresponding ejaculation, and the climax is not at all essential for conception. Some women have been confused about this because they interpret the secretion of the lubricating substance within and at the entrance to the vagina during sexual excitement as an ejaculation.

In terms of the build-up of excitation or tension and its release, the orgasm could be likened to the release of the string on an archer's bow after it has been pulled tighter and tighter to the point where it is very taut, then suddenly released. This "release" is usually accompanied by pleasurable sensations and sometimes by rhythmic muscular contractions in the genital area, the experience being somewhat more general and diffuse in the female as compared with a more specifically genital focus in the male. It is very important to note that the experience varies tremendously from individual to individual, and from time to time with the same person. For some couples it may take several weeks, months, or maybe even years to acquire the experience, skills, and teamwork essential for the wife to reach this potential. In some cases she may never experience anything exactly of this nature and yet be very happily married and find considerable enjoyment in the sexual relationship. Everything else being equal, there seems a better chance that the enjoyment will be enhanced if both usually experience some sense of contentment and relaxation following their sex play; beyond this no further prescription should be given concerning the nature of the response for any particular couple or time. Unfortunately, husbands and wives have sometimes been led to believe that if both partners don't finish explosively and even at exactly the same moment, they are really missing the mark. Such might be the ultra-ideal, but it is not a reasonable or realistic expectation in many cases. The feeling of satisfaction and completion or relaxation of some sort may leave one or both partners in such a state of drowsiness that sleep is the natural aftermath. When this is the case, it should not be interpreted as a lack of love or caring. For other people the experience will lead to a period of closeness and loving which will be more directly expressed.

In striving for some sort of mutual participation and response, it is important for each partner to know what sorts of love-play are effective in arousing the other. (Note: Premaritally, *if* they are committed to limiting their physical intimacy, it is equally important to know this in terms of avoiding intense arousal.) In much literature there has been an emphasis on the husband's knowing how to arouse the wife, without much attention to what the wife can do to make it interesting for the husband. Beyond just the specific caresses, it is very important for both to sense each other's responsiveness to all kinds of cues. Monogamy does not need to be equated with monotony—despite popular misconceptions to the contrary—if husband and wife will make some effort and devote some attention to keep it from being so and if they avoid being so involved in other roles that they shove this potentially vital and enlivening part of their life into the closet of routine. Both should have not only the responsibility but the opportunity and privilege to make it otherwise. (See the chapter, "Being a Married Mistress" in *How to Be a Woman*, by Mary and Lawrence K. Frank, keeping in mind that the implications should hold for both.) Sex is not "something that one person does to another" or "a favor which the wife bestows on the husband" (or vice versa); it should be a delightful and fulfilling experience together.

In the human organism there are certain erogenous or sexually sensitive zones. Some are rather common to most of the species, but others are more individual; and it is for this reason that adequate communication between husband and wife is particularly important. Again, this is assuming that there is a backdrop of tender and devoted love in general and that love play or sex play is primarily another way of expressing this love for each other, even if there are times when the mood is frivolous or in some other way is not just a direct reflection of abiding love. In this chapter we are discussing persons, not machines or animals, and this should especially be kept in mind when we discuss anatomy, physiology, or techniques, lest we leave the impression that it is just a physical process. The passionate and partially animalistic element of sex should not be ruled out by any means, and an attempt to see it just in a spiritual sense may be questioned, for it is a combination of tenderness and wildness. The caution here is against a mechanistic, step one–step two, approach. Lips and tongue are usually sexually sensitive, and from there on, except for the more specifically erogenous areas common to most, there is the great individual variation suggested before. In the male, the glans or head of the penis is the most specific center. In women the breasts, particularly the nipples, are usually sensitive, although not always to the same extent from individual to individual; but the clitoris is the most sensitive organ for the majority of women. Unknown to many is the fact that this tiny organ is homologous to the male penis. In some respects it resembles a miniature penis, and in embryonic development it is this which develops into the penis in the male. In the female it remains largely imbedded or sheathed in tissue, with barely the head or glans protruding just at the point where the inner lips of the vulva come together. It is important for both husband and wife to be aware of this organ, for it is direct, though gentle stimulation of the protruding glans (head) which will be most effective in increasing most wives' sexual arousal. Some think that with greater maturity the vagina itself may become the center of sexual excitation, but at least in early marriage the clitoris usually has an important place in this function. The clitoris, like the penis, tends to become somewhat erect during sexual arousal.

When the woman reaches a certain point of arousal, the sexual parts will ordinarily be bathed in a lubricating or moistening secretion, much like saliva in consistency. Unless this secretion has taken place, even very gentle stimulation (fondling) of the clitoris or surrounding genital area may be irritating rather than pleasurable. In most cases the response to the general love-making and the whole atmosphere of anticipation will take care of sufficient arousal for the moistening to take place. In some cases, however, it is important for some other means of moistening to be used. Saliva is the most readily available substitute. Another possibility is a non-greasy material such as surgical jelly or hand lotion.

In all of this preparation for the sexual relationship, usually spoken of as "foreplay," husband and wife have equal opportunity for participation (with neither being more responsible than the other). Sometimes the playing is the end as well as the means. It would be most unfortunate to leave the impression that this is some sort of chore, the price to be paid for the final part of the experience. Couples who take delight in all aspects of this playing with, and responding to, each other, both broadly and specifically speaking, know the zest, the joy, and the meaning which it can add to marriage. This is only another way of saying that the true value of marriage is the love, understanding, affirmation, and appreciation which "this man and this woman" have for each other in this most intimate of human relationships.

SUGGESTED READING

Chesser, E. *Love without fear*. New York: Roy, 1947. (paperback: Signet Books, $.35).

Ellis, A. *The art and science of love*. New York: Lyle Stuart, 1960. (paperback: Dell Publishing Co., 1965, $.95)

Ellis, A. Myths About Sex Compatibility. *Sexology*, May 1962, *28*, 652–655.

English, O. S. Sexual love: Man for Woman. In E. M. Ashley Montagu (Ed.), *The meaning of love*. New York: Julian Press, 1953.

English, O. S. Sex adjustment in marriage. In Fishbein & Kennedy (Eds.), *Modern marriage and family living*. New York: Oxford University Press, 1957.

Fromm, E. *The art of loving*. New York: Harper, 1956. (paperback: Bantam Books, $.60).

Jourard, S. *Personal adjustment: An approach through the study of healthy personality*. New York: Macmillan, 1963. Revised edition: Chapter 9, Interpersonal Behavior and Healthy Personality; Chapter 10, Healthy Interpersonal Relationships; Chapter 11, Love and Healthy Personality; Chapter 12, Sex and Healthy Personality.

Kovinovky, N. Premarital medical examination. In C. Vincent (Ed.), *Readings in marriage and family counseling*. New York: Cromwell, 1957.

Levy, D., & Munroe, R. *The happy family*. New York: Knopf, 1938.

Lewin, S., & Gilmore, J. *Sex without fear*. New York: Medical Research Press, 1953.

McGinnis, T. *Your first year of marriage*. New York: Doubleday, 1967.

Montagu, A. *The meaning of love*. New York: Julian Press, 1953.

Overstreet, H., & Overstreet, B. *The mind goes forth*. New York: Norton, 1956.

Stone, A., & Stone, H. *A marriage manual*. New York: Simon & Schuster, 1952.

Street, R. *Modern sex techniques*. New York: Wehman, 1959. (paperback: Lancer Books, 1966, $.75).

Walker, K. The art of love. In A. M. Krich (Ed.), *Men: The meaning and variety of their sexual experience*. New York: Dell, 1954. (paperback).

CHAPTER 24

Romantic Love: Neurosis
or Rational Ideal?

Nathaniel Branden

The concept of romantic love has a very short history. Throughout most of man's past, the concept was unknown; it is still unknown in many cultures of the world. As an ideal of the man-woman relationship, it has gained wide acceptance principally in North America. In Europe, its acceptance as the proper basis of marriage has never been so widespread. Its popularity has been growing steadily. During the past several decades, many members of the educated classes of India and Asia have been rebelling against the tradition of marriage arranged by families and have looked to America and to its concept of romantic love as a preferred ideal—paradoxically, at the very time the ideal has come under attack by American psychologists, sociologists, and anthropologists.

Primitive man had no notion of romantic love. The life of the earliest societies known to us was dominated by the tribal mentality. Little or no importance was granted to individual attachments. Little or no importance was granted to the worth of the individual personality. Individualism, as we understand that concept, was an entirely alien view. The individual was subordinated to the tribe—to tribal needs, rules, and taboos—in virtually every aspect of his life.

A major source of our knowledge of such societies comes from anthropological studies of primitive societies still in existence—such as Margaret Mead's study of the Samoans. Deep emotional attachments between individuals are very foreign to the Samoans' psychology and pattern of living. Sexual promiscuity, and a short duration of sexual relationships, is sanctioned or encouraged; whereas any tendency to form strong emotional bonds between individuals is actively discouraged (Mead, 1949).

In *The Natural History of Love*, Morton Hunt writes: "... by and large, the clanship structure and social life of most primitive societies provides a wholesale intimacy and a broad distribution of affections; ... most primitive people fail to see any great difference between individuals,

A paper delivered at the 1970 Annual Convention of the American Psychological Association, Sept. 3rd, Miami, Florida, and reprinted with permission.

and hence do not become involved in unique connections in the Western fashion; any number of trained observers have commented on the ease of their detachment from love objects, and their candid belief in the interchangeability of loves (Hunt, 1960). Dr. Audrey Richards, an anthropologist who lived among the Bemba of Northern Rhodesia in the 1930s, once related to a group of them an English folk-tale about a young prince who climbed glass mountains, crossed chasms, and fought dragons, all to obtain the hand of a maiden he loved. The Bemba were plainly bewildered, but remained silent. Finally, an old chief spoke up, voicing the feelings of all present in the simplest of questions: 'Why not take another girl?' he asked (Hunt, 1960)."

The principal purpose of marriage in primitive societies—indeed, in virtually all agricultural societies—is economic. The family is a unit established for the purpose of optimizing the chances of survival. Since survival in a pre-industrial society depends so crucially on physical strength and physical skills, the division of labor between man and woman is predominantly determined on the basis of their respective physical capacities. Man-woman relationships are conceived and defined not in terms of the need for emotional intimacy or fulfillment, but in terms of the practical needs associated with hunting, fighting, raising crops, child-rearing, etc. While it is reasonable to assume that at least in some instances men and women who live together develop feelings of warmth and affection—feelings which we might characterize as "love"—the notion of "marrying for love" is entirely absent from their thinking.

Among the Greeks—I am speaking now of Classical Greece—the upper classes, those who lived off the labor of slaves, tended to regard sexual or "love" relationships as an enjoyable game; a diversion of no deep importance which, as a matter of course, took place outside the marriage. Marriages were arranged between families for social, financial, and property reasons. As for the development of passionate and sustained sexual love between a man and a woman, when this occurred it was commonly regarded as a form of tragic madness, a ruinous disease, an affliction from the gods—a view not unlike that held by some contemporary psychologists, as we shall see.

When Rome was a great empire supported by its provinces, the city aristocrats had no occupations and no diversions except politics and extramarital sexual adventures. As with the Greeks, the Romans did not marry for love. Among the upper classes, marriages were arranged between families. A man married to acquire a housekeeper. Adultery, on the part of both sexes, was widespread and virtually taken for granted; it was regarded as a "sport" necessary to relieve the tedium of existence.

With the disintegration of the Roman Empire, a new cultural and historical force began to make its impact felt in the Western World: Christianity. What was the Christian view of sex, marriage, and the man-woman relationship?

Sex is evil, sex is sinful. It is good for a man not to touch a woman, taught St. Paul, but if men lack the necessary self control, "let them marry, for it is better to marry than to burn." Sexual abstinence was the moral ideal. Marriage—described as a "medicine for immorality"—was Christianity's reluctant concession to the depravity of human nature that made this ideal largely unattainable. Clement of Alexandria announced that "it is disgraceful to love another man's wife at all, or one's own too much." He announced further that "he who too ardently loves his own wife is an adulterer."

Christianity denied to women the legal rights and privileges they had won under the Romans; they lost all legal status, all right to own property. They were regarded, in effect, as vassals of the male, to whom they were to be entirely subordinate. This was justified on the ground that Eve had been the cause of Adam's downfall, therefore the cause of all the suffering men had to endure thereafter.

Marriage was still regarded essentially as an economic institution. Sex, even with marriage, required moral justification in the eyes of the Church; the sole justification was held to be the production of offspring; the purpose of offspring was to provide God with a plentiful supply of worshippers—it was evidently believed that He needed all He could get.

Given the brutally inhuman sexual repressiveness of the Middle Ages—when the influence of Christianity was at its most powerful—it is not surprising that the first major rebellion, the first blind groping toward a better view of the man-woman relationship, should emerge in the form of that strange concoction known as "the doctrine of courtly love."

Originating in the south of France toward the end of the 11th Century, this doctrine did not challenge the grey, dismal view of marriage that had been accepted for hundreds of years, but it upheld an exalted passion which was to exist between a man and someone else's wife. "Love" was identified specifically with extramarital involvements. I shall not attempt to recapitulate the many absurdities contained in the doctrine of courtly love, such as the proposition that "love that is known publicly rarely lasts," or that "every lover turns pale in the sight of the co-lover," or that "real jealousy always increases the worth of love," or that passion between husband and wife is impossible (Langdon-Davies, 1927). I wish merely to draw attention to three elements in this doctrine which are of profound and enduring importance, and which have relevance to the concept of romantic love as we understand it today: (a) authentic love between a man and a woman rests on and requires the free choice of each, and cannot flourish in the context of submission to family, social, or religious authority; (b) such love is based on admiration and mutual regard; (c) love is not an idle diversion, but is of supreme importance to one's life.

The concept of romantic love as the ideal basis of marriage, and as a widely-accepted cultural value, had to wait approximately seven centuries. It had to await the Industrial Revolution, the birth of a philosophy of individualism and the creation of the United States of America.

That which was distinctive about the American outlook, and which represented a radical break with the past, was its intransigent individualism, its doctrine of the supremacy of individual rights, and, more specifically, its belief in man's right to the pursuit of happiness. Few people today fully appreciate the revolutionary significance of the American concept of man's right to the pursuit of happiness. His own happiness. Here on earth. Man was not seen as the servant of the state or of society. For the first time in history, his right to exist for his own happiness was politically recognized. America is the first truly secular society men have ever known.

On the economic level, with the birth of the Industrial Revolution and the emergence of a capitalistic society, men and women were freed from dependence on the land as their sole means of survival. This was the beginning of woman's freedom from economic dependence on the male. In an industrial society, intellectual rather than physical skills are of paramount importance; physical strength as such has very little survival value; it became possible for a woman to earn her own living. Worshippers of the Middle Ages cried out that capitalism had destroyed the institution of family life. They stated that the legal rights women were winning under capitalism would lead to the end of civilization. They were correct to this extent: a new civilization, radically different from any that men had ever known, was in the process of being born—and one of its characteristics was that men and women were choosing to marry, not on the basis of economic necessity, but on the basis of their expectation of finding happiness and emotional fulfillment with one another.

Romantic love contains or entails the following precepts: (a) a man and a woman choose each other freely and voluntarily, without external compulsion or pressure; (b) they choose each other on the basis of values they believe the loved object to embody, that is, they choose on the basis of admiration and mutual regard; (c) they expect to achieve sexual fulfillment within the relationship rather than outside of it; (d) they commit themselves to mutual fidelity.

As I indicated at the start of this discussion, in the 20th Century the concept of romantic love has come under severe attack. Some three decades ago, Ralph Linton, an anthropologist, declared: "All societies recognize that there are occasional violent, emotional attachments between persons of the opposite sex, but our present American culture is practically the only one which had attempted to . . . make them the basis for marriage. Their rarity in most societies suggests that they are psychological abnormalities to which our own culture has attached an extraordinary value (Linton, 1936)."

Before considering the various attacks on romantic love, I propose to turn from an historical to a psychological examination of this subject. Is there a need for love? If so, what are the factors within man's nature that generate this need? What are the psychological factors that cause two people to fall in love? What is the relationship between love and sex? These are some of the questions I will now proceed to consider.

The Psychology of Romantic Love

I wish to mention at the outset that in the discussion of romantic love that follows I shall borrow rather heavily from my discussion of this subject in my book *The Psychology of Self-Esteem* (Branden, 1969).

The experience of romantic love answers a profound psychological need in man. But the nature of that need cannot be understood apart from an understanding of a wider need: man's need of human companionship—of human beings he can respect, admire and value, and with whom he can interact intellectually and emotionally.

Man's desire for human companionship may be explained *in part* by the fact that living and dealing with other men in a social context, trading goods and services, etc., affords man a manner of survival immeasurably superior to that which he could obtain alone on a desert island or on a self-sustaining farm. Man obviously finds it to his interest to deal with men whose values and character are like his own, rather than with men of inimical values and character. And, normally, man develops feelings of benevolence or affection toward men who share his values, and who act in ways that are beneficial to his existence.

It should be apparent, however—from observation and by introspection—that practical, existential considerations such as these are not sufficient to account for the phenomenon in question; and that the desire for and experience of friendship and love reflect a distinct *psychological* need. Everyone is aware, introspectively, of the desire for companionship, for someone to talk to, to be with, to feel understood by, to share important experiences with—the desire for *emotional closeness* with another human being. What is the nature of the psychological need that generates this desire?

Two events were crucial in leading me to the answer.

One afternoon, while sitting alone in my living room, I found myself contemplating with pleasure a large philodendron plant standing against a wall. It was a pleasure I had experienced before, but suddenly it occurred to me to ask myself: What is the nature of this pleasure? What is its cause?

The pleasure was not primarily esthetic: were I to learn that the plant was artificial, its esthetic chracteristics would remain the same, but my response would change radically; the special pleasure I experienced would vanish. Essential to my enjoyment was the knowledge that the plant was healthily and glowingly *alive*. There was the feeling of a bond, almost of a kind of kinship, between the plant and me; in the midst of inanimate objects, we were united in the fact of possessing life. I thought of the motive of people who, in the most impoverished conditions, plant flowers in boxes on their window sills—for the pleasure of watching something grow. *What is the value to man of observing successful life?*

Suppose, I thought, one were left on a dead planet where one had every material provision to ensure survival, but where nothing was alive; one would feel like a metaphysical alien. Then suppose one came upon a living plant; surely one would greet the sight with eagerness and pleasure. *Why?*

Because—I realized—all life; life by its very nature, entails a struggle, and struggle entails the possibility of defeat; and man desires, and finds pleasure in seeing, concrete instances of successful life, as confirmation of his knowledge that successful life is possible. It is, in effect, a *metaphysical* experience. He desires the sight of successful life, not as a means of allaying doubts or of reassuring himself, but as a means of experiencing and confirming on the perceptual level, the level of immediate reality, that which he knows conceptually.

If such is the value that a plant can offer to man, I wondered, then cannot the sight of another human being offer man a much more intense form of that experience? This is surely relevant to the psychological value that human beings find in one another.

The next crucial step in my thinking occurred on an afternoon when I sat on the floor playing with my dog—a wire-haired fox terrier named Muttnik.

We were jabbing at and boxing with each other in mock ferocity. What I found delightful and fascinating was the extent to which Muttnik appeared to grasp the playfulness of my intention; she was snarling and snapping and striking back while being unfailingly gentle in a manner that projected total, fearless trust. The event was not unusual; it is one with which most dog-owners are familiar. But a question suddenly occurred to me, of a kind I had never asked myself before: Why am I having such an enjoyable time? What is the nature and source of my pleasure?

Part of my response, I recognized, was simply the pleasure of watching the healthy self-assertiveness of a living entity. But that was not the essential factor causing my response. The essential factor pertained to the *interaction* between the dog and myself—the sense of interacting and communicating with a living *consciousness*.

Suppose I were to view Muttnik as an automaton without consciousness or awareness, and to view her actions and responses as entirely mechanical; then my enjoyment would vanish. The factor of consciousness was of primary importance.

Then I thought: Suppose I were left on an uninhabited island; would not the presence of Muttnik be of enormous value to me? Obviously it would. Because she could make a practical contribution to my physical survival? Obviously not. Then what value did she have to offer? Companionship. A conscious entity with whom to interact and communicate—as I was doing at the time. *But why is that a value?*

The answer to this question—I realized—would explain much more than the attachment to a pet; involved in this issue is the psychological principle that underlies man's desire for *human* companionship, the principle that would explain why a conscious entity seeks out and values other conscious entities—*why consciousness is a value to consciousness*.

When I identified the answer; I called it "the Muttnik principle"—because of the circumstances under which it was discovered. Now let us consider the nature of this principle.

My feeling of pleasure in playing with Muttnik contained a particular kind of self-awareness, and *this* was the key to understanding my reaction. The self-awareness came from the nature of the "feedback" Muttnik was providing. From the moment that I began to "box," she responded in a playful manner; she conveyed no sign of feeling threatened; she projected an attitude of trust and pleasurable excitement. Were I to push or jab at an inanimate object, it would react in a purely mechanical way; it would not be responding to me; there could be no possibility of it grasping the *meaning* of my actions, of apprehending my *intentions*, and of guiding its behavior accordingly. It could not react to my psychology, that is, to my mental state. Such communication and response is possible only among conscious entities. The effect of Muttnik's behavior was to make me feel *seen*, to make me feel *psychologically visible* (at least, to some extent). Muttnik was responding to me, not as to a mechanical object, but as to a *person*.

What is significant and must be stressed is that Muttnik was responding to me as a person in a way that I regarded as objectively *appropriate*, that is, consonant with my view of myself and of what I was conveying to her. Had she responded with fear and an attitude of cowering, I would have experienced myself as being, in effect, *misperceived* by her, and would not have felt pleasure.

Now, why does man value and find pleasure in the experience of self-awareness and psychological visibility that the appropriate response (or "feedback") from another consciousness can evoke?

Consider the fact that normally man experiences himself as a *process*—in that consciousness itself is a process, an activity, and the contents of man's mind are a shifting flow of perceptions, thoughts, and emotions. His own mind is not an unmoving entity which man can contemplate objectively—that is, contemplate as a direct object of awareness—as he contemplates objects in the external world.

He has, of course, a sense of himself, of his own identity. But it is experienced more as a feeling than a thought—a feeling which is very diffuse, which is interwoven with all his other feelings, and which is very hard, if not impossible, to isolate and consider by itself. His "self-concept" is not a single concept, but a cluster of images and abstract perspectives on his various (real or imagined) traits and characteristics, the sum total of which can never be held in focal awareness at any one time; that sum is *experienced*, but it is not *perceived* as such.

In the course of a man's life, his values, goals and ambitions are first conceived in his mind, that is, they exist as data of consciousness, and then—to the extent that his life is successful—are translated into action and objective reality; they become part of the "out there," of the world that he perceives. They achieve expression and reality in material form. This is the proper and necessary pattern of man's existence. Yet a man's most important creation and highest value—his character, his soul, his psychological self—can never follow this pattern in the literal sense, can never exist apart from his own consciousness; it can never be perceived by him as part of the "out there." But man *desires* a form of objective self-awareness and, in fact, *needs* this experience.

Since man is the motor of his own actions, since his concept of himself, of the person he has created, plays a cardinal role in his motivation—he desires and needs the fullest possible experience of the reality and objectivity of that person, of his self.

When a man stands before a mirror, he is able to perceive his own face as an object in reality, and he finds pleasure in doing so, in contemplating the physical entity who is himself. There is a value in being able to look and think: "That's me." The value lies in the experience of objectivity.

Is there a mirror in which man can perceive his *psychological* self? In which he can perceive his own soul? Yes. The mirror is another consciousness.

Man is able, alone, to know himself conceptually. What another consciousness can offer is the opportunity for man to experience himself perceptually.

To a very small extent, that was the opportunity afforded me by Muttnik. In her response, I was able to see reflected an aspect of my own personality. But a human being can experience this self-awareness to a full and proper extent only in a relationship with a consciousness like his own, a consciousness possessing an equal range of awareness: another human being.

A person's intelligence, his manner of thinking, his basic premises and values, his sense of life, are all made manifest in his personality. A person's psychology is expressed through his behavior, through the things he says and does, and through the way he says and does them. It is in this sense that a person's self is an object of perception to others. When others react to a man, to their view of him and of his behavior, their reaction (which begins in their consciousness) is expressed through *their* behavior, through the things they say and do relative to him, and through the way they say and do them. If their view of him is consonant with his own, and is, accordingly, transmitted by their behavior, he feels perceived, he feels psychologically visible. And he experiences a sense of the objectivity of his self and of his psychological state; he perceives the reflection of himself in their behavior. It is in this sense that others can be a psychological mirror.

Just as there are many different aspects of a man's personality and inner life, so a man may feel visible in different respects in different human relationships, and to different degrees.

All the forms of interaction and communication among people—intellectual, emotional, physical—can serve to give a person the perceptual evidence of his visibility in one respect or another; or, relative to particular people, can give him the impression of invisibility.

A significant mutuality of intellect, of basic premises and values, of fundamental attitude toward life, is the precondition of that projection of mutual visibility which is the essence of authentic friendship. A friend, said Aristotle, is another self. It was an apt formulation. A friend reacts to a man as, in effect, the man would react to himself in the person of another. Thus, the man perceives himself through his friend's reaction. He perceives his own person through its consequences in the consciousness (and, as a result, in the behavior) of the perceiver.

This, then, is the root of man's desire for companionship and love: *the desire to perceive himself as an entity in reality—to experience the perspective of objectivity—through and by means of the reactions and responses of other human beings.*

The principle involved ("the Muttnik principle")—let us call it "the *visibility* principle"—may be summarized as follows: Man desires and needs the experience of self-awareness that results from perceiving his self as an objective existent—and he is able to achieve this experience through interaction with the consciousness of other living entities.

The extent to which he is able to achieve it depends most crucially on the degree of mutuality of values between another person and himself.

The desire for visibility is usually experienced by men as the desire for understanding, that is, the desire to be understood by other human beings. If a man is happy and proud of some achievement, he wants to feel that those who are close to him—those he cares for—understand his achievement and its personal meaning to him, understand and attach importance to the reasons behind his emotions. Or, if a man is given a book by a friend and told that this is the kind of book he will enjoy, the man feels pleasure and gratification if his friend's judgment proves correct—because he feels visible, he feels understood. Or, if a man suffers from some personal loss, it is of value to him to know that his plight is understood by those close to him, and that his emotional state has reality to them. It is not blind "acceptance" that a normal person desires, nor unconditional "love," but *understanding*.

Let me mention, without further elaboration here, that a psychologically healthy person, a person of self-esteem, expects others to *perceive* his value, not to *create* it. He does not desire approval indiscriminately or for its own sake; the admiration of others is of value and importance to him only if he respects the standards by which others judge him, and only if the admiration is directed at qualities which he himself regards as admirable.

The desire for visibility does not mean that a psychologically healthy man's basic preoccupation, in any human encounter, is with the question of whether or not he is properly appreciated. When a man of self-esteem meets a person for the first time, his primary concern is not, "Am I visible to him?"—but rather, "What do I think of him?" His primary concern, necessarily, is with his own judgment and evaluation of the facts that confront him.

As I have indicated, a man can feel visible in different respects and to varying degrees in different human relationships. A relationship with a casual stranger does not afford man the degree of visibility he experiences with an acquaintance. A relationship with an acquaintance does not afford man the degree of visibility he experiences with an intimate friend.

But there is one relationship which is unique in the depth and comprehensiveness of the visibility it entails: romantic love. What is the unique nature of romantic love?

Contained in every human being's self-concept is the awareness of being male or female. One's sexual identity is normally an integral and intimate part of one's experience of personal identity. No one experiences oneself merely as a human being, but always as a male human being or a female human being.

While one's sexual identity (one's masculinity or femininity) is rooted in the facts of one's biological nature, it does not consist merely of being physically male or female; it consists of the way one psychologically *experiences* one's maleness or femaleness. More broadly, it consists of one's personal psychological traits *qua* man or woman.

For example, if a man is characteristically honest in his dealings with people, this trait pertains to his psychology as a human being; it is not a sexual characteristic. If, on the other hand, he feels confident in his sexual role relative to women, this trait pertains to his psychology specifically as a man.

What, then, are the various psychological attributes whose sum constitutes one's specifically psycho-sexual identity, that is, one's psychological identity as a man or as a woman.

One's psycho-sexual identity (one's sexual personality) is the product and reflection of the manner in which one responds to one's nature as a sexual being. To what extent is one aware of oneself as a sexual entity? What is one's view of sex and of its significance in human life? How does one feel about one's own body, not esthetically, but rather as a value, as a source of pleasure? How does one view the opposite sex? How does one feel about the body of the opposite sex? How does one identify the respective sexual roles of man and woman? How does one evaluate one's own sexual role—and does one feel confident in regard to it? His answers to such questions determine (for good or for bad) a human being's sexual psychology.

A person's attitude toward these issues is not formed in a psychological vacuum. On the contrary: in sex, more than in any other realm, the greatest range of one's premises and psychology tend to be involved. The single most pertinent factor in determining a person's sexual attitudes is the general level of his self-esteem: the higher the level of self-esteem, the stronger the likelihood that his responses to his own sexuality will be appropriate, that is, that he will exhibit a healthy sex psychology.

A healthy masculinity or femininity is the consequence and expression of a rationally affirmative response to one's own sexual nature. This entails: a strong, affirmative awareness of one's own sexuality; a positive (fearless and guiltless) response to the phenomenon of sex; a perspective on sex that sees it as integrated to one's mind and values (*not* as a dissociated, mindless, and meaningless physical indulgence); a positive and self-valuing response to one's own body; a strong, positive response to the body of the opposite sex; a confident understanding, acceptance and enjoyment of one's own sexual role.

This last point requires elaboration. The difference in the male and female sexual roles proceeds from differences in man's and woman's respective anatomy and physiology. Physically, man is the bigger and stronger of the two sexes; his system produces and uses more energy; and he tends (for physiological reasons) to be physically more active. Sexually, his is the more active and dominant role; he has the greater measure of control over his own pleasure and that of his partner; it is he who penetrates and the woman who is penetrated (with everything this entails, physically and psychologically). While a healthy aggressiveness and self-assertiveness is proper and desirable for both sexes, man experiences the essence of his masculinity in the act of romantic dominance; woman experiences the essence of her femininity in the act of romantic surrender.

Both roles require strength and self-confidence. A self-doubting man experiences fear of romantic self-assertiveness; a self-doubting woman experiences fear of romantic surrender. An unconfident woman fears the challenge of masculine strength; an unconfident man fears the challenge of the woman's expectation that he be strong.

Healthy masculinity requires a self-confidence that permits the man to be free, uninhibited, and benevolently self-assertive in the role of romantic initiator and aggressor. Healthy femininity requires a self-confidence that permits the woman to be free, uninhibited, and benevolently self-assertive in the role of challenger and responder to the man.

(The foregoing is intended only as a general indication of the masculine and feminine sex roles, not as an exhaustive analysis; the latter is outside the scope of this discussion.)

Just as one's sexual personality is essential to one's sense of oneself, so it is essential to that which one wishes to objectify and to see reflected or made visible in human relationships. The experience of full visibility and full self-objectification entails being perceived, and perceiving oneself, not merely as a certain kind of human being, but as a certain kind of man or woman.

This applies to persons with a neurotic sex psychology as much as to persons whose sex psychology is normal. For instance, the relationship of a sadist and a masochist rests on the fact that each senses and responds positively to the weaknesses, flaws, secret doubts, and neurotic fears of the other. A major difference, however, is that, unlike a healthy couple, the sadist and masochist would dread to conceptualize and face consciously the nature of that which is being made visible between them.

From the above discussion, it should be clear why the optimal experience of visibility and self-objectification requires interaction with a member of the opposite sex. A close friend of the same sex, with whom one enjoys a mutuality of mind and values, perceives and responds to those traits which pertain to one's psychology *qua* human being, but not *qua* sexual being. One's sexual personality can be perceived and appreciated *abstractly* by one's friend, but it cannot be of great *personal* importance to him. A member of the opposite sex, with whom one enjoys a strong mutuality of mind and values, is capable of perceiving and personally responding to one in *both* areas, that is, *qua* human being and *qua* sexual being. The difference in the way one is viewed from the perspective of the same sex and from the perspective of the opposite sex is thus crucial to the issue of experiencing full visibility.

Romantic love involves one's sense of visibility, not merely as a human being, but as a *man* or a *woman*.

A man and a woman may be in love while not enjoying a full unity of mind and values, if there are major and basic areas of affinity and mutuality between them. Even if they do not feel optimally visible to each other, they may feel visible to a significant and enjoyable extent.

Love is an emotional response that involves two basic, related aspects:

one regards the loved object as possessing or embodying qualities that one values highly—and, as a consequence, one regards the loved object as a (real or potential) source of pleasure. This applies to any category of love, not only romantic love.

In the case of romantic love, which is the most intense positive emotional response one human being can offer another, one sees the loved object as possessing or embodying one's *highest* values, and as being crucially important to one's personal happiness. "Highest," in this context, does not necessarily mean noblest or most exalted; it means: most important, in terms of one's personal needs and desires and in terms of that which one most wishes to find and experience in life. Further, one sees the loved object as being crucially important to one's *sexual* happiness. This last is one of the defining characteristics of romantic love.

More than any other relationship, romantic love involves the objectification of one's *self-value*. (I am speaking of genuine romantic love, not its counterfeit, infatuation. Infatuation is an exaggerated, out-of-context response which consists of selectively focusing on one or two aspects of a total personality, ignoring or being oblivious to the rest, and responding as though the person were only those particular aspects.) Romantic love involves *fundamental* visibility. The essence of the romantic love response is: "I see you as a person, and because you are what you are, I desire you for my sexual happiness."

To understand why this is the most profound personal tribute one person can pay another, and why romantic love involves the most intense expression and objectification of one's self-value, we must consider certain facts about the nature and meaning of sex.

Of all the pleasures that a person can experience, sex is, potentially, the most intense. Other pleasures can last longer across time, but none is comparable in strength and intensity. Further, sex is a pleasure, not of the body alone nor of the mind alone, but of the *person*—of the total entity. The pleasure of eating or walking or swimming, for instance, is essentially physical; psychological factors are involved, but the pleasure is primarily of the body. On the other hand, the enjoyment of productive work or of a stimulating discussion or of an artistic performance is essentially intellectual; it is a pleasure of the mind. But sex is unique among pleasures in its integration of body and mind; it integrates perceptions, emotions, values and thought—it offers an individual the most intense form of experiencing his own total being, of experiencing his deepest and most intimate sense of his *self*. (Such is the *potential* of sex, when and to the extent that the experience is not diluted and undercut by conflict, guilt, alienation from one's partner, etc.)

In sex, one's own person becomes a direct, immediate source, vehicle, and embodiment of pleasure. Sex offers man the most intense and immediate form of experiencing *life* as a value; experiencing the reality of the fact that happiness is possible to him.

In sex, more than in any other activity, man experiences the fact of being *an end in himself* and of feeling that the purpose of life is happiness. (Even if the motives that lead a person to a particular sexual encounter are neurotic, and even if, immediately afterwards, he is tortured by shame or guilt—so long as and to the extent that he is able to enjoy the sex act, life is asserting itself within him, the principle that a human being is an end in himself is asserting itself.) In sex, man escapes from any malevolent feeling of life's futility or drudgery, of his own senseless servitude to incomprehensible ends, which, unfortunately, most men experience too often. Thus, sex is the highest form of *selfishness* in the noblest sense of that word.

In light of the above, it is not difficult to understand why, throughout the centuries, the mystic-religionist enemies of man, of man's mind, of his self-esteem and of his life on earth, have been so violently hostile to the phenomenon of human sexuality.

The celebration of self and of life is so implicit in the act of sex that the person who lacks the self-esteem which such a celebration requires and implies often feels driven to fake it, to enact a neurotic substitute; to go through the motions of sex, not as an expression of his sense of self-value and of the value of life, but as a means of gaining a momentary feeling of personal worth, a momentary amelioration of despair, an escape from anxiety.

In the act of sex, the participants experience a unique and intense form of self-awareness—a self-awareness that is generated both by the sex act itself and by the verbal-emotional-physical interaction between them. The nature of the self-awareness, in any given experience, is crucially conditioned by the nature of the interaction, by the degree and kind of visibility they project and are made to feel. If and to the extent that the parties involved enjoy a strong sense of spiritual affinity (by "spiritual" I mean: pertaining to one's mind and values) and, further, a sense that their sexual personalities are harmoniously complementary—the result is the deepest possible experience of self, of being spiritually as well as physically naked, and of glorying in that fact. Conversely, if and to the extent that the parties involved feel spiritually and/or sexually alienated and estranged, the result is that the sexual experience is felt as autistic (at best), or frustratingly "physical," or degradingly meaningless.

Sex affords an individual the most intensely pleasurable form of self-awareness. In romantic love, when a man and woman project that they desire to achieve this experience by means of each other's person, *that* is the highest and most intimate tribute a human being can offer or receive; *that* is the ultimate form of acknowledging the value of the person one desires and of having one's own value acknowledged. It is in this sense that romantic love involves an intense objectification of one's self-value; one sees that value reflected and made visible in the romantic response of one's partner.

A crucial element involved in this experience is the perception of one's efficacy as a source of pleasure to the being one loves. One feels that it is one's *person* , not merely one's body, that is the cause of the pleasure felt by one's partner. One feels, in effect: "Because I am what I am, I am able to cause her (or him) to feel the things she (or he) is feeling." Thus, one sees one's own soul—and its value—in the emotions on the face of one's partner.

If sex involves an act of self-celebration—if, in sex, one desires the freedom to be spontaneous, to be emotionally open and uninhibited, to assert one's right to pleasure and to flaunt one's pleasure in one's self—then the person one most desires is the person with whom one feels most free to be oneself, the person whom one (consciously or subconsciously) regards as one's proper psychological mirror, the person who reflects one's deepest view of oneself and of life. *That* is the person who will allow one to experience optimally the things one wishes to experience in the realm of sex.

Such, in briefest essence, is the nature and meaning of romantic love.

Critics of Romantic Love

It can hardly be disputed that a passionate and sustained emotional sexual involvement between a man and a woman, reflecting intense mutual regard and an appreciation of each other's person, represents a relationship of romantic love. Yet it is difficult to believe that this can be what the critics of romantic love are attacking.

The policy of such critics seems to be to observe certain irrational or neurotic processes occurring between persons who profess to be "in love"—and then generalize to an indictment of romantic love as such.

For example, some men and women experience a strong sexual attraction for each other, and conclude that they are "in love," and proceed to marry on the basis of their sexual attraction, ignoring the fact that they have no interests in common, are bound to each other solely by neurotic values and neurotic needs, have incompatible personalities and temperaments, and, in fact, have little or no interest in each other as persons. Of course, such a relationship is doomed to failure. But it is surely unreasonable to take such a relationship as representative of romantic love. To love a human being is to know and love his or her *person.*

Another common argument against romantic love is the claim that lovers have a strong tendency to idealize or glamorize their partners, to misperceive them, to exaggerate their virtues and blind themselves to their flaws. Does this sometimes occur? Of course it does. Is it inherent in the nature of love that it must occur? Certainly not. Many men and women are fully able to be aware of their co-lover's weaknesses as well as strengths—and still love passionately. To argue that love *must* be blind is to argue that no one can be objectively worthy of being loved—in effect, that love is always a mistake. In such a matter, I can only suggest that one should speak for oneself.

It is sometimes argued that the experience of romantic love is generated solely by sexual frustration—and therefore must perish shortly after marriage. Can sexual frustration foster a tendency to endow the desired object with imaginary qualities he or she does not possess? Certainly. Is this inevitable? Certainly not. Moreover, fewer and fewer couples who feel themselves to be in love are enduring sexual frustration prior to marriage. Often, couples marry after having maintained a sexual relationship for a year or two; their passion for each other cannot, therefore, be accounted for in terms of sexual frustration.

It is sometimes argued that since most couples suffer feelings of disenchantment shortly after marriage, the experience of romantic love must be a delusion. Given the immaturity of most human beings, given the multitude of psychological problems they bring to the marital relationship, given their doubts, their fears, their lack of adequate self-esteem—given the fact that they have never learned that a love relationship, like every other value in life, requires rational thought and effort to be sustained—it is not astonishing that most marriages lead to disenchantment. But this is not an indictment of romantic love: it is an indictment of the psychological state of those people who, having no knowledge of themselves, no knowledge of love, no knowledge of what a love relationship requires, decide to marry on the blind assumption that "love"—that which they choose to call "love"— will somehow find a way.

As to anthropologist Ralph Linton's assertion, quoted earlier, that the rarity of romantic love in other cultures indicates that it may be a "psychological abnormality," let me point out that there are many aspects of American civilization which are peculiar to this country and which are found no where else in the world. I refer to the Bill of Rights, a greater degree of political freedom than any other country has ever known, and a higher standard of living than any other country has ever known. Electric refrigerators are also a rarity in most other cultures.

If a couple are not to marry on the basis of romantic love—if they are not to marry on the basis of a passionate emotional and sexual involvement with each other and an intense appreciation of each other's person—then on what basis are they to marry? This is the question for which, to the best of my knowledge, the critics of romantic love have supplied no answer.

Do the attacks on romantic love simply reflect a misunderstanding, a failure to appreciate the actual nature and meaning of romantic love as distinguished from the unrealistic notions of "love" that some people harbor? Doubtless in some cases that is all that is involved. But in *all* cases? I wonder.

A few years ago, two authors—John F. Cuber and Peggy B. Harrof—wrote a book called *The Significant Americans*, which is "a study of sexual behavior among the affluent." In this study, the authors contrasted two types of marriages which they encountered: "Utilitarian marriage," characterized by an absence of mutual involvement or passion, held together by social, financial, and family considerations, made tolerable by long separations, immersion in "community activities" and sexual infidelity—and "Intrinsic marriage," characterized by passionate emotional and sexual involvement, a policy of sharing life experiences to the fullest extent possible, and an attitude of regarding the relationship as more interesting, more exciting, more fulfilling than any other aspect of social existence. Partners in an "Intrinsic marriage" tend, according to the authors, to be very selfish with their time: they are reluctant to engage in social, political, community, or other activities that would cause them to be separated, unless they are convinced there are very good reasons for doing so; they are clearly not looking for excuses to escape from each other. While this type of relationship tends to provoke some degree of envy from those who exist in a "Utilitarian marriage," it also provokes a good deal of resentment and hostility. The authors quote such hostile sentiments as that "these immature people" must somehow "be brought into line." They quote a man trained in psychology as declaring: "Sooner or later you've just got to act your age. People who stay to themselves so much must have some psychological problems—if they don't, they'll soon develop them." They quote another psychologist as vigorously asserting: "Any man or woman who has to live *that* close is simply *sick*. He must need a mate as a crutch! He's too dependent! There's just something unhealthy about it (Cuber and Harrof, 1965)."

Is envy all that is involved here? Doubtless envy is a large part of it. But a wider issue is involved also: resentment of the self-esteem and spiritual self-sufficiency necessary to sustain a romantic relationship of this kind—resentment of the individualism of such couples who turn their back on the "group-mindedness" of couples whose empty lives are desperately in need of being filled—resentment of those who find their happiness in themselves and in each other rather than in absorption into the tribe.

I have said that romantic love is intimately connected to a philosophy of individualism and a respect for the individual's right to happiness. We are living in an age and in a culture increasingly antagonistic to individualism and to the ideal of personal autonomy. One manifestation of this antagonism is the hostility unleashed against the ideal of romantic love.

REFERENCES

Branden, N. *The psychology of self-esteem*. Los Angeles: Nash Publishing Co., 1969.
Cuber, J. F. & Harrof, P. B. *The significant Americans*. New York: Appleton-Century, 1965.
Hunt, M. *The natural history of love*. London: Hutchinson & Co., 1960.
Langdon-Davies, J. *A short history of woman*. New York: Literary Guild of America, 1927.
Linton, R. *The study of man*. New York: Appleton-Century, 1936.
Mead, M. *Coming of age in Samoa*. New York: New American Library, 1949.

CHAPTER 25

Love and Aggression: The Perils of Loving

Ben N. Ard, Jr.

One of the major tasks ahead for us in our society today is making the world safe for love. That is, we need to cut down on the aggression which is so frequently involved in love relationships. As Abraham Maslow (1954) has said, "We *must* understand love; we must be able to teach it, to create it, to predict it, or else the world is lost to hostility and to suspicion [p. 236]."

If we are to understand the etiology of love clearly, then we need to know the causes of love, how it starts, how it grows and is sustained, how it flowers, and how it dies. We need to know what factors help love to develop and what factors hinder the development of love.

Love is a very basic part of the human condition, as we know from cross-cultural studies of love. Such studies also show us that there are many different kinds of love, and not all of the various kinds of love are good—some kinds of love are very self-defeating.

The background from which I shall view love and aggression is that of a psychologist, sexologist, and marriage counselor. (I have been a psychologist in the student health service of a university in the Midwest as well as having a private practice in San Francisco.) I have seen the consequences of various mixtures of love and aggression in many people's lives.

During the following discussion, then, I shall be talking about *love* and *aggression*, two concepts which are very difficult to talk about with clarity unless we define our terms rather carefully. The concept of love has been treated so extensively in both poetry and prose that we shall have to delimit ourselves if we are to make any reasonable progress in our discussion.

Presented at the University of California, Davis campus, symposium on "The Etiology of Love," February 13, 1968.

That delightful poetess, Dorthy Parker, once penned four lines which pretty well sum up the matter:

TWO VOLUME NOVEL

The sun's gone dim, and
  The moon's turned black;
For I loved him, and
  He didn't love back.

Dorothy Parker. In the *Viking Portable Library*, p. 355

Dorothy Parker spoke in her poem about the crux of the matter I wish to discuss: the love of a maid for a man, and vice versa. So we shall leave to others the discussion of all other kinds of love, such as love of nature, love of God, love of old wine, tasty food, or stimulating books.

Therefore, I shall primarily be discussing the concept of love which deals with the feelings and ideas obtaining between men and women which involve some sexual connotations. (We shall leave so-called Platonic love to others to discuss.) I shall concentrate mostly on love between the sexes; in colloquial parlance that is sometimes referred to as "the battle between the sexes."

As has been pointed out by Dr. Albert Ellis, (1963)

Many males in our culture are so thwarted by our sex codes and become so sex-hungry that they begin to see females only as sex objects and to depreciate any nonsexual attributes that they may have. In their turn, millions of our women become so resentful of the fact that the men's interest in them is almost primarily sexual that they become misanthropic and after a while find it almost impossible to love any man [p. 208].

These are some of the reasons why the battle between the sexes can be so bitter. As Ellis also stated,

Again largely because of our different ways of raising males and females, the former are usually mainly obsessed with having premarital and adulterous affairs, while the latter are intent on confining their sex relations to monogamous marriage. This means that the sex goals of men and women are quite different in many instances, and that the men begin to resent the women for not, as they say in the vernacular, "putting out," while the women resent the men for being sexually exploitative and for not being as interested in marrying as they are [p. 208].

What does it really mean when one person says to another: "I love you"? It obviously means many different things to different people in various situations. Meerloo (1952) has described some of the different meanings as follows:

Sometimes it means: "I desire you" or "I want you sexually." It may mean: "I hope you love me" or "I hope that I will be able to love you." Often it means: "It may be that a love relationship can develop between us." . . . Often it is a wish for emotional exchange: "I want your admiration in exchange for mine" or "I give my love in exchange for some passion" or . . . "I admire some of your qualities." A declaration of love is mostly a request: "I desire you" or "I

want you to gratify me" or "I want your protection" . . . or "I want to exploit
your loveliness."

Sometimes it is the need for security . . . for parental treatment. . . . It may
be self-sacrifice and a masochistic wish for dependency. However, it may also
be a full affirmation of the other, taking the responsibility for mutual exchange of feelings. . . . [It may be] wish, desire, submission, conquest; it is
never the word itself that tells the real meaning . . . [p. 83].

Heterosexual love, then, as I shall mean it in this context, is a reasonably strong or intense attachment, involvement, or favorable attitude, to
say the least, between a male and a female. (Cf. Ellis, 1958, p. 160.)

What I shall mean in this context by *aggression* is the tendency of a
person to do something harmful to another person or to himself. As used
here, the word *hostility* might be considered a synonym. As Leon Saul
(1956) has noted,

Many people like to believe that hostility is inherited, and therefore should be
dismissed as something about which nothing, for the present at least, can be
done. Others believe, falsely, that hostility is a strength, that without it men
and women would be left defenseless in a world all too ready to attack and
exploit the weak [p. 5].

In this sophisticated, psychological age, when Freud's ideas (understood or not, right or wrong) are accepted by perhaps most of the
educated set, we need to look at Freud's concepts most critically, since
they are seemingly accepted without question by too many so-called
educated people. (Cf. Suttie, 1935.)

For example, Freud held that "the tendency toward aggression is an
innate, independent, instinctual disposition in man and that it constitutes
the most powerful obstacle to culture [Saul, 1956, p. 8]." I shall present
a minority opinion that aggression or hostility is a disease to be cured and
prevented like cancer, tuberculosis, or smallpox. (Cf. Saul, 1956, p. 8.)

Now, having suggested that not all of Freud's ideas are correct, let it
be acknowledged that Freud and other psychoanalysts have given us some
insights as to why we humans act the way we do in our relations with one
another, particularly where these relations involve love and sex. For
example, an English psychoanalyst, Melanie Klein (1964) has pointed out:

The reason why some people have so strong a need for general praise and
approval lies in their need for evidence that they are lovable, worthy of love.
This feeling arises from the unconscious fear of being incapable of loving
others sufficiently or truly, and particularly of not being able to master aggressive impulses towards others: they dread being a danger to the loved one
[pp. 62–63].

Melanie Klein has also noted that hatred

leads to our establishing frightening figures in our minds, and then we are apt
to endow other people with unpleasant and malevolent qualities. Incidently,
such an attitude of mind has an actual effect in making other people unpleasant and suspicious towards us, while a friendly and trusting attitude on our
part is apt to call forth trust and benevolence from others [p. 115].

That the road to love is not always smooth is a part of our folklore.

Many of our most famous stories of the greatest loves have ended in mutilation, separation, and/or death for the lovers—e.g., Abelard and Heloise, Romeo and Juliet, Tristan and Isolde. (Then, perhaps, one may recall from American folklore what happened to Frankie and Johnnie.)

Wisdom about the perils of loving is available in unsuspected places. For example, in one of the famous blues songs sung by Joe Turner, entitled "Cherry Red," Joe says,

> I ain't never loved,
> And I hope I never will,
> 'Cause the loving proposition
> 'Gonna get somebody killed.

Part of the perils of loving, I should like to suggest, arise from the *romantic concepts* which are so common in our culture but which lead to unrealistic and false expectations, and therefore to subsequent disillusionment. These false romantic notions must inevitably cause disillusionment because of the frustration of the romantic, over-idealized *expectations*. But if one takes a more rational, realistic attitude toward love, then one can face even the end of that love as no catastrophe. As an illustration of this latter kind of attitude I am recommending, consider these lines from a sonnet:

> "Well, I have lost you; and I lost you fairly;
> In my own way, and with my full consent.
> Say what you will, kings in a tumbrel rarely
> Went to their deaths more proud than this one went.
> Some nights of apprehension and hot weeping
> I will confess; but that's permitted me;
> Day dried my eyes; I was not one for keeping
> Rubbed in a cage a wing that would be free.
> If I had loved you less or played you slyly
> I might have held you for a summer more,
> But at the cost of words I value highly,
> And no such summer as the one before.
> Should I outlive this anguish—and men do—
> I shall have only good to say of you."

Edna St. Vincent Millay, in *Collected Sonnets*, p. 116

Young men are, in general, less likely to be romantic than young women in our culture, but young men also build up unduly high hopes about the young women they love. Sometimes when these young women merely look at other men, they get beat up, along with the "other man."

Attempts to justify such aggressive behavior can frequently be reduced to the unquestioned assumptions about jealousy as a natural, normal, expected response—even an indication of "real, true, deep love" (Ard, 1967c)! Here again is an illustration of the detrimental aspects of the conventional, romantic concepts of love which are still very much in evidence in our culture to this day.

These conventional notions about romantic love are fed and nurtured by Hollywood movies, romantic novels, romantic magazines and television shows, as well as many parents (with other, ulterior, motives).

But romantic concepts of love originated many years ago, under the influence of the Christians. "Not until the Christian era, however, did the idea of romantic love, as we know it, put in its appearance [Farnham, 1953, p. 180]."

> Romantic love, as it appears in the Middle Ages, was not directed at first toward women with whom the lover could have either legitimate or illegitimate sexual relations; it was directed toward women of the highest respectability who were separated from their romantic lovers by insuperable barriers of morality and convention [Krich, 1960, p. 11].

Our romantic concepts of love have arisen, then, because our religious teachings have defined sex outside of lifelong, monogamous marriage as sinful, dirty, and wrong.

Donald Day (1954), in his history of the evolution of love between the sexes over sixty centuries, concluded:

> There is little doubt that the United States is still in a stage of extreme reaction to fantastic puritanism. The country has not yet finished its "fling" and may not as long as the "sterile" panderers of spirituality continue as they have for thousands of years to set themselves up as arbiters of nature's most powerful force—sex [p. 517].

What can be done to encourage good, healthy, sex-love relationships between men and women, in a society with such strange, mixed-up notions about sex and love? Some things can be done:

> By changing some of our more idiotic sex customs, as well as by learning to live sanely with them while they are still unchanged, we can significantly reduce the hate-creating aspects of sex while notably increasing its love-enhancing aspects. . . . In our own sexually inhibited society, there is some evidence that sexual blocking—even when it causes considerable hostility between the sexes . . . —also may foment a particular kind of romantic or obsessive-compulsive love. Romantic love . . . has its clearcut disadvantages, and is not necessarily a particularly good harbinger of mature, marital love [Ellis, 1963, pp. 205, 207].

That love and sex are frequently mixed up with aggression and hostility is known to most people. I would only like to document this fact for those people who still tend to look at the etiology of love through rose-colored glasses. One cannot study the consequences of love between the sexes without also touching on rape, violence, beatings, sadism, masochism, and murder. Pick up practically any newspaper on any day. The facts are available for anyone to see.

"Do you know that in New York City, a woman is raped every four and a half hours? [Herb Caen, San Francisco *Chronicle*, December 28, 1967]" Think about that. One response to that statement was: "She must be the happiest woman in the world."

Of course, many women have certain expectations about sex which involve some aggression. Some women seem to want to be raped, in effect.

Rape has even been defined as "assault with a friendly weapon [in the film *Waterhole Number Three*]."

Also in the San Francisco *Chronicle* for December 28, 1967, was a report of a slaughter over a wedding. In Istanbul a twenty-three–year–old youth allegedly killed his fiancée and eight members of her family after an argument about their wedding date.

On page one of the same paper was the report of the disenchantment of a battered bride in Mexico City. It took the young bride only a few hours—and three beatings—to decide she was disillusioned with marriage. Three hours after the wedding, at the wedding reception, the husband administered her first beating, in front of the guests, as a sign of married bliss. A donnybrook ensued. The police broke it up only to have another free-for-all break out again after the party resumed. After the third time around, the young wife went to the hospital suffering multiple bruises. So, one may really see, there are indeed perils involved in loving.

I would contend that aggression is essentially learned as the result of frustration, but it is also learned as "acceptable behavior," particularly in certain males in certain subcultures. The mass media help teach people that aggression is an acceptable form of behavior, even "manly."

Berkowitz (1962, p. xiii), in his studies of aggression, suggested that frequent portrayals of hostility in the mass media can affect the audience's attitude toward aggression, and that under certain specified conditions the portrayed violence may *evoke* as well as *shape* hostile responses. There seems to be a greater likelihood that media violence will increase the probability of subsequent aggression rather than provide a cathartic lessening of hostile energies.

How can one check out the possibilities of aggression in one's partner? There are no guaranteed ways of ruling out the possibility of aggression in any love relationship, but there are some possible hints in some recent research.

Drinking alcohol is frequently a release for aggressive tendencies in people who already possess strong aggressive inclinations. Observing the prospective partner under the influence of alcohol might not be a bad idea.

Humor preference in cartoons could be a measuring stick for determining these aggressive impulses, too, as has been demonstrated by Professor Hetherington of the University of Wisconsin (San Francisco *Chronicle*, December 22, 1967). Cartoons depicting aggression seem funnier to people with inhibited aggressive tendencies than to people lacking these impulses. So check out the prospective partner regarding what seems funny in aggressive cartoons.

That ideas about love between the sexes are changing should be no surprise to anyone in our culture who is the slightest bit aware of what is happening (Ard, 1967a). There is much discussion of the so-called "new morality" (Aiken, 1968).

If we can summarize these observations of moralists in the younger generation, we can say that "the new moralists are more 'cool' toward sex than their elders [Aiken, 1968, p. 70]." What does this mean (for those who aren't "hip")? It means, for one thing, that the young people who live by this "new morality" have fewer rules about sexual immorality.

> Furthermore, the young are less disposed than their elders to confuse questions of manners with questions of morals, questions of conventional rudeness or incivility with questions of immorality. And since questions of etiquette interest them little or not at all, they tend to be less full of resentments, less disposed to take umbrage, less exposed to affronts, to conventional jealousy, to the whole emotional paraphernalia of conventional sexual relations [Aiken, 1968, p. 70].

The new attitudes toward sex and love are developing among several subgroups in our society, not merely among the hippies or flower children. There is a type of affection-oriented permissiveness that has been developing among the new middle classes, particularly within the professional occupational groups (Reiss, 1967, p. 178).

As Aiken (1968) has pointed out, "Perhaps the most disturbing attitude among some of the new moralists is a pervasive failure of discrimination . . . [p. 70]." I would like to urge upon you the basic idea that if a person wants to avoid some of the perils of loving, one of the first principles he or she will have to learn well is to *discriminate* in the choice of partners.

One of the things about which one needs to be very perceptive in one's choice of partner is the amount of *dominance* he has, i.e., the degree to which he will tend to try to dominate in the relationship. Maslow (1963) has found in his studies that "people who are secure show no sadism-masochism at all, nor do they seek to dominate or be dominated . . . [p. 108]."

In a study of male sex aggression among college undergraduates, Kanin (1967) found that the most sexually aggressive males, although the most "successful" among their peers in terms of frequency, also tend to be sexually the most *dissatisfied*. Again it is the *expectations* which seem to explain these findings. "Exploitation of the female for erotic gratification permeates the entire approach of the aggressive male [p. 431]." Corroborative evidence along these lines is also offered by Kirkendall (1961) in his study of premarital intercourse among college males.

Kanin's (1967) study might lead one to conclude that many aggressive males seek a high frequency of sexual outlet because of the influence of their *peers* (the significant other males' evaluations) rather than from the satisfaction gained from sexual relations per se. The "stud" self-concept does not seem to pay off in much real sexual satisfaction for the aggressive male, no matter how much of a ladies' man he considers himself to be.

Mate selection, which in our culture usually assumes some sort of love to be a factor, has been "explained" by the various scientists who study such matters through such theories as homogamy, heterogamy, complementarity, values, role theory, and psychoanalytic theory.

Homogamy means, briefly, that people tend to choose partners with traits *similar* to their own.

Heterogamy means, briefly, that people tend to choose partners with traits *different* from their own.

Complementarity means that the traits or needs of the partners dove-tail, e.g., a sadist marrying a masochist.

The point about *values* is that people tend to marry partners with similar values.

Role theory explains why, for example, women are more likely to "marry up" (above their role or social class) than men are.

The *psychoanalytic theory* explains choice influenced by unconscious factors, e.g., unresolved oedipal complexes, etc.

Notions about romantic love influence what sorts of partners are chosen. And, as is well known, "The romantic orientation of females is noticeably different from that of males [Kephart, 1967, p. 470]." It has been said that women want love, and use sex to get it, while men want sex, and talk of love to get it. This is obviously an oversimplification and an overgeneralization, but there would seem to be an element of truth in it. Some women, of course, do not have the conventional romantic orientation, even some who write sonnets about love. Consider this sonnet by Edna St. Vincent Millay:

> I shall forget you presently, my dear,
> So make the most of this your little day,
> Your little month, your little half a year,
> Ere I forget, or die, or move away,
> And we are done forever; by and by
> I shall forget you, as I said, but now,
> If you entreat me with your loveliest lie,
> I shall protest you with my favorite vow.
> I would indeed that love were longer lived,
> And oaths were not so brittle as they are,
> But so it is, and nature has contrived
> To struggle on without a break thus far,
> Whether or not we find what we are seeking
> Is idle, biologically speaking.

> In *Collected Sonnets*, p. 11

However, Edna, one must agree, was a most unusual woman. Not very many women in our culture would take such a view of their love relationships.

In a study of some of the correlates of romantic love among college students, Kephart (1967) found that the young people he studied *invariably* described their *current* experience as *love* rather than *infatuation*, the latter term usually being used in the *past* tense. This finding perhaps illustrates the absurd lengths to which many people in our culture go to maintain the illusions of romantic love, no matter how illogical or impossible it is, on the face of it.

Many problems result from the conventional views of man-woman relations in our culture.

The kind of monogamous, monopolistic sex relations that we value in our society encourages members of both sexes to become insecure about winning and retaining the exclusive affections and sex favors of the individuals in whom they are interested. Consequently, lovers and married partners tend to become exceptionally jealous of their loved ones for presumably causing them to be so jealous and insecure [Ellis, 1963, p. 209].

The *romantic* concept of love, the idea that there is a "one and only love" for each person (aren't such marriages "made in heaven"?) is obviously *not* in accord with the scientific facts. I have elsewhere (Ard, 1967a) referred to this concept of romantic love as the "needle in the haystack" theory.

A less self-defeating approach—a more rational, hopeful, and scientific approach—would at least open up the possibility that one may love more than one person in a, hopefully, long lifetime (and without feeling guilty about it, or being accused of being "promiscuous"). What men and women will seek in their sexual partners will, of course, vary from person to person, and at different points in their life (Ard, 1967b). Men, on the whole, do seem to be more concerned, relatively speaking, about their partner's physical appearance (Kephart, 1967).

If we ask what is the fundamental reason people seek love relationships, other than the obvious reason of desire for sexual satisfaction (which, by the way, is perfectly natural, normal, and desirable), it might be said that the fundamental desire is for *understanding*. As Nathaniel Branden (1967) has pointed out, "It is not blind 'acceptance' that a normal person desires, nor unconditional 'love,' but *understanding* [p. 7]."

What are some of the conclusions that one can draw about the etiology of love and the relationship of love and aggression, in order to cut down on some of the perils of loving?

Melanie Klein (1964) in her book *Love, Hate and Reparation*, concluded that "the more true satisfaction we experience, the less do we resent deprivations. ... Then we are actually capable of accepting love and goodness from others and of giving love to others; and again receiving more in return [p. 118]." Another very basic point, overlooked by many (with the exception of Erich Fromm), is that "a good relation to ourselves is a condition for love, tolerance and wisdom towards others [p. 119]." Melanie Klein has also pointed out that

if love has not been smothered under resentment, grievances and hatred, but has been firmly established in the mind, trust in other people and belief in one's own goodness are like a rock which withstands the blows of circumstance. ... If we have become able, ... to clear our feelings to some extent towards our parents of grievances, and have forgiven them for the frustrations we had to bear, then we can be at peace with ourselves and are able to love others in the true sense of the word [p. 119].

Finally, we need to distinguish between *sick* and *healthy* love. Some of the main characteristics of the person who loves in a healthy fashion are as follows: (Because of the nature of the English language, I have to say "he," but I am just underlining my reminder that "he" refers to either male or female.)

He is unusually accepting and understanding of his partner's failings and lapses; but he does not permit her to step on or walk all over him. He desires a considerable degree of companionship with his beloved; but he is not desperately lonely and miserable without her. He is willing to compromise with the desires of and to make distinct sacrifices for his mate or his child; but refrains from being a love slave or surrendering his basic individuality. He *dislikes* his loved one's unresponsiveness or unfairness to him; but never connects this with his personal worth and severely hurts himself by it. He is seriously involved with his beloved, but has much room for fun, merriment, and gaiety with her. He is saddened by the departure or death of those he loves, but does not go into a deep, prolonged period of depression because of their loss. He is *interdependent* with rather than totally independent or thoroughly dependent on his love partner. . . .

He becomes attached to another person because he *likes* and *enjoys* loving, and not because he has to compensate for some terrible feelings of inadequacy or worthlessness of his own. He is *eager* but not over-anxious to enter a love relationship [Ellis, 1963, p. 23].

What sort of society do we need in order to have the right sort of sex-love relationships? Albert Ellis (1963) has offered some suggestions:

It is possible, however, for a civilized society to arrange sex-love relationships so that hatred stemming from sex drives would be reduced while love which results from sexuality would be enhanced. In general, such a society would have to be enormously more liberal than ours. . . . Because of their lessened frustration, restriction, inhibition, and inadequacy, the inhabitants of a sexually liberal community are much less likely to hate themselves and their potential or actual sexual partners than are those of a highly restrictive community [pp. 210–211].

Insofar as these observations make sense, we can all work toward that kind of society wherein there would be less aggression and more love.

REFERENCES

Aiken, H. D. The new morals. *Harper's*, February, 1968.

Ard, B. N. Do as I do, be as I am: the bruising conflict. In S. M. Farber & R. H. L. Wilson (Eds.) *Sex education and the teenager.* Berkeley: Diablo Press, 1967. Pp. 78–88. (a)

Ard, B. N. Gray hair for the teen-age father. In S. M. Farber & R. H. L Wilson (Eds.) *Teenage marriage and divorce.* Berkeley: Diablo Press, 1967. Pp. 95–104. (b)

Ard, B. N. How to avoid destructive jealousy. *Sexology* Dec. 1967, *34*, 346–348. (c)

Berkowitz, L. *Aggression.* New York: McGraw-Hill, 1962.

Branden, N. Self-esteem and romantic love. *The Objectivist* December 1967, *6*, 1–8.

Day, D. *The evolution of love.* New York: Dial, 1954.

Ellis, A. On the myths about love. In A. Ellis, *Sex without guilt.* New York: Lyle Stuart, 1958. Pp. 159–167.

Ellis, A. *If this be sexual heresy.* New York: Lyle Stuart, 1963. Pp. 204–221.

Farnham, M. F. Sexual love—woman toward man. In A. Montagu (Ed.), *The meaning of love.* New York: Julian Press, 1953. Pp. 179–221.

Kanin, E. J. An examination of sexual aggression as a response to sexual frustration. *Journal of Marriage and the Family,* Aug. 1967, *29*, 428–433.

Kephart, W. M. Some correlates of romantic love. *Journal of Marriage and the Family,* Aug. 1967, *29*, 470–474.

Kirkendall, L. A. *Premarital intercourse and interpersonal relationships.* New York: Julian, 1961.

Klein, M. & Riviere, J. *Love, hate and reparation.* New York: Norton, 1964.

Krich, A. M. (Ed.) The anatomy of love. New York: Dell, 1960.

CHAPTER 26

A Rational Approach to Premarital Counseling

Albert Ellis

People come for premarital counseling obviously because they have problems; and people with problems, as has been stressed by Ellis (1956), Harper (1953, 1955), Laidlaw (1950), and Lawton (1958), can often best be helped by some form of marriage counseling which not only presents a solution to their present circumstances but also goes to the root of their basic problem-creating disturbances. They need, in other words, some type of psychotherapy.

Although I see a few clients for premarital counseling who have simple questions to be answered, which can sometimes be resolved in one or two sessions, the majority come for deeper and complicated reasons. Their typical presenting questions are: "Is my fiancée the right person for me?" "Should I be having premarital sex relations?" "How can I find a suitable mate?" and "How can I overcome my sexual incompetence or my homosexual leanings before I marry?" These and similar questions usually involve deep-seated personality characteristics or long-standing emotional problems of the counselees.

When put in more dynamic terms, the real questions most individuals who come for premarital counseling are asking themselves are: "Wouldn't it be terrible if I were sexually or amatively rejected? or made a mistake in my sex-love choice? or acted wrongly or wickedly in my premarital affairs?" And: "Isn't it horribly unfair that the girl or fellow in whom I am interested is unkind? or un-understanding? or overly-demanding? or too selfish?"

In other words, the vast majority of premarital counselees are needlessly anxious and/or angry. They are woefully afraid of rejection, incompetence, or wrongdoing during courtship or marriage; and they are exceptionally angry or hostile because general or specific members of the other sex do not behave exactly as they would like them to behave. Since, according to the principles of rational psychotherapy which I and Dr. Robert A. Harper have been developing for the past several years,

Reprinted with the permission of the author and the publisher from *Psychological Reports*, 1961, *8*, 333–338.

feelings of anxiety and resentment are almost always needlessly self-created, and inevitably do the individual who experiences them more harm than good, my psychotherapeutic approach to most premarital counselees is to show them as quickly as possible how to rid themselves of their fear and hostility, and thereby to solve their present and future courtship and marital difficulties.

The main theoretical construct and counseling technique which I employ in extirpating a client's shame and anger is the A-B-C theory of personality, which has been outlined in several articles and books (Ellis, 1957, 1958, 1960a; Ellis & Harper, 1960a, 1960b; Harper, 1960). This theory holds that it is rarely the stimulus, A, which gives rise to a human emotional reaction, C; rather, it is almost always B—the individual's system of beliefs regarding, attitudes toward, or interpretations of, A—which actually leads to his reaction, C.

Take, for example, premarital anxiety—which is usually the main presenting symptom of young people who come for counseling before marriage. I have recently been seeing a girl of twenty-five who, in spite of her keen desire to marry and have a family, has never been out on a date with a boy. She is reasonably good-looking and very well educated, and has had a good many opportunities to go with boys, because her entire family is concerned about her being dateless and will arrange dates for her on a moment's notice. But she always has found some excuse not to make appointments with boys, or else has made dates and then canceled them at the last minute. At the very few social affairs she has attended, she has latched on to her mother or some girl friend and has literally never left her side and never allowed herself to be alone with a male.

Although it is easy to give the girl's problem an impressive "psychodynamic" classification and to say that she is pregenitally fixated or has a severe dependency attachment to her mother, such labels, even if partially accurate, are incredibly unhelpful in getting her over her problem. Instead, she was simply helped to understand that her phobic reaction to males, at point C, could not possibly be caused by some noxious event or stimulus at point A (such as her once being rejected by a boy in whom she was interested); but that her own catastrophizing sentences at point B must be the real, current cause of her extreme fear of dating boys.

"What," I asked this client, "are you telling yourself at point B that makes you react so fearfully at point C?" At first, as is the case with many of my clients, she insisted that she wasn't telling herself anything at point B; or that, if she was, she couldn't say what she was telling herself. In my now distant past as a psychoanalyst, I used to take this kind of denial seriously, tell myself some of my own nonsense at point B to the effect that the patient was not yet ready for deep interpretation, and spend the next several months helping her avoid the main issue by demonstrating to her that she had some kind of an Electra complex which she was repressing and that she now, by long-winded processes of free association and dream analysis, had to dig up and face. Being, at the present stage in the game, a less naive and wiser psychotherapist, I now refuse to take a simple *no* for an answer and keep insisting that the client must on theoretical grounds be telling herself *something* at point B. Now what—and let's have no nonsense about this—is it?

My persistent questioning soon paid off. The client, on urging, found that she was telling herself that it would be perfectly awful if she went with boys and, like her two older sisters before her, was seduced sexually before marriage but (unlike these sisters) didn't actually marry her seducer. These internalized sentences, in their turn, were subheadings under her general philosophy, which held that marriage rather than sex was the only real good in life and that any girl who failed to achieve the marital state was thoroughly incompetent and worthless. Perversely enough, as happens in so many instances of neurosis, by overemphasizing the necessity of her marrying, my client literally drove herself into a state of panic which effectively prevented her from achieving the goal she most desired.

What was to be done to help this client? In my psychoanalytic days I would have encouraged her to transfer her love and marital needs toward me and then, interspersed with a great deal more free associational and dream analysis evocation and interpretation, I would have tried to show her that because I accepted her, she could fully accept herself and then presumably feel free to go off and marry some other male. Maybe, after a few thousand hours of analysis, this would have worked. Or maybe she would have become just as parasitically attached to me as she now was to her mother and would have finally, at the age of 65, realized that I was not going to marry her, and would have been pensioned off to a home for ex-analysands, which I sometimes fondly think of organizing.

Not being willing any longer to risk this dubiously fortuitous outcome of therapy, I very directly took this girl's major and minor irrational philosophies of life and directly challenged them until, after three months of counseling, she decided to give them up. More specifically, I vigorously attacked her notions that premarital sex relations are wicked and shameful; that marriage is the only good state of female existence; and that anyone who fails in a major goal, such as the goal of having a good relationship with a member of the other sex, is completely inept and valueless as a human being. I induced this client to believe, instead, that sex-love relations can be worthwhile in themselves, quite apart from marriage; that marrying may be a highly *preferable* but hardly a *necessary* goal for a female; and that failing in a given purpose is a normal part of human living and proves nothing whatever about one's essential worth.

In miracles or any other supernatural influences I passionately disbelieve. But the changes that took place in this patient concomitant with her reorganizing her sex-love and general philosophies of life were almost miraculous. It needed relatively little urging on my part to get her to make several dates with young males; she thoroughly enjoyed petting to orgasm with some of these partners; a few months later she entered into full sex-love relationship with one of them; and she is now engaged to be married to her lover. Moreover, although we rarely talked about some of the other important aspects of her life, she has also gone back to college, which she had left in despair because of her poor social life there, and is intent on becoming a nursery school teacher. Quite a constructive change, all told!

Let us consider another case of premarital counseling along rational psychotherapeutic lines. A 28-year-old male came for counseling because he kept becoming angry at his fiancée, ostensibly because she continually "unmanned" him by criticizing him in public. On questioning, he also admitted that he had never been fully potent with a female and had acute fears of whether he would succeed sexually with his fiancée after they were married. According to psychoanalytic interpretation, he was really not afraid of his fiancée's unmanning him in public, but of unmanning himself when he finally got into bed with his bride; and her so-called attacks on him were actually a projection of his own castration fears.

So I would have interpreted in my psychoanalytic youth. Fortunately, however, I had the good sense to call in this client's fiancée; and I quickly found that she was a querulous, negativistic woman and that she did, figuratively speaking, often castrate my client in public. Whereupon I quickly set about doing two nonpsychoanalytic and highly directive things. First, I talked the fiancée herself into becoming a counselee, even though she at first contended that there was nothing wrong with her, and that the entire problem was the result of her boyfriend's inconsiderateness and ineptitude. When I saw her for psychotherapy (in all, forty-eight sessions of individual and a year of group therapy, since she proved to be a rather difficult patient), I set about showing her that her anger, at point C, stemmed not from her boyfriend's inept behavior, at point A, but from her prejudiced and grandiose interpretations of this behavior at point B.

I showed this woman, in other words, that she kept saying to herself: (a) "John is doing these inept and inconsiderate things to me"; and (b) "He *shouldn't* be acting that way and is a no-good sonofagun for doing so." Instead, I insisted, she would do much better by saying to herself: (a) "John is doing these things, which I consider to be inept and inconsiderate to me"; and (b) "If I am correct (which I may or may not be), then *it would be much nicer* if he could be induced to stop acting this way; and I should be doing everything in my power to help him see what he is doing, without blaming him for his behavior, so that he changes his actions for the better."

When I convinced this client that no one is logically ever to blame for anything, and that people's errors and mistakes are to be accepted and condoned rather than excoriated if we are truly to be of help to them, she not only stopped berating her boyfriend in public but became a generally kinder and less disturbed individual in her own right (cf. Ellis, 1960b).

Meanwhile, to flashback to my original client in this pair, whom we left gnashing his teeth at his fiancée and shivering in his pajamas about the spectre of his sexual impotence, he proved to be a relatively easy convert to the cause of rational thinking. After sixteen sessions of highly directive counseling he was able to see that, whatever the verbal harshness of his intended bride, her words—at point A—could only hurt and anger him—at point C—if he kept telling himself sufficient nonsense about these words at point B.

Instead of what he had been telling himself at point B—namely, "That bitch is castrating me by her horrible public criticism, and she has no right to do that to poor weakly me"—he was induced to question the rationality of these internal verbalizations. After actively challenging his own unthinking assumptions—particularly, the assumptions (a) that his fiancée's critical words *were* necessarily horribly hurtful; (b) that she *should not* keep repeating her criticism of him; and (c) that he *was* too weak to hear this criticism and not be able to take it in his stride—this client began to believe in and tell himself a radically different philosophy of sex-love relationships, namely: "There goes my poor darling again, making cracks at me because of her own disturbance. Now let me see if any of her points about me are correct; and, if so, let me try to change myself in those respects. But let me also try, in so far as she is mistaken about her estimates of me, to help her with her own problems, so that she doesn't need to keep being nasty to me in public." When this change in his internalized sentences was made, my client improved remarkably in his ability to take his fiancée's criticism; and his hostility toward her largely vanished.

He was then also able to face the matter of his own impotence—which proved to be, as it so often does, a result of his worrying so greatly over the possibility of his failing that he actually tended to fail. When he was able to acquire a new sexual and general philosophy about failing, he became more than adequately potent.

In his new philosophy, instead of saying to himself: "If I fail sexually, it will be terrrible, and I will be totally unmanned," he began to say: "It is highly desirable, though not necessary, that I succeed in being potent; and in the event that I am impotent for the present, there are various extra-vaginal ways of satisfying my partner; so what's the great hassle?" Losing his acute fear of his fiancée's publicly criticizing him, he helped her to be much less critical.

The main aspects of rational therapy which are usually applied to premarital counseling, then, include the counselee's being taught that it is *not* horrible for him to fail in his sex-love ventures; that there is no reason why his love partner *should* act the way he would like her to act; and that any intense unhappiness that he may experience in his premarital (or, later, marital) affairs almost invariably stems from his *own* self-repeated nonsense rather than his partner's attitudes or actions. Rational therapy, in these respects, directly forces the patient to accept reality, particularly in his relations with his sex-love partner.

REFERENCES

Ellis, A. A critical evaluation of marriage counseling. *Marriage and Family Living*, 1956, *18*, 65–71.
Ellis, A. Outcome of employing three techniques of psychotherapy. *Journal of Clinical Psychology*, 1957, *13*, 334–350.
Ellis, A. Neurotic interaction between marital partners. *Journal of Counseling Psychology*, 1958, *5*, 24–28. (a)
Ellis, A. Rational psychotherapy. *Journal of General Psychology*, 1958, *59*, 35–49. (b)
Ellis, A. Marriage counseling with demasculinizing wives and demasculinized husbands. *Marriage and Family Living*, 1960, *22*, 13–21. (a)

Ellis, A. There is no place for the concept of sin in psychotherapy. *Journal of Counseling Psychology*, 1960, 7, 188–192. (b)

Ellis, A., & Harper, R. A. *Creative marriage*. New York: Lyle Stuart, 1961. (a)

Ellis, A., & Harper, R. A. *A guide to rational living*. Englewood Cliffs, N. J.: Prentice-Hall, 1961. (b)

Harper, R. A. Should marriage counseling become a full-fledged specialty? *Marriage and Family Living*, 1953, *15*, 338–340.

Harper, R. A. Failure in marriage counseling. *Marriage and Family Living*, 1955, *17*, 359–362.

Harper, R. A. A rational process-oriented approach to marriage counseling. *Journal of Family Welfare*, 1960, *6*, 1–10.

Laidlaw, R. W. The psychiatrist as marriage counselor. *American Journal of Psychiatry*, 1950, *106*, 732–736.

Lawton, G. Neurotic interaction between counselor and counselee. *Journal of Counseling Psychology*, 1958, *5*, 28–33.

CHAPTER 27

A Counselor Looks at Contraceptives for the Unmarried

Lester A. Kirkendall

In 1962 a book on thermonuclear warfare was published with the title, *Thinking about the Unthinkable* (Kahn, 1962). This might well serve as a subtitle for this article, for certainly in the area of sexual behavior "thinking about the unthinkable" has become our task.

While this discussion revolves around sex standards, changing sexual ethics represents only one turbulency in a rapidly changing world. Our age is one with many problems which are interrelated and interacting, and all of which have moral implications and aspects. Thus the rising demand that recognition of personal worth be based upon individual merit, as against status derived through birth or membership in some particular group, requires an alteration in racial relations with attendant alteration in moral concepts. The applications of technology which have resulted in an ever-increasing abundance of material goods, greater comforts and conveniences, better health and longer life have raised moral questions about how to utilize and distribute these benefits. The linkage of thermonuclear power to weapons of fearful destructiveness raises tremendous moral questions about how to deal with our hostile and aggressive impulses. The growing availability of leisure time, control of the reproductive processes, and changing concepts about the purpose and place of sex in life have raised a multitude of issues concerning the moral use of sex.

These changes and others are world-wide in scope. Practically no aspects of our lives are left untouched.

Neither did the current debate about sexual standards arise with the advent of "the pill." It has been developing for a long time, and the pill only serves as a convenient symbol around which to focus discussion. Furthermore, the debate involves much more than a simple, straight-line relationship between contraceptive methods and ethical conduct (Kirkendall & Ogg). The increased accessibility and effectiveness of contraceptive-methods, changing sex roles, an increasing reliance on secular authority, the greatly decreased need to use sex always in the interest of reproduc-

This article is based on a paper entitled "Contraception and the Unmarried—Sense and Nonsense," presented at a conference on "The Pill and the Puritan Ethic," sponsored by the Faculty Program Center of San Francisco State College, February 10–12, 1967.

tion, and the greater openness with which sex is discussed in our society—these forces and others have, over a period of time, produced the problems and intensified their nature. There are even further complexities. Thus the title of this article is "A Counselor Looks at Contraceptives for the Unmarried," but how the questions relating to this issue will finally be resolved is tied to such complex matters as our beliefs as to what constitutes morality, what the nature of sex is, the character of male-female nature, and in what manner the sexes should relate to each other. Until we come to terms with these matters, all we can hope for in the sexual realm is contradiction, confusion, and trouble.

To focus on the moral issue is realistic, for our traditional concepts concerning morals baffle and impede all our efforts to arrive at more rational and constructive ways of dealing with human sexuality. If we could come to terms with the moral issue, a major accomplishment would have been achieved.

The first task in "thinking about the unthinkable" is to be starkly realistic. In the interest of realism, I wish first to set forth six premises upon which I am basing my discussion, and then note some of the forces which are bringing us to the inevitable confrontation with the issue of contraception and the unmarried. I hope this will aid in arriving at a point of mutual understanding, if not agreement.

1. *In dealing with sexual matters or with any human relationship, we are properly concerned with morals and standards.*

2. *Contraceptive information will surely become increasingly available.* At the present time it is available in printed form to anyone who has the money to purchase a paperback from a book stand. And those who haven't the money can stand behind the upright racks to read. Securing this information verbally still comes harder, but willingness to discuss contraceptive devices and practices openly is increasing, too.

3. *Contraceptive devices are presently available to the unmarried and will, without doubt, become increasingly accessible and effective.*

4. *Neither contraceptive information nor devices can be kept from those who want them, excepting perhaps the most ignorant, immature, and confused.*

5. *We have always had, and will continue to have, nonmarital sexual intercourse.* In fact, I would expect the amount might increase substantially in the future, particularly among those who have once been married but are later found among the divorced or widowed in middle or late life. The high rates of marital breakup and the marked degree of mobility in our society suggest, too, that postmarital and extramarital intercourse will increase significantly in the future.

6. *The sexual patterns of individuals are influenced much more profoundly by many other factors than contraceptive knowledge or the availability of contraceptives.* I have no convincing evidence that knowledge or ignorance of contraceptive devices has much to do with the sexual practices currently followed by an individual. Over a span of time and in combination with other factors, however, I do believe knowledge and availability of contraceptives will help influence standards.

Discussion almost invariably concentrates upon unmarried youth, rather than including the many middle-aged or elderly persons who are unmarried, and the divorced. This is, of course, a reflection of our culture's obsessive concern with premarital intercourse. But the problem of obtaining contraceptive information and devices is much less for these older, experienced individuals than it is for those who are younger, more naive, and relatively inexperienced. The latter are, therefore, in a very real sense the proper objects of our concern.

Considering the realities we face, I should like to propose a three-pronged program.

1. *Our first need is to strip away the hypocrisy and deceit with which we have surrounded sexual matters.* Our need is to recognize realistically what exists and what is happening. So far as contraception is concerned, this calls for an acknowledgment that devices are now available, and will continue to be, and are being used by many unmarried. Consideration of their use by the unmarried must be related to moral issues, sound medical and health practices, and educational programs. The moral issue cannot be approached in the traditional sense; rather it must be placed in the context of the quality of the relationship, the responsible expression of feeling, and the incorporation of sexuality into growing, developing relationships. This right must be acknowledged.

Many questions on specific details relating to this point will be raised. To many of them I shall have simply to reply that answers will come from the knowledge gained through the experiences of other cultures and from our own.

2. *Contraceptive information should be provided as an integral part of a broad sex education program which is itself contained within the context of learning about human growth and development, human relations, or family life.* Education about contraception needs always to be contained within such a framework. We need much more effective teaching than we now get in regard to all aspects of human sexuality, and information about contraception should be a part of such instruction.

3. *Effective advisory-counseling services need to be set up to which young people can go to discuss various kinds of human relations problems, including personal problems involving sex.* Few schools have the kind of service I envision, and in the present state of public thinking, few can. So far as counseling on sex matters is concerned, a special competence and capacity on the part of the counselors would be required. They would have to be objective and nonjudgmental, and have a climate of freedom which exists hardly anywhere in the public schools. Incidentally, such services should be available to all persons, not just young people.

In this connection I was interested in the "family planning clinics for the unmarried" which were being developed in London when I was there in August, 1965. There are now four such clinics in England. These clinics were planned specifically for the unmarried with the dissemination of contraceptive information and devices a major function. They were also prepared to do counseling and educational work concerning sex with their clients. This latter purpose should be a major one, and in any advisory service of this kind it probably will become a major function if the staff is alert to the needs of the clientele and prepared to do this kind of counseling.

The Netherland's organization, NVSH, which combines family planning and sex education functions, prescribes contraceptives for "engaged" couples. Denmark and Sweden very frankly include teaching about contraceptives as a part of their educational program, and communities provide openly for the dissemination of contraceptives without making marital status a requisite.

I mention these circumstances, for I wish to emphasize that developments elsewhere foreshadow what I earlier called the "inevitable confrontation." It is in fact already here. Our alternatives are to deal with the issues rationally, objectively, and within a *moral* context, or to maintain our *immoral* stance of hypocrisy and duplicity. This, in turn, leads to disastrous outcomes for innumerable young people and their families. Reiss (1966), looking at the same contradiction, phrases it another way. He says, "What we are deciding is which sources of contraceptive information we will promote and how important it is to us to make coitus safer— we are not deciding . . . whether or not there will be premarital coitus. There will be premarital coitus regardless of what decision we make on the dissemination of contraceptive information."

At this point we face at least four interesting contradictions, four strange illogics. These represent the "nonsense."

First is the serious lack of logic with which the subject is discussed. In England in 1965, I witnessed a television debate over the desirability of establishing a family planning clinic for the unmarried in Birmingham. As might have been expected, the reaction of some of the participants was highly emotional, and assertions were made that this was the equivalent of "condoning promiscuity." It was further predicted that the presence of such clinics would result in unwanted pregnancies ("there will be pregnant girls all over the place") and forced marriages. That these were the very evils the clinics hoped to combat was never acknowledged. Rationality was completely discarded; logic was tossed to the winds. This is typical of the kind of thinking we find on this emotionally highly charged subject.

A second illogical position has already been mentioned: the assumption that we have a choice of giving or not giving contraceptive information and devices to the unmarried. Even my good friend, Dr. Mary Calderone, Director of the Sex Information and Education Council of the United States (SIECUS), sometimes makes this assumption. In one article (1966) she asks, "How will you answer my first question: should contraception be made available to teenagers? I'll be frank and immodest and give you my own answer, which is *no*"

Here Dr. Calderone assumes that we have a choice in this matter. This is not the case, and neither she nor I can do anything about it. We can only choose, as she says, between alternatives:

> I would suggest to you that there are, in honesty, only two courses open to us: One is to throw up our hands, say sex is good for every one at every age, hand out the contraceptives, and go into our own bedrooms and close the doors.

> The alternative, of course, is more difficult, more painful, and much more work: it is to take stock of ourselves and our attitudes before we can answer, really answer, the questions (regarding contraception and teenagers) posed earlier... [pp. 38–39].

We not only make contraceptives quite available to males particularly (thus perpetuating the double standard), but we make them available in such a way as to bring youth into the transaction as full-fledged partners in the duplicity and hypocrisy with which we have surrounded sex. We could scarcely have done better at this if we had consciously and conscientiously planned for this result. Let me illustrate what I mean.

Americans are often critical of the "openness" which they understand to exist in the Scandinavian countries. During a visit to the family planning clinic in Stockholm in the fall of 1965, I saw a classroom which I was told was used for high school classes coming to the clinic to learn about contraceptive methods and devices. Also I understood that sometimes parents asked that their teenage youth come to the clinic for contraceptive information. I have mentioned this situation to American audiences and have had in return expressions of shock and strong disapproval. Americans see this as a flagrant "condoning of immorality," i.e., of premarital intercourse.

Let us contrast this "immorality" with our own. As I returned from Scandinavia in 1965, I drove across the United States from New York. In one of the states I traversed, I found in every filling station restroom from one to three condom vending machines. In one I found seven such machines. The purchaser could buy long or short condoms under several brand names.

Situations of this kind abound, but our concepts of morality and our sex attitudes require us to pretend they do not exist.

A third contradiction arises from the fact that American youth are continually being extended both privileges and responsibilities which recognize their increased knowledge and social autonomy as compared to their parents' and grandparents' generations. Youth have been taught to ask questions, to search for answers based on evidence, to test solutions, and to seek new ones if the first ones do not work. We approve this state of mind in most areas, but are distressed with it when it comes to sex.

In the area of sex, however, we seem to wish to deny youth the right even to think about their sexuality, to say nothing of giving them control over it. Here we have chaotic confusion for everyone, especially youth. On one hand sex is portrayed as natural, fun, exciting, and glamorous; on the other, sex is dangerous, wrong, degrading, immature, and to be denied and repressed except in marriage. We ask denial of youth yet bombard them with erotic enticements and stimulation.

"... our society, despite its skill in the techniques of communication, seems unable to deal in a forthright manner with the conflict we impose upon the adolescent. We do not sanction his overt sexuality, yet we have no alternative to propose [*Health Tips*, 1966]." The adult generation has, for the most part, been unable even to set up a meaningful, constructive dialogue with the younger generation. This would seem to be the most elementary requirement in dealing with our confusion, yet we are unable to do even this much. How much longer must this continue? How can we learn to deal with human sexuality more maturely?

A fourth illogic resides in our attitudes toward protection as they relate to sex in comparison with other aspects of living.

Anything we do in life has some risk involved in it. In all other areas of risk than sex (and apparently drug usage), we may seek to prevent certain behavior, but at the same time if the behavior occurs, we seek to minimize the risks by providing protections which reduce the hazards. Along with the reduction of hazards commonly goes detailed teaching designed to explain the situation and to help an individual weigh and evaluate threats. He is taught how to cope with the hazards if he chooses to accept them. But in the matter of sexual behavior we seek to reduce the risks by increasing the hazards, and also by refusing to weigh and evaluate them.

When youth drive automobiles, the risks may entail serious property damage, severe injury of one or many persons, and most serious of all, death. Here we enact legislation to keep immature and unsafe drivers off the road. But we also provide whatever safeguards we can. We build safety devices into the roads, make insurance policies available, put driver education into the schools, ask for periodic checkups on the autos—in short, we try to cut down on the hazards at the same time that we try to obtain responsible driving.

In body contact athletics such as hockey or football, where injuries are frequent and deaths do occur, we require physical examinations to insure proper conditioning, provide shields and pads which will buffer blows, provide a team physician; in short, we do all we can to insure safety while accepting the fact that risks are an inevitable aspect of participation.

When it comes to sex, what happens? Recently I was party to a discussion which centered around the development of an educational program for pregnant teenage girls in a home for unwed mothers. I found the board of directors split on the question of whether these girls should be given any contraceptive information. Apparently the division occurred over the moral issue. Undoubtedly the provision of contraceptive information was construed by some as "condoning premarital intercourse."

But was not the denial simply condoning more illegitimacy, more forced marriages, unwanted children, and abortions? Is not this clearly a situation in which the moral decision would be to provide both these girls and society badly needed protection against these likely outcomes?

A number of young people are extending the principle of protection against hazards to their sexual relationships on their own volition and in a rational systematic way. A number have discussed with me the study they have made of contraceptive procedures before they obtained contraceptive devices and initiated intercourse. More and more will probably follow this practice. I find still others who in frank discussion with one another have agreed upon extended sex play to the point of orgasm as their way of dealing with the threat of pregnancy. And, of course, many decide to forego sexual participation at either of these levels. They have made these decisions as a consequence of their own study and discussion. For these young people, those organizations such as schools and churches, those adults who refuse to discuss with them views concerning contraceptives and sexual practices and standards are simply becoming irrelevant (Hettinger, 1966).

I have cited the educational programs of several other countries which have included contraceptive education. Actually we have been edging toward a similar position in the United States. I know of a few high schools in which contraception is discussed, but such instruction at the high school level is clearly not widespread.

At the college-university level the most widely quoted statement on the sexual dilemma is probably the report put out by the Group for the Advancement of Psychiatry (GAP, 1965). This report comments that the provision of contraceptive information or materials is not usually considered to be within the scope of the university health service. The report goes ahead to say:

> The broad, over-the-counter availability of contraceptive pills, diaphragms, condoms, and foams indicates the need for a reexamination of this position and suggests possible modification. . . . To those who might advocate dispensing contraceptive materials, we would say that this cannot be done routinely or casually. Prescription of contraceptive devices requires as much judgment as does any other medical decision. It should again be noted that many students will interpret the dispensation of contraceptive devices as sanction for their use.
>
> We believe, however, that silence is not the only alternative to dispensing diaphragms and pills. Providing contraceptive information in the college setting seems to us tenable and appropriate, either on an individual basis in response to requests or in the context of sex education. It is also proper that such resources provide information about the public health aspects of venereal disease. A decision to dispense contraceptive information but not contraceptive devices would be consistent with respect for the autonomy of the student and would place the responsibility for the use of the information in his own hands [pp. 134-135].

What must come, in my opinion, is what I have already suggested—a broad, thoroughly honest and frank discussion of sex in relation to all aspects of life. This instruction should be set firmly in a framework which assumes that in their sex life youth will be weighing, evaluating, and finally choosing among alternatives. Recognition must be given to the inevitability of some form of sexual expression throughout childhood and youth. It is with this that I am primarily concerned. The issue of contraceptive procedures as they relate to the unmarried can then be dealt with rationally and in the context of a meaningful view of sex and life.

Perhaps we could think our way through this morass with more assurance if we were more certain as to the forces and factors which motivate sexual behavior. We are prone to think that every situation in which intercourse might occur will be pressed to the hilt for just that outcome.

It also indicates the fear we have of the overwhelming and all-encompassing power of sex.

The expectation that students in coeducational dorms would engage in profligate intercourse if they had the opportunity has been the basis of much opposition to this innovation in our colleges and universities. And, of course, in these conditions intercourse has, does, and will occur, but it is also clear that under conditions of open recognition of feelings, of frank discussion of possible alternative behavior patterns, and an enlistment of the student's help in obtaining desirable living conditions, the abandon which is envisioned does not occur.

Let me share a portion of a personal letter written by Ken Jacob, advisor for a coeducational dormitory at the University of Washington.

> I am definitely in favor of coeducational residence halls as a means of increasing the potential for social, intellectual, and personal development. It seems natural that men and women should eat, talk, relax, and study together without inheriting all the pressure that we associate with a "date," i.e., what to wear, where to go, what to say, how to impress. As a result of men and women living in the same halls, much of the mystery about sex seems to disappear. These contacts seems to produce more relaxed, more honest and open relationships.
>
> We have men and women in the same wing and on the same floor with an unlocked door separating the two wings. When I go to conferences or when visitors note this arrangement, they are appalled and accuse us of irresponsibility. They feel we are asking for trouble because the physical arrangement makes it so easy for men and women to get together. But I am convinced there is no significant difference in the sexual behavior between a coeducational hall and a noncoeducational hall. The sexual behavior of the students is apparently controlled by factors other than the physical facilities; possibly peer group influence, fear of social ostracism, or their own ethical and moral beliefs.

Dr. Ira Reiss (1966), a recognized authority on sex standards says:

> Rubber condoms came in almost immediately after the vulcanization of rubber in the 1840's, and the female diaphragm came into use starting in the 1880's. These methods hardly seem to have produced immediate radical changes in premarital coital participation. The changes in sexual standards and behaviors in America during the eighteenth and nineteenth century seemed much more related to more basic parts of our social and cultural structure than to any available contraceptive techniques. As in so many other technological areas, the reception and use of an innovation depends on the values of the society. The attitudes of a society must be ready for a technological change to be accepted.
>
> On an individual level, I believe we have enough social scientific evidence to say that the basic values of an individual determine the use to which he will put new technical information, just as one may raise the basic question whether the development of a "pill" type cure for alcoholism (which is now being worked on) is likely, in and of itself, to make heavy drinking more attractive than it is now. I think the removal of the negative consequence of heavy drinking is likely mainly to encourage those who already have strong motivations in that direction [pp. 51–57].

I agree with the observations of Mr. Jacob and Dr. Reiss. I do not believe a policy of greater openness, more readiness to disseminate contraceptive information and devices to the unmarried in the context of a concern for their responsible use, would immediately result in reckless promiscuity, or that patterns of sexual behavior would be greatly and quickly changed. We often evoke visions of some disaster such as this when we are faced with change. Racial integration of schools and public facilities, it was predicted, would be followed by bloodshed and violence. While this did occur in some communities, there were others in which it did not. The experiences in the latter made it clear that when education for understanding took place, when openness and honesty characterized proceedings, and when there was a desire on the part of leaders to reach an honest and humane accommodation, disaster did not follow.

I do expect that in the future there will be an increasing number of unmarried youth who experience intercourse in affectional relationships. But I think this will happen quite independently of what is done with respect to openness about contraceptives. I also think that with the right kind of teaching about sex, sex roles, and personal responsibilities, and with a stabilization of family life (please note this last phrase), there may be a decline in the kind of irresponsible sexual expression which is presently the source of most of the evils about which we are concerned. I do believe, too, that many of the disasters which result from that kind of out-of-marriage intercourse, which will inevitably occur, can be averted by knowledge and use of contraceptives.

Acceptance of the suggestions I have offered could have further important consequences. It might relieve our intense preoccupation with premarital intercourse as the focal point of moral concern. If we could accomplish this, we could then begin to assess the significance of such immoralities as the double standard and other inequalities based simply upon the fact of sex membership; the misuse of sex in commercialization and the mass media; and the hypocrisy and dishonesty with which we have enveloped sex.

We should be able, too, to deal more effectively with other social problems as they relate to contraceptives. We have witnessed, and are still involved in, the battle as to whether unmarried women on welfare should have access to contraceptive information. When this was first attempted, public outcry forced a retraction of that policy. Nevertheless, there has been a gradual growth in the extent to which welfare agencies do dispense contraceptive devices, though public opinion probably remains strongly opposed to this.

The same condition exists with reference to the dissemination of contraceptives through college health services. Witness the outcry which arose some time ago when college authorities acknowledged that this was occurring at Pembroke. Yet as I move about the country, I hear that various colleges are following this policy on a *sub rosa* basis. I have talked with health service and private physicians who are giving prescriptions to "the pill" on request, without making any definitive inquiries as to marital status, but ostensibly to "regulate the menstrual cycle," and actually to get off the hook on which they find themselves.

In other words, our procedures are making hypocrites and deceivers out of more and more persons, including even professional people. What happens is that we reject a straightforward effort to work out a reasonable public policy, then we shut our eyes, turn around, and walk backward into the very practice which has just been renounced. I am not arguing that one view in these matters is all wrong, the other unqualifiedly right. But I am arguing that in the matter of sexual behavior and the development of public policies on contraception we need to be realistic and honest, reevaluate our traditional concepts, devise approaches and criteria for testing them, and ultimately come to some conclusions about the relative effectiveness of various procedures.

Time is too short to go into the relation between attitudes toward sex and public policy concerning contraceptives as they relate to population control, but Lee Rainwater (1965) has made it clear that a close relationship does exist. Efforts to do the most effective work in population control are hampered by ignorance and inhibited, hypocritical attitudes toward sex, and a resulting incapacity to teach either about sex or the use of contraceptive methods and devices.

The development of a reasoned, realistic attitude toward the existing and growing body of knowledge about contraception and its techniques is clearly connected with effective methods of dealing with a good number of the other problems we face.

But now I must turn to a major issue, namely to our concepts of morality. We have dwelt so long and with such intensity on premarital intercourse as the central moral concern that we have largely ignored other sexual immoralities in our culture—in fact, even other nonsexual immoralities. Our principal concern has focused on premarital penile-vaginal penetration. Virtue, or the lack of it, in youth is determined by counting how many have or have not had this experience. If we could go beyond this preoccupation, we might realize that the conception and birth of unwanted children to parents neither mature enough nor equipped to care for them is a far greater immorality. Yet we insist upon assuring the latter consequence upon the assumption that a lack of knowledge or inaccessibility of contraceptives will keep some penis from entering some vagina, and that this offsets all other evils.

Our neurotic fixation on premarital intercourse as the central issue in sexual morality was illustrated by an article by Robert Moskin in *Look* (November 15, 1966) on "Sweden's New Battle over Sex." From reading the article one would assume that the Swedish battle was entirely over premarital sex standards. No other aspect of sexual activity was discussed. The article itself mentioned a book, *Sex and Society in Sweden* by a Swedish author, Brigitta Linner (1967). The impression was left that this book dealt with premarital intercourse as the central moral issue. It so happened that in October of 1966, Random House, Mrs. Linner's publishers, had asked me to write a preface for the book. I had completed this just a few days before the article appeared. The major moral concern in Sweden, as Mrs. Linner sees it, is not premarital intercourse but how men and women may *relate* themselves honestly, responsibly, and with equality to their family, business, social, and civic roles. She discusses, for example, the possibility that in the case of divorce and the payment of alimony, the wife might, in the interest of fairness, have to pay alimony to the husband. That has occurred in Sweden. But scarcely a hint of equalitarian and responsible role adjustments as a moral issue appears in the article. News of a battle over premarital intercourse suits our preconceptions and our obsessive preoccupation. And it calls for us to maintain the fiction that youth can be frightened away from premarital intercourse if they know nothing of contraceptives.

We must rethink our concepts of sexual morality. Joseph Fletcher (1966) has written of the movement away from legalism and of the "situational ethics" approach. I find myself sympathetically allied with him, but making a somewhat different approach. However, Dr. Fletcher's feeling that it is necessary to move in the direction of dealing with morals on another basis than divine authority and revelation is shared by me and many others. Thus James H. Burtness (1966), of the Lutheran Theological Seminary in St. Paul, Minnesota, writes, "The shift from space to time and the shift from absolutes to situations is also a shift from a sex ethic centered in legal permission to one centered in relational responsibility." To this quotation could be added many others, which emphasize that our primary moral concern must be for responsible relationships rather than with an act itself.

We can deal with the issue of sexual morality in a constructive way only as we move away from our concentration on acts to a concern for "relational responsibility." Dr. Fletcher (1966) writes of the "law of love." I am in essential agreement with that, though I have been speaking in other terms. I can spell out my views more clearly when I speak of a concern for interpersonal relationships based upon genuineness and integrity, and provide specific illustrations from everyday experiences of what I mean.

But regardless of whether you accept Dr. Fletcher's terminology, that of Mr. Burtness, or mine, I nevertheless am sure of one thing: the time has passed when we can start and end our moral concern by focusing simply on an act which must be either accepted or renounced. We must be concerned with those attitudes, experiences, and that behavior which enable us to relate honestly and genuinely with one another and with all others, as human beings, capable of giving and receiving love.

We can and do get into all kinds of absurdities as a consequence of focusing on participation in, or renunciation of, the premarital sex act as the determinant of moral worth. The individual who has never had this experience is virtuous; the one who has had is immoral. In the January 1967 issue of *Cavalier* appeared an article entitled "The New Puritans of the Sexual Establishment" (Collier, 1967). In it I am described as "a small benign man, one of the important figures in the Sexual Establishment"

who speaks liberally and seemingly in accepting terms, but who always
winds up by saying *no* to premarital intercourse.

After my son, a university senior, read the article, he consoled me by
putting his arm around me and saying, "Poor Pop! He can't win for losing.
First he is that evil-minded advocate of free love who is leading all our
youth to hell; then he's that mean old Puritan who won't let them have
their fun."

And he is correct in that I have had both criticisms. This contradiction, however, becomes quite understandable when one remembers that
the starting point and the focus of my concern is the development of
interpersonal relationships based on genuine honesty, integrity, and respect. The starting point and focus of my critics is the premarital sex act.
Those who feel it should never occur premaritally under any condition are
disturbed that I don't spend my time condemning it. They see me as "an
advocate of free love" and write the university president requesting my
dismissal. Those who feel the act should occur quite without let or hin-
drance, see me as a "New Puritan," and they write for *Cavalier*.

Finally, new developments often bring with them subtle and unex-
pected consequences. Thus I think the widespread use of effective contraceptives will force us to a re-examination of the purpose and place of sex
in our culture and in individual lives. The central, and in fact the only
acceptable, use of sex has for ages been in the service of procreation. Any
use of sex which did not include the possibility of reproduction has been
regarded as unworthy—even sinful. This concept is implicit in those teachings of the Catholic Church concerning the natural and unnatural uses of
sex.

But with a burgeoning population, the need for a widespread and
fervent use of sexuality in the service of procreation has completely disappeared. An attempt to confine sexual expression entirely to procreative
needs would curtail sexual expression most sharply. This is a curtailment
very few persons would be willing to accept—or have accepted. At the
same time the old insistence that this is the only proper use of sex is still
strong.

It cannot remain strong, however, and future developments, of which
the pill is only one, will force us to a thoroughgoing reassessment of the
meaning and purpose of sex. How heavily shall the play—pleasure function
be weighted? Can sex be used to develop warmth, cordiality, and love in
relationships, within and outside of marriage? How can sex be used in
improving communication and in developing unity? What can be the contributions of human sexuality beyond procreation, to the enrichment and
fulfillment of individual potentialities and the strengthening of relationships? The increasing effectiveness of contraceptive procedures is making
it necessary that we address ourselves to questions such as these.

The use of the pill makes the woman a conscious and premeditated
participant in the sexual relationship. We have been told many times that
girls did not wish to carry contraceptives or to participate in the use of
contraceptive methods for the reason that they could no longer pretend

that they were swept away by the passions of love. This attitude has been an integral part of the double standard. It cast the male in the role of the aggressor and the seducer; the female in the role of the innocent one swept away with passions of the moment. What will be the net effect of an increasing use of the pill? My guess is that the pretense and shame which went with the double standard will further deteriorate as more and more women turn to the pill.

This should be, in the long run, a benefit to women. They should be relieved of the need for pretense and dissembling. The behavior of both sexes could then be appraised fairly by the same standards. Instead of being faulted because they are women, women can be regarded and respected as individuals, having the same privileges and assuming the same obligations in relationships as men.

And how will this affect males? Traditionally, the man has been all too ready to shift responsibility for the decisions relating to the consequences of sexual associations to the female. The girl has been the one to draw the line; males have said, "Any girl can stop me any time she wants." The girl has been made the keeper of the morals. This attitude was well typified by one of the male subjects in my study *Premarital Intercourse and Interpersonal Relationships* (Kirkendall, 1966). He described a situation in which he and four other boys had picked up a girl, plied her with beer, then taken her to the woods and one after another copulated with her. This chap closed his comments about the incident with the observation, "She just didn't have any morals."

The point is that with women openly taking over the responsibility for contraceptive procedures, the male may be further freed for a carefree existence in sexual matters.

I am not asking the sexual experiences be laden with guilt or a somberness which denies the desirability of enjoyment, but I do feel that the heart of our sexual problem is male–female associations in which the responsibilities accompanying them are somewhere nearly equally distributed and equally accepted.

And consequence of eliminating pregnancy as a probable outcome of intercourse is that older persons, reared with the traditional attitudes of the early twentieth century, are being forced to a reassessment of their views about sexual standards. After all, the continual weakening of the threat of possible pregnancy as a motivating power requires reanalysis.

In my files is a letter from Richard Hettinger (1966), a well-known religious writer, himself an author in this field. He asks, "*Does* premarital intercourse have harmful effects upon the personalities of the people concerned and upon their capacity for mature relationships then or later—any more, for example, than heavy petting? Or is it in itself harmless, and only when virtually promiscuous, a symptom of a more basic disorder? In other words, are we old people against it just because we are jealous of the freedom and pleasure of the young?"

This is a question which realistic adults are having to face more and more as a consequence of the head-on collision between "the pill and the Puritan Ethic."

We have come to the point where the older generation has much to learn from the younger generation, not only about arithmetic and space travel, but about sex as well. They stand to learn both from what youth have read and studied about sex and from what they have learned from their experiences. We often speak of the abysmal ignorance of youth about sex, and in a certain sense and with respect to some aspects of sex this is true. But in the last decade our youth have grown up in an atmosphere in which a free access to sexual information and experience was definitely greater than was the case when their parents and/or grandparents were young. For them as youth an open and frankly expressed interest in sexuality as an aspect for study was looked upon askance. For today's youth this barrier is far, far weaker.

In my discussions with youth I have become aware, too, that the sexual experiences of those couples who are able to communicate freely, who have a sense of responsibility and feeling toward one another, and who approach their sexual relationships as equals is quite different from the double-standard, guilt-ridden, boy-loses-respect-for-girl sexual experiences so common in my college generation. This is extremely hard for many adults to understand.

The concern which is sometimes expressed over the sexual ignorance of youth is at least partially misplaced. The sexual ignorance of adults is also an important factor in the situation. But even this is not the focal point of my concern. My deep concern is the almost unbridgeable communication gap which exists between the generations, of which the knowledge differential is but one aspect. Until we can bridge this gap, I see little hope of the present generation of middle-aged and older adults being able to help the generation just coming into maturity. In a very real sense the perfection of contraceptive techniques which effectively remove the threat of pregnancy as a consequence of nonmarital intercourse may be the final test of whether effective cross-generational dialogue can be developed. The older generation must learn to discuss sex in a more open, more accepting way, rather than orienting all thinking toward threats. Either that or there will be no dialogue.

The perfection of contraceptives means that whether or not a sexual relationship will occur and what its consequences will be are much more than ever before in the realm of conscious, deliberate, serious, and purposeful choosing. Sex education, then, needs to become the kind of education which will contribute to wisdom, integrity, and humaneness in choice. This kind of education cannot be based simply upon the patterns of the past, but must take into realistic account the developments and conditions of the present. Members of the older generation cannot in this matter afford to be cultural dropouts.

The very ease with which sexual relationships can now be experienced may contribute to a strengthening of the sense of need for individual responsibility and integrity, and of the importance of finding and respecting a caring relationship.

Myron B. Bloy, Jr., (1966) provides us with a realistic challenge when he says, "We must stop simply wailing through the shambles of the past and learn to use our expanded freedom as the occasion for new growth towards our adulthood. This is clearly a highly bruited moment in history, for the only alternative to using our freedom for fresh maturation is to allow it to dissolve into mere anarchy—an end that many traditionalists actually seem to desire as they passively wring their hands over the present simply because it confounds so much of the past. Freedom is not simply our release from captivity, but, more fully, the occasion, the elbowroom, to lay hold of our destiny as men [p. 20]."

If we are to meet this challenge we must accept as our goal a full and joyous life in which sex is an integral part, but subordinate to a deeper need—that of individual realization and meaningful relatedness to others. Sexual expression and its denial must be ordered in the interest of these larger goals. William Saroyan expressed it vividly in the play *The Time of Your Life*, when he wrote:

> In the time of your life, live—so there shall be no ugliness or death for yourself or for any life your life touches. . . . In the time of your life, live—so that in that wondrous time you shall not add to the misery and sorrow of the world, but shall smile to the infinite delight and mystery of it.

REFERENCES

Bloy, M. B., Jr. *Crisis of cultural change*. New York: Seabury Press, 1966.

Burtness, J. H. The new morality: Some bibliographical comment. *Dialog* Winter 1966, 5, 10–17.

Calderone, M. S. Contraception, teenagers and sexual responsibility. *The Journal of Sex Research* April 1966, 2, 37–40.

California Medical Association. Rx for health, growing up sexually. *Health Tips*, 1966.

Collier, J. L. The new Puritans of the sexual establishment. *Cavalier*, January 1967.

Fletcher, J. *Situation ethics*. Philadelphia: Westminster Press, 1966.

Group for the Advancement of Psychiatry (G.A.P.) *Sex and the college student*. New York: G.A.P., 1965.

Hettinger, R. The irrelevance of religion. In *Living with sex: The student's dilemma*. New York: Seabury Press, 1966.

Kahn, H. *Thinking about the unthinkable*. New York: Horizon Press, 1962.

Kirkendall, L. A. *Premarital intercourse and interpersonal relationships*. New York: Matrix House, 1966.

Kirkendall, L. A., & Ogg, E. *Sex and our society*. New York: Public Affairs Pamphlet No. 366.

Linner, B. *Sex and society in Sweden*. New York: Pantheon Books, 1967.

Moskin, R. J. Sweden's new battle over sex. *Look*, November 15, 1966.

Rainwater, L. *Family design*. Chicago: Aldine Press, 1965.

Reiss, I. Contraceptive information and morality. *The Journal of Sex Research*, April 1966, 2, 51–57.

Saroyan, W. *The time of your life* (A play).

Stanford Observer. Colleges and contraceptives: The physicians' dilemma. January 1967.

CHAPTER 28

Counseling Cases Involving Premarital and Extramarital Pregnancies

Clark E. Vincent

The physician who assumes the counseling role with patients having sexual problems or questions will need to keep in mind the social contexts out of which such problems and questions arise. This is especially true of counseling in cases of extramarital pregnancy, where the physician is quickly confronted with some of the contradictions in social attitudes concerning illicit sexual behavior.

The most persistent of these contradictions is to be found in the social practices and attitudes by which our society *inadvertently encourages, if not implicitly condones, the cause (illicit coition), and explicitly censures and condemns the result (illicit pregnancy)*. I have illustrated this contradiction at length elsewhere (Vincent, 1961), and will only note here in passing that the physician is confronted directly by it in such cases as that of the mother who confidently brings her teen-age daughter in for a diaphragm fitting, but who subsequently and angrily brings that same daughter in with a premarital pregnancy.

The remainder of this chapter is an attempt to balance the physician's knowledge about the anatomic and physiologic aspects of sex with information concerning some of the social and emotional aspects. It is also an attempt to highlight several unique opportunities the physician has for counseling with different categories of unmarried mothers.

Physicians, more so than any other professional group, have long been aware that many of the commonly accepted stereotypes of unmarried mothers are erroneous. Prior to the late 1950's the predominant image of unmarried mothers was that they were poor, uneducated, very young and emotionally disturbed females. Such an image had been derived over the years from published accounts of premaritally pregnant females who had come to the attention of therapists and psychiatric social workers and/or who had been attended at a county hospital, maternity home or charity institution. The physician has attended these mothers, but he also has attended in private practice the upper and middle-class females in the

Reprinted with permission of the author and the publisher from R. H. Klemer (Ed.), *Counseling in Marital and Sexual Problems*. Baltimore: Williams and Wilkins, 1965. Pp. 149–160.

older age groups bearing children out of wedlock. Because of his exposure to a broad cross-section of unmarried mothers from all walks of life, the physician has been in a unique position to develop counseling techniques and procedures that are not limited to any one socioeconomic or age group of unmarried mothers.

COUNSELING WITH THE YOUNG UNWED MOTHER

If the physician is to be helpful in his counseling relationship with the unmarried mother, particularly the very young one, he will need to be very clear in his own mind and to make it clear to the young girl that *she* is the patient, not the parents who brought her into his office or the couple who may be waiting to adopt the child.

This distinction is undoubtedly not an easy one to make when the parents or the adoptive couple are paying the bill, but it is a crucial one if a bona fide counseling relationship is to be established with the unmarried mother.

The very young unwed mother who is brought to the physician by her parents is already in a very awkward and potentially rebellious position vis-à-vis her parents. When the physician fails to explicate to her and to her parents that she is the patient, she will tend to see him as only an extension or tool of her parents and his efforts to be of other than medical help to her will be quite unsuccessful.

The physician's failure to establish and maintain her status as the patient was the most frequently expressed criticism of the several hundred unwed mothers interviewed in my own study several years ago. (Vincent, 1961). Many felt the physician had simply been a tool in the hands of the parents or adopting couple. Some indicated this as the reason they never returned to a given physician after the initial visit to ascertain pregnancy. There is a very viable grapevine among single females who become pregnant and who pass the word very quickly concerning the kind of treatment received from given physicians—thus accounting, in part at least, for the fact that over a period of time certain physicians build up quite a clientele of unmarried mothers.

When the single girl comes alone for her initial visit to ascertain pregnancy, the physician has not only a unique opportunity, but also a responsibility, to make sure that she does not become "lost" until the onset of labor pains. For the health and welfare of both the unmarried mother and the child to be, it is important that the physician be able to communicate the importance of regular medical checkups and proper care during pregnancy. Too frequently, young females of inadequate means disappear after the visit to ascertain pregnancy and reappear only when the baby is about to be born. If proper care is to be provided for those females who do not become private patients, the physician will need to have and to impart accurate and up-to-date information about other resources in the community, and to follow through on referrals to such other resources.

Whether she becomes his private patient or never returns, her initial visit is a particularly impressionable experience for her. The very manner in which the physician confirms that she is indeed pregnant may very well be indelibly etched upon her mind and emotions, and thereby, for that moment, assign him the role of counselor—regardless of his desire or intent to have such a role. The manner and the words he uses to convey the information that she is pregnant need to be chosen carefully. Her anxiety and her needs at that moment may be such that an offhand remark or the most casual of comments may be interpreted either as complete approval of her sexual behavior or as utter rejection of both her and her behavior.

Some of the young unwed mothers with whom I have talked manifested all too clearly the failure of their parents to distinguish between the doer and the deed. Some parents reject both in so devastating a manner as to preclude ever being of future help to their daughters. Other parents are so accepting and "understanding" that they encourage their daughters to "con" themselves into believing that no mistake was made, thereby precluding the learning experience and dignity that can accrue from admitting one's mistakes and accepting responsibility for them.

The girls with whom I have talked indicated in a variety of ways their parents' failure to provide them with a learning experience. Some denied any self-responsibility and were quite convinced that their illicit pregnancies were entirely the fault of their male partners, or their parents who were either too rigid or too permissive. Others, who did assume some responsibility for their pregnancies, did not perceive them as mistakes but as inconveniences—inconveniences which were viewed as worthwhile by some girls because they received a parent financed sojourn to another state during the later months of pregnancy, and were able to provide a childless couple with an adopted baby. They were explicit in their belief that they would not have come by such a trip had they not become pregnant. They also reported that their younger sisters thought their parents would provide them a similar "fun" trip when they were older.

Counseling the Unwed's Parents

The confirmation of the young female's pregnancy is also a highly impressionable moment for her parents, and perhaps is the time when they are most likely to express to her those thoughts and judgments they will later regret having expressed with so much destructive hostility and bitterness. The physician can be of considerable help to parents at such a time by encouraging them to vent some of their anger and disappointment before talking with their daughter in the hope that their subsequent discussions with her will be more constructive than destructive. He may also be able to help them examine the degree to which their attitudes toward their daughter involve a projection or displacement of their own feelings of failure as parents.

Should There Be a Marriage?

The question of whether the young girl should marry the father of the child-to-be is almost inevitable. The young girl is less likely to ask it in the form of a question; more likely she will try to demonstrate adult status by stating either that she does or she doesn't plan to marry the male involved—hoping, perhaps, that someone will question her statement. In their haste to state their own pro or con position about marriage, the parents may overlook her need to act as if she had already thought through this decision; their arguments with her then influence her to crystalize a decision she really wasn't ready to make. The physician can help the parents to understand the girl's need to act as if everything had been thought of and planned for, and can help both the girl and her parents recognize that the fact of pregnancy is only one of many variables to be considered in reaching a decision about marriage.

Decisions Concerning the Baby

Physicians attending unwed mothers in private practice are in a highly strategic position to influence the mother's decisions about whether she keeps or releases her baby, and which channels to use if the baby is to be released for adoption. Such physicians are the primary source of information about adoption for the older, out of state unwed mothers, and are the initial source of such information for many of the younger unwed mothers of middle and high socioeconomic status. Unwed mothers in the latter category usually obtain information initially from their parents who frequently have derived their information from physicians rather than social workers or adoption agency personnel. The strategic position of the physician in influencing the mother's decisions about her baby (Vincent, 1961) imposes a responsibility to be informed and objective about various adoption procedures and agencies.

The following excerpts from three case histories illustrate unwed mothers' differential interpretations and usages of adoption information provided by physicians and social workers.

UNWED MOTHER A:

"I'm placing the baby for adoption. . . . Our family doctor recommended a doctor here who could handle it very quietly. . . . I won't even see it, but that's best. It's a closed chapter in my life. Besides, there are more people out here wanting (to adopt) babies than they have, so I know it will get a good home. . . . My parents would never forgive me if I didn't leave it here. They can forgive me as long as no one finds out about why I'm here. . . . To bring the baby home would make liars of them. . . . It would be unfair to the baby to grow up with me and know that it was an illegitimate child. . . . If I kept the baby I'd probably never be able to find a man who would marry me."

UNWED MOTHER B:

"I'm not going to lose my baby forever. My aunt and uncle out here will keep it for me until I finish college. . . . I won't marry until I find a man who will accept it as our child, but in the meantime it would only hinder my college work if I kept the child with me and it will be better for the baby in the meantime to be in a home with two people who love children as much as they (aunt and uncle) do. . . . My doctor told me there were lots of opportunities to give my baby to a couple who really wanted one and would give it all the love it needed and the best home imaginable. But I know how I would feel when I grew up if I found out that my own mother gave me up for adoption and didn't want to raise me. . . . This way the baby will always know I did the best thing possible for it. . . . When she gets older I'll be able to explain that I loved her too much to give her away."

UNWED MOTHER C:
"I planned when I left home to have the baby adopted, but I can't do it. . . . The social worker explained that it was my decision, but that I should feel they had enough people to choose from to be really able to select a good home. . . . Mother will be furious and Dad will probably disinherit me when I come back with the baby, since they gave clear instructions I was to have it adopted, but I can't do it. . . . What kind of a person would I be if I let someone else have my baby? What would the baby think of me when it grew up if it knew I deserted it for just anyone to have? . . . . I really think that after a while my parents will respect me more for keeping the baby, and what would a future husband think of me as a mother if he knew I gave my child away even if it wasn't his? [Vincent, 1961, pp. 216–17]."

On interpreting these statements, will some girls hate themselves later for giving their babies away? We have no way of knowing, given the paucity of follow-up studies, but such statements do illustrate the unwed mother's need for the most informed and competent counseling possible in making the extremely difficult decision about what to do with her baby and in implementing that decision.

The physician attending the unwed mother may or may not have another responsibility, depending on how he views the professional ethics involved. This possible responsibility pertains to those attitudes and wishes concerning the baby which the mother may express during delivery and/or while partially anesthetized. Should the physician share with other professional personnel who might be involved in helping the unwed mother, the feelings and attitudes expressed during delivery if such feelings and attitudes are strongly and consistently contraindicative of the already announced decision about the baby? Many, if not most, physicians may ignore, or perhaps compartmentalize, such expressions from the patient as being unrelated and irrelevant to their medical role. But does the professional ethic concerning the patient's confidences uttered during periods of extreme stress or while partially anesthetized always supercede consideration of the future welfare of both the mother and the child?

"UNMARRIED FATHERS"

The concentration upon the female in studies and public concern about illegitimacy tends to obscure the biologic fact that the male is half the cause. The readiness with which they take advantage of the protective anonymity and irresponsibility preferred by society and by unwed mothers may too easily deceive us into believing that unmarried fathers go merrily on their way without remorse or guilt. And although many such fathers are quick to assert either that they had no feelings of guilt and responsibility, or that they quickly resolved such feelings, they just as quickly supply explanations which suggest the contrary.

If he is married, the male may emphasize that the female involved preferred no help or further contact for fear of becoming known as the "other woman"; or he may excuse himself by expressing suspicions that his wife has previously been similarly involved. If single, he may readily cite the advice of the family physician and/or that of the girl's parents to the effect that it is to the advantage of all concerned to sever all ties, including any financial help that might imply future marital obligations. Valid and quasi-soothing as such types of reasons may be, they inwardly distress the male reared in a society where the masculine role is to protect, and not to be protected by, the female.

The fathers who do maintain contact with their illicit sex partners are further demasculinized when unable even to see, much less take pride in, their offspring. And although it might commonly be thought they have no interest in doing so, the comments, questions, and implicit wishes expressed to me by unmarried fathers lead me to believe that a sizable proportion of them do. Whether it be called the male ego, the deep-seated desire to create and produce, or the showing of virility, there is something in a man of all walks of life which exacts a price when he is denied identification with that which he has helped to create, even when the denial is of his own choosing.

There is another category of rationale which the unmarried father employs in convincing himself and others that he has no guilt or obligations. This consists of his derogatory evaluations of his sex partner. His mildest portrayal will include such statements as the following taken from case histories: "She was old enough to know what she was doing." "She encouraged it as much as I did." "She went into it with her eyes open." "She could have said *no*."

A far more disparaging picture is painted by other unmarried fathers, some of whom one suspects are struggling less successfully with their feelings of guilt and/or inadequacy; it is these descriptions which, over the years, have undoubtedly contributed to, and prolonged, the misleading and negative stereotyping of unwed mothers:

"Why should I think it's mine when I know half a dozen guys who've had her?"

"She asked for it, always teasing everybody in the office. If it hadn't been me, it would be someone else sooner or later."

"Why shouldn't she take the consequences? She got paid for it twice over in all the parties, trips, and good times and even clothes I bought her. She has a hell of a lot more now than when I met her."

It is true that the male does not have to endure the physical discomforts of nine months of pregnancy and the labor pains of birth. Nor does he have to face the censorious comments and stares of others and wrestle with the decision about whether to keep or to release the baby for adoption. In fact, the enormity of what the unmarried mother must face is such as to usually make us forget that the physical discomfort of pregnancy and the pain of birth may afford her a form of "punishment," a degree of atonement, unavailable to the unmarried father. Also, for some unmarried mothers there is a feeling of retribution derived from having supported the traditional concepts of motherhood; for example, courageously completing pregnancy even though afraid, away from loved ones and censured. And difficult as the decision may be, many unwed mothers experience a sense of at least partial retribution to society when their illicit pregnancies subsequently make it possible for childless couples to achieve the cherished goal of having a family.

My intent is not to minimize the lopsidedness with which the burdens of stigma, hardships, and responsibilities in illegitimacy are borne by females. Rather, it is to illustrate the extent to which we have ignored the counseling needs of the males involved. It is also to suggest that counseling with the unmarried mother may be facilitated when her sexual mate is also seen by the physician.

MARRIED AND DIVORCED "UNWED" MOTHERS

A counseling opportunity available more frequently to physicians than to any other professional group involves the married and the divorced "unwed" mothers. Census data do not differentiate among married, divorced and single unwed mothers; therefore, we have no way of knowing how many of the *estimated* 245,000 illicit births in the United States in 1962 were to divorced women or to married women impregnated by men other than their husbands. In fact, we have no way of knowing how many of the more than 4,000,000 births recorded as legitimate in 1962 were the result of extramarital intercourse.

We do know from census reports that in the twenty-year period from 1940 to 1960, the illegitimacy rate increased five times as much among women aged 25 to 29 (538 percent), as among those aged 15 to 19 (108 percent).

The higher rates and greater increases in illegitimacy among older women, as shown in Table 1, give us reason to suspect that extra- and postmarital intercourse may be responsible for a considerably greater proportion of illicit births than is commonly assumed. Adulterous illegiti-

TABLE 1

INCREASE OF ILLEGITIMACY RATE

Age of Unmarried Mother	Illegitimacy Rate*		Percentage of Increase
	1940	1960	
10–14	0.4	0.6	50%
15–19	7.4	15.3	108%
20–24	9.5	39.3	314%
25–29	7.2	45.9	538%
30–34	5.1	28.0	449%
35–39	3.4	14.4	323%
40–44	1.2	3.6	217%

*Number of illegitimate births per 1,000 unmarried females.

macy is easily concealed from official records, of course, and is probably only reported in the minority of cases. Thus, in the absence of census data breakdowns for *pre-*, *extra-*, and *post*marital pregnancies, we are left with very tentative information from only a few individual studies that have differentiated among these types of illicit pregnancies.

As shown by the following information from 1,062 "unwed" mothers, there was a higher proportion of divorced and married mothers among those attended and reported by physicians in private practice, than among those attended in maternity homes and a county hospital where they were reported by social caseworkers (Vincent, 1961). The fact that few studies are made of "unwed" mothers attended in private practice helps maintain the emphasis on the young, single, never married ones who go to maternity homes and county hospitals where studies are usually conducted.

TABLE 2

STUDY OF 1,062 UNWED MOTHERS

Marital Status of "Unwed" Mother	Reported by Physicians in Private Practice*	Reported by Social Caseworkers	
		Maternity Home†	County Hospital††
Single—never married	65%	82%	76%
Divorced or widowed	23%	11%	18%
Married	11%	4%	0%
No answer	1%	3%	6%
	100%	100%	100%

*Total number of cases —425.
†Total number of cases—265.
††Total number of cases—372.

The minimum attention given to adulterous and postmarital pregnancies is also consistent with society's tendency to emphasize only selected aspects of a given social problem in such a way that perspective is distorted, and other forms of that same social problem are obscured. But the fact remains that each year there are a conservatively estimated 45,000 to 75,000 divorced and married "unwed" mothers who are in potential need of counseling, and that physicians are the major contact with these females.

Perhaps the most striking question concerning adulterous pregnancies is: "Why does a married woman ever reveal that it was not her husband who impregnated her?" The answer in the case of those seeking counseling help is frequently that either the marriage is threatened because the husband knows, or the wife seeks help in resolving her own feelings and course of action without her husband's awareness of the problem. In the case of women who inform their physicians that their pregnancies are adulterous, the answer may be that they need at least one confidant and/or fear they will reveal such information anyway while under the effect of anesthesia during delivery.

In an effort to be of aid to physicians counseling divorced and married women involved in illicit pregnancies, I should like to share a few impressions based on questionnaire data from 256 such women, and on interview and counseling sessions with 35 such women.

The Divorced Unmarried Mother

The sexual caution of divorced women tends to be reduced by their desire to escape the socially stigmatized category of the divorcee as soon as possible, and by their openness in male-female conversation as learned while married. Not only is the divorcee frequently perceived by men as easy sex prey (as William Goode notes in *After Divorce*), but she herself may unintentionally foster such a view. Previously accompanied by her husband and protected by marriage, she became accustomed to open and frank discussions of sex in mixed groups; now she has to relearn some of the coyness that traditionally accompanies courtship. Without such coyness, and tacitly pressured by society and friends to prove via a successful marriage that it was not she who failed in the first marriage, her involvement with men tends to progress at a much faster and less cautious pace than even she recognizes—until she is pregnant and the man is no longer interested or returns to his wife.

An unknown proportion, perhaps the majority, of divorces involve a period of continued, somewhat sporadic, sexual intercourse between the ex-partners. In the cases of so-called "friendly" divorces, the continuation of coition is frequently regarded as mutually enjoyable, with no love or family obligations expected; and abortion may be a frequent solution when pregnancy occurs. Even when this solution is unavailable or unacceptable to the mother, she is reluctant to affix paternal responsibility on the former husband, in part perhaps because of her feeling that others would think her foolish for continuing sex relations with her ex-husband.

In cases where the divorce was not mutually desired, the wife may perceive intercourse as a potential means for reclaiming her husband. She may also, as one stated, "want a memory of him. . . . I hope it's a boy that looks just like him. . . . That way a part of him will always be with me." There is also the case of the ex-husband who desires a reconciliation and who, after considerable effort that often includes the argument of "for old times' sake," impregnates his ex-wife, only to find this makes her even more adamantly opposed to reconciliation.

MAINTAINING THE CONTEXT

One of the counseling needs common to a wide variety of cases involving premarital coition and illicit pregnancy is the need of the counselee to maintain an historical and contextual perspective of their sexual experience. Adult women may unceasingly condemn themselves by imposing adult judgments upon those sexual acts they experienced during adolescence. Married women may judge too harshly in retrospect their earlier "love" affairs involving coition with other men. Knowing now, at 35, the depth and quality of love they have for their husbands, they may continually reinforce guilt feelings about earlier sex unions with other men with whom they fell in love while single. It is not always easy to maintain the context within which a given event or experience took place years previously, but it is important to try to do so. This does not mean that all early or prior sexual experiences should be lightly excused. It does mean that the woman of 45 should not judge her experiences at 18 as if she at that time had the wisdom, judgment, and values she now has at 45.

The physician may frequently find opportunity to provide both ameliorative and treatment types of counseling in helping his patients maintain perspective concerning the context in which given sexual behavior occurred. The single female who has coition with a male during the time she thinks they are in love and are going to be married, may need help in remembering that at the time of their sex union the context was one of love and planning for marriage. Too often in those cases where the couple later fall apart and decide not to marry, the girl takes the sex experience out of the context in which it occurred and may either feel she has to proceed with the marriage to preserve her self-image as a nice girl, or may regard herself overly harshly as less worthy of her future husband as yet unmet.

The married woman impregnated during an affair with another male may also need help in maintaining the total context within which her affair took place. Her own guilt and self-condemnation may propel her to project too much blame on either herself or her husband and thereby reduce the chances for a strengthening of the marriage. Again, this is not to say she should completely absolve herself of any blame, but that the physician can help her understand the totality of events and circumstances that almost imperceptibly led to the illicit coition.

Physicians are already overworked and spread too thin, but the members of no other professional group have quite the same unique opportunities to become "significant others" in times of sexual crises. Physicians who are genuinely concerned about illegitimacy and the price it exacts from youth will find much to do: (1) in providing the community with a more accurate perspective of illegitimacy, (2) in reaffirming confidence in youth and in not being afraid to point up the adult and community contributions to illegitimacy, (3) in contagiously educating parents to cherish the individual without condoning his mistakes, and (4) in being sensitive to those young men and women who are desperately in need of a significant relationship and identification with at least one adult with whom they can discuss their own sexuality as a mental and physical health entity.

REFERENCES

Goode, W. *After divorce*. Glencoe, Illinois: The Free Press, 1956.
Vincent, C. E. *Unmarried Mothers*. New York: The Free Press of Glencoe, 1961.
Vincent, C. E. Divorced and married "unwed" mothers. *Sexology*, 1962, *28*, 674–679. (a)
Vincent, C. E. Spotlight on the unwed father. *Sexology*, 1962, *28*, 537–542. (b)

Special Techniques in Marriage Counseling

He that will not be counseled cannot be helped.
THOMAS FULLER

Marriage and family counseling is a field where, because of the particular needs of the clients and the problems they face, special techniques have been developed by the various professionals that are involved in marriage and family counseling. Some of these techniques are still controversial in the field but are included in this section so that both professionals and laypersons may learn more about them in order to decide whether or not they want to consider using them in their professional or private lives.

In Chapter 29, Shirley Gehrke Luthman and James Moxom, two social workers, focus on the marriage relationship itself and explain a method they have termed "relationship counseling." They discuss both diagnosis and treatment techniques for five diagnostic classifications: conflict in the area of masculine-feminine roles, the sadomasochistic conflict, the detached-demanding conflict, the oral-dependent conflict, and the neurotic illness conflict.

Vincent Foley, in Chapter 30, offers some observations on roles, communication, and techniques in family therapy with black, disadvantaged families. Is color more important than competence? There are conflicting ideas in the field of just who should be helping whom. Foley's article should provide some helpful insights.

One of the most prevalent and recurring problems in marital relations is quarreling. George R. Bach and Peter Wyden, in Chapter 31, discuss marital fighting and offer some suggestions or rules for making these fights "pay off," as they say. Dr. Bach and Peter Wyden share with the reader some ideas about what they call "constructive aggression" from their book *The Intimate Enemy* (1968). Several basic issues are raised by this article. Should marriage and family counselors encourage quarreling among clients who come for marriage and family counseling? Will the expression of aggression help or harm marriages? Is what is needed "training in marital fighting"? Do lovers and spouses who don't fight actually miss a great deal, as Bach and Wyden suggest?

Some professionals in the field would disagree with Bach and Wyden, and say that marriage and family counselors need to help clients fight and quarrel *less*, to *reduce* hostility rather than encourage its expression. To find out the basic cause of expressed or repressed hostility and aggression, and to help clients reduce the frequency and the heat of quarrels might seem to some professionals (and some marital partners) as a worthier goal. Each reader will have to come to his or her own conclusion on these matters. Professional ethics and personal values as well as one's theoretical and personal philosophy of life obviously enter into the final conclusion. The reader will also want to compare the point of view expressed by Bach and Wyden with those expressed in the chapter which follows, Chapter 32, by Ben N. Ard, Jr. Dr. Ard discusses whether more batacas or more civility would be best in improving communication in marriage.

Dr. Albert Ellis, Chapter 35, discusses neurotic interaction between marital partners, some of the irrational ideas, values, and assumptions that get in the way, and how a marriage and family counselor could introduce some more rational ideas into the interaction between marital partners. Dr. Ellis sets forth five common neuroticizing ideas which cause difficulty among marital partners: the dire need for love, perfectionism in achievement, a philosophy of blame and punishment, catastrophizing frustrations, and the belief that emotion is uncontrollable. He discusses the effect upon marriage of these neurotic irrationalisms, and presents a method of treating neuroticism in marriage—a rational approach—using a case illustration of this approach.

In Chapter 34, Aaron Rutledge discusses husband-wife conferences in the home as an aid to marriage counseling. Erik H. Erikson has also made use of home visits in his attempts to help families in trouble. Maybe marriage and family counselors need to consider something more than merely sitting back in their offices as the only conceivable consultation room. This home conference idea of Rutledge's is, indeed, a radical, controversial, provocative suggestion but the idea is certainly still worthy of consideration.

John Williams, a psychologist in private practice in Seattle, offers in Chapter 35 a feedback technique for improved communication among married couples. This "stop-repeat-go" technique can be used in the marriage counselor's office during counseling sessions and also be assigned as "homework" between sessions. A case example provides a clear illustration of how this technique actually works.

CHAPTER 29

Diagnostic Classifications and Treatment Techniques in Marriage Counseling

Shirley Gehrke Luthman and James Moxom

In marital counseling, the approach used by many caseworkers has been to treat the individuals involved in terms of their respective neuroses, with change in the marital relationship coming as a byproduct of improved individual adjustment. This method really amounts to treating an individual who happens to have a marital problem rather than treating the marriage relationship itself. The same approach would be used whether the person, married or single, was requesting help about a problem in his job, school, marriage, or other relationships.

Such an approach undoubtedly has its merits and is in some cases one answer, in others the only answer. However, with this method, long-term treatment is often necessary before there is any improvement in the presenting marital problem. Many clients may not sustain treatment to this extent, because their request is for relief of conflict in the marriage and not reconstruction of their individual personality patterns.

We have focused our treatment approach on the marriage relationship itself, because we see a difference in treating an individual who has a marital problem and in treating the problem in the marital relationship. In explanation, it is our contention that people marry each other to have certain needs met through marriage, and as long as these needs are met, the marriage can be stable, even with an extreme degree of neurosis in one or both partners. When something happens to upset the balance in this mutually satisfying relationship, conflict results. To illustrate:

A equals the husband and his total personality adjustment.
B equals the wife and her total personality adjustment.
C equals the marriage relationship, which contains both A and B but also something different and apart, which is the result of the interaction of A and B and their effect on each other.

It is C on which we focus.

Reprinted with permission of the authors and the publisher from *Family Process*, 1962, *1*, 253–264.

In these situations, casework can be used to help restore the balance lost in the relationship without resolving the individual neuroses, and this is often really what the clients are requesting. It may happen that a person initially requesting marital counseling may decide to focus mainly on his problems as an individual rather than as a marriage partner. However, we then believe that help becomes something other than marital counseling.

The first principle in the use of this method is that the same caseworker must see both partners. Sharing a caseworker focuses attention on the binding factor in the marriage, the relationship between the partners. This focus becomes the first bridge in communication, sustaining the relationship until husband and wife gain some ability to communicate with understanding.

The use of one caseworker is reassuring to clients if they want the marriage. It demonstrates the caseworker's role of strengthening the relationship rather than separating the partners through assignment to two different caseworkers. If they do not want the marriage, this approach encourages a quick recognition of this fact, as it forces clients to try to get their needs met through each other, to recognize what each can expect from himself and his partner, and to make a choice as to whether or not he can tolerate the relationship on this basis.

We have chosen to term this method "relationship counseling." The first step is a joint interview unless one or both partners refuse. If they do, this has diagnostic implication in terms of the degree of their estrangement and inability to communicate. In this instance the first step is to help the clients reach the point where they can share a joint interview.

In the joint interview the caseworker recognizes certain facts with the clients:

1. They have reached an impasse, in having tried without success many different ways of handling their problems.
2. The purpose of counseling is to help them break through this impasse.
3. A third person is necessary to assist in bridging the gap by enabling meaningful communication through increased understanding of themselves and their effect on each other.
4. Therefore, the end result of counseling is that the third person is not needed.

The main purposes of the first interview are to familiarize the clients with the counseling method and to give them an opportunity for mutual commitment to an exploratory period of two or three interviews. This period enables them to learn how the caseworker functions so that they can judge whether this is the type of help they want and need. It affords the caseworker an opportunity to diagnose the problem and as much as possible to help the clients to diagnose it also. Another joint interview is offered at the end of the exploratory period. This allows clients to commit themselves to continuing treatment based on the diagnostic understanding that clients and caseworker have reached at that point and gives clients some indication of the length of time necessary for treatment. The use of structure in this manner acts out the caseworker's conviction of the mutual responsibility of husband and wife in solving a marital problem and allows each to be encouraged by the other's expressed willingness to expend effort in solving their problems.

An accurate diagnosis of the relationship problems as well as an appraisal of the individual strengths and weaknesses of the marital partners is important for the caseworker. To effect more immediate and accurate diagnosis, we have devised the following diagnostic classifications and treatment techniques, which we have successfully applied in "relationship counseling."

I. A CONFLICT IN THE AREA OF MASCULINE-FEMININE ROLES

A. Diagnosis

In this relationship, both are in conflict about being married and having a sexual partner because of doubt about their adequacy in their respective male and female roles. The result is that the wife acts more masculine and the husband acts more feminine than usual. The wife chooses a dependent, passive male who she feels is inferior and not demanding sexually. The man is generally withdrawn, inadequate and has a severely impaired ego. He may be alcoholic, enuretic or obese. He is sexually apathetic and makes infrequent demands. Almost without exception, the woman, although frigid, complains of insufficient sexual interest on the husband's part; and even though she doesn't enjoy sex, she is usually the aggressor, and the sex life is geared toward her needs. The roles are reversed here as in every other area.

This wife controls in order to be sure her own dependency needs are met, and the husband submits to maintain his dependency. This relationship frequently resembles that of mother-child, as she indulges him because she needs his passivity to maintain her semblance of independence and to prevent excessive demands being made on her as a woman. She has high expectations of herself and glories in her independence. As long as she tolerates her husband's "shortcomings," he is satisfied with the marriage. If the husband becomes ill or unemployed, she may go to great lengths to help out, but if this incapacity extends over a long period of time, she feels unloved and unprotected, and becomes excessively controlling in a more hostile, frantic way.

If she becomes too controlling or demanding, the husband becomes upset and withdraws, both to protect himself from her demands for more masculinity than he has and to maintain a semblance of independence. He may also both defend himself and retaliate by becoming critical of her in the area of her feminine identification. She is, of course, especially sensitive in this area, particularly with regard to her appearance. She feels unattractive and frequently does not make the most of her physical attributes—her attire may be masculine and she gives little attention to make-up or hair styling.

This couple gives the impression of a stable family group active in the community. The wife has a history of being active socially but mostly with groups. There is a striking absence of intimate relationships with either men or women. Her success in work or community activity masks her uncertainty about her desirability as a feminine woman and serves as a substitute for meaningful one-to-one relationships. She talks about wanting a "real man," meaning one of impervious strength and perfection; and she is always disappointed and castrating when her husband does not meet her expectations. She is in conflict because she is really frightened of very masculine men as she cannot control them. They threaten her shaky feminine identification, but she cannot appreciate the more passive male who is the only kind she could possibly marry. This relationship is characterized by many separations, violent arguments, and divorce.

B. Treatment

Movement in this relationship stems from the wife's ability to gain insight into her controlling ways and what this represents—her need to defend her femininity by aggressive masculine ways. This often is best done by going over incidents she brings to the interview in which she has exerted this control until she is able to recognize the pattern. Once she sees the pattern, she can give it up.

Goals are slight with the man because of his lack of ego strength, and he is seldom able to gain understanding of what is involved. He is often uncertain as to what the male role is, or does not have enough conviction about it to know in what ways to assert himself. The caseworker simply needs to support the strengths in the man and encourage any effort he makes toward self-expression. The wife, in giving up her controlling pattern, leaves a vacuum for him to enter. If she doesn't attack when he moves in, he will stay there. He moves as a result of the changes she makes. The caseworker makes a mistake if he gives the impression that the husband should try to push the wife out. Once the wife sees the results of her efforts, she is ready for continued change but is still critical. Then it is important to emphasize the positives in the relationship, pointing out the feminine or more attractive qualities in the wife to her husband, and helping her recognize the better qualities in her husband so that she can be more appreciative of her choice. When the caseworker establishes a good relationship with both, he can be more directive about this. In the continuing course of treatment, further elaboration on the wife's control pattern can often help her gain real insight into her need for this pattern.

II. THE SADO-MASOCHISTIC CONFLICT

A. Diagnosis

In this relationship the man uses marriage to express his hostile, rivalrous feelings toward women. She submits because her severely limited self-regard convinces her that this is the best she can do in a relationship and she doesn't deserve anything better.

He is aggressive, sadistic, and humiliating in his behavior toward her. She is dependent, submissive, and enduring, with great tolerance for his belittling treatment. However, she is also provocative and subtly hostile. Her helplessness and subtle hostility encourage excess in her husband's expression of feeling. The marriage is characterized by "living in conflict."

These people need each other, however, and will seldom terminate the relationship permanently. The wife is disorganized and often unable to pursue homemaking activities. The man is deeply insecure and hostile, finds it difficult to be magnanimous in marriage, nags and interferes even in the housework. The wife is given to hysterical outbursts, usually provoked by her husband, who needles and harangues her until she is completely unstrung. She plays into this to get release for her feelings and be punished for her hostile feelings toward him.

In the sexual relationship he is often rough, always the aggressor. She retaliates with frigidity and subtle castrating behavior such as disinterest, delaying tactics, tacit disparagement of husband's techniques, disgust, or martyr-like endurance. Often she compels him to adopt deviant measures to elicit sexual satisfaction from her. Her actions, plus his hostility to women, often provoke a potency problem on the part of the man.

He may disparage his wife by philandering, rationalizing that she is disinterested. He then disparages his paramour by leaving her for his wife and may use the same mechanism by leaving his wife for his mother. He deals with the marriage problem by blaming others and forcing his will in a demanding, depreciating manner. She is usually a patiently enduring martyr about the whole thing, or accepts all the blame in a self-depreciating manner.

B. Treatment

Most of the time, in these relationships, contact with an agency will be initiated by the wife because of difficulty with a child, or because she has reached even her masochistic limits in terms of the amount of punishment she can take. The husband will usually come also because he desires to establish more control and will gladly use help in doing this. If he initiates contact, as sometimes happens, it is because the marriage is threatened and he is seeking to re-establish controls. This man, more than any other type, needs this marriage. Therefore, when this couple comes for help, change has to be initiated by the wife because she has something to gain. Very often, the husband sees himself as assistant to the caseworker in gaining better understanding of the wife in order to bring about his own desired results.

With this couple, transference must be used in that the caseworker becomes the ideal parent—firm but warm, forgiving, noncondemning. It is necessary to clarify the limits of the caseworker and the casework process and to reaffirm these constantly. These partners will use the caseworker to attack each other. They frequently misinterpret what the caseworker says, have very little tolerance for each other, and want the caseworker to do things they feel they cannot do. It is necessary to constantly reaffirm focus, by recognizing that this problem has existed for years, that there are certain things the caseworker can and cannot do, the most important of which is that changes are made by them, not the caseworker. If limits are not firmly set, the couple will go in circles, get into heated arguments, constantly dredge up the past.

In addition to preventing manipulation by the clients, treatment involves firm support of the strengths of each partner. It is important to help the wife gain a more realistic view of herself, recognizing the part she plays in provoking punishing situations for herself, and to help modify her need to do this. She needs encouragement to seek recognition and satisfactions for herself without extreme guilt and self-depreciation. As she makes changes, it is necessary to establish a new balance in the marriage. In some instances, the husband may not be able to accept her as a more assertive person, and change may mean the dissolution of treatment or the marriage or both. In most instances, however, the change is not drastic and slight change may be reassuring to the husband as he can then get some of his dependency needs met by his wife. The sado-masochistic pattern is not discontinued. It is simply reduced in degree to a point where outbursts are fewer and less intense. The neurotic pattern is maintained but in a much more tolerable degree, allowing room for some healthier satisfactions. The result is greater stability and a more constructive balance in the marriage.

III. THE DETACHED-DEMANDING CONFLICT

A. *Diagnosis*

The partners in this relationship are markedly dependent. Each wants a parent who can meet his needs without demanding anything in return. The relationship is characterized by emotional detachment on the man's part and an intense open demand for love on the woman's part. Each is disappointed and disillusioned in his expectations of what the other can do.

The man appears the strong, silent type—sturdy, reliable, individualistic. His wife interprets his detached calm as emotional strength. She gets the father she needs, who generally works hard, provides an adequate living, and handles financial matters. However, he has nothing to give in a relationship except dependability, so that his wife is in conflict because she got what she wanted and finds it is not enough. Her own father was rejecting and inconsistent, and unconsciously she expects her husband to reject her also. Therefore, she demands constant proof of his love and acceptance, and he reacts to these demands with further withdrawal. Usually the women in these marriages are socially charming, vivacious, and effervescent. The husband misinterprets the wife's vivacity as independence, assuming she will require little from him. He has unrealistic attitudes about what a relationship is, marries a demanding woman because this is the only type who will take the trouble to hammer away at his protective shell long enough to involve him in a marriage. She has a need to prove she can win love from a man, and from past experience with her father, she is convinced it is necessary to demand and push if she wants to get it. The woman has usually been more active in bringing about the marriage. There is frequently a history of premarital relations and pregnancy. Both are asking for the same thing—unconditional love and approval—but express this need in different ways.

There is almost no giving in the relationship. Both are markedly sensitive to criticism and interpret the slightest expression of negative feeling on the part of the other as personal criticism even though it may obviously be directed at no one.

Early in the marriage the wife tries very hard. When she doesn't get the results she wants, she deteriorates rapidly. Housekeeping and child care become overwhelming burdens, and her work becomes disorganized. She is prone to hysterical outbursts far out of proportion to the stimuli, and frequent lack of emotional control. Her increasing disorganization frightens her husband, who withdraws even more or attacks critically. He may even withdraw physically in "socially acceptable" ways—working on hobbies, business trips, extra jobs, etc. This is a further and often unbearable threat to the wife's unmet dependency needs.

There is usually trouble from the beginning of the marriage as the normal stress and strains of marriage reveal the deep dependency needs of each partner.

B. Treatment

Treatment in this relationship, more than any other, must be geared toward direct handling of the extreme ambivalence on the part of the man. He is in conflict as to whether or not he really wants this or any other relationship. On one hand he sees relationships as demanding more than he is prepared to give. On the other hand he sees a lonely barren existence without people. It is necessary to face him directly with the choice. As this man often has the idea that demands will never end if he once lets go enough to give of himself, the caseworker can help him in his choice by presenting a more realistic picture of the amount of change necessary. Once he makes the decision to involve himself in treatment in an effort to save his marriage, the treatment goal is to help him relax and risk communication and giving of his feelings. It is necessary to point out that he has to make conscious efforts to give as it will not come naturally. Once a relationship is established with this man, the caseworker can often be quite directive as to what conscious effort the man might try.

By the time this couple get to the point of requesting treatment, he is getting more satisfaction outside of his home, and she is drawing more into the home with increasing hostility and panic. Housekeeping deteriorates, which infuriates the husband as he is often compulsive. Sexually, she becomes frigid. This woman feels undeserving and guilty about taking satisfactions. She needs help in recognizing that satisfactions are necessary and important to her but will not come just because she may deserve them. She needs help in recognizing her hostility and handling it more directly. Extremely important is an awareness on her part that her husband is never going to meet all her needs and that she will need to seek satisfactions in friends and community activities so that she will not need or expect so much from marriage.

The most difficult goal for this couple to achieve is communication with each other. They may show marked improvement, but this can be deceptive. They may be exerting conscious efforts toward change but be reporting back to the caseworker about any changes rather than discussing them with each other. They can achieve a better adjustment this way, but it won't last. It is necessary to point this out and help them develop incentive for effort from each other to sustain benefits rather than depending on the caseworker to do this. The goal of treatment is to help this couple achieve an emotional exchange which will help satisfy their dependency needs in the marriage. The prognosis is poorer in this group than others because often the man has little invested in the relationship, needs only a semblance of normality, and may not choose to do more. If the man really decides to involve himself in treatment, then the prognosis is good.

IV. THE ORAL-DEPENDENT CONFLICT

A. Diagnosis

In this relationship both partners are passive, dependent people striving for immature childish gratifications. There is a mutual attempt at domination resulting in stormy quarrels. Each exhibits "temper tantrums" frequently accompanied by physical violence on the part of both. This is not of a sadistic nature but resembles a sibling rivalry type of fighting. There is no emotional giving at all in these relationships. Neither has ever achieved a satisfactory adjustment on his own, away from parents. Therefore, both are still tied to parents and at the slightest provocation will run home.

The relationship is characterized by emotional emptiness and an intense longing for affection. Each wants complete victory over the other at any cost and because of strong dependency needs is alarmed at the prospect of losing the other. Each exhibits little interest in the well-being of his partner. The man frequently adopts activities generally associated with adolescence—motorcycle clubs, sports car racing, skin diving—preferring to be with "the boys." The wife bitterly complains about this although guilty of the same adolescent behavior.

They both feel like hurt, neglected children, become hostile to each other, exhibit irresponsible and unreliable behavior and look elsewhere for sympathy. Flight is characteristic—home to mother, retreat within self, desertion.

B. Treatment

In this relationship, there should be no attempt on the caseworker's part to change the situation. All this couple is requesting is the reestablishment of a tranquil balance without individual personality change. It is necessary to deal directly with the precipitating factor, which may involve environmental manipulation or, if no concrete action is possible, simply soothing the clients as you would excited animals until the crisis is past.

Because treatment goals are limited, contact should be short term for the purpose of handling the immediate problem, with the door left open for these clients to contact the caseworker when another crisis arises. There is no need or point in attempting to set up a sustained, long-term treatment plan. The prognosis is good if the caseworker remains with the environmental situation which precipitated the contact. Successful treatment is impossible if the caseworker gets involved with the oral dependency problem.

V. THE NEUROTIC ILLNESS CONFLICT

A. Diagnosis
In this relationship, the woman is helpless in manner, chronically ill, and expects her mate to be omnipotent and to relieve her suffering. Always disappointed, she expresses unconscious resentment through depression and exacerbation of symptoms. The considerate mate is patient and stays in the marriage because of his extreme sense of inadequacy. He is strengthened by the idea of helping a weaker one. He always fails, resulting in further loss of confidence. The sick person's tacit disappointment and criticism leads to intense resentment. The man's limited self-regard and inability to enjoy the good things in life cause him to handle his resentment by redoubling his efforts to meet his wife's needs.

B. Treatment
This relationship is not treatable on a marital counseling level even though the marital problem is apparent and at the root of whatever difficulty they are presenting.

It may appear that these categories are overlapping. It is true that a couple may seem to show characteristics of several of the categories, but it has been our experience, without exception, that these are surface similarities and that deeper probing reveals the basic conflict falls clearly in one of these areas and varies only in matter of degree, not type.

Within each classification, the degree of disturbance varies, but even so the same treatment applies. The degree simply determines the goals—the more extreme the degree, the more limited the goals. The greater the strengths evident, the greater the goals.

If the caseworker accurately evaluates the strengths and establishes appropriate goals, then help is possible for any who apply. If, as sometimes happens, one partner in the marriage wants to continue and the other does not, then help can be given but becomes counseling to a person with a marital problem rather than marital counseling per se. This needs to be spelled out with the client.

In all of these diagnostic classifications, joint interviews may be used intermittently in the following instances:
1. Contradictory stories from the husband and wife point out the need for clarification.

2. One or both express the desire to discontinue treatment.
3. A plateau is reached and there is no movement.
4. It seems advisable to pause for review and consensus of accomplishments to date and determination of future goals.
5. There is need to encourage greater communication; this is especially useful when the problem falls within classification IV.
6. A conclusion is reached in the treatment process; also for follow-up in one to six months after termination.

We have found that by focusing our diagnostic thinking and treatment goals on the marital relationship rather than the individuals, clients are involved in treatment much more quickly and sustain the treatment process to an appropriate termination. Treatment time usually lasts six to nine months. This means that there is no serious attempt to change the personality make-up of the individuals involved but simply to help them establish a marital balance.

In this article, we have presented a brief description of a marital counseling method with the diagnostic classifications and treatment techniques which we have used successfully. It is our expectation and hope that this presentation will stimulate questions and explorations which will further develop the body of knowledge in "relationship counseling."

CHAPTER 30

Family Therapy with Black, Disadvantaged Families: Some Observations on Roles, Communication, and Technique

Vincent D. Foley

This paper puts together some observations made over the course of fifteen years experience in dealing with black, disadvantaged families in areas as diverse as Topeka, Kansas; Roxbury, Massachusetts; and Brooklyn, New York. Based on clinical work rather than statistics, it focuses on the relationship of roles and communication within a system concept of family therapy and applies this to black, disadvantaged families. A system concept sees the family as the patient and the identified client only as a symptom of a sick system.

What emerges when we apply such a concept to a black, disadvantaged family? The paper offers observations which are, at best, tentative and by no means applicable only to such families. However, in our experience, therapy with white families of similar economic backgrounds yield either different dimensions or if similar, less extensive. For example, there is a need for immediate success with a black family which is not usually present in a white disadvantaged family. This is due to the fact that the former frequently, and correctly so, sees the therapist as part of an establishment which is hostile to it, whereas the latter sees him more as a helping agent. Even where similar observations can be made as the role of the oldest daughter is noted, there is a difference. In black families she is given a much greater part in the upbringing of her siblings than in white families of similar economic status.

For too long therapists have given lip service to cultural dimensions, and then proceeded to act as if differences of color, economics, education, or social class had relatively little to do with therapy. If we examine the interactions within any family system there will be certain similarities that

Reprinted with permission of the author and the publisher from the *Journal of Marriage and Family Counseling*, January, 1975.

repeatedly occur, such as the critical importance of the marital dyad and sibling rivalry. These are present in all families.

But what about the differences? Are the role expectations the same? Are there differences in the ways in which communication, especially nonverbal communication, takes place? Obviously such differences exist. It is our contention that these differences are critical and essential elements in successful therapy. Dimensions important for the therapist are outlined in this paper.

Not only are there differences between the ways which black and white families operate, but also among various kinds of black families. For example, among urban blacks there is a frequent pattern of dominance of the mother due in large measure to an absent father. However, among blacks with rural ties, one must be aware of the grandmother and a network of aunts who give such families a more extended pattern and lessen, to some extent, the mother's role of dominance. One often notes among West Indians a neat division of authority, the mother ruling the functioning of the home and the father controlling discipline and decision making.

The key idea to be kept in mind by a therapist is that a black system operates according to certain rules just as a white one, but that the ingredients are not necessarily or even usually the same. This means that he should realize that he is not necessarily concerned with changing the way the system is structured but with helping it operate more smoothly. His task as therapist is to help the family clarify roles and role expectation and facilitate communication within the system. To do this effectively he need not introduce his own value system but only be aware of how the family wishes to operate.

ROLES

The first major concept is the place of family roles. John Bell says that one of the specific aims of family therapy is "to make the family conscious of the roles that the various members play in relation to one another (Bell, 1961)."

Therapeutically, the concept of role involves two levels: first, the delineation of roles within the family structure, and, second, the attempt by the therapist to get the family to perceive someone's role in a different light. The frequent phenomenon of scapegoating is the result of role confusion or perception. In many instances a family comes into therapy with the idea that a certain person in the family has a problem and is the identified client. The purpose in seeking help is to get the therapist to straighten out the member in question.

The concept of disharmony in role fulfillment leads us to make some observations about black families in which the extent of disharmony is of special note. In dealing with disruption in the black family there are four areas of special consideration for the therapist.

The Need for Immediate Success
Most black families have a multiplicity of problems. They have been

seen often by social workers, school counselors, visiting nurses, and others. To tell such clients that therapy will be long and difficult is self-defeating. What is needed is to pick out a problem that has a workable solution and to set about accomplishing it. This may mean working on an increase in welfare allowance, getting an appointment at a public clinic, or having the house police investigate vandalism. If possible, the therapist should assist and not replace the family in doing this; for example, not going with a member of the family to the welfare office but allowing the person to experience success by his own effort.

From a psychological point of view success in such an endeavor takes away the frequently used defense of global generalizations such as, "All public officials are corrupt," or "Whitey is against me." This gives the therapist an opening into the family, because he has helped them accomplish something concrete, and thus opens up the possibility of hope.

Most therapeutic relationships contain an aspect of hope and despair. One seeks help because one has a wish of changing yet at the same time there is the deeply felt fear of failure, i.e., things will never change substantially. This ambivalence is part of most therapy but in black families tends to be more of an issue as one encounters a hopeless outlook with the disadvantaged. The view of the world as hopeless and one's life space as a dull and fixed thing is often realistic. Experience most often supports the contention that life is a losing struggle, especially for black families.

Again it should be noted that families are not often self-referred but are sent by the court, school, or some other social agency. Consequently, the therapist is seen not so much as a helping agent but as one who is used by the establishment to keep an errant child or family in line. The therapist then must work hard to disengage himself from this position and establish a different kind of contract. His contract ought to be to listen to the family and help them help themselves.

An immediate success can help restructure the relationship and allow both the therapist and the therapeutic contract to be viewed in a more favorable light.

The Critical Need for Self-observation

That self-observation is critical in any kind of change seems obvious. This means being able to see one's self in action and yet at the same time, be able to make a judgment on how one is acting or relating. This is perhaps the most important issue in all of therapy regardless of one's theoretical concepts. Psychoanalysts, for example, are quick to point out that the ability to use one's observing ego is a *sine qua non* in judging a client's ability to undergo analysis.

Something akin to a working alliance is also needed in family therapy. Without it there can be no realistic hope of change. What we are emphasizing is not that the family needs to have insight in the technical sense of the term, but that members must be able at least to see how they interact with each other. This kind of perception or awareness is possible even with relatively uneducated people as the following case illustrates.

Mr. and Mrs. T. had been fighting over a number of issues for several sessions. Their relationship could be characterized as a "Come here, go away" one, that is, Mrs. T. would constantly pick on Mr. T. who would finally become angry and leave. With much crying she would plead for him to return to the family. When he returned the pattern would be repeated again.

We tried to point this out to Mrs. T., but she skillfully backed away saying she did not understand what was meant. However Mr. T. understood quite well, and more importantly, was able to put the relationship into colorful and communicable language. After one involved explanation Mr. T. turned to his wife and said:

> Mr. T: Baby what the man is trying to say is if you don't like my features how come you shake my tree.

Mrs. T. got the point immediately and we were able to focus on Mrs. T's pattern and eventually why Mr. T. tolerated such a relationship. This illustrates the kind of awareness or perception that is needed in family therapy.

For those who do not have access to videotape equipment or a co-therapist, other dramatic techniques can be usefully employed.

One effective example of the dramatic occurred in a situation where Mrs. G. kept talking to her husband as if he were a child. I made this observation twice verbally but to no avail, and finally I asked Mr. G. to change places with me. Mrs. G. kept talking as if nothing had happened. After a few minutes I slouched lower in my chair and finally sat on the floor at her feet. Mrs. G. looked puzzled and said:

> Mrs. G: Why are you sitting there?
>
> T: That's the way you make me feel.
>
> Mrs. G: You look a little boy who's been scolded.
>
> T: Well?
>
> Mrs. G: You mean that's the way my husband feels?
>
> Mr. G. (with feeling): You always talk like I'm a kid.

This dramatization enabled Mrs. G. to get some awareness of her interaction where words alone were not effective.

Assigning Family Tasks

This is closely related to the concept of self-observation. Through a division of labor it allows various family members to get some awareness of their interaction. It helps to clarify attitudes and permits a better focus on critical family issues. A recent example may be illustrative.

> In an initial interview Mrs. J. complained that she was overburdened with her two school-age boys. Mrs. J. went to work from seven to three as a nurse's aide. As a result she was not able to prepare lunch for the children. Mr. J. worked as a night watchman from twelve to eight. After some discussion Mr. J. agreed to get up and prepare lunch for the children. A few sessions later Mrs. J. complained that her husband was not the most creative cook in the world.
>
> I made the observation that Mrs. J. wanted help but when it was offered criticized it. I asked her if she really wanted help or not. She nodded yes and I added that she would have to support her husband's efforts to help rather than undercut them. To this she replied, "I don't want him to push me around."

This opened up the whole area of how she wanted to relate to her husband and led us into a fruitful discussion of how authority and responsibility gets delegated in their family.

An attempt to get at some kind of self-observation would not have been possible without first making a division of labor. It should be noted that such a division is most important in the kind of disadvantaged family that Salvador Minuchin has labelled the "enmeshed family." He characterizes such a family system of interaction as one in which the mother has "an overwhelming need for continued hold on the children (Minuchin, 1967)."

The J. Family is a good case study of an enmeshed family. The therapeutic strategy was to divide the family tasks which would allow some of Mrs. J's ambivalence to come out. This enabled her to see both ends of the spectrum and hopefully to realize that her relationship with Mr. J. did not have to be a struggle for absolute power, i.e., a zero-sum game with only one winner. When the self-defeating game was pointed out, the "stakes were lowered" sufficiently so that some of Mrs. J's fears about losing control could be talked about. She could then allow Mr. J. to play a more active role as father without being overly threatened. This finally permitted us to work on the issue of tenderness which Mrs. J. had equated with vulnerability.

The Role of the Oldest Daughter

This point is connected with the idea of family tasks but holds a special place in black families and so is treated separately.

My experience has shown that the oldest daughter is treated more often as a surrogate parent than as a sibling. As a consequence too much responsibility is delegated or thrust upon an adolescent girl. Her needs for structure and support are not acknowledged and she looks for it outside. It is our feeling that much of the reason for the high rate of illegitimacy among black adolescents is attributable to this factor. What seems to be "crazy behavior," namely, getting pregnant or trying to, is in fact only a poor solution to a vexing problem. However, when seen within the context of a given situation it makes sense. Therefore, in an initial family interview, it is always wise to check out the amount of obligation given to this child, and if overburdened, to suggest a more equitable division of labor.

These observations bring us to some general considerations of how one gets at roles and relationships in family therapy. To a large extent this seems to depend on the style of the therapist. For example, some seem to work mostly with the roles of husband and wife and less with those of the children. Our own feelings are that this is generally preferable in black families. The role of husband-father has long been ignored to the detriment of the family. By dealing with the husband-wife dyad the therapist implicitly restores the role of the male.

On the other hand, others prefer to start with the children as individuals and later work with the parents and finally with the whole family. This offers some interesting possibilities with black parents who frequently feel defensive about their children. One might begin by siding with the parents and picking up some of their embarrassment and pain. This is another source of entry into the family. The choice of point of entry will be determined largely by circumstance rather than by any general idea of how one ought or must function. This brings us to the question of role discrimination, i.e., "How do roles and relationships get redefined in the family?" The answer to this question leads us to what we consider the second critical dimension of family therapy, communication.

COMMUNICATION

The concepts of role and communication can be separated for purposes of study but in fact are interrelated. As Jurgen Ruesch noted long ago, roles define the kinds of action and communication that take place between two people because they indicate the identity of the other in relation to self and self in relation to the other (Ruesch, 1961). Clearly one does not speak to the boss, a co-worker, or an underling in the same way, because in each case the relationship is different.

Similarly the communicational patterns are different in families because of cultural nuances. What are some of the more recurring, observable patterns of communication among black, disadvantaged families which are critical for the family therapist? One notes a high percentage of incomplete messages, a frequent neglect of metacommunication, a need for relabelling, and a tendency to neglect the adjectives when talking about the affective level; i.e., one is either loved or not loved in a relationship without gradations of love being noted.

Incomplete Messages

Communication among black families tends to be in generalities more than in specific instances. When questioned about a particular situation one is likely to receive an answer such as, "He's always jivin' me," or "My brother likes to rank me." These expressions allow for many kinds of interpretation, some of which are mutually exclusive.

Such generalizations need to be made concrete. For example, if Mrs. X. says that she fights continually with Mr. X., the therapist should ask her to show him how it happens. It is very helpful if the couple are asked to stage a typical fight. The therapist can then stop the fight at critical intervals and ask Mrs. X. what she thinks Mr. X. means by a certain comment or action and then check with Mr. X. about it. This approach helps them to see, and more importantly, to experience the vagueness of their messages.

This can be done in the form of homework, such as asking the couple to gather for five or ten minutes a day to talk about any subject of their choosing but requiring of each the following: Every sentence of Mr. X. must be followed by his wife's saying what she heard him say and then Mr. X's confirming or denying it. Only when there has been a complete exchange of messages can the dialogue proceed. This exercise is an attempt to make the communicational concepts complementary and symetrical.

Usually initial attempts will have little success. This failure allows the therapist to role play and become a model of communication without seeming to be obtrusive or condescending. This technique has the advantage of making a potentially provocative situation into a game, and thus taking some of the excess feeling from issues. This gives emotional distance and permits the therapist to get at some underlying problems.

Also the use of nonverbal homework can be effective. For example, each partner is instructed to notice three things about the spouse which reveal different states of mind. In one instance a woman said she knew her husband was angry when he smoked cigarettes only half-way, a fact of which he was unaware. However, care must be taken that the game does not deteriorate into an attempt to get something on the other party.

Frequent Neglect of Metacommunication

The Greek preface of meta means to go beyond something as in the word metaphysics which means to go beyond the physcial to the philosophical. To understand one needs both information and how the information is to be handled.

A computer needs data but it also needs to know how the data are to be processed. It needs information but also metainformation which tells it what to do with the information. Likewise human beings cannot understand unless they have both information and instructions on how to interpret the information. Family therapists call these two aspects communication and metacommunication. The former supplies the data and the latter tells one how to read it.

The process of understanding what is being said, the relationship of communication and metacommunication, is a struggle for all families. Black, disadvantaged families frequently are less verbal than white ones. This means that nonverbal aspects of communication are more predominant. Yet, at the same time, one observes a frequent neglect of metacommunication so that certain critical factors in familial interaction are overlooked as the following case illustrates.

> Mr. and Mrs. R. were locked in battle over their relationship but neither was willing or able to articulate it. One of their children, John, was constantly getting into fights at school and the R's were seeking help with the problem. As they talked about the boy Mrs. R. would say that she was upset about his behavior and her husband would agree although he would add, "Of course I don't want him to be a baby." It seemed to the therapist that the child's behavior was only a cover for some other problems in the marriage, in particular the marital relationship.
>
> The therapist picked up a number of nonverbal cues sent out by Mr. R., such as the way he sat (slightly turned from his wife), while shaking his head from side to side as he claimed to be upset at the boy's behavior (a seeming denial of her verbal assertion). The therapist fed back to Mr. R. the discrepancies he noted as a way of checking out their truth or falsity. In addition, he kept repeating, "Mr. R. it seems to me you are saying that you agree with your wife but at the same time I get the feeling that you also disagree to some extent with her thinking about John." Mr. R. admitted this might be true. In time the therapist was able to suggest that perhaps there were

some problems between Mr. and Mrs. R. in addition to John. By citing the ways in which Mr. R. delivered his information, i.e., the tone of his voice and body language the therapist was getting the metacommunicative level. With support from the therapist Mr. R. was then able to voice some of his negative feelings about his wife focusing about the issue of control in the family. The therapist was teaching the Rs the necessity of looking not only at what is said but also how it is said both verbally and nonverbally and then checking out the accuracy of the perception.

The first rule of communication is that one cannot not communicate because there is no such thing as nonbehavior. Whether I speak or remain silent I am communicating. However, the manner or way in which I communicate is not always easily understood or deciphered. This level, the metacommunicative, is frequently overlooked or misread in black, disadvantaged families and is a potential source of rich exploration for the family therapist. Understanding the metacommunicative is a task for any family because the ways in which data is processed in families will differ due to cultural dimensions. Black, disadvantaged families have distinct ways of communicating which both they and the therapist must examine.

Relabelling

Relabelling refers to the fact that there is more than one way of looking at things. For example, one can look out the window and say it is partly cloudy (a negative view) or say it is partly sunny (a positive view). Both are equally correct. Family interaction likewise can be labelled in a variety of ways. Due in large part to social factors black, disadvantaged families tend to label behavior in negative ways. The therapist, therefore, must be alert to the possibility of relabelling as a way of getting the kind of feedback into the family system which allows it to change as the following example illustrates.

Mr. and Mrs. T. had been quarreling for some time over the behavior of one of the children. Mr. T. was complaining that his wife was always yelling at the boy to do his homework, i.e., he was labelling her behavior as negative. The therapist nodded in agreement, but at the same time said, "One could also say it shows real concern about how well he is doing in school," i.e., labelling it positively. This was acceptable to Mr. T. and at the same time made his wife feel understood. Later in the session it was possible to talk about Mrs. T's anger and how, despite her best intentions, she was ineffective. The relabelling, however, made it evident that the therapist was trying to help her deal more effectively with her son.

Mention should also be made of the necessity of relabelling an entire situation. In a given case it may be necessary to restructure the entire relationship.

Some time ago the Cs were offered the choice of having one of their sons committed to a youth house for six months or seeking help. Mrs. C. called and asked if I would act as a club to keep her son in line. I tried to explain how I operated but she would or could not listen. I asked if she would arrange to have the whole family, i.e., Mr. and Mrs. C. and the two sons, come for an appointment.

Several days later she called again to say that Mr. C. didn't want to come but she would make sure he was present. She also suggested that I might straighten him out in addition to straightening out the son.

At the appointed time for our session I heard a knock and was greeted by a large, imposing woman. She entered the room followed by a teenage boy and a man. The woman extended her hand and said:

Mrs. C: I'm Mrs. C., Doctor.

T: I'm glad to meet you Mrs. C. (I looked puzzled and went to the door and looked up the hall. As I closed the door I shook my head).

Mrs. C: Is there something wrong?

T: I think so. I thought you had two sons.

Mrs. C: Oh the other boy didn't want to come. He said he didn't have no problems.

T: (Pause) I see. He's the boss in the family.

Mrs. C: Oh no. I am.

T: (Looking surprised) And what about Mr. C?

Mrs. C: He earns the money.

T: I see. You're the boss; Mr. C. does the work and you call the shots.

Mrs. C: (Flustered) No, not exactly. We both are in charge.

T: I notice Mr. C. you're smiling. You seem to be enjoying this.

Mr. C: Yeah man, I mean who is the boss? I tell the kids something and then she turns around and tells them to do what the hell thing they please. But when things blow up I'm to blame.

Such a confrontation obviously can backfire. I wanted to accomplish several goals in this case: first, to get the son labelled other than as the identified client; second, to get a browbeaten husband involved; and third, not to totally alienate Mrs. C. but shake her up.

To do these things required something dramatic. When the other son did not show up I was able to use the incident and relabel the entire situation. The father and son responded warmly to what I did. Mrs. C., of course, did not but I got around the anger by congratulating her on the interest she showed in the family and the son in particular.

This use of relabelling got us into the family situation immediately by enabling us to change the feedback going into the system. After only one session each family member had a different perception of self and a new way of looking at their interaction.

Affective Exchange: All-or-nothing

Minuchin (1967) has observed that transactions among disadvantaged blacks and Puerto Ricans tend to have an all-or-nothing quality about them. Extremes of involvement or total lack of interest are common. The nuances one might expect in human relations are not found.

This general observation leads to three practical therapeutic considerations.

First, the therapist must be on guard to notice changes, in behavior or attitude. He must identify them, label them, and credit positive effort. This offsets the tendency to demand complete shifts or changes in others while ignoring small but significant ones.

Second, the therapist must use his own feelings to make a point. For example, a common pattern of interaction is one in which the mother has a secret alliance with one or more children against the father, as was seen in the case of Mrs. C. and her "good son." Covertly, such mothers encourage the children to undermine the father's authority. It can be helpful if the therapist not only makes this observation but does so with sufficiently strong feeling so that the offending parent gets the point.

Third, the therapist must note an inappropriate lack of affect as, for instance, when a child has been suspended from school or a husband is in danger of losing his job, or a wife is becoming visibly more depressed. Often, such critical situations will be met with indifference or apathy. To note the improper feeling response and to act as a model for the family can be instructive, the care and concern of the therapist demonstrating to the family that the situation is serious and demands a strong response. In this way the therapist acts in a re-educative fashion, not only being cognitive but affective as well, showing the family that the heart and the head must both be used to deal effectively with problems in living.

What we are saying about the affective could be summarized under the general rubric of lack of variety in response, i.e., an all-or-nothing attitude.

TECHNIQUES

Throughout these pages in passing I have suggested ways of dealing with roles and communication within the system of a black, disadvantaged family. The use of a co-therapist, if possible, the use of audio and video tape, if available, have proven to be effective. However, the most dramatic results have been found to occur when a multiple family approach has been utilized. This seems to defuse whatever racial bombs that may be ticking. The fact that a therapist is white and the family is black is a factor that cannot be ignored nor disregarded. Any therapist is necessarily in the "one-up position." When the dimension of color is added to his therapeutic advantage the resistance can be immense. However, when one black family can see itself reflected in another and identifications can be made, the racial barrier becomes permeable. Time and again I have observed a lessening of hostility, an increase in verbalization, and a general "loosening up" of the family when a multiple family approach is used.

The advantages noted also operate in multiple family therapy with white families. Perhaps the diminution of the therapist's power here enables the family to move, whereas in conjoint family therapy the family's fantasy of the therapist paralyzes it. At times, this paralysis in black families becomes total.

Within a system concept the role of therapist is to carry information across boundaries without rupturing those boundaries. Since boundaries between blacks and whites are at best delicate, rupture of them is a constant hazard. Experience has shown that these boundaries are best protected by the use of multiple family therapy wherein each family acts as a cushion for the other. In such an atmosphere information can be transmitted and change is possible.

CONCLUSIONS

If family therapy as a distinct approach to family problems is still in its infancy, family therapy with the disadvantaged is in an incubator. The concepts we have articulated are only tentative and involve an attempt to conceptualize our experience using the notions or roles and communication within a system concept. Is this approach a true reading of the realities of black, disadvantaged families or not? The answer is by no means certain.

Some readers conversant with other ethnic groups may say that family therapy with black, disadvantaged is not basically different than therapy with lower-class Italian, Polish, or Irish families, arguing that economics is the key factor in determining family structure and that the roles and communication outlined here are found also in white families. On the other hand, the sociologist Robert Staples (1971), after observing the lack of research among black, middle-class families which would allow one to isolate economic variables, concludes his study by saying that "... the black family had evolved a unique structure and style to cope with the circumstances that it has confronted." He seems to be suggesting that despite similarities, black families have "a unique structure."

Clearly then the matter of the black, disadvantaged family is open to debate. There are similarities between such families and white families. But the question remains, "Are these differences essential or accidental?" At this stage of research there is no definite answer.

However, this paper has been an attempt to outline some observations from work with black, disadvantaged families. In our work we have observed roles and patterns of communication which seem to be distinctive of black, disadvantaged families. We are not able to say that they are only found in such families as our experience with white, disadvantaged families is limited. We can say, however, within those limitations that we feel there are unique factors in role relationships and communication as found in black, disadvantaged family systems.

Perhaps, the best conclusion to make on the issue is to remind the reader of the ancient wise man who observed that God gave man one mouth and two ears so that he could listen twice as much as he spoke. Having spoken, we are now ready to listen.

REFERENCES

Bell, J. Family group therapy. *Public Health Monograph*, 1964, *64*, 5.
Minuchin, S., et al. *Families of the slum*. New York: Basic Books, 1967, 359.
Ruesch, J. *Therapeutic Communication*. New York: Norton, 1961, 430.
Staples, R. Toward a sociology of the black family: a theoretical and methodological assessment. *Journal of Marriage and the Family*, 1971, *33*, 38.

CHAPTER 31

Marital Fighting: A Guide to Love

George R. Bach and Peter Wyden

In one of their public-opinion surveys some years ago the pollsters of the Louis Harris organization asked couples across the country, "Most of the time, what is the biggest single source of friction between you and your spouse?" The two main fight issues mentioned by husbands and wives were money spending and child-raising. However, as a close third they listed a variety of remarkably trivial-sounding complaints. Husbands objected to too much petty criticism from the wives. Wives complained because their husbands were too sloppy around the house.

One husband remarked: "My wife is always after me over nothing: clothes, cleaning up the yard, this and that. I stopped listening years ago."

This typical fight evader had elected to tune out on a vast amount of strategic intelligence about his marriage. But so, strangely enough, do most intimates who daily engage in epic battles about such matters as burning the toast, misplacing a car key, setting the clock, airing the dog, forgetting an errand, arriving late, arriving early, and so on and on.

There are four psychologically important reasons for this amnesia:

1. In the heat of battle, intimates cannot think as clearly as they usually do; or they may react to an angry voice like an ostrich sticking his head in the sand.

2. Shame represses memory. In the calm of dawn's early light it is easy to recognize the disproportion of the emotional stress that the partners experienced over such *apparent* trivialities. The embarrassment during the Monday-morning quarterbacking goes so deep that partners frequently apologize for each other ("Oh, he was so mad he didn't know what he was saying"). They may even seek escape in after-the-fact evasion ("I didn't mean it. Don't mind me. I was so mad I don't even remember what I said").

3. A trivial issue may be a decoy. It may be part of a broader—but usually not consciously schemed—battle plan. It may be an excuse to get angry just to scare the partner; or to make a big impression on him; or test the limits of the bond snap-line (how much anger can he take?). More likely, the trivial issue camouflages a signal that calls for sensitive decod-

Reprinted with permission of the authors and the publisher from the *Ladies Home Journal*, September 1968, page 76.

ing. Forgetting to run an errand may actually mean to a partner, "You don't interest me anymore"; telling an off-color story at a party may be interpreted as, "You deliberately try to humiliate me." These messages are often exaggerated by injustice-collectors. They lie in wait, prepared to seize upon any trivial act as proof of deeper villainy. To them, being seven minutes late to an appointment proves habitual neglect; talking to another woman at a party is taken as evidence of secret philandering.

4. The substance of the trivial issue itself really is trivial and therefore isn't worth remembering! Often it is so absurdly trivial that it would be downright embarrasing to remember having been so upset over "nothing."

Why, then, do intimates experience so much anguish when they fight over "trivia"? Why does a pair of pants turn into a "federal case"? Why do *strangers* often fight violently (perhaps even lethally) over important matters, but almost never over trivial ones? There are three explanations:

1. Intimates care deeply about each other, while strangers rarely do. Intimates are forever scanning each other for information about the "temper" or the "good" or "bad" nature of each other. They hold hypotheses about where they stand with each other and, like scientists, they like to check them out. This is an intuitive technique and a constructive one as long as it is not overdone in the exaggerated, vindictive manner of the people we call spouse-watchers, who silently gather evidence against their partners, much like peeping Toms or FBI agents.

2. The intensity of fighting over trivia is often the result of the cumulative effect of quietly "gunny-sacking" one's grievances instead of arguing them out. Between intimates and non-intimates alike, a minor disappointment is an equally trivial drop in the bucket of life's frustrations. The crucial difference is that the bucket into which intimates drop a trivial grievance is often already full. Any new stress, however small, will increase the reservoir of tensions until something has to spill over. Trivial bickering, therefore, functions as a safety valve in enduring intimate relationships. If trivia is dismissed often enough as "not worth having a fight about" and all minor frustrations are suppressed in the interests of domestic peace and harmony, there is eventually bound to be a major explosion, perhaps over trivia, perhaps over something far from trivial. In either event, there is bound to be too much heat and not enough light.

3. Between intimates, as the discerning reader will have gathered, trivia often is anything but trivial. It is a kind of emotional shorthand that intimates develop in the course of thrashing out an enduring relationship. With important exceptions, a specific fight over trivia can be a clue to a more basic underlying conflict. Only the apparent fight issue is trivial; the emotions it arouses are quite likely to be serious.

What serious message is being conveyed in the following seemingly absurd domestic tiff?

It is Friday morning. Sam Rhodes, a certified public accountant, is about to leave for work. His wife, Hope, is making the beds.

HE: I hope I can get away for a game of golf with Charlie tomorrow.

SHE: Why not? Let me help you get ready for it. Is there anything you need?

HE: Say, do you mind taking my golf pants to the cleaners this morning and have them done on the "one-day special"? I have to have them back tonight if I'm going to play tomorrow.

SHE: Sure. It'll be fun for you tomorrow. You always enjoy playing with Charlie.

HE: Be sure to have the pants back. They're the only ones I'm comfortable in.

SHE (annoyed): Why do you always worry about those silly things? Please leave everything like that to me. You should keep your mind free for the office.

Now it's Friday evening. Sam comes home after work. Hope is fixing dinner.

HE (cheerful): Hello, honey! Oh boy, am I glad this week is over! I sure look forward to a good game of golf tomorrow. Did the pants come back from the cleaners?

SHE (shocked): No.

HE (more alarmed than angry): Should I run down to get them? Maybe you better phone the cleaners so they don't close before I get there!

SHE (devastated): Oh, I'm so sorry, darling! I completely forgot to take them! Wasn't that stupid of me? I had to go shopping anyway, and I could have done it so easily. I even went by the cleaners this morning. I just forgot. I really am so sorry!

HE (very angry): That's great. In other words, you don't keep your promises. That's really irresponsible! You just don't care about me anymore. You just ruined my weekend. Thanks loads!

SHE (shouting): How can you say that! You know how much I love you! You're cruel! You hurt me very much by what you just said. (She cries.) I don't know why I put up with a selfish, ungrateful man like you!

Good fighters don't fan the flames of such a conflagration, as these contenders did, thereby setting off an appalling explosion that ruined their weekend; nor would they find it rewarding to pour water on the fire by resignedly accepting the wife's forgetfulness as "sloppy housekeeping." After they learned to level with each other in our fight training sessions, Sam and Hope took up the issue of the not-so-trivial pants again. Here is how it went the second time around:

HE (stating position and making demand): I hope you don't mind if I spend tomorrow with Charlie playing golf. If I'm going to play tomorrow, I need these pants cleaned today.

SHE (checking out): You really want to play golf tomorrow?

HE (confirming): Yes, I think it's a reasonable request, after a week's hard work. I want the exercise, and Charlie is fun to play with.

SHE (stating her position and making counter-demand): Well, it's reasonable *if* you would also spend some of your spare weekend time with me and the kids.

HE (checking out her proposal): Can I play golf with Charlie tomorrow if we do something together as a family Sunday?

SHE (leveling about what she's really after): Yes, I want you to take all of us to the beach and out to dinner. I think that's a reasonable distribution of your leisure time, don't you?

HE (pinpointing areas of agreement and disagreement): Well, to be perfectly honest, I prefer staying home Sundays and watching the ball game on TV to milling around on the beach or in restaurants.

SHE (probing): Under what conditions *would* you spend some time in family activities? Or can't you stand to go out with us? I know I like for us to go out and you like to stay home. Who is going to have his way?

HE (proposing conditions of agreement): Let's alternate between my way, your way and then develop a third way: a new way of spending family time that might be fun for all of us.

SHE (checking him out): In other words, every third weekend I have my way, and you will really cooperate?

HE (committing himself to a position for time being): Yes, but this weekend I want to play golf with Charlie on Saturday, watch baseball on Sunday—

SHE (interrupts): And take us out to dinner Sunday night! That's great, and I will have your golf pants clean and ready for your game tomorrow.

When this couple made a systematic, good-willed attempt to get to the bottom of the pants issue, they found that the pants could hardly have mattered less. The real issue was a conflict between the wife's and the husband's differing notions over how to spend their leisure time. Once they recognized the true issue, they could settle their differences by open negotiation.

On other occasions, the bone of contention may be less obvious. Suppose the husband tells his wife, "Why in hell can't you match the socks in my drawer?" This explosion may hide the dark husbandly suspicion that she is applying the strategy of deliberate "disorder" and is telling him, "You don't love me enough" or "You like to torture me" or even "I think you like me to depend on you just so you can let me down." She may indeed be using "disorder" to signal him, "I'm tired of you being a helpless little boy" or "I don't respect you for expecting me to do this; you should be beyond this sort of thing." More likely, the fight is really trivial. She is only signaling him, "I'm sick and tired of being your servant."

The only way to find out whether the socks issue is trivial or not is to ask for a formal fight engagement. The husband can then flush out the underlying trouble: "What is it, darling? Are you just trying to keep me irritated?" If the answer is that the wife has a maid complex, a solution can be sensibly negotiated. Perhaps she should have some paid help for a few hours a week. The husband should realize that this solution only reduces the source of the wife's irritation. It won't eliminate it. Now it is up to him to show his wife in new ways that she rates as a person with him, not just as a maid; that being a maid in the socks department doesn't make her a maid anywhere else.

Suppose the sock is on the other foot. Suppose the husband litters the house with socks, cigar stubs, newspapers and tools, and is then upset if the house is in disarray and tells his wife, "You're a lousy housekeeper!" Then it's up to the wife to do the decoding. Does it mean he feels she doesn't love him enough?

Chances are that the issue is not as serious: the husband is probably only signaling that coming home at night is no fun for him; that he had to take orders at the office all day and now wants to have somebody to boss around. Perhaps she should let him have this pleasure up to a reasonable point. At any rate, she shouldn't—as some frustrated housewives do—leave the vacuum cleaner and ironing board well displayed in the evening by way of demonstrating silently to him, "See, I'm doing my best!"

Actually, in investigating fights that break out when husbands come home from work at night, we found that many men get plenty of aggression release through conflicts on their jobs, while housewives only have the kids to yell at and usually feel guilty about getting too angry at them too often. It is rewarding for a husband in these cases to make adequate listening and sympathizing allowances for wifely carping about what a "terrible day" she had at home while he was having an interesting time with the fellows at the office.

Among major fight issues that are more serious than they appear and are therefore often erroneously downgraded as trivial are what we call nesting fights. Man is a territorial animal, and the maintenance of cooperative nesting behavior is an intricate art. If a wife says, "I'm sick of apartments, I want a house in the suburbs," she is probably not talking about real estate but about her image of herself and her joint image with her husband. Furniture fights ("I don't want wall-to-wall carpeting; I don't want our house to look like a hotel lobby!") also provide admirable illustrations of why nesting is a danger zone.

Each partner usually has his own taste in furniture. He is likely to be cagey about disclosing it. If his taste turns out to be tasteless, it becomes embarrassingly visible to the partner and even outsiders. He may therefore maneuver the partner into becoming responsible for a particular purchase; or at least try to make the partner co-responsible for getting an item he himself wouldn't quite have guts enough to get. The trouble is that most people's nesting image tends to be fuzzy. Also, most people tend to be error-phobic; instead of learning from a mistake, they prefer to avoid the experience and find a scapegoat for any ensuing problems. Finally, for many people such items as tables, lamps and (especially) pictures are really extensions of themselves. So furniture can become an adult security blanket that is sometimes more important than clothes—a fact that is well known to furniture salesmen.

Not infrequently, a ridiculously tiny annoyance becomes a conditional stimulus and serves to ignite a disproportionately serious conflict. This happens when a trivial point reminds a partner of a nontrivial issue that is gnawing at him. In such a case the trivia becomes a cue to him that the partnership is out of balance.

This is what happens in the fights for "optimal distance." Intelligent fighting regulates the intensity of intimate involvement by occasionally creating relief from it. It makes intimacy controllable. It enables partners to locate the optimal distance from each other—the range where each is close enough not to feel "left out," yet free to engage in his own thoughts and autonomous activities, uncontaminated by the other's encroachments.

Almost nobody realizes that some fights have no issue except: "Keep your distance!" These seemingly mysterious encounters often occur after love-making.

Many couples tell us that the morning after their love-making was particularly and mutually satisfying, a fight will break out over "nothing." Perhaps the husband gets up and can't find any clean underwear. Or the coffee is too weak. Or the kids are too noisy. Or the wife wishes out loud that he would say a pleasant word at breakfast, for once. Anyway, he gets furious. The wife becomes enraged. He growls. She blows up and reminds him that she not only made a special effort to make love nicely the night before; she had also lately done *this* for him and *that* for him and why does he have to be so ungrateful and ill-tempered?

This is one of a never-ending series of fights that helps partners to find and to reset their optimal range—the psychological distance from each other that makes them most comfortable. Unconsciously they designed the fight to find out how close an intimate can come without making the partner feel engulfed; and how far he can move away without making the partner feel rejected.

Once we had learned to interpret these fights correctly, we advised our trainees not to be too vexed by them. We also cautioned clients not to be envious when somebody said of another couple, "They're very close, you know." Optimal distance or, if you prefer, optimal closeness, is the ideal goal—not *extreme* closeness. Of course, what's optimal for one partner may be uncomfortable for the other. But this difference can be adjusted, and we teach trainees how to measure—and how to make up for—such a natural disparity.

One amusing but useful at-home exercise begins with the partners conversing while they face each other about 15 feet apart. As they continue to talk, Partner A walks up to Partner B until they make physical contact. Then Partner A slowly backs away until he reaches the right distance to make conversation comfortable for A. At that point A stops and the partners measure the distance between each other with a tape measure. The experiment is repeated with Partner B doing the walking and backing up. Almost invariably, the partners' distance preferences differ. These measurements, although inexact, suggest each partner's tolerance for closeness. The partner who requires more distance to be comfortable is the one who will be more likely to start fights for optimal distance.

"Don't come too close to me" is the message he is signaling.

Every intimate sends such a signal from time to time because true intimacy is a state of entwinement that occasionally proves exhausting. We advise couples to take this fatigue seriously and to study each other's limits.

We tell trainees to develop their own distancing techniques. If they are having a lot of optimal distance fights they may find it advisable to take a vacation with another couple to dilute intimate contacts; or they might vacation separately.

Usually, however, optimal-distance problems subside after periodic solitary self-confinement at home. We call those pauses "refueling." Some people establish a private music corner, where they listen to Beethoven or to The Beatles while they allow their recuperative forces to take hold. Others meditate over a book or a stamp collection. Our trainees know that when a partner puts up a sign (either figuratively or sometimes literally) that says, "Do not disturb—refueling!" nobody needs to feel guilty or angry. The refueling partner is only taking a break to make intimacy work better in the long run. According to the outmoded romantic model of marriage, it may not be "nice" to pull up one's drawbridge and withdraw into Fortress Me. In realistic intimacy, it is necessary and desirable as long as it is not misused as a cover-up for habitual withdrawal.

Sometimes it is fruitless to look for serious motives behind a trivial fight, because such motives may not exist at all. In such cases it may be destructive to dig into a partner with investigative questions. Indeed, the word "why?" is the most overused word in marriage. Much of the time nobody could uncover the real, way-deep-down answer to why a partner did something; and if anybody did find out, it might not help. Lively participation in the give-and-take of the here-and-now pays off best.

How can anybody know when a trivial fight doesn't need to be decoded for underlying causes? Our first suggestion is that students learn to recognize, and to ignore, the useless volcanic eruptions of the type of temper outburst that we call The Vesuvius. This is just blowing off steam—a spontaneous irrelevant sounding-off of free-floating hostility. It is an adult tantrum that does not involve a partner directly, although it is advisable to have an intimate on hand as an audience. A Vesuvius unleashed against no one and on the open street would lead to curious glances and conceivably to arrest on charges of disturbing the peace.

A beautiful Vesuvius was delivered by one husband who came home from work and yelled at his wife, à propos of nothing in particular, "If that S.O.B. Jones does it just once more, I'll punch him in the nose, and that goes for your Uncle Max, too!" (Nobody had mentioned Uncle Max for weeks; he functioned here only as a free-floating kitchen sink handy for throwing into the Vesuvius.)

The Vesuvius is never directed at anybody who is at the scene of the explosion or nearby. It never involves issues that are pending between partners. It doesn't deal with anything that the partner who is witnessing the Vesuvius could be expected to do anything about. And it evaporates as quickly as a puff of smoke. The best way to make certain that a Vesuvius is not, in fact, a bugle call to a serious fight is to listen sympathetically to a partner's outburst and to wait a bit for what happens next. In an authentic Vesuvius, nothing does.

One of our trainee husbands came home from work and found a written Vesuvius posted to the door. It was from his wife. It simply said,

"I've had it." The husband became quite upset. He started searching for his wife, and found her almost immediately at her girl friend's house next door. The women were having some drinks in the kitchen. When the husband appeared, his wife brightened up and said, "Hey, look who's here!" Her Vesuvius had blown up—and over.

The worst way to handle the Vesuvius is to take it at face value and "hook in." Suppose a husband suddenly shouts, "I'm going to take this lousy lawnmower and throw it into the swimming pool!" the trained wife would never say, "Yeah? You and who else, you pipsqueak?" She would wait for the squall to subside.

Trivia can also be dismissed as trivial when it becomes the subject of a fun fight. This is a fight without real issues, as when two puppies tease each other aggressively but without a bone. A gesture or inflection may be the giveaway as to whether a fight is for real or for fun. The husband may say, for example, "You *mean* it?" If the wife says, "Sure I *mean* it" in a certain way, both are likely to recognize that there is no issue.

Most fun fights, however, rage over pseudo-issues. Are the 1967 cars better than the 1968 cars? Did Adlai Stevenson lose the Presidency in 1952 because he wasn't married? Did the husband (or wife) miss the point of last night's movie? These are fun fights because nobody has a great stake in the outcome.

Fun fights have sensible functions. They help prevent boredom. They can entertain an audience. They may serve to get others—especially children—involved in a family activity ("What do you think, Jimmy?"). They may also provide vicarious exercise and release for everybody's natural aggressive proclivities; typically, such an exercise surfaces as what we call "good-willed sadism" in a game of wits.

The bridge table is a fine place for such a game because almost everybody enjoys a hostility-releasing laugh at somebody who is losing. Incidentally, our trainee couples are always urged to play *against* each other. This allows for a healthy aggression outlet and minimizes the far more cutting hostilities of a partnership situation. ("What's gotten *into* you? How *often* have I told you not to . . .")

Lovers and spouses who don't fight over "nothing" actually miss a great deal. Especially they miss out on the erotically rejuvenating powers of the revived courtship pattern where attraction and repulsion alternate in the familiar cycle of realistic romance: attraction-repulsion, counter-attack-chasing, refusing-forgiving, calling back-resistance, surrender, etc. In general, the redundant sameness of rituals doesn't serve the cause of realistic leveling, but this is an exception. We found out the hard way that long-term intimates can ill afford to dismiss trivial fighting as something that is beneath them.

Exactly how does trivial fighting stimulate love? The cause-and-effect process operates because the aggressive chase and the assertive claim of the partner as "mine" are themselves a strong stimulus to the arousal and release of love emotions. Conversely, attraction wanes when couples no longer chase or claim each other because they take each other for granted. The security of belonging—and being spoken for—is enjoyed by stable couples at the price of a less intensive love-releasing experience. Contrary to folklore, both sexes like to chase and to be chased at various times, to seduce and be seduced, to claim and to be claimed. And the partner who is always available, always accommodating, robs himself and the pursuer of considerable pleasure—although there are times in an authentic intimate relationship when easy availability can become a comfortable insurance against sexual frustration.

It is fortunate that sometimes the very absence of major fight issues makes intimates "pick" fights. They may bicker to upset the marital applecart just to be sure there are no rotten apples in the load.

Trivial fighting, then, deserves encouragement as long as the issues are current, the style is spontaneous and neither partner attempts to be hurtful or depreciating.

CHAPTER 32

Communication in Marriage:
Batacas or Civility?

Ben N. Ard, Jr.

Within the context of marriage, probably one of the most serious problems is *inadequate communication* (Ard, 1976a). Despite the view that marriage is an institution that forces someone to listen to you, it seems that too few spouses really listen, these days. As a marriage counselor and psychologist, I hear many spouses complain about the lack of communication between the marital partners. Wives complain that their husbands do not talk to them anymore. Husbands say that about all they hear from their wives is what the kids did, or what the milkman or butcher said, or the bridge club gossip or other trivia.

It would seem that some of the important factors that are sorely needed within the context of marriage are such things as knowing *when* to talk; when to appreciate silence and respect privacy, detachment, or solitude; *how* to say what is really meant; and perhaps most important of all, how to *disagree agreeably*. Within the context of marriage, then, we need to work out mutually-agreed-upon "rules of the game" when it comes to settling differences. In some fights no holds are barred, anything goes, and there is apparently no time limit. (Even the Roller Derby has a time limit). I have known some married couples who have been fighting for twenty years or more. And they frequently continue to bring up the same old *past events* that occurred twenty years before. All this is despite the fact that there is one thing certain about the past: we can never change it.

Quarreling is one of the most devastating things that I see among married couples. Despite the popular view nowadays that quarreling is inevitable and therefore to be expected in marriage, I believe that quarreling is more detrimental than helpful to marriage.

What one *assumes* about marriage is very influential in what actually turns up in a person's own marriage. If one assumes that quarreling is to be expected, that the battle between the sexes is inevitable, that marital fighting is just part of the context of marriage, then perhaps one had

This chapter is a much expanded and revised version of an article entitled "Communication in Marriage" which previously appeared in *Rational Living*, Vol. 5, No. 2, Spring, 1971.

better learn to fight well or vigorously. In this case, the manly art of self-defense and how to dodge the pots and pans should be, perhaps, prerequisites to obtaining a marriage license.

If aggression is innate in all of us, if we are born evil or, according to a more recent theory, born with an id (an unconscious) which is constantly seething with aggressive impulses which must come out in some way, then it would seem to follow that we indeed need to learn to make marital fights "pay off" and learn how to deal with that most intimate of enemies, our spouse. It has been suggested by some authorities in the field (Bach & Wyden, 1976) that we do, in fact, need training in marital fighting; that spouses who do *not* fight actually miss a great deal.

I shall attempt to swim against this current and suggest that we need to help marital partners fight and quarrel *less*, to *reduce* hostility and aggression rather than encourage its expression (Ard, 1976b). It seems a worthier goal to *question* the *assumption* that aggression is "natural" in mankind (Fromm, 1973; Montagu, 1968), to find out the basic causes of expressed hostility and aggression (Saul, 1956), and to help marital partners *reduce* the *frequency* and the *heat* of their quarrels, rather than to assume without question that people are helpless in the face of their strong emotions.

The clients' *cognitive orientations* affect their emotional responses, as has been shown by Schacter and Singer (1962), as well as Ellis (1973). Therefore, as Straus (1974) has so clearly put it,

> "To the extent that this is the case, it would seem as though the most efficient means of avoiding physical aggression in disputes between husband and wife is to maintain some of those 'outmoded notions of etiquette,' thrown out by Bach and Wyden. These are, in my opinion, the rules of civil behavior which mankind has evolved through the ages to deal with the arousal level problem (Straus, 1974)."

It would seem that the ventilationist school of therapy is part of a larger movement which might be called the counter culture movement; and "the conscious or unconscious goal of much recent social science, and of leaders of therapeutic-aggression movement, is really to change society and to drastically restructure the family, . . . (Straus, 1974, p.24)." However, "aggressiveness is not the only alternative to passive acceptance of the status quo. One can be *assertive* without being *aggressive* (Straus, 1974)." (my italics)

Just as many followers of the ventilation school confuse all use of the intellect with "intellectualization" (it should be obvious that they are not one and the same); they also are confused about the differences between aggression and assertiveness. As Straus said:

> "... there is a vast difference between asserting that humans have the *biological capacity* for aggression and asserting that they have an *innate tendency* to *exercise* that capacity which can be thwarted only at the risk of an explosive outburst of aggression at some later time (Straus, 1974, p. 24)." (my italics)

The extensive research cited in Straus (1974) fails to support the supposed value of the aggression-release or "ventilationist" type approach.

"In fact, the weight of the evidence suggests that such an approach may be dangerous because, rather than *reducing* subsequent aggression (as argued by the ventilationists), expressing aggression against others probably tends to *increase* subsequent aggressive acts (Straus, 1974)." (my italics)

On the basis of Straus' (1974) review of previous research and the results of his own study, one can concur with him that

". . . much of the new therapy and advice literature, and especially much current encounter group activity, is almost exactly opposite to what the scientific evidence suggests is appropriate for reducing physical aggression and bringing about satisfying interpersonal relationships (Straus, 1974)."

One of the best ways to reduce the heat in many quarrels is to eliminate the philosophy of *blame* which is so prevalent in our culture (Ard, 1975). Too many married couples frequently assume without question that in any disagreement or quarrel someone is "right" and someone is "wrong," and further that the one who is "wrong" must be *blamed* and *punished* in some way. We need to learn to distinguish between *responsibility* (or *accountability*) and *blame*. They are not equal or synonymous. Each person in a marriage relationship is, of course, responsible for whatever he or she does, in some ultimate sense. But the person need not be blamed every time he makes a mistake.

Although it is apparently a very difficult task for people reared in our culture, people can *divest* themselves of this philosophy of *blame* and *guilt* (Kaufmann, 1973) and, instead, accept the idea that we are indeed responsible or accountable for our acts but not to take blame for them (Ellis, 1973). This latter philosophy makes it easier for married couples to learn from their mistakes, rather than just blaming themselves or the other for past mistakes, and continue to feel guilty indefinitely. Instead of always trying to establish who is to blame for past actions, we can adopt a different stance and learn to ask how we can act in the future to better achieve the goals we mutually desire. And the best way to achieve mutual goals is through an understanding of your partner's objectives—an understanding that is best achieved through a *sane dialogue* rather than through childish emotional outpourings ("vesuvius" or temper tantrums).

Currently a view exists that suggests (or at least implies) that in communication between marital partners one should say whatever is on the tip of one's tongue, to always be completely and totally "honest" or, in other words, to talk "spontaneously," right off the top of one's head, so to speak. This is thought to be "gut-level" communication (which is *assumed* to be better than any other kind). In the "leveling" or "vent-the-spleen" (or "instinct of aggression") approaches, there is a rejection of the intellect, reason, the rational, scientific approach. This anti-rationalism and its corollary emphasis on emotions rather than reason or intellect takes many forms. Fritz Perls, for example, the founder and leader of the gestalt approach, states that ". . . the intellect is the whore of intelligence. It's a drag on your life (Straus, 1974)."

Once again I am going to take a minority view and suggest that in many serious marital discussions *considerate, thoughtful,* and even *planned communication* can frequently be more helpful than merely saying whatever one "feels" like saying. When important matters are being discussed between married couples, I would go so far as to suggest, if you will pardon the temerity, that some *thought* be given to questions raised, to possible alternative positions, and *why* one "feels" the way one does. And all this *before* one talks to one's spouse. I have even suggested something akin to "position papers" being *written out before* an important discussion (for example, whether or not to get a divorce, have another child, indulge in a bit of wife-swapping, move one's mother-in-law into the family home, move to another state, etc.).

One can always benefit from questioning one's own basic premises. After giving considerable thought to one's position, and writing down the pros and cons and weighing them carefully, one may then be in a better position to decide troublesome issues. There is no reason that an individual cannot present one's position or case in *carefully thought-out sentences* rather than spewing out one's guts in a kicking, screaming, yelling scene. Some people assume that the latter approach is somehow more "honest," more "spontaneous" than the former, since it is "at the gut level." In this day and age "feelings" are frequently *assumed* to be sufficient *in themselves* to base one's actions upon. I would emphasize here that one needs *more* communication in marriage than that which is merely at the gut level; and that one should consider where the gut level reactions or "feelings" come from and what *causes* them, rather than just "spontaneously" reacting to them.

With the recent emphasis on "sensitivity" training groups or encounter groups (I might suggest that they be called *insensitivity* training groups), some people might begin to suspect that the hostile and aggressive behavior there is the "natural" way for human beings to interact, *without realizing* that *healthy* individuals can and do learn to communicate, in marriage and out, with *compassion, thoughtfulness, considerateness, gentleness,* and *tenderness,* without at the same time feeling unduly restricted or unnatural.

The changes that the ventilationists seem to want, as Malcolm (1975) has stated, appear

> "always to be in the direction of disinhibition, rejection of the values of the inclusive society, and the belief that the real human being, the really creative human being, is the one who dislikes competence, integrity, and self-control, and who admires the spontaneous expression of feeling regardless of the circumstances (Malcolm, 1975)."

The techniques fostered by the ventilationists, with the use of batacas (or encounter-bats made of foam rubber with which clients are urged to flail away at each other, *supposedly* not causing any harm), are designed, as Malcolm (1975) has observed, to promote childish behavior. "They facilitate regression in adults. They are intensely opposed to the conscious operation of the intellect (Malcolm, 1975)."

The intense anti-intellectualism of the counter culture movement and the emphasis on *feelings* in the "here and now" in the ventilationists' therapeutic approaches is potentially threatening to the mental health of this society of ours (Malcolm, 1975).

"The gratification is limited to the experience of the high feeling in the immediate present; and as soon as it is over the seeker-after-experience must begin his search again just as though nothing had happened to him at all. For this reason he will move constantly in a more radical direction until only the extremes of experience will be satisfying to him. To promote a system of belief that has at its center such an impoverished state of mind is to do injustice to the dignity of man (Malcolm, 1975)."

Communication between marital partners need not be, or in fact, should not be restricted to verbal communication. Knowing *when* to talk is frequently as important as knowing what to say and how to say it. In this respect some of the *nonverbal* cues exchanged between mates are often the best guides as to when to talk and when to respect and appreciate the other's legitimate desire for privacy and solitude. Of course, there are dangers in misleading or misunderstood nonverbal communication. If a wife notices a pained expression flicker across her husband's face during the table conversation at dinner, she might assume that he was expressing (nonverbally) a negative reaction to the topic or situation being discussed. And she might be right. However, there is a danger here, if she does not check out her assumption: her husband may merely be having gas pains. If so, she would be *over-psychologizing* and that can get people into trouble very quickly! The antidote to over-psychologizing is to *stop assuming* and *start asking*. Use the nonverbal cues as an indicator, but when in doubt, find out through the verbal channels what he or she is really experiencing.

In summary, I have presented what is quite possibly a minority viewpoint among marriage counselors and psychologists today. To reiterate: (1) quarreling is an extremely destructive form of behavior in the marital relationship, (2) a *reduction* in quarreling is *not* accomplished by urging the expression of "gut feelings" or talking "off the top of one's head" but on the contrary, aggression and quarreling are only *accentuated* by these methods, and (3) major differences between the marriage partners can be resolved better by each person being more fully aware of his own objectives and then communicating these objectives in a *rational* way, by knowing *when* to talk, when not to talk, *what* to say, and *how* to say it.

REFERENCES

Ard, Ben N., Jr. Communication theory in marriage counseling: a critique. [In this text, Chapter 20].

Ard, Ben N., Jr. Love and aggression: the perils of loving. [In this text, Chapter 25].

Ard, Ben N., Jr. Nothing's uglier than sin. In B. N. Ard, Jr. (Ed.) *Counseling and Psychotherapy: classics on theories and issues*. (2nd ed.) Palo Alto: Science & Behavior Books, 1975.

Bach, G. R., & Wyden, P. Marital fighting: a guide to love. [In this text, Chapter 31].

Ellis, A. *Humanistic psychotherapy: the rational-emotive approach*. New York: Julian Press, 1973.

Fromm, E. *The anatomy of human destructiveness*. New York: Holt, Rinehart & Winston, 1973.

Kaufmann, W. *Without guilt and justice*. New York: Wyden, 1973.

Lederer, W. J., & Jackson, D. D. *The mirage of marriage*. New York: W. W. Norton & Co., 1968.

Malcolm, A. *The tyranny of the group*. Towata, N. J.: Littlefield, Adams, 1975.

Maslow, A. H. Synergy in the society and in the individual. *Journal of Individual Psychology*, 1964, *20*, 153–164.

Maslow, A. H. Toward a humanistic biology. Unpublished manuscript, 1968.

Montagu, M. F. (Ed.) *Man and aggression*. New York: Oxford University Press, 1968.

Saul, L. J. *The hostile mind*. New York: Random House, 1956.

Schachter, S., & Singer, L. J. Cognitive, social and physiological determinants of emotional state. *Psychological Review*, 1962, *69*, 375–399.

Straus, M. A. Leveling, civility and violence in the family. *Journal of Marriage and the Family*, 1974, *36*, 13–29.

CHAPTER 33

Neurotic Interaction between Marital Partners

Albert Ellis

A recent book, *Neurotic Interaction in Marriage* (Eisenstein, 1956), includes several interesting papers by eminent psychoanalytic therapists; but I could not find anywhere in its pages a simple, cogent definition of neurosis. A neurotic, to my way of thinking, is simply an individual who is theoretically capable of acting in an intelligent, flexible, self-constructive manner but who is actually behaving in an illogical, inflexible, self-defeating way. Neurosis does not consist merely of unintelligent or highly disorganized behavior. Some individuals who act in this way, such as mentally deficient or brain-damaged persons, are truly incapable of acting differently and are therefore defective rather than neurotic. But when a man or woman is capable of remaining undisturbed and flexible when faced with difficult situations and that person does not fulfill his or her own potentialities—then, I say, neurosis is evidenced. Or, stated more concretely, any individual who needlessly suffers from intense and sustained anxiety, hostility, guilt, or depression is neurotic.

If this definition of neurosis is reasonably accurate, then we can say that a husband or wife neurotically interacts in marriage when either, or especially both, of them becomes needlessly disturbed or disorganized, or suffers unnecessary anxiety, hostility, guilt, or depression in his or her relations with the other partner. Stated differently: neurotic interaction in marriage arises when a theoretically capable husband and wife actually behave in an irrational, marriage-defeating way with each other.

IRRATIONAL IDEAS OR BELIEFS CAUSING NEUROSIS

Human neurosis, as I have contended in several recent papers on the subject of rational psychotherapy (Ellis, 1956; Ellis, 1957a, 1957b, 1958, in press), invariably results from the individual's having illogical or irrational ideas, beliefs, assumptions, or philosophies. For if he is theoretically capable of acting in a non–self-defeating way, and he actually defeats

Reprinted with the permission of the author and the publisher from the *Journal of Counseling Psychology*, 1958, 5, 24–28.

himself and brings unnecessary anxiety and hostility into his relationships with himself and others, he must have some biased, unrealistic, irrational beliefs or value systems which block his potentially sane thinking, emoting, and behaving.

The Dire Need for Love

The first main neuroticizing idea I found in a study of the unrealistic beliefs of fifty-nine clients (Ellis, 1957a) was the notion that it is a dire necessity for an adult human being to be approved or loved by almost everyone for almost everything he does; that it is most important what others think of one instead of gaining one's own self-respect; and that it is better to depend on others than on oneself. Applied to marriage, this means that the neurotic individual firmly believes that, no matter how he behaves, his mate, just because she is his mate, should love him; that if she doesn't respect him, life is a horror; and that her main role as a wife is to help, aid, succor him, rather than to be an individual in her own right.

When both marriage partners believe this nonsense—believe that they must be loved, respected, and catered to by the other—they are not only asking for what is rarely accorded an individual in this grimly realistic world, but are asking for unmitigated devotion from another individual who, precisely because he demands this kind of devotion himself, is the least likely candidate to give it. Under such circumstances, a major marital holocaust is certain to occur.

Perfectionism in Achievement

The second major irrational belief which most neurotics in our culture seem to hold is that a human being should or must be perfectly competent, adequate, talented, and intelligent in all possible respects and is utterly worthless if he is incompetent in any way. When married, these neurotics tend to feel that, as mates and particularly as sex partners, they should be utterly successful in achieving. The wife therefore berates herself because she is not a perfect housewife, mother, and bedmate; and the husband because he is not an unexcelled provider and sex athlete. Then, becoming depressed because of their supposed inadequacies, both husband and wife either compulsively strive for perfection or hopelessly give up the battle and actually make themselves into poor spouses and lovers. Either of these maladjusted choices of behavior usually soon incenses the other mate, and another marital holocaust ensues.

A Philosophy of Blame and Punishment

A third irrational assumption of the majority of neurotics is that one should severely blame oneself and others for mistakes and wrongdoings; and that punishing oneself or others for errors will help prevent future mistakes. Married neurotics, in consequence, particularly tend to get upset by their mates' errors and stupidities, spend considerable time and energy trying to reform their spouses, and vainly try to help these spouses by sharply pointing out to them the error of their ways.

Because, as we previously noted, emotionally disturbed human beings already have the tendency to blame themselves too much for their imperfections; because even healthy men and women tend to resist doing the so-called "right" thing when they are roundly berated for doing the so-called "wrong" one; and because criticized humans tend to focus compulsively on their wrongdoings rather than calmly face the problem of how they may change their behavior—for many reasons such as these, one partner's blaming another for this other's imperfections does immense harm in just about one hundred percent of the cases. Even the counselor—who quite obviously is on his client's side—rarely can get away with blaming an individual; and spouses—who were often wed in the first place mainly because the bride or groom felt that he or she would not be criticized by this spouse—can virtually never do anything but the gravest harm to their relationships by criticizing their mates. But this is precisely what most neurotics are driven, by their basically false philosophies of living, to do.

Catastrophizing Frustrations

A fourth idiotic assumption which underlies and causes emotional disturbance is the notion that it is terrible, horrible, and catastrophic when things are not the way one would like them to be; that others should make things easier for one, help with life's difficulties; and that one should not have to put off present pleasures for future gains. In their marriages, neurotics who consciously or unconsciously espouse this I-cannot-stand-frustration system of values invariably get into serious difficulties. For marriage, of course, is an exceptionally frustrating situation in many instances, involving considerable boredom, sacrifice, pleasure postponement, doing what one's mate wants to do, and so on.

Neurotic individuals, consequently, bitterly resent their marriages and their mates on numberless occasions; and, sooner or later, they clearly show this resentment. Then, neurotically feeling that they are not loved or are being frustrated in their desires, the spouses of these neurotics get in a few or a few hundred counterlicks themselves, and the battle is again on. The ultimate result can be a hellish marriage—or a divorce.

The Belief That Emotion Is Uncontrollable

A fifth and final irrational belief which we shall consider here—since we do not have enough time at present to examine all those revealed in the original study—is the mythical supposition that most human unhappiness is externally caused or forced on one by outside people and events and that one has virtually no control over one's emotions and cannot help feeling badly on many occasions. Actually, of course, virtually all human unhappiness is self-caused and results from silly assumptions and internalized sentences stemming from these assumptions, such as some of the beliefs which we have just been examining. But once a married individual is convinced that his own unhappiness is externally caused, he inevitably blames his mate and his mate's behavior for his own misery; and, once again, he is in a marital stew. For the mate, especially if she is herself neurotic, will contend (a) that she does not cause his unhappiness; and that (*b*) he, instead, causes hers. Such silly beliefs, again, are the stuff of which separations are made.

EFFECT UPON MARRIAGE OF NEUROTIC IRRATIONALISMS

It is my staunch contention, then, that a seriously neurotic individual possesses, almost by definition, one might say, a set of basic postulates which are distinctly unrealistic, biased, and illogical. Consequently, such an individual will find it almost impossible to be too happy in an utterly realistic, everyday, down-to-earth relationship such as modern marriage usually is. Moreover, being unhappy, this mate will inevitably jump on his or her partner—who, if reasonably well adjusted, will tend to become fed up with the relationship and to want to escape from it; and, if reasonably neurotic, will return the spouse's resentful sallies in kind, thus leading to neurotic interaction in marriage.

No matter, therefore, how irrational the beliefs of one spouse may be, it takes a double neurosis to make for true neurotic marital interaction. Suppose, for example, a husband believes that he must inordinately be loved by his wife, no matter how he behaves toward her; that he must be competent in all possible respects; that he should blame others, especially his wife, for errors and mistakes; that he must never be frustrated; and that all his unhappiness is caused by his wife's behavior and other outside events. If the spouse of this severely neurotic husband had virtually no similar illogical beliefs of her own, she would quickly see that her husband was seriously disturbed, would not take his hostility toward herself with any resentment, and would either accept him the way he was, or would calmly try to see that he got professional help, or would quietly conclude that she did not want to remain married to such a disturbed individual and would divorce him. She would not, however, neurotically react to her husband herself, thus causing a mighty conflagration where there need only be a nasty, but still limited, flame.

A METHOD OF TREATING NEUROTICISM IN MARRIAGE

If what has thus far been said in this paper is reasonably accurate, then the solution to the problem of treating neurotic interaction in marriage would appear to be fairly obvious. If neurotics have basically irrational assumptions or value systems, and if these assumptions lead them to inter-act self-defeatingly with their mates, then the marriage counselor's function is to tackle the problem not of the marriage, nor of the neurotic interaction that exists between the marital partners, but of the irrational ideas or beliefs that cause this neurosis *à deux*. And this, as I have insisted in a previous paper (Ellis, 1956), and as Harper (1953) has also previously shown, can only be done by some form of intensive psychotherapy.

My own marriage counseling is part and parcel of the technique of rational psychotherapy which I have been developing in recent years. It consists largely of showing each of the marital partners who is neurotically interacting (*a*) that he has some basic irrational assumptions; (*b*) precisely what these assumptions are; (*c*) how they originally arose; (*d*) how they are currently being sustained by continual unconscious self-indoctrination; and (*e*) how they can be replaced with much more rational, less self-defeating philosophies. More concretely, each neurotic spouse is shown that his disturbed behavior can arise only from underlying unrealistic beliefs; that these beliefs may have originally been learned from early familial and other environmental influences but that they are now being maintained by internal verbalizations; that his marriage partner, in consequence, is never the real cause of his problems; that he himself is actually now causing and perpetuating these problems; and that only by learning carefully to observe, to question, to think about, and to reformulate his basic assumptions can he hope to understand his mate and himself, and to stop being unilaterally and interactionally neurotic.

A Case Example
Let me cite an illustrative case. A husband and wife who had been married for seven years recently came for marriage counseling because the wife was terribly disturbed about the husband's alleged affairs with other women, and the husband was "fed up" with his wife's complaints and general unhappiness, and thought it was useless going on. It was quickly evident that the wife was an extremely neurotic individual who believed that she had to be inordinately loved and protected; who hated herself thoroughly for her incompetency; who severely blamed everyone who did not love her unstintingly, especially her husband; and who felt that all her unhappiness was caused by her husband's lack of affection. The husband, at the same time, was a moderately disturbed individual who believed that his wife should be blamed for her mistakes, particularly the mistake of thinking he was having affairs with other women, when he was not; and also believed that it was unfair for his wife to criticize and sexually frustrate him when he was doing the best he could, under difficult circumstances, to help her.

In this case the somewhat unorthodox procedure of seeing both husband and wife together at all counseling sessions was employed—largely because I found this method to be time-saving, in that the main difficulties between the mates are quickly arrived at, and because I feel that the witnessing of one mate's emotional re-education by the other spouse may serve as a model and incentive for the second spouse's philosophic reformulations. The husband-wife-therapist group, in this sense, becomes something of a small-scale attempt at group therapy.

In any event, because the husband in this case was less seriously disturbed than the wife, his illogical assumptions were first brought to his attention and worked upon. He was shown that, in general, blame is an irrational feeling because it does neither the blamer nor his victim any good; and that, in particular, although many of his complaints about his wife's unrealistic jealousy and other disturbances might well have been justified, his criticizing her for this kind of behavior could only serve to make her worse rather than better—thus bringing more of the same kind of behavior down on his head. He was also shown that his assumption that his wife should not excoriate or sexually frustrate him was erroneous: why should disturbed individuals not act in precisely this kind of manner? He was led to see that even though his wife's actions were mistaken, two wrongs do not make a right—and his reaction to her behavior was equally mistaken, in that instead of getting the results he wanted, it was only helping make things worse. If he really wanted to help his wife—as he kept saying that he did—then he should, for the nonce, expect her to act badly, stop inciting himself to fury when she did so, and spend at least several weeks returning her anger and discontent with kindness and acceptance—thereby giving her leeway to tackle her own disturbances.

The husband, albeit with some backsliding at times, soon began to respond to this realistic approach to his wife's problems; and, in the meantime, her irrational assumptions were tackled by the therapist. She was shown how and why she originally acquired her dire need to be inordinately loved and protected—mainly because her mother had not given her the love she required as a child—and how necessarily self-defeating it was for her, as an adult, to continue to reinfect herself with this nonsensical belief. Her general philosophy of blaming herself and others was ruthlessly revealed to her and forthrightly attacked. She, like her husband, was shown just how such a philosophy is bound to alienate others, rather than win their approval or get them to do things in a different and presumably better manner. Finally, her notion that her unhappiness was caused by her husband's lack of affection was particularly brought to conscious awareness and exposed to the merciless light of rationality. She was shown over and over again how her unhappiness could only come from within, from her own attitudes toward external events such as her husband's lack of love, and that it could only be expunged by her facing her own integral part in creating it.

As the husband in this case started accepting his wife's neurosis more philosophically, she herself was more easily able to see, just because he was not goading and blaming her, that she was the creator of her own jealousies, self-hatred, and childish dependency. She began to observe in detail the sentences she kept telling herself to make herself unhappy. On one occasion, when the counselor was explaining to the husband how he kept goading his wife to admit she was wrong, ostensibly to help her think straight but actually to show how superior to her he was, she interrupted to say: "Yes, and I can see that I do exactly the same thing, too. I go out of my way to find things wrong with him, or to accuse him of going with other women, because I really feel that I'm so stupid and worthless, and I want to drag him down even below me." This, in the light of her previous defensiveness about her jealousies, was real progress. After a total of twenty-three joint sessions of counseling, the fate of the marriage of this couple was no longer in doubt, and they decided to go ahead with childbearing and rearing, which they had previously avoided because of their mutual uncertainties. They also solved several other major problems which were not necessarily related to their marriage but which had previously proved serious obstacles to happy, unanxious living.

In conclusion: neurotic interaction in marriage results when an emotionally disturbed husband and wife think and act illogically, not only in their own right but with each other. If their individual and mutual neuroses are forthrightly attacked by uncovering, challenging, and working through, the fundamental irrational beliefs and assumptions which underlie their neurotic interaction can be replaced by self- and mutual understanding that is a prime prerequisite to lasting marital love.

BIBLIOGRAPHY

Eisenstein, V. W. (Ed.). *Neurotic interaction in marriage.* New York: Basic Books, 1956.

Ellis, A. A critical evaluation of marriage counseling. *Marriage and family living*, 1956, *18*, 65–71.

Ellis, A. Rational psychotherapy. *Journal of General Psychology*, 1958, *59*, 35–49.

Ellis, A. Outcome of employing three techniques of psychotherapy. *Journal of Clinical Psychology*, 1957, *13*, 344–350. (a)

Ellis, A. Rational psychotherapy and individual psychology. *Journal of Individual Psychology*, 1957, *13*, 38–44. (b)

Ellis, A. Hypnotherapy with borderline schizophrenics. *Journal of General Psychology*, in press.

Harper, R. A. Should marriage counseling become a full-fledged speciality? *Marriage and Family Living*, 1953, *15*, 338–340.

CHAPTER 34

Husband-Wife Conferences
in the Home

Aaron L. Rutledge

In his office in Iran everything usually went well for the thirty-year-old oil company employee, but at home the end of the day brought restlessness, sleepless nights, and mental torture. He felt that he deserved to die for he knew not what. His social life (that which was available) was uninteresting. His head ached incessantly. His back, his chest—any part of his anatomy was subject to aches and pains. Sometimes he desired his twenty-nine-year-old wife sexually, but often all desire left him for weeks, and even months.

The company doctor had found it impossible to help, except through sedation at periods of most acute stress. He recommended requesting an early furlough to the States, and suggested consultation with a psychiatrist in Boston.

The wife wondered if her failure to conceive was a factor in his disturbance. She believed that her sterility was of emotional origin, and also her failure to menstruate for several months, in spite of medical care.

There had been fun again, after two years of boredom, as they rediscovered the thrills of relaxation and sexual satisfaction on the freighter voyage home. But then, back in his parental home, there was renewed bickering and tension. The familiar chasm separated them again, and his symptoms reappeared. He remembered, resented, but then agreed to consult a psychiatrist as suggested by the company physician.

After listening for an hour, the psychiatrist said: "Your marriage is the cause of your trouble. If a man has love and acceptance waiting at the end of the day, returning home will be a refreshing experience. The fact that you tense up there means your home life is not adequate. You won't be well until you do something about it."

In the next quarrel he flared: "Well, that does it! Divorce is the answer! The marriage is no good, and I'll never be well so long as we live together!" The wife was shocked at this first hint that he wished to end the marriage. Later she reasoned: "I've tried everything I know to please you, even to forcing myself into different personality types to fit your

Reprinted with permission of the author and the publisher from *Marriage and Family Living*, 1962, *24*, 151–154.

ever-changing moods. Sure, I'm not pleasant to live with a great deal of the time now because I've crawled into a shell to keep from being rejected again. I can't take it like this either. If the psychiatrist feels our marriage is the cause of all this, let's go see the 'marriage doctor'." He laughed at the idea, but a few days later asked if she wanted to buy the double bed they had discussed to replace the company-owned twin beds.

They found the marriage counselor nearest her parental home, where the remainder of the vacation was to be spent. There was time to see each of them separately four times, and they were seen together in a final session. In these interviews saving the relationship had become their major goal. She had a better picture of her "shell," and he realized that there would be only unhappiness with any woman until he understood himself better.

He saw himself as an overprotected boy who had run away to early independence and self-sufficiency. A chain of events had led to exemption from armed service. His first major physical symptoms and anxiety attacks had grown out of unconscious assumption of responsibility, with its attendant guilt, for the death of a brother in action. Soon a promotion had doubled job responsibility, reactivating repressed feelings of inadequacy and dependent needs, but all ties with home had been cut and there was no one upon whom to lean. At this point the attractive army nurse showed up and they were married. She failed to relieve his anxiety; in fact, the added responsibility increased it. Resentment, escape from responsibility, and other needs found expression in chronic illness and unusual demands upon her for care. Her cooking, housekeeping, and talking were upsetting to him, and openly he compared her to his mother, who had warned him against marrying a person of a different religion.

Everything the wife knew as a nurse failed; she could not be mother and wife when he didn't know which he wanted. She offered all she had as a woman, to be rejected more often than accepted, and finally withdrew into a protective shell. The conferences helped tear away the shell, revealing the hurt little girl loved by no one, who had worked her way through nurses' training only to be imposed upon by selfish relatives. She had enlisted in the Army for unconscious as well as conscious reasons. When they met, his needs clicked with her need to be needed, and that was sufficient for a while. But she needed to be loved and cared for, too, and he could only receive and demand more; not so much a husband as a son. After a noble trial she had run away again; this time into herself.

With encouragement these new insights were shared, they began labeling residual childhood needs, recognizing personality strengths in themselves, and started responding to the wholesome needs of each other.

The short stay in the United States necessitated putting this couple on their own much too soon in terms of conventional counseling. Obviously, they would have profited by long-term therapy, but the only way to continue the process was by means of planned husband-wife conferences in the home with the follow-up assistance of the company doctor. In the final conference, together, they were given home conference instructions, the gist of which follows.

THE HOME CONFERENCE PLAN

Your relationship "got this way" through the action and reaction of two personalities, and together you can undo the damage and grow a meaningful relationship.

Ordinarily each of you would be seen separately for a longer time, working toward a progressive understanding of (1) yourself, (2) your mate, and (3) the marriage relationship; how each reacts, feels, behaves, and why. With hurt feelings and bitterness drained off and the total situation seen in better perspective, you would be expected to carry on most of the work on your own.

The suggestions being made to you now would be made even if we could work together for several months. You are an exception only in that you are to be on your own earlier than is usual.

Since a major barrier in your marriage is lack of understanding, and since understanding is dependent upon communication, the biggest single task is learning to express true feelings and attitudes toward each other and toward the relationship.

You have concluded that a satisfying marriage relationship must be equalitarian, with neither person being the boss nor the bossed. Your relationship will grow as the individuality of each is made secure and meaningful. The goal is neither to find fault nor to place blame, but to evaluate and understand. When disturbed feelings are buried inside, they grow and abcess; and yet when they burst out, there is hurt and confusion. The goal is to prevent both, by finding another way of handling feelings.

The following suggestions may seem rigid and arbitrary; but unless temporarily you go "by the book", you may find yourselves dropping out along the way, cutting it short, or developing the process in a one-sided manner.

Arrange two conference periods a week for several weeks. Set an hour—say 8:00 p.m., Tuesdays and Fridays—and permit only the gravest emergency to interfere, and even then use the next evening. In each conference—

1. Mrs. B. talks 20 minutes;
2. Mr. B. talks 20 minutes;
3. she has 10 minutes for questions to clarify feelings;
4. he has 10 minutes for questions to clarify feelings;
5. Conference ends on the hour.

At the next conference, he talks first, etc., alternating. Agree that if tempers flare, you will wait a few minutes, then begin again. If you cannot cool off, postpone the discussion until the next evening. Remember, you are giving each the right to express feelings, whatever they are, in an effort to understand. If either has harsh or confused feelings inside, they will do both of you less harm if brought into the open, with agreement not to nurse grudges.

Agree in advance not to raise voices, but feel both the right and the obligation to express your feelings frankly. When one is talking, the other will listen just as attentively as I have listened to each of you, and you will not interrupt the speaker. Talk about all the feelings you have discussed with me, but never quote me to each other or in any way try to pit me against the other. I am interested equally in you.

Devote the first two periods to "bad" feelings out of the past and present. During the second and subsequent weeks give one period to "bad" feelings and the next to "what's right with us," things you have enjoyed, liked about each other, and had fun doing together. Part of this latter period might well be given to planning the family life to allow for a balance of work, social and recreational interests, relaxation, and worship, although you go to separate churches.

Don't be in a hurry to change the content or frequency of these periods, but eventually you may have only one conference a week, and will give it to both "good" and "bad" feelings. You may want to retain this "family hour" long after you cease to need it for straightening out confused feelings. Every family could use at least an hour a week on serious sharing and planning. When children come along they can be incorporated into the discussions, giving them an early taste of real democratic living.

Some of the things to be discussed positively at these sessions would be your place in the community, sex, your religious beliefs and your individual places in your church, some outstanding issues of your way of life, etc. The primary goal is not to change the other, but to learn to communicate openly and freely all your feelings, with a view to understanding more fully each other, yourself, and your relationship. This can become the means of making marriage so meaningful that minor adjustments will begin to fall into place.

Between these conferences you may have hurt feelings. If one loses control, the other will listen until the tempest is over, and then calmly suggest: "We have a time to discuss such matters, so let's postpone this." The other well may respond: "Yes, now we will get busy at other things in order to get our minds off it until then."

If things pile up unbearably for either of you, back off into a corner and write out your thoughts just as if you were talking to me; seal the envelope, lay it aside for mailing to me, and walk off from it just as you walk out of my office. Later, in your conference, you can discuss it quietly and objectively with each other.

I am counting on your doing this in a wholehearted manner for the sake of each of you and your marriage. Here is a copy of these suggestions so that each of you may become thoroughly acquainted with the plan before you undertake it.

A follow up over several years has demonstrated the effectiveness of the plan for this couple, both in terms of a meaningful marriage and the clearing up of psychosomatic symptoms in both.

MODIFICATIONS

The aid to marriage counseling illustrated in this case has been used regularly with a variety of clients over the past twelve years, usually during the final phases of counseling. The possible modifications of the plan are limited only by the needs of the individuals and the insight and ingenuity of the counselor.

1. Some couples may need to attempt these discussions in the counselor's presence until they get accustomed to handling hurts together, although trying the procedure on their own with instructions is preferable for many from the beginning.

2. The amount and degree of structuring may vary, and the length of time before initial rigid requirements can be relaxed, will be determined by their progress in communication. It may be necessary to continue the controls to guarantee somewhat equal production and emotional release;

otherwise the conferences can deteriorate to the level of previously unsuccessful communication.

3. Discussion can be limited to specific problem areas. On the other hand, some couples might need to begin discussing subjects about which there is little stress, establishing a pattern of participation before moving into ego-involved areas. They might be temporarily limited to the past, or to contemporary events, until the counselor feels that the relationship can survive facing the real conflict areas.

4. Bibliotherapy may prove effective, either as a beginning place, or as a means of stimulating understanding of human motivation in general. Books or pamphlets with pertinent information may be used to advantage on prescription of the counselor.

5. Although the method has been illustrated in the context of a democratic marriage, it is equally applicable in other systems so long as respect for an individual is a vital value.

6. Many couples with little or no counseling assistance can adapt this to their own needs as a "do it yourself" way of facilitating healthy marital interaction.

LIMITATIONS AND PRECAUTIONS

1. At least an average level of maturity seems essential to this method, or certainly a fairly equal emotional balance, and some desire on the part of both to make the relationship work. There must be mutual acceptance of the method.

2. There could be destructive consequences with psychopathic personalities, or those subject to strong paranoid trends, deep depressions, or uncontrolled impulses or compulsions.

3. Enough time must be spent in individual therapy to drain off intensive hostilities if the process is not to degenerate into mere quarreling or even fisticuffs. Each must be helped to avoid using confidences revealed here as psychological weapons later in their experiences together.

4. The rigid structuring makes it seem artificial and unreal for a while.

5. Often one spouse refuses to verbalize, although willing to listen to the other. This can be a passive expression of hostility, saying, "See, it's you who has the bad feelings; it's your problem."

6. There is some risk of uncovering feelings difficult to control, or too severe for the other to accept, by shocking confessions or release of pent-up contempt.

7. Some tend to dwell too persistently upon old hurts, making the past an escape from or justification for the present.

8. Others tend to stop the process much too soon—"nothing more to discuss"—which leads to further piling up and renewed resistances and misunderstanding.

9. This procedure may strip bare a personality previously held together by various defense mechanisms, leading to serious emotional disturbance.

All of this is to say that the counselor uses the method by prescription based upon his diagnostic understanding of each personality and of the marriage relationship.

VALUES OF THE METHOD

1. Planned home conferences afford a further opportunity to ventilate pent-up feelings, can reduce the frequency of counseling interviews, and well may decrease the number of professional conferences necessary.

2. Re-living disturbing experiences a second time, after they have been excavated in counseling sessions, provides further clarification, assimilation, acceptance, and re-integration. Facing oneself where he lives—in the area and with the person where stress is felt—can facilitate integration and personal growth, and speed the healing of the relationship illness.

3. It can bring about growth in understanding of how the mate feels, and lead to increasing respect for him as a person. Understanding has a way of awakening dormant love in a previously embittered mate, and being understood is the most therapeutic of experiences.

4. It prevents the accumulation of feelings of anger, hate, fear, loathing, shame, resentment, and guilt which poison a relationship. It calls for facing up to hurtful experiences while fresh, rather than evasion or repression, while at the same time minimizing the need for destructive types of quarreling.

5. When only one of a couple is undergoing psychotherapy, the growth process may be one-sided, which can broaden the gap between the mates and lead to divorce. In such a case these husband-wife conferences in the home make the individual counseling process a mutually shared effort toward self-determination of their marriage relationship.

6. Improved communication, along with the development of honesty, frankness, and spontaneity in the conferences, spreads to daily life, affording a stimulating variety of responses to each other, and creating an environment more in keeping with reality. Long-term repression as a means of controlling dangerous feelings toward the mate often results in burying or overcontrolling *all* feelings, including love and affection. Only as one is permitted to express in words his "bad" feelings and have them accepted can he learn to "let go," giving wholesome feelings of affection, love, and tenderness a chance to develop and find expression.

7. A couple can be led to work over any or all major areas of their life together, resolving problems not acute enough to take to the counselor, and developing a more meaningful family image to guide them.

8. As new conflict areas emerge in daily life, and the couple find themselves confused in their own attempts at solution, private conferences with the counselor are made more specific and meaningful if they have been working according to this plan.

9. This puts the couple in a position of accepting responsibility for the major part of the adjustment process much earlier than is possible

otherwise, avoiding excessive dependence upon the counselor. Adjustment may be desirable as a temporary goal, but initiative and creativity, which must emerge from mutual efforts, are necessary to a growing meaningfulness in marriage.

10. Such conferences may provide the basis and motivation for continued regular discussions long after the presenting problem is resolved. This guarantees that subsequent hurtful experiences and feelings will be handled, rather than allowed to accumulate. Without regular conferences as part of the family plan, one might feel that an "incident" was not serious enough to call a special session. If regular sessions are being held, it is easy to handle the difficult occasion together. Often this is the means of reactivating the significance of previous individual therapy and marriage counseling sessions long after they have ceased, affording the insight necessary to resolving the new crisis. A regular family conference can provide the setting for week-by-week examination of family interests, whether legal, economic, spiritual, social, recreational, or otherwise. This becomes the working center into which each of the children can be drawn as he learns to participate in discussions, decisions, and the sharing of family—and hence life—responsibilities.

CHAPTER 35

Feedback Techniques in Marriage Counseling

John Williams

The husband stated that although he really enjoyed sex with his wife, he felt he could enjoy it more if she would just relax, would be willing to experiment with some new ways to achieve satisfaction, and could possibly challenge some of her overly strict ideas about sex with which her frigid mother had indoctrinated her during her childhood.

"All you ever think about is sex," Mary Rogers said through clenched teeth, her voice dripping with sarcasm. "Sex and fun and that damn bedroom. You just think I'm no good in sex, and you hate me. You've always blamed the failure of everything in this marriage on me. And especially about sex. It's all my fault. Oh, why did we ever...," she started crying and hid her face in her hands.

Jack Rogers tried to pat her hand, saying, "That's not what I'm trying to tell you, Dear. You don't understand."

His wife jerked her hand away and shouted at him, "Oh, just shut up. There you go again, blaming me and saying it's all my fault and that I never listen to you." She turned away from him, sitting back in the corner of the big easy chair in my office, dabbing at her eyes with a wadded piece of tissue and staring out the window, sniffing and sniveling and feeling very sorry for herself.

I thought to myself how many hundreds of couples I have heard go through this typical way of trying to communicate with each other. The Rogers, like the others, certainly had a lot to learn before they were going to be able to talk to each other, and to other people, in a sane, rational way.

I frequently use (as have many other therapists) a special form of communication practice with a couple like this which I call the "feedback" technique, or "stop-repeat-go" talking. I have found that, although the process is fairly laborious, when I can get couples to practice using it in my office and also to use it as homework during the week, some fairly dramatic results can be obtained quickly.

Ellis (1962; Ellis & Harper 1961a, 1961b) has frequently stated how important communication is, not only in the sexual sphere of a relationship but in a person's total adjustment to life. Most of the people I see

really do not know how to say clearly what they are thinking and feeling—in addition to their having numerous neurotic motivations that cause
them to block and be afraid of saying the wrong thing, to talk too much
from anxiety, to say things to purposely cloud issues and confuse the
other person, or to express hostility which generally breaks down any
attempt at communication. Furthermore, most people are really very poor
listeners. They "hear" with preconceived prejudices; they generally twist
and misinterpret much that is said to them and often only hear what they
want to. It seems to me, therefore, that an essential part of therapy—
particularly when one is working with two people as in a marriage, a
parent-child relationship, or some form of partnership—is to aid individuals to say clearly what they mean and to learn to listen openly in order to
hear accurately what the other person is attempting to say.

I ask couples seen in joint therapy sessions, to use the "feedback"
technique repeatedly to facilitate understanding each other and to get
their messages across.

"We're going to try an experiment," I told the Rogers. "Obviously,
the two of you aren't getting anywhere the way you're going at talking,
and I have found a method that really proves helpful to people. I imagine
that most of the talking at home between the two of you is just like you
were doing here a minute ago, right?"

Both people nodded vigorously. "Oh, yes," Mary said. "Why even last
night . . ." her eyes started to fill with tears, and I could tell we were in
for another angry tirade.

"Hold it," I said firmly. "Continuing to blame each other for faults
and shortcomings is, as we've discussed before, the opposite of rationally
accepting the things other people say and do, even when what they do is
admittedly poor. We don't have to *like* what people do, but we do have to
accept what they do and say because that's reality. Then we can go ahead
and try to change some of the ways that other people act, to see if we can
get the world to be more the way we'd like it. But the way the two of you
are trying to change each other doesn't seem to me to be bringing you the
kinds of results that you both have repeatedly told me you want. So let's
try something new, OK?"

I went on then to outline the ground rules for the "feedback" technique. First, one spouse could say anything he or she wanted—bring up a
problem, "bitch" about something, etc. I instructed them to try to keep it
fairly brief; during the time one person was talking the other was not
allowed to interrupt or say anything. When the first person had had his
say, then the other person was to say back to him the gist of what had
been communicated. He did not have to use exactly the same words or
terms, but what was important was to try to say back the *meaning* of
what the first person had said. The original speaker was then either to
agree (yes, that was what he had been trying to say) or disagree (no, that
was not quite what he really had meant, or even that was *definitely* not
the correct interpretation). If the second person did not "feed back" what
had been said to the satisfaction of the first person, then the first party
was instructed to repeat his message. The second person was told that he

or she was to refrain from making faces or emoting in any negative way (a deep sigh at the right time can get across beautifully the message that you think someone is a real jackass); the listener was to try to listen and interpret as carefully as he could.

When the first person had repeated his message, the second person was to try again to feed back what had been said. The first person was also instructed to refrain from any negative criticism of what the second person was saying (since a well-timed "Dummy!" can again frustrate opening channels of communication).

This "stop-repeat-go" technique was to continue until the first person agreed that the feedback did, indeed, say what he had been trying to say. Only when the first person was relatively satisfied was the second person permitted to answer the statement of the first person.

It has been my experience that when the first person is given uninterrupted freedom to make a statement, he seems to be more *willing* to try to really say what he means and is more likely to be *able* to do so because of a lessening of frustration and anxiety (he knows he is not going to be interrupted). Also, the establishment of ground rules and getting a commitment from the two people that they will try to follow those rules "forces" the second party to focus on *what* is being said and not on his *reaction* to it. As a result this technique tends to short-circuit the usual prejudicial comeback that many people think up and have ready to fire when the first person stops to draw a breath. Patients later tell me in check-up sessions that they feel a responsibility to get accurately the message of the first person, and that occasionally an aspect of their neurosis is working, in that they know that I, too, am listening carefully for them to "say back."

That is the real message I am trying to get him to learn. Even if the person goes on and tells himself the typical, irrational sentences that he uses to disturb himself and create the negative sustained emotions and philosophies that constitute his neurosis (Ard, 1966; Harper, 1959; Ellis, 1961), I feel that he is now doing the correct thing (trying to listen carefully) though possibly for the wrong reason.

Since I too believe that it can be helpful at times to use the person's neurosis against itself (Seabury, 1968), I do not mind too much if he listens carefully to his wife partly because he is afraid of my disapproval. At least he is listening. I would hope that later, with practice and sustained effort, I could get him to do the correct thing for the appropriate reason (that is, to listen because he really wants to communicate with his wife).

Now it's the second person's turn to talk. Usually what happens is that he answers back, hostilely, to the original "charges," giving facts and history to prove or disprove certain points. (I instruct the second person, too, to try to keep it fairly brief so that we can apply the feedback technique. If a statement is too long, we easily forget what was said, and confusion once again reigns.) When the second person has had his short say, I instruct the first person to feed back what was said. Again, he need not use the same terms the other person has used, but only try to explain the gist of what was said. If the second person agrees right off, "Yes, that's pretty much what I meant," then the first person has his turn to speak again.

In practice, this rarely happens (unless the second person, in hostilely trying to get the first person to upset himself, says, "You are a rat"; here the first person may be able to ferret out the exact meaning of what the second person said, and *is* able to accurately feed back the meaning: "You really think I *am* a rat!"). Most of the time there will be a slow interchange between people: the second person's having his say over and over again, the first person's attempting to feed back what he had said, and the second person's repeating it over and over. But usually, with persistence, the second party finally says, "Yes, that's what I'm trying to tell you."

By now, a half hour may have elapsed, and everyone present (including the therapist) can feel the strain of belaboring each point. There is certainly some feeling of frustration on the part of the people involved, but I usually find a marked reduction in anger and hostility, a sort of "caught-up-in-the-process" feeling; and because I am constantly interrupting and reminding them of the rules, they agree to follow. Doing this often in a humorous fashion, I find that by this point in the session there may be a few smiles or even laughs as the couple begins to communicate with each other—maybe for the first time in years.

In a single therapy session, we may not cover more than one or two points. But this, as I explain to them, is not significant. As they learn to communicate more accurately, they can speed up the process. What we are now interested in is *quality* of communication, not quantity. Then I often assign them homework—to continue where we left off in the office; to keep talking, first one, followed by feedback, then the other, followed by feedback, on and on. (Homework assignments are an integral part of the rational-emotive psychotherapeutic technique; see Ard, 1966, Ellis, 1962, Harper, 1959.)

Granted, there are times when patients "need" to ventilate. But I have found that usually when they are allowed to talk on and on, they simply repeat themselves, continue to reindoctrinate themselves with nonsensical sentences, and feel more and more sorry for themselves, concretizing their poor self concepts. If I feel that a patient needs to talk at length, I do not encourage joint sessions.

Now, back to the Rogers. After the instructions were laid out and questions of procedure carefully answered, Jack Rogers again stated what he had first said at the start of their session—namely, that he liked sex with his wife, but that he felt he could possibly like it even more and get greater satisfaction, as he hoped she would, too. He said he wasn't demanding anything of her, but just preferred her to be more open, experimental, less inhibited, and more sexy.

Immediately, when Jack had stopped talking—in fact even before he had finished—his life had begun to cloud up, and her first words were, "Damn—he and his sex . . ."

I interrupted her in a loud voice, "Illegitimate! Illegal! No just answering how you feel. You are to feed back what Jack is trying to say to you. Now please go ahead and try."

She gave me a look that made it appear she had doubts about the legality of my parent's marriage, thought a minute, and said to Jack in a disgusted voice, "You just want more oral sex."

I asked Jack, "Is that what you are trying to say?"

"No, he replied, it wasn't."

"Try it again," I said. "Tell Mary again."

Jack repeated, in essence, what he had already stated twice before. As they tried to talk, his wife would either give him an irrelevant answer or say he was blaming her for all their failures; occasionally, as they progressed, she would touch on a point he had made and get part of it.

Jack was having his difficulties, too, since he was repeatedly getting frustrated, found it hard to sit and listen to his wife be hostile, sarcastic, and self-pitying, and was quite humanly getting tired of repeating himself over and over.

To avoid giving a verbatim account of the long, detailed interchange that followed, let me simply state that by the end of the session, after much crying and display of hostility on the wife's part, accompanied by some, though less, hostility on her husband's part, the talking gradually changed in its tone and content. At one point, Mary said to Jack, "Well, I guess what you're trying to say is that you'd like me to question some of the ideas I have about sex, and maybe if I were freer, I could enjoy it more and so could you."

Jack gave both her and me a huge grin. "Yah, damn, that's exactly what I'm saying—at least in part. Hey, how about that, we finally did really talk to each other!"

Our time was up. I encouraged each of them to keep on trying, to use the method at home, and to pick out some more areas to discuss. Next week we would do the same thing again—in fact for weeks and weeks to come, until they had really learned how to listen, interpret, and talk. As the Rogers left, I jotted a note in my notebook that I felt there had occurred a marked reduction in the level of hostility that they had shown to one another when they had come in for that particular session, and I had high hopes that this feedback method would be even more helpful to them in the future.

REFERENCES

Ard, B. N., Jr. (Ed.). *Counseling and psychotherapy.* Palo Alto, Calif.: Science and Behavior Books, 1966.

Ellis, A. *Reason and emotion in psychotherapy.* New York: Lyle Stuart, 1962.

Ellis, A., & Harper, R. A. *Creative marriage.* New York: Lyle Stuart, 1961. (a)

Ellis, A., & Harper, R. A. *A guide to rational living.* Englewood Cliffs, N. J.: Prentice-Hall, 1961. (b)

Harper, R. A. *Psychoanalysis and psychotherapy: 36 systems.*. (Paperback) Englewood Cliffs, N. J.: Prentice-Hall, 1959.

Seabury, D. *The art of selfishness.* (Paperback) New York: Cornerstone Library, 1968.

Counseling Regarding Sexual Problems

I regard sex as the central problem of life. And now that the problem of religion has practically been settled, and that the problem of labor has at least been placed on a practical foundation, the question of sex—with the racial questions that rest on it—stands before the coming generations as the chief problem for solution.

HAVELOCK ELLIS

As Havelock Ellis noted in the quotation introducing this section, sex may be the central problem of life. But even if sex is not viewed as that important, it is certainly a central problem for many of the clients who consult marriage and family counselors. Therefore it deserves a separate section in a handbook on marriage counseling.

In Chapter 36, Dr. Ben N. Ard, Jr. discusses different sexual patterns in marriage among various subcultures. In a pluralistic, changing society such as ours, marriage and family counselors need to get beyond the limitations of their own personal backgrounds and learn to view sexual behavior from a broad, cross-cultural perspective, if they are to be of optimal help to clients from all walks of life and diverse cultural and racial backgrounds.

Walter Stokes, a psychiatrist, in Chapter 37, discusses inadequate female orgasm, probably one of the most pressing and recurrent problems counselors will face in their practice. Dr. Stokes raises two questions: Is the current image of Miss America actually much improvement over her grandmother? And where did Miss America get her narcissistic, unloving view of sex? Dr. Stokes discusses just what can be done about the problem of inadequacy of female orgasm and gives specific suggestions that will be of help to marriage counselors as well as interested husbands and wives.

In Chapter 38, Helen Singer Kaplan, gives an overview of sex therapy as it has blossomed since the advent of the Masters and Johnson's innovative work, and discusses the implications for some of the older ways of treating psychosexual dysfunction, psychoanalysis, for example.

In Chapter 39, Thea Snyder Lowry and Thomas P. Lowry, a husband-wife team (she is a marriage counselor and he is a psychiatrist both of whom trained with Masters and Johnson), provide a much needed and very fundamental discussion of ethical considerations in the fast burgeoning field of sex therapy.

CHAPTER 36

Different Sexual Patterns in Marriage

Ben N. Ard, Jr.

Sex means different things to different people, so it should be obvious that there are many different sexual patterns in marriage. There are many subcultures in the United States and each has a somewhat different effect upon marital sexual relationships. Different sexual patterns are found among the poor, among the Latin-Americans living in various parts of the United States, among the middle-class, among the upper-class (or jet-set), and among the newer "hippie" elements who are trying out group marriages or communal living patterns.

The *ideal* of the middle-class pattern is still derived from the Judaic-Christian code and it may be the pattern to which the most *lip-service* is paid in our culture. The Judaic-Christian model might be said to be: no interest in sex before puberty, premarital chastity (no sex before marriage, no matter how long delayed), marriage conceived as a sacrament ordained by God, with the idea of permanence (lifelong monogamy), or sexual exclusiveness (one does not even think or fantasize about any other woman or man), with sex being thought of as for the purpose of procreation (the purpose of marriage being the rearing of children) (Christensen, 1964). Sex after marriage in this ideal middle-class model may be largely a matter of something that is never discussed, but takes place at night, with the shades drawn and the lights out, under the covers, and with as many clothes on as possible.

The frequency of intercourse is perhaps greatest in this pattern early in the marriage. The husband is usually, if not always, the initiator, the wife going along with his desires, as it is her wifely (conjugal) duty. The frequency of intercourse frequently tapers off to something of a plateau during the middle years of the marriage and gradually diminishes thereafter. Sometimes with the menopause there is a sharp decline in sex and many couples live together for many of their later years without any sex. This may seem like a pitiful, sad scene and yet it still occurs in many a "good Christian home" throughout the land. It may be more common in rural America, in the Bible Belts, and in the Midwest and the South, and less so in the large urban centers on either coast or the larger metropolitan areas.

A revised version of an article reprinted from The Marriage & Family Counselors Quarterly, Vol. 9, No. 1, Fall, 1973.

The range of behavior in this middle-class sexual pattern is rather limited with not much variety of position or technique, as compared with the upper-class jet-set or the pattern among some of the "hippie" element. The position most frequently used is that of the male on top, the female on the bottom (what is sometimes called the "missionary" position). There is rarely much oral-genital contact and not much imagination shown with regard to foreplay, olfactory factors (perfumes, body lotions, etc.), music (as background), or the use of literature as an erotic stimulant. Sex in this middle-class pattern is rather routine.

When discussing sexual patterns among various groups, such as lower-class, middle-class, or upper-class, it should be obvious that there are many different patterns among a particular subgroup. But if any generalities are to be drawn, certain types of themes or patterns can be analyzed for these groups. For example, among the affluent upper-middle-class (or the elite), at least five different patterns of marital relationships have been distinguished (Cuber & Harroff, 1965): (1) the conflict-habituated, (2) the devitalized, (3) the passive-congenial, (4) the vital, and (5) the total. These five types of marital relationships among the affluent are different kinds of adjustment and different conceptions of marriage.

The conflict-habituated type of relationship is very prevalent in our culture. It is something like a running guerrilla fight. In such a relationship, the sexual aspect of the pattern can vary from very little sex to lots of kissing and making up after fights. The overall pattern of sexual adjustment can hardly continue to be good in such a relationship. Going to bed to resolve other conflicts does not work well for very long.

The devitalized type of relationship is really very dull; a void, the zest is gone, there is an apathetic, lifeless quality about these couples. And yet this kind of relationship is exceedingly common in our culture. Some people in our culture even believe that this is an *appropriate* mode for people in the middle years and later.

The passive-congenial sort of relationship is where the passivity is there from the start. These people drift along and get where they do primarily by default.

The vital type of relationship is one that is intensely bound together psychologically. Their sharing is genuine. This type is definitely in a minority in our culture. These couples settle disagreements quickly and seek to avoid conflict. Despite a lot of contrary folk belief, such marriages are possible.

The total relationship is like the vital one except that the intermeshing of interests and life foci are more numerous. Few areas of tension exist. This kind of relationship is very rare. It seems, in one sense, that in these relationships neither spouse has a truly private existence.

Infidelity occurs among most of the five types, with the exception of the total relationship, although it means different things in different contexts. In the conflict-habituated the women used for sex outside of the marriage are symbols of the resentment of the wife. A husband who strongly resents his wife can hardly have good sex with her, or even with any other woman that he strongly identifies with his wife. Among the passive-congenial types the man strays out of sheer boredom. The devitalized man may be seeking to recapture a spark. Some of the vitals are involved in adultery sometimes, some of them are simply very emancipated, almost "Bohemian." Some of these latter see sex as a human right for both men and women (both inside and outside of marriage) (Ard, 1971).

There are various ways of describing the sexual pattern among the affluent. In what Cuber and Harroff (1965) have described as intrinsic marriage among the elite, sex is usually important for these men and women. Not only that, it is fun. Sex seems to get better all the time. Sex pervades their whole life. People in these intrinsic marriages are remarkably free of the well-known sexual disabilities, such as frigidity, impotence, menopausal or menstrual disorders. Even the sexual joking that takes place among these couples is free of the "sick" themes (involving perversions, impotency, or senile difficulties). To an outsider they might appear to be too affectionate and too frank about sex.

Among some circles in the upper-middle-class there seems to be a growing tolerance for the idea that some men and women need or want enduring sexual as well as platonic relationships with more than one person concurrently. Sometimes these other involvements are explained as beneficial to both husband and wife. Some people recognize that certain individuals cannot be encompassed in any one relationship; compelling relationships can arise after marriage as well as before. One conclusion from much research on human sexuality has been fairly well documented: men and women vary enormously in the amount and kind of sexual expression they need and desire (Cuber & Harroff, 1965).

Turning to another element in our culture, the "hippie" or youth scene, these more "liberated" members of our society (according to some) have been developing what amounts to a new pattern of sexual behavior, mostly on their own and in defiance of their elders (Simmons & Winograd, 1966).

Many different patterns can be seen in these young people. The traditional distance between the sexes has lessened; there is more frankness and openness. Some evidence points out that there is less guilt about sex. The new scene is not all mass debauchery, although some of the mass media reports would seem to indicate this to many people. More people among this group are becoming sexually more experienced in both numbers of partners and in varieties of sex performed. The unisex idea is confusing to many, but each sex among these pioneers feels freer now to have attitudes, interests, and tastes which were formerly assumed to be the exclusive property or characteristic of one sex or the other.

Some evidence indicates that the capacity to enjoy sex may be greater among some of these youths than their parents. Competence can and frequently does increase with experience. One learns to love through loving; one becomes a more proficient sexual partner or lover through practice. And these young people are starting earlier. One hopes there is less sexual teasing and game playing among some of these young people.

All is not perfect among them, however. It is still a moot question as to how many young people really approach sex with a freer, unmitigated sense of enjoyment and a feeling of responsibility to the other partner.

These contemporary lovers may move to complete intimacy with a swiftness that shocks and disconcerts their elders, but these elders are wrong when they judge this to be nothing but widespread promiscuity. Many of these couples who live together without being married are actually very monogamous and true to each other. And this living together is not like "shacking up" for an evening. Many of these young people are not interested in one-night stands, either.

Conflicting bits of evidence about sexual patterns can be found among the poor or lower-class elements in our culture (Rainwater, 1969), such as contrasting views about sex among Black people, for example. Blacks in the lower class or ghettos have been described by some as having a naturalness and greater sexual freedom, and among whom, therefore, sexual gratification is far greater than in the more respectable middle class. Other authorities have seen this view as a myth.

Some evidence shows that as one moves from higher to lower social status the proportion of men and women who show strong interest in sex and enjoyment of sex declines. Foreplay is less elaborate at lower educational levels; there is less use of oral techniques. Less educated wives view sex as more of a duty (and therefore refuse their husbands less often). At the same time, as the years pass reduced frequency of intercourse occurs and the lower-class man is likely to express reduced interest in and enjoyment of sexual relations with his wife. At the lower educational levels less versatility in positional variations in intercourse is found; in fact, lower-class men abandon variety in position more rapidly than do more educated men. This same pattern between the lower and middle classes applies for nudity in marital sexual relations.

This lower value placed on sex by lower-class wives, and to a lesser extent by lower-class husbands, can be seen as a result of the high degree of segregation in their conjugal role relationship. Such couples live separate lives in other areas and this separateness also affects their sexual relationship. A good, satisfying sex relationship is difficult to achieve or maintain without some degree of intimacy, sharing, and empathy; where role relationships are highly segregated, communication between the sexes is difficult and sex relations suffer. A high degree of conjugal role segregation seems to interfere with achieving maximum sexual gratification (Rainwater, 1969).

The cultural double standard seems to operate at all class levels and perhaps contributes to the difficulties of communication between the sexes, particularly about sexual matters. Sex sometimes is seen as essentially a hostile act between the sexes and where this is assumed by the participants, there naturally can be less open acceptance of sex.

Some evidence shows a "sexual renaissance" in marital sexuality among the modern working class, but there is no such evidence in the less prosperous lower class (Rainwater, 1969).

Among the Latin-American or Spanish-American groups who live in

Latin America or in the United States, a pattern of sexual behavior which is related to the concept of "machismo" or manliness is still seen. This concept of the Macho is a concept of masculinity that affects the pattern of sexual relations found in marriages that subscribe to this concept. We do not have an English language equivalent of this concept, but we do have many related concepts such as stud, Don Juan, ladies' man, lover-man, etc. These latter concepts are not limited to the Latin subcultures, but may be found in many subcultures in the United States (Ard, 1972).

The masculinity of the macho pattern in some Latin cultures includes an aggressive pride on the part of the male, particularly in his relations with women. The machismo concept stresses both having many partners and insists that the male should take his own pleasure in each relationship. This exaggerated masculinity may be understood as an overcompensation for the difficulty the young man has in developing a masculine identity in cultures where the machismo concept exists.

In the context of the machismo concept, sex is thought of as a man's pleasure and a woman's duty. Sex exists, in this view, for the pleasure of the man. Women are assumed either to have no sexual desires (as a man does) at all, or at most to have much weaker sexual desires. A frequent assumption is that a woman's sexual desires are not ordinarily aroused without stimulation from a man. This may be a most comforting thought for a husband in a society where the women are carefully controlled and kept in the family compound, but it is just not in accord with the facts. When any women appear, as they do in every culture, who are passionate and actively seek out sex, such women are thought of in the machismo cultural context as crazy, or "loco."

Under the machismo concept, it is assumed that man's nature demands sexual experience and if he is not given this sexual satisfaction at home, he will seek it elsewhere. What's more, this is assumed as natural and normal. What is interesting about this part of the machismo concept is that the same assumptions are not made about the woman.

A husband wrapped up in this machismo concept may even not wish to employ many different sexual techniques with his wife (but which he may indeed use with other women), because he does not want to stir up any "unnatural sexual desires" in her that might lead her to seek sexual satisfaction elsewhere, once aroused.

This machismo concept divides all women into two categories: the immoral or loose women and the good or virginal women. Such a highly vulnerable concept would seem likely to break down under the secularization and urbanization trends in our society today.

So it would seem that not only men, but women also are short-changed under the machismo concept and both are put into a situation which could hardly be called healthy. "Nice girls" are carefully chaperoned and guarded ("protected") so that they will not have any sexual opportunities or experience before marriage. They are also, unfortunately, not given adequate or even minimal sex education, for the same reasons.

One of the results of the machismo concept and the related assumptions about women's sexuality (or lack thereof) is that women (the "good" wives) develop unhealthy attitudes toward sex (understandably), and the husbands (also understandably) turn to prostitutes and other "loose" women for sexual satisfaction. This arrangement, wherein the sexual relationships within marriage become less involved and satisfactory (and more automatic) after the first few years of marriage (if they are ever very good), means that the men turn increasingly to relationships which by their very nature cannot prove very satisfying. Prostitutes do not provide very good sexual experiences for many men.

The interpersonal implications of the machismo concept are not healthy and can only lead to unfortunate results in the sexual relationships between men and women. Basically, the machismo concept leads to very segregated and uninvolved interpersonal relationships between the sexes. This can hardly lead to good sexual relations which bring the pleasure and satisfaction which are possible under different concepts of masculinity and femininity (Ard, 1974).

Men and women do not share conjugal role relationships that are compatible with healthy sexual relationships under the machismo concept. Segregated role relationships, with men largely associating with other men, and women associating with other women, are not conducive to healthy relationships in marriage, and certainly are detrimental to healthy sexual relations. Mutuality helps good sexual relations; segregated role relations do not help men and women have better sexual relations.

The segregated, isolated role relations between men and women, which derive from the machismo concepts, do not lead to empathy or mutual helpfulness between the sexes. On the contrary, the machismo concept leads to poor communication between the sexes in a very fundamental sense. This is true in more than several subcultures.

The machismo concept leads to a lack of intimacy between the sexes. And while all sexual relations do not have to be deeply involved and intimate to provide some satisfaction, in the long run better sexual satisfactions are obtained where a man and a woman at least have some chance of interacting intimately with mutual respect and affection and some mutual accommodation and empathy. This is very difficult under the machismo concept wherein the aggressive, strutting male gets his sexual satisfaction from women who are defined as beneath him. A lot of the sadism and masochism occurring between men and women under this cultural concept of machismo is "excused" by the basic concepts of the lordly male or macho. But the man who is really a man does not have to prove his manhood by fighting or taking his pleasure from women without any effort to satisfy them. Rape is not an ideal concept of good sex and yet tinges of this sort of sexual relations are inherent in the machismo concept. Men and women who go along with the machismo concept expect that sexual relations will be sort of a fight scene with the man taking his pleasure regardless of whether or not the woman gains any satisfaction in the process. This sort of concept of masculinity cannot help but ultimately deprive both men and women of many of the joys and pleasures that a healthier concept of masculinity and femininity would provide.

A brief look at sex among psychologically healthy (or self-actualizing) people might serve to round out this survey of some of the different sexual patterns in marriage. In Maslow's (1970) study of self-actualizing people, his data definitely contradict the age-old theory of intrinsic hostility between the sexes. This suspicion of the "opposite" (rather than the other) sex is found in many people, but not in self-actualizing people. One of the other major findings was that the quality of the love and sex satisfaction may improve with the length of the relationship. Even the strictly sensual and physical satisfactions can be improved by familiarity with the partner (rather than by novelty) in these healthy people. These people are exceedingly rare, of course, comprising about one percent of the population.

Sexual pleasures are found in their most intense and ecstatic perfection in self-actualizing people. The orgasm is described as having a revivifying effect upon them. They enjoy sex wholeheartedly. For these people sex can be, on occasion, a delicate pleasure rather than an intense one, sometimes gay and lighthearted, playful rather than always a serious (or even sacred) experience.

These self-actualizing people are free to admit sexual attraction to others, but they actually do less about it than other people. There seems to be less compulsion for sexual affairs with outsiders.

Among these self-actualizing people, no real sharp differentiation is made between the roles and personalities of the two sexes; they did not assume that the female was passive and the male active, either in sex or love or anything else. In other words, both sexes among these couples could be both active and passive lovers, and they revealed this clearly in the sexual act and in physical love-making. Taking the initiative, or being above or below in the sexual act was found in both sexes. Thus, among psychologically healthy people (or self-actualizing people) the sexual pattern in marriage is considerably different from other groups considered above. The fact that these self-actualizing people developed their sexual patterns in the same culture where the other patterns appeared offers hope for the future. Evidently it is possible to live a rational, sane, enjoyable sex life, even in an irrational, largely sex-negating culture.

REFERENCES

Ard, B. N., Jr. Sexuality as a personal and social force. In Otto, H. A. *The new sexuality*. Palo Alto: Science & Behavior Books, 1971.

Ard, b. N., Jr. Machismo: when men rule women. *Sexology*, *38*:68–70, February, 1972.

Ard, B. N., Jr., *Treating psychosexual dysfunction*. New York: Jason Aronson, 1974.

Christensen, H. T. *Handbook of marriage and the family*. Chicago: Rand McNally, 1964.

Cuber, J. F., & Harroff, P. B. *The significant Americans: a study of sexual behavior among the affluent*. New York: Appleton-Century, 1965.

Maslow, A. H. *Motivation and personality*. New York: Harper & Row, wnd ed., 1970.

Rainwater, Lee. Sex in the culture of poverty. In Broderick, C. B. & Bernard, J. *The individual, sex & society*. Baltimore: Johns Hopkins Press, 1969.

Simmons, J. I. & Winograd, B. It's happening: a portrait of the youth scene today. Santa Barbara: Marc-Laird Publications, 1966.

CHAPTER 37

Inadequacy of Female Orgasm as a Problem in Marriage Counseling

Walter R. Stokes

At the outset it seems appropriate to have a look at the question: Just how important, in the course of marriage counseling, is the attainment of orgastic response by the wife? I am aware that there is considerable diversity of opinion among us on this issue. Some tend to minimize the importance of mutual sex enjoyment or to feel that adjustment will automatically follow if the overall interpersonal relationship can be improved. A few even go so far as to question whether orgastic capacity in the wife is really of much importance to the success of a marriage. Others see a high rate of passionate sex activity and orgastic response as utterly essential to a good marriage and view it as the touchstone to satisfactory married life.

It is well to acknowledge that there exists among therapists and counselors a marked difference of opinion as to which comes first: poor sex adjustment (often involving inadequate female response) or poor interpersonal adjustment at nonerotic levels.

Before moving into closer examination of the questions I have raised, it is necessary to set a few things straight. Living in a culture such as ours we are enormously handicapped in our efforts to understand and to develop the best potential of either sex. We simply do not have much of a store of reliable information or experience about the expression of female sexuality at its guiltless, happy optimum. In a great measure this must be attributed to the unfortunate cultural heritage of sex mores in our society. I wish to document this briefly, particularly as it relates to women and female orgastic response.

Our sex mores are heavily influenced by the doctrines of Hebraic-Christian morality. In this mystical system there is a basic assumption that enjoyment of sex is sinful, nothing better than bait in the Devil's cruel trap. It is conceded in the Book of Genesis story that Eve was a natural, curious, sex-enjoying creature but for following her inclinations she is pictured as turning loose all the misfortunes of mankind. In a considerable sense she represents both the first and the last sexually responsive woman.

Reprinted with permission of the author and the publisher from the *Journal of Sex Research*, 1968, *4*, 225–233.

All her female descendants are supposed to be so terrified by the results of Eve's bad judgment that they are to regard erotic emotion with horror and aversion. This ideal reaches its full flower in the Christian myth of the Immaculate Conception and the character of the Virgin Mary. Her awesome, desexualized, icily frigid personality is the female image every little girl must emulate if she wishes to become a "lady" in the Christian sense. Therefore girls find themselves under enormous pressure to deny their instinctual erotic feelings or to express them only in sublimated, symbolic, or furtive ways. The effect of this upon the development of orgastic capacity in intercourse is painfully obvious. It is strikingly summarized in a couple of stories told me early in my practice by a cultured, elderly woman who had been reared in the strictest Victorian tradition, as a member of one of the First Families of Virginia.

She commented that up to the time of her marriage her mother had never directly mentioned sex in any way. But as her wedding approached the mother took her aside and grimly instructed "You are about to be married and must be thinking of having children. To do this a woman must submit to revolting physical contact with her husband. She must summon all her courage and endure this, as she does childbirth. It is said that there are women who enjoy sexual contact with a man, but this has never been known in the history of our family. I am sure you will not enjoy the sex act but if you should, never let your husband know, for no decent man can respect a woman who does."

The second story told by this daughter of Victorianism had to do with a visit she made to a burlesque show with one of her early boy friends. They went there for a daring lark. But when the lewd jokes of the comedians began to register the boy was humiliated and apologetically begged her to leave at once. She drew herself up and replied acidly "No! Do you think I would permit these ruffians the satisfaction of knowing that I understand their vile jokes?"

It may appear that I am belaboring a dead horse in these references to the past. Someone may justifiably point to the recent progress made by all three of our major religious faiths in moving away from the old sex puritanism. In so far as this is really true I rejoice over the change and am happy to see religious morality letting up on sex. But I raise two serious questions about the change that is taking place.

First, is the current image of Miss America actually much improvement over her grandmother? When I observe Miss America's superficial, empty glamour values; her cultivated narcissism; her seductive use of phoney sex appeal to win prestige and material rewards; and her poor record in marriage, I wonder whether she is a great deal closer to appreciating and expressing sex in a sound, functional way than was her grandmother.

This brings me to my second question: Where did Miss America get her narcissistic, unloving view of sex? Why did not her family and others give her a biologically and socially sound conception of sex? My suspicion, backed by much clinical observation, is that, just as in the old days, the family and society of today are still pretty much taken in by the ancient myths and are still feebly capable of giving children rational, humanly understanding support in the realm of sex development.

I would not wish to imply that there has been no progress in this century. But I suggest that much of the so-called progress is in the empty, unloving directions of glamour sex, thrill sex, and pornography rather than coming more in tune with affectionate human relatedness or operating as the magnificent creative and social force which I believe it should be.

I am much disturbed by the role of television and all forms of commercial advertising in cementing the false image of female sexuality which I have ascribed to Miss America. Also I am distressed by the fact that television and Madison Avenue advertising are peculiarly dominated by the voices of censors who can not tolerate sex as a warm, functional human reality. To put it bluntly, a glamorized image of the Virgin Mary is still being held before our children.

Here I shall return to the question "Just how important is orgastic enjoyment in the personal and marital life of a woman?" Judging from the testimony of the relatively few women of excellent orgastic capacity with whom I have explored this critically and carefully I surmise that it is of overwhelming importance if a woman is to know the fullness of life and the peculiar joys and satisfactions that are experienced in affectionately sharing her erotic emotions with a man of like capacity. I am not denying that a woman may find a good deal of pleasure and meaning in life without orgastic enjoyment. But I am led to believe that no other experience gives her so much happiness when enjoyed in an affectionate, genuinely mutual relationship.

It seems significant to note that my personal observations are derived from thirty-five years of private practice in the field of marriage and family counseling. Last Spring, upon my retirement from clinical work, I found, in the course of sorting and destroying case records, that there were nearly 9,000 of them, involving almost as large a number of other persons, mostly spouses and children. I have saved for study 1,500 records of cases on which I have extensive information, many with prolonged follow-up ranging from 10 to 35 years.

Throughout this considerable clinical experience, devoted to premarital preparation, marriage counseling, child guidance, and psychotherapy, I have been constantly alert to the significance of female orgasm as a factor relevant both to a woman's personal happiness and the general state of her family life. It is my carefully weighed conclusion that although some women may endure marriage without orgastic satisfaction such a marriage is, at best, of poor quality compared with those in which the wife is erotically alive and regularly reaches orgasm in intercourse with her husband. I am convinced that for a woman to function at her best as either wife or mother she must have the rich emotional experience of guiltless capability to enjoy orgasm in intercourse. However, as a clinician experienced in our culture, I wish emphatically to stress that I do not consider it wise for a marriage counselor to set this goal for all clients. Some are incapable of attaining it because of unfavorable early life conditioning while others face the reality of a hopelessly inadequate husband who refuses to seek help or cannot respond to it. Thus if some marriages are to continue (and it may be, for many reasons, necessary that they should) the wise counselor will not always make too much of female orgastic attainment. Nevertheless I feel deeply certain that a marriage of high quality and enduring satisfaction is not possible without orgastic response on the part of the wife.

Some clinical highlights bearing upon this come to mind. I think of the countless times that women who could not reach orgasm have sought my help, desperate and fed-up over pretending a good erotic relationship with the husband; I recall the large number of women with impotent husbands who have achieved satisfaction in extramarital relations and the transforming happiness (as well as conflict) it has brought them; and I am impressed by the capability of sexually responsive women to give their children a superior kind of support and guidance in all that relates to sexual development. The latter observation stems from much long-term observation of families, particularly the many instances in which I have given premarital preparation to the mother and years later to her daughter also.

I find something deeply significant in the fact that during all of my clinical experience I encountered only two instances in which a woman who regularly achieved orgasm with her husband came to me contemplating divorce. In each case there was a staggering discrepancy in the cultural backgrounds of the spouses and the husband was unable to provide enough financial security to undertake the responsibility of children. When divorce was finally decided upon, in each of these marriages the spouses wept bitterly and parted with reluctance. I am glad to report that it was not long before each entered a new and more suitable marriage. Against these two cases I have seen many hundreds of marriages break up in the face of poor sex response by the wife, even though in most instances the cultural backgrounds of the spouses were reasonably compatible.

In order to be sure of what we are talking about it seems essential to offer definitions of both adequate and inadequate orgastic response. I choose to define adequate female orgasm as regular or frequent attainment, during intravaginal intercourse, of a high degree of erotic excitement culminating in a spasmodic pelvic and generalized reaction attended by intense sensation of pleasure and followed by feelings of fulfillment and a state of relaxation.

I exclude from my definition of satisfactory orgasm that which can be attained only by means of manual or oral stimulation of the clitoris or other parts of the body. I flatly reject the widely known dictum of my esteemed colleague and friend, the late Dr. Robert L. Dickinson, that "orgasm is orgasm, however won." I have encountered convincing evidence that female orgastic experience is fully satisfactory only when there is enthusiastic, unrestrained acceptance of intravaginal intercourse. Even then it may not be satisfactory if accompanied by a compulsion to draw upon morbid fantasies.

The common clinical forms of inadequate female response may be summarized and defined as follows.

1. Fearful early marriage response based upon ignorance and inexperience and sometimes coupled with actual physical pain.

2. Chronic aversion to any kind of genital stimulation.

3. Passive acceptance of intercourse without erotic arousal or with insufficient arousal to reach orgasm.

4. Compulsive preference for various kinds of clitoral or breast stimulation, linked with rejection of intravaginal participation.

5. Ability to reach orgasm in intercourse only through mental detachment from the partner and substitution of morbid fantasies, usually pornographic and sado-masochistic in nature.

6. Mention must be made of inadequate female response due directly to chronic inadequacy in the male.

In addition to my attempt at defining adequate orgastic response I would like to add something about degrees of inadequacy. I suggest the following gradations.

1. The situation where the wife has a generally good relationship with the husband and experiences some erotic arousal but can not gain orgasm during intercourse. This is probably the complaint most often heard. I have observed that in cases of this kind, especially when seen early in marriage, the difficulty tends to disappear spontaneously with continued marital experience. However, improvement may usually be hastened by counseling and reassurance, involving both husband and wife. This is the mildest form of our problem.

2. The frequently seen cases in which the wife has orgastic response on some occasions but where the husband's sex need is much more active than hers, resulting in a degree of sexual incompatibility that induces mutual hostility. Here is a situation that often lends itself to successful counseling, employing techniques of education, reeducation, mutual discussion and sensible compromise.

3. The case where intercourse is attended by little or no erotic arousal and the general personal adjustment with the husband is poor. Usually such a woman is unconsciously rejecting a sound female role and the problem is a grave one, unlikely to respond to the counseling approach. Deep-level psychotherapy is indicated as soon as a firm diagnostic opinion can be formed. The prognosis is variable. Sometimes excellent results are attained but often a patch-work of improvement is the best that can be done. In some of these cases, with more severe personality disturbance, both counseling and psychotherapy may fail or achieve meagerly limited success.

4. A situation, either with or without erotic response, in which there is chaotic personality disturbance, as in severe obsessive-compulsive neurosis, prepsychotic states, chronic alcoholism, and psychosis. Some of these cases are readily identifiable while others must be observed for some time before a diagnosis can be made. Counseling is quite ineffective. Psychiatric referral is generally advisable. These women have suffered the severest kinds of early traumata in both basic human relatedness and sex related-

ness. The female role is either rejected or accepted only in a false, unrealistic, unworkable form. Even under the best of contemporary psychotherapy it is often difficult to correct the major pathology fully. Notwithstanding, it is a rare case in which some stabilization can not be achieved if the therapist is geared to the realities of the situation and can make appropriate compromise with his preferred goals. I have treated a few persons of each sex, psychotically disturbed, who have learned to enjoy sex relations under limited circumstances but have come to recognize and accept it that they were not stable enough to handle the responsibilities of marriage and parenthood.

Those whose training is largely in counseling and limited in regard to psychotherapy are likely, when dealing with the more complicated types of inadequate female sex response, to consider referring the client to a psychotherapist, perhaps a psychiatrist. Judgment about this must derive from training and experience and take into account the referral resources that are available. If such a referral is to be made I caution against overselling to the client the results to be expected. It is best to make a modest, guarded estimate about the probable benefits of deep-level psychotherapy. Often the client solicits extravagant reassurances of magical results but it is in the interest of all concerned to give a sober, factual appraisal of what lies ahead.

It is prudent for nonmedical counselors, when confronted by a problem of inadequate female sex response, to require a gynecological consultation or to get an opinion from a physician who has already given the client a pelvic examination. This is a routine step that protects the interests of both client and counselor. In a vast majority of cases nothing will be found that is relevant to the sex response problem but certainly there are anatomical or disease conditions that might account for all the difficulty or contribute heavily to it. Obviously there are situations in which failure to insist upon a pelvic examination could result in a suit for malpractice.

Now I wish to take a close look at the proposition "Which comes first, good sex response or a good generally affectionate relationship?" Much as I value the experience of good sex, I hold that the mutually trusting, affectionate relationship comes first and that without it sex is reduced to an unsatisfactory caricature.

The strength of my feeling about this has grown with the years of personal and clinical experience. As I have dealt with people in great sexual difficulties: the neurotic, the compulsive sex deviant, the juvenile delinquent, the criminal, and the psychotic I have been impressed by the failure of all of them to achieve a basis for trusting, affectionate human relatedness in early life. Also for most of them their early sex interests were associated with their worst experiences of rejection and guilt. Thus I am persuaded that first there must be an adequate degree of trusting, affectionately toned human relatedness and that erotic relatedness must be successfully superimposed upon this without creation of serious emotional trauma.

This concept has support in the work of Harry Harlow and associates on affectional responses and sex behavior of our cousin, the rhesus monkey. In essence Harlow's work demonstrates that unless the young monkey is able, at a critical early age, to experience affectionate relatedness to others of his kind he will grow up incapable of normal social adjustment, including incapability to follow an adequate pattern of sex interest and behavior.

The plight of many young human beings is worse than that of Harlow's deprived monkeys for they suffer not only affectional deprivation but are also subjected to a barrage of terrifying interpretations regarding any display of erotic emotion. Small wonder that they seek refuge in the phony world of romantic glamour sex or its opposite number, the world of pornography and sado-masochism. Here appears to be the genesis of schizophrenic process: a deep defect in trusting human relatedness coupled with desperate grasping at weird ideals that can never integrate with basic emotional needs. Under such circumstances the best adjustment that can be hoped for is a kind of anxious pseudo-mutuality that dooms any human being to failure as a spouse and as a parent. Such a person, as a parent, will try desperately to administer his false values to his child but the harder he tries the more confused and unloving the child becomes, even though on the surface a deceptive semblance of stability is presented to the world.

As I see it, we are reaching a point in our cultural evolution where we are rapidly gaining insight into the morbidities that afflict our emotional lives and which are manifested as defects in both general human relatedness and sex relatedness in particular. I believe, however, that some of us are groping in the right direction. I believe, too, that as we are able to discard our traditional irrationalities more and more of us will do better and better at understanding the inescapable emotional needs of children and will meet them with increasing affection and greater skill. It is only through such a process of slow cultural evolution that I am able to visualize substantial solution of the plague of inadequate sex response in both sexes.

Meanwhile, as counselors and therapists, we are confronted with the daily problem of what to do about the complaints of female unresponsiveness that are pouring in in increasing volume. I suggest that the first thing a counselor should do is to feel and to display genuine concern and not to brush the problem aside or minimize it unduly, which some have a tendency to do. Next, in taking a comprehensive life history of the client, sexual aspects should be explored as completely as the sensibilities of the client will permit at the time. If possible, the husband should be interviewed in the same thorough manner, with equal attention to sex attitudes and behavior. Out of these interviews relatively simple and successful remedial measures may emerge. In other instances it may seem best to do some tentative experimenting through educational and conjoint interview techniques.

I trust that we shall never overlook how very much the sex response of one spouse is likely to be affected by that of the other. Since the heterosexual relationship involves two people any examination of their sex difficulties must take each into account in a deeply inquiring and emphatic way. If there is to be understanding and satisfaction between men and women concerning sex it can be achieved only through mutual concern and respect.

CHAPTER 38

Sex Therapy: An Overview

Helen Singer Kaplan

The objective of this paper is to present an overview of the new techniques for the rapid treatment of sexual disorders, which have been termed "sex therapy." The discussion will be organized around three questions:

1. *What is sex therapy?* What are its distinguishing features? How does it differ from psychoanalysis and in what ways, if any, is it similar?

2. *How effective is sex therapy?* What is the current evidence? Is sex therapy a passing fad or will it stand the test of time and prove to represent a significant advance?

3. *Does the success of sex therapy invalidate psychoanalysis?* This last question entails a comparison of the presumed mechanism of actions of psychoanalysis and of sex therapy.

WHAT IS SEX THERAPY

The new approach to the treatment of sexual disorders differs from other forms of therapy in two respects: first, *its goals are limited* essentially to the relief of the patient's sexual symptom; second, it represents a departure from traditional techniques in that it employs a combination of prescribed *sexual experiences* and psychotherapy to achieve its primary objective.

Limited Goals

Sex therapists differ somewhat in the way they define their therapeutic goals. All workers in this field focus on fostering better sexual functioning, but some espouse broader objectives, including improvement in the couple's mode of communication and their relationship in general, as well as resolution of intrapsychic conflicts which may underlie their sexual problems. However, the overriding objective of the new treatment of sexual disorders is to cure the patient's sexual symptom. All therapeutic interventions—psychotherapy, couples therapy, etc.—are ultimately in the service of this goal.

Reprinted with permission from the author and the publisher of *Sexuality and Psychoanalysis*.

It is this admittedly limited objective which distinguishes the new sex therapy from other treatment modalities, such as psychoanalysis and marital therapy. Although the patient's problem may appear to be limited to his inability to function adequately in the sexual sphere, psychoanalysts tend to regard the presence of a sexual dysfunction as a manifestation of psychological illness. Proponents of this position contend that all sexual disorders, regardless of their nature and severity, are expressions of unresolved intrapsychic conflicts and/or destructive interpersonal interactions. The patient's conflicts and his interpersonal difficulties invariably exert their noxious influence on other aspects of his behavior as well. The aim of treatment, therefore, necessarily extends beyond alleviation of the patient's sexual difficulty; rather, its main objective is the resolution of the patient's deeper intrapsychic and interpersonal problems, and the concomitant reconstruction of his neurotic personality.

Psychoanalytic treatment techniques reflect this theoretical orientation. First, sexual problems are never treated in isolation from the patient's other problems. Second, the sexual symptom is not treated directly, that is, no attempt is made to modify the immediately operating, "here and now" causes of the patient's sexual dysfunction. Instead, the psychotherapist proceeds on the assumption that the intrapsychic and/or interpersonal causes of the patient's sexual dysfunction are invariably embedded in the developmental matrix of the past. Third, since, as noted above, the patient's sexual disorder is regarded as a manifestation of his deeper psychological problems, any symptomatic improvement which may occur in the course of treatment is considered a "by-product" of the resolution of his more basic personality problems and/or the modification of his pathological pattern of interpersonal relationships. Therefore, when the impotent man becomes able to have intercourse, or the inorgastic woman has an orgasm, treatment is not terminated. Therapy ends only when the psychotherapist feels that the basic oedipal conflicts and/or the marital power struggles which have presumably given rise to the patient's sexual problems have been resolved.

Sex therapists, when they are dynamically oriented, do not dispute the fact that some sexual symptoms can be traced to intrapsychic conflicts and destructive interpersonal relationships, and can best be understood in terms of the patient's childhood experiences. However, the sex therapist is concerned, first and foremost, with the immediate causes of the patient's sexual problem and the specific defenses he has erected against sexuality. In contrast to the treatment modalities described above, the remote determinants of the problem are dealt with in sex therapy only to the extent necessary to cure the sexual target symptom and prevent a recurrence of the disability. Psychodynamic and transactional factors are interpreted, and neurotic behavior modified, only if these are directly operative in impairing the patient's sexual functioning, or if they obstruct the progress of treatment. Therefore sex therapy is concluded when the patient's sexual functioning has been restored. This is not to say, of course, that treatment is terminated precipitately, as soon as the impotent patient, for example, manages to have intercourse on one or two occasions. Treatment is terminated, however, when in addition to alleviation of the sexual dysfunction, the factors which were immediately responsible for its onset have been identified and sufficiently resolved to warrant the assumption that sexual functioning is now reasonably permanent and stable.

The following case is presented to illustrate the influence on therapy of the limited objective of relieving the sexual symptom, and the manner in which psychodynamically oriented sex therapists generally handle related intrapsychic and marital problems. In addition, the ways in which clinicians of other orientations might be expected to manage certain aspects of this case will be discussed briefly in order to underscore the unique features of sex therapy.

Mr. and Mrs. A., both of whom were in their early twenties, came to the clinic to seek help for Mr. A., who suffered from severe premature ejaculation.

Formulation. It became apparent in the course of the initial interview that Mr. A. harbored a good deal of unconscious hostility toward his wife. At the same time, however, he seemed to be quite dependent on her. Although he was not aware of these feelings, it was the therapist's impression that Mr. A. was afraid that he would be abandoned by his wife if he did not "perform."

In all probability, Mr. A.'s conflicts had their roots in disturbances in his interactions with crucial members of his family in early childhood. It is also possible that these conflicts played a role in the genesis of his sexual problems. Certainly, it is safe to assume that a psychoanalyst confronted with this case would proceed on this premise. Accordingly, he would attempt to help the patient resolve his residual oedipal conflicts and gain insight into the unconscious sources of his anger at women and his fear of abandonment by maternal figures, with the expectation that he would thereby gain ejaculatory competence. The marital therapist, on the other hand, would try to identify and resolve the transactional causes of Mr. A.'s problem, i.e., the hostilities between the couple, which very possibly might be reinforcing the husband's prematurity. And this approach would be no less valid, for it was obvious that this couple had serious marital problems. As mentioned above, the quality of their relationship reflected Mr. A.'s ambivalent feelings toward his wife. Moreover, Mrs. A.'s fears, on some level of awareness, that if the husband were to function well sexually he would abandon her for a more attractive woman, had also had an adverse effect on their relationship. The interpersonally-oriented therapist would, therefore, consider the resolution of this couple's destructive marital interactions as his first order of business.

As noted above, in contrast to these approaches, the sex therapist's initial objective is to attempt to modify the immediate cause of prematurity, which, presumably, is the patient's lack of awareness of his erotic sensations prior to orgasm. Thus, in such cases, during the first therapeutic session, the patient and his wife are instructed in the Semans procedure, which enables the achievement of ejaculatory control without producing insight into the intrapsychic or interpersonal dynamics which may play a role in the genesis and perpetuation of that dysfunction. Essentially, the therapist instructs the wife to stimulate her husband's penis, and instructs the patient to focus his attention on the premonitory cues to orgasm. This is not to imply that therapeutic interventions are limited to the prescription of such behavioral tasks. On the contrary, the psychodynamically oriented sex therapist must be an extremely skilled psychotherapist and couples therapist. However, those skills are employed in order to implement the top priority objective, namely, the relief of the sexual target symptom. Once again, psychodynamic and/or transactional material, i.e., the remote causes of the sexual symptom, are dealt with skillfully and effectively, but only insofar as these variables present immediate obstacles to the couple's sexual adequacy and/or give rise to resistances which interfere with the implementation of the essential therapeutic tasks.

Treatment. In this case, such obstacles to treatment did not arise initially, with the result that after four sessions Mr. A. was able to exert good ejaculatory control in the female superior position. However, at this point treatment reached an impasse. The couple managed to avoid the sexual tasks for a whole week. Mr. A. rationalized his behavior on the grounds that he was extremely involved with business and could not find the time to devote to the exercises. His wife felt irritable and tired, and did not pursue the issue. It was apparent, of course, that this avoidance of the sexually therapeutic tasks was a manifestation of resistances which had been mobilized by treatment. Therefore the therapist's efforts now focused on the clarification and resolution of these resistances. Specifically, therapeutic emphasis was shifted to the husband's hostility toward his wife, and the wife's anxieties which seemed to have been mobilized by his improvement. Inasmuch as treatment of the husband's dysfunction could not proceed in the face of the resistances created by these problems, this shift in therapeutic emphasis was mandatory at this point. But apart from the fact that it would ultimately serve to foster ejaculatory control, it also afforded the therapist an opportunity to identify and explore important marital and intrapsychic problems. In this case the therapist was able in the next four sessions to foster sufficient resolution of these resistances—by confronting the couple with their avoidance of sex and by active interpretation of the unconscious problems which had given rise to their resistances to treatment—to enable the husband to achieve excellent ejaculatory control.

Treatment was terminated when the husband's ejaculatory competence appeared to be stable, although, of course, many of the couple's marital and intrapsychic problems remained unsolved.

Relief of the sexual dysfunction is the crucial criterion for the termination of sex therapy, unless it becomes apparent that severe marital difficulties or neurotic conflicts preclude satisfactory sexual functioning—even though the patient's symptom no longer presents an impediment to the achievement of this goal—or unless the couple want further treatment for other problems which have come to light in the course of sex therapy.

Sexual Tasks Combined with Psychotherapy

The case also points up the crucial technical difference between the new sex therapy and traditional treatment modalities, namely, the synergy of sexual tasks and the psychotherapeutic procedure. In other forms of psychotherapy the events which occur in the therapist's office provide the setting for the therapeutic process. Thus, in traditional treatment based on the psychoanalytic model, the analyst does not intervene directly in the patient's life, except perhaps to admonish him against the self-destructive "acting out" of his conflicts and resistances. He generally refrains from making specific suggestions, and certainly he never instructs him to engage in specific experiences outside the clinical setting. Such behavioral prescriptions would be interpreted as an attempt on the part of the therapist to "manipulate" the patient, which is considered by many authorities to be contraindicated in psychoanalytically-oriented psychotherapy. Instead, the psychoanalyst relies exclusively on the events which transpire during the therapeutic sessions—and particularly on the patient-analyst relationship—to achieve his results.

The marital therapist, who generally employs conjoint sessions in which husband and wife, as well as the therapist, participate to resolve marital discord, also considers the couple's experiences during these sessions to constitute the primary cure-producing agent. Similarly, the various techniques employed by behavior therapists to extinguish the fears and inhibitions which impair the patient's sexual response are generally administered in the therapist's office under his direct guidance. For the most part behavioral therapists also do not exploit the therapeutic potential of extra-office experiences.

This exclusive reliance on the office session is in sharp contrast to the approach of sex therapy. Sex therapists consider specific experiences suggested by the therapist, but conducted by the patient and his partner while they are alone together, to be a crucial feature of the therapeutic process; indeed, these prescribed tasks are regarded as essential change-producing agents. The rational use of these therapeutic experiences enhances the effectiveness of psychotherapy enormously.

However, if it is psychodynamically oriented, the new therapy does not rely exclusively on prescribed sexual interactions. Rather, it employs an integrated combination of sexual experiences and psychotherapy. This combination constitutes its main innovation and is probably largely responsible for its impressive success. Psychotherapeutic intervention, in itself, whether it is conducted on an individual basis or addresses itself to the joint treatment of husband and wife, alleviates sexual problems to some extent. It is also safe to assume that highly stimulating and concomitantly reassuring sexual experiences have enabled some persons to overcome their sexual difficulties. However, the judicious combination of prescribed sexual interactions, which are systematically structured to relieve specific sexual difficulties, and psychotherapeutic sessions, which are designed to modify the intrapsychic and transactional impediments to adequate sexual functioning, is the most effective and far-reaching approach to the treatment of sexual difficulties devised to date. As such, the new sex therapy may be considered to constitute a major advance in the behavioral sciences.

The therapeutic sessions and prescribed sexual experiences act in synergism to reveal and resolve the personal and marital problems which impede the couple's free and healthy sexual expression. Thus, on the basis of his initial evaluation of the couple, the therapist formulates a provisional concept of their sexual problem, and of its psychodynamics. In prescribing the initial sexual tasks he is guided by this formulation. The couple's response to these tasks further clarifies the dynamics of their difficulty. For example, the case presented earlier was formulated as follows: The presenting problem was the husband's ejaculatory incontinence. The immediate cause of the problem was his apparent inability to experience the high surges of erotic sensation prior to orgasm. On a deeper level, his problem presumably had its roots in his unconscious hostility toward women in general, and his wife in particular, which made him ambivalent about giving her pleasure. A contributory factor, which created a pressured sexual system between the couple and reinforced the patient's premature ejaculation pattern, was his wife's fear that a sexually adequate man would abandon her for another, more desirable woman. The strategy adopted in this case, on the basis of this provisional formulation, was to attempt to modify the immediate cause of the husband's dysfunction and to circumvent the conflicts which had given rise to his problem to the extent that this was possible. Thus the initial sig. was the Semans exercise, and the couple was instructed in the implementation of this procedure. After they had conducted the prescribed experiences at home, they returned to the clinic to discuss their reactions in detail with the therapist. Usually, a wealth of psychodynamic material is evoked by these experiences. With these data the therapist can correct and refine the concept of the deeper structure of the couple's problem, and devise and prescribe additional relevant sexual tasks. Concomitantly, this psychodynamic material becomes available for psychotherapeutic intervention during the therapeutic sessions. Thus, in actual practice, although relief of the sexual problem is the prime objective of the new sex therapy, the dynamically oriented therapist invariably works with the couple on related intrapsychic and dyadic difficulties, to varying degrees.

Specifically, in the case cited above the wife's dormant anxiety, which centered on her fears of being abandoned, was mobilized by her husband's rapidly growing control over his ejaculatory reflex. She manifested this anxiety by being generally unpleasant and by her resistance to treatment, i.e., her reluctance to carry out the assigned sexual tasks. Although these resistances impeded treatment temporarily, they also provided the therapist with an opportunity to deal with this significant material during the therapeutic sessions. The wife's fears of abandonment had to be dispelled before the couple could achieve satisfactory functioning. But apart from fostering ejaculatory control, the resolution of this long-standing problem also had an extremely beneficial effect on the wife's general psychological functioning.

The Treatment Format

The treatment formats used by various sex therapy clinics and therapists have one feature in common—they all provide for the combined use of prescribed sexual experiences and psychotherapeutic sessions. Within this general framework, however, workers in this field differ considerably with respect to the specific format they employ.

Therapists who follow the Masters and Johnson format see patients daily for a period of two weeks. Other programs, including our own, see couples one to three times per week for as long as is necessary to restore and stabilize sexual functioning. Some sex therapists follow Masters and Johnson in employing mixed gender co-therapy teams. Others, including ourselves, have found this unnecessary and get very good results with well trained solo therapists of either gender. Some programs insist that one member of the therapy team be a physician, others have no such requirements. Programs also differ as to the specific tasks which they employ in treatment. However, the most significant differences among sex therapy programs arise from differences in the conceptualization of the therapeutic process, which are ultimately reflected in the conduct of the psychotherapeutic aspect of sexual treatment. Some of the clinicians who practice sex therapy have had no prior instruction in the theory of psychopathology; nor have they had clinical training in psychotherapy. They lack the theoretical conceptualization of the therapeutic process which is an essential prerequisite of clinical competence; consequently, they are forced to work empirically and to deal only with surface causes. They rely exclusively on sex education and counseling and the prescription of erotic tasks to achieve their therapeutic objectives. In sharp contrast, our own program, as well as some others, places heavy emphasis on psychotherapy. Although the sexual experiences are crucial to the success of treatment, they constitute only one aspect of the total therapeutic process. They are of value primarily when they are integrated with the psychotherapeutic sessions.

Our own program is conducted strictly within a psychodynamic conceptual framework. An attempt is made to understand the causes of the patient's problem, and to relate treatment to this formulation. Both the immediate and the deeper causes are considered, and each task and each therapeutic maneuver is based on a rational consideration of its impact on the couple's psychopathological structure. Resistances, unconscious motivations, and the pathological dynamics of the couple's relationship—all these factors are considered and dealt with in therapeutic process.

The counterpoint between the prescribed sexual interactions and the psychotherapeutic experience is exploited fully. The sexual tasks reveal individual conflicts and marital pathology far more rapidly and dramatically than do mere discussions, and this material is worked with extensively and intensively in the psychotherapeutic sessions.

Essentially, we view sex therapy as a task-centered form of crisis intervention which presents an opportunity for rapid conflict resolution. Toward this end we employ the various sexual tasks, as well as the methods of insight therapy, supportive therapy, marital therapy, and other psychiatric techniques as indicated.

We believe that the treatment format must be flexible and rational and psychodynamically oriented if it is to meet the specific needs of the diverse patient population who suffer from sexual dysfunctions. At the same time, however, it must retain the essential ingredients of sex therapy, i.e., the combined and integrated use of prescribed sexual experiences and psychotherapeutic intervention within a basic psychotherapeutic context.

This brief overview raises certain crucial questions: Can sexual dysfunction really be alleviated with any degree of permanence by such direct intervention which, essentially, is limited to modifying their surface causes without resolving the conflicts which underlie such disorders? Can sexual symptoms be treated in relative isolation from other neurotic symptoms? Can the intrapsychic conflicts which give rise to sexual symptoms be circumvented in the treatment of such symptoms? Not surprisingly, those who subscribe to traditional psychoanalytic theories predicted early on that an approach to the treatment of sexual disorders which incorporated such premises would not be effective. These questions raise the second major issue to be considered in this paper: What is the evidence for the efficacy of sex therapy?

HOW EFFECTIVE IS SEX THERAPY?

Sex therapy promises rapid and permanent relief of distressing sexual symptoms which have heretofore been regarded with therapeutic pessimism. However, many of the claims and optimistic preliminary impressions have not yet been scientifically substantiated.

The efficacy of any therapeutic modality, be it psychotherapy, drug therapy, behavior therapy, or the new approach to the treatment of sexual dysfunctions, can be established with confidence only if that modality has been tested under controlled conditions. The well designed evaluation study provides an opportunity for comparison of the outcome of a given therapeutic approach with the effects of various other treatment techniques which have some demonstrated value. It will be designed to guard against the possibility that the findings derived therefrom will be contaminated by experimenter bias, and such common error as attribution of "false positives," i.e., cures which result from the therapist's enthusiasm for, and the patient's suggestibility to, the treatment procedure under investigation. Inasmuch as studies of sex therapy conducted to date have not provided controls against such errors, our current enthusiasm for this approach is unfortunately not based on solid evidence of its effectiveness. Instead this enthusiasm stems, for the most part, from admittedly impressive findings which, however, derive from uncontrolled outcome studies.

The new therapy is not unique in this respect. None of the other methods, including psychotherapy and psychoanalysis, currently used in the treatment of sexual disorders have been adequately evaluated under controlled conditions. Consequently, claims regarding their efficacy also await scientific validation. Thus, the results of sex therapy will be discussed on the basis of preliminary impressions and the reports of uncontrolled studies, with the understanding that these may have to be revised in future, when the definitive data yielded by controlled outcome studies are published.

The discussion of outcome will consist, first, of a report of the effects of the new treatment on the sexual target symptom, and these data will be compared as far as possible with the results reportedly achieved by psychoanalysis.

The Effects of Treatment on the Sexual Target Symptom

Masters and Johnson carefully evaluated the effects of their two-week-long intensive sex therapy on the sexual symptoms of the couples they treated over a ten-year period. The results were excellent. In addition, the scientific committee was impressed by their meticulous five-year follow-up which revealed a small relapse rate. Masters and Johnson reported that with a total of 510 dysfunctional couples they attained an 80% success rate, with a relapse rate after five years of 5%.

The different dysfunctional syndromes differ to some extent with regard to their prognosis. The following are the Masters and Johnson outcome figures as reported in their book, *Human Sexual Inadequacy* (1):

Male Dysfunctions: Primary impotence—60% cured
                       Secondary impotence—74% cured
                       Premature ejaculation—98% cured
                       Ejaculatory incompetence (retarded ejaculation)—
                          78% cured
                       Total: 80% cure

Female Dysfunctions: Vaginismus—100% cure
                       Primary orgastic dysfunction—83% cure or im-
                          provement
                       Absolute orgastic dysfunction—78% cure or im-
                          provement
                       Total: The sexual symptoms of 80% of patients
                          were cured or improved after two weeks of sex
                          therapy.

While Masters and Johnson did not conduct their studies according to a controlled model, the work is unique in the size of their sample, and in the fact that they conducted five-year follow-ups. It is difficult to find comparable data on the effects of other treatment modalities, notably psychoanalysis, on sexual dysfunctions. The best outcome study in this area to date is that of John O'Connor, who studied the effects of psychoanalytically oriented psychotherapy and psychoanalysis on the sexual symptoms of patients seen at the Columbia Psychoanalytic Clinic during a period of two years. The data represent the opinions of the treating doctor regarding his patients' symptoms. With 96 patients included in the survey, the results were as follows:

Male Dysfunctions: 57% cured, 17% improved
Female Dysfunctions: 25% cured, 36% improved
                       Total: The sexual symptoms of 66% of patients
                          were improved or cured after two years of
                          psychotherapy or psychoanalysis.

The two populations, that studied by Masters and Johnson and that studied by O'Connor, are not comparable on several grounds. For one, the patients seen at the psychoanalytic clinic were suffering from various personality and neurotic disorders, while the Masters and Johnson population presumably contained many couples who were healthy in all other respects except for their sexual symptom. Nevertheless, one cannot fail to be impressed by the 80% cure rate (with only 5% relapses after five years) obtained by two weeks of treatment, versus the 66% cure rate obtained after two years of intensive insight therapy.

Our own experience at the Cornell Sex Therapy and Education Program, while by no means definitive, tends to support Masters and Johnson's contention that one can expect approximately 80% cure rate with brief, intensive, experientially oriented treatment which involves the active participation of both sexual partners. Again, however, it is too early for any definitive claims to this effect.

Effects of the Rapid Relief of Sexual Dysfunction on the Psychological Status of Patient and Partner

Apart from improvement of the sexual disability, the new techniques afford us an opportunity to observe the effects of the rapid relief of long-standing sexual disabilities on the general psychological and emotional status of the symptomatic patient and his partner, and on the quality of their relationship.

Two major conceptual models of human behavior predict that rapid symptom-focused therapy will have diametrically opposite results. On the one hand, psychoanalytic theory predicts that direct removal of a symptom, when not accompanied by concomitant resolution of the conflict which underlies that symptom, will result in the psychological deterioration of the patient and/or the formation of substitute symptoms which serve the psychological needs hitherto served by the "cured" symptom.

In contrast, learning theory considers the symptom to *be* the disorder, and discounts the possibility that its removal will engender the formation of substitute symptoms. On the contrary, it is predicted that the patient's consequent sense of mastery will result in enhanced self-esteem and a decrease in anxiety. This generalization of improvement to other aspects of the patient's functioning has been described as the "ripple effect."

In our own clinical experience we have observed that the rapid treatment of sexual problems may affect the patient's overall functioning in one of three ways: there may be no change in his psychic status; there may be a positive change; or negative changes in his psychic status may occur as a result of treatment. In the great majority of cases, no permanent significant changes in the patient's psychic status seem to occur as a result of the successful rapid treatment of his sexual dysfunction. In rare instances, however, profound positive changes, as well as profound negative changes are seen.

While most patients tend to respond to the rapid treatment of sexual symptoms as predicted by learning theory, i.e., without the development of substitute symptoms, clinical experience has also yielded evidence in support of the psychoanalytic position which states that sexual dysfunctions have their genesis in the patient's unconscious unresolved conflicts, and further hypothesizes that sexual symptoms have a symbolic meaning and serve a defensive function. The mobilization of anticipatory anxiety prior to symptomatic improvement, which is a very common phenomenon, and the adverse reactions to treatment which are observed at this stage, albeit in rare instances, provide compelling evidence in support of the validity (but not the universality) of this theoretical formulation.

Almost invariably, patients manifest a good deal of anxiety and resistance just before their symptom yields to treatment. In fact, this reaction is so predictable that the trainees at our clinic anticipate the third and fourth treatment sessions, at which point the anxiety-resistance phenomenon usually occurs, with some trepidation. These feelings of trepidation are not without justification. In fact, the way in which the anxiety aroused by the prospect of relinquishing sexual dysfunction is handled largely determines the outcome of treatment. Clinical competence at this crucial stage can make the difference between a favorable outcome and treatment which is interrupted prematurely and/or reaches a stalemate.

According to psychoanalytic theory, relinquishing a painful neurotic symptom arouses anticipatory anxiety because that symptom once served as an important defense against the emergence of dangerous impulses and wishes, which were adaptive during the patient's childhood. This material now lies outside the patient's conscious awareness. Nevertheless, acute anxiety is experienced when the loss of the old defense, i.e., the symptom, appears to be imminent, to the degree that some transient substitute symptoms may develop during this period.

Psychoanalysis and psychoanalytically-oriented treatment modalities seek, first and foremost, to clarify the nature of the patient's conflict, for only then can the defensive function of the symptom be fully understood. To illustrate, if it becomes apparent in the course of treatment that the patient's impotence is based on the persistence of an unconscious sexual attachment to his mother, and the concomitant existence of the unconscious belief that such feelings are extremely dangerous, the meaning of his symptom becomes self-evident. Specifically, in such cases impotence serves as a defense against the emergence into consciousness of "dangerous" incestuous wishes. Once the patient senses that the cure of his impotence is imminent, that he will soon be capable of normal sexual functioning, the infantile sexual aims which had been warded off are activated, and there is a concomitant mobilization of the fears which were once associated with these infantile sexual aims. In short, unconsciously, the patient believes that sexual intercourse is connected with an intense danger which, according to classical analytic theory, is believed to take the form of castration. In essence, this is the source of his anticipatory anxiety. In psychoanalysis this type of material is discussed, and an attempt is made to resolve the patient's basic oedipal conflict.

In sex therapy the therapist does not usually make such interpretations, but may point out to the patient that he is behaving as though he anticipated some punishment if he should have intercourse. In some instances the childhood roots of such fears and the former importance to the patient of his defenses are also discussed. However, the therapist does not rely solely on interpretation of unconscious material but usually attempts to deal with this kind of anxiety by actively confronting the patient with the irrational nature of his fears, and reassuring him that his ability to have intercourse will not result in injury. These rather simple and direct tactics are frequently effective in helping the patient rapidly to resolve the anxiety engendered by his improvement and imminent cure. At times, however, these simple supportive strategies are not sufficiently effective to permit treatment to proceed in the face of the patient's anticipatory anxiety. In that event, the therapist may attempt to resolve the deeper issues which underlie the patient's response by identifying and clarifying the genetic roots of his unconscious fears and the defenses he has employed against the emergence of feared impulses into conscious awareness in accordance with the principles of psychoanalytic treatment.

As mentioned above, usually, as soon as the symptom is cured and the patient finds that the anticipated injury does not occur, his anxiety tends to disappear rapidly and permanently. However, in the psychologically fragile patient, anticipatory anxiety represents a more serious hazard in that it poses a potential threat to his ability to maintain his psychic integrity. Consequently, it is at this point, immediately prior to the achievement of symptomatic relief, that adverse reactions to treatment are most likely to occur.

Thus, as a general rule, the patient manifests adverse reactions to treatment before his symptom has been cured. Occasionally, however, adverse reactions emerge after relief of the symptom enables the patient to function well sexually, often for the first time in his life. For example, this is not uncommon among premature ejaculators, who may experience transient episodes of impotence following the rapid attainment of ejaculatory control.

Effects of the Rapid Relief of Sexual Dysfunction on the Marital Relationship

The sudden attainment of sexual adequacy seldom leaves the partner unaffected. The effects of sex therapy on the psychologic status of the partner of the symptomatic spouse also range from highly beneficial to dangerously disruptive. It is most beneficial where treatment affords an opportunity for effective psychotherapeutic intervention in the problems of both spouses.

As is true of the symptomatic patient and his spouse, the brief treatment of sexual problems may have no discernible effect on the marital relationship; it may have a positive effect; or it may affect the relationship adversely.

There is a difference, however, in the frequency with which these specific effects occur. As stated earlier, as a general rule, rapid relief of sexual dysfunctions has little discernible permanent effects on the psychological status of the individual patient or his partner. In contrast, successful sex therapy usually has a decidedly beneficial effect on the marital relationship.

Sex therapy usually entails changing the insecure, guilt-provoking, and constrictive sexual system which the couple has created for themselves. They must learn to be open, to trust, to communicate on a more authentic level, at least in their sexual transactions, if they are to be able to abandon themselves to their sexual feelings when they are with each other. The benefits of this new openness often generalize outside of the bedroom, with a salutary effect on the relationship as a whole. Unfortunately, this is not always the case, and a couple may find that, although they now enjoy an excellent sexual relationship, their other difficulties and hostilities continue to plague them.

Sometimes the changes entailed in the sex therapy process are threatening to the relationship. In most cases the crisis is temporary and ultimately salutary. In rare cases, sex therapy reveals serious marital difficulties which cannot easily be resolved.

Adverse Reaction to the Rapid Treatment of Sexual Disorders

Psychiatric crises occur when the individual is overwhelmed by anxiety or rage and concomitant feelings of low self-esteem, helplessness, and despair. The rapid treatment of sexual disorders may, in rare instances, precipitate such psychiatric casualties.

Sometimes these adverse reactions occur in the symptomatic patient; at other times, the partner is the victim. When the sexual dysfunction serves an important defensive function in a psychologically fragile patient, the anticipatory anxiety which often occurs prior to symptomatic improvement presents a hazard to the maintenance of psychological integrity. When the sexual symptom serves as a defense for the partner, then he or she may react with panic to the patient's rapid improvement.

Adverse reactions may result not only from the threat of the removal of a defensive sexual symptom, but from the anxiety which may be evoked by the very process of sexual therapy. During the course of treatment, couples must discuss previously hidden feelings and wishes which were never disclosed before; they must touch each other in intimate ways which had always been forbidden; and they must allow themselves to experience sensuous, sexual, and intimate feelings which they have avoided all their lives. Old defenses against emotion and openness must be relinquished. Such new and previously avoided experiences are apt to engender severe anxiety and anticipation of humiliation and rejection. It is incumbent upon the therapist to remain alert to the potentially disruptive emotions evoked by his or her directions and suggestions, and to deal with these actively and supportively. However, in the extremely fragile patient, even the most skillful and sensitive psychotherapeutic management cannot prevent an occasional adversive reaction to these threatening new experiences.

In summary, on the basis of pilot studies and the clinical data accumulated to date at various clinics, it can be stated that the new rapid treatment of sexual dysfunction seems to produce excellent results in terms of relieving the specific sexual sumptoms of the great majority of patients. Certainly this approach merits the attention of the investigator. Furthermore, on the basis of comparing the outcome statistics of alternative treatment methods, one may even venture to claim, until evidence to the contrary is published, that sex therapy constitutes the treatment of choice for the sexually dysfunctional patient who is free of major psychopathology and who is involved in a stable and affectionate relationship with his sexual partner. Successful treatment of the patient's sexual dysfunction does not necessarily mean that a concomitant improvement in his psychological and emotional status will occur. Although the effects of the new treatment seem to be impressive for the most part, its benefits are limited to the patient's sexual functioning. There are exceptions. For example, when sexual conflicts are central to the patient's psychic economy, the alleviation of the sexual disorder may result in a dramatic improvement in overall functioning. And, similarly, although sex therapy usually improves a couple's communication and intimacy to some degree, the quality of their marital relationship may be greatly enhanced as a result of treatment if the couple's sexual difficulties have been the sole cause of marital discord. In brief, the new sex therapy seems to constitute a major advance in our understanding and treatment of the difficulties which impair sexual functioning. It is not a panacea; it cannot cure a neurosis, or a sick marriage, or improve the quality of life.

DOES THE APPARENT SUCCESS OF SEX THERAPY INVALIDATE PSYCHOANALYSIS?

Yes. But only if one adheres strictly to a monocausal view of psychopathology. If the psychoanalytic position maintains that unconscious conflicts which derive from childhood maladaptations are the *only* cause of sexual disorders, it is seriously undermined by a treatment method which is successful in relieving sexual symptoms without resolving deep unconscious conflicts. If psychoanalysis insists on the view that *only* insight into and resolution of unconscious conflict can lead to the permanent remission of psychopathologic symptoms, then the success of the sumptom-focused sex therapy would threaten to invalidate psychoanalysis.

Fortunately, however, psychoanalysis rests on firmer or more flexible ground. The survival of psychoanalysis depends on its accommodation to a multidetermined model of pathogenesis. Deep unconscious conflicts which derive from childhood are of course very important causes of sexual symptoms and of other disorders as well. However, they are not the only causes. More immediate anxieties and learned reactions may also produce sexual and other symptoms. In addition, making conscious the previously unconscious, which is the major strategy of psychoanalysis, is an important but *not* unique way of modifying human behavior. Experiential methods, behavioral therapy, and transactional techniques are also highly effective in bringing about therapeutic changes. However, the symptom-focused methods seem more useful for changing isolated symptoms, while insight methods seem more suitable when broader therapeutic changes are indicated.

Analysis and sex therapy are not in opposition. They intervene at different levels and are indicated for different problems. Sexual dysfunctions can be the product not only of deep unconscious conflict and profoundly rooted disturbances in the marital relationship, but also of surface anxieties such as the simple fear of failure to perform. Psychoanalysis has addressed itself solely to the former, and has ignored the latter. On the other hand sex therapy, when it is not practiced within a psychodynamic context, runs the danger of ignoring the deeper roots of a couple's sexual problem and becoming mechanical by focusing only on the surface or immediate antecedents. Optimally, sex therapy works both dynamically and experientially in counterpoint. The two approaches do not represent a dichotomy. The prescribed sexual experiences evoke sensitive material, which is then dealt with in an analytic manner during the sessions. The couple's experience of previously avoided feelings and actions evokes insights and conversely, the insights gained during the sessions foster the experiencing of new and freer modes of sexual expression. Thus sex therapy without analytic orientation is limited and sterile, and a psychodynamic viewpoint enriches it and extends its scope. And perhaps analysis can also gain from sex therapy. New experiences and improved communications can be a powerful stimulus to promote insight into previously unconscious and repressed material. Resistances tend to melt in the face of rationally prescribed transactions. Also, analysis might profitably free itself from its exclusive concern with great depth. The roots of problems do not always run so deep and the optimal focus of intervention does not always involve probing into the foundations of the patient's psyche. Immediately operating factors are also potent psychopathogenic elements in many disorders. These are frequently overlooked in psychoanalytic treatment.

The behavioral and experiential methods of sex therapy do not displace psychoanalysis. Rather they place at our disposal additional and alternative strategies which can extend our therapeutic spectrum.

REFERENCES

Kaplan, H. S. *The new sex therapy*. New York: Brunner/Mazel, 1974.

Masters, W. H. & Johnson, V. E. Human sexual inadequacy. Boston: Little, Brown, 1970.

O'Connor, J. & Stern, L. O. Results of treatment in functioning sexual disorders. *New York State Journal of Medicine*, 72:15, 1927–1934, August 1972.

CHAPTER 39

Ethical Considerations in Sex Therapy

Thea Snyder Lowry
Thomas P. Lowry

Sex therapy has for its goal the reversal of such problems as premature ejaculation, impotence, and ejaculatory incompetence in males; vaginismus, anorgasmia, and dyspareunia in females; sexual aversion in either sex; differing levels of sexual interest in a couple; and other concerns that patients may identify as undesirable when present. Although its major focus is the relief of the presenting symptom, responsible sex therapy usually also includes attention to patients' self-esteem, the marriage relationship, communication skills, and the partners' personal and mutual growth.

Beginning with Semans and the monumental work of Masters and Johnson, sex therapy is no longer subject to bystanders' hints and folklore. Now there are literally hundreds of sex therapy centers, at least two consortia of medical school sex therapy programs, and in 1973 a corporation (Male Potency Centers of America) was arranging regional franchises. Inevitably in all this proliferation, there are self-appointed experts and evangelical sexual messiahs, whose motivations and credentials vary widely, but who seem to share the common features of self-confidence, modest training, and low interest in the statistics of cure rates or long term follow-up studies. This too is probably inevitable considering the current resurgence of anti-intellectualism and the increased reliance upon experimental therapy techniques such as encounter groups, instant intimacy, Z therapy, primal scream, and so forth, but just being able to "relate" to the problem may not be enough for the patient's welfare.

PSYCHOLOGICAL INTIMACY AND TRANSFERENCE

The ethical considerations in sex therapy will be discussed in two contexts: a universal problem (with two facets) and the problems relating to specific dysfunctions.

The universal problem is intimacy, both psychological and physical,

Reprinted by permission from the author and the publisher of *Journal of Marriage and Family Counseling,* July 1975.

between therapist and patient. Psychological intimacy is in some ways a necessary and inescapable aspect of all psychotherapy. Shearer's valuable discussion of history taking in sex therapy states:

> As the interview progresses, the patient should feel able to be increasingly vulnerable to the therapist, in terms of accepting the therapeutic recommendations. If, after a reasonable time, the patient is not becoming increasingly vulnerable, something is amiss. Why should the patient guard his flank from the person he sought out to help him with his problems? The questions need to be understood and dealt with by the therapist. The greatest pitfall in the history is not recognizing the non-vulnerable patient and not dealing with the situation properly (Shearer, 1973).

Clearly the patient must reveal something of himself, or the therapist's efforts will be crippled by inadequate facts. Yet, as is true in all skills requiring discretion and judgement, there are degrees. The surgeon cuts, but only as deeply as necessary; so, also in eliciting a psychosexual history.

Therapists should know their business well enough so that they ask all the questions necessary, but no more. Only questions which surface the patient's sexual value system, clarify the origin and evolution of the symptom, and demonstrate the practitioner's skill, understanding, and objectivity are necessary questions. Pursuing a line of inquiry which has even a hint of personal curiosity or voyeurism is unnecessary and demeaning. Equally undesirable are "fishing expeditions" in interviewing, either by use of a rigid questionnaire or by reliance upon free association. Phrasing questions in a style foreign to the patient's vocabulary, or allowing either oneself or one's patient to sidestep pertinent questions dealing with specific sexual behaviors (which is necessary to understand in order to help the patient get his goal) are other ways to forfeit credibility. The questions should yield tactically useful information and should establish the therapist as trustworthy and knowledgeable. Skillful, goal-directed psychosexual history taking is usually not provided by most training programs, nor is it adequately conceptualized in current texts.

Patients' fantasies are especially sensitive areas. For many persons, their daydreams, secret erotogenic stories, and mental images are more carefully guarded than information about overt behaviors. Yet a history which neglects fantasy is incomplete. Quite logically, the patient may fear that the sharing of his secret will cause it to lose its magical potency; if there is hesitation in the patient's response to questions about fantasy, the therapist may tactfully add, "I don't need to hear all the details, just the relationships between the participants." It is sufficient to comprehend a patient's imaginary interest in being dominated, for instance; the exact scenario may be of little further value.

Another aspect of psychological intimacy long discussed in psychiatry is transference, in which the patient relates to the therapist emotionally in a manner which parallels the patient's relationship with other significant figures in his or her life. Unfortunately, most patients with psychosexual concerns have their symptoms in the context of a relationship with a significant other, and any technique which diverts emotional energy away from that relationship is probably counter-productive; we certainly concur with Carl Whitaker's assertion that the therapist who sees only one spouse in a distressed marriage contributes directly to divorce. The task of the therapist is to promote the relationship between the spouses, not one between one spouse and the therapist. A useful approach for accomplishing this is to treat both spouses together with a male and female therapist present, each the advocate, interpreter, and critic for the same sex client. This four person therapy format seems to promote rapid therapeutic change, keep the emotional bonding within the marriage, and to avoid the pitfalls of a person of one sex attempting to interpret the sexuality of a person of the opposite sex. In situations where the use of a co-therapist is not practical, the next best technique is probably one in which a male therapist says, for instance, "I have been told by other women that . . ."

SURROGATES

A patient with sexual difficulties who is unmarried or has difficulty making friends may have no partner to bring to treatment. A frequently used method is the provision of surrogate or replacement partners, a concept which has now evolved to include surrogates in private practice who participate in the treatment by providing sexual opportunities and then later consulting with the psychological counselor.

While the use of surrogates appears to have been helpful in many situations, two other approaches might also be considered for treatment of the partnerless patient. The first is the case of a socially inept person who cannot make friends. A man who cannot say "Hello" effectively or invite a woman to join him for a cup of coffee is not likely to be able to manage the intricacies of a sustained sexual liaison. A paid partner may only postpone his acquring the skills necessary for social and emotional maturity. Assertion training and socialization therapy programs described by Salter, Ellis, and Marquis might be more relevant interventions for the painfully shy misfit than surrogate therapy.

The second situation is that of the obsessive impotent male with rigid standards. We recently saw a 64-year-old upper-middle-class bachelor with a decade of worsening psychogenic impotence. He had recently been treated by a psychologist-surrogate team; by the third session, his feelings of depression, nausea, and sexual aversion were so intense that he terminated therapy. He told us that he was preoccupied during each session with such thoughts as, "I'm just case number thirty-four. She's only in this for the money. If it doesn't work it won't prove anything. This isn't like a social situation." His self-fulfilling prophecies of failure and embarrassment at finding himself in a situation which was inadmissible in his value system completely overcame the potential sexual opportunity with the female surrogate. Giving this man the courage to locate a voluntary partner and using a relationship format would seem to be a more productive counseling avenue.

Thus the problem of psychological intimacy in sex therapy may best be handled by enhancing the relationship that the patient has with his or her natural sex partner, decreasing emotional involvement with the therapist, and allowing the patient to retain a significant portion of fantasy life inviolate. The trust and vulnerability needed for effective psychotherapy are provided by skilled, incisive history gathering, coupled with a benign but encouraging professional distance, all consonant with the patient's personal, moral, and religious psychosexual value system.

PHYSICAL INTIMACY WITH CLIENTS

The second aspect for ethical consideration in sex therapy is physical intimacy. At least three forms are identified: the standard, chaperoned, diagnosis-focussed physical examination; examinations emphasizing sexuality (including "sexological" examinations); and overt sexual behavior (petting, intercourse) between therapist and patient.

The usual physical examination should present no problem, as the format and style are neither provocative nor is there a goal of sexual interaction. Performed correctly, a routine physical examination (including pelvic and prostatic) should be painless, brief, reassuring, and devoid of behavior which could be interpreted as seductive.

Sexuality examinations take several forms. First are those prescribed for couples who seem unable to perceive their bodies accurately, despite being shown anatomical drawings and attempting to show one another their unclothed selves in privacy in a well-lighted "learning" environment. Such couples (in the format used by Masters and Johnson and by us) are given a "geography lesson" in the standard examination room, with both therapists and both spouses present. All relevant body parts are identified and explained, until both partners seem to be crystal clear about anatomy.

Other centers utilize a "sexological" examination more or less routinely. In the examination room, in addition to identification of various structures, the patients are asked to note that their perceptions of one body area (especially genitally) differ from their perceptions of other areas. One advocate of this approach (a male gynecologist), uses a cotton applicator to touch the patient, so that any sexual sensation she perceives is attributed not to the therapist but to an agent at least one step removed from the examiner. This system allows the pleasurable sensations derived from direct touch to be associated only with the appropriate sexual partner. These examinations often include instruction in increasing the patient's pelvic muscle perception and control, especially through the introduction of Kegel exercises.

A third type of "sexological examination" is recommended by a wellknown therapy center. In this approach the male therapist stimulates the wife to sexual excitement, calling her attention to vaginal lubrication, pleasurable sensations, and so forth, meanwhile teaching the husband, who is present during part of the examination. Some patients reportedly experienced orgasm in the examining room, much to their surprise. The success rates of this center are not published, so it is difficult to assess the efficacy of their method.

OVERT SEXUAL ACTIVITY WITH CLIENTS

Overt sexual behavior between therapist and patient is the third category of physical intimacy which may be an ethical concern. It will perhaps astound some therapists that this issue should even be addressed; the ethical codes of 3000 years have explicitly prohibited doctor-patient sex. However, at least two recent medical publications have recommended such activities and the issue must be faced.

In the first major assessment of the problem, Kardener (1973) mailed questionnaires to 1,000 male Los Angeles physicians, asking for anonymous responses about their behavior with patients, including activities "... primarily to arouse or satisfy sexual desire." Four-hundred-sixty physicians responded. Seventy-five percent were between the ages of 40 and 60. Eighty-six percent were currently married. About one third of the respondents occasionally or frequently engaged in non-erotic hugging, kissing, or affectionate touching of their patients. The specialists most likely to provide this response were internists and general practitioners. Regarding specifically erotic behavior, there were some differences between specialities; 14% of the responding surgeons stated that erotic behavior might occasionally or frequently be beneficial to the patient. Ninety-five percent of 358 respondents answering the question averred that they had never had intercourse with a patient, four percent had "rarely," and one percent said that they did so "frequently."

In another study (Wagner, 1972), of freshmen medical students, 25% reported that intimacies with patients might be acceptable if the doctor was "genuine" and "authentic." Thus sex between doctors and patients is no longer viewed as a question of "Never!" but of "Why not?"

One reason "why not" is the psychological asymmetry in the usual doctor-patient relationship. The physician symbolizes a benevolent and honorable parent; the patient, a trusting child. When the two become lovers, the relationship then represents (in the view of T. S. Lowry) a symbolic violation of the incest taboo—humankind's oldest and most respected limitation on behavior. Kardener (1973) points out that when the "parent" abandons that role, the patient becomes psychologically orphaned; if a physician stops being a care-taker and becomes a lover, the loss is serious, since good lovers are much easier to find than good care-takers.

Another set of reasons "why not" is suggested by the philosopher Marx Conkling (1973). If the therapist has sexual interaction with his patient and accepts a fee, the relationship is social, not professional. If the therapist has sexual pleasure from the encounter, is he doing it for himself, or for the patient? If the therapist refrains from pleasure in the encounter, he has two choices: he can remain emotionally neutral and non-orgasmic and run the risk of the patient (usually female) thinking "He cannot value me as a person, he's only working on me," or he can seem to appear involved (although faking an ejaculation might be quite a feat) and pretend sexual pleasure, thereby making the proceedings inauthentic, and once again, much like the usual prostitute-client encounter. If the therapist finds that attractive patients need his "reassurance" more, he should question his motives to make sure that he provides sexual services to the elderly, ugly, to the crippled, to the incontinent, to the same sex, and to all races, creeds, and religions. We are not aware of a direct intervention sex therapist who meets these criteria.

In short, we believe it useful for a therapist (preferably of the same sex) to give "permission" and gender-specific information to the client, including the identification of genital structures if that is a problem, and that it is inappropriate and indefensible to provide intentional sexual stimulation.

TREATMENT OF SPECIFIC PSYCHOSEXUAL DISORDERS

In discussing treatment, we make two assumptions: first, ethical treatment is that method shown to be most effective and least costly; second, treatment must deal with both the relationship and the sexual symptom.

In psychotherapy, there are varying opinions about the most effective therapy approaches. From our years of work in the field of psychosexual dysfunction, our training of other professionals, and our reviews of the literature, it is our conclusion that the therapies described here are the most effective known. We look forward to the data of the proponents of alternative treatment methods.

Premature ejaculation is the commonest male problem. The most efficacious treatment is the squeeze technique as used by Masters and Johnson. Widespread and quite understandable misreadings of *Human Sexual Inadequacy* (Masters & Johnson, 1961) by some practitioners and alternative methods (such as prolonged penile compression, relaxation therapy, and recommendations of very frequent intercourse) have led to disillusionment and exacerbated dysfunction, in our experience. Applied correctly, with adequate attention to the psychology of the woman's role, the Masters and Johnson squeeze technique appears to surpass other documented approaches; further research should clarify the relative efficacy of other rational techniques, such as the Semans start-and-stop technique, and its derivative, the Zilbergeld eight-step method.

Impotence is the most difficult male dysfunction to treat, because it tends to appear in men who are obsessive and rigid, or fearful and worrisome. When such men develop erective failure, a powerful downward spiral of fear and self-depreciation begins. Usually the client hopes for a medical explanation, but after eliminating iatrogenic medication-based impotence (not rare), diabetes (relatively uncommon), and low plasma testoserone (quite rare), the usual cause is found to be psychological.

Treatment methods: about 80 percent of short-duration uncomplicated cases of reactive impotence may respond to affirmative suggestions and placebos, usually hormone injections. When effective, such methods offer a simple and inexpensive route to restored function (Fellman, 1973).

In the therapy experience of one of us (T. P. Lowry) with Masters and Johnson, most impotent males had already undergone years of psychotherapy, hormones, vitamins, and encouragement. Each failure to respond to treatment had deepened the client's despondency and he needed extremely directive and supportive measures to break repetitive patterns. Our experience agrees with Cooper (1971), in that the St. Louis dual-sex-therapy team model is, so far, the most effective approach to long-term impotence problems. This form of counseling is both difficult to provide and to teach others.

In our current state of knowledge, the team treatment attention-refocussing Masters and Johnson approach, including emphasis on rechanneling anger and "throwing away" erections, seems to be the most helpful approach for men with both primary and chronic erective insecurity.

Vaginismus is involuntary spasm of the vaginal muscles. The approach described by Masters and Johnson (the daily use of vaginal dilators, under the direction of a dual-sex-therapy team, in which the woman therapist is both strongly supportive and somewhat confrontive) seems to continue to be the most helpful, with a 100 percent cure rate. Some therapists working in the field have modified the method insofar as substituting either plastic disposable hypodermic syringe cases, which are manufactured in various diameters and lengths; or having the woman independently acquire a number of paraffin candles she has personally selected, in graduated sizes ranging from birthday candle size to about plumber's candle size, and she is encouraged to "make friends" with them, with her husband's help. This method has the dual advantage of low cost and the fact the patient may keep forever her own dilators. English investigators at the Tavistock Clinic have reported on a series of 700 virgin wives, amply confirming this experience.

Dyspareunia needs to be approached in a problem-solving manner; it is quite likely that pain reflects a physical cause. If pain stems from insufficient lubrication due to poor sexual communication, however, or because of the tension and apprehension the woman experiences when she is approached, a sensitive and helpful female therapist is able to elicit a fearful patient's expectations and most quickly reassure the wife after allowing her full expression of her negative feelings. It is our theoretical construction that females "receive permission to be sexual beings" from their mothers, and acquire validation of their role from fathers (and the opposite is true for males). Thus the woman therapist provides a type of knowledge and emotional support for the wife which no male therapist can. The work of Tunnadine, also at Tavistock, powerfully confirms these observations.

Secondary anorgasmia may reflect either cause or effect of a disappointing marriage relationship. In either case, the most effective treatment centers use Masters and Johnson's approach, with a female therapist who assists the wife in identifying what she needs in order to have function restored and a male therapist who coaches the husband in providing the emotional feedback needed to change the marital balance to healthy mutuality.

Primary anorgasmia seems to have the highest therapeutic success rate (orgasm experienced by about 91 percent of clients during treatment) in the goal-oriented group method developed in the San Francisco Bay Area by a consortium of women during the past two years. The groups consist of four to seven preorgasmic (preferred term) women, who may be single, married, heterosexual, or homosexual; there are two meetings per week for five weeks. The group experience is one of caring and sharing, and the leaders facilitate growth by homework assignments, some personal revelation, use of a movie and feminist readings, and some consciousness-raising and gestalt techniques. During the acute treatment phase the women are encouraged to continue their usual sexual activities with partners, "as it is too soon to try to put it all together."

Research and follow-up have been carried out by Lonnie Barbach (1975), a woman psychologist whose coordinating and training efforts have maintained continuity and uniformity. The dual-sex team approach to couple counseling of primary anorgasmia has a success rate of 83 percent, and seems the treatment of choice where the relationship is bad.

We have tried to emphasize here that ethical treatment of sexual dysfunction is that mode which gets the clients to their goal as quickly, inexpensively, and effectively as possible, while keeping in mind the relationship in which the dysfunction was manifest. An essential element in such ethical behavior is that the purpose of therapy is to obtain the patient's goal, not the therapist's. We have experienced great difficulty in training psychiatrists (especially those of psychoanalytic persuasion), who want to explore at length all the possible byways and unconscious backgrounds of symptoms, which usually become irrelevant after the symptoms disappear.

While this problem may seem bizarre to non-psychiatric therapists it is not at all unusual in our experience. We recently saw a couple, a physician and his wife. He had grown restless and bored in the marriage; the therapist he consulted insisted on spending the first ten months of the psychotherapy exploring how the husband felt about the therapist! Meanwhile, the couple separated, each took lovers, and the husband, who tends to be ambivalent, introspective, and withdrawn anyway, drew further into his shell. The situation changed when his wife entered a woman's group to deal with her own orgasmic incapacity and rediscovered her potential for self-responsibility and affirmative action. This took the form of, "I want you and I want our marriage, and you and I are going to get some therapy *together*." They did.

Preliminary steps in defining ethical behavior in sex therapy have been taken by the American Association of Sex Educators and Counselors, who have published a monograph outlining what they believe to be appropriate training for professionals who will provide sex therapy. Legal aspects of sexual therapies are discussed carefully by Perr (1975). EAST, a consortium of East Coast medical school sex therapists, plans publication of ethical standards and therapist qualification recommendations.

We believe it is time for the formation of a task force on ethics in sex therapy. Such a group should include professionals in psychology, family therapy, psychiatry, marriage counseling, urology, gynecology, women's self-help groups, and educators. It should draw upon the experience of those clinicians and researchers whose work can stand public scrutiny, in terms of both effectiveness and lasting results. The guidance of such a task force could be helpful to providers of grant money, patients seeking treatment, counselors seeking ethical therapists to refer to, malpractice insurance carriers, and licensing bodies who must distinguish "innovative" from "unethical" in this rapidly evolving field.

REFERENCES

Barbach, L. *For yourself: The fulfillment of female sexuality*. New York: Doubleday, 1975.

Conkling, M. Personal communication, 1973.

Cooper, A. J. Treatment of male potency disorders: the present status. *Psychosomatics*, 1971, *12*, 235.

Ellis, A. *The art and science of love*. New York: Stuart, 1960.

Fellman, S. L. *Medical World News*, 1973.

Kardener, S. H. Sex between doctor and patient. Unpublished manuscript, 1973.

Kardener, S. H., Fuller, M., & Mensh, I. N. A survey of physicians' attitudes and practices regarding erotic and non-erotic contact with patients. *American Journal of Psychiatry*, 1973, *130*, 1077.

Masters, W. H. & Johnson, V. E. *Human sexual inadequacy*. Boston: Little, Brown, 1961.

Perr, I. N. Legal aspects of sexual therapies. *Journal of Legal Medicine*, 1975, *3*, 23.

Semans, J. H. Premature ejaculation: a new approach. *Southern Medical Journal*, 1956, *49*, 353.

Shearer, M. Unpublished manuscript, 1973.

Wagner, N. Ethical concerns of medical students. Presented at the 1972 Western Workshop of the Center for the Study of Sex Education in Medicine, Santa Barbara, CA.

Professional Issues and Ethics

One of the principal reasons which makes the eradication of quackery forever impossible is to be found in the fact which finds expression in the proverb "Stupidity is a hardy perennial."

WILHELM EBSTEIN

In the field of marriage and family counseling many professional issues and ethical problems exist which deserve underscoring and discussion, if professionally qualified marriage and family counselors are to supplant "quacks" in the field. These issues must be explicitly dealt with and clarified for the sake of the profession and the public who uses these professional services.

Professional marriage and family counseling has finally "come of age." In order to gain some historical perspective on this growing profession, Emily Mudd and Ray Fowler have presented in Chapter 40 a two-part chapter which provides a history of the national organization.

In Chapter 41, the American Association of Marriage and Family Counselors' Code of Professional Ethics is presented. This is the document that is expected to guide the professional marriage and family counselor.

Dr. Richard Kerckhoff, in Chapter 42, discusses the profession of marriage counseling as viewed by members of four allied professions: clergymen, physicians, social workers, and attorneys. In this study in the sociology of occupations, Dr. Kerckhoff deals with several related questions: What do members of these professions think about marriage counseling? What relationship do they see between marriage counseling and their own professions? In what ways do they react as members of interest groups? One finding was that members of each of these professions chose their own profession as best equipped to do marriage counseling.

In Chapter 43, William C. Nichols, Jr. provides an extensive discussion of legislative considerations regarding marriage and family counseling. He discusses the relevant laws in various states and discusses a model law as well as practical suggestions for those professionals in states where such a law regulating marriage and family counselors have not yet been passed.

Dr. Ben N. Ard, Jr., in Chapter 44, discusses providing clinical supervision for marriage counselors, specifically giving a model for supervisor and supervisee. This is one professional's conception, however, and the interested reader is also referred to Appendix 2 on The Approved Supervisor, which outlines the AAMFC policies on this matter.

CHAPTER 40

The AAMC and The AAMFC:
Nearly Forty Years of
Form and Function

Emily H. Mudd and C. Ray Fowler

This article is divided into two sections. Section A entitled "AAMC: The First Twenty-Five Years, 1942–1967," is the work of Emily H. Mudd, Professor Emeritus of Family Study in Psychiatry and Director of Marriage Council of Philadelphia: 1933–1966. It was especially prepared by Dr. Mudd for the celebration of the twenty-fifth anniversary of the founding of the Association. Section B, entitled "The Association Enters Adulthood," is authored by C. Ray Fowler, Executive Director, AAMFC. In it, Dr. Fowler brings up to date the history of the AAMFC since 1967.

SECTION A – AAMC: THE FIRST TWENTY-FIVE YEARS, 1942–1967

This short summary will describe the origin, growth, and functioning over a twenty-five year period of a relatively new national, clinically-oriented organization—The American Association of Marriage Counselors. The purpose of the Association is to foster the exchange of pertinent information, and promote and maintain standards at a professional level in a new field of clinical specialization. Its special focus is upon the interpersonal relationships between men and women, and how these may be constructive, mutually supportive, and a source of strength to the family group. This approach is useful within the practice of the recognized "helping" professions: medicine, psychology, social work, law, the ministry, and teaching.

Sources of information consist of the written records of committee and annual meetings, correspondence, and the recorded recollections of the charter members. Many of these documents were utilized in the statement entitled "The American Association of Marriage Counselors," prepared in 1957 by Lester Dearborn and others, which serves as an appendix

Reprinted with permission of the author and the publisher from *American Association of Marriage Counselors: The First 25 Years*. Dallas: American Association of Marriage Counselors, 1967.

to the volume *Marriage Counseling, A Casebook* (Association Press, 1958). These materials, together with subsequent annual reports and documents prepared by Dr. and Mrs. David Mace, executive directors of the association during the years 1960–67, have provided the base on which this survey rests.

The experience of studying this material quickened the writer's appreciation of the gap between the written reports, calmly recording what is now a *fait accompli*, and the emotionally laden interchanges so familiar to all A.A.M.C. members that often accompanied its evolution. But after all, what other kind of interchange could realistically be expected of strong-minded individualists, in an interdisciplinary association dedicated to new and pioneering approaches to old problems?

The reader unfamiliar with this story cannot hope to catch these subtle nuances. But for those who have been part of the story's unfolding, as for the writer, memories will be reactivated and the voices of friends and associates, audible now only to the inner ear, will restore the rich overtones and undertones, rounding out the inevitable shortcomings of this necessarily brief factual record.

MATTERS OF FACT—THE WAY AND THE HOW

The American Association of Marriage Counselors developed out of the confluence of at least two streams of activity and interest.

One was a committee organized by Dr. Robert L. Dickinson on "Socio-Sexual Relations of Men and Women," which met irregularly in New York City to exchange data and information. It had a strong core of medical members but included others, such as Mrs. Marion Bassett, who was a particularly active member of it.

Concurrently with the exploration of this group, some members of the Groves Conference (originated by Dr. Ernest Groves) were also moving toward action. As early as 1934 and again in 1939, Mr. Lester Dearborn had discussed with Mrs. Stuart (now Dr. Emily) Mudd and Dr. Abraham Stone the formation of a group "for the purpose of establishing standards, exchanging information, and helping in the development of interest in marriage counseling." In 1939, as a step in this direction, Dr. Groves appointed a Committee on the Protection of Professional Standards.

Dr. Robert W. Laidlaw and Mr. Dearborn, members of both groups, invited the following persons to meet with them in New York on June 20, 1942: Dr. Robert L. Dickinson, Dr. and Mrs. Ernest R. Groves, Mrs. Stuart Mudd, Dr. Valeria Parker, and Dr. Abraham Stone. A second meeting was held with a small, carefully expanded invitation list in October of that year. On April 30, 1943, the first clinical session of the group took place.

For two years, up to the spring of 1945, Mr. Lester Dearborn chaired the group. In April, 1945, the following officers were elected: president, Dr. Ernest Groves; first vice-president, Mr. Lester Dearborn; second vice-president, Mrs. Stuart Mudd; secretary-treasurer, Dr. Robert W. Laidlaw.

It is worth noting that out of this small group of professional persons, who had become so deeply interested in the problems of sex and marriage, no less than fifty percent came primarily from the medical specialties, while the rest represented such fields as social work, psychology, and sociology. The group was at first informally organized, its purposes being almost exclusively to exchange clinical experiences, to aid in the development of counseling techniques, and to study the results of their use.

By 1943 the group had become more organized, aware of the need to define membership requirements more closely and to produce a formal statement of purpose. Of particular importance to the thirty-one dues-paying members in 1944 was the sense of mutual support and challenge gained through their shared professional interest. The association was formally incorporated in 1947.

Those who have served as presidents of the association have been, in order: Dr. Ernest R. Groves (from November, 1945), Dr. S. Bernard Wortis (November, 1946), Dr. Abraham Stone (November, 1947), Dr. Robert Laidlaw (May, 1950), Dr. Emily Mudd (May, 1952), Dr. Lewis Sharp (April, 1954), Mr. Lester Dearborn (May, 1956), Dr. Lawrence Crawley (May, 1958), Dr. Robert Harper (May, 1960), Dr. Sophia Kleegman (acting president from January, 1962), Dr. Aaron Rutledge (May, 1962), Mrs. Ethel Nash (October, 1965), Dr. Gerald Leslie (November, 1966), Dr. James Peterson (October, 1967), and Dr. Gerhard Neubeck (1968).

PHASES OF DEVELOPMENT

History is made by plans which are first projected, then carried into effect. But these plans may be accomplished, or frustrated, by the impact and impetus of divergent views and experience, emerging from the biases of individual attitudes and feelings—the unpredictable variations of human personality. Plans are also greatly conditioned by the hard-core reality of available financial resources—a factor which inevitably sets the stage upon which creative and basic pioneer work plays out its richly divergent roles.

A careful review of this twenty-five year period suggests to the writer five major phases in the development and activities of the association. These may be described as: the Beginning Years, 1942–47; the Golden Years, 1948–55; the Years of Anxiety, 1956–60; the Years of Consolidation, 1960–63; the Years of National Expansion, 1963–67.

The Beginning Years, 1942–47

According to a statement by its formally elected secretary and later president, Robert W. Laidlaw, M.D., "The American Association of Marriage Counselors is a professional organization which concentrates its work specifically on marriage counseling. It has this stated purpose in the by-laws: to establish and maintain professional standards in marriage counseling. This purpose shall be furthered by meetings, clinical sessions, publications, and research. Membership in it is open to those who meet its detailed requirements for clinicians in the field or for affiliates whose work in this or related fields is outstanding, and for associates whose background, training, and beginning practice are sufficiently advanced to enable them to gain professionally by meeting with the more experienced counselors." Under the influence of the second president, Dr. Samuel Wortis, in 1947, the association first discussed certification, courses on marriage education, bibliotherapy, and even mass education. Financially, those were carefree days. There was a budget of $1,427.00 and a balance at year's end of $30.00!

The Golden Years, 1948–55

The second phase was ushered in by the leadership of Dr. Abraham Stone, president, and Dr. Robert Laidlaw, secretary. As a team they exhibited enthusiasm, mutual respect, and dedication. They believed that marriage counseling was important to the healthy development of our society and that dignified, intelligent means would be found for its successful launching.

The association's announced concern for establishing and maintaining professional standards was implemented by two special projects during this period. In 1948, together with the marriage counseling section of the National Council on Family Relations, the A.A.M.C. released a joint statement of standards for acceptable and recognized marriage counselors. These were presented in terms of (1) academic training, (2) professional experience and qualifications, (3) personal qualifications.

Later, in 1954, at its annual meeting in Philadelphia, the association formally accepted the report of the Committee on Criteria for Marriage Counseling Centers. This report made specific recommendations for minimum standards to apply to organizations which, either exclusively or as a specialized part of their total service, offered marriage counseling. The recommendations dealt with matters relating to organization and structure, qualifications of professional staff, provision for staff case-conferences, supervision, consultation, and referral. They also dealt with the question of confidentiality of records, and with that of fees. An appropriate committee was appointed to explore ways and means of implementing these recommendations.

Earlier, in 1949, a Legal Committee had been appointed and had cooperated with a committee from the NCFR to explore possibilities of *licensing* counselors and marriage counseling clinics. Active in this investigation was Mrs. Harriet Pilpel, a distinguished member of the legal profession. Mrs. Pilpel has served continuously since, with enthusiasm and great helpfulness, as legal counsel to the association, which owes a great deal to her keen insight, clarity, and vision.

At this time, too, there was increasing interest in the national aspect of A.A.M.C. responsibility, and a Committee on Regional Groups was established. Meanwhile, an association member, Dr. Janet Nelson, registered for a year of in-service supervised training at the Marriage Council of Philadelphia, and by doing so initiated the concept of specialized advanced training in the field.

With the association's activities thus rapidly multiplying, the officers and Executive Committee could no longer handle the organizational details from their own offices. Part-time help was employed and paid for by generous contributions from individual members. But diminishing resources both of energy and of pocketbooks would undoubtedly have curbed enthusiasm if Dr. Robert Laidlaw had not communicated to a patient some of his own enthusiasm for the work and goals of the A.A.M.C. This kind lady most generously left to the association its first and, to date, its only legacy.

The advent of this sizeable source of income served as a powerful and practical catalyst to action. The beginning groundwork of ideas and possibilities had already been laid. An office and a paid administrative officer were now acquired. Funds were allocated to the making of a systematic survey of the then functioning marriage counseling services. By 1954, as a result of the field trips made by Dr. Janet Nelson, it was possible to obtain an objective picture of the services currently available in the United States in this specialized field and to compare it with the criteria already established and accepted by the association. These investigations laid the groundwork for national expansion and served as a stimulus to local agencies to improve their services. Because of the wide divergences in actual standards, there was no attempt at that time to undertake the accreditation of clinics, although this possibility was explored with related national associations.

As early as 1950, the association had accepted the idea of publishing a casebook, and a contract had been signed with the Association Press by 1952. This project, supported with necessary funds allocated from the treasury, involved the officers, the Casebook Committee, and many of the members in close communication and effort for seven years until the manuscript went to press in 1958 under the title *Marriage Counseling—A Casebook*. A decade later, the volume is still in demand.

During this period the Executive Committee had been meeting regularly, and its members were elected, by design, from different geographic regions. Expenses of travel were available to encourage full attendance without undue personal deprivation. Budgets naturally increased with expanding activity. The legacy, Dr. Laidlaw had declared, "was given to be spent wisely."

The board accepted Dr. Laidlaw's stated philosophy, and during 1952–54 with Emily Mudd, president, and Janet Nelson, secretary, the work of the existing committes was extended and intensified. In addition a Committee on Training was appointed. One of its primary tasks was to seek ways and means to provide in-service supervised training, which was now increasingly in demand by young professional men and women who wished to supplement their basic skills in order to specialize in marriage counseling. The Fellowship Committee, under the able guidance of Evelyn Duvall, and later of Dr. Luther Woodward, drew up criteria, processed applications, and investigated services with good training potential. Twelve or more fellowships were conferred, amounting in all to approximately twelve thousand dollars of A.A.M.C. legacy funds.

It was also during 1952–54 that the A.A.M.C. subsidized a section devoted to articles on marriage counseling, in the journal *Marriage and*

Family Living. The subsidy ran to $750.00 per issue, and these articles appeared in some six or seven issues of the journal, until the arrangement unhappily terminated in a disagreement about editorial authority.

A definition of marriage counseling generally acceptable to association members at that time was presented by the Criteria Commiteee in the 1950s. This may still seem appropriate to many members in 1967. Marriage counseling was considered a specialized field of family counseling, primarily concerned with the interpersonal relations of husband and wife, wherein the clients are aided to reach a self-determined resolution of their problems. A further distinction was made in 1955 by one of the officers (Mudd) who wrote:

"...the focus of the counselor's approach is the relationship between the two people in marriage rather than, as in psychiatric therapy, the reorganization of the personality structure of the individual."

Without attempting to resolve the complicated area of the relationship between psychotherapy and counseling, the association made it clear at that time that psychotherapy and counseling were not considered synonymous. Members of the A.A.M.C. might do psychotherapy—many of them did—but this was not essential to their work in marriage counseling. This activity derived from their own individual basic training and qualifications. The marriage counselor *per se* was not considered to be a psychotherapist. This issue was of special importance in relation to the question of the private practice of non-medical counselors. With these differences in mind, in 1955, the association appointed a Private Practice Committee to study and explore this controversial subject.

A Program and Development Committee, chaired by Dr. Abraham Stone in 1953–54, sought to relate program potential to the association's available financial resources. In 1955 Dr. Lewis Sharp, president, and Dr. Janet Nelson, secretary, encouraged an assortment of existing committees to continue active work, and new committees were added: on grievances, on ways and means, and on fund raising.

The Years of Anxiety, 1956–60

When Mr. Lester Dearborn became president in May of 1956, the work of the association was rapidly expanding. For example, the Committee on Training and Standards had embarked upon a survey of three of the then-existing training centers—those at the Marriage Council of Philadelphia; at the Menninger Foundation in Topeka, Kansas; and at the Merrill-Palmer Institute in Detroit. Data were obtained by means of a prepared questionnaire, administered during an official site visit by Dr. Janet Nelson. After study of the results of this investigation, the training programs at these centers were officially approved.

However, the association was beginning to face problems inevitable to its extended program. The funds provided by the earlier legacy were running out. Financial resources available from dues were quite inadequate to meet the growing demands. Marriage counseling was arousing increasing interest, on the part of both the public and members of the helping professions. The New York office was swamped with requests for counseling help and inquiries of many kinds, and the time of the administrative office was being consumed in meeting these demands. The available resources of the A.A.M.C. were clearly becoming over-extended.

By early 1960 Dr. Lawrence Crawley, who was then president, was faced with a crisis following the resignation of the administrative officer. He appointed a special committee to formulate plans for the future of the A.A.M.C. The approved plan recommended inviting Dr. and Mrs. David Mace, who has successfully built up a national organization in this field in England, to honor the A.A.M.C. by becoming joint executive directors. Their acceptance moved our association from near annihilation to a more optimistic consolidation.

The Years of Consolidation, 1960–63

Dr. Robert Harper assumed the presidency at a time of drastic transition. He strongly supported bold new policies. The New York office was closed, and the Maces transferred the national headquarters of the association to their home community in New Jersey, with a dramatic reduction in costs. An attempt to augment membership by requiring less clinical experience, which had been adopted by constitutional amendment, was terminated. As the years passed, the trend was decisively in the direction of tightening membership standards. Dues were, with the loyal support of the members, substantially increased. A three year grant totaling $24,000.00 was procured from the Pathfinder Fund by an A.A.M.C. board member to supplement the budget, while financial aid for special projects was provided by the Mary Duke Biddle Foundation.

These and other promising developments were achieved with the continued support of Dr. Harper, and later of Dr. Sophia Kleegman, who filled out the unexpired term during which he was unable to continue to serve. A Code of Ethics for Marriage Counselors, initiated earlier by Dr. Maurice Karpf, was at this time developed by Dr. Walter Stokes, and given formal acceptance at the annual business meeting of 1962. A general overhaul of the association's entire administrative structure resulted in the framing of the new constitution and by-laws, which were approved at the annual business meeting of 1963. Both of these documents are printed in the annual directory of members.

The Years of National Expansion, 1963–67

The steady guidance of presidents Aaron Rutledge (1962–65), Mrs. Ethel Nash (1965–66), and Dr. Gerald Leslie (1966–67), and the vitality, imagination, and able organization and leadership of David and Vera Mace, have proved a revitalizing dynamic for the association.

No marriage counseling service *per se* functions under A.A.M.C. auspices, nor does the association perform any certifying procedures. However, a directory of members listed alphabetically and geographically is now published yearly and is available at $2.00 per copy from the headquarters office. A nationwide mail referral service is also operated. The association makes referrals only to its clinical members or to agencies of high repute.

Since its inception, the association has taken consistent interest in the definition and redefinition of membership standards. These have now been firmly established for some years. There are three categories of "clinical" members: *fellow, member,* and *associate member.* In addition, there are the categories of *affiliate* and *associate-in-training.*

The composition of the A.A.M.C. membership reflects the interdisciplinary character of marriage counseling. In 1955, an investigation of clinical members indicated that the medical profession was in the majority, representing 31 percent (gynecology, 12 percent; general medicine, 9 percent; psychiatry, 9 percent; urology, 1 percent). In addition, 18 percent were ministers, 16 percent, social workers; 13 percent, psychologists; 11 percent, educators; 11 percent, sociologists. (The indicated profession refers to the academic field in which initial training and advanced degrees were obtained.) However, in 1966 the structure of the clinical membership showed a decisive shift. According to the directory, "in rough percentages psychology claims 26 percent; social work, 25 percent; ministry, 15 percent; education, 8 percent; medicine, 8 percent; sociology, 5 percent; law, 1 percent." The remaining 12 percent could not be identified exclusively with one specific discipline. Some were qualified in as many as three separate fields.

Although in no way offering "accredited" standing, membership in the association is meaningful insofar as it represents a screening in terms of training, experience, and personal qualifications. According to a statement made by Dr. David Mace in July, 1967, "... membership of the A.A.M.C. has now come to mean, for all practical purposes, the possession of the only recognized credential in the field of professional marriage counseling, a kind of guarantee of dependable service to the general public." Training and experience initially stem from the original disciplines in which the member is qualified. In addition, there is a common body of knowledge, techniques, and qualifications that cross-cuts the professions involved.

To provide in-service training which supplements existing skills and is focused on marriage counseling is the responsibility of the Committee on Training and Standards, which has continued its work since 1952. There are currently eight training centers in North America which have met the A.A.M.C. standards. Others are likely to emerge in the future.

The association owes a great deal to the strenuous and time-consuming toil of its Admissions Committee, which thoroughly investigates all new applications for the various categories of membership. There has in recent years been encouraging regional development. Some of the now eleven regional associations function with spirit and efficiency, others with less vitality. The newsletters regularly circulated by the executive directors have proved invaluable as a means of communication between members and with outside groups.

Before their retirement as executive directors in October, 1967, David and Vera Mace listed the special needs of the association, in addition to the maintenance of the basic present services, as follows:

1. To develop all possible ways and means of increasing A.A.M.C.

membership, without endangering the high standards of clinical competence which have built up respect for our organization.

2. To coordinate more closely the work of our training programs, and to encourage and develop further training programs (the National Institute for Mental Health, which already gives grants to two of the programs, might be persuaded to subsidize others); and to provide all possible means, in the form of workshops and arrangement for approved supervision, to enable professional persons already clinically qualified to get the additional orientation and training needed to give them the specialized competence to meet our membership requirements.

3. To explore fully the promising idea of closer cooperation, and even possible merger, with the Family Therapy movement, and in the process to secure for the A.A.M.C. the professional journal it so badly needs.

4. To explore actively possible sources of financial support which will put the A.A.M.C. operation thoroughly on its feet, and enable the association to do the work and exert the influence that will further its goals at this time of great opportunity.

SECTION B — THE ASSOCIATION ENTERS ADULTHOOD

The twenty-fifth year of the A.A.M.C.'s life in 1968 was the occasion for a celebration and a transition: The celebration of a quarter century of progress, and the passing of the Executive Office from the Maces to Edward J. Rydman. It was the plan of the Association in contracting with Dr. Rydman, that he would be the full time Executive Director. It was expected that the membership growth of the Association combined with anticipated Foundation support, would underwrite the costs of this expanded operation. In order to establish a base from which to launch a drive for Foundation support, the A.A.M.C. initiated a Development Fund drive within its own ranks. The goal of that drive was to raise $50,000.00 from the members—an ambitious goal for an organization with less than 500 Clinical Members.

The leadership of the A.A.M.C., faced with the limits placed on it by the small number of members in the Association, determined to combine the drive for new members. Setting a goal of tripling the membership in three years, the Board of Directors was nonetheless determined to maintain the high quality of professionals admitted to the Association.

The problem of membership growth confronted the A.A.M.C. with several important issues. First, the parallel, but largely separate development of the family therapy movement during the late 50s and early 60s posed for the A.A.M.C. a challenge and an opportunity. Second, the enactment of state licensing laws for marriage counselors which had begun in California in 1963 based on standards different from those of the A.A.M.C., appeared to be the wave of the future. Finally, the development of regional or national organizations of both marriage counselors and/or family therapists appeared imminent.

The first of these challenges, that of the family therapy movement, was met by a dual strategy, A.A.M.C. leaders initiated conversations with leaders of the family therapy movement. Simultaneously, outstanding family therapists were invited to Clinical Membership in the A.A.M.C. It was possible to do this without arousing organization of family therapists. Family therapy had a journal, *Family Process*, but no formal organization. The A.A.M.C. was a formal organization without a journal. As discussions progressed between the A.A.M.C. and the leaders of the loosely identified "movement" of family therapists, it appeared for a time as if the initial rapprochement might be formalized. However, the consensus of the leadership within the family therapy movement resisted, and continues to resist, the formalization of the movement into an association. The distinguished journal, *Family Process*, continues to be independently published.

The growth of the family therapy movement also prompted the A.A.M.C. to consider whether it ought to expand the focus of its professional organization to include "family" as well as "marriage" counseling. Since the identification of family treatment had been as "therapy" rather than as "counseling," the discussion of including family in the title of the A.A.M.C. raised another philosophical/semantic issue. Wheras "therapy" is associated with the medical model, the context in which the family therapy movement germinated, "counseling" implies a growth model in which the client is unstigmatised by imputed illness. This discussion continues in the A.A.M.F.C. today, just as it does within the more general fields of medicine and psychotherapy.

In the end, the discussion of the name was concluded on the grounds that an already cumbersome title for the Association should be increased as little as possible. Therefore, only the words ". . . and family . . ." were inserted in the already existing title of the Association.

Meanwhile, the campaigns for new funds and new members were under way. Each member of A.A.M.C. was asked to recruit two well qualified professionals to become new members of the Association. Each member was also asked to make a cash contribution and a pledge of future contributions toward the three year program to raise $50,000.00. Much time and effort was expended on the part of the leadership of the A.A.M.C. in those dual campaigns. Each was moderately successful. However, neither goal was fully achieved. Partly as a result of the difficulty of these efforts, an already dawning awareness was painfully emphasized. As expressed by A.A.M.C. President Ethel Nash, it was ". . . a danger that our Association, which calls itself the American Association of Marriage Counselors, might in fact be shutting out most of the people who are really doing the marriage counseling . . . If we keep our doors closed to the people who are doing the day-to-day marriage counseling, we can hardly blame them if they create an organization of their own. Surely it would be far better, before it is too late, to find a place for them within our ranks." (Minutes of the A.A.M.C. Board of Directors meeting, 4/16/66.) At the time, this is exactly what was happening. For, in the State of California, the number of licensed marriage and family counselors was twice the total of A.A.M.C. members nationwide! A California State Marriage Counseling Association had been formed and had already recruited nearly as many members as the national organization.

An historic decision was being thrust upon the A.A.M.C. For the first twenty-five years of its life it had steadfastly maintained its allegiance to the highest possible academic and clinical standards for membership. It had proudly borne the consequences of that noble commitment—a commitment entered into before the founders realized that they were establishing the guidelines for a new profession. Now the A.A.M.C. must decide whether to continue its elitist stance and make a virtue of its numerical weakness, or to recognize that most of the bonafide marriage and family counseling was being provided in the United States by reasonably well-qualified professionals whose academic and clinical credentials did not meet A.A.M.C. minimum standards.

Accustomed to rejecting more applicants than it accepted, the A.A.M.C. now courageously, but cautiously faced the task of recruiting rather than resisting new members. By the end of 1969 it became clear that neither the membership drive nor the fund raising efforts of the Association would render the A.A.M.C. self-supporting before the "Laidlaw legacy" was exhausted. Drastic measures were the order of the day. Fortunately, during his two-year tenure as full time Executive Director, Dr. Rydman had begun to develop a part-time private practice. It was therefore possible for him to voluntarily reduce his work commitment to the A.A.M.C. to one-quarter time. Further, the Board voted to present to the membership a proposal for a significant dues increase for Clinical Members. This was to be done at a special meeting of the membership called for March, 1970. At this time it was also proposed to present the modification of minimum membership requirements, as well as the change of name to include Family. It is interesting to note that in each of these crucial decisions, the Board was in close touch with the thinking of the membership as witnessed by the fact that of those voting in the special election, either in person or by proxy, nearly 90% favored the change in name and in membership requirements, and nearly 80% favored the increase in dues.

In revising the minimum membership standards to accept Master's degrees in the behavioral sciences and two years of clinical experience, the A.A.M.F.C. as it had now become, initiated a new category of membership, Associate. This new category was understood to be for those persons who were minimally qualified, but who very soon were expected to meet full clinical membership standards. The pre-clinical category of membership, Associate-in-Training, was retained as the basic title for those who were under supervision or in training to become Clinical Members of the A.A.M.F.C. These categories of membership remained in effect until 1974.

After lagging behind expectations for nearly two years, applications for membership began to increase sharply. By the end of 1970 there were more than a thousand A.A.M.F.C. members in all categories. Associate members who had at first been accepted without the right to vote or hold office were granted full electoral privileges.

Just as the membership recruitment strategies were beginning to pay off, so were the efforts at improving the financial condition of the Association. The reduction of expenses combined with the increase in dues resulted in a significant surplus at the end of 1971. Perhaps the most active A.A.M.F.C. committee during the late 1960s and early 70s was the Training and Standards Committee. Its long-standing responsibility for the review and approval of training programs continued during this period with numerous institutions showing an increasing interest in being approved by the A.A.M.F.C. During these years nearly a dozen centers were formally visited and evaluated. By now, institutions from coast to coast as well as in Canada were becoming recognized as Approved Training Centers for marriage and family counselors. These institutions represented a variety of academic and professional training specialties—psychiatry/family studies, child development/family relations, pastoral psychology, sociology, and interdisciplinary programs.*

In addition to approved training programs, the A.A.M.F.C. recognized the need for identifying senior supervisory clinicians experienced in marriage and family counseling who could provide appropriate supervision for established practitioners in related professions who wished to meet the clinical practice and experience requirements necessary for A.A.M.F.C. membership. In response to this demand the A.A.M.F.C. inaugurated the special status of Approved Supervisor.

There had been selected individual members scattered throughout the country almost from the beginning of the Association. There also had been a few pockets of local activity for many years. Following the years of national expansion during the mid-60s, an increasing number of regional divisions came into being. By the end of that decade there were nearly a dozen well-established regional units of the A.A.M.F.C. functioning as metropolitan, statewide, or multi-state divisions.† Most of these regional divisions had a formal structure including officers, dues, and regular meetings. Although the frequency of programming varies from region to region, the emphasis is primarily on presentations of clinical and professional interest to those involved in the field of marriage and family counseling, psychotherapy, and clinical education. These regional meetings provide one of the most effective ways to recruit new members for the A.A.M.F.C.

In addition to its traditional annual meeting held in the fall of each year, the A.A.M.F.C. initiated a Spring Topical Conference. The purpose of this Conference was to focus the entire meeting on one particular issue such as divorce, human sexuality, licensure, marital health, etc. Geographical locations for this Spring Topical Conference were selected in relation to the annual fall meeting, so that, insofar as possible, there would be geographical balance from north to south, and from east to west. In recent years this Spring Topical Conference has been expanded to provide three

---

*A current list of A.A.M.F.C. accredited graduate training programs and approved clinical training programs in marriage and family counseling appears at the end of this chapter.

†Northern California	Massachusetts	New Jersey	Southwestern
Southern California	Mid-Atlantic	New York	Utah
Illinois	Minnesota	North Carolina	

such Conferences during the spring months in various parts of the Continent.

After nearly five years as Executive Director, Dr. Edward J. Rydman announced his intention to conclude his work with the A.A.M.F.C. and devote his full time to the private practice he had been developing in Dallas, Texas. By the time he concluded his work as A.A.M.F.C. Executive Director in the summer of 1972, he had helped successfully to guide the A.A.M.F.C. through five of its most turbulent years. The Association has faced serious financial and philosophical crises with skill and wisdom. A grateful Board and Association honored Dr. Rydman for his distinguished service.

By mid-1972, the A.A.M.F.C. had expanded its membership sufficiently to provide an effective financial base for a full range of Association activities. The newly appointed Executive Director, Dr. C. Ray Fowler, began his full time service to the Association with the relocation of the Executive Offices from Dallas, Texas, to Claremont, California, a small New England type college town near Los Angeles. Dr. Fowler had been a leader in regional activities, having served as an officer of the Southern California A.M.F.C. and also of the California State Association. In addition to his private practice, he had both teaching and administrative experience with University of California Extension.

Several major tasks confronted the A.A.M.F.C. and its new Executive Director. First, there were important organizational issues facing the Association. The organizational structure of the Association had not been changed since its original incorporation in the State of New York in 1948. At that time it was organized as a tax-exempt non-profit educational and research foundation. While it continued to conduct such activities, its operations had been broadened considerably in recent years. Therefore it seemed necessary, while retaining the corporate foundation structure, to initiate a slightly different form of corporate structure along the trade or professional association model, also tax-exempt and non-profit. When such an organization was incorporated in 1974, it was decided to establish its legal home in the District of Columbia where many other such national professional organizations are domiciled. It was not intended that the Association would conduct its headquarters operation in Washington. However, it does maintain a very active program of representation there under the Washington Counsel For Governmental Affairs.

Organizational issues were also being raised by the conversations being carried on between the A.A.M.F.C. and the California Association of Marriage and Family Counselors. These were begun in 1971. At the beginning of the present decade, there were three independent and autonomous state associations of marriage counselors. These were in Oregon, Michigan, and California. Of these, Oregon has voted to merge with the A.A.M.F.C. and become its official state division. Negotiations continue in 1976 with the other two Associations on a variety of organizational questions related to amalgamation. During the first half of the 1970s the number of regional divisions of the A.A.M.F.C. nearly tripled so that only three or four of the least populous states are not covered by a regional division of the

A.A.M.F.C. There are also two strong regional divisions in Canada—the Ontario and the Quebec Associations of Marriage and Family Counselors.

Almost every year since the A.A.M.F.C. was organized the leaders seem to have discussed in at least one of their meetings the critical need for a professional and scientific journal to be sponsored by the Association. Time after time, the issue was raised, studied, and finally shelved because there was not enough money available to produce a journal of uncompromising quality. The archives of the A.A.M.F.C. contain a hand-lettered mockup of a Journal of Marriage Counseling enscribed as Volume I, Number 1, and dated June, 1954. Almost exactly twenty years to the day after that early prototype was presented to the Board, the Board received a proposal and voted to authorize Dr. William C. Nichols, Jr. to implement his proposal as Founding Editor of the Journal of Marriage and Family Counseling. The new Journal was launched with its premier issue published in January, 1975, featuring articles by Jay Haley and James Framo. Response to this new Journal was so enthusiastic due to the high quality of the contents as well as the fine editorial work of Dr. Nichols that unlike most scientific and professional journals in the field, it is expected to be self-supporting before the publication of the four issues in Volume II is completed. In addition to more than 1500 paid subscriptions from non-A.A.M.F.C. members and institutions, the Journal is provided to every A.A.M.F.C. member as one of the membership benefits.

In addition to the critical issue of organizational structures, a second major challenge to the A.A.M.F.C. during the 1970s is membership benefits. Every organization must effectively answer the question, "What do I get for my annual payment of dues?" As was true of its consideration of a Journal, so it was that for many years the Board of Directors of the A.A.M.F.C. considered the need for providing professional and business services to A.A.M.F.C. members. In the early 1960s the A.A.M.F.C. made arrangements for its members to obtain professional liability insurance as marriage and family counselors. In addition to this coverage, the A.A.M.F.C. now provides for its members at special group rates, a variety of insurance coverage including accidental death and dismemberment, hospitalization, and income continuance plans. Such benefits as these are increasingly essential as the marriage and family counselor becomes widely recognized as an independent professional and consequently growing numbers of A.A.M.F.C. members are developing full time private practices. This is in contrast to the earlier patterns of professional involvement by A.A.M.F.C. members, wherein only a tiny fraction of the entire membership was primarily engaged full time in the private practice of marriage and family counseling.

Public recognition of the profession through state licensure is another professional issue in which the A.A.M.F.C. has been engaged. While licensure laws have been passed in only a few states, the A.A.M.F.C. through its regions and individual members, has been actively involved in the introduction and support of licensing laws since the beginning of the decade of the 1960s. Its minimal record of success in this field is a testimony to the difficulty of such campaigns and the resistance with which legislators face the licensure of a newly identified profession. It is interesting to note that the six states in which licensure has been achieved run the gamut from urban, secularized, industrial environments (Michigan, New Jersey, and California) on the one hand, to the rural and traditional environments (Nevada and Utah), as well as a combination of the two types (Georgia). So the difference between those states in which licensing has been achieved and those in which it has not is the peculiar complex of circumstances under which legislation is introduced, opposed, and implemented. The A.A.M.F.C. continues to work vigorously for the passage of laws regulating the practice of marriage and family counseling in those states where no law now exists.

While state licensure is essential for the recognition of marriage and family counselors as independent health practitioners, much that affects the profession is decided at the federal level. Therefore a long-time goal of the A.A.M.F.C. has been to establish some kind of representation in Washington, D.C. which would be formal, effective, and sustained. The financial resources of an increased membership made it possible for the A.A.M.F.C. to inaugurate such a program in 1974. The many years of successful experience which the A.A.M.F.C. had accumulated with its New York legal counsel, Harriet Pilpel, Esq., influenced the Board of Directors to select for the A.A.M.F.C. Washington representative, Steven L. Engelberg, Esq., an attorney with an impressive record of service "on the Hill" as well as with federal regulatory agencies. In the fall of 1974, Mr. Engelberg assumed his part-time duties for the A.A.M.F.C. While the priorities for A.A.M.F.C. action in Washington were still being ranked in preparation for a major effort, the A.A.M.F.C. was presented with a massive challenge to the very existence of the profession of marriage and family counseling.

The challenge to the profession came in the form of an announcement by the U.S. Department of Defense that it was suspending all payments to CHAMPUS beneficiaries for treatment by marriage and family counselors. As background for this decision, the Civilian Health and Medical Program for the Uniformed Services (CHAMPUS) was instituted by the Congress following World War II as a means of upgrading service men's benefits and thereby encouraging them to voluntarily remain on duty. The original program was later expanded to include not only the minimum levels of physician and hospital care but also the numerous types of non-medical care deemed essential to health maintenance. Marriage and family counselors were included by Congressional enactment in these programs beginning in 1966, so that U.S. military personnel and their dependents, upon referral by a physician, could receive treatment from a marriage and family counselor whose services would be paid for by CHAMPUS. This coverage represented the most liberal benefit package available to any segment of the U.S. population. The inclusion of marriage and family counseling services was justified by the Congress on the grounds that the particular demands of military life put exceedingly heavy pressures on the individuals and families subjected to its rigors.

On February 28, 1975, the Department of Defense made an administrative decision to terminate payment for marriage and family counseling services when rendered by marriage family counselors, while continuing to reimburse for those same services if provided by other health professionals. Although very few A.A.M.F.C. members were actually involved as CHAMPUS providers, the Association determined that this action manifest a symbolically lethal attack on the profession. Therefore, an immediate response was authorized by the Board. Key Congressional leaders who were contacted by the A.A.M.F.C., persuaded CHAMPUS administrators to open talks with A.A.M.F.C. representatives in an effort to negotiate. After two months of fruitless conversations, the intractability of the Pentagon became clear. Recourse was sought by the A.A.M.F.C. through the Federal District Court of Washington, D.C. In June, 1975, the A.A.M.F.C. was granted a preliminary injunction by the Federal Court prohibiting the Department of Defense from implementing its termination order for marriage and family counselors. Further, the Department was ordered to reinstate recognition of these providers exactly as it had been prior to its termination and to pay all back claims for service rendered since the termination notice. Effectively blocked by the Courts, the Department of Defense now turned to the legislative process. The Congress has not yet authorized appropriation of the military budget for fiscal year 1976, even though that time period had begun July 1, 1975. Therefore, when the Military Appropriations Bill was introduced into the House of Representatives by the Department of Defense in September, it contained a provision specifically deleting the services of marriage and family counselors. The Bill was quickly passed through Committee and acted upon favorably by the House before any effective representation could be made by the A.A.M.F.C. It was therefore decided that the A.A.M.F.C. strategy should concentrate on the Senate. For, if the Senate passed a version retaining the services of marriage and family counselors, there would still be a chance of a compromise in the final legislation agreed to by both Houses. A.A.M.F.C. members in each of the states having a Senator on the key Committee were mobilized to make personal contact with the Senator and provide information on the A.A.M.F.C. point of view. The same basic facts which had carried the day in Federal Court were presented to the Senators, (1) the Congress has mandated the services of marriage and family counselors and the Department of Defense has no authority to terminate them, (2) this decision is arbitrary, capricious, and exceeds the Department's equivalent cost, so the Department's argument of economy is fallacious, (4) termination of access to these providers will be extremely detrimental to military personnel and their dependents, etc. The characterization of the Department's action as fundamentally unfair and unwise, as well as uneconomical, impressed the Senators on the Committee as well as their colleagues when the final vote was taken in the Senate to retain the services of marriage and family counselors.

It now remained for the House version terminating marriage and family counselors' services and the Senate version retaining them to be reconciled in conference. Having won this much, the A.A.M.F.C. faced the prospect of losing everything if the House conferees remained uninformed or unimpressed by the facts in favor of the A.A.M.F.C. position established in the Federal Court. Again, every A.A.M.F.C. member in the districts represented by key Congressmen made personal contacts to get the A.A.M.F.C. story across.

Of the 122 separate issues brought to the Conference Committee on which the House and Senate versions differed, it was reported that the item on the services of marriage and family counselors was debated longer and more hotly than any other in this huge Military Appropriations Bill. In the end, the Senate version mandating the continued service of marriage and family counselors in the CHAMPUS program prevailed, and was signed into law February 9, 1976.

In addition to mounting a tremendous effort to make individual personal contacts with their own Senators and Representatives, the members of the A.A.M.F.C. contributed over $20,000.00 to finance the legal and legislative efforts to retain CHAMPUS coverage for marriage and family counselors. Once again the A.A.M.F.C. had proved itself a highly committed organization capable of mobilizing its members to take effective action on a particular issue. Largely as a result of its successful efforts in the CHAMPUS affair, the A.A.M.F.C. was invited to join the Liaison Group for Mental Health, a working group of staff members from all of the major Washington based associations of mental health professionals. In numerous other ways also the establishment of a staff representative of the A.A.M.F.C. in Washington, D.C. has led to increasingly closer working relationships with the larger and more traditionally identified mental health associations.

To the inter-association cooperation which the A.A.M.F.C. has enjoyed for many years with the National Council on Family Relations and the American College of Obstetricians and Gynecologists through its Committee on Family Life Education, has been added the American Psychological Association, the National Association of Social Workers, the American Home Economics Association, and the National Association for Mental Health. Although as yet licensed in only a few states, marriage and family counselors are increasingly identified by the public as an appropriate resource in time of trouble. This increased recognition is the basis for the recent growth and continued expansion of the A.A.M.F.C., as well as in part a result of the Association's efforts on behalf of the profession. Due to the increasing rate of divorce during the decade of the 60s, some observers of the American scene predicted the impending demise of marriage and the family. However, in spite of the divorce statistics, serious interest in marital and family relationships including their maintenance and improvement, appears likely to remain a high priority for Americans throughout this century and well into the next.

Therefore, the well trained clinical mental health professional who focuses his/her work on marital and family relationships can expect an increasing demand for services from the American public. This increased demand for marriage and family counselors will be a product in part of A.A.M.F.C. efforts, as well as a basis for increased membership and activity by the A.A.M.F.C.

SUMMARY

In summary, we have seen something of the vision that brings a new organization into being. We have surveyed the why and the how of the A.A.M.C. which later became the A.A.M.F.C. We have followed the excitement of infancy, the joys of childhood, the struggles of adolescence, and finally the increasing strengths and maturity of adulthood.

What in an overall sense has been accomplished? With no apologies, we can claim the advent of a new specialization of use to all helping professions—medicine, psychiatry, the ministry, teaching, social work, the law, and community mental health. We have united together in membership individuals within these professions who focus a substantial part of their clinical work on the interpersonal relations of marriage and the family. Further, we have seen marriage and family counseling emerge from a specialty of use to many professions into an increasingly clearly identified profession of its own.

Minimum standards in professional preparation and practice, necessary to qualify for membership and to protect adequate practice, have been agreed upon and publicized, as have standards for adequately functioning marriage counseling services and for accredited training in this field. A few fellowships have been available to approved persons desiring training. Certain training centers have been officially approved, others disapproved, and still others are under investigation.* A pioneering volume, *Marriage Counseling: A Casebook*, edited by E. H. Mudd, Abraham Stone, Maurice J. Karpf, and Janet F. Nelson, based on the actual clinical work of Association members, was published by Association Press in 1958 and is still widely used for teaching. A.A.M.F.C. members now lead the field in publishing clinical and scientific works on marriage counseling and family therapy, including this text.

Regional groups representing most areas of the United States and most of the members in Canada are active in sharing with the A.A.M.F.C. the continuing process of education of members and would-be members through meetings, conferences, and publications. Consultation is offered to individuals and groups wishing to develop resources in the field. The Association is providing active leadership in assisting states with the difficult task of regulating this profession by encouraging adequately trained marriage and family counselors and excluding persons practicing in the field who do not meet minimum standards and who are potential hazards to the public.

Based on its nearly 40 years of pioneering leadership in the field of marriage and family counseling, the A.A.M.F.C. promises to uphold and extend those high professional standards of membership, performance, ethics, and community relationships of which the Association can be justly proud.

*   *   *   *

---

*These informational materials are available from the A.A.M.F.C., 225 Yale Avenue, Claremont, CA 91711.

ACCREDITED GRADUATE TRAINING PROGRAMS

Brigham Young University — Provo, Utah

Colgate Rochester/Bexley Hall — Rochester, New York

Syracuse University — Syracuse, New York

University of Southern California — Los Angeles, California

APPROVED CLINICAL TRAINING PROGRAMS

Family Service of Milwaukee — Milwaukee, Wisconsin

Indiana Counseling and Pastoral Care Center — Indianapolis, Indiana

Institutes of Religion and Health — New York, New York

Marriage Council of Philadelphia — Philadelphia, Pennsylvania

Marriage and Family Consultation Center — Houston, Texas

Mental Hygiene Institute — Montreal, Quebec

Onondaga Pastoral Counseling Center — Syracuse, New York

Westchester Institute — Rye, New York

REFERENCES

Dearborn, L. The American Association of Marriage Counselors. In *Marriage counseling: A casebook*. New York: Association Press, 1958.

Mace, D. Annual report, Association of Marriage Counselors, 1960 through 1967.

Mudd, E. H. Psychiatry and marital problems. *Eugenics Quarterly*, 1955, 2, 110–117.

CHAPTER 41

AAMFC: Code of Professional Ethics

Preamble
Members of the A.A.M.F.C. are professional counselors trained in dealing with marriage and family problems. They are conscious of their special skills and aware of their professional boundaries. They perform their professional duties on the highest levels of integrity and confidentiality and will not hesitate to recommend assistance from other professional disciplines when circumstances dictate. They are committed to protect the public against, and will not hesitate to expose, unethical, incompetent and dishonorable practices. To maintain these high standards of service, members of the A.A.M.F.C. have imposed upon themselves the following rules of conduct and will earn highest public confidence.

Section I. Code of Personal Conduct
1. A Counselor provides professional service to anyone regardless of race, religion, sex, political affiliation, social or economic status, or choice of life-style. When a Counselor cannot offer service for any reason, he or she will make a proper referral. Counselors are encouraged to devote a portion of their time to work for which there is little or no financial return.

2. A Counselor will not use his or her counseling relationship to further personal, religious, political, or business interests.

3. A Counselor will neither offer nor accept payment for referrals, and will actively seek all significant information from the source of referral.

4. A Counselor will not knowingly offer service to a client who is in treatment with another counseling professional without consultation among the parties involved.

5. A Counselor will not disparage the qualifications of any colleague.

6. Every member of the A.A.M.F.C. has an obligation to continuing education and professional growth in all possible ways, including active participation in the meetings and affairs of the Association.

7. A Counselor will not attempt to diagnose, prescribe for, treat or advise on problems outside the recognized boundaries of the Counselor's competence.

Reprinted with permission of the A.A.M.F.C. from the *A.A.M.F.C. Code of Professional Ethics* and the *A.A.M.F.C. Standards on Public Information and Advertising*, (Claremont, California, 1975).

8. The Association encourages its members to affiliate with professional groups, clinics or agencies operating in the field of marriage and family life. Similarly, interdisciplinary contact and cooperation are encouraged.

Section II. Relations With Clients

1. A Counselor, while offering dignified and reasonable support, is cautious in prognosis and will not exaggerate the efficacy of his or her service.

2. The Counselor recognizes the importance of clear understandings on financial matters with his or her clients. Arrangements for payments are settled at the beginning of a counseling relationship.

3. A Counselor keeps records of each case, and stores them in such a way as to insure safety and confidentiality, in accordance with the highest professional and legal standards.

    a. Information shall be revealed only to professional persons concerned with the case. Written and oral reports should present only data germane to the purposes of the inquiry; every effort should be made to avoid undue invasion of privacy.

    b. The Counselor is responsible for informing the client of the limits of confidentiality.

    c. Written permission shall be granted by the clients involved before data may be divulged.

    d. Information is not communicated to others without consent of the client unless there is clear and immediate danger to an individual or to society, and then only to the appropriate family members, professional workers or public authorities.

4. A Counselor deals with relationships at varying stages of their history. While respecting at all times the clients' right to make their own decision, the Counselor has a duty to assess the situation according to the highest professional standards. In all circumstances, the Counselor will clearly advise a client that the decision to separate or divorce is the responsibility solely of the client. In such an event, the Counselor has the continuing responsibility to offer support and counsel during the period of adjustment.

Section III. Research and Publication

1. The Counselor is obligated to protect the welfare of his or her research subjects. The conditions of the Human Subjects Experimentation shall prevail, as specified by the Department of Health, Education and Welfare guidelines.

2. Publication credit is assigned to those who have contributed to a publication, in proportion to their contribution, and in accordance with customary publication practices.

Section IV. Implementation

1. In accepting membership in the Association, each member binds himself or herself to accept the judgment of his or her fellow members as

to standards of professional ethics, subject to the safeguards provided in this section. Acceptance of membership implies consent to abide by the acts of discipline herein set forth and as enumerated in the Bylaws of the Association. It is the duty of each member to safeguard these standards of ethical practice. Should a fellow member appear to violate this Code he or she may be cautioned through friendly remonstrance, colleague consultation with the party in question, or formal complaint may be filed in accordance with the following procedure:

a. Complaint of unethical practice shall be made in writing to the Chairperson of the Standing Committee on Ethics and Professional Practices and to the Executive Director. A copy of the complaint shall be furnished to the person or persons against whom it is directed.

b. Should the Standing Committee decide the complaint warrants investigation, it shall so notify the charged party(ies) is writing. When investigation is indicated, the Standing Committee shall constitute itself in an Investigating Committee and shall include in its membership at least one member of the Board and at least two members (other than the charging or charged parties or any possible witnesses) from the local area involved. This Investigating Committee or representatives thereof shall make one or more local visits of investigation of the complaint. After full investigation following due process and offering the charged party(ies) opportunity to defend him or herself, the Committee shall report its findings and recommendations to the Board of Directors for action.

c. The charged party(ies) shall have free access to all charges and evidence cited against him or her, and shall have full freedom to defend him or herself before the Investigating Committee and the Board, including the right to legal counsel.

d. Recommendation made by the Committee shall be:
1. Advice that the charges be dropped as unfounded.
2. Specified admonishment.
3. Reprimand.
4. Dismissal from membership.

2. Should a member of this Association be expelled he or she shall at once surrender his or her membership certificate to the Board of Directors. Failure to do so shall result in such action as legal counsel may recommend.

3. Should a member of this Association be expelled from another recognized professional association or his/her state license revoked for unethical conduct, the Standing Committee on Ethics shall investigate the matter and, where appropriate, act in the manner provided above respecting charges of unethical conduct.

4. The Committee will also give due consideration to a formal complaint by a non-member.

Section V. Public Information And Advertising
All professional presentations to the public will be governed by the Standards on Public Information and Advertising.

* * * * * * * *

STANDARDS ON PUBLIC INFORMATION AND ADVERTISING

The practice of marriage and family counseling as a mental health profession is in the public interest. Therefore it is appropriate for the well trained and qualified practitioner to inform the public of the availability of his/her services. The membership standards of the A.A.M.F.C. provide the public with the assurance of competence in this field, relieving the individual member of the need to "advertise" his/her services to the public.

However, much needs to be done to educate the public as to the services available from qualified marriage and family counselors. Therefore the members of A.A.M.F.C. have a responsibility to the public to engage in appropriate informational activities in keeping with the following standards.

I. TELEPHONE DIRECTORY LISTINGS

Yellow Pages. All listings should be governed by the principles of dignity, modesty and uniformity.

A. Special type (boldface, etc.) and lined boxes or any other technique tending to make one individual or firm's listing stand out from other listings in the directory is a breach of professional ethics.

B. A proper listing will include no more than the following:
  (1) Name
  (2) Highest earned relevant degree (one only)
  (3) State licensure (including license No.)
  (4) A.A.M.F.C. clinical membership
      (Diplomate status if attained)
  (5) Address
  (6) Telephone number
  (7) Designated specialty

C. Office hours (or the statement "By Appointment Only") may be listed if permitted by the local telephone company.

D. Any title including words such as "Institute," "Center," "Clinic," "Service" is acceptable only if a group practice includes at least three professionals. Other A.A.M.F.C. members of such a group may choose to be listed under the identifying group practice name as well as separately in the proper alphabetical location.

E. When titles utilizing the name of a city, county, or state are employed, care should be taken to indicate the private nature of the enterprise.

Sample Individual Listing.

Jones, John J.
M.A.
Member, American Association of Marriage and Family Counselors
By Appointment Only
123 N. Main 672-3903
Res 324 S. Adams 674-2811

Sample Group Practice Listings

(a) Jones, John J. and Associates
   Patricia Adams, Ph.D.
   John J. Jones, M.A.
   Richard Williams, D. Min.
   123 N. Main 672-3903
(b) North Main Family Institute
   Patricia Adams, Ph.D.
   John J. Jones, M.A.
   Richard Williams, D. Min.
   123 N. Main 672-3903
(c) North Main Family Institute
   John J. Jones, M.A.
   123 N. Main 672-3903
(In this example Patricia Adams and Richard Williams will be listed alpha-
betically elsewhere with the same address and phone number as North Main
Family Institute.)

A.A.M.F.C. Insignia

A regional division or a chapter of the A.A.M.F.C. may use the
A.A.M.F.C. insignia to list its members as a group. When all members
practicing within a telephone directory district have been invited to list,
any three or more members may do so.

Sample Insignia Listing

American Association
of Marriage and Family Counselors
(Nevada
Division)

Baxter, Arthur W.
   MSW
   81 S. Rushford 832-9481
North Main Family Institute
   Patricia Adams, Ph.D.
   John J. Jones, M.A.
   123 N. Main 844-6377
Smith, Roberta
   MSW
   2345 Hartdale 943-5656
Williams, Richard
   D. Min.
   123 N. Main 844-6377

II. PRINTED PROFESSIONAL MATERIALS

A. Stationary, Business Cards and Announcements. Dignity and good
taste should characterize the printed professional materials of an
A.A.M.F.C. member. Select paper stock, type and composition suitable to
the presentation of a professional practice. Imprinting should be limited
to a minimum of simple, clearly legible information:

1) *Name and degree.* Listing more than the highest earned relevant degree rarely adds information and detracts from the dignity. Listing an honorary degree (D.D., D.Sc. etc.) is a violation of professional modesty. Using the title "Dr." in front of one's name, in place of or in addition to initials of a doctoral degree following the name, is considered improper.

2) *Type of practice.* The A.A.M.F.C. member will ordinarily identify himself/herself as a Marriage and Family Counselor. Related professional identification may be included (Licensed Clinical Social Worker, Licensed Psychologist, etc.)

3) *Specialty.* Should a member wish to emphasize a single specialization within marriage and family practice, he or she may do so provided the designation reflects an exclusive emphasis.

4) *A.A.M.F.C. membership.* Persons holding clinical membership in the A.A.M.F.C. may designate this by the following statement: "Member, American Association of Marriage and Family Counselors."

5) *Address and telephone.* The location of the professional practice may be designated by appropriate address and telephone number(s).

6) *Insignia.*

   (a) A.A.M.F.C. Insignia. The A.A.M.F.C. insignia may NOT be used on printed professional materials of a member, a group of members practicing together, nor a training center approved by the A.A.M.F.C. It may be used by regional divisions in the course of their bona fide activities as divisions of the A.A.M.F.C.

   (b) Other Insignia. Professional insignia intended to convey the orientation focus of professional practice may be proper if the design and content is simple and informational.

B. Brochures. The production and distribution of public informational materials is an appropriate activity of the marriage and family counselor. The purpose of such material is to inform the public, not to "promote" the individual's practice. Therefore the emphasis should be on simple statements of services offered, factual presentations of the practitioner's relevant training and experience, and accurate information about contracts and conditions for service.

CHAPTER 42

The Profession of Marriage Counseling as Viewed by Members of Four Allied Professions

Richard K. Kerckhoff

Within the last twenty years, marriage counseling has been assuming some of the characteristics usually associated with a new profession. Previously, the only marriage counseling done by professional people was that practiced as an unofficial side-line by clergymen, physicians, teachers, attorneys, and others. Since these latter groups, along with social workers, psychologists, and psychiatrists, still give most of the marriage counsel that is given in a professional setting, a question arises about their reaction to the emergence of a specialized profession of marriage counseling. Also, since the new profession of marriage counseling is still not very strongly established as a separate profession, it might be assumed that the reaction of the more established professions, as expressed through their organized "pressure groups," will be an important factor in the future structure, function, and status of the new profession.

That assumption was made in this study. It was hypothesized that there are areas of ignorance and antipathy concerning marriage counseling and the marriage counseling profession among members of four of these allied professions: clergymen, physicians, social workers, and attorneys. An attempt was made to discover what members of these professions think about counseling, what they think it is and should be. What relationship do they see between marriage counseling and their own professions? In what ways do they react like members of interest groups?

The main instruments used in this study to test the hypothesis and answer the questions were personal interviews with professional people in the four chosen occupations and a 77-item questionnaire. Prior to the building of the final questionnaire, hundreds of interviews and open-end statements were gathered and two trial questionnaires were tested. One thousand and ten copies of the final questionnaire were mailed to random samples drawn from membership lists of organized bodies of the four

Reprinted with permission of the author and the publisher from *Marriage and Family Living*, 1953, *15*, 340-344.

professional groups in Detroit, Michigan. When a return of 120 social worker questionnaires and 80 of each of the other three professions had been received, the sampling was "closed" and these 360 questionnaires were analyzed. The statistical analysis was composed of percentages for the various responses and critical ratio analysis to determine the statistical significance of the differences between percentages.

An estimate of the probable differences between those who replied to the questionnaire and those who did not was made, although in this study there was special interest in people who have strong opinions and who might feel like expressing them via the questionnaire. The study includes an analysis of "first wave" and "second wave" questionnaires compared with each other and with replies to a short, three-item questionnaire filled out by persons who refused to fill out the large questionnaire. It was also possible to make a telephone study of thirty attorneys who failed to return any questionnaire and to compare the results of these interviews with the responses made by those attorneys who did return questionnaires. Although differences are found in these various comparisons, they are not clear-cut unidirectional differences. In general, however, they lead one to believe that people who returned the questionnaire differed from people who did not largely because of the *intensity* of their acceptance or rejection of marriage counseling, rather than because they were as a group either more likely to be accepting or more likely to be rejecting.

Although no well-established measuring device could be found with which to compare the questionnaire to test its validity, it was possible to note comparisons on specific areas of the questionnaire with other studies and with the author's professional experience as a marriage counselor as well as with the personal interview results. Some confidence in the validity of the instrument was gained through these "tests." The reliability of the instrument was tested by test-retest, comparison of responses to similar items within the questionnaire, comparison of responses to certain items which appeared on both the final questionnaire and on the earlier questionnaire, and by split-sample tests of responses to specific items on the final questionnaire. In the last-mentioned test both odd and even samples made responses within one standard error of the responses of the total sample; for example, while 45 percent (S. E. of 2.6) of the 360 respondents said they knew where to find a good marriage counselor, 43 percent of the 180 odd-numbered respondents said so and 47 percent of the even-numbered ones agreed.

It was found that a third of the 360 respondents claimed to have made referrals to a marriage counselor in the past; this ranged from 10 percent of the attorneys to almost half of the clergy. About 17 percent claimed to have heard of a national organization of marriage counselors. Almost all of the respondents said that they came into contact with cases of marital difficulties in their professional work, and half the social workers and more than nine-tenths of the three other professional groups claimed to have done some marriage counseling during the past year. Twenty-eight percent, mostly clergymen and social workers, replied that they had had some formal training in marriage counseling; 23 percent considered themselves marriage counselors. Only 16 percent of the questionnaire respondents would say that marriage counseling today is a profession; 42 percent believed it is becoming a profession, and 16 percent said it would be a mistake to professionalize marriage counseling. More than four-fifths of the clergy, social workers, and physicians claimed that marriage counseling today is either "worthwhile" or "very worthwhile," and two-thirds of the attorneys agreed. Nine percent of the total respondents felt that marriage counseling is "of little or no worth," and two percent said it is "harmful or dangerous." Fifty-eight percent said they would refer cases to a marriage counselor if a capable one opened an office nearby. Very few (usually less than 10 percent) of the respondents said marriage counseling is quackery or pseudo-science or strictly "advice to the lovelorn" material for newspapers. The specific objections to counseling were more often based on ignorance that counseling of a professional nature exists or confidence that the respondents themselves could do adequate marriage counseling. The personal interviews also discovered a vague feeling that marriage counseling is too "loose," not organized, not really a profession, and so, not acceptable for referral relations. In items wherein the respondents' conceptions of the relationship between counseling and their own professions were examined, it was definitely found that most opposition to a separate profession of marriage counseling centered in that area where the new profession might compete with, or infringe upon, the established professions' prerogatives. However, very few respondents except some of the lawyers actually claimed marriage counseling is a threat to their profession. When asked which professional group today—including the separate profession of marriage counselors—is best equipped to do marriage counseling, each of the four sub-samples chose its own profession as best equipped. All four groups chose "full-time marriage counselors" as second best, however, and a great deal of interest in, and desire to know more about, this newer professional group was expressed. All of the above ideas about counseling are amplified by various other questionnaire responses and by the personal interview material which is quoted in the study.

To become a professional body, the questionnaire respondents claimed, marriage counselors must do a better public relations job, create better relations with other professional groups, become better organized, establish more rigid professional standards, and license practitioners. They tended to expect future marriage counseling to be practiced both by a separate group of counselors and by members of the "allied" professions. They said that a person who practices marriage counseling should have a great many personal virtues not usually demanded in most occupations; both personality traits and social characteristics such as marital status and religious affiliations were included in their specifications. As for the training of counselors, the respondents almost all agreed that a graduate or professional degree is needed for this work. Psychology, theory and techniques of counseling, social work, sociology, human biology, theology, and medicine were chosen as the most important subject matter fields for the counselor trainee; and again each professional group considered its own academic preparation as most important for marriage counseling.

The respondents tended to choose "mental hygiene" goals as most important for marriage counseling rather than "traditional" goals. Most frequently chosen from a 13-point checklist were: "To help the couples understand and appreciate each other's personality, to safeguard the welfare of children, to help the counselee grow in emotional maturity, to help people enjoy their marriages more, to help the counselee understand himself." The clergy leaned more strongly toward "traditional" goals, such as "to prevent divorces, to impress the counselee with the seriousness of his marriage vows, and to help make marriage the sacred institution it once was." In stating their views on the functions a counselor should and should not perform, the respondents showed considerable agreement with the professional literature on marriage counseling. In general, the social workers were more in agreement with the views of professional counselors as expressed in the literature than were the other three groups. As for the method of counseling, 31 percent of the 360 respondents chose a response which indicated that they favored a "directive" role on the part of the counselor, 20 percent chose a "non-directive" role, and 42 percent chose a middle-of-the-road course; the clergy split almost evenly on the three courses but leaned toward the two extremes, the physicians favored the middle-of-the-road and the directive relationship, especially the latter, and the attorneys were mostly "directive."

In personal interviews, as well as in numerous other questionnaire items not mentioned herein, it was found that the professional groups being tested had many other specifications for the profession of marriage counseling. Defining goals and eliminating publicity-seeking quacks in the field were often suggested by social workers; attorneys most often suggested licensing or other legal controls on the new profession; and the clergy were most interested in the adequacy of the marriage counselor's spiritual or religious views.

In comparing the replies made to the questionnaire by the four professional groups, the conclusion was made that the clergy were the most enthusiastic about marriage counseling but were also most suspicious of the counseling done by persons not closely associated with organized religion; they tended to see counseling as religious work. The Catholic clergy failed to reply to the questionnaire to such an extent that the clergy sample is almost entirely Protestant (the Jewish sample was small to begin with). Of all the clergy, however, the Catholic respondents were most confident that the counseling being done by their church is adequate.

The social workers tended throughout the study to "talk the same language" as that used by marriage counselors. However, few social workers would make referrals to the average marriage counselor who is not himself a social worker or psychiatrist, since most of these social workers expressed a preference for family case workers. Some interesting data were discovered by examining the social worker responses closely enough to compare case workers with group workers, and psychiatric social workers with medical social workers.

The physicians in this study showed some traditional conservatism about the new marriage counseling profession and tended to view marital problems in medical terms. Few of them had any formal training in counseling and almost all of them do counseling in their work. General practitioners were compared with obstetrician-gynecologists in this study.

The attorneys were the most outspoken of the four groups against the new profession of marriage counseling; they, along with the physicians, were least well acquainted with counselors or with where to find a marriage counselor. The attorney sample was analyzed in terms of those who had handled the most divorce cases compared with those who had handled the least, to see if significant differences appeared in their questionnaire responses.

The data were also examined to see what relationship certain views of marriage counseling had with personal characteristics such as age, sex, marital status, length of professional practice, religion, and income. Some interesting differences were noted when these categories were subdivided, but the resulting samples were so small that relatively few statistically significant differences were found.

In conclusion, a good deal of ignorance and some antipathy to the new profession were found among people who are in a good position to know about marriage counseling and to influence its future as a profession. Very little concrete opposition to the newer profession was found, but a large amount of distrust was expressed. The author's general impression is that this distrust, along with the normal vested interests of the older professions and the present inadequacies in the field of marriage counseling itself, will tend to be a deterrent to the future growth of the profession of marriage counseling.

CHAPTER 43

Marriage and Family Counseling: Legislative Considerations

William C. Nichols, Jr.

THE CURRENT AND FUTURE SCENE

Marriage and family counseling legislation is a need and cause whose time has arrived. A majority of the states have made attempts—some repeatedly—during recent years to pass laws regulating the practice of marriage counseling or marriage and family counseling (terms used interchangeably in this handbook). By early 1973 five states had succeeded in enacting such statutes. California was the first, providing for the licensure of marriage, family, and child counselors in 1963. Michigan followed with an act to certify marriage counselors in 1966. New Jersey's law licensing marriage counselors was passed in 1968 and became effective in 1969. The movement toward state licensure gained momentum in 1973 when two more states enacted legislation covering marriage and family counseling, Nevada with a certification act and Utah with a licensure statute. Other bills in 1973 missed legislative enactment, some very narrowly, in states as widely separated as Texas and Connecticut. These are among the scores of bills that have appeared in state legislatures during the past decade.

For the states that have not yet enacted statutes it appears to be less a matter of whether they will pass licensing or certification laws concerning marriage and family counseling than a matter of when and what kind of law they will eventually place on the books. Those who identify with professionalization in marriage and family counseling are faced with the choice of taking the lead in advancing the cause of adequate and appropriate legislation or having laws devised and passed by others who are less knowledgeable and dedicated to the cause of sound standards and effective legislation in this area.

The need for marriage and family counselors to become involved in legislative and other political activities in an organized, group way has been recognized at the national level by the American Association of Marriage and Family Counselors. The 1973 chartering of an A.A.M.F.C. organization in Washington, D.C., as a trade organization rather than as a tax-exempt foundation type of organization, had several consequences. The action made it possible for marriage and family counselors as an

organized group to work for legislation and to lobby and engage in other
political activities on issues—such as national health insurance—which
affect the profession at the national level. Further, the action made it
possible for the new national structure to assist groups and individuals
seeking legislation at the state level, and, equally important, it provided a
pattern for functioning in the legislative and political area for the present
and future that can be duplicated in the various states.

All states could benefit from the organization of marriage and family
counselors within the state into a structure similar to that of the
A.A.M.F.C.-D.C. There is a serious impediment to effective political
action when marriage and family counselors are either unorganized or
organized under provisions that provide a tax-exempt status that would be
jeopardized by group involvement in legislative or other political activity.
Such actions necessarily have to be conducted on an individual basis in
which marriage and family counselors act as individual citizens rather than
as an organized entity when the group enjoys the tax-exempt status. This
impediment needs to be removed so that marriage and family counselors
not only can work for original and improved licensure laws, but also so
that they can continue to function in an organized way at the state level
on matters of periodic and perennial concern to the profession.

Standards may be a national concern, but licensure is a state matter. It
is at the state level that marriage and family counselors must obtain their
license to practice under law and the public must secure its protection
against the untrained and the unscrupulous practitioner that the passage
and enforcement of good laws can provide. Practically speaking, in order
to protect the public good and advance the cause of professional marriage
and family counseling, it is sometimes necessary not only to write and
support sound legislation but also to oppose and defeat poorly conceived
and unsound laws and actions.

None of this should be construed as indicating or implying that marriage and family counselors should engage in what is commonly referred
to as "fence building," i.e., setting up requirements that keep out other
qualified individuals. Laws affecting the public good should not be written
so restrictively as to carve out a domain of special privilege for a favored
small group any more than they should be written so permissively as to
admit practically any person who wishes to enter.

There will be debates here and there for some time into the future as
to who should be licensed to perform marriage and family counseling. A
tension will continue to prevail between those who would view marriage
and family counseling as a completely open domain for any lay or professional person to enter without any need of specialized training, and those
who assert that it is a kind of endeavor requiring specialized knowledge
and training. Another tension will be found between those who would
require marriage and family counselors to be trained specifically in marriage and family counseling as an addition to their basic orientation and
skill and those who would either permit or require graduate or professional training directly and entirely within the framework of the new,
younger discipline of marriage and family counseling.

During much of its existence the old American Association of Marriage Counselors required its members to be trained in an established profession or graduate discipline and then to obtain specialized training in marriage counseling on top of the basic work in an academic discipline or profession. More recently developments have occurred that make it possible today to obtain training in marriage and family counseling as a graduate field of study and to earn academic degrees in the specialty. Consequently, more than one kind of path exists through which individuals may move toward competence and professionalism in marriage and family counseling, some coming along the old route of training in an outside discipline followed by specialization and some along the newer route of training in marriage and family counseling as such, without first going into psychology, social work, or some other allied field. The tensions between different orientations concerning what is the best or even the permissible kind of training for marriage and family counselors probably will continue for an extended period into the future.

Given both the background out of which marriage and family counseling has developed and the current mixture of multidisciplinary and single discipline streams feeding practitioners into the field, it appears the course of both necessity and reason to provide for liberal definitions of marriage and family counseling preparation requirements. This does not mean that standards in training and supervised clinical experience or academic preparation must be compromised. What it does mean is that individuals and groups of individuals who enter the field from both streams need to work together for strong legislation and conscientious implementation of the statutes enacted.

Professional imperialism of the type that would seek to bar qualified professional persons from the field or to limit licensure to individuals belonging to a given profession or holding membership in a given organization is not in the public interest and is self-defeating for the profession. For example, assuming that they would be able to do so, it would be as wrong and ill-advised for marriage and family counselor professionals to engage in that kind of professional imperialism and fence building as it would be for psychologists, physicians, social workers, or clergymen to seek to stake a claim on marriage and family counseling and keep all others from practicing in the area.

The laws that are written should protect the complete rights of qualified professional persons to perform marriage and family counseling services so long as they do so within the discipline, ethics, and accepted procedures of their own profession. At the same time, it is reasonable and equitable, as well as in the public interest, to require that professional persons who wish to advertise and hold themselves out to the public as marriage and family counselors and to function primarily as marriage and family counselors—in contrast to merely performing such services in a manner incidental to their customary professional services to their clientele—meet the qualifications for licensure and be licensed before they practice as marriage and family counselors. Although a good law will provide for appropriate exemptions, it also will demand adequate training and licensure for those functioning primarily as marriage and family counselors.

Marriage and family counselors have not completed their task when a strong statute has been passed. There is a continuing need to monitor the actual implementation of the law, discovering the shortcomings and inequities and working to remedy the deficiencies, and to work with the state licensing board and regulatory agencies, as well as directly with individuals, on matters of ethical advertising and practice. Equally important is the need to recognize that legislation is no panacea, that it can only require given levels of education and experience of those licensed and can only protect against certain kinds of incompetence and poor practice. Competence can be obtained only through proper and appropriately devised and executed training. In brief, the profession protects by legislation and provides for competent service by training. The supervision of the work of marriage and family counselors needs support long after the best possible bill has been placed on the books, continuing as a perennial concern for the profession.

Effective group effort, organized action supported by the largest number of persons and resources that marriage and family counselors can bring together in a responsible way is needed long after passage of state legislation and national legislation, for matters that can be dealt with at a national level. Cooperative efforts between national and state organizations are needed now and will be required now for dealing with many things. The formation and promulgation of this handbook on state licensure represents but one step in that direction.

PROFESSIONALIZATION AND LICENSURE

Marriage and family counseling, as mentioned above, is relatively young as a separate and distinct professional service. The first centers for service and training in the United States were established approximately 40 years ago, in the early 1930s. The American Association of Marriage Counselors was formed in 1942 as a multidisciplinary or interdisciplinary organization composed of representatives from sociology, psychology, social work, law, religious ministry, medicine, and education. The early members of the organization were trained in varying degrees to deal with marital and family problems, many being self-trained.

The generally accepted criteria for professionalization in a field had been met by the time that the organization changed its name to the American Association of Marriage and Family Counselors in 1970. As noted in the reports of others, both individual and group, over the years, the organization has promulgated a code of ethics that is binding on its members, conducts numerous national and regional meetings, encourages research on marriage and family counseling which is published in a number of national and regional journals and books, approves training centers and programs, and encourages the establishment and maintenance of professional standards for clinical competence. There has been, therefore, for more than 30 years an established national organization setting the pace in the marriage and family counseling field.

One of the more significant aspects of the movement into professionalism in the field has been the establishment and operation of training centers approved by the A.A.M.F.C. (formerly the A.A.M.C.). Among such centers have been Columbia University, the Merrill-Palmer Institute in Detroit, the University of Minnesota, the Marriage Council of Philadelphia (the University of Pennsylvania), the University of Southern California, Purdue University, and others, including the Marriage Counseling Centre of Montreal in Canada. Programs currently are in operation in college and university settings, as well as in freestanding clinical facilities, from one coast to the other, from the Florida State University to the University of Southern California. By 1973 the field was developing at such a pace that it was becoming increasingly difficult and, indeed, virtually impossible, to keep track of the emerging academic and clinical training programs in the field.

Simultaneous with the development of an organization, an ethical code, a body of knowledge, training programs both clinical and academic, and legislation in some states has emerged an unprecedented and ever-growing demand from the public for marriage and family counseling services. The multiple and complex problems that contribute to that large and growing demand for services include the changing roles of males and females, the expectation of greater personal fulfillment and satisfaction from the marital relationship and family living, and other more remote sociocultural factors. The remarkable surge upward in divorce rates between 1960 and 1970 also highlights the need for qualified marriage and family counselors who can help to prevent the development of irreconcilable differences between spouses and can help other persons to handle such problems in the best ways possible in the event that they do arise.

The public needs guidance in finding adequately trained practitioners who can help in working with marriage and family problems. In states that do not provide for licensure or certification of marriage and family counselors, the public is faced with an undefined situation in which marriage and family counseling is being offered on three quite different levels. As noted in interprofessional and multidisciplinary reports of the past, these include:

Non-Professional, Untrained Practitioners.

Friends, relatives, neighbors, hairdressers, bartenders, and other untrained individuals including phrenologists, palmists, and undifferentiated charlatans offer marriage and family counseling with or without a fee attached.

Professional, Non-Specialized Practitioners.

Professional persons such as clergymen, attorneys, physicians, psychologists, and others offer marriage and family counseling as an incidental part of their primary professional service. Their qualifications vary, but the major thing that they have in common is a lack of specialized training, including supervised experience, in marriage and family counseling.

Professional, Specialized Practitioners.

Marriage and family counseling services offered by professional persons who are trained to perform such services within an agency setting or in an independent or private practice setting represent a third and distinct level of assistance for a troubled public. Some of these practitioners were trained first in one of the older disciplines, adding their specialized work in marriage and family counseling to their original theory and practice base, while others learned their theory and obtained their practice entirely within the framework of the new profession. As noted above, qualified persons trained through either of these routes can provide good professional marriage and family services to the public.

The need for legal control in the marriage and family counseling field is twofold: on the one hand, the public needs and deserves protection from exploitation and damage, intentional or unintentional, by quacks or well-meaning individuals who are untrained or inadequately trained for the practice of this complex clinical skill and specialty; and, on the other hand, persons seeking assistance require and deserve the assurance of a reasonable level of competence and accountability on the part of the practitioner insofar as those things can be provided by legal controls.

Quackery. Examples of quackery may be turned up in any state in which legal controls are lacking. Occasional articles in the mass media highlight bizarre examples of exploitation of the public from all sections of the United States. Among the common types of occurrences are sexual exploitation of unwary individuals, especially females, under the guise of providing professional help; and misrepresentation of qualifications, i.e., individuals without adequate or appropriate training represent themselves to be qualified professional marriage and family counselors. Absence of legal regulation makes it difficult, and often impossible, to find, investigate, and prosecute fraudulent counselors and to correct abuses in the field.

Competence and Accountability. As is true with other professions the most effective way of providing legal control over marriage and family counseling is through the enactment and enforcement of well designed legislation. Such laws should aid the public to discriminate in at least a general way between authentic and spurious practitioners and services. Laws at best, however, can only screen out the unqualified and spurious and provide guidelines for the enforcement of minimal standards of practice, holding practitioners accountable in essentially general ways for what they do or fail to do with their clientele and in regard to the public. Legislation does not replace the responsibility of the profession itself for working to produce competent practitioners and striving to make certain that they remain accountable for their professional actions, but it does provide a framework in which the profession's task is made much easier and the public good is served.

Legal regulation of marriage and family counseling may be of two kinds: licensing or certification. It is important that the differences be understood by those seeking regulatory laws.

Certification. Certification restricts the use of a title. If the law is a certification law, no one may use the restricted titles—e.g., "marriage and family counselor" or "marriage and family therapist" or other restricted titles—unless he or she meets the requirements set forth in the statute and

obtains a certificate under its provisions from the designated state board
or office.

Licensure. Licensure laws, on the other hand, restrict function. An
individual may not engage in the practice of marriage and family counseling, for example, as it is defined in the law unless he or she meets the
requirements set forth in the law and obtains a license, regardless of the
title used. As an important practical matter, sections on certification and
protection of title are included in licensure laws.

To paraphrase a task force report rendered a decade ago:

> Licensing is more restrictive. All that needs to be done to assure that licensing
> will be effective is to enforce the licensing statute. More is needed in the case
> of certification. Not only must the certification requirement or statute be
> enforced, but also the public must be educated to use the services only of
> those who are certified, because under a certification act, other, uncertified
> persons can provide marriage and family counseling, so long as they do not use
> the restricted title or titles.

A good licensure bill would not only provide for the exclusion of
unqualified persons, but also would make provision for the close, explicit
control of those who are qualified to practice in order to encourage the
highest quality service.

Exemptions from Licensure. Legislators may have a genuine concern
that the public good be served by any proposed legislation and also may
need to be convinced that the purposes of those seeking passage of the bill
are not simply those of economic advancement or self-aggrandizement in
other ways for marriage and family counselors. Hence, it is important not
only to draft a bill that provides for the exclusion of the unqualified and
the control of the qualified, but also to inform and educate members of
the marriage and family counseling profession and the legislature with
regard to the role and meaning of public need, exclusion, control, and
other factors in legislation.

The laws enacted to date have been concerned essentially with the
private practice of marriage counseling, marriage and family counseling, or
marriage, family, and child counseling, the exact title of the counselor
depending on the particular state statute considered. Those enacted in the
future probably will be focused essentially on private practice. Individuals
who have worked for legislation in marriage and family counseling as well
as persons who have dealt with licensing laws in other fields generally
seem to be in agreement that it is necessary to exempt from legal control
in the licensure bill practitioners who perform their services in the
employment of certain categories of institutions and agencies. As a practical matter, it generally does not appear possible to secure passage of a
law without providing such exemptions, the collective lobbying power of
the concerned institutions, agencies, and professional groups being too
powerful to overcome.

The first five states to enact legislation in this field all made specific
and clear provision for the exemption of practitioners performing their
services in the employment of certain categories of agencies and institutions. California exempted workers in nonprofit and charitable agencies

and all educational institutions meeting accrediting standards, issuing waivers to such practitioners. Michigan exempted practitioners in governmental and reputable social agencies. New Jersey widened the scope, exempting workers in accredited educational institutions, nonprofit community agencies, and governmental agencies (federal, state, or local), and provided that those working in proprietary agencies could be exempt if they functioned under the supervision of a licensee. Nevada provided exemption for public agencies and accredited educational institutions offering the regulated services. Under the Utah law those working in governmental and social service agencies and students who are in training under supervision need not be licensed for the practice of marriage and family counseling. Provision for exemption of students is generally stipulated, provided they practice under supervision in approved settings and are designated by a title that clearly indicates their student or training status.

The other factor that has to be considered with regard to exemption is whether legislation will exempt certain categories of practicing professionals from the requirement that they be licensed as marriage and family counselors if they offer such services as part of their independent professional practice. The first five states to regulate marriage and family counseling ran the gamut on this point from Nevada which provides only student and institutional employee exemptions and none for practicing professionals from other fields to Utah which exempts professional persons deemed qualified to practice including specifically psychiatrists, attorneys, clinical psychologists, certified social workers, and certain pastoral counselors in addition to those who qualified under the grandfather clause. The others fall somewhere between Nevada and Utah. California exempts lawyers and clergymen who provide marriage counseling as part of their professional duties. Michigan's act indicates that consulting psychologists, attorneys, and physicians who do not advertise or charge for marriage counseling and ordained ministers who do not advertise or charge a fee and who provide marriage counseling incidental to their usual duties are not affected. New Jersey exempts psychologists, attorneys, ministers, guidance counselors, and physicians who provide such services within the accepted standards of their professions. Most states passing licensure laws in the future probably will find it necessary to give careful attention to the claims of clergymen, attorneys, psychologists, and psychiatrists for some exemptions, particularly if they do not advertise themselves specifically as marriage and family counselors and perform such services in a manner that is consistent with practice in their professions and in a way that is incidental to their usual services to their clientele.

Hanging out a shingle for private practice in marriage and family counseling and performing such services for a fee, monetary or otherwise, is a different matter from working in an institutional setting or performing such actions as an incidental part of normal professional services to clientele, and one that should be subject to legal regulation because it does affect the public interest and is not subject to legal regulation and control under other existing laws.

THE MODEL BILL

The model bill presented here represents an attempt to combine in one document a model that could be used to draft a bill for either certification or licensure as well as a model that could be used to draft a bill for legal regulation of either marriage counseling or marriage and family counseling. The term marriage counseling was used in two of the early acts—in Michigan and New Jersey, but the descriptions of what was regulated covered marriage and family counseling. The model bill, in other words, could be used—with proper deletion and placement of wording—as a guide for drafting bills for:

1. Licensure of marriage and family counselors
2. Licensure of marriage counselors
3. Certification of marriage and family counselors
4. Certification of marriage counselors.

If, for example, one wished to draft a bill for the licensing of marriage counselors, it would be necessary only to delete the underlined materials between bars—i.e., /certified/, /certification/, and so forth—and the words "and family" in the "marriage and family counseling" references. On the other hand, if the desire were to write a bill for the certification of marriage counselors—instead of the licensure of marriage and family counselors—it would be necessary only to replace references to license, licensure, and so forth with the proper form of certify, certification, et cetera, and to remove the words "and practice" in section 4 and "or practices marriage and family counseling" in section 19.

Portions of the bill undoubtedly would have to be modified in order to make it conform to requirements of particular states. For example, the word "state" may be replaced by "commonwealth" in some jurisdictions; board of marriage and family counselor examiners by some other term; and other sections relating to procedures altered so as to meet state requirements.

The staff of the legislator introducing the bill generally can be counted on to provide some assistance in making certain portions of a bill conform to the pattern followed in that state. Bills customarily are sent from the office of the sponsoring legislator to the appropriate state office for final drafting and checking. In Florida, for example, the Office of Legislative Services handles such details.

The major concerns of professional marriage and family counselors will be that the qualifications for practice, definitions of the activity permitted and prohibited, the composition and qualifications of the board, and other related matters are preserved in a manner that will produce a statute consistent with sound standards and practices.

If a bill at any step along the way is so drastically altered as to undercut markedly the intent of the profession—i.e., if it is so altered that the result is a poor bill that would harm the public and the profession—it may be better to try to kill it and start all over again in the next legislative session than to permit the passage of a bad bill. The particular strategy employed depends on the peculiarities of the state involved, as well as on the judgment of the supporters of the legislation, some feeling that it is better in some instances and states to get whatever law is possible on the books and then to work diligently to get it amended and improved. This is a matter that should be carefully considered in the light of all the facts available, there being no universal principles applicable to all situations.

The chapter following the model bill will include discussion of some specific sections and items within the bill.

MARRIAGE AND FAMILY COUNSELING MODEL BILL

A bill to be entitled

AN ACT relating to marriage and family counselors; requiring licensure/certification/ of certain individuals who carry on the practice of marriage and family counseling in the state of _____

_____ ; providing definitions; providing exceptions; creating a board to be known as the state board of marriage and family counselor examiners; prescribing the membership, duties, and powers of said board; providing for issuance and revocation of licenses/certificates/; fixing penalties for violation; providing an effective date.

Be it enacted by the Legislature of the State of _____ :

Section 1. SHORT TITLE. This Act shall be known and may be cited as the "Marriage and Family Counselor Licensing/Certification/Act."

Section 2. PURPOSE. The practice of marriage and family counseling in the state of _____ is hereby declared to affect the public safety and welfare, and to be subject to regulation and control in the public interest in order to protect the public from the unprofessional, improper, unauthorized, and unqualified practice of marriage and family counseling and from unprofessional conduct by persons licensed/certified/ to practice marriage and family counseling. This Act shall be liberally construed to carry out these objects and purposes.

Section 3. DEFINITIONS. As used in this Act, unless the context clearly requires otherwise and except as

(1) "Licensed/certified/ marriage and family counselor" means an individual to whom a license/certificate/ has been issued pursuant to the provisions of this Act, which license/certificate/ is in force and not suspended or revoked as of the particular time in question.

(2) "Marriage and family counseling" means the rendering of counseling services or therapy to individuals, either singly or in groups, for the purpose of resolving emotional conflicts within marriage and family relationships, modifying behavior, altering old attitudes, and establishing new patterns in the area of marriage and family relationships, modifying behavior, altering old attitudes, and establishing new patterns in the area of marriage and family life including premarital counseling and post-divorce counseling.

(3) "Advertise" means, but is not limited to, the issuing or causing to be distributed of any card, sign, or device to any person, or the causing, permitting, or allowing of any sign or marking in or on any building or structure, or in any newspaper or magazine or in

any directory, or on radio or television, or by advertising by any other means designed to secure public attention.

(4) "Board" means the state board of marriage and family counselor examiners established by this Act acting as such under the provisions of this Act.

(5) "Recognized educational institution" means any accredited educational institution which grants the bachelor's, master's, and doctor's degrees, or any one or more thereof, and which is recognized by an accrediting body acceptable to the state board of marriage and family counselor examiners.

Section 4. PROHIBITED ACTS. Beginning January 1, 19___ , no person who is not licensed/certified/ under this Act shall advertise the performance of marriage and family counseling services or represent himself to be a licensed/certified/ practicing marriage and family counselor, use a title or description, including the following titles: marriage counselor, advisor, or consultant; family counselor, advisor or consultant; family guidance counselor, advisor, or consultant; marriage therapist, advisor, or consultant; or any other name, style, or description denoting that the person so advertising engages in marriage and family counseling. Except as otherwise specifically provided in this Act, only a person licensed/certified/ under this Act shall advertise himself, purport or describe himself as offering marriage or family counseling or advice; marriage or family guidance services or advice; marriage or family relations advice or assistance; services in the alleviation of any marital or family problem; or service of like import or effect, or offer to practice, or practice marriage and family counseling as defined in this Act, except as otherwise permitted in section 5.

Section 5. EXCEPTIONS. This Act does not apply to:

(1) a person who practices marriage and family counseling solely as part of his duties as an employee of:

    (a) an accredited academic institution, or a federal, state, county, or local governmental institution or agency, or a bona fide research facility while performing those duties for which he was employed by such an institution, agency, or facility;

    (b) an organization which is nonprofit and which is, in the opinion of the board, a bona fide community agency, while performing those duties for which he was employed by such an agency.

    (c) a proprietary organization while performing those duties for which he was employed by such an organization, provided his marriage and family counseling duties are under the direct supervision of a licensed/certified/ practicing marriage and family counselor under arrangements approved by the board.

(2) a student of counseling, a marriage and family counseling intern or person preparing for the practice of marriage and family counseling under qualified supervision in a training institution or facility or supervisory arrangement recognized and approved by the board, provided he is designated by such titles as "marriage

counseling intern," "family counseling intern," or others, clearly indicating such training status.

(3) a qualified practicing member of another profession such as law, medicine, religious ministry, psychology, social work, or school counseling and guidance, when his practice is clearly within his profession and consistent with the accepted standards of his profession; provided, however, that he does not purport to the public by any title or description stating or implying that he is a marriage and family counselor or is licensed/certified/ to practice marriage and family counseling.

Section 6. STATE BOARD OF MARRIAGE AND FAMILY COUNSELOR EXAMINERS.

(1) There is hereby created the State Board of Marriage and Family Counselor Examiners which shall consist of seven members who are residents of this state. At least five members shall be licensed/certified/ practicing marriage and family counselors; each shall have been for at least five years immediately preceding appointment actively engaged as a marriage and family counselor in rendering professional services in marriage and family counseling, or in the education and training of doctoral or post-doctoral students of marriage and family counseling deemed substantially equivalent thereto, and shall have spent the majority of the time devoted by him to such activity during the two years preceding his appointment, in this state; shall hold from an accredited institution so recognized at the time of granting of such degree at least a master's degree in family life education, marriage and family counseling, psychology, social work, or sociology of the family, or a closely allied field, or shall be a practicing attorney, clergyman, or physician whose transcripts establish that he has completed an appropriate course of study in a closely allied field; and shall be a member of or have professional standing equivalent to that required for clinical membership in the American Association of Marriage and Family Counselors. At least one member shall be a representative of the general public who has no direct affiliation with the practice of marriage and family counseling. The initial appointees, with the exception of citizen members, shall be deemed to be and shall become licensed/certified/ practicing marriage and family counselors immediately upon their appointment and qualification as members of the board.

(2) The members of the board shall be appointed by the governor. The governor shall appoint the members of the initial board on the effective date of this Act, designating two members for terms expiring on June 30, 19____ ; two members for terms expiring on June 30, 19____ ; and three members for terms expiring on June 30, 19____ . Thereafter, each member of the board shall be appointed for a term of three years.

(3) Each appointee shall, upon accepting appointment to the board, take and subscribe to the oath or affirmation prescribed by law and file same in the office of the secretary of state.

(4) If before the expiration of his term any member shall die, resign, become disqualified, or otherwise cease to be a board member, the vacancy shall be filled by the governor by appointment for the unexpired term.

(5) The governor shall have power to remove from office any member of the board for incompetence, neglect of duty, unprofessional conduct, or moral turpitude; but no member may be thus removed until after a public hearing of the charges against him, and at least 30 days' prior written notice to such accused member of the charges against him and of the date fixed for such hearing.

Section 7. BOARD ORGANIZATION AND MEETINGS.

(1) The board shall, at its first meeting, to be called by the governor as soon as may be following the appointment of its members, and at all annual meetings, to be held in June of each year thereafter, organize by electing from among its members a chairman, vice-chairman, and secretary. Such officers shall serve until the following June 30 and until their successors are appointed and qualified.

(2) The board shall hold at least 1 regular meeting each year, but additional meetings may be held upon call of the chairman or at the written request of any 2 members of the board.

(3) Four members of the board shall constitute a quorum and no action at any meeting shall be taken without at least 3 votes in accord.

Section 8. POWERS AND DUTIES OF THE BOARD.

(1) The board shall administer and enforce the provisions of this Act. The board shall from time to time adopt such rules and regulations and such amendments thereof and supplements thereto as it may deem necessary to enable it to perform its duties under and to carry into effect the provisions of this Act.

(2) The board shall examine and pass on the qualifications of all applicants for licenses/certificates/ under this Act, and shall issue a license/certificate/ to each successful applicant therefor, attesting to his professional qualification to engage in the practice of marriage and family counseling.

(3) The board shall adopt a seal which shall be affixed to all licenses/certificates/ issued by the board.

(4) The board may authorize expenditures deemed necessary to carry out the provisions of this Act from the license fees and other sources of income of the board, within the limits of available appropriations according to law, but in no event shall expenditures exceed the revenues of the board during any fiscal year.

(5) The board shall be empowered to hire such assistants as it may deem necessary to carry on its activities pursuant to this Act.

(6) Board members shall serve without compensation but shall be reimbursed for actual expenses reasonably incurred in the performance of duties as a member of the board or on behalf of the board.

Section 9. LICENSE/CERTIFICATION/ APPLICATION. Each person desiring to obtain a license/certificate/ as a practicing marriage and family counselor shall make application therefor to the board upon such form and in such manner as the board shall prescribe and shall furnish evidence satisfactory to the board that he:

(1) is at least 21 years of age;

(2) is of good moral character;

(3) has not engaged or is not engaged in any practice or conduct which would be a ground for refusing to issue a license/certificate/ under this Act;

(4) qualifies for licensing/certification/ by an examination of credentials or for admission to an assembled examination to be conducted by the board.

Section 10. APPLICATIONS BEFORE JANUARY 1, 19____. Any person who applies on or before January 1, 19____, may obtain a license/certificate/ to be issued by the board by an examination of credentials if he meets the qualifications set forth in subsections (1), (2), and (3) of section 9 and provides satisfactory evidence to the board that he:

(1) meets educational and experience qualifications as follows:

(a) Educational requirements: at least a master's degree from an accredited institution so recognized at the time of granting of such degree in marriage and family counseling, family life education, psychology, social work, or sociology of the family, or a clearly comparable field emphasizing marriage and family counseling, or shall be a practicing attorney, clergyman, or physician whose transcripts establish that he has completed an appropriate course of study in a closely allied field.

(b) Experience requirements: at least three full years of full-time counseling experience or its equivalent of a character approved by the board, subsequent to the granting of a degree described in Section 10 subsection (1a), two years of which experience must have been in marriage and family counseling; and pays the original license/certification/ fee prescribed by this Act; or

(2) is already licensed January 1, 19____, in this state in a discipline cited in subsection (1a) of Section 10 and deemed qualified as a marriage and family counselor under the provisions of subsection (1) of Section 10; and pays the original license/certification/ fee prescribed by this Act.

[Note: An optional third subsection may be added . . . or;

(3) is a legal resident of this state and has been principally employed in the practice of marriage and family counseling in this state for at least 5 years prior to the effective date of this Act and submits satisfactory proof of the duration of his practice; and meets the requirements of subsections (1), (2), and (3) of Section 9 and subsection (1) of Section 10, except that in lieu of an advanced degree the applicant may, at the discretion of the board, substitute 10 years of experience, satisfactorily substantiated, as a marriage and family counselor; and pays the original license/certification/ fee prescribed by this Act.]

Section 11. APPLICATION AFTER JANUARY 1, 19____. Any person applying to the board after January 1, 19____, may be licensed/ certified/ if he submits satisfactory evidence to the board that he:

(1) is at least 21 years of age;

(2) is of good moral character;

(3) has not engaged and is not engaged in any practice or conduct which would be a ground for refusing to issue a license/certificate/ under this Act;

(4) meets educational and experience qualifications as follows:

    (a) Educational requirements: at least a master's degree from an accredited institution so recognized at the time of granting of such degree in marriage and family counseling, family life education, psychology, social work, or sociology of the family, or a closely comparable field emphasizing marriage and family counseling, or shall be a practicing attorney, clergyman, or physician whose transcripts establish that he has completed an appropriate course of study in a closely allied field.

    (b) Experience requirements: at least three years of full-time counseling experience or its equivalent of a character approved by the board, subsequent to the granting of a degree described in subsection (1) of Section 11, two years of which experience must have been in marriage and family counseling under supervision approved by the board. [Note: The following may be added: The two years' professional experience in marriage and family counseling required by this subsection shall include not less than 20 hours a week devoted to the specialized practice of marriage and family counseling under the direct supervision of a licensed/certified/ practicing marriage and family counselor acceptable to the board and who has had at least 5 years' experience in the practice of marriage and family counseling, and shall include at least 200 hours of consultation between the supervisor and the applicant concerning the applicant's marriage and family counseling activity.]

(5) files an acceptable application for a license/certificate/;

(6) passes a written and/or oral examination administered by the board, if, at the discretion of the board, such examination is deemed necessary in order to determine the applicant's qualifications for the practice of marriage and family counseling;

(7) pays the original license/certification/ fee prescribed by this Act.

Section 12. EXAMINATION.

(1) The board may conduct an examination at least once a year at a time and place designated by the board, if, at the board's discretion, such examination is deemed necessary in order to determine any applicant's qualifications for the practice of marriage and family counseling.

(2) Examinations may be written and if the board deems advisable, oral. In any written examination each applicant shall be desig-

nated so that his name shall not be disclosed to the board until examinations have been graded.

(3) Examinations shall include questions in such theoretical and applied fields as the board deems most suitable to test an applicant's knowledge and competence to engage in the practice of marriage and family counseling.

(4) An applicant shall be held to have passed an examination upon affirmative vote of at least four members of the board.

Section 13. ADMISSION TO SUBSEQUENT EXAMINATION. Any person who fails an examination conducted by the board shall not be admitted to a subsequent examination for a period of at least 6 months.

Section 14. RECIPROCAL LICENSES/CERTIFICATES/. The board may issue a license/certificate/ by examination of credentials to any person licensed/certified/ as a marriage and family counselor in another state whose requirements for the license/certificate/ are equivalent to or exceed the requirements of this state, provided the applicant submits an application on forms prescribed by the board and pays the original license/ certification/ fee prescribed by this Act.

Section 15. FEES. A fee of_____ dollars shall be paid for the original licensure/certification/. Licenses/certificates/ shall be valid for one year and must be renewed annually, the renewal fee being _____ dollars. Any application for renewal of a license/certificate/ which has expired shall require the payment of a reregistration fee of_____ dollars.

Section 16. RENEWAL OF LICENSE/CERTIFICATE/. On or before _____ of each year the secretary of the board shall forward to the holder of a license/certificate/ a form of application for renewal thereof. Upon the receipt of the completed form and the renewal fee on or before _____ , the secretary shall issue a new license for the year commencing _____ .

Section 17. PROCEDURES FOR DENIAL, SUSPENSION, REVOCATION, OR CANCELLATION OF A LICENSE/CERTIFICATE/.

(1) A license/certificate/ may be denied, suspended, or revoked if the applicant or licensee/certificate/ has:

(a) been convicted of a crime involving moral turpitude;

(b) secured a license/certification/ by fraud or deceit;

(c) advertised, practiced, attempted to practice, or aided another in advertising, practicing, or attempting to practice under the name of another licensee/certificatee/ under this Act;

(d) violated or conspired to violate the provisions of this Act or rules or regulations or code of ethics promulgated by the board pursuant to this Act;

(e) been found by the board to be addicted to the use of any narcotic drug or to the excessive use of alcohol;

(f) been found by the board to be negligent or guilty of professional misconduct in the performance of his duties as a marriage and family counselor.

(2) The board shall not refuse to grant and shall not revoke or suspend the license/certificate/ of any person for any of the reasons listed in subsection (1) of section 17 until after a hearing of the charges against the accused (which shall be public unless the accused requests a private hearing thereon).

Section 18. REINSTATEMENT. Application may be made to the board for reinstatement at any time after the expiration of one year from the date of revocation of a license/certificate/. Such application shall be in writing and shall be accompanied by the reinstatement fee of_____ _____ dollars. The board shall not reinstate any applicant unless satisfied that he is competent to engage in the practice of marriage and family counseling, and if it deems same necessary for such determination, may require the applicant to pass an examination, written and/or oral.

Section 19. PENALTIES. Any person not a licensed/certified/ practicing marriage and family counselor under this Act, who on or after January 1, 19___, represents himself to be a licensed/certified/ marriage and family counselor or offers to practice or practices as a marriage and family counselor in violation of this Act shall, upon conviction, be guilty of a misdemeanor and be punished by a fine not exceeding_____ _____ dollars for the first offense and_____ dollars for each subsequent offense.

Section 20. INJUNCTION. As an additional remedy the board may proceed in the circuit court to enjoin and restrain any unlicensed/ uncertified/ person from practicing in this state as a marriage and family counselor. The board shall not be required to post bond to such proceeding.

Section 21. PRIVILEGED COMMUNICATION. Any communication between a marriage and family counselor and the person or persons counseled shall be confidential and its secrecy preserved. This privilege shall not be subject to waiver, except where the marriage and family counselor is a party defendant to a civil, criminal, or disciplinary action arising from such counseling, in which case, the waiver shall be limited to that action.

Section 22. SEVERABILITY. If any provision of this Act or the application thereof to any person or circumstances is held invalid, such invalidity shall not affect any other provisions or applications of the Act which can be given effect without such invalid provision or application and to this end the provisions of this Act are declared to be severable.

Section 23. EFFECTIVE DATE. This Act shall take effect on January 1, 19___ .

THE MODEL BILL:
DISCUSSION AND EXPLANATION

The introductory portion of the model bill contains two words that may require some brief explanation. A document that is submitted for consideration by the legislation is termed a bill. (There are other terms for other things that come up for legislative consideration, such as resolution and memorial as well as others, but bill will suffice for present purposes.) Once the bill has been passed and become law it is termed an act or a statute.

The introductory paragraph is a summary of the contents of the bill.

The opening sentence of the bill may require modification in some jurisdictions, the term "Legislature" being replaced by "Assembly" or other term as is appropriate and "State" by "Commonwealth."

Section 1. SHORT TITLE. This section is common to legislative acts. In the New Jersey statute on marriage counseling the section on title is placed at the end of the act, whereas in others it is found at the beginning.

Section 2. PURPOSE. Not all of the statutes contain a section on purpose, but it seems sensible and important to set forth the reasons why a law is deemed necessary. The wording employed in this section is fairly standard.

Section 3. DEFINITIONS. All laws on licensure contain definition sections. The definition of marriage and family counseling used here is taken from the Texas bill that got through both houses only to get lost in the end-of-session logjam. The definition is simpler than the one used in the New Jersey act and others, but covers the essential elements of marriage and family counseling. Subsection (4) may need to be changed if another term is used to designate the state board of marriage and family counselor examiners.

Section 4. PROHIBITED ACTS. This section, in brief, provides that after a given date an individual may not advertise and use certain titles and either offer to practice as a marriage and family counselor or practice as a marriage and family counselor unless he is either licensed under this act or specifically exempt from its provisions. It is worth noting at this point that the model bill uses the term "he" and various other forms of masculine pronouns. If it is deemed desirable to do so, those who are drafting bills may add such terms as "her" or "herself" whenever such wording is appropriate in order to eliminate sexism from the bill.

Section 5. EXCEPTIONS. This is one of the most important sections of the bill. It makes explicit the exemption of employees of certain kinds of institutions, agencies, and facilities, eliminating the necessity of their being licensed in order to perform their duties as employees of the institution, agency, or facility. They are not exempt if they move into private, independent practice.

Employees of proprietary organizations—as in the New Jersey act—are included under this section, but with the proviso that nonlicensed individuals who practice marriage and family counseling in such proprietary organizations do so under the *direct* supervision of a licensed counselor *under arrangements approved by the board*. The intent here is to avoid penalizing proprietary organizations while protecting the public interest at the same time. This section allows individuals to work in proprietary organizations while gaining supervised experience leading toward licensure for themselves. Importantly, the board must approve of the arrangements under which such individuals are supervised in proprietary organizations. This section is drafted so that the board can devise procedures for overseeing the arrangement by which such supervision is conducted. If a good board is appointed the supervision can be supervision in fact and not merely on paper and the supervisor can, in truth, be accountable to the board.

The subsection pertaining to the exemption of students, interns, and persons preparing for the practice of marriage and family counseling under qualified supervision contains a significant change from earlier bills and acts. In the model bill such students and other learners are exempt not only if they are working under qualified supervision in training programs located in institutions or agencies, but also if they are working in a *supervisory arrangement recognized and approved by the board*, provided they are properly titled. This addition to earlier provisions clearly recognizes that individuals may be trained under the supervision of a qualified supervisor who functions outside a formal training program or agency, institution, or facility, i.e., under the supervision of a qualified supervisor who works in independent private practice. At the same time, it provides that the trainee shall be clearly labeled a trainee, a provision that forbids misrepresentation, and calls for the supervision to be under an arrangement recognized and approved by the board.

The section does not contain an explicit mention of prior approval, although this is the intent. It would be possible to add a subsection on prior approval without too much difficulty if it were considered important to do so. A subsection such as the following could be inserted:

> Any person desiring to fulfill the supervised professional experience requirement for licensure under the provisions of this Act may apply to the board for advance approval of the situation in which he intends to gain his supervised professional experience. Prior to approval the board may require an examination to establish the educational qualifications of the applicant. Experience gained in an approved situation shall be credited toward the supervised professional experience requirements of this Act. The board may revoke its approval at any time, but experience gained by an applicant up to the time that notice of the board's revocation of approval shall have been mailed to him by registered or certified mail at his last known address, shall be credited toward the supervised professional experience requirement.

A section or rather subsection such as the above—which has been adapted from the Michigan Psychology Law—could be inserted at an appropriate point in the model bill, specifically in Section 11 subsection (4b).

The third category of exempt individuals consists of practicing professionals in specified professions so long as their practice is clearly within the confines of their profession and consistent with the accepted standards and ethics of their profession. Such individuals as attorneys, clergymen, physicians, psychologists, school guidance and counseling personnel, and social workers are exempt under these circumstances, specifically provided they do not indicate to the public that they are marriage and family counselors or that they are licensed to practice marriage and family counseling or do not practice as such.

This subsection needs to be completely understood by marriage and family counselors who are advocating the passage of licensing laws and adequately explained by them to the exempt professionals. It needs to be made clear that this subsection does not prevent a psychologist, physician, or certain others from performing their legitimate duties or doing marriage and family counseling work of a type that comes about as a natural part of the legitimate professional endeavors of such professionals, but that it does prevent them from advertising and performing essentially as marriage and family counselors, unless they meet the requirements for licensure and obtain a license to do so as others must do in order to have those privileges.

Section 6. THE STATE BOARD OF MARRIAGE AND FAMILY COUNSELOR EXAMINERS. The board that is required by this bill contains both professional and citizen-public representative members. This can be changed to an all professional board by making simple changes in wording, if an all professional board is desired. The professional members are required to be practicing marriage and family counselors who could qualify for licensure under the statute.

This section could be made less restrictive without seriously harming the bill. Utah's act which calls for a "committee of marriage and family counselors within the department of business regulation" has a committee or board that consists of "five persons from the counseling field who are residents of the state and have had at least seven years of experience in their profession." Nevada's board, according to the law, is to consist of five members. In addition to some specific requirements, the law states that "*If possible*, at least one examiner will be appointed in each of the following three specialties: Psychiatry, psychology, social work." (Emphasis added) New Jersey's act provides for professional and citizen representation. If this section is modified and the citizen representatives deleted, it would be necessary to modify the final sentence in Section 6 subsection (1), deleting the clause "with the exception of citizen members."

One part of this section may or may not be retained. This is the proviso that the professional board members "shall be a member of or have professional standing equivalent to that required for clinical membership in the American Association of Marriage and Family Counselors." To require that board members were members of the A.A.M.F.C. or had equivalent professional standing would ensure a certain level of professional standing and a continual reference to the standard setting organization in the marriage and family counseling field, it is true. It would seem, however, that if such a proviso were to become the focal point of heated controversy and were regarded as a kind of special pleading for an organization—even though such is not the intent—it would be better to drop that part of the bill, adjusting the wording and punctuation of the subsection accordingly.

There are other possibilities for structuring the composition of the board. Nevada's certification law, for example, provides with regard to its five man board:

> If possible, at least one examiner will be appointed in each of the following three specialties: Psychiatry; psychology; social work. All examiners must be in good standing with, or acceptable for membership in their local or state societies and associations when they exist . . .

In addition to the requirements cited above, the Utah act states that the initial committee (board) shall consist of:

> ... three persons who are eligible for membership in the American Association of Marriage and Family Counselors, a psychiatrist, and a clinical or counseling psychologist. These members shall comply with any licensing provisions of this act in the same manner as other practitioners.

Further, the law specifies:

> After the appointment of the initial committee members, any licensed practicing marriage and family counselor may be appointed.

The requirement that the members of the board of examiners be able to meet the qualifications and requirements for licensure under the act seems to be a common and reasonable one, as does the requirement that they be able to qualify for membership in the appropriate professional organization.

Sections 7–8. BOARD ORGANIZATION AND MEETINGS, POWERS AND DUTIES. The goal in drafting these sections was to find the golden mean between specifying too little with regard to board organization, meetings, powers, and duties and spelling things out in minute detail. In some instances it may be necessary to make special adaptations to the administrative, financial, and other procedures peculiar to a particular state. The offices of the legislators sponsoring the bills and the legislative service office that checks bills for appropriate wording and articulation with existing state laws and procedures would be sources for assistance in making necessary adjustments.

Section 9. LICENSE/CERTIFICATION/ APPLICATION. This section is largely self-explanatory. Subsection (4) is a general statement in which it is indicated that an applicant for licensure shall furnish evidence satisfactory to the board that he qualifies for licensure on the basis of an examination of his credentials or that he qualifies on the basis of evidence he presents to the board for admission to an examination administered by the board. In the latter case, applicants would be required to pass successfully the examination in order to demonstrate qualification for licensure as practicing marriage and family counselors.

This section does not specifically require an applicant to be a resident of the state as, for example, does the Michigan law. It would be a simple matter to add a subsection between the present subsections (3) and (4) that specifies "is a resident of the state" if this requirement were considered important to the bill.

Section 10. APPLICATION BEFORE JANUARY 1, 19____ . This section pertains to "grandfather" applicants. Many acts passed to regulate the practice of a profession or vocation contain a grandfather clause. This means that certain categories of individuals who were providing the newly restricted service prior to the passage of the legislation will be given some opportunity to obtain licensure under reduced regulations and requirements for a limited period of time. After expiration of the specified time for the grandfather clause all applicants must meet the full requirements of the bill that has been passed.

The period of grandfathering frequently covers one year past the effective date of the act, i.e., after the time that the bill actually goes into effect. The time allotted for the grandfather clause could be less than one year, but rarely is it longer than one year. The dates in the model bill could be arranged so that the grandfather's period is one year or less. If the effective date of the act in Section 23, for example, is specified as immediately and the bill becomes law on June 30, 1975, and the date January 1, 1976, specified in Section 4 (Prohibited Acts), Section 10, and elsewhere when appropriate, the period of grandfathering would encompass six months. Six months or even one year does not appear to be an unreasonably long period of time in which to permit application under a grandfather's clause, whereas more than one year does seem too much time to delay full operation of the standards and requirements of the legislation.

The second subsection of this section pertains to those professionals who are already licensed or certified by the state in specified professions before a given date, deeming them qualified as marriage and family counselors. This is a rather liberal provision that can be removed if desired. There is no question but that it will result in some unqualified persons being granted license, but this will happen on a one-time basis and will not be repeated once the grandfather period has passed.

The model bill contains an even more liberal subsection (3) that is put in the model bill as an option, because it is not recommended. Under this subsection any individual who can prove to the board through providing it with satisfactory evidence that he or she is a legal resident of the state who has been earning a living primarily as a marriage and family counselor for at least five years prior to the effective date of the act, and who is at least 21 years of age, of good moral character, and who has not engaged or is not engaged in actions that would be a ground for refusing to issue a license under the act and either has the required minimum educational preparation or 10 years of fulltime practical experience in marriage and family counseling can be licensed if such satisfactory application is made prior to expiration of the grandfather's date.

Having such a liberal grandfather's clause as the inclusion of subsection (3) would provide will not meet the desires of those who would try to use the law to screen out all of the ill-prepared, unprepared, and incompetent. This section may permit the licensure of some individuals who would not be licensed subsequently, but it is not likely to prevent any moderately competent person from practicing—a point that should be made clear to those who would oppose licensure on the ground that it would "take away the livelihood" of individuals not trained in a given pattern or path. It probably would screen out some charlatans while letting some others get through to obtain a license.

The argument is realistic and sometimes persuasive that granting a license to some such individuals who are not well-trained does not allow them to do anything that they were not doing previously—i.e., they were already practicing—and letting some of them through may be necessary in order to get a bill passed, state legislators being somewhat reluctant in some cases to flatly "take away the means of livelihood" of any category of individuals, including the incompetent. A further argument that is advanced is that granting a license to such borderline qualification practitioners does bring them under the control of the board. The decision on this point will have to be made by those urging passage of legislation in the light of the perceived realities of their political situation.

There is some consolation for the competent and concerned marriage and family counselor in the realization that licensure per se does not insure that a given individual will secure clients and actually engage in practice. There is the possibility that in an open market situation under licensure, particularly if there is public education as to the kind of services and training to be expected from competent practitioners, the marginally competent will find their own level. Although charlatans and incompetents fall into different categories generally, education of the public and the careful training of practitioners are, in the final analysis, the twin sources of protection of the public that will enable the law to work effectively. These triplets—training, legislation, and education—must work together in order to provide public protection and effective service.

It is exceedingly important to realize that the grandfather's clause covers only a limited period of time. After a given date, individuals seeking to qualify for licensure must meet higher standards. While the practice of grandfathering may give some added degree of respectability to some individuals, it does so only for a limited number and evidently is a necessary part of securing legislation in many of the as yet unlicensed states.

It is not necessary in providing a grandfather's clause to take in all who would insist that they have a claim on a given area.

Section 11. APPLICATION AFTER JANUARY 1, 19____. This section is concerned with individuals who apply for licensure after the period covered by the grandfather's clause has expired. In practical terms, it covers the majority of individuals who eventually will be licensed under a given law.

It may be considered desirable in some instances to insert a provision that an individual "is a resident of this state" as an additional requirement.

Under subsection (4a) the educational requirement is identical to that set forth in preceding sections. It is worth noting that the phrase "or a closely comparable field emphasizing marriage and family counseling" is included. What constitutes a closely comparable field emphasizing marriage and family counseling must be determined by the board. The integrity of the board and the integrity of the act of legislation are inextricably bound together on this question, as in other instances.

The educational requirements follow fairly closely the requirements for clinical membership in the American Association of Marriage and Family Counselors at the time of writing.

Subsection (4a), as similar sections, indicates that a practicing attorney, clergyman, or physician is considered eligible for licensure if he or she has transcripts that establish completion of an appropriate course of study in a field closely allied to marriage and family counseling. The background of some attorneys, clergymen, and physicians does not equip them to do any kind of clinical work and certainly not the specialized work of a marriage and family counselor. Where their training does provide adequate background, they are eligible for licensure under this bill. It should be pointed out to members of such professions who are concerned about the effect of the proposed legislation on their practice that they are exempt from the act under subsection (3) of Section 5, so long as they practice within the confines and established standards of their profession and do not advertise or represent themselves to be marriage and family counselors.

Setting the educational degree required for marriage and family counselors at the master's level does not align very closely with the assessment of many individuals as to the necessary and desired level of academic training for qualified practitioners in the field. Some would restrict license and practice to those holding a doctorate in one of several behavioral science fields or a master's degree in social work plus supervised experience of several years' duration. The educational requirements in the bill can be raised. Certainly they should not be lowered.

Moving the requirement to the master's level in several fields—and not simply in social work—inevitably elicits questions and some confusion from those who were accustomed to the old pattern in which a doctorate was the normative degree. This change reflects not only alterations that have taken place in recent years in the mental health and counseling field generally, changes in which more emphasis has been on experience and less on formal academic training than formerly—for better or worse—but also changes that are taking place in marriage and family counseling itself and in public demands for personal and marital-family assistance that exceed the supply of practitioners holding a doctor's degree.

Part of the change is related to the fact that now a body of knowledge that can constitute a sound academic program in marriage and family counseling or psychotherapy is available and can be tapped and utilized in various kinds of educational programs. The rapid growth of curricula in this field is one of the remarkable phenomena in the academic world of recent years. Thus, it is now possible to talk about a degree in marriage and family counseling or a closely comparable field emphasizing marriage and family counseling. Similarly, it is more realistic today than formerly to require that a practicing attorney, clergyman, or physician who would seek to practice as a marriage and family counselor be licensed and required to have taken some coursework in a field closely allied to that expected of behavioral science graduates, given some of the changes that are occurring in graduate and professional education.

In brief, there is more specialized and focused knowledge and material in marriage and family counseling available today at the graduate and professional levels than previously, enough so that it is no longer necessary to rely primarily on certain older disciplines to provide the basic education for marriage and family counselors.

The educational requirement is, of course, only one part of the skill and knowledge area. Adequate experience, qualitatively and quantitatively, is vital to the development of a sound professional in marriage and family counseling. The model bill, following the requirements in the field generally, calls for at least three years of full-time experience or its equivalent—meaning part-time experience spread over a longer period of time—after the individual has secured his or her terminal degree or requisite academic degree, two years of which experience must be in marriage and family counseling.

For all practical purposes, the experience requirement of the bill is written so that individuals must secure a minimum of three years of professional experience, two in marriage and family counseling, after gaining their degree before they can be licensed. An individual may not secure the requisite degree and move immediately into independent practice. He or she can work in a proprietary clinic under the supervision of a licensed marriage and family counselor under arrangements approved by the board of examiners. Such provisions protect the public without unduly restricting the beginning practitioner.

The provision for allowing proprietary clinics to be so operated and their practitioners exempt under the stated conditions makes explicit a practice that often prevails in professional fields, puts the arrangement under the discretion of the board in that the arrangement must be board approved, and prevents the possibility of an interpretation of the law that would require newly graduated professionals to work for a non-profit agency for three years while they secured the required post-degree experience, an inequitable interpretation but one that has been attempted in some instances under other laws. The need is not to force individuals to work in non-profit agencies or to keep them from securing fees while they work in a governmental agency for a salary for a certain number of years, but to make certain through legislation and cooperation between the board of examiners and professional groups, insofar as this is possible, that they work under adequate supervision until they gain the necessary or required minimum of practical clinical experience subsequent to completing their academic degree work. The key issue is not public or private practice but supervised or independent practice.

Two years of the post-degree experience in marriage and family counseling must be *under supervision approved by the board*. This is a most important phrase. How it is interpreted and implemented by the board and by the marriage and family counseling profession will be a major factor in determining the quality and quantity of supervision that occurs in a state and ultimately the kind of service its people receive.

A major shortcoming of most of the early laws in this field has been the emphasis on the initial groups or categories of persons to be qualified and licensed under the statute and the failure to provide adequately for the regulation of supervision in later years. To put it more succinctly, most of the laws have dealt inadequately with supervision and the matter of a continuing supply of supervised practitioners once the initial bill has been passed. The qualifications for those whose supervision of trainees qualifies the trainees for subsequent licensure should either be established in the original law or the bill should be drafted in such a way that those qualifications can be set by the board in accordance with some recognized guidelines.

Not all persons licensed as marriage and family counselors are capable of providing adequate supervision for persons in training. While it is a mistake to leave the matter so open in drafting a bill that all licensees are automatically eligible to provide supervision and to set up no provision for board approval of such supervision, it may be unduly restrictive and too limiting to the needs of the various states to try to write into the bill all the qualifications of those who would be designated or approved by the boards as supervisors. It seems sensible to give the board some guidance as well as the responsibility and privilege of approving the supervised experience, and to work for consistent and responsible interpretation and implementation of the statute by the board. Such guidelines as those formulated by the A.A.M.F.C. for the Approved Supervisor procedures that it has implemented in recent years may be promulgated and followed by a given board.

The experience subsection in the model bill includes an optional portion that would provide boards with some guidance regarding the quantity of supervision. The 20 hours per week spent in marriage and family counseling is a guideline that has already been accepted in several of the licensing states, 20 hours per week for 50 weeks or so being considered a year's specialized work in marriage and family counseling to meet experience requirements, twice that being acceptable for two years of experience, and so forth. The 100 hours of supervision or consultation around cases would, of course, allow for approximately one hour of supervision per week over a two year period.

Although one hour of supervision or consultation per week on cases does not appear to be very much when compared with the 1:5 ratio of supervision to treatment or client contact hours recommended in A.A.M.F.C. Approved Training Programs, it is not to be compared with the supervisory-treatment ratio in a formal training program. The A.A.M.F.C. guidelines for approved training programs were devised at a time when all or nearly all of the specialized training in marriage counseling was gained at the post-degree, generally post-doctoral, level. It is anticipated now that by the time individuals are obtaining their post-degree experience and supervision to qualify for licensure, they will have received not only more specific and explicit academic education in marriage and family counseling than had their forerunners at the same stage in their careers, but also that they will have received a considerable amount of supervised experience while pursuing a graduate degree. Having started specialization earlier than their predecessors, they should have reached the point or level of development by the time they are into post-degree work that they can function with weekly consultation or supervision.

The optional portion of the subsection also contains the proviso that the supervisor—who shall be a licensed practitioner—shall have had at least five years of experience in the practice of marriage and family counseling. This, of course, would by an additional guideline or directive to the board. Some may wish to increase the amount of professional experience the supervisor would be required to obtain before beginning supervision. The five year requirement is essentially in line with provisions in the New Jersey law and with the A.A.M.F.C. guidelines for Approved Supervisors. This surely does not set the requirements of professional experience for those designated or accepted as supervisors at too high a level.

Section 11, subsection (6) deals with the written and/or oral examination of applicants for licensure. The question of whether applicants should be required to undergo a written and/or oral examination in addition to furnishing the board with their credentials is left to the discretion of the board. Written and/or oral examination in addition to examination of credentials is not made mandatory and, on the contrary, is provided for in case it is "deemed necessary in order to determine the applicant's qualifications"—as an additional factor to be considered along with his or her transcripts, letters of recommendation, reports of supervision, and other completed forms customarily and routinely required by a licensure board. The intent, in other words, is to provide for written and/or oral examination as a fine screening device to be used when broader screening devices do not answer adequately the board's questions concerning a particular applicant, rather than as a routinely employed screening device. The board could decide to exercise its discretionary power to require a written and/or oral examination of all applicants, but it is not required to routinely examine in this way and is left with the flexibility to follow the path deemed most appropriate to the needs of its state and situation. It would seem unnecessary and wasteful of time and effort to routinely put all applicants through such additional qualifying hurdles as examinations.

Sections 12 and 13 also pertain to examination and require little additional explanation. Where examination has been provided for in other laws, passing has been based on either a numerical score or percentage of correct answers or by a vote of the board members. The model bill provides for a decision by the board members, an affirmative vote by four of the seven indicating that an examination has been passed satisfactorily. The provision that a score of 75 percent, the score used in some other places, or whatever score considered appropriate could be put in place of the provision that the vote of the board would determine passage or failure, but vote by the board seems less cumbersome when all factors are considered.

Section 14. RECIPROCAL LICENSES/CERTIFICATES/. Some arrangement for reciprocity is common to licensure acts. Reciprocity sets up ways which an individual licensed in one state may gain licensure in another by virtue of already being a license holder.

Fence building in which the practitioners of a particular skill seek to protect their domain by making it difficult for others having the same skill to enter practice in their state occurs when the licensed practitioners use legislation to build fences around the borders of their states or around the doorways to practice within their state.

The attitude behind the drafting of this section of the model bill is that such fence building is detrimental to the profession and to the public good. Once it is determined, for example, that the requirements for licensure in a skill in State A are equal to or superior to those in State B, there is no reasonable basis for refusing to accept such licensure in State B or for compelling holders of valid licenses in State A to repeat all of the rites of initiation. In brief, there appears to be no reason in the public interest for not accepting licensure from another state whose requirements are equal to or superior to those of one's own state and doing it with minimum of redtape. Certainly, it seems adequate to require an applicant who is so licensed in another state to complete reasonable forms and to give information such as his license number that can be checked to determine his standing with the board or licensing office in his state of licensure.

This section is written so that it is permissible for the board to issue reciprocal licenses without examination to licensees from states whose requirements are equal to or superior to those of the board's state. This provision could be broadened if desired by adding "or nation" after the word state. It could be amended in several ways in addition to the foregoing. For example, it would be possible to add a clause or statement to the effect that a license could be denied if the person were in violation of Section 17 subsection (1), something that is clearly intended. Also, this section does not require that the person seeking licensure by reciprocity be a resident of the state in which he is seeking the new licensure.

The requirement of state residency as a prerequisite to licensure appears to create more problems than it solves. What is lost in flexibility does not seem to be regained in additional protection for the public or the profession. There do not appear to be sufficient numbers of persons who would to through the process of applying and paying for licenses in states in which they have no intention of practicing to give boards legitimate cause for concern about that kind of abuse of this section. At the same time, there are numerous border situations in which a city or metropolitan area crosses state lines, and it appears counterproductive to individual and public good in many instances to require an individual to reside in a state in order to practice there when the state line constitutes an artificial boundary across a natural community.

Section 15. FEES. Fees for an original license, renewal, or reinstatement vary among the licensing states. Michigan's act provides for a fee of $25 for an original certification and an annual renewal fee of $25. Nevada's law calls for a $30 examination fee, a $15 certification fee, an application fee of $15, a biennial registration fee of not less than $20 or more than $80, as determined by the board. Interestingly, it requires payment of a $50 fee for certification by endorsement under the reciprocity section of the act, a fee that presumably would discourage any tendency toward casual "shingle collecting" that might otherwise appear among individuals licensed or certified in other states. New Jersey's act requires the following, for: examination of credentials, $25; renewal of license, $25; registration, $10; and reinstatement, $50.

Notable is the fact that acts typically provide for fixed fees, but that there are ranges of "not less than, not more than" in at least one statute.

Section 16. RENEWAL OF LICENSE/CERTIFICATE/. The model bill calls for annual renewal of the license. The secretary of the board would be responsible for forwarding an application of renewal in the late fall months and the applicant responsible for returning the form with the renewal fee at a date set before or on the end of the year, the renewal beginning on January 1. This could be changed to a biennial renewal if desired.

Section 17. PROCEDURES FOR DENIAL, SUSPENSION, REVOCATION, OR CANCELLATION OF A LICENSE/CERTIFICATE/. This section follows the wording of similar sections in existing laws and is a fairly standard provision of model bills drafted by various professional and interprofessional groups in the past. One feature of subsection (1) that requires mention is the part pertaining to a "code of ethics promulgated by the board pursuant to this Act."

In the practical implementation of legislation, it will be extremely helpful to both the state board of marriage and family counselor examiners and to the profession itself if the board does promulgate a code of ethics. Otherwise, the desire to have practitioners present themselves and function in the most ethical fashion may be undercut by a diminished ability to guide or correct the occasional individual whose advertising or other behavior falls outside the desired standards.

New Jersey has set a sound example in adopting a "Code of Professional Ethics for Marriage Counselors Licensed by the State of New Jersey Board of Marriage Counselor Examiners." The six principles set forth in a 1971 copy of the code were accompanied by a procedure for implementing the code. The procedure included the provision that the board issue in writing to each licensed marriage counselor in the state a copy of the code of ethics.

Section 17 does not provide a mechanism by which an individual may seek to have an action of the board denying him or her a license, suspending or revoking a license reviewed by an appropriate court. In drafting this section, it would be important to have the legislator's office and the office of legislative services that puts bills into final form make certain that if such a mechanism is included it is the correct one. The Nevada statute spells out some appeal procedures in detail, ending with a statement indicating that "the certificatee is entitled to review pursuant to the Nevada Administrative Procedures Act." Utah, on the other hand, makes no mention of any appeal mechanism or procedure.

Section 18. REINSTATEMENT. This section is largely self-explanatory. Such a section is necessary to a law.

Section 19. PENALTIES. The New Jersey law provides for a fine of $200 for the first offense and $500 for each subsequent offense in which an individual not a licensed practicing marriage counselor has so represented himself or offered to practice or practiced. The Michigan statute states that violation is a misdemeanor without specifying penalties. Violation of the Nevada and Utah laws also constitutes a misdemeanor, without specific dollar penalties being named. The Utah act states simply that "Any person who engages in marriage and family counseling or advertises in violation of this act shall be guilty of a misdemeanor." The Nevada law specifies that "Each violation shall be deemed a separate offense."

This section on the model bill could be altered in order to eliminate the dollar amounts simply by putting a period after "misdemeanor" and deleting the remainder of the sentence. If this is done, the sentence quoted above from the Nevada law could be added in order to give additional strength and clarity to the section.

Section 20. INJUNCTION. Section 20 is another of those portions of the model bill that may require some slight alterations of wording in order to make it conform to the needs of various states. The comparable section in the Michigan law reads:

> In addition to any other proceedings provided in this act, whenever any person has engaged, or is about to engage, in any acts or practices which constitute or will constitute a violation of this act, the circuit court of the county where the acts or practices have taken place, or are about to take place, may issue an injunction or other appropriate order restraining such conduct on application of the attorney general or the county prosecuting attorney upon complaint of the board.

New Jersey's law provides for an even broader base of action:

> The Superior Court may prevent or restrain an action at the suit of the Attorney General or the board, or of any citizen of the same county, any person from representing himself as a licensed practicing marriage counselor or from practicing marriage counseling in New Jersey who is not licensed under this act or excluded from its application by sections . . . Through the same means the Superior Court may prevent or restrain any person from violation of any provision of this act.

Section 21. PRIVILEGED COMMUNICATION. Because of the peculiar nature of marriage and family counseling in which the counseling work or psychotherapy is performed with members of a marriage or even with an entire family group, the tendency has been to provide for the communications made to the counselor to be privileged, waiver being allowed only when the marriage and family counselor is defending himself in a civil, criminal, or disciplinary action arising from such counseling, the waiver in that case being limited to that particular civil, criminal, or disciplinary action. The model bill is constructed with a provision for privileged communication and waiver only in the circumstances just described. This is consistent with the New Jersey statute. The New Jersey professional code of ethics for professional marriage counselors spells out some of the procedures and safeguards to be followed with respect to confidentiality of communications and keeping of records. It is in the principles of the code of ethics that such matters as release of records are discussed.

The following sentences are added in the Michigan law:

> Notwithstanding any other law to the contrary, if cases are counseled upon court referral, the marriage counselor may submit to the appropriate court a written evaluation of the prospects or prognosis of a particular marriage without divulging facts or revealing confidential disclosures. Attorneys representing spouses who are the subjects of such evaluation shall have the right to receive a copy of the report.

Such a provision makes it possible for the counselor to serve the court without compromising his professional relationships, carrying a behavioral science perspective into an arena that often can profit from such assistance, but with protection against being compelled to testify concerning the counseling.

The intent in the laws is to protect the clients ultimately and to protect the integrity of the marriage and family counselor and his counseling or psychotherapeutic work with the clients by giving him the privilege of holding in confidence all such communications made to him in the course of such work.

The meanings of privileged communication and confidentiality are very important and should be clearly understood by marriage and family counselors who are advocating legislation, as well as by the legislators who are supporting such legislation. It may be helpful to consult a standard dictionary for definitions, e.g., confidential is defined as "told in confidence, imparted in secret;" whereas, privileged communication, law, is defined as "a communication that one cannot legally be compelled to divulge;" but it would seem even more helpful and necessary to consult a lawyer who can explain precisely what is meant by privileged communication.

Sections 22 and 23, pertaining to severability and an effective date for the act respectively, are fairly standard for licensing acts. The effective date can be set as immediate or future. Here it is set for the next January 1 occurring after passage of the bill. Any change here would require changes in other sections of the bill in which dates are included, as in Sections 4, subsection (2) of 6, 10, 11, and 19.

SOME MISCELLANEOUS PROVISIONS

This chapter will list several provisions that could be included in a licensure bill. Some will be offered with comment and others without commentary.

Section___. BOARD REVIEW OF ACT. This Act shall be reviewed by the board at least every three years for the purpose of recommending appropriate amendments, revisions, changes, additions, deletions, or rewriting.

Section___. MEDICAL DISCLAIMER. Nothing in this Act shall authorize the practice of medicine and surgery by any person not licensed to do so pursuant to (the appropriate state statute).

(The medical disclaimer essentially appears to be an anachronism, stemming from earlier days, but can be included if necessary to effect passage of a licensure act, particularly in those instances in which statutes are on the books that give sweeping protective powers to the medical profession as did some of those passed long ago.)

Section___. DISPOSITION OF FEES AND OTHER MONEYS. All fees, fines, penalties, and other moneys derived from the operation of this Act shall be paid to the board by it remitted to the State Treasurer.

Section___. RECOGNITION OF EDUCATIONAL INSTITUTIONS. The board shall determine which schools in and out of this state have courses of study for the preparation of marriage and family counselors which are sufficient and thorough for licensure purposes. Published lists of

educational institutions accredited by recognized accredited organizations
may be used in the evaluation of such courses of study.

Section ___. NONRESIDENT PRACTITIONERS. A marriage and
family counselor not a resident of _____ and not
licensed in this state who meets the requirements for licensure in this Act
is not subject to the provisions of this Act if he does not practice marriage
and family counseling in the state of _____ for more
than 10 days in any one calendar year, and if he is invited as a consultant
by a marriage and family counselor licensed in this state.

Section ___. EXCEPTIONS. Any person who is not a licensed practicing marriage and family counselor shall not be limited in his activities as
a practicing marriage and family counselor for a period not exceeding 3
years under the direct supervision of a licensed practicing marriage and
family counselor designated by the board as an eligible supervisor, if he
has a temporary permit therefor which the board may issue upon his
completion of all the requirements for licensing under this Act except the
supervised experience requirement.

(Both of the above two provisions seem to have been handled in more
efficient and desirable ways by the model bill. The model bill makes
provision for supervision under arrangements approved by the board. To
add the "temporary permit" seems to open the way for public and professional confusion and for a considerable amount of potential abuse. As
noted elsewhere, the issue is the integrity of the board and its carefulness
in carrying out the provisions of the act, devising and policing the supervision rendered in cooperation with the professional practicing marriage
and family counselors. Nonresident practitioners who wish to practice in
the state for any period are required under the model bill to be licensed in
order to do so, but are not discriminated against by the provisions of the
bill because they are not residents of the state. The section given above on
nonresident practitioners is not recommended, but is given as a kind of
additional concession that could be made in order to provide for a particular kind of problem and situation.)

Section ___. ADVANCE APPROVAL OF SUPERVISED PROFES-
SIONAL EXPERIENCE. Any person desiring to fulfill the supervised professional experience requirement for licensure under this Act
may apply to the board for advance approval of the situation in which he
intends to gain his supervised postgraduate professional experience. Prior
to the approval the board may, at its discretion, require an examination to
establish the educational qualifications of the applicant. Experience
gained in an approved situation shall be credited toward the supervised
professional experience requirements of this Act. The board may revoke
its approval at any time, but experience gained by an applicant up to the
time that notice of the board's revocation of approval shall have been
mailed to him by registered or certified mail at his last known address,
shall be credited toward the supervised professional experience requirement.

(If this section is not added to the model bill, it could be implemented
as an action of the board. The arrangement has proven to be a workable
and desirable one in other fields in the past.)

Section ___. DESIGNATION OF SUPERVISORS. Any person designated a supervisor of marriage and family counseling practice pursuant to this Act shall be eligible for or licensed under the provisions of the Act and shall have completed not less than 5 years of full-time professional experience acceptable to the board as a marriage and family counselor subsequent to earning his terminal professional or graduate degree.

Section ___. SUPERVISION REQUIREMENTS. The board shall establish minimum requirements for the number of hours of supervised practice in marriage and family counseling and for the number of hours of supervision of such marriage and family counseling practice required to fulfill the experience requirements of section ___ subsection ___ that equal or exceed the hours of supervised practice and hours of supervision recommended by the American Association of Marriage and Family Counselors.

GUIDELINES FOR LEGISLATIVE ACTION

The guidelines that are spelled out in the pages that follow have been formed from contacts with numerous individuals and groups that have worked toward securing legislation for professional practice in states from all over the country. Those who have not been successful as well as those who have succeeded in getting bills passed have learned from their efforts and have been generous in sharing their experiences. These guidelines are offered with the awareness that all parts may not fit all states and that some adaptations may be necessary to the particular situations in given states, but efforts have been made to devise and offer an outline that has a high degree of usefulness in all states contemplating legislative activity in the marriage and family counseling area. Where state associations of marriage and family counselors are mentioned, it is assumed that such organizations will be formed so that they are not forbidden by the terms of their charter from engaging in lobbying and other legislative-influencing activity or that the membership will set up organizational structures that will permit such activity.

1. *Organize the Membership for Legislative Action.*
   Group support is needed. One person working alone generally cannot carry through effectively the multi-faceted task of securing the passage of good legislative acts. A well organized network of representatives of the organization throughout the state is needed. One effective pattern that has worked for others has been the use of committeemen, an organizational pattern similar to that employed by political parties, with the structure set up along county lines and, where possible, within senatorial and representative legislative voting districts. Such committeemen have liaison responsibility with the local situation, coordinating the efforts of their legislative representatives and the state organization of marriage and family counselors. In many states it may be necessary to operate with a partial framework, leaving some counties or areas without such organization, given the shortage of marriage and family counselors in some parts of states. Wherever possible, however, committeemen who are well-informed, competent, and active

should be recruited, whether or not they are members of the state association of marriage and family counselors. As will be noted subsequently, the assistance of many persons who are outside the professional field as well as the help of many who are inside it may be necessary to the passage of sound legislation covering the practice of marriage and family counseling.

2. *Make the Organization Visible.*

Making the state organization of marriage and family counselors visible to legislative persons and other politicians is important and may be accomplished through a number of actions and channels. These include sending a representative to the annual fund-raising function given by the political parties or by individual legislators, providing recognition to officials whose actions benefit marriage and family counseling, and family life, offering the benefit of the organization's professional knowledge and expertise to legislative committees for assistance with problems they are dealing with, whether or not they use it in all instances, and others.

3. *Keep the Membership Informed.*

The entire membership of the state organization of marriage and family counselors should be kept informed as to what is happening with regard to legislation as frequently and directly as possible. Personal contacts through face-to-face conversations, telephone, or written communication seem to be the most desirable methods, but printed mailings and newsletters are also useful. The major need is to keep the membership aware of what has happened, its meaning, and what is forthcoming.

4. *Know the Legislative Process.*

Probably no other guideline deserves as much emphasis as this one does, because ignorance of the legislative process in one's state can defeat efforts to get a legislative act passed in such myriad ways. It is necessary not only to know the formal steps involved in getting a bill through the legislative process but also to be aware of the informal factors that operate and help to determine the success or failure of a legislative effort. For example, in one state, as a correspondent has written, the process goes as follows:

> The bill is drafted, the "right legislative sponsor is induced to sponsor it, and then it goes to the legislative service office and any changes they introduce, including commas, must be modified. After that, sponsors of the bill have to attend hearings, get people to talk to their legislators, and continually check at each hurdle along the way to see what has happened.

In some states a bill that is prefiled has a better chance of passage or going through the legislature without extensive change than does one introduced later, after the legislature convenes. A bill introduced early in the session, before frustrations have arisen and time and political demands become as significant as they tend to become during the course of the session, frequently has a better chance of passage than one introduced later, after the regular session has gotten well under way. The logjam that results in the last days of legislation, as hurried efforts are made to get bills through before adjournment, can cause the loss of a bill that has successfully passed all hurdles up to that point. Knowledge of the legislative process and of specific developments within the legislature also may lead to the decision to kill a bill or let it die in some instances, e.g., if it has been changed so that it has become an undesirable bill. Information on the formal steps in the legislative process can be secured from the appropriate office or agency of the state government. Generally, such information would include references to the manner in which bills are drafted, placed on the calendar, amended, checked for conformity to proper legal form, and so forth.

5. *Know the Legislators.*

Who are the legislators who are friendly to marriage and family counseling or can be influenced to support appropriate legislation? What contacts with them already exist through members of the state organization of marriage and family counselors? Once such legislator-friends have been identified, it is important to ascertain the possible influence they may have on members of the legislative committees that will deal with the proposed bill. What kind of influence will they have on the leadership of the political parties and state legislature? Sometimes it is equally important to determine, when possible, the legislative members who are likely to be unfriendly toward the proposed legislation and to seek to influence them toward neutrality if not outright support of the measure. Knowing the legislative process and the legislature helps to determine the most appropriate strategy and tactics to be used in seeking to get a bill enacted. For example, one state group using in part knowledge gained from past failures lined up their sponsors long before the legislature began its session, had the bill introduced at the first opportunity to do so in the chamber in which support was known to be weaker, worked hard to secure speedy passage there, and subsequently guided the bill through the more favorably disposed chamber of the legislature to the governor's signature. A considerable amount of information on legislators can be secured either at no cost or at nominal cost from an appropriate state office, or perhaps through a legislator, in most states. For example, Florida provides brochures that have a considerable amount of personal data on legislators, including such things as photographs, hobbies, organizational memberships, family, religious affiliation, and so forth, in addition to information on committee assignments, telephone numbers, home address, and office address.

6. *Use the Membership Talent.*

Determine which members of the state organization are most effective in presenting the case of marriage and family counseling, encourage and assist them in reading widely in the area and being well-prepared to answer questions that may be asked of them, and then organize the time of such members so that they can spend some time lobbying and dealing with legislators in personal, face-to-face discussion. The knowledge such spokesmen have including awareness of the kinds of concerns that legislators have will be important along with an acquaintance with all phases of the bill, the need for such legislation, the national picture, and so forth. For example, according to one correspondent:

> Legislators most frequently ask who is going to be in opposition to any particular piece of legislation. From their point of view, they are quite concerned about the amount of opposition they will face.

In order to work effectively and persuasively with legislators and to provide them with the kinds of materials that they need, therefore, it is necessary that the members of the organization do their own homework assiduously and patiently. It is a good idea to keep copies of all materials furnished legislators, because they are busy persons and may lose the material.

7. Hire a Lobbyist.

Securing the passage of legislation will require the expenditure of considerable amounts of time and talent, obviously. No better expenditure of money toward such ends can be made than that used to secure the services of a professional lobbyist. On a parttime or even a consultative basis, the lobbyist can be of considerable assistance in helping the organization to learn how to proceed in the practical political world in which it is seeking to function. If funds dictate a choice between a poor lobbyist or no lobbyist, however, the option to go without a lobbyist probably makes more sense. A small piece of the time of a good one is preferable to more of the time of a poor one, it would seem. The need, to paraphrase a correspondent, is to hire a good one who is perceptive and sensitive to the kind of image that marriage and family counselors wish to project and who is aggressive and persuasive in making the necessary contacts and presenting the case. A lobbyist may be particularly helpful in discovering the opposition on the legislative committees as well as in identifying potential friends. As is the case in selecting individuals who provide services in other areas, the reputation of the lobbyist among those who are familiar with where he works is probably as good a guide as any in determining which lobbyist to consider hiring. Some members of the state organization may have had contact with lobbyists through their participation in other organizations and may have some suggestions. Personal interview time spent in getting to know a lobbyist and time spent in educating him or her to the organization's purposes and image is usually worth the effort. The lobbyist is the person who can stay on the capital scene and shepherd the bill along. As several individuals who have worked to get legislation enacted have pointed out, nearly total support from key individuals is needed and it helps to have a cooperative governor. A lobbyist even on a consultative basis can provide invaluable guidance in the organization's efforts to learn how to deal with such state officials.

8. *Obtain Outside Support.*

Support from individuals and groups outside of the profession of marriage and family counseling is not only desirable but also necessary if the effort to secure passage of a sound bill is to be successful. Groups that consider themselves to be affected by the proposed legislation especially need to be contacted, again if not to obtain their endorsement at least to neutralize their opposition insofar as this is possible. Whatever fears such individuals and organizations have concerning the proposed marriage and family counseling legislation should be allayed to the extent possible through extensive educational work with them. Frequently, it is sufficient to get across the message clearly that the bill carefully and explicitly exempts them, and how and under what conditions it does so, in order to allay the fears of those professionals who are concerned that the proposed legislation would restrict their practice of marriage and family counseling within their fields of law, medicine, religious ministry, or social work. With some established professionals it is necessary to provide reassurance concerning their fears that they may not qualify for practice under the proposed bill if they should seek licensure as marriage and family counselors, pointing out what the realities are in the proposed bill. The endorsement of the proposed legislation by respected professional organizations and influential individuals also may be helpful in buttressing the case for licensure of marriage and family counselors. These may include representatives from psychology, social work, psychiatry and other fields in medicine, law, and religion, as well as from the general field of mental health. From the national office of the American Association of Marriage and Family Counselors, assistance may be solicited in terms of statements of endorsement and some information and guidance concerning resources and procedures. As various states are successful in obtaining passage of marriage and family counseling legislation and in forming licensure boards that gain experience in administering and implementing the laws, a pool of experience continues to develop. The knowledge accrued by individuals involved in such endavors may be helpful to persons and organizations in states seeking to pass their own legislation. The A.A.M.F.C. office may be helpful in providing contacts with such knowledgeable individuals who can help the novice to avoid unnecessary work and wasted effort. The mass media in a state may be particularly helpful and their support should be actively sought. Newspapers played a major role, for example, in demonstrating the need for marriage counseling legislation in Michigan. In that state the effort to secure a bill was an interprofessional one in which representatives from several different professional fields worked cooperatively in order to hammer out a proposed bill that, in modified form, eventually passed the legislature. If there are individuals within the state organization of marriage and family counselors who have had experience in working with or dealing with the mass media, their experience may be utilized in effecting cooperative relationships for the purpose of securing appropriate legislation. The newspapers, as well as other media, may be especially concerned with the passage of the bill that would provide for the licensure of qualified practitioners unless there is extensive work done with them to secure their understanding of what is needed to bring about good practice and to protect the public through legislation.

9. *Persist Until the Job is Completed.*
More than one effort may be required to effect passage of marriage and family counseling legislation. For example, a marriage and family counseling bill was introduced in three successive sessions of the Utah legislature before passage was obtained. Legislatures in other states have seen more than one attempt to get a bill passed end in failure, frequently because there was either strong opposition or inadequate preparation for the endeavor. In still other states in which statutes have not yet been enacted, attempts to get licensure bills passed may be regarded as learning exercises or trial runs preparatory to eventual successful effort, although adherence to the first eight of these guidelines will tend to reduce the possibility of continuing futility and speed up the date of eventual successful effort.

THE WORK IS NOT COMPLETED

The passage of legislation does not end the work of a state's marriage counselors in matters of public policy and professional practice. In a larger and very practiced sense the task of a concerned and responsible organization of marriage and family counselors becomes that of seeing that what they have worked to accomplish for the profession and for the public is implemented as it was intended. After passage of the bill there still remain the important matters of helping to see that the bill serves as it was intended, sometimes meaning that considerable cooperative work with the licensing board is needed and sometimes meaning that amendments to the law are required. Not the least of the needs is that of assuring a continuing supply of competent, well-trained, and ethical marriage and family counselors. Training and supervision, as well as ethical advertising and practice, become matters of perennial concern following passage of licensure laws, assuming places that they did not occupy previously. The strong state organizational structures required for passage of sound licensure laws are needed even more after a bill becomes a statute.

William C. Nichols, Jr., Ed.D., is Professor of Home and Family Life and Director of Family Counseling in the Interdivisional Doctoral Program in Marriage and Family Living at Florida State University. Certified as a marriage counselor and also as a consulting psychologist in Michigan, he was in private practice there for several years and trained postdoctoral students in marriage counseling at The Merrill-Palmer Institute. A founder and first president of the Michigan Association of Marriage Counselors, he also is a Fellow and former member of the Board of Directors of the A.A.M.F.C. Editor of *The Family Coordinator*, he has recently been named founding editor of the A.A.M.F.C.'s *Journal of Marriage and Family Counseling.*

CHAPTER 44

Providing Clinical Supervision for Marriage Counselors: A Model for Supervisor and Supervisee

Ben N. Ard, Jr.

In the professional education and training of qualified marriage counselors, clinical supervision would seem to be a central, basic core. Yet little has been published to date that a supervisor might use to help give himself some guidance and which a supervisee might use to see if he is getting his money's worth, so to speak (Ekstein and Wallerstein, 1958; Johnson, 1961; Mueller and Kell, 1972). The term "supervision" is not even found listed in a comprehensive dictionary of psychological and psychoanalytical terms (Enlish and English, 1958). Perhaps it might prove helpful if we discuss the who, what, when, where, and why questions regarding the clinical supervision of marriage counselors. Specifically, these questions might be spelled out as follows:

> *Who?* Who is the supervisor? Who is the supervisee? Who are the clients?
> *What?* What is "supervision?" For the supervisor? For the supervisee?
> *When?* When is supervision done? How often? For how long? Can it be done from a distance?
> *Why?* Why is supervision necessary?

Before getting into the detailed answers to these questions, a logically prior matter needs to be determined: We need to be clear about what "marriage counseling" is before an examination of the supervision of marriage counselors can be reasonably discussed.

Marriage counseling may be considered in this context as any counseling with one or more clients dealing with problems relating to marriage, including getting married (premarital counseling), staying married, or resolving problems related to marriage (sexual, money, children, in-laws, communication, etc.), or getting out of marriage (divorce counseling).

Essentially marriage counseling is a form of *psychotherapy* (although some would disagree with this statement and prefer to consider it something less than psychotherapy, maintaining a distinction between coun-

---

Reprinted from *The Family Coordinator*, Vol. 22, No. 1, pp. 91–97, January, 1973.

seling and psychotherapy which this writer does not believe will hold up under rigorous analysis). Marriage counseling, then, is a form of psychotherapy which deals with problems centering around marriage (Nichols, 1968). Training and educating marriage counselors is, therefore, training psychotherapists in how to handle or cope with the problems clustering around marriage and man-woman relationships. Supervision in this context is one aspect of the overall professional education and training of marriage counselors. In a sense, clinical supervision may be the core of the professional training and education of marriage counselors.

An increasing number of people are going into the practice of marriage counseling despite the fact that there seems to be a dropping off of training centers. More people are getting licensed to do marriage counseling but still need to get the supervision specified in some state laws. Therefore it would seem appropriate at this time to examine some of the concepts revolving around supervision.

Who?

Who is the supervisor? The supervisor, if we are to consider the ideal situation, would ordinarily be a professionally trained marriage counselor who has had considerable experience not only in marriage counseling but also in the supervision of marriage counselors in training. If he meets the requirements of the American Association of Marriage and Family Counselors for the title of "approved supervisor" he will have had several years of supervisory experience. The A.A.M.F.C. requirements may be obtained by writing to the national office of the Association. The present discussion will not limit itself to the A.A.M.F.C. requirements, however. The supervisor may have been through a marriage counselors training program which has been approved by the American Association of Marriage and Family Counselors. (It should go without saying that whenever "he" is used in this context, it obviously refers to the person, who may be either male or female.)

Who is the supervisee? Obviously any marriage counselor in training who is seeing clients under the supervision of the supervisor. The supervisee may have largely completed the academic aspects of his education, having finished perhaps most of his course work, including history courses, background courses, and perhaps even some practica.

The clients whom the supervisee is seeing may be people concerned about any of the problems referred to earlier; that is, the clients may be coming in for premarital counseling, marital counseling, divorce counseling, or any of the particular problems that may arise around the general field of "marriage counseling."

If we add an administrator of the clinic who is "over" the supervisor in the organization, we can have a complex relationship between the therapist or counselor (supervisee or student), the supervisor, the client(s), and the administrator. The complex matrix of relationships among the four members mentioned has been named the clinical rhombus by Ekstein and Wallerstein (1958). This four-way relationship was named the clinical rhombus because of the kite shaped figure or diagram the above authors used to illustrate the nature of the possible relationships involved. All the above staff members are concerned about the clients. The supervisee may be able to appeal to the administrator if he feels his supervisor is "unjust" or "unfair" to him as a student.

What?

What is supervision? Traditionally, and unfortunately, supervision too often became contaminated with overseeing, directorial, and inspecting functions so that it too frequently has been diverted from its *teaching* objective (Wolberg, 1954). In the present context, supervision means looking over the shoulder, so to speak, of the supervisee by the supervisor, while the supervisee is learning to practice the skills of marriage counseling.

The supervisor's goal is seen by Dean Johnson (1961) as helping the supervisee clarify and sharpen his perceptive powers to the end that his analysis of clients and their problems may become more accurate.

> "The supervisor's goal also includes helping the counselor to learn to use himself more fully and appropriately in the counseling process. The focus is upon how the counselor perceives his task and his clients and their problems and how he attempts to provide help. The supervisor enables the counselor to stimulate his perceptive functions and provides ego support as the counselor applies his perceptive, organizing, and calculating powers toward appropriate execution of his counseling task (Johnson, 1961, 220)."

Dean Johnson, in his book *Marriage Counseling* (1961, 219–224) has suggested several principles of supervision. They include: (1) The primary focus of supervision should be upon the professional growth and development of the counselor. (2) The teaching role of the supervisor should be quite clear to him and easily discernable to his counselors-in-training. (3) Supervisory hours in which the central focus is upon the development of counselor self-awareness and professional growth, rather than wholly upon the client and his problems offer the most rewarding experience in learning. (5) Anxiety associated with a counselor's student status can be a useful stimulus to the learning process. (Cf. Mueller and Kell, 1972, who would agree with this point.) (7) In supervision, learning is facilitated far more by positive approaches than by negative ones.

Despite a statement that "supervision is not a disguised form of psychotherapy," (Ekstein and Wallerstein, 1958, 15) the whole tenor of much supervision influenced by the so-called psychodynamic or psychoanalytic tradition seems to regard much of the behavior that comes out of students in training as uniformly "sick" (Ekstein and Wallerstein, 1958, x).

This whole question of personal psychotherapy for marital therapists has been dealt with most clearly by William Nichols (1968). Nichols discusses the need for personal psychotherapy for marital therapists and how a carefully worked out separation and coordination of supervision and personal psychotherapy for interns was worked out in a program formerly conducted at the Merrill-Palmer Institute in Detroit. A psychotherapy training faculty member who was not involved in supervision with the intern was assigned as his psychotherapist (not chosen by the intern). Wives of interns occasionally were accepted into treatment by her husband's therapist under this system. As Nichols described the set-up, the supervisor often made it explicit that the historical and etiological aspects of the intern's difficulty were not appropriate for supervision but properly belonged in his therapy. Once again it needs to be underlined that the personal therapist under this system was *not involved in teaching the intern or evaluating his work at any point*. Also, the major aim was helping the interns become more effective professional persons, rather than reconstructing personality in a major way or changing some form of psychopathology.

The distinction between supervision and personal psychotherapy for the supervisee needs to be carefully maintained in the view of the present writer (Ekstein and Wallerstein, 1958). Whether a didactic analysis, or training analysis, or "control analysis" is *required* or *recommended* makes a difference. The present writer would agree with Ekstein and Wallerstein (1958) in making personal psychotherapy a *recommendation* rather than a requirement. Also, as Ekstein and Wallerstein (1958) say, the personal supervision of the psychotherapist-to-be should *not compete* with his personal therapeutic experience. The supervision should not be a hidden form of psychotherapy, in the opinion of the present writer.

Turning to more concrete and specific discussion of just what supervision is and how it may be accomplished, we may say that it may be accomplished in several ways; for example, by having the supervisee sit in on some marriage counseling the supervisor is conducting and learning by observing, so to speak; also by the use of tapes and video-tapes which the supervisor may provide for the supervisee, with the supervisor going over the material with the supervisee, pointing out some of the things the supervisee may have missed, correcting possible errors (which even qualified supervisors make), making critical suggestions, and raising questions with the supervisee. Going over, together, verbatim case reports which have been published (Ellis, 1971; Wolberg, 1954) and discussing alternative responses, can be helpful.

The supervisor may sit in on some sessions the supervisee conducts and observe the supervisee in action at the time; this may be accomplished with one-way screens or mirrors so that the supervisor does not have to be physically present in the same room with the supervisee and his client(s). Video-tapes are becoming increasingly used and are excellent for getting at the non-verbal as well as the verbal communication taking place both in the clients and in the supervisee.

A phone set-up may facilitate the supervisor calling in to the supervisee and helping him handle particularly touchy topics or problem situations at the time they occur (where the supervisor has recording equipment set up and/or one-way screens or mirrors and can follow along right with the supervisee, rather than discussing possible mistakes long after they have happened and therefore, have sometimes become uncorrectable). This phone set-up sometimes troubles supervisees when first encountered but it can be an effective teaching tool, if properly handled.

Probably, for most situations, the tape recorder and the critical analysis of tape recordings of the supervisee's sessions with his clients will continue to be the most basic tool of supervision (Ekstein and Wallerstein, 1958). The supervisor aids the learning process by listening carefully, teaching the supervisee to do the same, and also by making helpful, constructive suggestions, helping the supervisee by lending a "third" and/or fourth ear. Sometimes several supervisees can learn together and hear different things, so that a small group of several supervisees may help each other if they can overcome their possible anxiety at sharing their beginning efforts. Dean Johnson (1961) has provided a good illustration of just how such a group of supervisees might be handled with a good integration of dydactic and clinical training. The American Association of Marriage and Family Counselors has stated that of the 200 hours of supervision which constitute their minimum requirement, at least 50 hours must be individual.

Dean Johnson (1961) has stated that he believes that the supervisory process as experienced by the counselor-in-training typically proceeds by stages. He delineates these stages as proceeding in the following fashion (the counselor's perception of the supervisor): (1) judge-evaluator, (2) evaluator-helper, (3) evaluator-helper-confronter, (4) unjust judge-witholding "father," (5) fallible person like all others—faded omnipotence and omnisience, (6) teacher-helper rather than judge or all-giving object of dependency longings.

As another way of looking at the various roles through which supervision may develop, the present writer would like to suggest that supervision probably involves evolving roles, over time, for both the supervisor and the supervisee: Supervision would seem to involve two professionals as they move together through preceptorship, apprenticeship, mentorship, sponsorship, to, finally peership relationships.

Preceptorship may be considered the first form of learning wherein the novice is placed with a professional marriage counselor (perhaps early during the novice's advanced training) where he can, in effect, follow the marriage counselor through a typical day's work, sitting in on whatever the marriage counselor may be doing. This may better enable the novice to get a clearer idea of just what the profession is all about.

Later on, the supervisee may serve an *apprenticeship*, which has traditionally been considered the time during which an apprentice or novice serves, in this context, in learning his profession. This usually involves spending more time (at least more than one day per week) learning his new profession under the supervision of an experienced marriage counselor to whom he has been assigned. This apprenticeship is perhaps the beginning of an intensive relationship over some extended period of time.

The supervisor is a *mentor*, in a sense; he is a close, trusted, and experienced counselor or guide who can hold up a mirror, as it were, to the supervisee so that the beginner can learn to be critical of his own responses and, in particular, grow beyond the limitations of his own personal experience and background (in other words, begin to become a professional).

To use another analogy, the supervisor helps the supervisee learn to shoot his responses like a rifle rather than a shotgun. That is, the supervisee can begin to learn to ask penetrating, thoughtful, perceptive questions (in a Socratic fashion, if you will), that get to the core of the problem, rather than responding in shotgun fashion, spraying the client with vague, amorphous responses in the vain hope that some might hit the mark. This is not to say, of course, that open-ended questions may not prove helpful, on occasion. Many types of questions need to be learned, of course, by the supervisee (Branden, 1970).

The supervisor, if he is to do a thorough job, needs to teach the supervisee what to look for through the use of adequate theories (Ard, 1966; Harper, 1959). Hopefully, more than one theory can be of use to the supervisee. The basic idea is to stretch the supervisee's mind with helpful ideas, not to put theoretical blinders on him (which might make him more mulish if not blind to some things).

The supervisor can also help the supervisee by teaching the apprentice how to handle difficult dilemmas, how to deal with values, conscience, super-ego, etc. (Ard, 1969). Personal value problems of clients as well as the professional ethics marriage counselors need to know are basic matters the supervisor may well deal with, if he is to help the supervisee handle tough, difficult cases. These value dilemmas merge into another difficult task which the supervisor can be of great help to the supervisee with, namely helping the supervisee see what kind of person he wishes to be as a therapist (Ard, 1971). In addition to the kind of person the supervisee develops into, the supervisor must also help the supervisee develop a *professional identity* of the psychotherapist (Ekstein and Wallerstein, 1958).

The supervisor serves in the role of *sponsor*; his role is the sponsorship of the supervisee. In ancient Roman law, a sponsor was one who bound himself to answer for another's default. In a sense, we hold the sponsor responsible for the supervisee's later actions (at least his *professional* behavior). If the supervisee turns out to be a competent counselor, perceptive, insightful, and, all in all, a good counselor, we say he had a good training and praise his supervisor. We sometimes even ask: "Who did you study under?" This is a way of determining what kind of training and what kind of competence one might expect of the counselor in question. This putting such an emphasis on supervision is a heavy responsibility, indeed.

The sponsor is one who supports and confirms in the apprentice that which is best in the supervisee, without exacting an excessive price in terms of submission, initiation, emulation, or even gratitude. It is a fine line for the supervisor to walk.

Finally, ideally, the relationship becomes one of *peership*, where the supervisor treats the supervisee as an equal, a professional colleague, perhaps even as a friend. There is a mutual respect and warm feeling which remain after a successful supervision experience. So the supervision relationship evolves through preceptorship, apprenticeship, mentorship, sponsorship to peership.

When?

When is supervision done? Frequently it is done after the supervisee has largely completed his academic training (course work), although this may not be always true. There is some advantage to having the supervisee have some actual experience in marriage counseling before having completed all his course work, since that may make his course work, particularly the theory courses, more meaningful. A common pattern is for the supervisee to bring tapes of his session to his supervisor on a once-a-week basis, perhaps for an hour, and to raise at that time any questions he may have with the supervisor, playing portions of his tapes which seem troublesome to him.

Different state laws have different requirements for supervision for marriage counselors. For example, the Michigan law requires one year of specialized training in marriage counseling under the supervision of a certified marriage counselor in order to meet that specific part of the requirement. The law in Michigan calls for five years of post-degree experience of which one is to be of this type (Nichols, 1972, personal correspondence).

Some supervisors may require verbatim reports of every client response, along with the therapists's responses, for each hour or session. This can be a unique learning experience, although typing up the verbatim reports can be a very time-consuming process if the supervisee has to type up every case from a tape recorder himself. An occasional experience of this sort may be helpful but it is not routinely necessary where good tape recordings can be made.

When supervision should be done has to fitted in with two professional schedules, but if the supervision can follow the actual experience as soon as possible it is perhaps better for all concerned (the supervisee, the supervisor, and the clients). How often should the supervisory sessions be scheduled? Probably at the beginning, one hour each week would be ideal. (The A.A.M.F.C. states that they normally expect their required 200 hours to occur within two years.) If the supervisee seems to be getting along well, the weekly sessions might be changed to every other week. Once a month supervisory sessions would seem to be a minimum for at least a year.

The question of interminable supervision is one that needs to be faced. Some authorities in the field, particularly in social work, seem to suggest that supervision should indeed be interminable. Ekstein and Wallerstein, a psychologist and a psychiatrist, have stated with regard to social workers, that

> ". . . the other professions often experience the social workers as being unduly and even permanently dependent upon their supervisors. Supervision is not only an integral part of the training in social work school but remains a permanent pattern in most agencies. It is often maintained even for those who supervise . . . (Ekstein and Wallerstein, 1958)."

The same authors state (1958) that "This mistake of introducing a step in training too early is about as dangerous as the mistake of those social work agencies that maintain dependency on supervision forever."

A more realistic stance might be to suggest that whenever a marriage counselor, after finishing the professional training that should allow him to practice privately without supervision, has some difficult cases or some of his own reactions that he would like to check out, he would be wise to discuss such matters with a professional in the field from whom the therapist thinks he can learn something. So consultation sessions might occur several years after a marriage counselor had finished his professional training, but initiated at his own request. Later on consultation may cease and be replaced by the occasional sharing of clinical experiences with other experienced colleagues who are partners in clarification, rather than supervisors or consultants (Ekstein and Wallerstein, 1958). But certainly supervision, in the view of the present writer, should not be interminable.

Where?

Supervision can occur in a variety of settings. The old idea of two people at either end of a log is still a viable concept. The more usual situation, however, and in some sense even more ideal, is in a setting where one-way mirrors, video-tape facilities, tape recordings, etc., are readily available. The clinic or training institution would seem the more standard place for supervision to take place. Where possible, tape recording set-ups with phones in the counseling rooms and in the supervisor's office are certainly very functional.

The question of whether supervision can be done at a distance is one that needs to be realistically faced in view of the fact that not every marriage counselor has access to training facilities or clinics of the sort just mentioned. Tapes can be mailed (wrapped in aluminum foil to prevent accidental erasure) and running logs (or notebooks) with space for questions and answers can also be mailed back and forth. Long distance phone calls can be expensive but conference calls can be arranged and can prove helpful. Such long distance techniques may not be ideal but they may be the only possibilities in some instances.

Why?

The question of why do we need supervision at all should have perhaps been asked first rather than last but we can wind up our discussion of supervision by restating why supervision is deemed so necessary in the field of marriage counseling.

Since marriage counseling is a form of psychotherapy, and cannot be learned completely by sitting in a library, some form of supervision seems to be necessary in order to help teach the beginning marriage counselor the professional skills he needs.

In very practical terms, as the A.A.M.F.C. has spelled it out, supervision is assumed to have the following characteristics:

(a) It is face-to-face conversations with the supervisor.

(b) It is sustained and intense, usually once a week over a period of one or two years.

(c) It focuses on the raw data from the supervisee's current clinical work, this made directly available to the supervisor through such means as direct observations, written clinical notes and audio and television recordings.

(d) It is a process clearly distinguishable from personal psychotherapy and is contracted to serve *professional* goals.

It is expected by the A.A.M.F.C. that a trainee will have a minimum total of 500 hours of counseling, and will receive not less than 200 hours of supervision, to include at least 50 hours of individual supervision.

In conclusion, supervision provides that form of apprenticeship, mentorship, sponsorship and peership relationships that seems called for if the beginning marriage counselor is to round out his learning from books and become that sort of therapist who can become of helpful, constructive use to people with problems centering around marriage and man-woman relationships. If marriage counselors are truly to be professionals, as it would seem to be implied that they must be in view of the certification or license laws being passed in various states, then supervision would seem to be a necessary and very basic step in providing the finishing touches of their professional education and training.

REFERENCES

Ard, B. N., Jr. *Counseling and psychotherapy: classics on theories and issues.* Palo Alto: Science & Behavior Books, 2nd ed., 1975.

Ard, B. N., Jr. The conscience or superego in marriage counseling, *Marriage Counseling Quarterly*, 1969, 5, 1–8.

Ard, B. N., Jr. The therapist as a person (Or: The compleat counselor). *Marriage Counseling Quarterly*, 1971, 6, 1–5.

Ard, B. N., Jr. & Ard, C. C. *Handbook of marriage counseling.* Palo Alto: Science & Behavior Books, 1969.

Branden, N. *Breaking free.* Los Angeles: Nash, 1970.

Ekstein, R. & Wallerstein, R. S. *The teaching and learning of psychotherapy.* New York: Basic Books, 1958.

Ellis, A. *Growth through reason: verbatim cases in rational-emotive psychotherapy.* Palo Alto: Science & Behavior Books, 1971.

English, H. B. & English, A. C. *A Comprehensive dictionary of psychological and psychoanalytical terms.* New York: Longmans, Green & Co., 1958.

Harper, R. A. *Psychoanalysis and psychotherapy: 36 systems.* Englewood Cliffs, NJ: Prentice-Hall, 1959.

Johnson, D. *Marriage Counseling: theory and practice.* Englewood Cliffs, NJ: Prentice-Hall, 1961.

Mueller, W. J. & Kell, B. L. *Coping with conflict: supervising counselors and psychotherapists.* New York: Appleton-Century Crofts, 1972.

Nichols, W. C., Jr. Personal psychotherapy for marital therapists. *The Family Coordinator*, 1968, 17, 83–88.

Wolberg, L. R. *The technique of psychotherapy.* New York: Grune & Stratton, 1954.

Divorce Counseling

The land of marriage has this peculiarity, that strangers are desirous of inhabiting it, whilst its natural inhabitants would willingly be banished from thence.

MONTAIGNE

The question of whether or not to get a divorce is one of the most crucial questions which clients bring to marriage counselors. The professional marriage counselor has to have some perspective on divorce in our society in order to be of optimal help to clients considering whether or not to dissolve their marriage. As Max Lerner has said in his discussion of *America as a Civilization*:

"There are no people in the world who make greater demands upon marriage than Americans do, since they lay greater exactions upon it and also expect greater psychic satisfaction from it. They do not make the necessarily right demands, but whether right or wrong, they don't settle easily for a small fraction (1957)."

American attitudes toward divorce are shifting, as Lerner has also shown, with a more experimental attitude developing which might be described as no longer seeing divorce as a final disaster or a catastrophic failure but rather as a temporary setback in a continuing quest. At least this is a possibility among some people.

In Chapter 45, Laura Singer discusses divorce and the single life and also considers divorce as development, an intriguing concept. As more and more clients consult marriage counselors about divorce, perhaps this article can help the marriage counselors (and ultimately the clients) see divorce as a legitimate alternative.

Probably one of the reasons so many people in our culture have so much trouble in their thinking about divorce is that they have assumed without question that monogamy or lifelong marriage is the proper or appropriate way for people to live, if not the only acceptable way. Dr. Ben N. Ard, Jr., in Chapter 46, in an attempt to clear away some of the self-defeating attitudes in this area, discusses conventional ideas about monogamy and raises the fundamental question, paradoxical as it may seem, is monogamy destructive of marriage? Here, indeed, are some unconventional thoughts on a conventional topic. The thoughtful reader is not asked necessarily to agree with everything said in this article, but

509

merely to examine some of the common unquestioned assumptions in our society about marriage, monogamy, and whether or not marriage counselors need to have somewhat independent ideas about these matters than the man on the street.

CHAPTER 45

Divorce and the Single Life:
Divorce as Development

Laura J. Singer

Divorce can herald freedom, independence, growth toward self-actualiza-tion. It can also herald a variety of psychosomatic ailments, depression, despair, and, in some cases, even death. In most instances, it encompasses feelings of hurt, anger, pain, and loss as well as relief and liberation.

In our society, alienation in interaction seems to be a common experi-ence, as Goffman has indicated. Social theorists attribute this alienation to a variety of causes including

> the distortion of communication by the mass media, the shallowness of life styles in middle class ghettos, the unanticipated destructive consequences of technological innovations in the cities as well as in the countryside, the sense-less warfare machinery, the adjustment and readjustment of people to the values and standards of the Protestant ethic through the various socialization agencies in one of several forms. All this contributes to a general feeling of meaninglessness and estrangement in social life (Dreitzel, 1972).

In an attempt to counteract meaninglessness and estrangement in so-cial life—the frustrations engendered by a schizoid society—young people are propelled into marriage impulsively, and then gigantic and unrealistic demands are placed upon the marriage and upon the spouse. The marriage is expected to provide communication, understanding, personal fulfill-ment, eroticism, romantic love, ever-stimulating intellectual companion-ship, and ever-present emotional support and responsiveness. It is out of these unreasonable cultural expectations in concert with a multiplicity of personal psychological factors that divorce emerges from a breakdown in communications between the marital dyad or perhaps out of a deep atten-tion to what is being communicated both overtly and covertly. Divorce, like marriage, contains wishes, hopes, and fantasies that may be conscious but are largely unverbalized or, more likely, are unconscious.

Reprinted by permission of the author and the publisher of the *Journal of Sex and Marital Therapy*, Spring, 1975.

SOME SELECTIVE STATISTICS

Our statistics on divorce in the United States are most illuminating. The upward trend of divorce in recent years is continuing. For the 12 months ending in September of 1973, an increase of 26% in the rate of divorce was reported over a comparable period ending in September of 1970. In New York State, the number of divorces went from 24,157 in 1970 to 45,626 in 1973. Out of every five marriages, three end in divorce, and in some parts of California there is one divorce for each marriage (HEW, 1973).

The alacrity with which remarriages are instituted is also impressive. One-fourth of white divorced men remarry within 1 year, one-half within 3 years, and three-fourths within 9 years. For black men, the interval is about half as long again as that for white men, and all women tend to "wait" slightly longer than men to remarry.

For the first 5 years after divorce, the odds are 1 out of 5 that the divorced will remarry within a year's time; for divorces of longer duration the odds are only about one-half this high. *Three-quarters of all divorced people tend to remarry within 5 years* (Kargman, 1973). According to the statistics available at this time, persons who remarry are more likely to remain in their second marriages than persons who married only once are likely to remain in their first marriages (Glick, 1971).

PREVAILING ATTITUDES

Let us examine some of the prevailing attitudes toward divorce. These can be divided into four categories. The first is "The Moral Deterioration Theory," in which the proponents declare that people who seek divorce are irresponsible, that they lack moral courage, that their children are overindulged. This point of view seems to be based upon some of the more traditional aspects of the Protestant ethic, and some of its proponents would like to see the divorce laws tightened up as one way of coping with the burgeoning rate of divorce.

The second category is "The Ignorance Theory," in which the proponents declare that young people marry before they are ready; that they are too young and immature and insufficiently prepared; that they don't know what it means to take responsibility for themselves or others. This point of view is based upon the somewhat simplistic concept that all that is needed is a program of massive education—including "preparation for marriage" courses and more premarital counseling.

The third, "The Psychoanalytic Viewpoint," is based upon psychological and psychoanalytic theory in which some of the proponents declare that divorce is the result of neurotic patterns of relating to mother, father, and siblings; that it is the result of intrapsychic conflicts. Some further declare that even divorce doesn't help because people tend to repeat the same patterns over and over again and that what might be of help is some form of systematic intervention.

The fourth, "The Divorce is Inevitable" approach, is based upon the sociological doctrine that divorce is a mass phenomenon implicit in a culture that allows for freedom of choice of marital partner and, therefore, also freedom to get rid of one's partner if one so chooses. It appears to be based upon an ethic in which there is an injunction to pursue happiness and to actualize oneself. The implication here is that divorce, that is, the breakup of couples and families, does not seem to be undermining society, and that as a matter of fact, even if these breakups might be undermining society, it doesn't matter since between 85% and 90% of all divorced people eventually do remarry (Gee).

DIVORCE AS AN OPPORTUNITY
FOR GROWTH AND DEVELOPMENT

Because people who divorce tend to remarry within a relatively short period of time, I shall herein consider divorce as a crisis point and postdivorce and the single life as an opportunity for further growth and development. The period under scrutiny can last from 6 months to 9 years—before remarriage.

Postdivorce will be considered in terms of object relations as defined by developmental psychoanalytic stages and modified by the ego psychologists (Kernberg, 1966). More specifically, I shall attempt to view divorce as an adjunctive developmental period—growth producing in some instances, containing regressive features in most instances, and regressively fixated in still others. Gertrude and Rubin Blanck (1968) have offered some interesting hypotheses concerning opportunities for further development within marriage. I am utilizing and altering some of their constructs in an attempt to apply them to some clinical examples of the postdivorced. It is my contention that:

1. Divorce, like marriage, can provide an additional opportunity for psychological separation from the parents, or spouse as parent.

2. Divorce, like marriage, can provide an opportunity for working through of early sexual restrictions and inhibitions.

3. Divorce, like marriage, can aid in the development of a new level of object relations—the ability to relate to others with mutuality and a recognition of the needs of the other.

4. Divorce, like marriage, can provide an opportunity for the exercise of autonomy, for the ability to be close and at the same time retain a sense of one's own personal identity.

Although some people can spontaneously utilize the experiences of a first marriage and a subsequent divorce for the aforementioned kinds of growth, many need therapeutic aid in order to acquire these insights.

Let us address ourselves to separation which most, if not all, of us never fully complete. "Perhaps all anxiety stems from the ego's incapacity to accept separation which [to the infant] equals death," thus spoke Martin Grotjahn (1968). Anxiety around separation seems to be a universal Western reaction to the trauma of divorce. How is this anxiety mastered? How do divorced people deal with separation?

Case 1

Andrea, a psychologist and educator, married for 3 years then divorced, no children, describes her experience:

> I was the youngest of two children, younger by 4 years than my brother. I adored my father, a brilliant intellectual, and never seemed to be able to get close enough to my mother who was very self-involved and involved with other men. When I was 10, we left my father and my brother. I agonized over this separation, but leaving my father was less frightening than the thought of being separated from my mother. I always felt as if I had betrayed my father by going away with my mother.
>
> Because I was aware of the deep unhappiness between my mother and my father, I was determined that I would have a good marriage. I would be a devoted wife. I guess I had been brainwashed by the idea of an ideal marriage, if only I really wanted it to be that way. I was convinced that by really trying, I could make it work. I was not at all prepared for a relationship which was emotionally shallow with a narcissistic man who was an external charmer and who promised me the world, but demanded all and delivered nothing. Our sexual relationship, never good, was deteriorating. He preferred pornography and masturbation to sex with me. We tried for 3 years and then went through one of those divorces in which we were forced to say terrible things about each other. I learned how unrealistic and starry-eyed my expectations had been and how disappointed and disillusioned I had grown.
>
> I was one of the lucky women because I was prepared to earn a living. This helped me to feel a little better about myself—the knowledge that I could be self-reliant. One of the problem areas in divorce is for the woman who has been completely dependent upon a man and is faced with the necessity for earning her own living. I had to learn to stand on my own. I did, but I felt very lonely. Through therapy, I learned that I was looking for a good mother in my ex-husband; and selected someone who could barely take care of himself, let alone me. I was as big a disappointment to him as he was to me. The divorce, in making me seek therapy, helped me to grow to where I am now; involved in work that gives me gratification and in a relationship which provides many satisfactions; companionship and intimacy and an opportunity to grow; albeit with pain and anxiety.

Andrea's ability to move toward independence, to be involved in work that has given her satisfaction and in a new relationship of intimacy, seems to give evidence of the ability of the ego to have fairly successfully come to grips with symbiosis, partially able to deal with separation-individuation and to have moved toward object constancy. Her early experiences with a mother who was minimally available emotionally and a father who appears to have been emotionally present for her, although unable to deal with his own life, seem to have provided the matrix for development. Her anxiety around separation first from father and brother and then from husband seems to give evidence of unfinished business at the separation-individuation level with which she was partially able to deal during the postdivorce period, with therapeutic intervention.

Case 2

More bruising was the parental climate into which Janet was born. A tall, striking brunette of 29, Janet is the mother of two sons, one of whom is a 3-year-old and the other 18 months of age. Married for 3½ years, she has been divorced for 1 year. Her Swedish husband has custody of the two sons. She is a chronic depressive who had partially identified with an infantile, depressed mother, who was neither physically nor emotionally available through most of her childhood. She described her childhood in this fashion:

> As a child, I hated my mother, but I was very proud of her, because she was so pretty; I used to love to show her off. I was extremely unhappy. I'd never see my mother; she always had lots of boyfriends. For years I would have given anything for her to be a mommy. I hated her, she was so unfair. But I've always had this tremendous love for her and she's shit on us all. Jennie [her father's mother] brought me up morally; she was very strict. She and daddy lived near us and if I got sick, I'd go over to her house and she'd take care of me. Through the love she gave me, I was able to survive. We had lots of good moments together. She was an artist and she loved to sing. Daddy always wanted to be a doctor, but she wanted him to be a musician. And so he became a musician, like grandmother's two husbands, but he always hated it. Jennie was very tall and very strict and when daddy wanted to beat me and my sister, she would stand between us and daddy to save us. When daddy got angry, he would froth at the mouth and I would sit there, pee would run down my legs, and I would shake. When I was 12, Jennie died and I started being a naughty girl. I was the black sheep of the family.
>
> When I was 13, I had to call the police to get mommy's boyfriend out of the house; he was beating up on her and he said, "Your mother's a slut, she fucks around." I said, "Mommy, is that true?" and she said yes, and it made me feel awful. Then, when I was 15, he tried to make love to me, and I ran away. When I was 16, I had an abortion and after that I became very heavy, I weighed between 165 and 185 pounds, and I became a lesbian. My mother sent me to Menninger's and I was there for 3 years. They never allowed me to see mommy; they said she was a bad influence. I was a fighter, very rebellious. I've always felt that my father loved me. He always respected me; he was pretty pissed off at me, but somehow I've known that he cared.

Janet married a man who was quiet, nurturant, calm and patient, never seemed to worry, and was very fond of their sons. Her husband's patience did not carry into their sexual life. He enjoyed neither foreplay nor oral-genital contact, nor could he sustain an erection long enough to enable her to reach orgasm. Since he was a symbiotic mother substitute for her, it is hard to say whether it was fear of symbiotic merger and loss of identity that inhibited the orgasm or whether it was projection of her own aggression onto her husband that was an additional inhibiting factor.

She divorced him after he had confessed that he had taken a mistress while she was pregnant with each of her sons. The narcissistic injury, loss of self-esteem, repreated her earlier object losses. She came to live with her mother hoping for the elusive, magical love that she is so hungry for. Apparently, her mother was somewhat available to her during the very early months, during the 1st year of her life, but minimally available thereafter. Her grandmother, Jennie, provided some of the affection and care she needed, as did her father, who, though harsh and punitive, was also caring. When her sons were infants, Janet was able to enjoy the symbiotic attachment to them. When they started to rebel and to separate, she was unable to tolerate the aggression and divorced herself from her sons as well as from her husband, who became one of the 365,000 men in our country who were granted custody of their children between 1965 and 1972.

During the postdivorce period, with psychotherapy, she began to develop some of her own resources. She found and lost several jobs, finally remained with one in which she could put her propensity for order to work. At the same time, she completed a course in scuba diving, one of the few courses she has ever been able to successfully complete. Janet further describes herself thusly:

I'm a thinker, a planner aheader. I want to be my own boss. I've always resented people telling me what to do. I'm feeling more relaxed now. I never was able to have an orgasm; now I'm getting less inhibited. I can come forever. I see myself changing. I'm really getting good in bed. This is the first time I've made love and didn't think about myself. I can't believe it. I am enjoying sex for what it is. And only when I want it. For the first time, I've been able to say no. I feel an inner urgency to do something that's bigger and better ... not only for myself.

Janet is beginning to work through some of the restrictions and early inhibitions around sex. She is beginning to take some steps toward separation and individuation. She now says: "My mother is the best friend I have in the world. I do have a habit of draining. I want, I want, I want." It's still difficult for her to comprehend someone else's needs, but she seems to have more neutralized energy available for the unfinished development of object relations. During this postdivorce period, she controlled by selecting men with whom she would have sexual experiences, found men who enjoyed foreplay and oral-genital contacts, and discovered that she is well able to be fully orgasmic.

Here we have seen two young women in their late 20s, one whose development has been through partial completion of the phallic phase and into the phase of Oedipal conflict, and who has used the postdivorce period to further her development through separation-individuation and toward achieving object constancy. The other, whose family provided a far less favorable milieu, who suffered symbiotic deprivation, had partially worked through separation-individuation, and whose tolerance for frustration is very low indeed, was able to utilize the postdivorce period for working through some of the earlier sexual restrictions and inhibitions as well as to correct some of her distortions and heighten her self-esteem. During the postdivorce period, she received therapeutic support for her stubbornness, her orderliness, her choices, her judgement, and her courage to learn how to say no.

Many men who initiate a divorce seem to have someone else waiting in the wings (Lyman, 1971). Not so with Bill.

Case 3

Bill is a minister, a rather slender, attractive man, who was divorced when he was in his middle 30s. He fathered two daughters who at the time of the divorce were 12 and 14. He describes his experiences:

I very much enjoyed being admired by my congregation, and found myself spending more and more time absorbed in a variety of church activities. When I met Betty, she was nice and kind and very strong. At first she seemed happy to participate in the work of the church, but after the children were born, she became angry and jealous of the time spent away from her and the girls. It was more and more difficult for me to go home at night; it was always a hassle, with all kinds of accusations. I felt as if I were being torn to shreds. But I was able to put on a mask for my congregation. They thought we were really a happy pair. Until it got so bad I began to develop ulcers. And then I knew. I just had to leave. Everyone was shocked; some kept making sly references to another woman, or, in fact, a series of women. Everyone was terribly upset. My loving congregation was divided into factions, some siding with Betty and others siding with me. I felt terrible, and finally asked to be transferred. Then I went into psychotherapy to find out what went wrong with the marriage. I found out a lot about myself.

Bill had married Betty when he was 22. Although he was tentatively diagnosed as psychoneurotic rather than borderline, the crisis of divorce made psychotherapy the treatment of preference (Blanck & Blanck, 1974). It turned out to be a fortuitous decision, since further treatment began uncovering material that seemed to indicate that the early psychosexual development had not been as favorable as initially reported, and that there was more psychopathology albeit combined with neurotic features. Even though he had been able to advance to a phallic level of psychosexual development, he had not worked through some of his early symbiotic strivings, had a good deal of unfinished business at the separation-individuation level, and was barely along the road toward object constancy. The congregation, as well as his wife, initially provided some gratifications, but since he had not really worked through the early relationship with his mother, he began to be afraid that he would be swallowed up in the symbiotic bond with his wife. He projected his aggressions upon her and saw her as the bad, unloving, ungiving mommy. The congregation, on the other hand, symbolized all that was good and kind and loving, until the divorce. He describes the postdivorce period in this way:

I learned that I wanted closeness, but was deathly afraid I would be swallowed up in the process. I was scared, and I didn't date. It felt safer to relate to married couples, and some of my friends nurtured and supported me. I could relate much easier to married women than I could to single women. I have gradually begun to trust women, and I finally found one with whom I can be truly close and intimate without feeling that I'm losing part of myself. But it has taken me 5 years, much of the time spent in psychotherapy, to find out about myself and my marriage. Now, with Jane, I feel close and still feel like my own person. But we work hard at our relationship. It's worth it.

Bill's mother was rigid, stern, strict. She always did the "right thing." She was always at home, forever cleaning and working around the house. His father was an auto mechanic who worked long hours. He'd come home late and drink himself to bed. Bill speaks:

It was a nothing kind of life. The one thing we did together was to go to church on Sunday. That we all did together. When I was 2, my sister was born, and she was my father's favorite. When I was 3 I had a kidney infection and had to go to the hospital. I was scared, very scared. I screamed and cried for my mother to come. She came when she could. She had no one to leave my sister with. I've had funny feelings about hospitals ever since then. I always did well in school; I was not much for sports. I looked after my little sister a lot—sometimes that got to be a pain. Mother was very proud when I decided to go into the ministry. It was one of the few times she kissed me and told me how proud she was of me.

Bill was the victim of impaired object relations—a stern and demanding mother and a weak and impotent father. His gender identification was partially with his mother whose values he incorporated. His sense of masculinity was impaired because he experienced his father as passive and impotent. He married a woman who appeared to have the qualities of his mother except that he viewed her as "nice and kind" as well as strong. She appeared to approve of him, of his strivings to live up to his ego ideal, and then withdrew her warmth and approval. Bill idealized his mother, then his wife, and then the congregation. When the congregation became loving and good, he became very disappointed in his wife who withdrew her support and threatened his sense of identity. "Where identity is threatened, then aggression must be summoned to maintain it (Blanck & Blanck, 1968)." His aggression became so overwhelming that the anxiety made the marriage dysfunctional; distance through divorce became mandatory for him.

DISCUSSION

While Andrea, the young woman in the first example, was involved in a growth-inhibiting marriage, both Janet and Bill had a marriage in which growth might have been able to take place. It is important to be able to evaluate to what degree marriage is growth inhibiting and divorce thus becomes necessary in order to provide further opportunities for growth (Blanck & Blanck, 1968)." However, these decisions were made prior to seeking psychotherapeutic aid. It would seem that both Bill and Janet's marriages contained opportunities that could have been utilized for further growth, but Bill sought divorce as a defense against his fear of closeness and fear of loss of identity, and Janet as a defense against her fear of merging as well as her oral rage and disappointment. However, for Andrea, marriage, although it provided a chance for her to grow in a career, was, in the main, growth inhibiting. Had we had the opportunity to explore the marital parameters more fully, perhaps the decision for Janet, and perhaps Bill as well, would have been to explore ways for growth within the marital relationship.

I have attempted to show how divorce can provide an additional opportunity for psychological separation from the parents, or spouse as parent; how it can provide an opportunity for working through of early sexual restrictions and inhibitions; how it also might aid in the development of a new level of object relations; and how it might provide an opportunity for the exercise of autonomy, for the ability to learn how to be close and at the same time retain a sense of one's own personal identity.

It has not been within the scope of this paper to deal with many significant correlates of divorce and the single life, including the mourning aspects; the impact of our couple-oriented society upon the divorced-single (Burgess, 1970); the divorced swinging singles and all that this implies (O'Neill, 1970); the divorced pair who continue to have sex with each other (Krantzler, 1973); the divorced who enter into an instant attachment with another person; the children who are a third party to divorces in a way that is not visible and the increasing necessity for providing advocates for children of divorce (Stuart, 1972); co-parenting that continues beyond the divorce (Gardner, 1970); and the possible adverse effect upon the wife's prospects for remarriage when she is left with the major responsibility for the support of children (Citizen's Advisory Council, 1972). Hopefully these profound problems can be dealt with in future papers.

REFERENCES

Blanck, G. & Blanck, R. *Ego psychology theory and practice.* New York: Columbia University Press, 1974.

Blanck, R. & Blanck, G. *Marriage and personal development.* New York: Columbia University Press, 1968.

Burgess, J. K. The single parent family: A social and sociological problem. Family Coordinator *19*: 137, 1970.

Citizen's Advisory Council on the Status of Women: Memorandum. Washington, D.C.: Author, 1972.

Dreitzel, H. P. (Ed.) *Recent sociology,* NO. 2. New York: Macmillan, 1972.

Gardner, R. A. *The boys and girls book about divorce.* New York: Science House, 1970.

Gee, A. Personal communication.

Glick, P. & Norton, A. J. Frequency, duration, and probability of marriage and divorce. *Journal of Marriage and Family, 33*: 307, 1971.

Grotjahn, M. Dynamics of growth and maturation. In Rosenbaum, S. & Alger, I. *The marriage relationship.* New York: Basic Books, 1968.

Kargman, M. W. There ought to be a law: The revolution in divorce law. Family Coordinator, *22*:245, 1973.

Kernberg, O. Structural deriviates of object relationships. *International Journal of Psychoanalysis,* 47:246, 1966.

Krantzler, M. *Creative divorce.* New York: Evans, 1973.

Lyman, H. B. *Single again.* New York: McKay, 1971.

Monthly Vital Statistics Report. National Center for Health Statistics, HEW, Rockville, Maryland, 1973.

O'Neill, G. C., O'Neill, N. Patterns in group sexual activity. *Journal of Sex Research,* 6:191, 1970.

Stuart, I. R., & Abt, L. E. *Children of separation and divorce.* New York: Grossman, 1972.

CHAPTER 46

Monogamy: Is it Destructive of Marriage?

(Some Unconventional Thoughts on a Conventional Topic)

Ben N. Ard, Jr.

In these days of rising divorce rates, "sexual revolution" or "sexual renaissance" and communal living, perhaps it would not be entirely out of order for marriage and family counselors to think some unthinkable thoughts about monogamy. One presumption which underlies the following discussion is that professional marriage and family counselors are not out to maintain monogamous marriages at all costs. Rather, their aim might better be stated as that of helping their clients live optimal lives, not self-defeating ones, particularly with regard to their love and marital relationships.

In the average, conventional person's mind, it probably sounds like a contradiction in terms to ask if monogamy is possibly destructive of marriage, since to the conventional person, marriage and monogamy are thought of as synonymous. But as anyone who has studied marriage, sexual customs, and cultural anthropology in various cultures knows, marriage and monogamy are *not* the same thing.

By way of brief review, let us define some of the relevant terms here. *Polygamy* means having a plurality of wives or husbands at the same time. *Polygyny* is where a woman is permitted to have several husbands at the same time. *Monogamy*, or more specifically, the monogamous ideal, will be defined shortly. But first, I would like to offer for your serious consideration the thesis that the *monogamous ideal*, as it is conventionally understood in our culture, *is detrimental to marriage*. That is, the monogamous ideal tends to force people into unfortunate, poorly chosen marriages, and forces them to try and maintain these unfortunate marriages in spite of the fact that they never should have been contracted in the first place. The monogamous ideal makes people avoid divorce as a legitimate alternative. The monogamous ideal tends to make too many people feel that they are "failures" simply because they do not measure up to the monogamous ideal.

———————
Reprinted, with the permission of the author and the publisher, from *The Marriage and Family Counselors Quarterly*, Spring, 1972.

Let us be clear about just what is meant here. The *monogamous ideal*, as it is usually understood in conventional terms, means that *every* individual man and woman is expected to fall in love with, and marry *for life* (or, more accurately, *forever*), *only one* member of the other sex, *and to desire no other* from that moment on.

The monogamous ideal insists that love is forever and the real thing ("true love") only comes *once in a lifetime*. Lest you think that this is mere human belief, on mere human authority, St. John, speaking for the highest authority (1 Corinthians 13) says: "Love never ends." And there are heavy penalties for those who do not follow the monogamous ideal: they commit sins against God.

As an illustration of just how far this sort of thing can be carried, I shall quote the highest moral leader (of the Western world, at least): Jesus. He is reported to have said the following: "You have heard that it was said, 'You shall not commit adultery.' But I say to you that every one who looks at a woman lustfully has already committed adultery with her in his heart (Matthew 5, 27)." And Jesus is also reported to have said, a little further on in Matthew (19, 9): "And I say to you: whoever divorces his wife, except for unchastity, and marries another, commits adultery." As a psychologist and marriage counselor, I suggest to you that it would be very hard to conceive of any ideals, values (or laws, yet) that would be more detrimental to the possibility of happy marriages among a people than this monogamous ideal, which even includes one's fantasy life. I am going to suggest that this monogamous ideal is sick, twisted thinking. And yet millions of people in our culture subscribe to this sort of thinking without ever questioning the underlying assumptions. These people feel guilty and sinful if they do not measure up to this perfectionistic, self-defeating, mentally harmful nonsense.

I have had husbands as clients who felt they were "dirty dogs" merely because they saw an attractive woman who was not their wife, and quite understandably, thought about having sexual intercourse with her (or at least contemplated, in their fantasy, such a possibility). And I have seen in my marriage counseling practice many, many people who feel guilty and a "failure," simply because they are considering getting a divorce! In both instances, I think any fair, clear thinking done on these sorts of situations would force one to conclude that anyone who feels guilty or a "failure" over such things must be engaging in sick, twisted thinking.

If anyone else but Jesus had said these sorts of things they would have been relegated to the garbage heap a long time ago. But because Jesus did say them (according to many people's belief), we have had reams of paper expended on efforts to say what he really meant, to reinterpret him, to explain him, to make it fit in with later, more rational thinking about divorce and looking at beautiful women.

In anthropology, two schools of thought have been in active conflict with each other for a number of years, the one contending that the original nature of man was polygamous and the other that it was more or less monogamous (Calverton, 1931b). "As a result of the logic of this latter school, an entirely erroneous idea of the sexual nature of the human species has been foisted upon the social sciences (Calverton, 1931b)." These anthropologists of the "monogamous" school of thought were not content, for instance, with tracing the development of marriage through its various forms, but were equally concerned with "proving" that monogamy was the ultimate stage in marital evolution (Calverton, 1931a).

Despite contrary evidence, these anthropologists of the "monogamous" school of thought declared that monogamy was *the* basic form of marriage of the human species (Calverton, 1931a). "Anthropology was thus made to serve as an excellent prop for the support of middle-class ethics. It defended the *status quo* by giving so-called final scientific sanction to its essential doctrines (Calverton, 1931a). One famous anthropologist (Westermarck) stated that "The laws of monogamy can never be changed but must be followed much more strictly than they are now (Calverton, 1931a)."

What are the actual facts with regard to the question: is man monogamous by nature? Obviously American society formally recognizes only one form of sexual partnership, namely, monogamy (Ford & Beach, 1951). But, "In cross-cultural perspective this formal attitude toward sexual partnership is exceedingly rare (Ford & Beach, 1951)." In the most extensive cross-cultural survey made to date (Ford & Beach, 1951), where 185 different cultures were studied, the evidence reveals that formal restriction to single mateships characterizes only 29 of the cultures, or less than 16 per cent. "Furthermore, of these 29 societies, less than one-third wholly disapprove of both premarital and extramarital liasons (Ford & Beach, 1951)."

It would seem, then, that it might be fairly accurate to conclude, without fear of contradiction, that *man is not monogamous by nature*. In fact, if we confine ourselves to the recent, serious scientists of the subject, "no one has ever dared argue that man is genuinely monogamous by nature (Calverton, 1931b)."

However, some people have reluctantly accepted the fact that *men* are polygamous but still insist that at least *women* are monogamous. But I would like to suggest that women are by nature no more monogamous than men, and no less polygamous (Calverton, 1931b). The best evidence of this is to be found in those cultures where the conditions of life do not hamper the sex expression of women any more than of men. ". . . whenever conditions have allowed it, woman has rejected the monogamous relationships as frequently as man . . . granted equal freedom, she tends to be equally variational and multiple in her sex expression (Calverton, 1931b)." These are facts which practically every psychologist and marriage counselor has known, but has been unwilling to declare.

Where the element of "romance" is most stressed, as in America, there monogamy tends to be the greater failure (Calverton, 1931b). It would seem a fair conclusion, then, to say that monogamy, particularly the romantic, monogamous ideal as conceived in America, is destructive of the possibility of many happy, healthy marriages.

Unofficially and extra-legally, America actually might be said to be a polygamous country today. That is, about one in three married couples become divorced or legally separated, and many of these divorced or separated individuals carry on extramarital affairs for years before they actually part from each other. Among those who do not legally break up their marriages about a quarter of the women and a half of the men admit to having extramarital relations at some time during their lives (Ellis, 1962).

The monogamous ideal works in a negative fashion against marriage in that it puts unrealistic demands and expectations into people's minds which frequently work to their detriment in so far as achieving a satisfactory adjustment in marriage. A more realistic and rational view of human nature would allow for a variety of kinds of patterns of relationships between the sexes, rather than saying there is only one, legitimate sort of relationship, i.e., the lifelong monogamous one.

From the standpoint of freedom and democracy, the polygamous societies are more open-minded and uncoercive; whereas the monogamous societies, including our own, tend to be more dogmatic, authoritarian and restrictive (Ellis, 1962).

If we can get people to question the monogamous ideal and eliminate it as the *only* way to govern their lives, as far as sexual relationships are concerned, we would provide more people with the opportunity to work out a more satisfactory sexual adjustment with as many, or as few, people of the other sex as they realistically could.

Such a freer, pluralistic view would have several advantages over the monogamous ideal. For example, it would allow for those people who have what might be called a varietist's needs. If these people can arrange for multiple partners, why should they be denied? Such a freer view would also provide for the sex needs of surplus males and females. It would also permit maximum sex satisfaction, each person would seek his own level. It would minimize jealousy and possessiveness. Sex, under this pluralistic system, would become a free choice instead of a forced choice. Love could be freely given instead of restrictively and jealously monopolized. Human beings could become choosers of their own sex destiny rather than pieces of sexual property.

The basic statement here being made is that a more *pluralistic* arrangement should be freely permitted but not necessarily engaged in by all. Let us *allow* true sexual freedom to those courageous people who want it. Let us *not force* polygamy *or* monogamy on anyone, through laws, public opinion or the ideals we profess. The sanest society is the one which forces no one marital arrangement on anyone, while permitting all possible designs for mating for everyone (Ellis, 1962).

The basic argument here, then, is for *marital democracy*, with each individual being able to determine what sort of marital or non-marital arrangement he or she wants to have.

There is some evidence that such a suggestion may not be entirely out of the range of possibility. Gerhard Neubeck's recent book on *Extramarital Relations* (1969) offers some such evidence. As Albert Ellis, in a chapter in that book on "Healthy and Disturbed Reasons for Having Extramarital Relations," has said,

"Almost the entire history of mankind demonstrates that man is not, biologically, a truly monogamous animal; that he tends to be more monogynous than monogamic, desiring one woman at a time rather than a single woman for a lifetime, and that even when he acts monogynously he craves strongly occasional adulterous affairs in addition to his regular marital sex. The female of the human species seems to be less strongly motivated toward plural sexuality than is the male; but she, too, when she can have varietistic outlets with social impunity, quite frequently takes advantage of them (Ellis, 1969)."

A crucial question here would be: are human beings capable of loving more than one member of the other sex at the same time? As Ellis has noted, "Healthy human beings are generally capable of loving pluralistically, on both a serial and a simultaneous basis (Ellis, 1969)."

If a "new sexuality" is developing, as Herbert Otto (1971) has documented, perhaps this discussion can provide some guidelines as to how to help make the new sexuality more sane, rational and less self-defeating for those who wish to partake of it. But if this is to be, we will need to seek the answers to the questions Gerhard Neubeck has raised:

"Can we learn to understand that it is possible to love more than one person, to be loved by more than one person? Can we accept that? What it will mean is a reshaping of the total culture so that even the young child in the beginning of the socialization and conditioning process can learn this idea of non-exclusive love (Neubeck, 1969)."

And finally,

"Are we then headed for a society in which extramarital relationships will not occur in a clandestine fashion, but where married couples will make conscious choices, to be or not to be monogamous (Neubeck, 1969)?"

REFERENCES

Calverton, V. F. Modern anthropology and the theory of cultural compulsives. In Calverton, V. F. *The making of man: an outline of anthropology*. New York: The Modern Library, 1931a.

Calverton, V. F. Are women monogamous? in Schmalhausen, S. D. & Calverton, V. F. *Woman's coming of age: a symposium*. New York: Horace Liveright, 1931b.

Ellis, A. A plea for polygamy. *Eros*, Vol. 1, No. 1, pp. 22–23, 1962.

Ellis, A. Healthy and disturbed reasons for having extra-marital relations. In Neubeck, G. *Extra-marital relations*. Englewood Cliffs, NJ: Prentice-Hall, 1969.

Ford, C. S. & Beach, F. A. *Patterns of sexual behavior*. New York: Harper, 1951.

Neubeck, G. *Extra-marital relations*. Englewood Cliffs, NJ: Prentice-Hall, 1969.

Otto, H. A. *The new sexuality*. Palo Alto: Science & Behavior Books, 1971.

Technical Assistance for the Marriage and Family Counselor

> *There is nothing, Sir, too little for so little creature as man. It is by studying little things that we attain the great art of having as little misery and as much happiness as possible.*
>
> SAMUEL JOHNSON

In previous sections the content has dealt with deep and complex matters. In this section appear what may seem at first glance to be little things, relatively speaking. But the best marriage and family counselor needs to know about several matters of a technical and practical nature in order to be able to function efficiently in the profession.

The tools of the trade (forms, inventories, etc.) are matters rarely discussed in the more formal papers in the literature. In Chapter 47, Constance Callahan Ard examines the initial interview, intake interview forms, marriage counseling inventories, sex knowledge inventories, marriage prediction schedules, release forms, and other practical matters which may prove a valuable introduction for the beginning counselor as well as a review of available aids for the experienced counselor.

In Chapter 48, Albert Ellis discusses bibliotherapy as a technique in marriage and family counseling. There are many books available to consider; Albert Ellis has written many books in this particular area himself and gives his opinions of the available books in his usual forthright manner. Which are to be recommended? Ultimately, each reader will have to make the final decision, but Dr. Ellis gives frank, straightforward reasons for choosing his favorites. It is hoped that the reader will learn to recommend books for bibliotherapy on a sound basis, after carefully considering the wide variety available.

In Chapter 49, Constance Callahan Ard discusses information gathering techniques in marriage and family counseling: note-taking, ways of safeguarding confidentiality, tape-recording, video tape, one-way screens, and written communication.

In the final offering in this section, Chapter 50, Ben N. Ard, Jr. discusses basic professional books for the marriage and family counselor. This last chapter attempts to pull together the professional books which the marriage and family counselor may want to become familiar with, and with which the counselor may start a professional library. The books referred to in this last chapter are all listed in the Annotated Bibliography which immediately follows this last chapter.

The Appendices all contain information which will prove of help to the student and the counselor in the field..

CHAPTER 47

The Tools of the Trade

Constance Callahan Ard

In marriage counseling, as in most professions, there are certain "tools of the trade," such as inventories, forms, etc. which it behooves the practitioner to be aware of so that he can make the professional judgment as to when and *whether* to use them. This chapter will discuss some of the available materials which might be of value in marriage counseling and related problems. Space will not allow for a detailed illustration of each available form or inventory, but several examples will be presented for consideration.

Helpful though they are, the use of these "tools" should not become routine, or be expected to take the place of effective counseling, which is still the most basic tool of the trade.

INITIAL INTERVIEW

Available literature on the function and type of information secured in the initial interview is rather meager. A great deal of the material pertaining to the initial interview which could present some possible resource information for marriage counselors is discussed under headings such as "the psychiatric examination," "the diagnostic study," or "the case study."

The function of the initial interview is to provide an understanding of what the problem is, as the client views it. It marks the beginning of a unique interpersonal relationship for the client as well as the marriage counselor.

The marriage counselor may well benefit from being aware of his social manners and the nonverbal reactions or responses of his new client (cf. Ard, 1969; Beier, 1966; Ekman, 1965; Dittman, 1961; Fretz, 1966; Ruesch & Kees, 1970). After the counselor invites his or her client to be seated, he or she may begin the discussion by clarifying data—such as the client's phone call stating the reason for coming for marriage counseling, or the referral of the client by another professional. This provides an opportunity for both counselor and client to revise any incorrect data.

Throughout this chapter the term "client" may refer to the *couple* that has sought counseling, as well as to either husband or wife individually.

Initial stages of rapport will, it is hoped, begin to develop. If the counselor and client seem to be incompatible, this could be discussed during the first interview; or if it's the first time the client has ever seen a counselor or therapist, the counselor might want to wait until another session. This way both the counselor and client will have time to re-evaluate their feeling, etc.

Quite frequently, if a person has never seen a therapist or counselor he is really uptight, nervous, etc. and might need a session or two to work through this.

Also, a general overview of what the client wants to explore, re-examine and the goals and growth directions he wants to examine would help to determine the extent of motivation for counseling and the reasons for coming to see a marriage counselor.

Another area of importance which needs to be discussed is that of making and cancelling appointments. Whatever your particular guideline, it ought to be discussed so that each client knows what is expected in these areas. The counselor's time is just as important as the client's, so if a client can't keep the appointment, he ought to phone at least 24 hours ahead or be charged for that time. This also frees the counselor to see someone else.

INTAKE INTERVIEW FORM

Interviewer: (if in clinic situation)

Name: Sex: Age: Military Status: Date:

Address: Home Phone Number:

Occupation: How Long: Business Phone Number:

Amount of Income: Education:

Source of Income, If Not Employed:

Marital Status: How Long Married: Age of Spouse:

Education of Spouse: Occupation of Spouse:

    Amount of Income of Spouse:

Number and Ages of Children:

Any Previous Marriages:

Previous Therapy with:

Where: Length:

Reasons For Coming to Marriage Counseling:

How Long Has Problem(s) Existed:

How Has This Affected Relationship to Job, Family, Self, Friends, etc.:

Perhaps these ground rules or general expectations can be typed and given to each client. Suggestions and ideas will be presented following an example of an intake interview and a checklist of problems and feelings.

Certain pertinent identifying information can be included in an intake interview form, similar to the one on the facing page.

Another form listing a number of physical and pyschological symptoms could also be given to the client to fill out. He would check the terms which best describe how he is feeling and/or his current situation. If both spouses are present, each fills out a form independently.

CHECKLIST OF PROBLEMS AND FEELINGS*

Tension	Digestive symptoms
Depression	Sexual problem
Suicidal ideas	Impotency
Severe anxiety	Homosexuality
Hallucinations	Phobias
Delusions	Compulsions
Dangerous	Excessive use of sedatives
Excited	Insomnia
Physical symptoms	Nightmares
Fatigue	Stomach trouble
Headaches	No appetite
Dizziness	Obsessions
Unable to relax	Always worried about something
Unable to have a good time	Don't like weekends or vacations
Overambitious	Shy with people
Can't make friends	Can't make decisions
Can't keep a job	Inferiority feelings
Home conditions bad	Financial problems

No communication with spouse or children

Description (elaboration) of those checked:

MARRIAGE COUNSELING ETIQUETTE

A brief overview statement such as the following can be utilized as a guideline.

Marriage counseling, like any other human relationship, functions more smoothly if there are some ground rules. Counseling is a particular kind of human relationship, which is unique in its *professional* framework of closeness and intimate communication. In order to minimize misunderstandings between therapist and client, a code of etiquette ought to be discussed and also a typed copy presented to each client.

Have the client read it during the first session so that if any questions arise they can be dealt with at that time and future misunderstandings probably will be eliminated.

---

*Adapted from Wolberg, 1954, pp. 814 and 833.

HOMEWORK REPORT
Consultation Center
Institute for Advanced Study in Rational Psychotherapy
45 East 65th Street, New York, N.Y. 10021 / (212) LEhigh 5-0822

Name .... Date .... Therapist ....

Instructions: Please draw a circle around the number in front of those feelings listed in the first column that troubled you *most* during the period since your last therapy session. Then, in the *second* column, indicate the amount of work you did on each circled item; and, in the *third* column, the results of the work you did.

	Amount of Work Done				Results of Work		
	Much	Some	Little or none		Good	Fair	Poor
Undesirable Emotional Feelings							
1a Anger or great irritability	1b				1c		
2a Anxiety, severe worry, or fear	2b				2c		
3a Boredom or dullness	3b				3c		
4a Failure to achieve	4b				4c		
5a Frustration	5b				5c		
6a Guilt or self-condemnation	6b				6c		
7a Hopelessness or depression	7b				7c		
8a Great loneliness	8b				8c		
9a Helplessness	9b				9c		
10a Self-pity	10b				10c		
11a Uncontrollability	11b				11c		
12a Worthlessness or inferiority	12b				12c		
13a Other (specify)	13b				13c		
Undesirable Actions or Habits							
14a Avoiding responsibility	14b				14c		
15a Acting unfairly to others	15b				15c		
16a Being late to appointments	16b				16c		
17a Being undisciplined	17b				17c		
18a Demanding attention	18b				18c		
19a Physically attacking others	19b				19c		
20a Putting off important things	20b				20c		
21a Telling people off harshly	21b				21c		
22a Whining or crying	22b				22c		
23a Withdrawing from activity	23b				23c		
24a Overdrinking of alcohol	24b				24c		
25a Overeating	25b				25c		
26a Oversleeping	26b				26c		
27a Undersleeping	27b				27c		
28a Oversmoking	28b				28c		
29a Taking too many drugs or pills	29b				29c		
30a Other (specify)	30b				30c		
Irrational Ideas or Philosophies							
31a People must love or approve of me	31b				31c		
32a Making mistakes is terrible	32b				32c		
33a People should be condemned for their wrongdoings	33b				33c		
34a It's terrible when things go wrong	34b				34c		
35a My emotions can't be controlled	35b				35c		
36a Threatening situations have to keep me terribly worried	36b				36c		
37a Self-discipline is too hard to achieve	37b				37c		
38a Bad effects of my childhood still have to control my life	38b				38c		
39a I can't stand the way certain people act	39b				39c		
40a Other (specify)	40b				40c		

(please complete other side)

PLEASE PRINT! BE BRIEF AND LEGIBLE! ANSWER QUESTION C FIRST; THEN ANSWER THE OTHER QUESTIONS.

A. ACTIVATING EVENT you recently experienced about which you became upset or disturbed. (Examples: *"I went for a job interview." "My mate screamed at me."*) ....

rB. Rational BELIEF or idea you had about this Activating Event. (Examples: *"It would be unfortunate if I were rejected for the job." "How annoying to have my mate scream at me!"*) ....
....

iB. Irrational BELIEF or idea you had about this Activating Event. (Examples: *"It would be catastrophic if I were rejected for the job; I would be pretty worthless as a person." "I can't stand my mate's screaming; she is horrible for screaming at me!"*) ....
....

C. CONSEQUENCES of your irrational BELIEF (iB) about the Activating Event listed in Question A. State here the one most disturbing emotion, behavior, or CONSEQUENCE you experienced recently. (Examples: *"I was anxious." "I was hostile." "I had stomach pains."*) ....

D. DISPUTING, questioning, or challenging you can use to change your irrational BELIEF (iB). (Examples: *"Why would it be catastrophic and how would I become a worthless person if I were rejected for the job?" "Why can't I stand my mate's screaming and why is she horrible for screaming at me?"*) ....
....

cE. Cognitive EFFECT or answer you obtained from DISPUTING your irrational BELIEF (iB). Examples: *"It would not be catastrophic, but merely unfortunate, if I were rejected for the job; my giving a poor interview would not make me a worthless person." "Although I'll never like my mate's screaming, I can stand it; he or she is not horrible but merely a fallible person for screaming."*) ....
....

bE. Behavioral EFFECT or result of your DISPUTING your irrational BELIEF (iB). (Examples: *"I felt less anxious." "I felt less hostile to my mate." "My stomach pains vanished."*)..

F. If you did not challenge your irrational BELIEF (iB), why did you not? ....
....

G. Activities you would most like to *stop* that you are now doing...
....

H. Activities you would most like to *start* that you are not doing..
....

I. Emotions and ideas you would most like to change ....
....

J. Specific homework assignment(s) given you by your therapist, your group, or yourself ....
....

K. What did you actually do to carry out the assignment(s)? ....
....

L. Check the item which describes how much you have worked at your last homework assignment(s): ....(a) almost every day ....(b) several times a week ....(c) occasionally ....(d) hardly ever.

M. How many times in the past week have you specifically worked at changing and DISPUTING your irrational BELIEFS (iBs)? ....

N. What other things have you specifically done to change your irrational BELIEFS and your disturbed emotional CONSEQUENCES? ....
....

O. Check the item which describes how much reading you have recently done of the material on rational-emotive therapy: ....(a) a considerable amount ....(b) a moderate amount ....(c) little or none.

P. Things you would now like to discuss most with your therapist or group ....
....
....

Some suggestions that you might wish to consider are:

APPOINTMENTS—length of session and completion or wind-down of each session and cancellations.

USE OF THE TELEPHONE—give phone number and perhaps explain that it is to be used primarily for making and cancelling of appointments. If a client finds himself in an emergency situation then the phone can be utilized as the tool to facilitate the counselling session and they will be charged accordingly. It may be impossible to talk at that time so an alternative time can be established.

FEES—many therapists are finding that it is easier if they are paid each session, rather than sending out a monthly statement. This will vary for each therapist's organizational pattern.

TAPE RECORDINGS—Some therapists find it beneficial to tape each session. In fact, some clients tape each session and then review it during the week. (This can also be part of the homework assignment.) If tape recordings are made the purpose of such tapes ought to be explained to the client.

HOMEWORK ASSIGNMENTS—Each therapist has his or her own framework and theoretical orientation, therefore, homework assignments are optional.

As we all know, growing, changing and putting new knowledge and insights to work takes a great deal of hard work. Specific suggestions which the client can continue to work on outside the therapeutic hour will supplement and enhance his or her individual growth. This may be something very specific such as trying to overcome the fear of talking to someone one doesn't know, or by reading a book that may present some new and widening ideas which would help in reevaluating one's philosophy.

ABOUT THE THERAPIST—Present a summary of pertinent information.

SUPPLEMENTARY READINGS—If you require that specific books be read, they can be listed. Other books which you think could be of value could also be suggested.

These are just a few guidelines. Each therapist in his or her unique environment can make adaptations in accordance with his/her specific clientele.

MARRIAGE COUNSELING INVENTORIES

A brief discussion of the value and purposes of marriage counseling inventories and some examples of those available may prove helpful for the counselor. Before deciding which to use, if any, he may wish to familiarize himself with critical essays by Bernard (1933), Ellis (1948), Kelly (1941), and Terman & Wallin (1949).

The *Psychotherapy Inventory*, formally known as the *Individual and Marriage Counseling Inventory* (1967), was prepared by Aaron L. Rutledge. It consists of three sections: "Personal Data," "Your Parental Family," and "The Personal Relations in My Family." Examples of the questions asked are:

Personal Data
Sex, birth date, age, height, weight?
Religious preference?

Present marital status?
Any previous marriages?
Do you feel that you have lived a happy life?
List sources from which you received most of your sex information.
List problems or subjects, in order of their importance to you, which you
would like to discuss with the counselor.

Your Parental Family

Your parents' ages at marriage?
Nationality background?
Do parents live together? If separated or divorced, your age then?
Do you feel closest to your father or mother?
Rate your parents' marriage.
If you are married, did your parents approve of your marriage?

The Personal Relations in Your Family

Write several paragraphs about the following—
1. your father as an individual, including personality changes.
2. your mother as an individual, including personality changes.
3. your parents' relationship to each other.
4. your brothers and sisters.
5. both constructive and destructive influences upon yourself and
   upon the remainder of the family from both the short-range and
   long-term points of view.

The *Marriage Personality Inventory* (Form IV, Marriage), was constructed by Karl V. Schultz, Ph.D., and is published by the Psychological
Services Press, 364 Fourteenth Street, Oakland, California 94612.

Dr. Schultz has constructed an inventory which provides a means of
describing oneself, one's parents, one's mate and one's marriage. This
inventory consists of 200 questions (accompanied by an answer sheet)
covering the following areas: Marriage rating; Growing-up years—
childhood, teenage; Parents—background, personality; Personality; Health;
Vocation; Money and finance; Love, marriage, divorce; Sex, Child rearing;
Interests; Communication and decision making; Religion; Philosophy of
life.

The client is to mark the available rating space which best describes
the *degree of similarity or difference* between him and his mate. In the
second column space is available to rate these same questions as to the
effect on marriage—negative, neutral, or positive. Examples of statements
presented are:

Growing-up years

Unpleasant and unhappy
Pleasant and happy
Did not feel close to relatives
Felt close to relatives

Parents

Family income below average
Family income above average
Forced or sarcastic, cutting sense of humor
Easy, pleasant, relaxed sense of humor

Personality
    Changes personality depending on whom with
    Has distinct personality of own
    Blames self when things go wrong
    Blames others when things go wrong

Health
    Has important health-physical limitations
    Excellent physical health

Vocation
    Pay more important than personal satisfaction
    Personal satisfaction from job more important than pay

Money and finance
    Unconcerned about material things
    Ambitious for financial, material success

Love, marriage, divorce
    Love is something that is there or not—can't make it grow or die
    Love grows or dies depending on how much put into it
    Person shows love by giving, being, or doing what pleases mate
    Person shows love by being (him-/her-) self—and encouraging mate to be (him-/her-) self

Sex
    Sex is most important need-drive of life
    Sex is only one of the important need-drives of life

Child rearing
    Chances for good marriage better without children
    Having children important for a successful marriage

Interests
    Little interest in home upkeep and improvement projects
    Enjoys home upkeep and improvement projects

Communication and decision-making
    When senses disagreement, gets angry and blows
    Easy give and take in working out problems-differences

Religion
    Person should follow guidance of church and its leaders
    Up to each person to work out his own religion

Philosophy of life
    Environment, culture, religion, etc. makes people very different
    Underneath, people are very much same—wherever they are

SEX KNOWLEDGE INVENTORIES

One *Sex Knowledge Inventory* (Form X, Experimental Edition, for Marriage Counseling, 1950), was developed by Gelolo McHugh. It is published by the Family Life Publications, Inc., P.O. Box 6725, College Station, Durham, North Carolina.

The intended purpose of this sex knowledge inventory is to help the taker better understand the constructive part of sex in life. This inventory is a measure of what individuals know about sex. The Sex Knowledge Inventory consists of 80 questions and includes a glossary of unfamiliar terms (*cervix, circumcision*, etc.).

Some of the questions asked are:

What is the relation between sex attraction and love?

What kinds of sex play may be used by a couple before or during sex relations?

What should a couple do about sex relations on the first night of marriage?

How long should each act of sex relations last?

When a woman is sexually excited, which of her sex organs is usually enlarged and quite firm?

What position should be used for sex relations?

How much of the unsatisfactory sex relations in marriage is caused by differences in size of the male and female sex organs?

How do large differences in sex drive affect the possibility of a satisfactory sexual adjustment in marriage?

What should a man do if he consistently has premature ejaculations?

What do physicians say about the effects of modern birth control methods?

What is the effect of circumcision during infancy or childhood on sex relations of the adult?

What changes usually occur in menstruation after marriage?

What does the size of the female sex organs indicate?

What is the effect of eating foods such as oysters, raw eggs, olives, celery, etc., on sex desire?

What is the usual effect of masturbation on ability to become a parent?

A second *Sex Knowledge Inventory*, also developed by Gelolo McHugh, concerns itself with the vocabulary and anatomy related to sex. This too can be obtained through the Family Life Publications, Inc.

Part I asks for the identification of the proper names for male and female sex parts—organ or structure. Diagrams accompany it. Part II seeks the inventory-taker's knowledge regarding the male and female sex parts without knowing their names. For example, "What covers and protects the male reproductive glands?" Part III calls for matching of words that best fit the available definitions.

DATING, COURTSHIP, AND
MARRIAGE PREDICTION SCHEDULES

The Family Life Publications, Inc., also make available a *Courtship Analysis* and a *Dating Problems Checklist* accompanied by a Counselor's and Teacher's Guide. These checklists, too, were developed by Gelolo McHugh. The intended purpose of the Dating Problems Checklist is to help those couples who are contemplating becoming engaged. This checklist may be utilized as a communications device for couples who want to know each other better and who want to understand their needs for a good courtship and a successful marriage.

It has been suggested that after couples have completed the Courtship Analysis, they should openly and frankly discuss their responses. This seemingly would provide an excellent opportunity for a couple to communicate about traits, behaviors, etc., that might help or hinder an acceptance of each other or a long-term relationship.

A *Marriage Prediction Schedule*, constructed by Ernest W. Burgess (University of Chicago), was prepared for those persons who are seriously contemplating marriage. It was designed for engaged couples, but could be of interest to anyone who would like to better understand his probability of success in marriage. This prediction schedule consists of five parts with a total of 74 questions.

This is not a complete representation of the available inventories or schedules available to the marriage counselor, but a mere sample. For further reference, the interested counselor may consult Locke (1951), Burgess and Cottrell (1939), and Terman et al (1938). It is hoped these aids will remain as aids and not be relied on so routinely or so heavily as to take the place of the more valuable direct confrontation between the marriage counselor and those who are in need of premarital or marital counseling!

The authorization of the client's release of interview data, tapes, etc. needs to be mentioned. This is of great importance in maintaining professional ethics and confidentiality. Two suggested forms are as follows:

AUTHORIZATION FOR THE CLIENT'S RELEASE OF INTERVIEW DATA AND TAPES

Third Party Release

TO:
ADDRESS:

I would appreciate your releasing to
all interview data and tapes regarding my marriage counseling. I herewith grant permission for this release.

(Signature of client)

WITNESS:
DATE:

Direct Release to Counselor

I hereby permit   to utilize any case
(Marriage Counselor)
material or tape recordings in any professional manner desired. I understand that all personal, identifying information will be eliminated.

(Signature of client)

DATE..

REFERENCES

Ard, C. C. Use of nonverbal communication in marriage counseling. *Marriage Counseling Quarterly*, 1968–69, *3–4*, 32–45.

Astin, H., Parelman, A., Fisher, A. Sex roles: a research bibliography. Washington, D.C.: Center for Human Services, 1975.

Beier, E. G. The silent language of psychotherapy. Chicago: Aldine, 1966.

Bernard, J. An instrument for measurement of success in marriage. *Publications of the American Sociological Society*, 1933, *27*, 94–106.

Burgess, E. W. and Cottrell, L. S. Predicting success or failure in marriage. Englewood Cliffs, N. J.: Prentice-Hall, 1939.

Dittman, A. T. and Wynne, L. C. Linguistic techniques and the analysis of emotionality in interviews. *Journal of Abnormal Psychology*, 1961, *63*, 201–204.

Ekman, P. Communication through nonverbal behavior: A source of information about an interpersonal relationship. In S. S. Tomkins and C. E. Izard (Eds.) *Affect, Cognition and Personality*. New York: Springer Press, 1965, 390–442.

Ellis, A. The value of marriage prediction tests. *American Sociological Review*. 1948, *13*, 710–718.

Fretz, B. Postural movements in a counseling dyad. *Journal of Counseling Psychology*, 1966, *13*, No. 3.

Kelly, E. L. Marital compatability as related to personality traits of husband and wife as rated by self and spouse. *Journal of Social Psychology*, 1941, *13*, 193–198.

Locke, H. J. and Klausner, W. J. Marital adjustment of divorced persons in subsequent marriage. *Sociology and social research*, 1948, *33*, 97–101.

Locke, H. J. *Predicting adjustment in marriage*. New York: Holt, 1951.

McClelland, W. A. and Sinaiko, H. W. An investigation of a counselor attitude questionnaire. *Educational psychological measurement*, 1950, *10*, 128–133.

McHugh, G. S. *Courtship analysis*. Durham, N. C.: Family Life, 1966.

McHugh, G. *Dating problems checklist*. Durham, N. C.: Family Life.

McHugh, G. *Sex knowledge inventory*. Durham, N. C.: Family Life, 1950.

Mellinger, G. D. Interpersonal trust as a factor in communication. *Journal Abnormal Social Psychology*, 1956, *52*, 304–309.

Peterson, Severin. *A catalog of the ways people grow*. New York: Ballantine Books, 1971.

Ruesch, Jurgen and Kees, Weldon. *Nonverbal communication*, Notes on the visual perception of human relations. Berkeley: University of California Press, 1972.

Terman, L. M. and Wallin, P. The validity of marriage prediction and marital adjustment tests. *American Sociological Review*, 1949, *14*, 497–505.

Terman, L. M., et al. *Psychological factors in marriage happiness*. New York: McGraw-Hill, 1938.

Wolberg, L. R. *The technique of psychotherapy*. New York: Grune and Stratton, 1954.

CHAPTER 48

Bibliotherapy:
Books on Marriage for Clients

Albert Ellis

Many patients come to psychotherapy or to marriage and family counseling with specific sex, love, and marriage problems; and most therapists and counselors find it advisable, from time to time, to recommend supplementary reading material to these patients, particularly in regard to sex technique. The problem is: *Which* books, out of the literally hundreds of marriage manuals that exist, are to be recommended? I have a decidedly biased response to this question, as I have for many years found practically all the extant works sadly lacking. This is the main reason that I have written so many sex-marriage books myself, so that I could have texts for my own patients which I could unqualifiedly endorse. Let me forthrightly enunciate some of my prejudices.

First: Does the old, classical literature on sex—such as the works of Richard von Krafft-Ebing, Havelock Ellis, Iwan Bloch, August Forel, and Magnus Hirschfeld—have much usefulness today? No, not for most patients and counselees. Although this material is interesting for professionals and students of sex, and was very useful in its day, it is largely antiquated and misleading, and can do as much harm as good. Havelock Ellis's one-volume *Psychology of Sex* is not too bad today; but even its range of information leaves much to be desired.

How about the oriental classics, such as K. Malla's *Ananga Ranga*, Mohammed Nefzawi's *Perfumed Garden*, and Vatsyayana's *Kama Sutra*? Again, no. A few decades ago, these works were far ahead of their day and made interesting reading for inhibited westerners. But they are full of mysticism, religious fanaticism, and antiscientism, and are only safe in the hands of highly sophisticated, selective readers who will not take whole sections of them very seriously.

What can be said for the work of Freud and his disciples, such as Karl Abraham, Edmund Bergler, Helen Deutsch, Sandor Ferenczi, J. C. Flugel, Ernest Jones, Theodor Reik, and Wilhelm Stekel? Very little. The libido theory of personality growth and development is almost unadulterated

Reprinted with permission of the author and the publisher from *Voices*, 1966, 2, 83–85.

hogwash; the Freudian views of pregenitality and later fixation and regression are brilliant fantasies for which there seems to be no scientific verification; the psychoanalytic notions of love and hate are highly speculative and still unsubstantiated; and the Freudian dogma on female sexuality is a holy horror. One of the most execrable marriage manuals of our time, Marie Robinson's *The Power of Sexual Surrender*, typically emphasizes the pernicious Freudian view that women must have a so-called vaginal orgasm in order to be sexually well-adjusted; and innumerable other psychoanalytically-inspired works (including Wilhelm Reich's semi-psychotic *Function of the Orgasm*) uncritically accept this position, which has probably had more to do with sabotaging the sex life of innumerable couples than any other doctrine in recent times. A psychotherapist who recommends any sex-marriage book to his patients which has even a moderate flavor of Freudianism does so to their great peril.

How about the standard marriage manuals of the last thirty years, some of which have sold millions of copies? Of the older manuals of this sort, a few, such as W. F. Robie's *The Art of Love*, were unusually frank for their day and are still usable, though a little outdated. The most popular one of the lot, T. H. Van de Velde's *Ideal Marriage*, is great in regard to its description of intercourse positions, but it is romantically puritanical in many respects, and takes the unscientific position that sexual relations have to be finished off with penile-vaginal copulation leading to orgasm if they are to be considered normal and natural. Its (and many other sex manuals') deification of the glories of simultaneous orgasm has done enormous harm to the sex-love life of untold numbers of couples during the last several decades; and for all its good points, it nonetheless serves as a monument of sexual stupidity. Abraham and Hannah Stone's *A Marriage Manual*, which has also been fabulously popular for many years, is not as puritanical as *Ideal Marriage*, but it omits many salient, down-to-earth attitudes and much information, and is definitely on the namby-pamby side.

Several recent sex-marriage manuals are much better than the older books, in that they less inhibitedly delineate ideas and facts that the former omitted and pretty fully accept the point that sex *relations* are much broader and more inclusive than sex *intercourse*. They show sex partners how to achieve *some* forms of satisfaction that are individually tailored for *themselves*, and that are not necessarily "normal" or "natural" to *all* couples. They also face the fact that orgasm is orgasm, however achieved, and that there is nothing sacred about penile-vaginal copulation. These books acknowledge the scientific findings of modern researchers, such as Alfred C. Kinsey and his associates, and William H. Masters and Virginia E. Johnston. Included in this category are Inge and Sten Hegeler's *An ABZ of Love*, Phyllis and Eberhard Kronhausen's *The Sexually Responsive Woman*, G. Lombard Kelly's *Sex Manual*, and Robert Street's *Modern Sex Techniques*. The most popular of the up-to-date marriage manuals is my own *The Art and Science of Love*, which I wrote because of the deficiencies of most of the other works in the field, and which has helped hundreds of my own patients to achieve far better sex-love lives.

Because sex is hardly the only part of a love or marital relationship, the question also arises: What books can be recommended for a couple who want to thoughtfully consider the emotional aspects of marriage? Years ago, I recommended John Levy and Ruth Munroe's *The Happy Family*, but this book has been out of print for some time now. Most of the other books in the field I view dimly, since they tend to be psychoanalytically oriented and/or basically puritanical. Two books that I can largely accept are Rudolf Dreikurs' *Challenge of Marriage* and Richard Robertiello's *Sexual Fulfillment and Self-Affirmation*. For the most part, I have had to write my own books to use with my patients in this respect—especially, *The American Sexual Tragedy* and (in collaboration with Robert A. Harper) *Creative Marriage* (published in paperback form as *The Marriage Bed*). Even more important, I have found that in the area of love relations people do much better with each other when they understand themselves and others in general psychological ways, and when they realize what nonsense they are telling themselves to interfere with their love relationships and to create needless hatred and dissension. To this end, I have found my books *How to Live with a Neurotic* and (again in collaboration with Robert A. Harper) *A Guide to Rational Living* most helpful in helping save many love relationships that otherwise seemed to be going on the rocks.

I have often been asked whether I use any kind of anatomy atlas or other special visual aids to teach techniques of intercourse. The answer is no, although I sometimes draw a sketchy diagram for my patients to show them where the female clitoris is, as distinct from the vaginal opening. No book that I know of has adequate pictures of sex positions, though Dr. Sha Kokken's recent volume published in Japan, *A Happier Sex Life*, has some interesting illustrations of puppets in different poses (and also has much puritanical nonsense in its accompanying text). I find that if couples read the details of sex positions and then open-mindedly experiment with their own variations, that is all that is necessary for their achieving proficiency.

More to the point, I think that bibliotherapy can be used to help males and females loosen up in their sex attitudes, so that they are then willing and eager to try anything in and out of the books that may be useful in their own sex-love relations. To this end, I often recommend fictional works, such as John Cleland's *Fanny Hill*, Marquis de Sade's *Complete Justine and Other Writings*, and the novels of Henry Miller. On the nonfictional side, I especially find that Rey Anthony's *Housewife's Guide to Selective Promiscuity* is a useful book for inhibited females to read. Although the edition of this book published by Ralph Ginzburg has been banned from the mails, the original manuscript edition can still be obtained (for five dollars) from Seymour Press, Box 12035, Tucson, Arizona 85711.

Other nonfictional works which I find very helpful in undermining the puritanical blockings of patients which prevent them from having a full sex-love life include Rene Guyon's *The Ethics of Sexual Acts*, Hugh Hefner's *Playboy Philosophy*, Alfred C. Kinsey's *Sexual Behavior in the*

Human Female, Lawrence Lipton's *The Erotic Revolution*, Lars Ullerstam's *Erotic Minorities*, and Wayland Young's *Eros Denied*. I have made quite a contribution to the field of sexual liberalism myself, and among my own books which I find most helpful in getting patients to loosen up in this respect are *Sex Without Guilt, The American Sexual Tragedy, If This Be Sexual Heresy...*, *The Case for Sexual Liberty, The Search for Sexual Enjoyment*, and (edited in collaboration with Albert Abarbanel) *The Encyclopedia of Sexual Behavior*.

A final word on bibliotherapy and nonmarital sex relations. Up until quite recently there were virtually no good books for unmarried individuals who wanted sexual guidance, since the extant literature was firmly preoccupied with the sex lives of married couples. Ira S. Wile edited a pioneering book on the *Sex Life of the Unmarried Adult* in 1934; but this has long been out of print. A few years ago Helen Gurley Brown made quite a stir with her *Sex and the Single Girl*—a fairly wishy-washy text, but one which at least fully espoused premarital sex relations for women. Since that time, several other books dealing with the problems of single people have appeared, most of them ultra-sensationalistic or else, like Evelyn M. Duvall's *Why Wait Till Marriage*, incredibly naive and puritanical for today's world. Seeing that nothing to my own liking existed, I wrote *Sex and the Single Man* and *The Intelligent Woman's Guide to Man-Hunting*, both of which, I am happy to say, have helped thousands of unmarried individuals to achieve a higher degree of sex-love fulfillment.

To sum up: Innumerable books exist which purport to be helpful to single and married individuals who desire to enhance their sex, love, and marital relationships. Most of them are puritanical, over-romantic, or sensationalistic, and may do their readers more harm than good. A few of them are objective and liberal, and can be selectively used by psychotherapists and marriage and family counselors with their patients and clients. This article gives a highly personal view of some of the wheat and chaff in the field.

CHAPTER 49

Information-Gathering Techniques in Marriage Counseling

Constance Callahan Ard

If marriage counseling is to develop and progress as a scientific profession, the counselor needs to be familiar with techniques of gathering objective information on what happens in marriage counseling. Several techniques are of value—note-taking, tape-recording, the use of the video tape, one-way screens, and written communication. The initial interview data, questionnaires, and inventories, discussed in Chapter 45, "Tools of the Trade," are also useful.

NOTE-TAKING

Perhaps the most common information-gathering technique—and the least threatening, not only to clients but also to the marriage counselor—is note-taking. One advantage is that it can be continued throughout the session if it does not interfere with the therapist's active participation.

Sigmund Freud waited until the end of each day to write up his notes on the various patients he had seen during the day. Authorities who object to taking notes during therapeutic sessions might feel this is the only feasible way to make a record of their cases. However, there are obvious flaws in making notes at the end of the day—the possibility of distortions, the blurring of details, and simply the failure to remember accurately due to the time lapse between the occurrence and the recording. Other professionals (e.g., Sullivan, 1954) have suggested it is better to make notes immediately after each therapeutic session, but there is still the danger of leaving out important data.

The notes can be recorded on a specific note-taking form or ordinary paper. This would vary, presumably, according to personal taste or perhaps professional setting. The most important factor involved in the recording of personal and private information is *confidentiality*. Therefore, if notes are filed by client name, they should be kept in a locked file cabinet. As an alternative they might be filed under a coded system, with only an identifying number on the file folder and a separate card file to record number and corresponding name. The latter system might be advisable in an agency setting where other personnel have access to the files.

There is a difference between note-taking and interview summaries. Some marriage counseling clinics require that each counselor turn in a *summary* of every client seen. The information called 'for varies, but it usually consists of name, number of the visit, and several general statements describing the interview contents. Note-taking, in comparison, is a more detailed "log" of important ideas, feelings, growth, etc., which is kept in a *confidential* file of the counselor.

Confidentiality, respect for the integrity of each person seen, and guarding the welfare of those persons can hardly be overemphasized. Section 12 in the American Association of Marriage Counselors (1967) Code of Ethics states:

> "Except by written permission, all communications from clients shall be treated in complete confidence and never revealed to anyone. When a client is referred to in a professional case report, his identity shall be thoroughly disguised and the report shall so state [p. 84]."

Traditionally, both the client and society are of importance to the marriage counselor. For example, Wrenn (1966, p. 179) suggests as a principle that the counselor is primarily responsible to the client and ultimately to society. (This does not imply that the marriage counselor is out to "save" marriages for society's sake.) Wrenn (Ard, 1966) poses several interesting questions: What is confidential and what is not? How do you record information considered confidential? Under what conditions can the counselor be legally required to disclose information given him while in a counseling relationship?

The marriage counselor's legal position needs to be "checked out" according to the laws of the state where he practices, as there may be more legal leeway than is recognized.

> "For example, he does not have to release any personal or counseling records merely upon the request of an officer or a court, a state, or the federal government. In fact he probably should *not*, for the client can sue the counselor for failing to protect his interests. A warrant for the release of the records is necessary. Furthermore, the counselor may keep confidential notes on his clients in the form of personal memoranda and since these do not become part of the official records of the institution (or clinic) or of his office they do not have to be released when the personal records of an individual are taken into custody [Wrenn, in Ard, 1966, p. 174]."

Another point of interest regarding information supplied by the client is that it is almost always "hearsay" evidence and therefore not admissible in court [Wrenn, p. 175].

TAPE RECORDING

The tape recorder appears to be at present the most practical and helpful means of recording data. It leaves the marriage counselor free to observe more of the nonverbal as well as the verbal interaction and to take a more active role in the counseling session; furthermore, the tape is available for him to analyze more thoroughly at a later time.

Valuable use of the recorded sessions could also be made by the married partners themselves. For couples who do not think much progress or growth has occurred in counseling, an available tape may provide evidence of positive change and growth. Again, the counselor might ask the couple to listen to a specific tape at home as a "homework assignment," providing "listening proof" of how they speak to each other and what they are really communicating. They may even find in it clues to why they react as they do to some of their spouse's comments. As additional "homework," the couple could write (or perhaps tape-record) their reactions to the recorded session. If a couple wants to keep a particularly significant tape, they could purchase it at cost.

Tape recording of interviews can also be an excellent self-improvement device for marriage counselors. Many counselors may have the tendency not to grow in their interviewing skills. One way of checking up on oneself is by listening to one's own work critically. For even greater professional stimulation, perhaps a tape could be sent to a colleague; or interested professionals might have a monthly meeting to discuss one another's tapes and related problem areas in counseling. Tape recordings are also of great value as training aids.

Harper and Hudson (1952) suggest that perhaps counselors are more frightened of possible deleterious effects of tape recording interviews than are clients, and that some clients may feel *more* secure in knowing that the marriage counselor has an accurate record of their discussion.

Like other material from counseling sessions, recorded tapes must be treated with complete confidentiality, except upon signed release by the client. (See page 433.) The tapes, too, should be housed under lock and key. Information such as speed of recording, date, number of interview, and a coded identification of the client should be placed on the tape box. Numbers, "blind" identifying labels such as "The Case of the Girl in the Red Coat," or simply initials might provide a code to fit a particular professional environment.

VIDEO TAPE

The newest and most intriguing form of information-gathering device is the video tape. It not only records verbal output but also the very important *nonverbal* interaction of each participant. The size, quality, and quantity of equipment needed varies among manufacturers. Unfortunately, however, all video equipment is still probably too expensive for most individual counselors in private practice.

Video equipment can be utilized effectively in both individual sessions and in groups. It can "zero in" on the individual speaker showing a close-up of facial expressions and body position. Or, if a husband is expressing a specific problem area, the focus can switch for a few moments to his wife's nonverbal reaction, then back to the husband.

The video tape appears to be a valuable and stimulating device when working with couples. It helps one spouse become more aware of what the other spouse is saying, both verbally and nonverbally. "A woman commented, 'I can see how smug I look when you are talking to me. You must feel like hitting me' [Alger & Hogan, 1967, p. 1426]." If one person does something nonverbally that his partner interprets as negative when the tape is replayed, the counselor can have him "check it out" verbally by asking what was meant by the action. In short, video tape can help both clients become more congruent in action and speech.

By the instant replay of video tapes, the counselor can present the "fresh" experience or interaction for discussion and observation, rerunning it as many times as necessary. As suggested by Alger and Hogan (1967), the video technique helps the client become more aware of his own and others' behavior and feelings, and he tends to remember the new insight.

The video tape seems to offer practically endless possibilities for stimulating professional growth. For instance: (1) The counselor may observe how he relates to the client, or how the client relates to him; he can no longer remain in his safe realm of "objectivity." (2) He may also observe his reactions to interaction between clients. (3) Video tapes could replace demonstrations of marriage counseling techniques at professional meetings, thus increasing the authenticity and avoiding the effects on clients of possible distractions, disturbances, or viewer reactions. Another advantage of the video tape is that it can be used regardless of the theoretical orientation of the therapists.

The research possibilities of video tape seem to be largely untapped as yet. Some research has been reported by Ekman (1964), Ekman & Friesen (1967), Alger & Hogan (1967), Krumboltz, Varenhorst and Thoresen (in press), Dittman (1962), Kagan, Krathwohl, & Miller (1963), Stoller (in press), Walz & Johnson (1963), and Rogers (1968).

ONE-WAY SCREENS

One-way screens provide a variety of uses. Fulweiler (1968, p. 187), for example views the family interaction of his clients from behind a one-way mirror and enters the consulting room only to make an intervention or interpretation. (As a variation, the therapist might make his interpretations via an intercom.) Also, because the participants are unable to see observers, interested professionals who are not personally involved in the session can observe the interaction of the participants.

This also provides an excellent learning device, in that students and beginning counselors may observe experienced counselors demonstrate various marriage counseling techniques.

WRITTEN COMMUNICATION

Visotsky (1965) maintains that a great deal of written material is usually presented by the client to the therapist. Instead of laying aside this information, why not encourage the client to write more? An individual or couple sees the counselor perhaps once a week for fifty minutes. It seems evident that more than fifty minutes per week is needed to change deep-lying values, attitudes, behavior, etc. By written communication the client may spend up to an hour or two every day thinking and doing something about his problems.

Burton (1965) agrees that "written production" may help to immerse the client into therapy. If a client finds it difficult to talk about a problem, the counselor may suggest that it be written out. Of course this may not necessarily continue as a standard procedure—perhaps should not—because it could offer the client a way to escape direct confrontation.

Burton (1965) has also used the keeping of diaries in marriage counseling. Frequently, the first interviews of a married couple are full of expressed hostility. If each of the partners keeps a separate diary, feelings and thoughts about the spouse and problem areas can be looked at more rationally outside the interview setting.

Ellis (1965) asks his clients to do some type of "homework assignment" throughout the week. This frequently consists of writing down some of the significant happenings of the week or some of the "mental sentences" the client has been telling himself.

Once again, with written communication, confidentiality should be maintained, and all identifying material should be coded or erased.

REFERENCES

American Association of Marriage Counselors, Inc., *Directory of Members*. Dallas: A.A.M.C., 1967.

Alger, I. & Hogan, P., The use of video tape recordings in conjoint marital therapy. *American Journal of Psychiatry*, 1967, *73*, 1425–1430.

Burton, A. The use of written productions in psychotherapy. In L. Pearson (Ed.), *The use of written communications in psychotherapy*. Springfield, Ill.: Charles C Thomas, 1965.

Dittman, A. T. The relationship between body movements and moods in interviews. *Journal of Consulting Psychology*, 1962, *26*, 480.

Ekman, P. Body position, facial expression, and verbal behavior during interviews. *Journal of Abnormal and Social Psychology*, 1964, *68*, 295–301.

Ekman, P. & Friesen, W. V. Nonverbal behavior in psychotherapy research. *Research on Psychotherapy*, 1967, Vol. 3 (A.P.A.).

Ellis, A. The use of printed, written and recorded words in psychotherapy. In L. Pearson (Ed.), *The use of written communications in psychotherapy*. Springfield, Ill.: Charles C Thomas, 1965.

Fulweiler, C. Personal communication. Cited in D. D. Jackson (Ed.), *Therapy, communication, and change*. Palo Alto: Science and Behavior Books, 1968.

Harper, R. A., & Hudson, J. W. The use of recordings in marriage counseling. *Marriage and Family Living*, 1952, *14*, 332–334.

Kagan, N., Krathwohl, D. R., & Miller, R. Stimulated recall in therapy using video tape: A case study. *Journal of Counseling Psychology*, 1963, *10*, 237–243.

Krumboltz, J. D., Varenhorst, B. B., & Thoresen, C. E., Nonverbal factors in the effectiveness of models in counseling. *Journal of Counseling Psychology* (in press).

Rogers, A. H. Video tape feedback in group psychotherapy. *Psychotherapy: Theory, Research and Practice*, 1968, *5*, 37–39.

Stoller, F. Focused feedback with video tape: Extending the group's functions. In F. M. Gazda (Ed.), *Basic innovations in group psychotherapy and counseling*. Springfield, Ill.: Charles C Thomas (in press).

Sullivan, H. S. *The psychiatric interview*. New York: W. W. Norton, 1954.

Visotsky, H. M. Foreword. In L. Pearson (Ed.), *The use of written communication in psychotherapy*. Springfield, Ill.: Charles C Thomas, 1965.

Walz, G. R. & Johnson, J. A. Counselors look at themselves on video tape. *Journal of Counseling Psychology*, 1963, *10*, 232–236.

Wrenn, G. The ethics of counseling. In B. N. Ard, Jr. (Ed.), *Counseling and psychotherapy*. Palo Alto: Science and Behavior Books, 1966.

CHAPTER 50

Basic Books for the Marriage and Family Counselor

Ben N. Ard, Jr.

The professional marriage and family counselor is one, presumably, who has made a special study of the problems and interpersonal relationships of marriage and family life—in brief, the stresses and strains involved in membership in a marriage and family, and the psychosocial factors and influences of such membership on the personality. Marriage and family counseling may be regarded as a specialized field because of the specialized knowledge the counselor is expected to have. Those who wish to enter the field require a common body of scientific knowledge, techniques, and qualifications. The American Association of Marriage and Family Counselors suggests that certain substantive content should include personality theory, human sexuality, marriage and family studies, marriage counseling, and family therapy.

This chapter is intended to provide an introduction to some of the major, basic books in these areas which would be of benefit to the professional marriage and family counselor. Obviously the fields covered are much too large to include all of the possible books in each area; therefore, some selection is necessary and inevitable. No doubt someone's favorite book will most certainly be left out. But the start of a professional library is indicated here; the professional marriage and family counselor probably will continue to add to his or her professional library as knowledge in the field grows. Wherever possible, an attempt has been made to select books of a scientific nature that are still in print. All of the books discussed here can be found in the Annotated Bibliography immediately following.

One additional comment might be worthy of attention: for this "professional library" as for any other, a bookplate might well be put into each of the books stating: "Possession does not imply approval"—certainly not of everything which appears in these books. All books should be read with a critical, inquiring mind, and the material checked against further evidence. With that disclaimer, let us proceed to the books that might prove helpful to the professional marriage and family counselor.

Several classified bibliographies of articles, books, and pamphlets on sex, love, marriage, and family relations have appeared in the literature, for example those of Ellis and Dunbar (1951, 1952), as well as previous efforts by Ard (1955, 1961). Aldous and Hill (1967) have published an *International Bibliography of Research in Marriage and the Family, 1900–1964*. Olson and Dahl (1975) have published the most recent inventory of marriage and family literature. Collections of papers on marriage counseling may be found in Silverman's two books (1965, 1972), Klemer (1965), Greene's *The Psychotherapies of Marital Disharmony* (1965), Fishbein & Burgess (1963), Mudd, et al, *Marriage Counseling: A Casebook* (1958), Abse, Nash & Louden's *Marital & Sexual Counseling in Medical Practice* (1974), and Mudd & Krich's *Man and Woman* (1956).

For the psychology of personality development, several books may serve—Hall & Lindsey (1957), Gordon (1963), McCary (1956), Witmer & Kotinsky (1952), Sahakian (1965), and DiCaprio (1974). Hall & Lindsey is a standard in the field, Gordon's book is more experimentally and research oriented. DiCaprio's is a practical guide to living survey of personality theories.

For the elements of psychiatry, the marriage and family counselor may find the following books profitable: Arieti (1959), Freedman & Kaplan (1967), Sullivan's *The Psychiatric Interview* (1954), Ruesch & Bateson (1951), Howells (1975) *Principles of Family Psychiatry*, and Beck's *Depression* (1967).

For the legal aspects of marriage and the family, one may profitably consult Pilpel and Zavin (1952), Haussamen and Guitar (1960), Kling (1963) or Slovenko (1965). Discussions of divorce and what follows may be found in Goode (1956), Krantzler (1974), Bohannan (1970), Jacobson (1959), Mindey (1969), Taves (1968) and Weiss (1975) on *Marital Separation*.

For the sociology of marriage and the family, some of the information needed may be gleaned from Christensen's monumental *Handbook of Marriage and the Family* (1964), Sussman (1963), Stephens (1968), Schur (1964) and Bell & Vogel (1960). Winch, et al, have published a collection of *Selected Studies in the Family* (1962). Two standard texts widely used in the field are those by Blood (1962) and Bell (1963). Saxton (1968) also has another widely used text. Research oriented books are those by Whyte (1956), Blood & Wolfe (1960), Cuber & Harroff (1965), Bernard (1966), and Komarovsky (1962).

For human biology, including the fundamentals of sex anatomy, physiology and genetics, there are a wide variety of books available. For sex anatomy, Dickinson's *Atlas of Human Sex Anatomy* (1949) is still a classic. Other references are Hastings (1966) and Clark (1963). Masters & Johnson have three books (1966, 1970, 1974) which deserve reading for their influence on the field.

Sexual problems and sexual behavior form a large part of the day-to-day concerns the marriage and family counselor faces in the profession. Unfortunately, the publications in this area are quite uneven, with many books of questionable scientific value. Among some of the better references available in this particular area are the two monumental volumes edited by Ellis & Abarbanel, *The Encyclopedia of Sexual Behavior* (1961).

Kaplan (1974, 1975) has two very popular books out on sex therapy. Other books in this area are those by Ard (1974), Hartman & Fithian (1974), Allen (1962), Milne (1976) and Belliveau & Richter (1970). McGrady (1972) has written a popular book on *The Love Doctors*. Ellis has contributed many volumes in this field (1951, 1960, 1962, 1963, 1965, 1972). Wahl (1967) and Oliven (1965) have also discussed sexual problems. The Kinsey volumes (1948, 1953) would seem a must, along with later publications such as Gebhard (1958, 1965).

Information about birth control should be available to every marriage and family counselor if he or she is to discuss such matters intelligently with clients, even though the actual instruction in birth control techniques is a function of the especially-trained physician. There are several books which might prove helpful, including Guttmacher (1969), Dickinson (1950), Rainwater & Weinstein (1960) and Tietze (1960).

Some historical, cross-cultural perspective is needed on the subject of sex, if the marriage and family counselor is to rise above the limitations of the narrower aspects of attitudes toward sex in our culture. Several books can help the counselor gain this needed perspective, including Ditzion's *Marriage, Morals, and Sex* (1953), Young's *Eros Denied* (1964), Lipton's description of the *Erotic Revolution* (1965), Bassett's fictional discussion of *A New Sex Ethics and Marriage Structure* (1961), Dingwall's critical look at *The American Woman* (1956), the penetrating book by Ellis on *The American Sexual Tragedy* (1962), Taylor's *Sex in History* (1954), Comfort's *Sexual Behavior in Society* (1950), Lewinsohn's *A History of Sexual Customs* (1958), Ford & Beach's *Patterns of Sexual Behavior* (1951), and Otto's *The New Sexuality* (1971).

To do an effective job in premarital counseling the marriage and family counselor today needs to have considerable background in scientific knowledge about dating behavior, including premarital sexual behavior. For this sort of knowledge, one can turn to Ehrmann's *Premarital Dating Behavior* (1959), Bell's *Premarital Sex in a Changing Society* (1966), Reiss's *Premarital Sexual Standards in America* (1960) and *The Social Context of Premarital Sexual Permissiveness* (1967), as well as Kirkendall's *Premarital Intercourse and Interpersonal Relationships* (1961). A book on *Premarital Counseling* has been written by Rutledge (1966). For books of practical help to the single person, two books by Albert Ellis are valuable: *Sex and the Single Man* (1963), and *The Intelligent Woman's Guide to Man-hunting* (1963). Albert Gordon has presented a study of *Intermarriage* (1964) which is relevant in premarital counseling, as is Locke's *Predicting Adjustment in Marriage* (1951).

Counseling techniques may be said to be one of the most important areas where marriage and family counselors need to be up to date. There are several general books on marriage counseling, such as Mudd, et al (1958), Eisenstein (1956), Johnson (1961), Silverman (1965, 1972), Abse, et al (1974), Klemer (1965), Taylor (1965), Cuber (1948), Herbert & Jervis (1959), Wallis & Booker (1958), Mudd (1952), Mudd & Krich (1956), and Skidmore, et al (1956).

The marriage and family counselor will find that more general books on different theoretical approaches to psychotherapy and counseling may prove helpful in working with marital, family and premarital problems. Some such books are those by Harper (1959, 1976), Ard's *Counseling and Psychotherapy* (1975), Frank (1963), Wolberg's two volumes (1967), Patterson (1966), Stein (1961), Greenwald's *Active Psychotherapies* (1967), Brammer & Shostrom (1968), Stefflre (1965), Watzlawick, et al (1967), McCary (1955), Ford & Urban (1963), Mahrer's *The Goals of Psychotherapy* (1967), and Greene's book on *The Psychotherapies of Marital Disharmony* (1965). Jackson's two volumes (1968) are also helpful.

Books which deal with specialized techniques or particular theoretical approaches are those by Rogers (1951), Herzberg (1945), Albert Ellis (1962, 1971, 1973), Satir (1967), Ackerman (1958), Bloch (1973), Erickson & Hogan (1972), Ferber (1973), Fitzgerald (1973), Foley (1974), Framo (1970), Glick & Kessler (1974), Green (1970), Greenwald's *Direct Decision Therapy* (1974), Haley (1971), Haley & Hoffman (1968), Knox (1971), Luthman & Kirschenbaum (1974), Martin (1976), Minuchin (1974), Nichols (1974), Papajohn & Spiegel (1975), Sager & Kaplan's *Progress in Group and Family Therapy* (1972) and Watzlawick, et al (1974). Rosenbaum & Alger's psychoanalytic perspective of *The Marriage Relationship* (1968), Wolpe, et al (1964), Wolpe & Lazarus (1966), Riesman, et al, *Mental Health of the Poor* (1964), Bellak & Small (1965), Phillips, et al (1966), Wolberg (1965), Eysenck (1964), Holland (1965), Stieper & Wiener (1965), Beier (1966), and Pearson (1965) are some additional useful books in this area.

Bibliotherapy, or suggesting particular books for clients to read, is a technique the marriage and family counselor may wish to consider. Some books have been specifically written for use with clients, such as Ellis & Harper's *Guide to Successful Marriage* (1961), Ard's *Treating Psychosexual Dysfunction* (1974), Lederer & Jackson's *The Mirages of Marriage* (1968), Satir's *Peoplemaking* (1972) to mention only a few.

The foregoing books will give the beginning marriage and family counselor some idea of the knowledge in the field which is relevant to the counselor's needs. The older, more experienced counselor may check over some of the familiar items and move on to some of the newer books to bring himself or herself up to date. All counselors need to keep reading critically so that they stay abreast of the constantly changing field called marriage and family counseling.

REFERENCES

Ard, B. N., Jr. Sex knowledge for the marriage counselor. *Merrill-Palmer Quarterly*, Winter 1955, *1*, 74–82.

Ard, B. N., Jr. Basic books on sex for family life educators. *The Family Coordinator*, July, 1961, *10*, 63–68.

Ellis, A. & Doorbar, R. R. Classified bibliography of articles, books, and pamphlets on sex, love, marriage, and family relations published during 1950. *Marriage and Family Living*, November 1952, *14*, 338–340.

Annotated Bibliography

Abse, D. W.; Nash, E. M.; Louden, L. M. (Eds.) *Marital and sexual counseling in medical practice*. Hagerstown, Maryland: Harper & Row, 2nd ed., 1974.
[A good text aimed at the medical practitioner.]

Ackerman, N. W. *The psychodynamics of family life*. New York: Basic Books, 1958.
[A classic by one of the early leaders in the field.]

Adelson, E. T. (Ed.) *Sexuality and psychoanalysis*. New York: Brunner/Mazel, 1975.
[A look at sex from the psychoanalytic point of view.]

Aldous, J. & Hill, R. L. *International bibliography of research in marriage and the family, 1900–1964*. Minneapolis, Minnesota: University of Minnesota Press, 1967.

Allen, C. E. *A textbook of psychosexual disorders*. London: Oxford University Press, 1962.
[A standard text by an English psychiatrist.]

Ard, Ben N., Jr. *Treating psychosexual dysfunction*. New York: Jason Aronson, 1974.
[A description and explanation of how a variety of sexual problems are dealt and resolved.]

Ard, Ben N., Jr. (Ed.) *Counseling and psychotherapy: classics on theories and issues*. Palo Alto: Science & Behavior Books, revised edition, 1975.
[A variety of approaches from the leaders themselves, contrasting theories and issues.]

Arieti, S. (Ed.) *American handbook of psychiatry*. New York: Basic Books, 1959.
[A monumental two volumes; a standard in the field.]

Bach, George & Wyden, Peter. *The intimate enemy*. New York: William Morrow, 1969.
[How to fight with one's spouse.]

Bassett, M. *A new sex ethics and marriage structure*. New York: Philosophical Library, 1961.
[A fictitious pair of college teachers, Adam and Eve, discuss a new sex ethic and marriage pattern.]

Beck, A. T. *Depression*. New York: Harper & Row, 1967.
[Clinical, experimental, and theoretical aspects of depression.]

Beier, E. G. *The silent language of psychotherapy*. Chicago: Aldine, 1966.
[A comprehensive, documented study of the crucial role of covert communication, persuasion, and social reinforcement in psychotherapy.]

Bell, N. W. & Vigel, E. F. (Eds.) *A modern introduction to the family*. New York: Free Press of Glencoe, 1960.
[An excellent standard text.]

Bell, R. R. *Marriage and family interaction*. Homewood, Illinois: Dorsey, 1963.
[A good college text on marriage and the family.]

Bell, R. R. *Premarital sex in a changing society*. Englewood Cliffs, N. J.: Prentice-Hall, 1966.
[A paperback which analyzes sociologically the changing nature of premarital sex in American society.]

Bellak, L. & Small, L. *Emergency psychotherapy and brief psychotherapy*. New York: Grune & Stratton, 1965.
[Experiences of the Trouble-Shooting Clinic in Queens, New York, which provided 24-hour emotional first-aid.]

Belliveau, Fred & Richter, Lin. *Understanding sexual inadequacy*. New York: Bantam Books, 1970.
[The clearest brief explanation of the Masters & Johnson approach.]

Bernard, J. *Marriage and family among Negroes*. Englewood Cliffs, N. J.: Prentice-Hall, 1966.
[A woman sociologist looks at Negro families.]

Bernard, J. *The sex game*. Englewood Cliffs, N. J.: Prentice-Hall, 1968.
[A sociologist discusses communication between the sexes—with words and without.]

Blanck, Rubin & Blanck, Gertrude. *Marriage and personal development*. New York: Columbia University Press, 1968.
[A psychoanalytic view of marriage.]

Bloch, Donald (Ed.) *Techniques of family psychotherapy*. New York: Grune & Stratton, 1973.
[A collection of new techniques in an expanding field.]

Blood, R. O., Jr. *Marriage*. New York: Free Press of Glencoe, 1962.

[One of the standard texts in the field.]

Blood, R. O., Jr. & Wolfe, D. M. *Husbands and wives.* Glencoe, Illinois: Free Press, 1960.
[The dynamics of married living; a sociological study of different classes and ethnic groups in Detroit; comparisons in farm families.]

Bohannan, Paul (Ed.) *Divorce and after.* Garden City: Doubleday, 1970.
[An excellent reference for professionals and laypersons dealing with divorce.]

Brammer, L. M. & Shostrom, E. L. *Therapeutic psychology.* Englewood Cliffs, N. J.: Prentice-Hall, 2nd ed., 1968.
[A comprehensive introduction to the field of psychological counseling.]

Broderick, C. B. & Bernard, J. (Eds.) *The individual, sex & society.* Baltimore: Johns Hopkins Press, 1969.
[A fine collection of papers from *Siecus*.]

Brown, F. & Kempton, R. T. *Sex questions and answers.* New York: McGraw-Hill, 2nd ed., 1970.
[Simple, direct, and authoritative answers to sex questions frequently asked.]

Burton, Arthur (Ed.) *Modern psychotherapeutic practice.* Palo Alto: Science & Behavior Books, 1965.
[Innovations in technique.]

Christensen, H. T. (Ed.) *Handbook of marriage and the family.* Chicago: Rand McNally, 1964.
[A team approach of 24 leading authorities, providing an extensive treatment of theory and research in the field of marriage and the family.]

Clark, L. (Ed.) *Illustrated sex atlas.* New York: Health Publications, 1963.
[A very practical paperback book with 287 illustrations, including glossary.]

Comfort, A. *Sexual behavior in society.* New York: Viking, 1950.
[A bold, serious discussion by a rational humanist from England.]

Constantine, Larry L. & Constantine, Joan M. *Group marriage.* Riverside, N. J.: Macmillan, 1973.
[A discussion of the pros and cons of group marriage.]

Cuber, J. F. *Marriage counseling practice.* New York: Appleton-Century-Crofts, 1948.
[One of the early texts.]

Cuber, J. F. & Harroff, P. B. *The significant Americans.* New York: Appleton-Century, 1965.
[A study of sexual behavior among the affluent by two sociologists.]

Curtin, Mary Ellen (Ed.) *Symposium on love.* New York: Behavioral Publications, 1973.
[Excellent compendium of different views on love by a variety of specialists.]

DiCaprio, Nicholas S. *Personality theories.* Philadelphia: Saunders, 1974.
[Guides to living in various personality theories.]

DeMartino, M. F. (Ed.) *Sexual behavior and personality characteristics.* New York: Citadel Press, 1963.
[Twenty four contributors discuss a wide range of topics.]

Dickinson, R. L. *Atlas of human sex anatomy.* Baltimore: Williams & Wilkins, 1949.
[The definitive book on the subject.]

Dickinson, R. L. *Techniques of conception control.* Baltimore: Williams & Wilkins, 1950.
[Includes various methods but not the pill; fifty excellent illustrations.]

Dingwall, E. J. *The American woman.* New York: Rinehart, 1956.
[An English anthropologist takes a controversial look at American women.]

Ditzion, S. *Marriage, morals and sex.* New York: Bookman Associates, 1953.
[A history of ideas from colonial times to the era of the Kinsey reports.]

Ehrmann, W. *Premarital dating behavior.* New York: Holt, 1959.
[A study of 1,000 male and female college students.]

Eisenstein, V. W. (Ed.) *Neurotic interaction in marriage.* New York: Basic Books, 1956.
[An authoritative study by 25 specialists.]

Ellis, Albert. *The folklore of sex.* New York: Charles Boni, 1951.
[An analysis of the conflicting attitudes found in the various media.]

Ellis, Albert. *The art and science of love.* New York: Dell paperback, 1960.
[A very popular marriage manual; a good book for clients, too.]

Ellis, Albert. *The American sexual tragedy.* New York: Lyle Stuart, 2nd ed., 1962.
[An unflinching account of the difficulties that result from our mores.]

Ellis, Albert. *Reason and emotion in psychotherapy.* New York: Lyle Stuart, 1962.
[The first basic text in the rational-emotive approach.]

Ellis, Albert. *The intelligent woman's guide to man-hunting.* New York: Lyle Stuart, 1963.
[A practical guide for women clients.]

Ellis, Albert. *Sex and the single man.* New York: Lyle Stuart, 1963.
[A practical, down-to-earth book for the single man.]

Ellis, Albert. *Sex without guilt.* New York: Grove Press, rev. ed., 1965.
[The frank and candid views one expects from this famous sexologist.]

Ellis, Albert, et al. *Growth through reason: Verbatim cases in rational-emotive therapy.* North Hollywood: Wilshire Books, 1971.

[Several rational therapists present transcripts of actual cases.]

Ellis, Albert. *Humanistic psychotherapy: the rational-emotive approach*. New York: Julian Press, 1973.
[The latest statement of rational-emotive therapy.]

Ellis, Albert. *How to live with a "neurotic" at home and at work*. New York: Crown, revised edition, 1975.
[A revised classic, very useful for clients.]

Ellis, Albert & Abarbanel, A. B. (Eds.) *The encyclopedia of sexual behavior*. New York: Hawthorn, 1961.
[Two volumes with contributions by 98 authorities. The most extensive work.]

Ellis, Albert & Harper, Robert A. *A new guide to rational living*. North Hollywood: Wilshire Book Co., revised edition, 1975.
[The best book for "bibliotherapy" for clients (from the rational-emotive approach).]

Ellis, Albert & Harper, Robert A. *A guide to successful marriage*. North Hollywood: Wilshire Book Co., 1961.
[An excellent bibliotherapy tool for marriage counseling clients.]

Erickson, Gerald & Hogan, Terrance (Eds.) *Family therapy*. Monterey, Ca.: Brooks Cole, 1972.
[An introduction to theory and technique.]

Eysenck, H. J. (Ed.) *Experiments in behavior therapy*. New York: Macmillan, 1964.
[Readings derived from learning theory.]

Farber, S. M. & Wilson, R. H. L. (Eds.) *Teen-age marriage and divorce*. Berkeley: Diablo Press paperback, 1967.
[A symposium of 14 contributors from various disciplines.]

Fishbein, M. & Burgess, E. W. (Eds.) *Successful marriage*. Garden City, N. Y.: Doubleday, rev. ed., 1963.
[Thirty eight contributors discuss various aspects of marriage.]

Foley, Vincent D. *An introduction to family therapy*. New York: Grune & Stratton, 1974.
[A good brief review of family therapy.]

Ford, C. S. & Beach, F. A. *Patterns of sexual behavior*. New York: Harper, 1951.
[The most comprehensive study yet made of 190 different societies.]

Ford, D. H. & Urban, H. B. *Systems of psychotherapy*. New York: Wiley, 1963.
[A comparative study of ten systems.]

Framo, J. L. (Ed.) *Family interaction*. New York: Springer, 1970.
[A dialogue between family researchers and family therapists.]

Frank, J. D. *Persuasion and healing*. New York: Schocken Books, 1963.
[A comparative study of the various schools of modern psychotherapy.]

Freedman, A. M. & Kaplan, H. I. (Eds.) *Comprehensive textbook of psychiatry*. Baltimore: Williams & Wilkins, 1967.
[An eclectic, multidisciplinary, comprehensive textbook.]

Gebhard, P. H., et al. *Pregnancy, birth and abortion*. New York: Harper, 1958.
[A study of approximately 7,000 women by the Institute for Sex Research.]

Gebhard, P. H., et al. *Sex offenders*. New York: Harper & Row, 1965.
[The results of the study of 1,500 sex offenders by the Kinsey researchers.]

Glick, Ira D. & Kessler, David R. *Marital and family therapy*. New York: Grune & Stratton, 1974.
[A good recent addition to a growing field.]

Goldstein, A. P., et al. *Psychotherapy and the psychology of behavior change*.
[Applies nonclinical research findings to psychotherapy.]

Goode, W. J. *After divorce*. Glencoe, Illinois: Free Press, 1956.
[What happens to mothers who divorce.]

Gordon, A. I. *Intermarriage: interfaith, interracial, interethnic*. Boston: Beacon, 1964.
[Presents statistical and case data on a variety of intermarriages.]

Gordon, J. E. *Personality and behavior*. New York: Macmillan, 1963.
[An integrated presentation of personality against a background of experimental research.]

Gorney, Roderic. *The human agenda*. Simon & Schuster, 1972.
[A penetrating look into the future by an observant psychiatrist.]

Green, Bernard. *A clinical approach to marital problems*. Springfield, Illinois: Thomas, 1970.
[A text which has been used at the college level.]

Greene, B. L. (Ed.) *The psychotherapies of marital disharmony*. New York: Free Press, 1965.
[Twelve contributors discuss topics presented before the American Orthopsychiatric Association on March 20, 1964.]

Greenwald, H. (Ed.) *Active psychotherapies*. New York: Atherton, 1967.
[Includes a wide variety of theorists on various approaches.]

Greenwald, H. *Direct decision therapy*. San Diego: Edits, 1974.
[Helps therapists help clients make better life decisions.]

Grier, W. H. & Cobbs, P. M. *Black rage*. New York: Basic Books, 1968.
[Two black psychiatrists discuss the inner dimensions of black men and women.]

Gross, Leonard (Ed.) *Sexual issues in marriage*. New York: Spectrum, 1975.

[Sixty contributors from articles published in the now defunct *Sexual behavior*.]

Group for the Advancement of Psychiatry. *The right to abortion: A psychiatric view*. New York: Scribner's, 1970.
[A discussion from social, legal, and ethical points of view.]

Guttmacher, A. F. *The complete book of birth control*. New York: Ballantine Books paperback, 1961.
[Medical techniques, the new pills, and popular myths are discussed.]

Haley, Hay & Hoffman, Lynn. *Techniques of family therapy*. New York: Basic Books, 1968.
[An excellent introduction to this field.]

Haley, Jay (Ed.) *Changing families: A family therapy reader*. New York: Grune & Stratton, 1971.
[An excellent reader edited by one of the outstanding leaders in the field.]

Hall, C. S. & Lindzey, G. *Theories of personality*. New York: Wiley, 1957.
[A standard classic in the field, widely used as a college text.]

Harper, Robert A. *Psychoanalysis and psychotherapy: 36 systems*. Englewood Cliffs, N. J.: Prentice-Hall, 1959.
[One of the best brief summaries of different systems of psychotherapy.]

Hartman, William E. & Fithian, Marilyn A. *Treatment of sexual dysfunction*. New York: Jason Aronson, 1974.
[A bio-psycho-social approach by a California dual-sex team.]

Hastings, D. W. *A doctor speaks on sexual expression in marriage*. Boston: Little, Brown, 1966.
['Written from a modern point of view, not the moralistic.]

Haussamen, F. & Guitar, M. A. *The divorce handbook*. New York: Putnam, 1960.
[A good handbook for the professional's library.]

Herbert, W. L. & Jervis, F. V. *A modern approach to marriage counseling* London: Methuen, 1959.
[An English team's approach to marriage counseling.]

Herzberg, A. *Active psychotherapy*. London: Research Books, 1945.
[Uses "tasks" assigned by the therapist.]

Holland, G. A. *Fundamentals of psychotherapy*. New York: Holt, Rinehart & Winston, 1965.
[Uses the explanatory and descriptive concepts of general psychology.]

Howells, John G. *Principles of family psychiatry*. New York: Brunner/Mazel, 1975.
[A text by a famous psychiatrist.]

Hunt, Morton M. *The world of the formerly married*. New York: McGraw-Hill, 1966.
[A writer surveys what happens after divorce.]

Jackson, D. D. (Ed.) *Communication, family and marriage*. Volume I. Palo Alto: Science & Behavior Books, 1968.
[The double-bind theory, communication systems and pathology.]

Jackson, D. D. (Ed.) *Therapy, communication, and change*. Volume II. Palo Alto: Science & Behavior Books, 1968.
[Psychotic behavior and interactional contexts; conjoint family therapy.]

Jacobson, Paul H. *American marriage and divorce*. New York: Rinehart, 1959.
[The facts and figures.]

Johnson, D. *Marriage counseling: Theory and practice*. Englewood Cliffs, N. J.: Prentice-Hall, 1961.
[A text by a counselor formerly on the staff of the Menninger Clinic.]

Kantor, David & Lehr, William. *Inside the family*. San Francisco: Jossey-Bass, 1975.
[An intriguing new look inside the family.]

Kaplan, Helen Singer. *The new sex therapy*. New York: Brunner/Mazel, 1974.
[An attempt to integrate traditional with newer approaches.]

Kaplan, Helen Singer. *The illustrated manual of sex therapy*. New York: Quadrangle, 1975.
[A brief book with beautiful art work.]

Kaufmann, Walter. *Without guilt and justice*. New York: Wyden, 1973.
[A philosopher questions our concepts of guilt and justice.]

Kinsey, A. C., et al. *Sexual behavior in the human male*. Philadelphia: Saunders, 1948.
[The most extensive research on the subject ever completed.]

Kinsey, A. C., et al. *Sexual behavior in the human female*. Philadelphia: Saunders, 1953.
[The results of interviews with nearly 8,000 women across the U.S.]

Kirkendall, L. A. *Premarital intercourse and interpersonal relationships*. New York: Julian Press, 1961.
[A research study based on case histories of 668 experiences.]

Klemer, R. H. (Ed.) *Counseling in marital and sexual problems*. Baltimore: Williams & Wilkins, 1965.
[A physician's handbook with chapter by 20 different specialists.]

Kling, S. G. *The complete guide to divorce*. New York: Simon & Schuster, 1963.
[A practical paperback in question and answer form.]

Knox, David. *Marriage happiness: A behavioral approach to counseling*. Champaign, Illinois: Research Press, 1971.
[A practical guide for marriage counselors.]

Komarovsky, M. *Blue-collar marriage*. New York: Random House, 1962.
[A portrayal of the working-class existence of value to the marriage counselor.]

Krantzler, Mel. *Creative divorce*. New York: Signet, 1974.
[A counselor discusses his trip through divorce.]

Lederer, W. J. & Jackson, D. D. *The mirages of marriage*. New York: Norton, 1968.
[The false assumptions of marriage and how to make a marriage work.]

Lewinsohn, R. *A history of sexual customs*. New York: Harper, 1958.
[A cross-cultural examination in objective terms.]

Lipton, L. *The erotic revolution*. Los Angeles: Sherbourne Press, 1965.
[An affirmative view of the new morality.]

Locke, H. J. *Predicting adjustment in marriage*. New York: Holt, 1951.
[A comparison of a divorced and a happily married group.]

Luthman, Shirley Gehrke & Kirschenbaum, Martin. *The dynamic family*. Palo Alto: Science & Behavior Books, 1974.
[Two followers of Satir develop a new look at families.]

Lyman, Howard B. *Single again*. New York: David McKay, 1971.
[Practical help for the divorced or widowed.]

McGrady, Patrick M., Jr. *The love doctors*. New York: Macmillan, 1972.
[A description of some of the leaders in sex therapy and their work.]

Mahrer, A. R. (Ed.) *The goals of psychotherapy*. New York: Appleton-Century-Crofts, 1967.
[The goals of psychotherapy as seen by various leading theorists.]

Marshall, D. S. & Suggs, R. C. *Human sexual behavior*. New York: Basic Books, 1971.
[An anthropological look at sex in several cultures.]

Martin, Peter A. *A marital therapy manual*. New York: Brunner/Mazel, 1976.
[A clinical handbook by a noted family therapist.]

Maslow, A. H. *Toward a psychology of being*. New York: Van Nostrand, 2nd ed., 1968.
[An excellent brief introduction to Maslow's approach.]

Maslow, A. H. *Motivation and personality*. New York: Harper, 2nd ed., 1970.
[Presents the basic data from Maslow's studies of self-actualizing people.]

Maslow, A. H. *The farther reaches of human nature*. New York: Viking, 1971.
[The last book Maslow wrote, published posthumously.]

Masters, W. H. & Johnson, V. E. *Human sexual response*. Boston: Little, Brown, 1966.
[A pioneer study; a research of eleven years into anatomy and physiology.]

Masters, W. H. & Johnson, V. E. *Human sexual inadequacy*. Boston: Little, Brown, 1970.
[The famous Masters & Johnson treatments of sexual dysfunction.]

Masters, W. H. & Johnson, V. E. *The pleasure bond*. Boston: Little, Brown, 1974.
[The philosophy behind Masters & Johnson's approach is spelled out.]

Milne, Hugo B. (Ed.) *Psycho-sexual problems*. Baltimore: University Park Press, 1976.
[A fine contribution from England.]

Mindey, Carol. *The divorced mother*. New York: McGraw-Hill, 1969.
[A helpful book for clients.]

Minuchin, Salvador. *Families and family therapy*. Cambridge, Mass.: Harvard University Press, 1974.
[Includes transcripts of family sessions and examples of effectively-functioning families and those seeking therapy.]

Mudd, E. H. *The practice of marriage counseling*. New York: Association Press, 1952.
[A text by one of the early leaders in the field.]

Mudd, E. H., et al (Eds.) *Marriage counseling: A casebook*. New York: Association Press, 1958.
[Includes 41 cases from the files of 38 leading marriage counselors.]

Neubeck, Gerhard (Ed.) *Extra-marital relations*. Englewood Cliffs, N. J.: Prentice-Hall, 1969.
[Discussions by several authorities with contrasting views.]

Nichols, William C., Jr. (Ed.) *Marriage and family therapy*. Minneapolis: National Council on Family Relations, 1974.
[A reader from NCFR journals.]

Oliven, J. F. *Sexual hygiene and pathology*. Philadelphia: Lippincott, 2nd ed., 1965.
[A comprehensive manual for the physician and the professions.]

Olson, David & Dahl, Nancy. *Inventory of marriage and family literature*. St. Paul: IMFL Project, University of Minnesota, 1975.
[Subject and author indexes of over 2,000 articles.]

Packard, V. *The sexual wilderness*. New York: McKay, 1968.
[The contemporary upheaval in male-female relationships.]

Papajohn, John & Spiegel, John. *Transactions in families*. San Francisco: Jossey-Bass, 1975.
[A new way of looking at interactions in families.]

Patterson, C. H. *Theories of counseling and psychotherapy*. New York: Harper & Row, 2nd ed., 1973.
[Presents a variety of viewpoints.]

Pearson, L. (Ed.) *The use of written communication in psychotherapy*. Springfield, Illinois: Thomas, 1965.
[Contributions by Arthur Burton, Albert Ellis, Molly Harrower, & Victor Raimy.]

Phillips, E. L. & Wiener, D. N. *Short-term psychotherapy and structured behavior change*. New York: McGraw-Hill, 1966.
[A theory closely tied to direct, observable behavior.]

Pilpel, H. & Zavin, T. *Your marriage and the law*. New York: Holt, Rinehart & Winston, 1952.
[A practical, helpful book for both the professional and the layperson.]

Rainwater, L. & Weinstein, K. K. *And the poor get children*. Chicago: Quadrangle Books, 1960.
[An excellent discussion of sex and family planning among the poor.]

Reiss, I. L. *Premarital sexual standards in America*. Glencoe, Illinois: Free Press, 1960.
[A sociological investigation with a lot to offer to the marriage counselor.]

Reiss, I. L. *The social context of premarital sexual permissiveness*. New York: Holt, Rinehart & Winston, 1967.
[The first national probability sample of premarital sexual standards.]

Riessman, F. et al (Eds.) *Mental health of the poor*. New York: Free Press of Glencoe, 1964.
[Readings on new treatment approaches for low-income people.]

Rogers, Carl R. *Client-centered therapy*. Boston: Houghton Mifflin, 1951.
[The definitive book on this approach.]

Rosenbaum, S. & Alger, I. (Eds.) *The marriage relationship*. New York: Basic Books, 1968.
[Some 25 psychoanalysts provide their views of marriage.]

Ruesch, J. & Bateson, G. *Communication: The social matrix of psychiatry*. New York: Norton, 1951.
[One of the early contributions which has greatly influenced family therapy.]

Rutledge, A. L. *Pre-marital counseling*. Cambridge, Mass.: Schenkman, 1966.
[Deals with wide-ranging information of value to the marriage counselor.]

Sager, Clifford J. & Kaplan, Helen Singer (Eds.) *Progress in group and family therapy*. New York: Brunner/Mazel, 1972.
[Fifty-two articles provide a comprehensive review of the field.]

Sahakian, W. S. (Ed.) *Psychology of personality*. Chicago: Rand McNally, 1965.
[Readings from 21 prominent psychologists.]

Satir, Virginia. *Conjoint family therapy*. Palo Alto: Science & Behavior Books, 1967.
[A guide to theory and technique by one of the famous leaders in the field.]

Satir, Virginia. *Peoplemaking*. Palo Alto: Science & Behavior Books, 1972.
[An excellent book for laypeople as well as professionals.]

Saxton, L. *The individual, marriage, and the family*. Belmont, Ca.: Wadsworth, 1968.
[An excellent text with a good glossary.]

Schur, E. M. (Ed.) *The family and the sexual revolution*. Bloomington, Indiana University Press, 1964.
[Selected readings from a variety of contributors.]

Shiloh, Ailon (Ed.) *Studies in human sexual behavior: The American scene*. Springfield, Illinois: Thomas, 1970.
[An excellent compendium of American sex research.]

Siecus. *Sexuality and man*. New York: Charles Scribner's Sons, 1970.
[A fine collection of articles from the Siecus organization.]

Silverman, H. S. (Ed.) *Marital counseling*. Springfield, Illinois: Thomas, 1967.
[A large volume presenting 36 nationally known specialists.]

Silverman, H. S. (Ed.) *Marital therapy*. Springfield, Illinois: Thomas, 1972.
[A comprehensive text with many contributors.]

Skidmore, R.; Garrett, H. V. S.; & Skidmore, C. J. *Marriage counseling*. New York: Harper, 1956.
[A standard text in the field.]

Slovenko, R. (Ed.) *Sexual behavior and the law*. Springfield, Illinois: Thomas, 1965.
[A comprehensive text with 47 contributors.]

Speigel, John P. & Machotka, Pavel. *Messages of the body*. New York: Free Press, 1974.
[Learning to read non-verbal communication.]

Stefflre, Buford & Grant, W. Harold (Eds.) *Theories of counseling*. New York: McGraw-Hill, 2nd ed., 1965.

Stein, M. I. (Ed.) *Contemporary psychotherapies*. New York: Free Press of Glencoe, 1961.
[Ten leading therapists discuss the theoretical orientations they use, with a case illustration.]

Stephens, W. N. (Ed.) *Reflections on marriage*. New York: Crowell, 1968.
[Represents a wide range of approaches and viewpoints.]

Stieper, D. R. & Wiener, D. N. *Dimensions of psychotherapy*. Chicago: Aldine, 1965.
[An experimental and clinical approach.]

Stone, H. & Stone, A. *A marriage manual*. New York: Simon & Schuster, rev. ed., 1952.
[One of the widely used marriage manuals.]

Stuart, Richard B. *Marital pre-counseling inven-*

tory: Counselor's guide. Champaign, Illinois: Research Press, 1975.
[A practical tool for the marriage counselor.]

Sullivan, H. S. The psychiatric interview. New York: Norton, 1954.
[A fine discussion of the basics by an outstanding leader.]

Sussman, M. B. Sourcebook in marriage and the family. Boston: Houghton Mifflin, 2nd ed., 1963.
[Seventy five articles on marriage and the family.]

Taves, Isabella. Women alone. New York: Funk & Wagnalls, 1968.
[Helpful hints for clients in this condition.]

Tayler, D. B. (Ed.) Human sexual development. Philadelphia: Davis, 1970.
[Basic information of a sexual nature for the marriage counselor.]

Taylor, D. L. Marriage counseling. Springfield, Illinois: Thomas, 1965.
[A brief introduction to nondirective marriage counseling with an emphasis on communication and feelings.]

Taylor, G. R. Sex in history. New York: Vanguard, 1954.
[An objective look at sex throughout history- a good perspective.]

Tietze, C. (Ed.) Selected bibliography of contraception 1940-1960. New York: National Committee on Maternal Health, 1960.
[For the serious student who really wants to get into the field.]

Vincent, Clark E. (Ed.) Human sexuality in medical education and practice. Springfield, Illinois: Thomas, 1968.
[One of the best texts on the subject.]

Vincent, Clark E. Sexual & marital health. New York: McGraw-Hill, 1973.
[Includes the "marital health check-up" idea, among many other fine concepts.]

Wahl, C. W. (Ed.) Sexual problems. New York: Free Press, 1967.
[Diagnosis and treatment in medical practice; contributions from 18 authors.]

Wallis, H. J. & Booker, H. S. Marriage counseling. London: Routledge, Kegan Paul, 1958.
[A contribution from English colleagues.]

Watzlawick, P., et al. Pragmatics of human communication. New York: Norton, 1967.
[A study of interactional patterns, pathologies, and paradoxes of human communication, with special attention to behavior disorders.]

Watzlawick, P., et al. Change. New York: Norton, 1974.
[Discusses paradoxical ways to help clients change.]

Weiss, Robert. Marital separation. New York: Basic Books, 1975.
[Coping with the end of a marriage and the transition to being single again.]

Whyte, W. H., Jr. The organization man. New York: Doubleday, 1956.
[A sociological study of a way of life that many Americans are now leading.]

Winch, R. F., et al (Eds.) Selected studies in the family. New York: Holt, Rinehart & Winston, 1962.
[One of the standard books of reading in the field.]

Witmer, H. L. & Kotinsky, R. (Eds.) Personality in the making. New York: Harper, 1952.
[The fact-finding report of the Mid-Century White House Conference on Children and Youth.]

Wolberg, L. R. (Ed.) Short-term psychotherapy. New York: Grune & Stratton, 1965.
[Nine theorists join Wolberg in discussing brief psychotherapy.]

Wolberg, L. R. The technique of psychotherapy. New York: Grune & Stratton, 2 volumes, 2nd ed., 1967.
[A comprehensive textbook with many practical suggestions. Good appendices.]

Wolpe, J. & Lazarus, A. Behavior therapy techniques. London: Pergamon Press, 1966.
[A guide to the treatment of neurosis from the behaviorist approach.]

Wolpe, J.; Salter, A.; & Reyna, L. J. (Eds.) The conditioning therapies. New York: Holt, Rinehart & Winston, 1964.
[Twelve contributors discuss the challenge of conditioning therapies.]

Young, W. Eros denied. New York: Grove Press, 1964.
[Sex in Western society discussed by an English scholar in a frank, open manner.]

Zubin, Joseph & Money, John (Eds.) Contemporary sexual behavior: Critical issues in the 1970s. Baltimore: Johns Hopkins University Press, 1973.
[Based on the proceedings of the 61st annual meeting of the American Psychopathological Association.]

Appendices

Appendix A

MEMBERSHIP STANDARDS
AMERICAN ASSOCIATION OF MARRIAGE
AND FAMILY COUNSELORS

CLINICAL MEMBER

1. Recognized graduate professional education with the minimum of an earned master's degree from an accredited educational institution in an appropriate behavioral science field, mental health discipline, or recognized helping profession.

2. (a) 200 hours of approved supervision of the practice of marriage and family counseling, ordinarily to be completed in a 2–3 year period, of which at least 100 hours must be in *individual* supervision. This supervision will occur preferably with more than one supervisor, and should include a continuous process of supervision with at least several cases.

(b) 1000 hours of clinical experience in the practice of marriage and family counseling under approved supervision, involving at least 50 different cases.

OR

3. (a) 150 hours of approved supervision of the practice of psychotherapy, ordinarily to be completed in a 2–3 year period, of which at least 50 hours must be *individual* supervision. *Plus*: At least 50 hours of approved *individual* supervision of the practice of marriage and family counseling, ordinarily to be completed within a period of not less than one nor more than two years.

(b) 750 hours of clinical experience in the practice of psychotherapy under approved supervision involving at least 30 cases. *Plus*: At least 250 hours of clinical practice of marriage and family counseling under approved supervision, involving at least 20 cases.

4. Applicants may be requested to have a screening interview with the national Membership Committee or a regional membership committee, or designated representative(s).

5. Demonstrated readiness for the independent practice of marriage and family counseling.

6. Upon completion of the graduate professional degree plus the required supervised clinical experience, the candidate will be expected to have mastered the important theory in the field of marriage and family counseling as defined in the document on supervision: "The Approved Supervisor is responsible for the supervisee's familiarity with the important and relevant literature in developmental psychology, personality theory, human sexuality, behavior pathology, marriage and family studies and marriage and family therapy."

FELLOW

A minimum of five years in good standing as a Member of the Association and significant contributions to the field of marriage and family counseling, as determined by the Board of Directors upon recommendation by the Honors Committee.

DIPLOMATE

A Member who demonstrates an advanced level of clinical competence and experience, as determined by the Board of Directors.

STUDENT

The designation "Student" may be given to a person who is currently enrolled in the graduate program of an accredited college or university in an appropriate discipline, or one who has completed such a program and is now serving on an internship basis in a training program approved by the Association or is under supervision arrangement with the Membership Committee. The Student category shall ordinarily be for a maximum of five (5) years, or until satisfactory completion of requirements for *Member*, whichever shall come first.

ASSOCIATE

The designation "Associate" may be given to a person who has already completed graduate studies and achieved professional competence in an appropriate behavioral science or mental health field and who is now receiving supervision by arrangement with Committee in order to become qualified as a *Member*. The Associate category shall ordinarily be for a maximum of five (5) years or until satisfactory completion of requirements for Member, whichever shall come first.

AFFILIATE

Upon recommendation of the Honors Committee the Board of Directors may, at its discretion, invite suitable persons to become Affiliates of the Association. Such persons shall be of high standing in a field related to marriage and family counseling, and shall be making an outstanding contribution to the field of marriage, the family, or counseling. The total number of Affiliates shall not exceed two percent (2%) of the total number of clinical members. All Affiliates shall be subject every five (5) years to re-election by the Board of Directors.

HONORARY LIFE MEMBERSHIP

Upon recommendation of the Honors Committee the Board of Directors may, at its discretion, invite suitable persons to become Honorary Life Members of the Association. Such persons shall be of high standing in a field related to marriage and family counseling, and shall have made an outstanding contribution to the field of marriage, the family, or counseling. The total number of Honorary Life Members shall not exceed 25.

* * *

Members, Fellows and Diplomates shall be required to meet the following standards:

ACADEMIC AND PROFESSIONAL STANDING. The Applicant shall be required to hold whatever graduate or professional degree is necessary for the practice of the recognized behavioral science or mental health profession for which he or she has been trained. The Board of Directors shall determine, for the guidance of the Membership Committee, and in consultation with authorities in the professional fields concerned, how this requirement is to be interpreted.

CLINICAL COMPETENCE AND EXPERIENCE. The applicant shall have had at least three (3) years of experience in marriage and family counseling, at least one (1) year of which has been under supervision deemed acceptable by the Membership Committee. This must be in addition to any general training he or she may have received in counseling or psychotherapy. This internship shall have been in a training program approved by the Association or other internship deemed acceptable by the Membership Committee. The applicant may be required to submit case material for evaluation, and to undergo an oral examination, in order to establish clinical competence. (This section from the A.A.M.F.C. Bylaws, adopted 1/74, is a broad general statement of the fundamental requirements. It has been amplified and modified by subsequent actions of the Board of Directors. The specifications for clinical training and supervision which are to be found elsewhere in this material are recognized by the Membership Committee as the current basis for membership.)

PERSONAL MATURITY AND INTEGRITY. The applicant shall possess the qualities of character and of personality deemed to be necessary for the task of marriage and family counseling. The Membership Committee shall carry out whatever investigation may be necessary to secure satisfactory evidence of this.

LICENSING. In those states which license marriage and family counselors, an applicant who holds such a license will ordinarily be deemed qualified for membership. Exception to this will be where state licensing standards do not meet minimum national A.A.M.F.C. clinical standards. In states which license marriage and family counselors, members of the Association will ordinarily be required to meet the standards for licensing in that state.

CONTINUING PROFESSIONAL EDUCATION. Clinical members of the A.A.M.F.C. are expected to document their participation annually in some significant continuing professional education experience, with a view to increasing self-awareness and updating professional skills.

Appendix B

THE APPROVED SUPERVISOR
AMERICAN ASSOCIATION OF MARRIAGE
AND FAMILY COUNSELORS

Meeting in Boston, Massachusetts on March 29, 1974, the Board of Directors of the AAMFC officially approved the following document on *Approval for Supervision* of Marriage and Family Counseling (after final revision). This document is a revision of an earlier statement on this subject, approved by the Board of Directors of the AAMFC at the annual meeting at Salt Lake City in October 1971.

The rationale behind this development initially was to provide a means of identifying what are believed to be clearly competent resources for supervision in marriage and family counseling, in light of the standards and commitments of the AAMFC. This is expected to be of use to the Membership Committee, as well as to students and potential members.

Certain members of the AAMFC were designated as Approved Supervisors under a grandfather provision, which expired on February 1, 1973.

I. COMMITTEE ON APPROVAL FOR SUPERVISION

A Committee on Approval for Supervision, functioning as a subcommittee of the Training and Standards Committee and appointed by the President of the AAMFC, receives and reviews applications for the status of Approved Supervisor and recommends to the Board of Directors for appointment, those candidates believed to be qualified.

The Committee will make available to the Board, as is necessary, documentation adequate to support its recommendations.

II. DEFINITION OF SUPERVISION

Supervision is expected to have the following characteristics:

a. It is face-to-face conversation with the supervisor, usually in periods of about one hour each.

b. The learning process is sustained and intense. Appointments ordinarily are scheduled once a week, three times weekly being the usual maximum and once every other week being the usual minimum. Supervision is normally completed over a period of one to three years, in blocks of at least 20 hours.

c. The total supervision experience of a student should include more than one supervisor, at least one block of 20 hours being with other than the primary supervisor, where feasible, and preferably one from a different discipline.

d. Supervision focuses on the raw data from the supervisee's current clinical practice, as this is made directly available to the supervisor through such means as direct observations, co-therapy, written clinical notes, and audio and video recordings.

e. Supervision is a process clearly distinguishable from (if in some ways similar to) personal psychotherapy, and is contracted in order to serve *professional-vocational* goals.

III. REQUIREMENTS FOR SUPERVISORY STATUS

A candidate for designation as an Approved Supervisor is expected to meet the following conditions:

a. Have achieved Clinical Membership in the AAMFC.

b. Have provided the Committee on Approval for Supervision with a statement of the nature and length of his *training for supervision*, and his previous experience as supervisor. An applicant is required to have received *supervision of his own supervision* of at least two students (ordinarily at least 36 hours), this normally to have occurred within a one-year period. Where possible a candidate for appointment as an Approved Supervisor should complete his training for supervision with an AAMFC Approved Supervisor.

c. Have at least *two* years experience supervising staff and/or students in marriage and family counseling in a clinic or educational setting, or have had at least *three* years of performing private supervision outside of a clinic or educational setting. (All candidates from either setting should list the number of supervisees supervised, and the average number of hours of supervision per student.)

d. Have been involved in actively supervising trainees for a significant period of time within the three years immediately prior to seeking appointment.

e. Provide the Committee on Approval for Supervision with an evaluation from the consultant who has *supervised his supervision*, plus supporting reference letters from two professional colleagues in a position to evaluate the candidates supervisory skills and experience.

f. Submit to the Committee on Approval for Supervision a written summary of the work he has completed of at least one training block with at least one supervisee. The purpose of this summary is to demonstrate some knowledge of and skill in the supervisory process, and to present his "philosophy of supervision."

g. Appear in person before the Committee on Approval for Supervision *if requested.*

h. In states which license or certify marriage and family counselors, state standards for designation as supervisor will be used in lieu of AAMFC standards, provided that they meet minimum AAMFC standards.

IV. RESPONSIBILITIES AND GUIDELINES FOR SUPERVISORS

The Approved Supervisor is expected to make a decision to accept a particular supervisee for training only if he believes him to have the potentiality to qualify subsequently for clinical membership in the AAMFC.

a. The supervisee accepted for training by an Approved Supervisor should be enrolled in or have already attained the appropriate graduate professional degree in his primary professional field.

b. The supervisee is expected to be a Student or an Associate while under supervision.

c. The Approved Supervisor is responsible for the supervisee's familiarity with the important literature in developmental psychology, behavior pathology, personality theory, human sexuality, marriage and family studies and marriage and family therapy.

d. The major emphasis in supervision is on the supervisee's work with marital and family processes, including pre-marital and post-marital processes, whether singly, conjointly or in groups.

e. It is the Approved Supervisor's responsibility to see that all work being supervised by him is conducted in appropriate professional settings and with adequate administrative and clinical controls.

f. The Approved Supervisor will provide whatever reports are required by the Membership Committee when a supervisee applies for AAMFC clinical membership. These reports should include such information as:

(1) The number of hours spent by the trainee in different areas of clinical practice under this supervision.

(2) The number and form of supervisory hours, individual and group.

(3) The number and nature of cases supervised.

(4) An assessment of the applicant's personal and professional readiness for clinical membership.

(5) Any other information deemed relevant to the evaluation of the application.

g. The Approved Supervisor is assumed to be available for consultation with the Membership Committee on any details of the applicant's record, personal adjustment, or clinical competence for membership.

h. The fee for supervision is a function of the private contract between the supervisor and the supervisee, including the amounts agreed to and the collection thereof.

V. TRAINING STATUS

There are two levels of training membership in the AAMFC—*Student* and *Associate.* Trainees are ordinarily expected to secure their training and supervision in an AAMFC Approved Training Center or under a supervisor who holds appointment with the AAMFC as an Approved Supervisor. However, under special circumstances trainees may be allowed to seek training or supervision from other than an Approved Supervisor. The trainee should write directly to the national office to see if training with the supervisor in question can be regarded as meeting AAMFC standards for supervision. The Committee on Approval for Supervision is empowered to make this decision.

VI. CONDITIONS OF APPROVAL FOR SUPERVISION

Persons approved are designated as "Approved Supervisor: AAMFC." Appointment is for a three-year period, subject to renewal or discontinuation, beginning on January 1 of the first year. After careful consideration, including consultation with the Approved Supervisor, the Committee on Approval for Supervision may recommend to the Board of Directors the revocation of the supervisory status of a given supervisor. Subsequent reinstatement will require reapplication to the Committee. The Committee may at any time request an up-to-date report of the supervisor's current supervisory activities and procedures.

At the end of each three-year period the appointment will be renewed on request, and subsequently renewed or terminated as the member continues to meet, or fails to meet, the conditions of appointment. A fee of $35.00, necessary to underwrite the administrative implementation of the program, is due on the occasion of initial request for appointment and at each subsequent renewal of appointment.

VII. PROCEDURES FOR CANDIDACY

Designation as an Approved Supervisor is by appointment of the Board of Directors of the AAMFC, in response to recommendations of the Committee on Approval for Supervision. However, this process can be initiated by a candidate as follows:

a. A candidate for designation as an Approved Supervisor may write to the Executive Director indicating why he believes he should be considered for appointment as an Approved Supervisor.

b. Members who believe they have the required qualifications will be sent a *Supervisor Candidacy Form*, which is to be completed and returned to the national office with the processing fee. When the file is complete, including all supporting documentation, the Committee on Approval for Supervision will receive the candidate's file and make recommendations to the Board of Directors for action. The Committee may first require a personal interview with the candidate.

c. Candidates will be processed once a year. The file for each candidate must be completed in the national office by *August 1* for action by the Board of Directors at the subsequent annual meeting. New appointments will take effect on January 1 following.

Appendix C

STANDARDS FOR TRAINING CENTERS
IN MARRIAGE AND FAMILY COUNSELING

A. ORGANIZATION AND STRUCTURE

There must be some established group (such as a marriage and family clinic, a social agency, a counseling center or a group practice) recognized as reputable and responsible, which operates the counseling service with a clear administration and accepts broad responsibility for the service.

Provision needs to be made for:

1. A Clinical Director (or Director of Training) who is administratively responsible for the clinical training and programs.

2. Employment of competent, paid, professional staff who meet minimum professional standards for the practice of marriage counseling and clinical *supervision.*

3. Establishment and supervision of a well-defined financial policy and a budget reasonably guaranteed for three years or more.

4. Development of accepted personnel practices.

5. Support and interpretation of the program to the community.

If the training center is part of a larger institution, then appropriate fiscal, administrative and organizational responsibilities must be assumed by the institution and in a way that is clearly understood.

B. PROFESSIONAL RESOURCES

The staff of the training center should consist of:

1. A professional staff, at least some of whom must be members of the AAMFC.

2. Supervisors who have training, experience and demonstrated ability in teaching and supervising trainees or staff in the practice of marriage counseling, with a substantial focus on interpersonal relations. It is expected that identified supervisors among staff members will be able to meet the requirements of the American Association of Marriage and Family Counselors for designation as an Approved Supervisor.

3. Experienced personnel from the fields of psychiatry, psychology and social casework (if not included on regular staff) should be available to staff as needed, and their participation regularized.

C. OPERATIONAL PROCEDURES

1. *Case Files and Record Keeping*

Systematic, confidential record-keeping is essential for teaching marriage and family counseling and for evaluating the service. This should include data with regard to:

    a. Intake process
    b. Identifying biographical information
    c. Source of referral
    d. Problems presented
    e. Records of all examinations and tests
    f. Staffing and assignments
    g. Consultations and case conferences
    h. Significant detail on the course of the counseling process (including referral or termination)
    i. Fees paid
    j. Summary of case at the time of closure

2. *Confidentiality*

Confidentiality of all clinical records is imperative and must be specifically provided for. This extends to teaching, training and educational assignments. (Confidentiality is ultimately the responsibility of the Clinical Director or Director of Training.)

3. *Fees*

The policy concerning the setting and collecting of fees should be clearly stated.

4. *Number and Variety of Cases*

The training center should be able to provide for the trainee a reasonable number and variety of cases, such as pre-marriage counseling, marriage counseling, divorce and remarital counseling, family therapy, and group couples' counseling.

D. TRAINING PROGRAM

1. *Usual Entrance Requirements for Trainees*

    a. *Academic requirements.* The trainee should be enrolled in (or have completed) a doctoral or a master's degree program in social work, sociology, or a closely related field—medicine, law, or the ministry.

    b. *Personal qualifications.* Consistent provision must be made by the staff of an Approved Training Center for the careful exploration of the personal qualifications of each applicant who fulfills the professional requirements for training (by direct interview, unless distance prevents).

    c. *Plans for professional utilization of training.* A candidate should submit a reasonably realistic plan for subsequent professional use of his counseling training.

  2. *Substantive Content*

It is expected that the program will expose the student to the important areas of theoretical competency. This would include personality theory, human sexuality, marriage and family studies, marriage counseling and family therapy.

  3. *Structures of Supervision*

In this context the concept of "supervision" is assumed to have the following characteristics:

    a. It is *face-to-face* conversations with the Supervisor.

    b. It is sustained and intense, usually once a week over a period of one to two years.

    c. It focuses on the raw data from the supervisee's current clinical work, this made directly available to the Supervisor through such means as direct observations, written clinical notes and audio and television recordings.

    d. It is a process clearly distinguishable from personal psychotherapy and is contracted to serve *professional* goals.

It is expected that a trainee in an Approved Training Program will practice during the training year a minimum total of 500 hours of counseling and will have received not less than 200 hours of supervision to include at least 50 hours of individual supervision.

It is further expected that group supervision (or else some other part of the curriculum) will provide for a regularized interprofessional-interdisciplinary case conference. Supervision should include instruction and practice in the uses of psychiatric consultation, as well as the giving and receiving of referrals.

  4. *Evaluation*

Evaluation is an ongoing process. It is the responsibility of the designated supervisor in consultation with the Clinical Director or Director of Training to systematically evaluate the progress and performance of each trainee and give appropriate feedback. A final evaluation is part of the process of termination of training.

Adopted by the AAMFC Board of Directors, 10/9/71.

Appendix D

FILMS

In the previous edition of the *Handbook* brief descriptions of some of the films then available were included. Since that time the number and variety of films has grown so that such a task does not seem feasible at this time. Instead, resources where information about films are mentioned so that the reader can contact the resource center and find out what are the latest films available.

The National Council on Family Relations, 1219 University Avenue Southeast, Minneapolis, Minnesota 55414, offers a film awards competition each year. The 1974 Sixth Annual NCFR Film Awards Competition was published in *The Family Coordinator*, Volume 24, No. 1, January 1975 and in this article are described not only the winners but the honorable mentions and some long films.

The National Sex Forum, 1523 Franklin, San Francisco, Ca. 94101, also produces and rents, as well as sells, films and puts out a catalog with descriptions of their films.

The *Journal of Sex Education and Therapy*, published by the American Association of Sex Educators and Counselors, 5010 Wisconsin Avenue, N. W., Washington, D. C. 20016, reviews films.

Sensate Media Service, 5436 Fernwood Ave., Los Angeles, Ca. 90027 also distributes films and provides technical media service.

Appendix E

AGENCIES FOR REFERRALS

The agencies listed below are only a few of the many responsible places where one may secure information about professional assistance for marriage and family counseling. Most cities of any fairly large size have a directory which lists local agencies (frequently available through the United Fund, Community Chest, or Red Feather offices). Colleges or universities sometimes are also good resources for referrals to clinics or training centers.

Abortion Counseling, Information and Referral Services, 160 West 86th Street, New York, New York, 10024

American Association of Marriage & Family Counselors, 225 Yale Avenue, Claremont, California 91711

American Personnel & Guidance Association, 1607 New Hampshire Ave., N. W., Washington, D. C. 20009, [Publishes a *Directory of Approved Counseling Agencies*, some of which provide marriage counseling.]

Board of Behavioral Science Examiners, 1021 "O" Street, Sacramento, California 95814

Family Service Association of America, 215 Fourth Avenue, New York, New York 10003

Institute for Rational Living, 45 East 65th Street, New York, New York 10021

National Association for Mental Health, 10 Columbus Circle, New York, New York 10019

Planned Parenthood Federation of America, 501 Madison Avenue, New York, New York 10022

Reproductive Biology Research Foundation, 4910 Forest Park Boulevard, St. Louis, Missouri 63108

Appendix F

PROFESSIONAL ORGANIZATIONS

The following professional organizations are a few of the ones that might prove particularly helpful for marriage and family counselors.

Academy of Psychologists in Marital Counseling, William R. Reevy, Ph. D., President, c/o Department of Psychology, New Mexico Institute of Mining and Technology, Socorro, New Mexico 87801

American Association of Marriage & Family Counselors, 225 Yale Avenue, Claremont, California 91711

American Orthopsychiatric Association, 1790 Broadway, New York, New York 10019

California Association of Marriage & Family Counselors, 10474 Santa Monica Blvd. (#8) Los Angeles, California 90025

National Association for Mental Health, 10 Columbus Circle, New York, New York 10019

National Council on Family Relations, 1219 University Ave., S. E., Minneapolis, Minnesota 55414

SIECUS (Sex Information & Education Council of the United States), 1855 Broadway, New York, New York 10023

Society for the Scientific Study of Sex, 12 East 41st Street (Suite 1104), New York, New York 10028

Appendix G
SAMPLE FORMS

Code No.____

Your name____

PSYCHOTHERAPY INVENTORY

AARON L. RUTLEDGE

Director of Psychotherapy Program, The Merrill-Palmer Institute

Confidential information for the use of your psychotherapist. For premarital or marriage counseling, each of the couple should fill out an Inventory.

Code No.____

Published by

THE MERRILL-PALMER INSTITUTE, 71 East Ferry Avenue, Detroit, Michigan 48202

© Aaron L. Rutledge 1967; revision of "Individual and Marriage Counseling Inventory" © 1956

The "Psychotherapy Inventory" is reproduced here by permission of the author and publisher.

A. PERSONAL DATA

Date today_____ Referred by:_____

                                                    Name   Position   Address

1. List problems, in order of their importance to you, which you would like to discuss:_____
_____
_____

2. INDIVIDUAL DATA:

Sex_____ Date of birth_____ Age_____ Height_____ Weight_____
Education completed (grades, degrees or courses)_____
Further study plans_____
Religious preference (denomination): In childhood_____ Now_____
Military service: (branches and dates)_____
Describe your life: Very happy_____ Happy_____ Average_____ Unhappy_____ Very unhappy_____
List sources from which sex information was received_____

3. OCCUPATIONAL DATA:

Type of employment and position or duties_____
_____
Previous employment_____
Annual income *before* deductions: Your income_____ Mate's income_____ Total_____

4. PHYSICAL HEALTH DATA:

Very good_____ Good_____ Average_____ Poor_____. List present illnesses, symptoms, including allergies
_____
List childhood and other illnesses, surgery, handicaps, etc., underlining any which caused serious difficulty_____
_____
When was last medical check-up?_____. Reason for this, and findings_____
_____
List or describe purpose of *medication* of any kind now being taken_____
_____
Your Physician_____

                                                    Name   Telephone

                     Address

5. EMOTIONAL HEALTH DATA:

Ever had serious mental disturbance or a "nervous breakdown"?_____ When?_____
Treated by_____
Hospitalized?_____ How long ill?_____
List all previous psychotherapy, counseling, or other treatment for personal and/or marital problems:

    Dates   Type of Problem   Name of Professional or Agency

_____
_____
Type of health insurance carried_____
(Does it cover emotional or mental problems?)_____

6. MARITAL AND FAMILY STATUS:

Single_____ Going Steady_____ Engaged_____ How long_____ Number previous engagements_____
Married_____ Date Married_____ How long dating mate_____ How long engaged_____
Mate's age_____ Occupation_____ Education_____ Religion_____
Children by present marriage:

    Name   Age   Comments (residence, custody, support, etc.)

_____
_____
_____

Separated_____ When separated_____; Widowed_____ When widowed_____
Divorced_____ When divorced_____ Divorce applied for_____ By whom_____
Previous marriages: How many_____ How terminated_____ Date_____
Children by *previous* marriages:

    Name   Age   Comments (residence, custody, support, etc.)

_____
_____

B. YOUR PARENTAL FAMILY

Your Father   *Your Mother*

1. Age now if living_____

   Age at death and date_____

2. Nationality background_____

3. Education completed (Circle)

   Grammar School   5   6   7   8   5   6   7   8

   High School   9   10   11   12   9   10   11   12

   College   1   2   3   4   1   2   3   4

   Graduate   1   2   3   4   1   2   3   4

4. Occupation_____

   (Father—major and minor:

   Mother—before and after marriage)_____

5. Religious (denominational) preference

   Present_____

   In Childhood_____

6. Age at Marriage_____

7. Rate your parents' marriage

   Very happy_____ Happy_____ Average_____ Unhappy_____ Very unhappy_____

8. Do parents live together? Yes_____ No_____ Separated_____ Your age then_____ Divorced_____ Your age then_____

9. Remarried? Mother_____ Your age then_____; Father_____ Your age then_____

10. Do you feel closest to your father?_____; Your mother?_____

11. If you are married, did your parents approve? Father: Before_____ Later_____ Mother: Before_____ Later_____

12. Data about your brothers and sisters in order of birth:

Age	Sex	Living (yes, no)	Education	Occupation	Health	Marital Status	Marital Adjustment (very happy, happy, average, unhappy, very unhappy)	Number Children

13. Describe other persons who lived in your parental home and their relationship to you_____

_____

_____

_____

Code No._____

Your name_____

Street address_____

City_____ State_____ Zip Code_____

Telephone: Residence_____ Office_____

Code No._____

C. THE PERSONAL RELATIONS IN MY PARENTAL FAMILY

For use *only* if specifically assigned; even then, if this portion of the Inventory causes undue anxiety, delay completing it until you have discussed the material with your psychotherapist.

Write several paragraphs about each of the following:

1. My father as an individual, including personality changes
2. My relationship to him through the years
3. My mother as an individual, including personality changes
4. My relationship to her through the years
5. My parents' relationship to each other:
   1) Which was dominant? By choice or by necessity?
   2) Which was submissive? By choice or by necessity?
   3) Describe what you know about their relationship:
      a) As two personalities
      b) As financial team, or otherwise
      c) As members of their community
      d) In handling problems
      e) In dealing with children
      f) Their affectional life, including sex relations
6. Discuss your brothers and sisters:
   1) Their reaction to parents
   2) Their reaction to each other
   3) Your relationship to them individually and collectively
7. Evaluate both constructive and destructive influences upon yourself and upon the remainder of the family from both the short range and long term points of view.

Do not write below this line

Code No._____; Psychotherapist_____; Fee_____

Dates Seen		Presenting Problems:
		Diagnosis and Revealed Problems:
		Outcome:

HOMEWORK REPORT

Consultation Center

Institute for Advanced Study in Rational Psychotherapy

45 East 65th Street, New York, N.Y. 10021 / (212) LEhigh 5-0822

Name .... Date .... Therapist ....

Instructions: Please draw a circle around the number in front of those feelings listed in the first column that troubled you *most* during the period since your last therapy session. Then, in the *second* column, indicate the amount of work you did on each circled item; and, in the *third* column, the results of the work you did.

		Amount of Work Done				Results of Work		
Undesirable Emotional Feelings			Much	Some	Little or none		Good	Fair	Poor
1a	Anger or great irritability	1b	....	....	....	1c	....	....	....
2a	Anxiety, severe worry, or fear	2b	....	....	....	2c	....	....	....
3a	Boredom or dullness	3b	....	....	....	3c	....	....	....
4a	Failure to achieve	4b	....	....	....	4c	....	....	....
5a	Frustration	5b	....	....	....	5c	....	....	....
6a	Guilt or self-condemnation	6b	....	....	....	6c	....	....	....
7a	Hopelessness or depression	7b	....	....	....	7c	....	....	....
8a	Great loneliness	8b	....	....	....	8c	....	....	....
9a	Helplessness	9b	....	....	....	9c	....	....	....
10a	Self-pity	10b	....	....	....	10c	....	....	....
11a	Uncontrollability	11b	....	....	....	11c	....	....	....
12a	Worthlessness or inferiority	12b	....	....	....	12c	....	....	....
13a	Other (specify)	13b	....	....	....	13c	....	....	....

Undesirable Actions or Habits

			Much	Some	Little or none		Good	Fair	Poor
14a	Avoiding responsibility	14b	....	....	....	14c	....	....	....
15a	Acting unfairly to others	15b	....	....	....	15c	....	....	....
16a	Being late to appointments	16b	....	....	....	16c	....	....	....
17a	Being undisciplined	17b	....	....	....	17c	....	....	....
18a	Demanding attention	18b	....	....	....	18c	....	....	....
19a	Physically attacking others	19b	....	....	....	19c	....	....	....
20a	Putting off important things	20b	....	....	....	20c	....	....	....
21a	Telling people off harshly	21b	....	....	....	21c	....	....	....
22a	Whining or crying	22b	....	....	....	22c	....	....	....
23a	Withdrawing from activity	23b	....	....	....	23c	....	....	....
24a	Overdrinking of alcohol	24b	....	....	....	24c	....	....	....
25a	Overeating	25b	....	....	....	25c	....	....	....
26a	Oversleeping	26b	....	....	....	26c	....	....	....
27a	Undersleeping	27b	....	....	....	27c	....	....	....
28a	Oversmoking	28b	....	....	....	28c	....	....	....
29a	Taking too many drugs or pills	29b	....	....	....	29c	....	....	....
30a	Other (specify)	30b	....	....	....	30c	....	....	....

Irrational Ideas or Philosophies

			Much	Some	Little or none		Good	Fair	Poor
31a	People must love or approve of me	31b	....	....	....	31c	....	....	....
32a	Making mistakes is terrible	32b	....	....	....	32c	....	....	....
33a	People should be condemned for their wrongdoings	33b	....	....	....	33c	....	....	....
34a	It's terrible when things go wrong	34b	....	....	....	34c	....	....	....
35a	My emotions can't be controlled	35b	....	....	....	35c	....	....	....
36a	Threatening situations have to keep me terribly worried	36b	....	....	....	36c	....	....	....
37a	Self-discipline is too hard to achieve	37b	....	....	....	37c	....	....	....
38a	Bad effects of my childhood still have to control my life	38b	....	....	....	38c	....	....	....
39a	I can't stand the way certain people act	39b	....	....	....	39c	....	....	....
40a	Other (specify)	40b	....	....	....	40c	....	....	....

(please complete other side)

PLEASE PRINT! BE BRIEF AND LEGIBLE! ANSWER QUESTION C FIRST; THEN ANSWER THE OTHER QUESTIONS.

A. ACTIVATING EVENT you recently experienced about which you became upset or disturbed. (Examples: *"I went for a job interview." "My mate screamed at me."*) ....

rB. Rational BELIEF or idea you had about this Activating Event. (Examples: *"It would be unfortunate if I were rejected for the job." "How annoying to have my mate scream at me!"*) ....
....

iB. Irrational BELIEF or idea you had about this Activating Event. (Examples: *"It would be catastrophic if I were rejected for the job; I would be pretty worthless as a person." "I can't stand my mate's screaming; she is horrible for screaming at me!"*) ....
....

C. CONSEQUENCES of your irrational BELIEF (iB) about the Activating Event listed in Question A. State here the one most disturbing emotion, behavior, or CONSEQUENCE you experienced recently. (Examples: *"I was anxious." "I was hostile." "I had stomach pains."*) ....

D. DISPUTING, questioning, or challenging you can use to change your irrational BELIEF (iB). (Examples: *"Why would it be catastrophic and how would I become a worthless person if I were rejected for the job?" "Why can't I stand my mate's screaming and why is she horrible for screaming at me?"*) ....
....

cE. Cognitive EFFECT or answer you obtained from DISPUTING your irrational BELIEF (iB). Examples: *"It would not be catastrophic, but merely unfortunate, if I were rejected for the job; my giving a poor interview would not make me a worthless person." "Although I'll never like my mate's screaming, I can stand it; he or she is not horrible but merely a fallible person for screaming."*) ....
....

bE. Behavioral EFFECT or result of your DISPUTING your irrational BELIEF (iB). (Examples: *"I felt less anxious." "I felt less hostile to my mate." "My stomach pains vanished."*)..

F. If you did not challenge your irrational BELIEF (iB), why did you not? ....
....

G. Activities you would most like to *stop* that you are now doing..
....

H. Activities you would most like to *start* that you are not doing...
....

I. Emotions and ideas you would most like to change ....
....

J. Specific homework assignment(s) given you by your therapist, your group, or yourself ....
....

K. What did you actually do to carry out the assignment(s)? ....
....

L. Check the item which describes how much you have worked at your last homework assignment(s): ....(a) almost every day ...., (b) several times a week .... (c) occasionally .... (d) hardly ever.

M. How many times in the past week have you specifically worked at changing and DISPUTING your irrational BELIEFS (iBs)? ....

N. What other things have you specifically done to change your irrational BELIEFS and your disturbed emotional CONSE-QUENCES? ....
....

O. Check the item which describes how much reading you have recently done of the material on rational-emotive therapy: ...., (a) a considerable amount ...., (b) a moderate amount ...., (c) little or none.

P. Things you would now like to discuss most with your therapist or group ....
....
....

Name Index

Subject Index